Finding Europe

Looking to the future, we dedicate this book

To our children, grand-children and students

And looking to the past, we also dedicate it

To the memory of Robert Wokler,
whose erudition, friendship, and gentle spirit
greatly enriched our discussions

Finding Europe

Discourses on Margins, Communities, Images
ca. 13th – ca. 18th Centuries

Edited by

Anthony Molho, Diogo Ramada Curto and Niki Koniordos

Berghahn Books
New York • Oxford

First published in 2007 by
Berghahn Books
www.berghahnbooks.com

Library of Congress Cataloging-in-Publication Data

Finding Europe : discourses on margins, images, communities ca. 13th – ca.
18th centuries/ edited
by Anthony Molho and Diogo Ramada Curto.
    p. cm.
Includes bibliographical references and index.
ISBN 1-84545-208-9 (hbk. : alk. paper) 1. Europe--Civilization.
I. Molho, Anthony. II. Curto, Diogo Ramada.
CB203.R485 2007
940--dc22

                                                    2006100352

British Library Cataloguing in Publication Data
A catalogue record for this book is available from the British Library
Printed in the United States on acid-free paper

ISBN 978-1-84545-208-7 hardback

Contents

Acknowledgements

Our warmest and most sincere thanks to all those who, generously and consistently, helped us on this project.

Yves Meny, Principal of the European University Institute and Joseph Connors, Director of the Harvard University Center for Italian Renaissance Studies at the Villa I Tatti gave us their support – both personal and material – from the very start.

Our colleagues at the Department of History and Civilization of the European University Institute, despite some intellectual disagreements with them, encouraged us to continue, even at times when the going got rough and the end was hardly in sight.

Gérard Delille, Gigliola Fragnito, Cemal Kafadar, Giovanni Levi, Sara Mathews Grieco, Lucia Nuti, Wolfgang Reinhard, Silvana Seidel and Christopher Wood participated actively in our two workshops, and contributed mightily to the discussions.

Paolo Viola, whose much too premature death was a blow to his many admirers and friends, joined us for a special meeting, when we talked about how, over the past few generations, the history of Europe had been conceived and written. Marcello Verga, Wim Blockmans, Sergio Romano, Gabor Klaniczay and Lucette Valensi were also present in this discussion, and their observations were precious in our own reflections on the topic.

Last, but by no means least, are our students, whose contributions to the realization of this project have been vital. We owe them a huge debt of gratitude for their seriousness, their critical engagement, and their willingness to help along the way. Serena Ferente, Massimo Rospocher, Gunvor Simonson, and Joanna Vadenbring took charge of a series of practical matters, handling them with the greatest tact and efficiency imaginable.

To all of these friends our warmest and most sincere thanks.

List of Illustrations

A Harlequin's Dress
Reflections on Europe's Public Discourse

Anthony Molho

*L'Europe n'est qu'un nom, qu'une 'expression géographique', comme disait
Metternich de l'Italie, si elle n'est pas une conception d' histoire.*
Ernst Robert Curtius[1]

Il faut, dans nos temps modernes, avoir l'esprit européen.[2] One hundred and ninety
years ago, when Mme. De Staël wrote these lines, *l'esprit européen* was perhaps
easier to identify than it is today. How would we, today, wish to come to terms with
this *esprit*? What exactly would we want to embrace or reject?

These are not new questions, of course. They were not new in the early
nineteenth century. They have persisted ever since. There is no need, here, to survey
the range of answers offered over the years by politicians, scholars, and intellectuals,
a task admirably fulfilled in their weighty anthology, *Europes*, by Yves Hersant and
Fabienne Durand-Bogaert.[3] For each one of the dozens of views contained in their
anthology – from Havel and Mitterand, back to Hesiod and Horace – an historian
would need to dwell upon texts and contexts in order to understand these writers'
fears and aspirations for the Europes they described, imagined, or yearned for.

Rather, for the purpose of these preliminary reflections, one can refer to two of
the authors included in this anthology. Both were famous historians, and belonged
to the generation of our own teachers. They are Federico Chabod and Lucien Fèbvre.
Within a year, unbeknownst to each other, each of them offered a university course
devoted to Europe: *Storia dell'idea d'Europa* was Chabod's course, and *L'Europe.
Genèse d'une civilisation* was Fèbvre's.[4] The materials for both courses were gathered
and published, but in both cases posthumously, a coincidence that has not gone
unnoticed. Chabod offered his course at the University of Milan in the academic year
1943–4, Fèbvre, at the Collège de France, in the academic year 1944–5.

Obviously, context, here, is key. The politics of Europe's nation states and
Europe's long civil war in the first half of the twentieth century frame both historians'
exercises. A recently published essay raises the possibility that even Chabod's decision
to stop his story with Guizot's ruminations about Europe and not to round it out to
the mid-twentieth century is inexplicable aside from other, hitherto unexamined

dimensions of the contemporary context.[5] Chabod's alleged urge to distance himself from the triumphalist discourses about Europe's *Neue Ordnung*, of Nazi and Fascist inspiration, is thought to have led to the interruption of his analysis. That may or may not be so. But this recent iconoclastic re-examination of Chabod's ideas forcefully underscores the importance of context. In his discussion of Fèbvre's lessons on Europe, Marc Ferro made very much the same point: Fèbvre's decision not to publish these lessons may not be unrelated to the echoes triggered by the term Europe during the Second World War. In 1944, when Fèbvre began his course, Pierre Laval's rhetoric on the *Nouvelle Europe* resonated through other, contemporary discourses on Europe, including Fèbvre's own.[6] To publish a book on Europe ran the risk of giving a false impression.

It seems that always – or nearly so – the term Europe reveals as much as it conceals. The messages are not always decipherable, at least not before the term is subjected to the sort of semantic and contextual excavation recently undertaken in Chabod's case. This strikes me to be the case even with a seemingly anodyne statement about Europe as the one contained in Pius II's *Commentarii* whose meaning only a careful understanding of context can convey. For the term Europe, as in 'Europae imperium', to which 'Mahumetes Turchorum imperator' aspired following his conquest of Constantinople, surely refers not simply to a geographic region of the world but rather evokes a range of other meanings (or images) of peoples, religions, and cultures.[7]

So, we come to this book and to the meetings that preceded it. Twice over a rather short period – in autumn 2003 and in late winter 2004 – two dozen or so mostly European scholars found their way to the European University Institute to discuss, in the course of two workshops indirectly funded by the European Community, questions related to Europe's past. In the months before these meetings, a series of other gatherings, some conducted with the assistance of a group of secondary school teachers and young journalists drawn from nearly two dozen European countries, had also addressed comparable issues, setting the foundations for the two workshops. What, if anything, did these occasions have to do with Mme. De Stael's *esprit européen*? What might the repetition in the preceding sentences of the terms Europe and European – defining at once actors, patrons, subject matter, and location – signify? What Europe (more appropriately what Europes) did this group have in mind, and what meanings (images) did these Europes evoke? Answers to these questions varied among the workshops' interlocutors, as they no doubt will among this essay's readers.

Discussions and arguments about contemporary Europe, broader notions regarding Europe's past, as well as methods used to study this complex topic constantly impinged on our discussions. In more than a casual way, they helped to shape this book. They are basic elements of the context in which it was conceived and produced, and, in the conviction that, for our project as well, context is key, we start with these.

Contexts: Europe

Writing in 1943–4, Chabod had ruefully noted: 'There is in these years a *gran parlare* about Europe and European civilization ... and of forces that are opposed to the *civiltà europea*'. And, reflecting on the meaning of the term Europe, he sceptically concluded: 'The exact value of this term remains unclear; one could actually repeat that "everyone says that it exists, but no one knows where it is" (*che ci sia ognun lo dice, dove sia nessun lo sa*)'.[8] Change the *dove* (where) in Chabod's statement to *che cosa* (what) and the second part of his statement could easily fit our times. But the first part will do just as it is. Rarely before our day has there been so much talk about Europe. Rarely have so many people – not simply statesmen and government officials, but regular, ordinary citizens – been so directly engaged with Europe. Will Europe have a constitution? Will Europe's governance limit the sovereignty of its member states? Has the *euro* benefited or hurt local economies? Will Europe have a foreign policy of its own? Should it? What about an army? A standardized university system? Every day, questions such as these fly back and forth, in all languages spoken in the European Union's member states, in newspaper columns, television programmes, solemn or silly pronouncements made by scholars and politicians.

To those gathered in Florence, it seemed that while the entire discussion was likely to arouse deep passions among many Europeans, some of its elements had a more direct bearing on their own immediate, scholarly preoccupations. Two of these took up a good deal of time and generated much discussion: the nation state and Europe's culture.

Participants in the current discussions on Europe's future – whether they argue for the creation of a federated United States of Europe, or for a *Europe des nations* – continue to be inspired by a nineteenth century vision of the state. For the federalists, in its deep structures, their new Europe will bear a striking resemblance to the nation state. It will be unified and its parts integrated into an organic unit; it will have a clear centre of authority, from where the new Europe's policies will be fashioned and enforced. At the spectrum's other end are those who insist that, whatever the new Europe's shape, the nation states that currently comprise it must occupy its core. For them, Europe will provide a broad institutional umbrella under whose protection economic interests, always carefully overseen by national governments, will be pursued by citizens of the Union's nation states. Between these two positions, there is a range of other proposals, shaped, nearly all of them it would seem, by the weight of the nation state's presence. Later in this Introduction, when our project's direction is more explicitly presented, we shall return to the importance of the nation state in our own discussions.

Alongside politics and the nation state, Europe's culture has received its share of attention in the broader civic dialogue about Europe. Right from the start, we were struck by a silence in this discussion. There is a weighty word that is hard to find in the current conversation on Europe, yet often associated with it until after the Second World War. This word is 'civilization'. In their meditations and pronouncements, scholars, and commentators – from Voltaire to Husserl, from

Burke to Croce to Elias – did not hesitate to combine the term Europe with the term civilization. Often, it was simply assumed that the semantic fields covered by the two terms – Europe and civilization – complemented and reinforced each other. To be sure, the term has not disappeared from current use. But references to it are less frequent, and one wonders about the reasons for this shift. As we noticed, in the cases of Fèbvre and Chabod, it has been suggested that the reluctance of one to publish his lessons on Europe, and the decision of the other to stop his lessons in the mid-nineteenth century probably reflected the discomfort that the term Europe may have provoked because of its appropriation by extreme right-wing political movements. One wonders if the link between Europe and civilization was in some way eroded for the same reasons. The unity and coherence implied by the term civilization, its status as repository of the more refined and elevated qualities of a society's spiritual accomplishments, may have further accentuated the reluctance of commentators to rely upon it and link it with Europe. For how could one insist on the expression European civilization, at a time when the Holocaust had erupted onto centre stage of public discussion and post colonial studies were responsible for a radical shift in the traditional views of Europe's relations with other parts of the world?

Attention has now shifted: from Europe's civilization to its values. Talk about European values is almost endless. Of course, this is not new. It goes back centuries if not millennia, and has continued unabated through the twentieth century's disasters. One could even suggest that a discourse about Europe has itself been part of Europe's intellectual landscape at least since the Renaissance, and that one of Europe's cultural traits is precisely this quality of self referentiality, and the recurring variations on the twin themes of Europe and its identity. Clearly enough, recent pronouncements on the question of Europe's culture are themselves deeply coloured by this continuous, and continuously unfolding discourse. If not necessarily more profound and original, the current interest in Europe's culture has been more diffuse and persistent than in the past.

Scholars are not the only ones to join this wide conversation on European values. Impressive arrays of intellectuals have somehow felt the need to do so. Vaclav Havel has reminded us that 'Europe is a community of destiny', whose 'fundamental values are based on tolerance, humanity, and fraternity'. In his recent best seller, *Le nouveau désordre mondial. Réflexions d' un Européen* (2003), Tzvetan Todorov listed the *valeurs européens*, which, according to him, are *rationalité, justice, démocratie, liberté individuelle, laicité,* and *tolérance*. For his part, in a front-page article in one of Italy's most widely circulated newspapers (*La repubblica*, 31 May 2003), Eco enumerated the *'principi fondamentali del cosidetto mondo occidentale: l'eredità greca e giudaico-cristiana, le idee di libertà e uguglianza nate dalla rivoluzione francese, l'eredità stessa della scienza moderna ... la forma di produzione capitalistica, la laicizzazione dello Stato, il diritto romano o la Common Law, la stessa idea di giustizia che si realizza attraverso la lotta di classe ...'* Having first become *un patrimonio della sola Europa*, they are now shared by peoples in nearly all parts of the world.[9]

Contexts: Method

Many of the interlocutors in the public discussion on Europe's values often construct their arguments, without always acknowledging it, on an implicit teleology. According to their position, the values that define European culture have been expressed and applied with increasing clarity and force over time. On occasion, and in contraposition to this view, some thinkers have feared for the worst. Especially during the first half of the twentieth century, thinkers such as Valery, Husserl, Croce, Zweig and others thought that time, and a set of unhappy circumstances, had pushed into the margins of public consciousness the basic values of European culture. But on the whole, and perhaps more so among historians than among other scholars, there has often prevailed an idea that European values have developed teleologically. One need not go back to the proponents of the traditional view of progress in the late nineteenth and early twentieth centuries to find expressions of this view. A very good example is contained in Jean-Baptiste Duroselle's *Europe: A History of its Peoples*, published simultaneously in several European languages in 1990. Duroselle was nothing but sanguine about Europe's past, even more so about its future. He was convinced that it was 'possible to discern in Europe's history a general if halting growth in compassion, humanity and equality'. The project of constructing a federated European Union 'is natural, realistic and legitimate, because there has long been a community of Europe – embryonic at first, but growing with time, despite centuries of war and conflict, blood and tears'.[10]

A variant of this view can be found in the work of some other scholars. Although they take their distance from teleological formulations, they often aggressively insist that a discourse on Europe is necessarily linked to its values. Theirs can be defined as the single track view of European culture. Its exponents single out *the* one intellectual or moral tradition with which they propose to associate the fundamental character of European history, and weave their account of Europe's past around that tradition. Time is also an important consideration in their discussions. But while for the teleologists time serves to give increasingly clear expression to a set of values, for those who embrace such single track views, time has a curiously neutral function. The passage of time notwithstanding, the value each of them singles out as the essence of European culture retains, over the ages, its full strength and importance.

In the recent fracas about the possible adoption of a European constitution, the place of Christianity in Europe's past received considerable attention, religious leaders insisting that this one tradition – Christianity – had to be especially acknowledged by the new Constitution's drafters. In their view, no other tradition could rival the cultural weight that religion had in Europe's culture. This argument is by no means new. Christopher Dawson wrote an important book on Christianity's capital contribution to the sense of a European community (a book, incidentally, that attracted some attention in Italy during the 1930s, and may have coloured Chabod's own thinking on Europe).[11] A little later, in 1943, Oskar Halecki argued that the Catholic Church expressed Europe's defining cultural value, a point that then entitled him to argue that Poland, firmly placed within the Catholic Church's embrace, could claim its rightful place in Europe.[12] Variations on this theme have been heard in recent decades, especially from east European scholars and intellectuals for whom an evocation of what they take to be Europe's values represented a powerful weapon with which to resist various oppressive regimes. Single track arguments have not always been accompanied by the smell of incense. Lay scholars have had their own ideas about *the* European tradition or value to be singled out for special attention. Recently, democracy and republicanism have been presented as holding place of pride in Europe's culture.[13]

'Single track' claims do hold their own interest. Yet, in the end, it would be difficult to accept them at their face value. Quite beyond their imbalance in singling out one strand in Europe's complex cultural web, they seem to open themselves to a double criticism: their unbalanced treatment, and their silence on recent epistemological and methodological proposals made in the wider realm of the human sciences. Most importantly, whether by intention or not, many of these interpretations are tinged by a triumphalistic rhetoric, or, to be less critical, they more often than not leave unaccounted what one can only euphemistically refer to as the dark side of Europe's history. One of the most recent historical disquisitions on Christianity's unrivalled importance in European history leaves unmentioned Christianity's role in the Holy Inquisition, the expulsion of Muslims and Jews from the Iberian Peninsula, the various Christian churches' intolerance toward new scientific discoveries, or, even, any reference to the currently debated question of the Papacy's alleged acquiescence to the Holocaust. Rather, its author, Giovanni Reale, objecting to the omission of any reference to Christianity in the draft of the European Constitution, insisted that Christianity has been *l' asse portante spirituale da cui è nata e secondo cui si è sviluppata l' Europa* (the basic spiritual axis from which Europe was born, and according to which it was developed).[14] More astoundingly, an impressive new collective book entitled *The Idea of Europe* and devoted to the history of republicanism from antiquity to the present contains no entry in its index for the Holocaust, as if such an event, with all its cultural and ethical implications, were extraneous to *the* idea of Europe.[15]

From the point of view of method, then, many recent discussions are striking for their conservative approaches. It is hard to find in them even distant echoes of the intense, epistemological clashes that, in the past few decades, have punctuated nearly all fields in the humanities and the social sciences. Schools such as the 'linguistic turn' and 'postmodernism' have injected a level of epistemological scepticism and a degree of complexity in nearly all fields of historical analysis. The metaphor of 'construction' has invaded nearly all historical inquiries, with scholars now intent on 'deconstructing' analytical categories that refer not only to political institutions and social categories, but also, and above all, to ideas and values. There is a paradox here. Although many historians and other social scientists have, since the 1970s, made capital contributions to epistemological discussions, they seem to forget ideas about 'construction' when they take up the subject of Europe. Then, in their pronouncements, past and present seem to coalesce into a seamless continuum, interrupted, to be sure, by wars, technological changes, and economic and political transformations, but basically commensurate in their essences. Thus, a powerfully, often exuberantly anti-teleological current has been introduced into historical studies, all the while an equally powerful but often implicit teleology continues to define current discourses about Europe's history.

There is one notable exception to these observations. A group of social scientists among whom one finds an occasional historian have been careful to weave into their analyses lessons they draw from new epistemological insights. They have been receptive to the category of 'construction', especially intent upon pointing to the shifting valences assumed by the term Europe in the past few generations. Equally, they have been highly critical of traditional discourses on European values, suspicious, as they often intimate, of political and ideological motives behind such approaches. An excellent example of this approach is a collective book, *The Idea of Europe. Problems of National and Transnational Identity*, published in 1992, coincident with the Treaty of Maastricht and the establishment of the European Union. In their Introduction, Brian Nelson and David Roberts write that Europe, 'the creator and creation of modernity, cannot be reduced to a historical or geographical entity. It has always been a contested concept, a future-oriented project, the Enlightenment utopia from Leibnitz to Kant of a pacified Europe, based on the civil religion of reason and law'.[16] The idea of construction has been picked up by several other scholars, for whom, as one of them recently wrote: 'Europe is not a fixed essence, but labile and in flux. European – and national – identities are always fluid and contextual, contested and contingent, and discursively shaped under various *forms of inclusion and exclusion*'.[17]

Although he is not mentioned by name, Chabod's shadow looms large over the work of these scholars, especially in their definition of the chronological limits they more often than not impose on their work. Chabod had insisted on one point. It was difficult to refer to a consciousness of Europe before the Enlightenment. Denys Hay, one of Chabod's principal Anglophone admirers, and translator of his ideas to English, had presented a variant of Chabod's views in a small book published in 1957: *Europe: the Emergence of an Idea*. There, Hay wrote that during the Middle Ages and the Renaissance, Europe was often identified with Christianity. Later, 'Christendom slowly entered the limbo of archaic words and Europe emerged for its peoples as the unchallenged symbol of the largest human loyalty'. Later still, the Enlightenment philosophers supplanted Christianity for Europe, as the universal civilization project, to which they juxtaposed the notion of a despotic East. This notion appears and reappears in much other work. In the words of Agnes Heller, the noted Hungarian philosopher, 'a specifically European identity was not formed before the eighteenth century... *Modernity, the creation of Europe, itself created Europe*' (her italics).[19]

For them, to talk about Europe, then, is to concentrate on the last two or so centuries, when notions of progress, and institutions such as the nation state and its attendant cultural and ideological attributes became central elements of Europe. Necessarily, therefore, the temporal focus of such studies has been the fraction of Europe's history from the Enlightenment to the present, from the birth of modernity to the advent of 'postmodernity', from the mid-eighteenth century to the turn of the twenty-first. In these studies, references to a more distant past tend to take the form of introductory comments, intended to frame discourses on Europe's much more recent history. In fact, the more distant past (say, the Middle Ages and the early modern centuries) is largely cut off from the present, with the past two hundred or so years considered largely an almost self contained historical period. One is tempted to ask these scholars: why rely on such traditional schemes of historical periodization? Why conceive of the past as if it comprised distinct historical periods? Can there not be cultural characteristics – forms of social organization, types of political allegiance, psychological perceptions, etc. – that traversed the course of European history from one historical period to another? Does 'modernity' (whatever exactly scholars such as Agnes Heller and others might mean by this term) necessarily imply a sundering of 'modern' from 'premodern' Europe? What bearing do experiences from before (even long before) the middle of the eighteenth century have on an understanding of our own, contemporary Europe?

For all these questions, how can one, today, reject these ideas out of hand? What historian, working in the early years of the twenty-first century, could deny them categorically? We all know that analytical terms, values, institutions – despite similarities in vocabulary between present and past – assume different meanings in different periods of time, and in different cultures. One of the first lessons students learn in any course on the history of political philosophy is that a word such as liberty carried different meanings at the times of Thucydides, Saint Augustine, Leonardo Bruni, and John Stuart Mill. The point is self evident, and we know that the cultural and philosophical meanings of the term and the significance imputed to it by contemporaries will become more easily comprehensible to us the more deeply and firmly we place it in the local contexts in which we find it. In this sense, a term such as liberty (or freedom, or democracy, or autocracy, or, of course, Europe) are always constructed, and our task as historians is to recover their historically specific meanings. By extension, how can one take at its face value the notion that permanent, timeless, transhistorical values – of the sort that Havel, Todorov and Eco almost proudly enumerated – could possibly define Europe, and its culture?

Summarizing, I would argue that the 'constructionists' have a weighty argument on their side. Yet, there is a point that remains unclear in their work. It is well and good to talk about construction and shifting meanings, but on the basis of what elements, one wishes to ask, does this construction take place? In short, to stick to the prevalent metaphor, what is lacking in many of these analyses is a sense of the building blocks with which the construction of Europe has taken place. In the end, what does it mean to say, as was recently said, that Europe 'is not a fixed essence but labile and in flux. European – and national – identities are always fluid and contextual, contested and contingent, and discursively shaped under various forms of inclusion and exclusion'?

Our project addresses some of our questions and uncertainties as we gradually discovered and reflected upon the current discourses on Europe. We share many ideas with scholars who have expressed themselves both on the 'essentialist' and the 'constructivist' fronts. Yet, without repeating the points made above, we think that these ideas are partial. We are convinced that while it is important to seek a common base and common elements in Europe's past, in two significant ways the values based discourse overdetermines (often with pernicious consequences) the history of Europe. It overlooks the 'dark' and negative sides of that history, and it embraces a teleology that simply cannot be supported by careful analysis.[20] Furthermore, it is undeniable that the concept of Europe has been manipulated and used in attempts to 'construct' various and not always easily reconcilable political and ideological programmes. Yet, the 'constructivist' approach is too intent on primarily teasing out of the tissue of European history and discussions about it this manipulative, instrumentally constructive process that coincides with the post-Enlightenment triumph of the nation state.

In our own project, we aspire to preserve the long temporal dimension of the values based approach, separate it from its teleology, and avoid the temptation of succumbing to essentialist formulations. We also wish to integrate into our analysis a sensitivity to the 'constructivist' interpretation without pretending that such construction could be carried out outside the framework of (or without reference to) long-standing European traditions. The questions, then, are two: What do we mean by traditions? How do we reconcile the tension between these and the construction of politically motivated and ideologically tinged definitions (or imaginings) of Europe?

Our answer is simple. It is that the continuities in Europe's history are evident in the persistence of a number of overlapping and intertwining discussions, or discourses. This is what we mean by *discursive traditions*. This book's contents conveys a sense of these. Centuries-long discussions about the law, about political authority, about resistance to that authority, about citizenship, about 'otherness', or civility, or heroism, or the relationship of the present to the past, or about an almost myriad other subjects, define the history of Europe – and not only in the relatively short *durée* of the past two or three centuries. Issues that, according to some, are at the very core of a collective European identity, were themselves contested, provoking individuals or groups to often violent verbal and physical clashes. Even in times of great upheavals (one thinks of the religious reformations of the sixteenth century, or of the English civil wars), these traditions provided a field of common understanding, composed of shared concepts and symbols, often elaborated before the term Europe was invested with its modern, eighteenth century valences. Two points emerge with some clarity from these chapters: the resilience of the discussions (the discursive traditions to which repeated reference is made by the authors); and the fragility of solutions (or resolutions) which were proposed, over time, to these discussions.

One key point about our initial project and the current book needs to be articulated explicitly. It is this: the goal of the overwhelming majority of recent books and articles about Europe, its history, and collective European identities is to present one or more conclusions of substance about Europe's past. What one means by 'substance' is that in each of these instances, a set of ideas, or institutions, or practices, or processes is identified as representing the core of European culture. There is a unity that is imputed to the history of Europe, a unity of direction, of meaning, of time. We have shied away from such an approach. We simply do not share the view that a reasonable consensus about any such topic could be teased out of an examination of European history – especially if this examination takes a long-term perspective as we do. Nor, as will be suggested below, do discussions based on a presumed unity imputed to the history of Europe help us to capture some of that history's tensions and contradictions.

Our ambition in this book is to make a different point. It is a point of method. The method is to move from things to words, from institutions to discussions about them, from reified values to discourses about ways of justifying and explaining actions. Some might think that our method places our project in a postmodernist camp, that by focusing on *discursive traditions* we forego the ambition of reaching back to the reality of the past. We resist this charge. We believe that historians must seek the reality of the past, and that such reality is, indeed, accessible to them. But we also believe that the reality of a European consciousness has, by necessity, to be sought at the level of discourses, of the ways in which Europeans of the past thought and wrote about their world. The connective tissues out of which a European consciousness was woven comprises the discourses – the words and verbal expressions which persisted over centuries across much of the continent.

In his eloquent essay, '*Europa, Europa* ...', Carlo Ossola made a point that, we think, is not far from our own. What is Europe, he asked? 'Today', he mused, 'we recognize her in us, memory of so many rustlings, of books, of heroes, of utopias, of regrets' (*la riconosciamo in noi, memoria di tanti brusìi, di libri, di eroi, di utopie, di rimorsi*).[21] For all the pedestrian quality of our own formulation, we suggest that Ossola's image of *brusìi* – those rustlings of past discussions, controversies, exhortations that, often at a subterranean level, left a mark on the consciousness of Europeans – are comparable to our *discursive traditions*.

It is hard to tease out of the tumultuous unfolding of Europe's history, a long-lasting agreement about many of these issues. Christianity itself, thought by some as occupying the very core of Europe's collective identity, provoked more controversy, and generated more violence than many other institutions and ideas. Yet, Christianity gave rise to a sense of a community – a community not necessarily based on a consensus but one that was rooted in an understanding of the issues over which it was worth (or so it often seemed) disagreeing, and of the words and expressions that were needed to define a position in one of these unfolding controversies. Edgar Morin, in a book that provoked much discussion when it was first published, referred to the *bouillonement dialogique permanent*, that, according to him, provided the key characteristic of la culture européenne. This comes fairly close to our own view, if only one adjusts Morin's 'dialogic bubbling' to our own expression discursive tradition, for a dialogue to take place requires the existence of common conceptual and linguistic elements shared by the interlocutors.

There is a further issue that needs to be mentioned here, not so much of method as of perspective. Earlier, we referred to the often celebratory and self-satisfied tone of many accounts of Europe's history, especially those written by historians. For all the wrong turns Europe may have taken, despite the record of suffering, injustice, and oppression, the dark side of its history is either overlooked or minimized. Instead, many historians are often intent on underscoring what they take to be that history's great accomplishments, in the world of ideas, in fashioning institutions, in forging social bonds, or generating productive tensions. This, surely, is an inadequate perspective. There is an indisputably 'bright' side to Europe's history, a record of accomplishment often emulated by non-European peoples; but alongside this, there is also a decidedly 'dark' side, of intolerance, violence, oppression, and destruction. Europeans and non-Europeans have been recipients of this destructive penchant, and to overlook or to minimize it seems to us just as short-sighted as is the occasional case of an exclusive attention on the 'dark' side. All, or nearly all, participants in our discussions shared this perspective, which is evident in their essays for this volume.

All this is at the level of method, or approach. The subjects of this book's essays encompass a large field, from the Iberian peninsula to the Ottoman Empire to the British Isles and several points in between. Although the major portion of the coverage is focused on the period from the fourteenth to the late eighteenth centuries, the chronological span in some instances reaches back to Antiquity, and, in others, to our contemporary world. In every case, each author has reflected upon the materials examined from the perspective of the point of method mentioned above. In each instance, a discursive tradition, sometimes perduringly resilient, in other cases fragile, has been at the centre of analysis. Our coverage of such different traditions does not aspire to be complete. Our aim is different, supported, as we think it is, by Lucien Fèbvre's injunction to *comprendre et faire comprendre*, as against an ambition *d'être complet*.[23] A project such as ours cannot aspire to completeness. But it can aspire to *comprendre et faire comprendre* by a systematic critical analysis, with a point of method at its core, collectively undertaken by a group of historians, each expert in her or his subject.

This approach still leaves a question open. Beyond the issue of method, what common themes can subsume such a numerous set of disparate essays. To be sure, our ambition was to suggest – above all to ourselves and to our students – new ways of thinking about the history of Europe. But beyond this ambition, a second aim has been to tease out of these disparate researches the idea of a European public discourse. It is around this very notion that a series of lively discussions was held among us. Is it possible to imagine that, especially in the period which is the chronological focus of many of the following studies, a European public discourse did exist? Could such discourse encompass regions as distant from each other as was Poland and Scandinavia from the Mediterranean region, Ireland from the Italian states, Spain from the Germanies? What were this discourse's unifying elements, and what was its European character? To be sure, these questions are not subject to ready responses. In our discussions, we came away with a conviction that the existence of such a European public discourse could serve as a useful working hypothesis to students of the European past. Our final, if necessarily provisional, position was that such a public discourse could be compared to a tissue composed of different fragments (our *discursive traditions*), and shared by several European peoples, their political divisions notwithstanding. As one of our colleagues put it, it was like a Harlequin's dress, a patch-like habit, whose patches retained their distinctiveness all the while connected to each other, forming a variegated whole. A Harlequin's dress: this could have perhaps been our book's title, with its subtitle being 'Elements of European Public Discourse in the pre-Modern Era'.

Thus, variety and pluralism are central images that emerge from this book. There is variety and pluralism in the approaches brought to bear by the authors in their own analyses. But we claim that the qualities of variety and pluralism are also central in the very substance of Europe's history. Here, as we noted earlier, we come to face one of the cornerstones of modern European historiography. From the early nineteenth century, the history of writing the history of Europe has developed along two complementary axes: the nation state and, necessarily, a centralizing and unifying perspective. This perspective was made necessary by the conviction that the nation state represented the highest form of historical development. Recent attempts to write the history of Europe, without always acknowledging their reliance upon the nation state's historiography, have moved very much in the same direction. In this recent tradition, Europe's history has been imagined as entailing an effort to unify, and centralize its political structures, its economies, and its cultures. Even in what, for the sake of argument, we define as the 'constructivist' tradition, there exists an assumption that those who have imagined the history of Europe have done so on the basis of such a unified, and centralized (or unifying and centralizing) perspective.

Our project moves away from this set of assumptions. It rather assumes the perspective that a patch-like landscape can be used as an organizing principle for (re)thinking the history of Europe; that different cadences of time, and a sensibility to non-linear trends, even contradictory ones, come closer to capturing the variegated and rich history of Europe, than does a narrative based on a linear, unidirectional, and centralizing set of assumptions. We like to think that our book, by virtue of the heterogeneity of the topics its sets out to cover, and by virtue of our collective determination not to distil these phenomena into one integrated and unified picture, proposes a new paradigm for studying the history of Europe.

In doing so, we at once address and take our distance from one of the major public issues of our time: Europe's current and future identity. Our project does have the ambition of adding a voice to this discussion. Yet, in our approach and our conclusions, we take our distance from what appears to be one of the dominant ideologies in Europe today. We propose that an examination of Europe's history in the pre-modern, pre-national era reveals variety rather than unity; a perduringly resilient localism alongside unifying forces such as Christianity and the law; the persistence of tradition (Christianity, magic, local customs) alongside novelty, in ideas and institutions. In short, the images of Europe that emerge from our project suggest that nothing in the 'pre-modern' (or early modern) centuries need lead to the conclusion that centralization and homogenization need be central principles of Europe's future identity.

What, then, of Europe's borders, or of its limits? To what extent does our own discussion of Europe's *discursive traditions* cast light on one of today's most hotly debated issues – subject of controversy and anxiety to citizens of the European Community as well as to those who aspire to join it? The answer will probably disappoint some readers, who may look into this book for arguments with which to support their positions for or against the European Union's possible enlargement. The answer for such readers is that the issues they wish resolved are exquisitely political, and that they require political answers. One could construct an answer for including, or for excluding, Turkey, or Romania, or Croatia from the European Union, just as comparable arguments could, in the past, have been constructed for or against Sweden's, or Greece's, or Poland's, or many other countries' membership.[24]

This book suggests that there is a basis for entertaining a broad, capacious definition of Europe. There is perhaps just as strong a case for calling for a more limited, restrictive definition. In some discourses examined in subsequent chapters, territories physically located in Europe's margins, were referred to as being well outside Europe's imagined boundaries. In other discourses, these same regions were unquestioningly treated as if they belonged to the moral universe which comprised Europe's very core. This is true no less for the lands of the Ottoman Empire (Turkey included) as of the Scandinavian regions, arguably also of Iberia. It is at this analytical level that our discussion meets the work of the 'constructionists', for the sort of Europe one aspires to promote today and in the future must be constructed by reference to elements found in the following pages. But such a construction must be the expression of a political will, and this is, perhaps, what is most strikingly absent in today's public discourse on Europe.

In short, if its non-teleological and non-celebratory perspectives colour our collective approach, an additional perspective is offered by the patch-like pattern that emerges from our enterprise. Variety, rather than unity, tensions and contradictions rather than homogeneity, change as well as resistance to it define Europe's history in the early modern centuries.

One final observation: indirectly, but no less sharply, in the course of our discussions, we faced the issue of historical periodization, which, in turn, led us once again to dwell upon the complex issue of historical time. The question was simple enough: each of the essays that follows deals with a different theme, and proposes the existence of a European *discursive tradition*, mostly in the early modern centuries. Should all these traditions be labelled 'early modern', and, if so, how should each be placed in relation to the presumed modernity that began in the eighteenth century? Were discursive traditions about 'others', or about physical phenomena, or about the law subject to the same cadences of change, as Europe made that presumably great leap into modernity? While struggling with this question, we came across a passage in Johan Huizinga's old but still wonderfully suggestive essay, 'The Problem of the Renaissance'. There, the great Dutch historian, musing on Burckhardt's view of the Renaissance, wrote that 'the image for the transition from the Middle Ages to modern times is ... not that of one revolution of a great wheel, but that of a long succession of waves rolling onto a beach, each of them breaking at a different point and a different moment. Everywhere the lines between the old and the new are different; each cultural form, each thought turns at its own time, and the transformation is never that of the whole complex of civilization'.[25] We should like to think that Huizinga's metaphor can be equally applied to our own enterprise. His reference was to a cultural movement, and ours is to a three-century long span of European history. Yet, in both instances, the metaphor helps to undermine the sense of uniform, lock step change over time, and sharpens the image of fragmentation and variety in Europe's history.

Postscript

The initial meetings on which this book is based were completed by spring 2004. The climate about Europe was positive at the time. It seemed then that citizens of the European Union's states were favourably inclined to the transformation of the Union into a stronger and more integrated organization. If anything, several participants in our meetings expressed their fear that the European Union would become too centralized, and too bureaucratic, that it would try to deprive Europe's culture of its variety and the diversity of its traditions. Whether well- or ill-founded, these fears have now receded, and have been replaced by other, perhaps contradictory ones. In June 2005, as these introductory pages were being written, the European Union seemed to have slid into a state of torpor, unable not only to sustain the process of adopting a Constitution, but even at a loss as to what budget to adopt for the coming years. Rather than fearing for the EU's excess of centralization and uncontrolled power, newspaper polls in various European countries suggest that a surprisingly high fraction of the population nurtures doubts about the Union's ability to survive even in the form it has taken in recent years.

At best, these issues are tangential to our own scholarly enterprise. Yet, it is perhaps understandable that they would suggest a set of reflections about how the themes contained in this book might add to the current, dispirited discussion about the European Union's future. What has happened in recent weeks (late spring and early summer, 2005) is that a process of institutional reinforcement has been arrested. The issues that produced this standstill are clear enough: budgets, subventions, diplomatic and military policies, the admission of new countries, a consequent generalized fear about the future. Yet, it is difficult not to recognize that, alongside these issues, deep processes that were set into motion long ago continue to function. For young people, especially, Europe is a reality in a way that it simply was not for their parents. Programmes of student exchanges have, for one, generated knowledge of Europe among millions of young Europeans, whose lives are coloured by this new knowledge. The 'Treaty of Schengen' has created conditions of travel that altogether have changed the meaning of national borders among huge numbers of travellers through Europe. Travel and study have generated new sensibilities about the environment, about work and leisure. Even in the absence of new institutions, and new treaties, Europe continues on its path, in directions that were at once imagined, and not. Europeans, drawing on old and new conventions of communicating with each other, continue to inhabit a symbolic space whose underlying unity is provided by these discursive habits.

A reading of this book should give rise to comparable views. For the synthetic image of Europe that emerges from the essays that follow is that of a fragmented unity held together by the Harlequin's dress of discursive traditions. No attention has been paid in this book to the history of diplomacy, not even (and on this point we should, justly, be criticized) to economic trends, little and then only hurried attention has been given to war, and to technology. These are subjects whose importance does not escape even this author. Another time, another workshop, another book – this could be one response to this observation. Yet, we dare to propose a different answer. For this book claims that a European public discourse, composed of fragments that were unevenly shared by societies across the European continent, did offer the basis of self-recognition among inhabitants of this continent. However patchy, and however unevenly distributed the patches might have been, the metaphor of a Harlequin's dress did provide then, as perhaps it helps to provide now, a sense of coherence to Europe. As Ernst Curtius suggested in this essay's very opening, for Europe to cease being merely a name and a geographic expression (and, one should perhaps add, a huge market), it must be rooted in a concept of history.

If not entirely mistaken, the preceding thought should help to dissipate some of the current gloom about Europe's future.

Notes

1. Quoted in French translation in Hersant and Durand-Bogaert (2000), p. 854. Note that in the English translation (Curtius, 1953, p. 6), the expression 'conception d'histoire' appears as 'historical entity in our conception'.
2. De Staël (1814).
3. Hersant and Durand-Bogaert (2000).
4. Chabod (2001); Fèbvre (1999).
5. See Verga (2004), pp. 93–6.
6. Ferro in Fèbvre (1999), pp. 16–17.
7. Book II, 1.
8. Chabod (2001), p. 8.
9. Havel (1995); Todorov (2003), pp. 87–102; Eco (2003), p. 1.
10. Duroselle (1990), p. 21.
11. Dawson (1934).
12. Halecki (1943).
13. Dunn (1992); Pagden (2002).
14. Reale (2003), p. xii.
15. Pagden (2002).
16. Nelson et al. (1992), p. 5
17. Malmborg and Strath (2002), p. 5.
18. Hay (1968), p. 116.
19. Heller (2002), p. 12.

20. A recent, eloquent antidote is Mazower (2002).
21. Ossola (2001), ix. Marc Bloch's point, made more than half a century earlier, seems not far removed from Ossola's own. Writing in 1937, Bloch reflected that 'les sociétés humaines sont douées d' une mémoire, pleine de trous, parfois, mais souvent aussi terriblement tenace … les generations se transmettent les unes aux autres des souvenirs qui s'incorporent à chaque cerveau individuel'.
22. Morin (1987), pp. 79, 129.
23. Fèbvre (1944), p. 11.
24. Pécout (2004) contains a set of very interesting ideas and approaches to the problem of Europe's frontiers.
25. Huizinga (1959), pp. 281–2.

References

Chabod, F. (2001; orig. pub. 1961), *Storia dell'idea d' Europa*, a cura di Ernesto Sestan e Armando Saitta (Bari).

Curtius, E.R. (1953), *European Literature and the Latin Middle Ages*, translated from the German by Willard R. Trask (Princeton).

Dawson, C. (1934), *The Making of Europe. An Introduction to the History of European Unity* (New York).

De Staël, G. (1814), *De L'Allemagne* (Uppsala).

Dunn, J. (ed.) (1992), *Democracy: the Unfinished Journey, 508 BC to AD 1993* (Oxford).

Duroselle, J.B. (1990), *L'Europe. Histoire de ses peuples* (Paris).

Eco, U. (2003), 'L'Europa incerta tra rinascita e decadenza', *La Repubblica*, 31 May, p. 1.

Fèbvre, L. (1944), *Autour de l'Héptameron, amour sacré amour profane* (Paris).

Fèbvre, L. (1999), *L'Europe. Genèse d'une civilisation. Cours professé au Collège de France en 1944–1945, établi, présenté et annoté par Thérèse Charmasson et Brigitte Mazon, avec la collaboration de Sarah Lüdemann*. Préface de Marc Ferro (Paris).

Halecki, O. (1943), *A History of Poland* (New York).

Havel, V. (1995), *Charta der Europäischen Identität*, Website: http://www.europa-union.de/fileadmin/files_eud/PDF

Hay, D. (1968), *Europe: The Emergence of an Idea* (Edinburgh).

Heller, A. (2002), 'Europe: an Epilogue' in Nelson, Roberts, and Veit, pp. 12–25.

Hersant, Y. and F. Durand-Bogaert (2000), *Europes. De l'Antiquité au XXe siècle. Anthologie critique et commentée* (Paris).

Huizinga, J. (1959), 'The Problem of the Renaissance', in *Men and Ideas. Essays. History, the Middle Ages, the Renaissance* (New York).

Malmborg M. and B. Stråth (eds) (2002), *The Meaning of Europe* (Oxford).

Mazower, M. (2002), *Dark Continent: Europe's Twentieth Century* (New York).

Morin, E. (1987), *Penser l'Europe* (Paris).

Nelson, B., D. Roberts and W. Veit (eds) (1992), *The Idea of Europe. Problems of National and Transnational Identity* (New York and Oxford).

Ossola, C. (2001), 'Europa, Europa …' in Carlo Ossola, a cura di, *Europa: miti di identità* (Venice).

Pagden, A. (ed.) (2002), *The Idea of Europe. From Antiquity to the European Union* (Cambridge).

Pécout, G. (2004), sous la direction de, *Penser les frontières de l'Europe du XIXe au XXIe siècle. Elargissement et union: approches historiques* (Paris).

Pius II (1984), *Commentarii rerum memorabilium,* edizione a cura di Luigi Totaro (Milan).

Reale, G. (2003), *Radici culturali e spirituali dell'Europa. Per una rinascita dell' 'uomo europeo'* (Milano).

Todorov, T. (2003), *Le nouveau désordre mondial. Réflexions d'un Européen* (Paris).

Verga, M. (2004), *Storie d' Europa. Secoli XVIII–XXI* (Rome).

Rethinking the History of Europe: Old and New Approaches[1]

Diogo Ramada Curto

Echoing Demosthenes' berating of his fellow Athenians for their complacency in face of the looming threat from Macedonia, Marc Bloch's scorching indictment of the failure of his contemporaries to rise to the occasion and rally in favour of alternatives to the growing menace of Nazism continues to resonate with us and to demand, as perhaps no other, our own response to the question of the political responsibility of historians as intellectuals and citizens.

In Europe, no less than in France, perilously verging on collapse into that 'strange defeat' Bloch sought to come to terms with, it was imperative, he felt, to denounce the dereliction of responsibility and lack of patriotism thanks to which evil triumphed because men stood indifferent or helpless on the sides. His own patriotism encompassed a defence of European civilization, both threatened equally by Nazism. Yet, Bloch did not imagine that the civic responsibility of historians could be reduced to a conception of history simply adapted to the present moment's political demands. On the contrary, Bloch was particularly wary of such reductionism.[2] Setting out the *Annales* project, Bloch had already then denounced the 'obsession with politics' in French schools' history teaching programmes. A more adequate pedagogic approach, he argued, required at once deepening the time span and broadening the social scientific context within which to frame historical understanding and explanation. Half a century has passed, and Bloch's reflections on the secondary school teaching of history still make for sobering reading. In his conception, there was no paradox or contradiction between historians' simultaneous political commitment and responsibility to the present and their warding off presentism by putting their present into historical perspective. Distance, Bloch suggested, was a lesson of history teaching.

The same principle can be said to inform this book. The current and ongoing political process of forging a European Union is no mere incidental background to the conception from which our project first emerged as a series of lectures, or to its publication as a book. Its origin lies in a summer course for high school teachers and young journalists first organized at the European University Institute in July 2002.

The association of the lectures and the book with the Institute would itself point to issues about the European nature of the project. Lectures and book both proceed from the conviction that rethinking the history of Europe demands going beyond the academic world's often overdetached and at times arcane discussions. The fact that high school teaching programs are still heavily oriented towards the construction of national memories was very much on our minds at the annual summer courses as we discussed the role of war, violence, social discrimination, and the more emotional forms of allegiance to national identities. Yet, the lively presentism of so many of our discussions led us to appreciate even more the importance of critical distance from contemporary disagreements.

To cultivate this critical distance historians have different tools at their disposal. One is offered by historiography itself – in our case, the critical examination of the rich tradition of histories of Europe. Analyzing the different ways in which the history of Europe has been written, and the contexts in which they were written, better equipped us to more critically assess our own perspectives. Henri Pirenne's and Federico Chabod's histories of Europe, analyzed in the first part of this chapter, are here chosen to illustrate this point. But if distance from merely presentist discussions of the image of Europe is indispensable, it is no less our conviction that proper historical distance can only be achieved by means of concrete historical analysis. The second part, therefore, turns to the examples offered in the chapters of this book, and reflects also upon the more general implications of putting together the scholarly 'conversations' of the fifteen historians assembled in the pages of this book.

A critical reflection on the writing of European history in the twentieth century must begin with the question of historical object and its identification. Some of the criteria represented here proceed from the choice and nature of the texts discussed and our strategies of reading them. Texts and reading strategies are in turn reflected in the corresponding choice of time frames, geographical focus, and stress accorded to the realm of ideas as against the political, economic or social dimensions. Other criteria are more contextual, emerging from the biographical trajectories of individual historians, or the institutional settings in which these histories were written. Indeed, twentieth-century historical practice is characterized by a process of academic institutionalization which defines its routines and imposes constraints on historical writing. The personal charisma of certain historians in particular moments of their lives is no less illuminating. Many of the historians who have since attained the status of heroes in our discipline were actively engaged in the struggles of the two world wars, were victims of persecution by authoritarian regimes, or suffered the experience of exile. The relationship we can discern between moments of crisis, war and violence and the general search for deeper regularities that underpin the histories of Europe is a striking feature of their work.

The Belgian historian Henri Pirenne's *Histoire de l'Europe* offers a good example. The relevant facts concerning the history of the making of the Histoire are known and easily summed up. This work was written while Pirenne was a prisoner of war in

Creuzberg between March 1917 and the Armistice (1918). The book, which only partly corresponded to the planned work which was to span a longer period, from the invasions of the Roman Empire to 1914, was published soon after Pirenne's death in 1936 by his son Jacques.[3] The war above all had dictated Pirenne's sense of urgency in writing this history of Europe; with the war's end, finishing the manuscript or publishing it ceased to be a priority for him. Though incomplete, the *Histoire* makes clear its author's intent to search for alternative ways of conceiving the period since the fall of the Roman Empire, so as to address contemporary political events. The marked anti-German stance evident from the very first page is a case in point. It can be read as the very *leitmotif* of Pirenne's thesis on the history of Europe. Its presence in the treatment of the Age of Reformation is evident, with Luther emerging as the champion of a conservative mysticism, cast here as a throwback to the Middle Ages, precisely at the moment when the Renaissance values of Erasmus, More and Rabelais were laying the groundwork for the creation of autonomous spaces leading to the development of modern individual values. Luther's theology of Justification by Grace by removing the outcome of individual fate from the individual to God allowed Pirenne to find in religion the explanation for the German proclivity to willingly submit to authority. Moreover, what really decided the success of Lutheranism was not so much a process of individual voluntary conversion, but an imposition determined by the State, through princely choice. The German Protestant states, in other words, launched the model for State Churches, thereby, here too, laying the course from which authoritarian regimes would later emerge. The return of serfdom in the sixteenth century, finally, provided an explanation for the emergence of the militarized state in Germany. A military state would always be antithetical to the values of citizenship. In religious, political, social and economic terms, therefore, German history since at least the sixteenth century appeared to foreclose the conditions required to nurture the growth and values of individualism. Nazism grew on deep roots.

Pirenne's anti-German attitude actually constituted a decisive break in an intellectual trajectory otherwise largely shaped by a German education and dependent on a large network of contacts with German historians. Pirenne's methodological agenda – especially his orientation towards an economic and social understanding of history – was heavily influenced by debates taking place in Germany, such as his friend, Karl Lamprecht's attack on the dominance of the philological and erudite approach to history, and his rejection of antiquarian perspectives in favour of a more sociological and psychological conception of history. Calling for the comparative study of collective groups it rejected a Rankian history centred on great men and politics. Werner Sombart's focus on the dynamism of social forces in the making of a modern world, and Otto Hintze's studies of the military and bureaucratic structures of the State were good examples. Writing economic and social history also sought to correct a Hegelian history oriented primarily towards the understanding of thoughts and ideas.[4] The *Histoire de l'Europe* then bears the mark of Pirenne's anti-German sentiment and threads his stance towards militarized Germany into the very fabric of his narrative of European history, while all the while drawing on a German influenced historiography. Though central and particularly instructive, this is by no means the only aspect of Pirenne's *Histoire* that is of direct relevance to our enterprise. Here, we must turn to the last complete chapter of the book.

In this chapter, Pirenne sketched a panorama of international relations between the second half of the fifteenth and the first fifty years of the sixteenth century. The rise of Catholic Spain, discussed here, with its close and orthodox relations between the Church and the State, including the Inquisition, constituted for Pirenne, another definitive moment of European experience and another reference from which we may elaborate what could be called Pirenne's counter model of European organization. Understood simultaneously as a close parallel to the militarized state in Germany and as an annihilator of nations, for Pirenne, emperor Charles V's reign represented yet another negative model. Despite his acknowledgement of the Emperor's great, nearly global authority – unparalleled since the time of the Romans – Charles V's politics were for Pirenne directly dictated by dynastic interests. From this followed the crucial distinction between him and his French rival, Francis I, as a matter, therefore, not of two opposed personalities, but of a fundamental antithesis between a supranational empire, as represented by the Habsburgs, and France, representing in Pirenne's narrative a sort of state that vested individuals and citizens with the responsibility to take charge of their national destiny. For Pirenne, the positive and progressive values of Europe lay in the emancipation of individuals, turned into responsible individuals who strove for the common good, as citizens of their nation states.

The most revealing example of Pirenne's contrasting judgments on different forms of political organization is found in his description of the Ottoman Empire. Although, through their involvement in the politics of Charles V and Francis I the Ottomans became part of what he calls the 'European community', they represent yet another authoritarian and oppressive state structure. If the Turks must be considered useful partners in the games of politics (in so far as politics could be separated from religion), they did so without sharing the values of European civilization and citizenry. The Ottomans, whom Pirenne could see only through the stereotyped paradigm of Oriental Despotism, only enslaved their population.

The Protestant States of Germany, Catholic Spain, the Habsburg Empire, and the despotic Ottoman regime thus represented a European counter culture – they collectively formed an image of what Europe must avoid becoming. Pirenne ascribed a positive valuation to the work of collective forces – the so-called 'civilizing forces', in his expression of the Church's Roman legacy – and collective values. Liberty, responsibility, intelligence and energy are the terms by which modern and civilized Europe is characterized, and the merchants of free cities were the group which best embodied and represented them. It is as well to remind ourselves that the reduction of Pirenne's historical narrative of Europe to a series of binary opposites, such as the ones here proposed, risk betraying the nature of Pirenne's authorial intent, for he rejected simple antinomies. It is nevertheless the case that the composite picture created from his articulation of the different dimensions – from the concept of State to economic and social forces, from Church and religion to new forms of thought – reveals an antinomian vision informed by and translating into a set of value judgements on the history of Europe.

Moving to a different context, Federico Chabod's *Storia dell'idea d'Europa* emerged out of lectures delivered at the University of Milan in 1943–44.[5] As with Lucien Fèbvre's *L'Europe. Genèse d'une civilisation*, based on the author's lectures at the Collège de France in the academic year 1944–45, the context of war and violence also shaped Chabod's approach.[6] In both cases we see a similar project of rescuing the notion of Europe from authoritarian appropriations. We also see how efforts to rethink the history of Europe outside the ideological values of a new order led both historians to a more explicit presentation of the methods and scholarly tools of historical research. Febvre's reference to historical psychology and Chabod's defence of the history of ideas demonstrate too that the writing of history would henceforth follow a more academic path of specialization. As with Pirenne, we can identify the disciplinary trends that inspired Chabod's historical writing. His defence of the history of ideas was heavily influenced by Meinecke and Croce, and in successive elaborations of his work, Chabod sought to justify the validity of his approach in face of what would, in the 1950s, become the more dominant approach of economic and social history.[7]

Chabod's *History of Europe* can be examined from the perspective of three particular points of his approach: the defence of an erudite and philological treatment of primary sources; a clear reference to his political motivation in writing this work; and the simultaneous need to avoid the risk of anachronistic projections of the present into the past. The latter is discussed with reference to two telling examples. Discussing Charles V and his Empire, Chabod explicitly dissociates Charles V's imperialism from any sort of European-wide project, thus distancing himself from a long historiographical tradition that glorified the emperor and his imperial mission.[8] Elsewhere, Chabod was quick to suggest that Edmund Burke's emphasis on noble and religious traditions rooted in the medieval past as features of European superiority in face of Asian despotism should be seen as a *political reaction* to the French Revolution – as a form of invention of tradition.[9] As in Pirenne, then, so too with Chabod, these examples work as counter-models of how to write the history of the idea of Europe while creating a safe and critical distance from both conservative values (Burke) and authoritarian ones (imperialism of Charles V).

Chabod's idea of Europe is unapologetically liberal. It is also firmly located in the domain of the history of ideas. The contrast between Europe and the rest of the world constitutes the main, and perhaps most controversial, part of his presentation. To tell the story, Chabod goes back to Isocrates' contrast between Greek liberty and Asian despotism and to Aristotle's positioning of Greece as a median between the extremes of Europe and Asia. The digression through classical antiquity, then, lays the foundation for the contrast between the values of European citizenship and liberty in the face of Asian serfdom and despotism, but it is only during the Age of Renaissance and Discoveries that the concept of Europe actually emerged. The discoveries – as opposed to the Renaissance and the Reformation, oriented as they were to the past – were predicated on a modern concept of time. Authors and writings inspired by the process of European expansion contributed to the construction of a sense of Europe vis-à-vis other, but contemporary, peoples and civilizations. In their more elaborate or refined expressions we find utopian and literary fictions opposing Europe to other societies, and historical works, geographical descriptions and travel accounts revealing a European perception of an 'othered' Rest – Chabod himself was particularly attentive to the critiques of Europe developed by writers inspired by and projected onto the New World, China, Japan and India.

For Chabod then, Europe's identity was in part created through this contrast with other societies and civilizations. One perspective which clearly lent itself to structuring this contrast was the tradition of European liberty versus Asian despotism. Elaborated in classical times, the topic had resonated through the works of Machiavelli, Botero, and Montesquieu. In Chabod's view, however, the question of the European perception of the rest of the world could not be reduced to this theme alone – and in this respect Chabod anticipates (and rebuts) the paradigm of Orientalism as it came to be defined by Edward Said some thirty years later.[10] Though unquestionably Eurocentric in his interpretation of the texts, Chabod's particular interest lay in exploring other dimensions of the European perception of the rest of the World. The emphasis on self-criticism developed by European writers at particular moments, as for example at the end of the sixteenth century, or during the 'crise de la conscience européenne', is one such dimension. This penchant toward self-criticism, Chabod argues, led more importantly to a *differentiation* between the spheres of knowledge and power. This is a dimension that clearly contradicts Said's thesis concerning European uses of knowledge about other societies in direct association with imperial or colonial powers. Similarly, the references, mostly in French texts from Lery and Montaigne to the Enlightenment, to life in society – ways of dressing, conversation, etc – also challenge the reductive collapsing of power and knowledge. The development of an autonomous sphere of sociability, born out of a comparison between Europe and other civilizations, created a 'factor of civility which was not dependent on politics or economics.'[11] By the same token, the view of progress – influenced by Botero's 'incivilmento' – laid the foundations for comparing different civilizations, while the attractions of an admittedly idealized Chinese civilization, led to a relativization of the importance of Europe as a model.

Besides the relations between Europe and the World, other elements in Chabod's history converge towards the creation of an image of Europe and a sense of European consciousness. For Chabod, the humanism represented by Piccolomini, Erasmus and Machiavelli, inaugurated in the cultural sphere a modern and secular view of Europe. The sense of European community – conceived as *respublica*, a space of civility and liberty – developed by these and other humanists from Italy to the Low Countries had very little to do with religion, whether in the medieval conception of *Christianity*, or that of the newly emerging religious movements oriented to a return to the original principles of the Bible.[12] Machiavelli, for instance, had nothing to say on *Christianitas*.[13] Certainly, one finds in Chabod's account a reference to a rupture with Christianity, but there is also a celebration of progress, intellectual connections, and a new consciousness of Europe. For Chabod, this emerging construction of a secular cultural sphere came to fruition with Erasmus and, then again, with Voltaire's notion of the 'république littéraire.'

Thus for Chabod, the history of the idea of Europe was a secular construction that arose out of the European Discoveries (and from the European discovery of the world); but it was also a political construction embodied in the rise of the State. In Machiavelli, Montesquieu, Voltaire and Rousseau, Chabod found exactly what he identified as the European values – individuality, liberty, republicanism, the notion of a European balance of power, and above all the emergence of national sentiment. Originally conceived (in the writings of the humanists) as national pride, it was only in the second half of the eighteenth century, and especially with Rousseau, that nationalism assumed its fuller emotive appeal. This, in turn, in the period immediately following the French Revolution, led to a crisis of that same European consciousness and unity that had been so carefully nurtured by Montesquieu and Voltaire. The Romantic response to this moment of crisis privileged a return to the peaceful religious values of medieval Christianity destroyed by the Reformation and the Enlightenment.[14] The crude and instrumental reduction of the idea of Europe to a balance of power, by conservative advocates such as Heeren and Metternich, in its turn left little room for the articulation of the ideas of nation and Europe.[15] Only by the middle of the nineteenth century, with Mazzini and Guizot, did patriotism once more come to relate sentiments towards the nation with a notion of Europeanness in the tradition of the Enlightenment.[16]

The end of the *Storia dell'idea d'Europa* was probably intended as a clarion call to Chabod's contemporaries. If the Second World War could be explained as a clash between European nations and an authoritarian understanding of Europe associated with a clear expansionist and imperial political project, it was possible to learn from Guizot's lessons and once again recover the old ideals of civic values and liberty ascribed to Europe. If Guizot could establish an intellectual basis for articulating a sense of Europe in harmony with national identities, Chabod's generation could do the same. This was the message of the Italian historian, and it helps to put in perspective one of the earliest discussions on the role of national memories in Europe.[17]

Pirenne and Chabod sought to identify the Europeanness of European history by distinguishing an inside from an outside. For the Belgian historian, political systems that did not correspond to the values of liberty and citizenship were relegated to the margins of Europe. Thus, Charles V's empire in the fifteenth and sixteenth centuries, the German territories under Luther's influence and later the Prussian Empire – as well as the Ottomans – could be branded as un-European, precisely because they were militarized societies. In this view of empire as evil, Pirenne resorted to the paradigm of Oriental despotism: it works as a counter-image, representative of what Europe is not; or better still, of what Europe should not be. Moving from great systems to the history of ideas, Chabod's greater interest in European perceptions of the world led him instead to historicize the same notion of Oriental despotism: he was able, however, to identify other discursive traditions within European perceptions of the Self and the Other – self-criticism, a step-by-step creation of an autonomous sphere of civility and the development of a comparative method in writing history.

The papers included in the first part of this book adopt a similar approach. They, too, analyze the relation between what was perceived as belonging to, and what was placed outside of Europe. However, our own context is very different from those of Pirenne and Chabod. Our past has been marked by totalitarianism, the Holocaust, and Europe's own post-colonial recognition of Empire and colonial wars, and our field transformed by the reflections of a number of powerful thinkers; one thinks, as examples, of Adorno, Arendt or Said. It is no longer possible to sustain with quite the same assurance certainties about the coherent nature of European values of liberty in opposition to those of an imagined despotic Orient. In place of simple contrasts we now have multiple, transversal complexities. The historiography of colonial societies and post-colonial literary criticism have bluntly exposed the contradictory features of European knowledge about other societies and the various forms of colonial knowledge. It is no longer possible to accept old dichotomies opposing home and abroad, metropole and colony, centre and periphery. Such thorough exposure not only poses a challenge to thinking about Europe and its colonies, but also proposes new methodological suggestions for the writing of Europe's own history.

The range of attitudes and perceptions suggested by Giulia Calvi, Stuart Clark, Giovanni Ricci, and André Stoll challenges any simple inventory. For some readers, the simple act of putting these articles together would have suggested a commitment to a fragmentary view – a deconstruction of older certainties concerning the relations between Europe and the rest of the world. This, however, is not our reading. All four articles are based on a careful and concrete analysis of primary sources: mostly texts, but also archival evidence related to people living on the margins of, or in the interstices of different European cultures. But what is clearly striking is how these authors have been able to raise a series of methodological questions based on exercises of contextualization. The particular role assigned to women and gender relations in sixteenth-century books of customs examined by Calvi, are compared, in respect to both text and image, to information contained in Giovanni Botero's *Descrizione universale* and in juridical treatises. Clark analyzes demonological treatises both by reference to their sources of inspiration, such as José de Acosta's *Historia natural y moral de las Indias*, as well as to images contained in books by Cesare Ripa or John Dee. Ricci's explicit aim of moving beyond the intellectual constructions embodied in galleries of noble texts, leads him to place ordinary people at the centre of his inquiry. He has focused on the traces of their behaviour, yet, he has also sought to compare their attitudes with those represented in prescriptions for ceremonies and other less well-known literary texts. Finally, though claiming expertise in literary analysis, Stoll is undaunted in approaching his subject through real people and their actions – including the itinerant story of Dona Beatriz de Luna, alias Gracia Nassi Mendes, the Jewish widow who journeyed from Portugal to Antwerp, Ferrara and Istanbul – before, in the second part of his chapter, discussing a variety of Spanish texts from the time of *El Quijote*. These telegraphic summaries of how the four chapters are structured provide enough examples of how these authors have combined different texts to shape their arguments. This is a simple enough point, but one much overlooked in the practice of a textual analysis that only too often tends to concentrate exclusively on a single type of discourse, forgetting that behind (or surrounding) each text there is a variegated social context, where other texts and actions play an active role.

What then may we retain from this first part of our collective effort? The fact that the starting point for any perception of otherness tends to be established by a process of analogy with the familiar is not a new argument. It has been well rehearsed by historians of the age of reconnaissance as they often doubted the ability of fifteenth and sixteenth-century observers to perceive and identify real difference. This point was also borne out by the thesis emphasizing the continuity of traditional culture throughout the early modern period. This argument was made on the basis of early printed books, a medium that largely contributed to the reproduction of older forms of knowledge, or of arguments that suggested that incredulity remained beyond the range of mental possibilities in the sixteenth century. Although they are provocative, these theses fit within a well-organized conception of European history: the age of discoveries was simply an age of reconnaissance; the new technology of printed culture turns out to be an instrument for reinforcing tradition; and the beginning of laicism and atheism may be downgraded by reference to the persistence of ecclesiastical institutions and a religious life shaped by Christianity. In short, visions of continuity and stability replaced, or at least curbed, the more celebratory view of modernity as rupture.

The papers comprising this first part seek to move us beyond simplistic contrasts between visions of rupture and continuity. The case studies and texts analyzed by Calvi, Clark, and Stoll give particular emphasis to the last quarter of the sixteenth, and the first years of the following century. The decision to narrow the focus to a single period allows the authors to recreate the pertinent context for their Italian custom books, Spanish and French treatises on demonology, and Spanish Moorophilic literature. In each case, lines of continuity with the past have been traced in order to identify models for dealing with otherness: visions of Amazons and classical mythology, Biblical literature meshed with popular culture on witches and sabbats; fears and feelings of insecurity that emerged during the period shadowed by the Black Legend. However, in each case, it is the balance of these shifting lines of continuity and break that creates an interesting tension. By the same token, it is also possible to understand Ricci's analysis of ordinary people as challenging an intellectual and top-down conception of individualism. In short, older certainties about European perceptions of the other or simply about relations between Europe and the rest, here give way to more experimental and tentative approaches. Fixed identities are displaced by more flexible notions of the self. The grand frames of Europe facing the Orient or of a European genealogy of values elaborated by intellectual history are substituted by an increasing reflexivity on case studies concerning the ways of conceiving the social fabric of meanings within what Jacques Revel has called 'le jeux des échelles'.[18]

The second part of this book, comprising seven articles, is concerned with the question of core European values, with the identification of competing discursive traditions associated with ways of conceiving – or imagining – communities. The old certainties summarized by Pirenne or Chabod recede much further before this polyphony. For those claiming that a static order existed before the great rupture created by the Enlightenment, these contrasting conceptions of communities and political societies suggest a rather different Europe. Pietro Costa places the pan-European tradition of *ius commune* (or the diverse readings of a patrimony of texts concerning Roman law, Canon law and the laws of different kingdoms) at the centre of his analysis. This was anything but a static juridical order that gave way to modern rationality. Since the twelfth century, the method or *habitus* of *ius commune* had formed a basis for interpreting social phenomena, it had provided academics an essential analytical tool, and had become an integral feature in the professional life of every magistrate. The traditional hegemony of *ius commune* was finally challenged only with the emergence in the seventeenth century of a body of natural law. The vitality of *ius commune,* however, persisted well into the nineteenth century, when constitutional regimes were established in new liberal societies.

Placing Costa's reading of Roman law aside, Janet Coleman's analysis of different conceptions of citizenship since St. Augustine, has the effect of bringing to the fore different ways of conceiving European community. In fact Coleman places at the centre of her analysis two different views of the self and the individual, his/her identification with a community, notably of believers, and his/her role *vis-à-vis* the state: in the thirteenth century, the neo-Augustinians came to believe that every individual was a potential sinner with a tendency to give in to passions; therefore, law – and above all, the law of God – needed to be imposed coercively. In contrast, since the neo-Aristotelians accepted that human beings were naturally oriented towards the common good, law in their view was a rational construct that corresponded to human expectations. The debate between these two differing views was part of Christian tradition, whose origins coincided with the end of the Roman Empire. Coleman argues that no other legacy, in the conceptual space of early modern Europe, not even the interpretations of Roman law, could compete with the impact of this theological and Christian debate. In light of this tradition, it also becomes possible to understand: (i) the dissemination of discourses on the virtues of princes, governors and citizens, which created a corpus on the basis of which the reputation of individuals was regulated according to their status; (ii) a first moment, from the thirteenth century onwards, when urban political cultures confidently modelled themselves as self-governing communities, in correspondence with the neo-Aristotelian attitude; and finally (iii) a shift towards the creation of a more coercive order, rooted in a neo-Augustinian position that, first, differentiated the elite from ordinary people in the Renaissance and led, later, to the Wars of Religion. This coercive order was expressed in civic humanism with its definition of people as an irrational multitude; in the emergence of forms of individual control and exclusion of heretics by the Inquisition; and also in the Hobbesian conception of a *Leviathan*. In this light, can the Enlightenment be understood as a return to a neo-Aristotelian perspective? This paradox is not Coleman's point. On the contrary, for her it was much more important to stress the consequences of the politics of disciplining inspired by a neo-Augustinian understanding of politics that colours our own modernity.

Starting with these two contributions, all the chapters in this part of the book contribute to break the celebratory approach to specific periods of European history. Indeed, instead of taking the Renaissance, the Scientific Revolution, the Hobbesian moment or the Enlightenment for granted as foundational moments of European identity, all seven authors opt instead for a *longue durée* perspective. They go back to the fourth century, when the Theodosian code of Roman Law was prepared, or to the sixth century when Justinian codified the *Corpus Iuris Civilis* (Coleman). They emphasize the role of the twelfth century, when the *usus modernus Pandectarum* took shape (Pietro Costa) and the commercial revolution of northern Italy occurred (Francesca Trivellato). They also consider the emergence of new languages of court society from the thirteenth and the fourteenth century onwards defining the individual (Rita Costa Gomes), or the examples of resistance to public violence by local communities in the second half of the fourteenth and the first half of the fifteenth centuries (Angela De Benedictis). The study of a network of scholars interested in botany and natural history during the sixteenth century challenges the most common view of the break in European history created by the Scientific Revolution (Florike Egmond). Finally, Robert Wokler's analysis proposes that the elite – from Britain and elsewhere – travelling in Europe and especially in Italy, opposed first, Greek and Roman ideals to the legacy of Christian fanaticism; second, 'a comparative anthropology of modern Europe's inhabitants and curiosity in the relics of Europe's achievement before the advent of Christianity' to the academic models of Oxford, Cambridge and Paris, still dependent on the interpretation of scriptures and doctrines. Therefore, the Grand Tour represented an opposition to the values of Christianity in the name of a classical legacy discovered by the Italian Renaissance and associated with the cultivation of bonnes manières – an exercise in sociability. The point, however, it is worth emphasizing, is not to develop a strategy of anticipation, where a development commonly attributed to one period is traced to an earlier age; nor, for that matter, to claim medieval origins for what was once considered modern and European. A more serious strategy of dealing with long periods of time in a non-linear perspective emerges as a common way of following continuities and ruptures through European history, thus disrupting the usual expectations of linearity and moral resonances of good or bad times.

Other traditional views are similarly challenged in the process. If these diverse views of how society, groups and individuals worked, or were represented, in early modern Europe actually hold together, it is because they share a methodology. There is a common inclination to avoid, and even to challenge, the most problematic generalizations of sociology. The simple opposition between community and society, to evoke Tönnies' celebrated juxtaposition, or between mechanic and organic solidarity, to use Durkheim's, gives way to the precision of historical analysis. Rita Costa Gomes, for instance, sets out to establish an explicit dialogue with social science models. Her reconstruction of the creation of court hierarchies stresses how the subordination of individuals to the rules and powers that controlled them did not necessarily entail the existence of a preceding community characterized by face-to-face relations and an anonymous power of the State. Francesca Trivellato challenges the same opposition between community and society, demonstrating that the creation of a cosmopolitan *republica mercatorum* did not correspond to the spread of an anonymous social rationality; on the contrary it implied the existence of often flawed, interpersonal relations. The same kind of argument is reinforced by Florike Egmond's analysis of the relation between humanists, scientists and enquiring men and women devoted to the study of botany: the creation of a really international society, she argues, is a consequence not only of personal interaction but also of gift exchanges usually associated with the tradition of small-scale communities. For her part, Angela De Benedictis explores the notion of political community, demonstrating how the values and practice of liberty shaped by forms of resistance should be ascribed to local dimensions, instead of being the result of an abstract state construction. Following her argument it would be possible to imagine a local tradition of liberalism – rooted in local communities well aware of their political interests, corresponding to a bottom-up conception of a moral economy (to use E.P. Thompson's famous notion) – and perhaps more able to influence the role of the State than to be influenced by it. In all these essays one notices a desire to challenge the sharp opposition between community and society, as well as the Weberian divisions between the modernity of the European, Protestant north, and the south characterized by an allegiance to Catholicism (Trivellato and Egmond).

The book's last section emphasizes the role of a limited number of images, predominantly visual images, in identifying European culture from the Middle Ages to the Enlightenment. The approach aims again to suggest future research and by no means intends to be exhaustive. Christiane Klapisch-Zuber analyses how the image of the tree was in constant use from the time of the Bible through the high Middle Ages, and then again from the Enlightenment to evolutionary theories of the nineteenth century. While the tree visibly embodies a way of thinking about the origins of Europe rooted in the language of the Bible, arboreal images have always been used to classify different forms of knowledge, many inspired by Cicero. Even more diffused but generic was the tree's use to make sense of family genealogies – an image of social integration equally applied to national dynasties or to state bureaucracies of the early modern period. The scope of this analysis is not only determined by the variety of fields or texts where it is possible to trace such images, but also by the careful analysis of the time dimension proposed by the author: behind the lines of continuity it is possible to identify moments of rupture such as a trend towards vegetalization of the tree around 1300, suggesting a bottom-up representation rooted in nature and breaking with ideas of a transcendent sphere. A second rupture comes with the intensification of the use of the tree in the age of print, demonstrating how the early modern period instead of breaking with the past, actually carried forward an intense reutilization of traditional imagery. It is only with the *Encyclopédie*'s criticisms of genealogical representations that doubts about the tree's function began to be heard.

There is, however, another and perhaps more important reason for considering this chapter exemplary: the careful study of the tree does not intend to suggest that we are dealing necessarily with 'a dominant figure at the heart of the dreams of our traditional societies'. With this statement, Klapisch-Zuber not only challenges other historians who claim paramount status for their individual fields of inquiry, but also suggests an implicit need to think about other important and comparable images. Her suggestion deserves attention in order to recall and integrate comparable (and contemporary) studies on images of Europe centred on the body (from anthropomorphic representations of European maps to custom books), emblem books, memory palaces, or on analogies from classical mythology to the fable of the bees.[19]

How did antique sculpture, collected and displayed, create a pattern of visual representation paradigmatically European, the seeds of an exhibitionary complex organized around the praise of Greece and Rome, their ruins and vestiges? This is the question guiding Edouard Pommier. Pommier charts how a European sense of patrimony first emerges through patterns of collecting and museum organization developed first in sixteenth-century Italy, the competition for these 'spoils' between rival cities, and their diffusion to other parts of Europe, in particular in German territories. The growth of an international art market in the seventeenth century was a natural corollary to the notions of prestige associated with the ownership of such collections that court culture had actively encouraged. But it was again in Rome in the eighteenth century that the work of antiquarians like Winckelmann met the Church's growing interest in preserving art, and firstly, of antiquity. Classical sculpture and museums of art, Pommier argues, offered a common language to Europe, and therefore, an opportunity to go beyond religious fractures and to create a lively practice of cultural tolerance.

If sculptures, particular objects from antiquity, were diffused by Rome and accepted in many parts as signs of a shared language of Europe, two other instruments also signified similar value: Latin and the Grand Tour. Latin, Françoise Waquet reminds us, was used in Catholic schools, in particular in Jesuit colleges, but also in the Lutheran world. In fact, Latin retained its vitality until the eighteenth century, not only in elite education and church ritual, but in the republic of letters and in domains of governance and diplomacy. Its substitution by vernacular languages, in an international sphere particularly by French, cannot be considered a linear process. In the case of botany, also studied by Florike Egmond in this book, the use of the vernacular in the sixteenth century as a tool of communication contrasts with Linnaeus' refusal to use 'barbarous' terms in the eighteenth. By the same token, the Grand Tour appears as one of the common features of Enlightenment classicism.

If the analysis of images and shared languages of classicism relativizes our vision of Europe, it nevertheless cannot erase the presence of Christ and Christianity. Yet, our collective approach to the various discursive traditions that create a history of Europe is in no sense an iteration of the currently popular discourse identifying Europe with Christianity. On the contrary, we have been explicitly searching for *loci* of religious relativism, exemplified by the presence of the so-called Moorophile literature of the Catholic Spain of Philip II (Stoll), the ambiguous forms used by Christians (dis)simulating their individuality as Turks (Ricci), or by the strong commercial activities of Jews linking Europe with the rest of the world (Trivellato). Even when the same languages are shaped by references to the Bible (as happens with the arboreal images studied by Klapisch-Zuber) or to Latin (used in ecclesiastical organizations and religious schools referred to by Waquet) this relativism is clearly evident. In his chapter, Denis Crouzet presents a series of case studies of S. Teresa de Avila, Inácio of Loyola, the French Catholic League, Martin Luther and Thomas Müntzer. His article, based on careful textual analysis, glosses the shift in models of sainthood in the sixteenth century: from heroic martyrdom resplendent with sacrificial blood and mutilation to the discovery of an inner space of sainthood by S. Teresa; from the image of Christ's sacrifice represented by a community of mystical body ready to perpetrate massacre in the Catholic League, to French catholic reform of the seventeenth century; or from the encouragement to violent sacrifices by Thomas Müntzer to a distance from the imagery of pain and achievement of everyday grace suggested by Luther. The shift proposed by Crouzet crosses the Protestant Reformation, the Counter-Reformation, and the different processes through which images of the Self were constructed and reconstructed in a Christian Europe. Violent fanaticism – inspired by Christ's sacrifice – appears only as a single aspect of a much more variegated reality of the Christian world.

Françoise Waquet evokes the wonderful image of Pedro, born in the Canaries, offered as a gift to the king of France, who ended up writing his autobiography in Latin. Yet, it is this image of integration, what may be considered a sign of savant culture, that in fact provides an angle of vision on a number of exclusions. A portrait of Pedro's daughter by Lavinia Fontana, for instance, shows her holding an Italian text: women were by and large excluded from the practice of Latin in early modern Europe, and therefore subordinated to a lower sphere *vis-à-vis* a hegemonic and more distinguished Latin culture. Class divisions such as this hindered the construction of the Self at every turn (see chapters by Ricci, Calvi, Coleman, Costa Gomes, and Trivellato). Yet, a sense of multiplicity of approaches and images of Europe could be once again evoked by the simple fact that though she represented Pedro's daughter as unlettered in Latin, Lavinia Fontana herself actively participated in the Bolognese circle of the Aldrovandi, whose collections of natural history remind us of other networks of scholars and another conception of museums and of displaying their objects.

This multiplication of images reinforces the claim to historical diversity and relativism for which we have been calling. This, we have proposed, is the best way of demonstrating a lively association between historical research and freedom of thought. Yet such freedom is not unfettered. In each chapter the focus on a limited variety of images or discursive traditions and the investment of a straightforward line of contextual inquiry reflect what we do believe is the strength of our profession: our capacity to understand the past, avoiding the pitfalls of anachronism, creating distance towards the construction of our object, reflecting on the effects of time, and proceeding analytically. However, the simple fact of presenting so many perspectives creates a variety of possibilities, difficult to reduce to a single unity. In other words, if concrete historical analysis provided by each chapter reveals the limits associated with any exploration of the images of Europe,[20] when we multiply these exercises it seems that we are not only multiplying the range of possibilities, we run the risk of disintegrating any claim about what really defines the most representative images of Europe. Therefore, the risk of an endless multiplicity cannot be avoided, and the only way to control it remains concrete historical analysis. Nevertheless, if we are to proclaim our freedom to pursue a relativistic view of the images of Europe we must also recognize the possibility that criticism may at once be directed to this relativism, just as it can (and should) be levelled at those apparently definitive views of European history: the Europe of the nations, the Europe of Christianity, the Europe of liberal republicanism, the Europe that sprang out of the Enlightenment.

As we survey the contributions of our fifteen authors and the resulting kaleidoscope of images and discursive traditions, what can we suggest are the main points of a constructive critique on current discussions about the history of Europe? One way to answer this question is to recall the position already suggested in this volume's introduction, which distances ourselves both from the postmodern notion that identities are largely constructed, and from Enlightenment progressivism. Neither of these notions should be allowed to stand unquestioned. As far as the second of these, the essays in the volume clearly establish that there are strong grounds for scepticism with regard to considering the eighteenth century as the necessary point of departure for the history of the concept of Europe. With regard to the constructivist position, the cumulative effect of the following chapters is indeed to reject notions of European identity fashioned entirely (or even largely) on constructivist premises. What, then, are we left with? Is this volume's contribution a bouquet of competing images whose selection is never other than random (to which one could justifiably retort that, in any case, this is not necessarily a conceptual advance of our postmodern age)? From the very start, our aim was never to arrive at an integrated, single, and comprehensive interpretation. We knew that such comprehensiveness would set us off in an illusory and ultimately frustrating search. Rather, in the spirit of Lucien Febvre's rumination 'je ne serai pas complet. Je voudrais, une fois de plus comprendre, et faire comprendre', our aim was not unity, but understanding.[21]

In these terms, the lesson of the fifteen essays that comprise this book should be sought not in what they add up to in terms of substance, but as a method for trying to understand the history of the idea of Europe, even the history of Europe, *tout court*. All of them challenge the hedgehog approach to the history of Europe. Each of them projects a reflective engagement with the challenge of writing history, which, at once, is borne out of an awareness of the historian, and the history teacher's civic responsibilities and refracts this engagement through a carefully constructed critical distance. By the same token, the localized and erudite exercises presented in each chapter, relying explicitly on concrete analysis of primary sources, also create a tension between images and discursive traditions, on the one hand, and specific and local social contexts, on the other. It is the force of this tension – reconstructing simultaneously the specificity of each image, language or discourse, and questioning its inscription in a concrete social structure, in a specific situation or in the performance of an actor – that suggests unity of method. At the risk of sliding into a more empirical and less theoretical approach, the chapters in this volume do, to borrow E.P. Thompson's ironic expression, demonstrate the 'poverty of theory'.[22] They also call into question the assumption that because structures of language presumably remain stable, social contexts themselves remain fixed and unchanged.

The book may be taken to task over its apparent lack of unity. Or for its bias for concrete analysis and its neglect of theory. Neither of these charges worries us particularly. Nor is it appropriate to impute to ourselves or our colleagues a sentiment of nostalgia for pre-Enlightenment or pre-modern times. All along, one of our overriding aims was to reject a celebratory attitude towards any period of European history. For this very reason, from the very start, we encouraged colleagues who participated in this enterprise to try out diverse scales of time, and to ponder new types of periodization. In our day, as Europe faces the grave challenges of an altogether uncharted future, we saw no need to indulge in any sort of nostalgia. But we do strongly believe that fragments of the past – in this instance comprising a set of images and discourses – may cast new and revealing light on the predicaments that we and our students – citizens and scholars that we all are – face today. It is for this reason that all seventeen authors represented in this volume collectively dedicate this book to their children, grand-children, and to our students. It is to them that Europe – past and future – belongs.

Notes

1. I thank Nicky Koniordos for assistance in the preparation of this text. Urmila Dé and Abdoolkarim Vakil helped me in formulating my ideas. The text was fully revised by Tony Molho.
2. Bloch (1946), p. 172.
3. Pirenne (1936).
4. Lyon (1974); Violante (1997).
5. Chabod (1995).
6. Fèbvre (1999).
7. Chabod (1995), p. 58.
8. Chabod (1995), p. 18.
9. Chabod (1995), p. 19.
10. Woolf (2002), p. 278.
11. Chabod (1995), p. 76.
12. Chabod (1995), p. 60.
13. Chabod (1995), p. 50.
14. Chabod (1995), pp. 127–130.
15. Chabod (1995), p. 132.

16. Chabod (1995), pp. 133, 137.
17. For a different interpretation of Chabod's work, see Verga (2004).
18. Revel (1996); Chartier (2005).
19. One of the best examples is offered by Adriano Prosperi (1993).
20. On the need to keep in mind a critical history of European images, see Pocock (1997), p. 311.
21. Fèbvre (1944).
22. Thompson (1978); Sarkar (1997), pp. 50–81.

References

Bloch, M. (1946), *L'Étrange Défaite. Témoignage écrit en 1940*, introduction by George Altman (Paris).

Chabod, F. (1995), *Storia dell'idea d'Europa* (Rome and Bari).

Chartier, R. (2005), *Inscrire et effacer. Culture écrite et littérature (XIe –XVIIIe siècle)* (Paris).

Fèbvre, L. (1944), *Autour de 'L'Heptaméron'. Amour sacré, amour profane* (Paris).

_____ . (1999), *L'Europe: Genèse d'une civilisation. Cours professé au Collège de France en 1944–1945* (Paris).

Lyon, B.D. (1974), *Henri Pirenne: a Biographical and Intellectual Study* (Ghent).

Pirenne, H. (1936), *Histoire de l'Europe des invasions au XVIe siècle* (Paris).

Pocock, J.G.A. (1997), 'Deconstructing Europe', in *The Question of Europe*, ed. by P. Gowan and P. Anderson (London, New York).

Prosperi, A. (1993), 'Europa "in forma virginia": aspetti della propaganda asburgica del '500', *Annali dell'Istituto storico italo-germanico in Trento*, vol. 19, pp. 243–75.

Revel, J. (ed.) (1996), *Jeux d'échelles. La micro-analyse à l'expérience* (Paris).

Sarkar, S. (1997), 'The Relevance of E. P. Thompson', in S. Sarkar, *Writing Social History* (New Delhi).

Thompson, E.P. (1978) *The Poverty of Theory and Other Essays* (New York).

Verga, M. (2004), *Storie d'Europa, Secoli XVIII–XXI* (Rome).

Violante, C. (1997), *Uno storico europeo tra guerra e dopoguerra, Henri Pirenne (1914–1923): per una rilettura della Histoire de l'Europe, la fine della 'grande illusione'* (Bologna).

Woolf, S. (2002), 'Reading Federico Chabod's *Storia dell'idea d'Europa* half a century later', *Journal of Modern Italian Studies*, vol. 7, no. 2.

Part I: Margins

If nothing else, it is perhaps a signal of our times that we start with a group of essays devoted not to unity and cohesion, but to margins and forms of exclusion. In our own uncertain times, migratory movements provide the single most compelling evidence of European unity and centrality. The massive migrations of the postwar decades – from the countryside of Europe's south and east to the factories of its north and west, and then from the lands of Africa and Asia to Europe – have generated overlapping discourses about Europe's identity and about its margins. Central points of these discourses are notions of European unity – what is it that defines Europe today? – and of difference – what is it that distinguishes Europe from other regions of the world, especially from regions considered to lie at its edges?

Comparable notions – of fragmentation, contrasts, dissimulation, and exclusion – emerge from this book's first group of essays. Take for example, Charles V's visit to Granada. It triggered an outburst of images about peoples who were excluded from Spanish society; most pointedly, it led to the construction in 1533 of a Roman-style palace, in sharp stylistic (but was it only stylistic?) contrast with the rest of the Alhambra. To evoke an antique Roman tradition in the construction of an imperial palace was much more than to express a preference for an architectural style. It was a way of marginalizing another style (and with it a culture and a people) that had left a deep Arabic imprint on this Iberian region. Another sort of cultural exclusion is illustrated in late sixteenth century Venetian custom books. Scandinavians and Turks were described as alien outsiders, even if in the case of the Ottoman Turks there existed another contemporary tradition that tended to integrate them in European thought as 'exotic' peoples, thus comprehensible to European authors and their audiences. By the same token, collections and representations of idols as symbols of a New World gave Europeans a sense of their own difference. Perhaps the same consciousnesses of difference that led to demonizing outsiders was also used to locate Europe's internal demons, groups that either belonged to different (enemy) confessional groups, or those who practised (or were thought to practise) witchcraft.

These fractures are probably easier to identify and analyse than it is to tease out diverse strategies of dissimulation used by groups or individuals, who, in different moments of Europe's past, either sought to survive in the midst of societies that did not welcome their heterodoxy, or who, simply enough, were trying to advance their careers and social status. At one end of our conceptual spectrum were people who, often in concealed form, maintained their diversity in the midst of an alien society. At the other end, there is the perhaps ironic case of peoples who, even in the face of persistent and militant hostility by Europeans, often insisted on their Europeanness. This was the case with some Ottoman Turks, a number of whose distinguished men of learning and high government functionaries thought of their empire as a continuation of its Byzantine antecedent, and their culture as a variation on preceding Byzantine themes.

It would be absurd to claim that the following fragments of past European discourses add up to a comprehensive, much less a cohesive, picture. What we have below is four essays, each of which, from a particular angle of vision, analyses and reflects upon the issue of Europe's margins. Nonetheless, for all the fragmentariness of this book's first section, it is possible to suggest that an attempt to rethink the history of Europe must necessarily contain (perhaps it might have to begin with) images and discourses of contrasts, exclusions, violence, dissimulation. The histories of peoples who have been marginalized and oppressed are always exceedingly difficult to capture. They are often concealed by opaque and coded discourses, fashioned over time, in historical contexts which could be limited to local and well circumscribed regions, or, on other occasions, they could extend to much wider geographic spaces and generate the interest of diverse groups of writers and thinkers.

One final, if difficult, question: How can fragments of the sort presented below be used to construct a comprehensive, and cohesive picture of Europe's past? What are the analytical and rhetorical strategies appropriate for moulding a vaster whole, a narrative, as it were, of European history, when cohesion and integration are not at the centre of one's analysis? This is a question that we do not address in this book. But we are deeply conscious of its importance and of the need to continue reflecting upon it.

Chapter 1

Crypto-identities
Disguised Turks, Christians and Jews

Giovanni Ricci

I shall consider the subject of crypto-identities not in abstract or universal terms, but rather by linking it with a specific and minor, though very complex topic: ethnic and religious disguise in early modern Europe. The point is to analyse the types and variety of disguise by taking account of the mutual relations among the three great religions of the Book, without however taking into consideration renegades, converts, Moriscos, Marranos, new Christians, etc, who were not disguised – though they may have changed clothes – and whose cases raise other well-known problems. Moreover, the disguises studied here (literally, putting on other people's clothes) will not be those tolerated at Carnival, but those illicit ones practised throughout the year. My point of observation takes us away from the world of ideas and leads us to people giving themselves up to often avid or dishonest material gestures. Yet it is possible that this quotidian aspect may, in the course of time and quite unexpectedly, have contributed to engendering a sophisticated discourse about individual identity. In that case, the resulting image of Europe would certainly have a less noble genealogy than others that have already been explored.[1] I shall, then, attempt to follow revelatory clues by tracing and giving value to relevant contexts. But before all else, the demonstrative and narrative framework must be set up.

Wartime Cunnings

Constantinople had been besieged by the Turks for four weeks. It was then decided that a Venetian brigantine would set off for the island of Negroponte to seek help. In order to do so it had to force the naval blockade, not an easy thing. Accordingly, on the night of 3 May 1453 the chain defending the Golden Horn was lowered, and, with no problem, the ship slipped out among the Turkish fleet. To that end, the strategy that was used was described by Nicolò Barbaro, a Venetian physician who saw everything, as follows: 'all the men on this brigantine were dressed in Turkish style, and the brigantine bore the ensign of the Turkish Lord, and with God's favour made a good voyage'.[2] The disguise must have been really convincing to score such a success, as well as the night very dark and the Turks rather distracted. Be that as it may, conceived and carried out, this project was within the limits of the possible. The whole history of the Mediterranean is shot through with this type of ruse, so we shall confine ourselves to selecting a few characteristic cases.

Christians disguised themselves as Turks to escape from Constantinople; elsewhere, Christians were obliged by the Turks to disguise themselves as Turks. This variant happened at Otranto on 10 September 1481. Thirteen months earlier, the fall of this town in Apulia, occupied by the Turks, had brought a wave of panic in Italy. Subsequently, the counter-attacks by the king of Naples, Ferdinand of Aragon, and the death of Mahomet II compelled the Turks to negotiate capitulation.[3] As always in these cases, it was stipulated what the vanquished would be able to take away. But the Neapolitan commander, who witnessed the parade of Turks toward the port, noted that these were 'dragging along with them women dressed in Turkish style to bring them on board, with little children (*figlioli*)'. Obviously, he had them freed, and punished the Turks by depriving them of the baggage they had been allowed. The confusion of this embarkation must have been great: otherwise, how could the Turks have hoped to get off with their forcibly disguised prisoners? This is what we are told by a late source, namely the history composed half a century later by Michele Laggetto, citizen of Otranto.[4] Yet the truth may perhaps be different. The account written immediately thereafter, in 1481, by Giovanni Albino, a man of letters at the Aragon court, gives us a glimpse: 'many girls from Puglia, who in two years had easily learned the barbarians' religion and language, were hidden on the vessels'.[5] Are we sure they were not consenting, or not fleeing in fear of being accused of collaboration? Did love or sex not perhaps also have something to do with it (the *figlioli*...) as happens whenever an enemy withdraws? The semantics of disguise are often deceitful, as much as its phenomenology is varied.

The disguises at Constantinople and Otranto were defensive. By contrast, a blow dealt by those redoubtable corsairs, the knights of Malta, was decidedly offensive. In 1601 they ventured a sally against Mahomedia (Hammamet) in Tunisia. Three hundred disguised men, with turbans, fanions and hautboys, penetrated the town; profiting from the effect of surprise, they put everything to the sack and carried off seven hundred slaves.[6] As for us, now that we have extended our scene to North Africa, we have to ask about the meaning of the expression 'disguised as a Turk' used by the sources. If at Constantinople and Otranto the false garments, in order to function, were those of Ottoman Turks, at Hammamet the clothes had to be those of the Maghreb, which were different. The fact is that to the Christian world Turk meant not an Ottoman subject in the narrow sense, but someone who belonged to 'the Mahometan sect'. In Italy that was certified by the normative dictionary of the language published by the Accademia della Crusca in 1691.[7] If all Musulmans were Turks, their clothes were Turkish, irrespective of place or time.

The official war thus intersected with the war of piracy, that little but bloody war that seethed in the Mediterranean whenever the frontal conflict died down,[8] involving individual actions, where disguise was very likely to be employed. There were camouflaged Christian boats approaching coasts on which Muslim travellers awaited embarkation, in order to capture them.[9] As for the Barbary corsairs, when they left for the course they flew a Christian standard, they charged a renegade to launch deceptive vocal signals, and masked the features of their vessels – which were often captured Christian ships.[10] The confusion of appearances reigned over the whole Mediterranean, a sea which displayed in its human landscape both unity and division, cohabitation and conflict.[11]

Trickery For All Seasons

In the context of spying actions, the range of disguises overlapped with comedy scenarios. Venice and its possessions, exposed for geopolitical reasons to contact with the Turks and regarded as centres for disseminating information,[12] offered considerable evidence of the phenomenon – sometimes of the psychosis that accompanied the phenomenon. While in 1501 an anonymous Turk dressed as an Armenian was arrested in Venice, on 1 October 1571 (one week before Lepanto) the corsair Kara Hodja disguised himself as a Greek fisherman to count the Christian galleys anchored at Igoumenitsa. When peace returned, the manoeuvres continued: in 1582 two Turks dressed as Christians were surprised in the course of poking around the arsenal in Venice, but managed to flee. The invasion of Candia in 1645 and the ensuing war saw large-scale resumption of the machinations. In 1646 at Traù in Dalmatia, two Turks dressed as Christian pilgrims were condemned; in 1649 in Istria a Turk was captured who was travelling disguised as a Greek monk; in 1658 two other Turks were expelled from Venice for entering in disguise that eternal object of desire, the arsenal, and the castles of Verona and Brescia; immediately after comes a mention of the sending to Venice of a 'cunning Turk' who spoke perfect Italian and pretended to be a merchant from a 'nation hostile to the Turks, in order to spy'. And so on, for as long as Venice and the Ottoman Empire remained rivals: as late as in 1759, some Turks pretending to be fishing were surprised making soundings in the lagoon, and moving around by night disguised as Slavs.[13] The intensity of exchanges between Occident and Orient, which no war ever managed to block,[14] supplied fertile ground for such conduct. All that ended by inspiring literature. In the epistolary novel *Turkish Spy* by the Genoese Gian Paolo Marana, first published in French in 1680 and then, over the next century, in several other languages, the protagonist is the Arab Mahmud who feigns to be a Christian abbé.[15]

One encounters such cheating disguises not just at the intersection of worlds and religions, but also within each bloc; here, the reasons were no longer political. For centuries, in the Christian world tales were told of impostors specializing in soliciting money by disguising themselves in Turkish style. The fraud is catalogued in the literature of roguery from early modern times, especially in Italy, a peninsula in the very front line against Islam; outside Italy, it is found in texts inspired by or translated from Italian. They span a period from the fifteenth to the seventeenth century, through such authors as Teseo Pini, Tommaso Garzoni, Giulio Cesare Croce. But the most analytical description can be read in the small treatise *Il vagabondo* by Rafaele Frianoro, published in 1621 and very soon translated into various languages. Here, then, is an appearance of these vagabonds in a village in old Italy (old Europe): 'when they arrive in a town or a castle they go to the middle of the squares, make a terrible noise with a sling, and when they have gathered enough people together begin to shout Allah, allah, allah, hebher, elhemdu, lillahi, la illah, illelach and other words in an unintelligible language, displaying chains that they say had long bound them ... at the hands of the infidel Turks, enemies of Christ'.[16] Before continuing, one linguistic observation is in order. The words used by the actors are perhaps 'unintelligible', but not invented, given that they are modelled on the Muslim profession of faith to a single god: 'Lâ ilâha illâ'llâh'. A truly imaginative way of fooling low people: speaking Turkish in order to pretend to be a victim of the Turks. Nevertheless, a suspicion arises. Were these false Turks all real Christians? Are we able to exclude that some real Turks (by origin or converts) might have passed as escapees from the Turks in order to earn their living? The game of mirrors knows no end.

Faced with these texts, it is hard to distinguish literary invention from social document. Judicial sources would seem to confirm the reality of the phenomenon, unless they too are victims of cultural stereotypes. This is certainly the case with the interrogation of a young beggar, recorded on 4 February 1595 in a Rome jail. Among the 'various secret companies' of beggars in the town were 'those bearing around their necks great chains of iron, speaking Turkish Bran Bran Bran Bre Bre Bre and asking for alms, saying they had escaped from the hands of the Turk'.[17] To be sure, here the problem of linguistic credibility does not arise. Ignoring the disappearance of the original manuscript, a police document like this is perplexing, since it is too rich and expressive: to the point of evoking the analogy of witches' confessions, which undoubtedly cannot be regarded as proof of the reality of the Sabbath.[18] It is a fact that collecting alms to ransom slaves aroused sympathy, but the events described could not be checked. We can, then, understand how fraud and trickery of all types flourished: false ransoms, false chains and false whips, invented or semi-invented words in Arabic. The forms of begging (and of madness)[19] underwent the influence of this dissemination of the languages of concealed appearance.

Playing (Sometimes) With Fire

Far from the village squares, princely courts also delighted in Turkish disguises. Take, for example, a farce that took place near the mouth of the Po in 1584; a contemporary Ferrarese man of letters, Annibale Romei, recounts it. Fifty or so ladies and gentlemen had gathered in the castle of Mesola. One morning they all boarded a 'sumptuous bark' and sailed 'delightedly upon the very calm sea'. All of a sudden 'two artillery shots were heard, a sign that two corsair hulls had been sighted; and at that very instant a boat full of fishermen arrived at full speed, fleeing to the port before being discovered by the corsairs'. Amid the terror of the excursionists, one gentleman organized a counter-attack, until the corsairs were brought to land 'in chains'. Then everything became clear. Under the Turkish garments were hidden some of the Duke of Ferrara, Alfonso II d'Este's 'principal knights'. The pretended corsair vessels belonged to the coastguard, and the Duke had personally thought up the farce.

Here again, in a different blend, we find Turkish disguises, followed immediately by the disguises of slaves. One noble lady pretended she wished revenge. 'Having looked at the prisoners, full of disdain and ill humour, she ordered them to be put to service ... and with their chains on their feet they served, thus dressed in their vile garments'.[20] Under the formalization of courtly behaviour, the farce stuck entirely to the dynamics of corsair incursions. None of these noble victims dreamed of doubting the false information, particularly because there had been a worrying precedent. A century earlier, at the time of the capture of Otranto, the Ferrara ambassador to Naples announced that the Turkish fleet 'was able to enter the Po'.[21] It never happened, but the strategic value of the permeable Po delta was obvious to all.

Alfonso d'Este's passion for Turkish themes derived from the traditional links between the Ferrara court and Burgundy. There, since the fifteenth century, chivalrous ideas and the myth of the crusades cohabited with Turkish fashions in tournaments and in literature.[22] In 1558 in Florence, Alfonso had indulged his passion when celebrating his wedding with Lucrezia de' Medici. One day a masquerade of Moorish women dressed in damask and veiled according to the Arab custom displayed themselves for the young couple. Then two teams of knights armed in Turkish fashion fought each other.[23] But the 1584 joke was much bigger; additionally, it fitted one of the duke's other passions for athletic, competitive and 'masculine' activities.[24] But we know that laughter and farce (for us, disguise) are among the most serious things in existence: they are precious instruments revealing deep and otherwise inaccessible strata. Let us say, then, that only the sovereign could permit himself to push the frontier of the comic so far as to make repressed material surface: namely that the 'Turks', real or false, might be everywhere and anywhere. A chronicler writes that in 1576, 'someone dressed in Turkish fashion' arrived in Ferrara and 'was widely believed to have been sent by the Grand Duke of Tuscany to trick Duke Alfonso'. In fact, after the death of Lucrezia in 1561, the relationship between the two courts had deeply deteriorated. Declaring himself to be a Sultan's ambassador, he offered Alfonso the crown of 'king of Jerusalem'. He was received with great ceremony and only accurate investigation in Constantinople made it possible to unmask him. After being arrested and questioned, he succeeded in running away, and 'what he had confessed was never divulged'.[25]

Purifying Oneself With Clothes

The return among Christians of a ransomed slave reminded everyone graphically of the danger. On such occasions complex ceremonies were staged. Often the ransomed presented themselves disguised as Turks or slaves, and were subjected to rites of undressing and redressing. They thus abandoned their Turkish clothes to resume their 'Christian' ones, proper to their rank and geographic origin, at religious functions, civil festivals or military parades.[26] The spectacular publicity makes one immediately think of an adaptation of a knightly dubbing or monastic vestiture;

thus, the public change of status reveals a first level of meaning. But apart from that, the hypothesis is that the point was to restore identities that had undergone involuntary contamination in the course of the stay among the infidel. Expurgated in principle of Christian theology, impurity was at work without being identified as such; the absence of formal apostasy called for surreptitious reconciliation.[27] The disguises, by serving as signals of social reintegration, once again revealed their seriousness and meaningfulness.

Throughout Catholic Europe, particularly in the Franco-Iberian area, festivals of this type had long been held. At Lisbon in 1559, 200 slaves paraded through the town raising up on sticks the little brown rolls on which they had for years been fed. In 1635 in Marseilles, 42 slaves freed by the Trinitarians paraded in chains and then repeated the procession in the towns they crossed until reaching Paris. In 1653 other ransomed slaves paraded at Leghorn and Pisa, displaying a chain on their shoulder; and in 1765 91 were seen in Venice. Sometimes the irons gave way to mere allusions, like silk cords or little golden chains; this softened version was presented at Marseilles in the seventeenth century, while at Bologna in 1722 plaster collars were seen. In Rome the people en masse watched the pious masquerades, thus gaining the indulgence granted by Sixtus V in 1585.[28] On occasions requiring special emotional investment, the spectacular aspect was magnified. After Lepanto, Don John of Austria accompanied to Loreto thousands of freed Christian oarsmen, who offered their chains to the Virgin.[29] Elsewhere it was typically theatrical models that were employed. In 1667 at Douai in Artois, a cart in the form of a galley paraded loaded with ransomed slaves dressed as prisoners, all this being done to honour an exceptional spectator, Louis XIV.[30]

But when the Enlightenment age arrived, attitudes to disguises and chains changed. High-level ransomed slaves kept away from public display, even though the ransom contracts specified their obligatory presence. At Lucca in 1783, one ransomed slave scandalously refused the ceremony of return. The custom was coming to an end, which in France happened in 1785. The organizers were accused of staging the spectacle: beards and hair were left uncombed to give a more wretched appearance; a false Arab burnous was worn, or chains were carried that had perhaps never been borne by the slave.[31]

As to the provenance of these Turkish garments, they were probably new, manufactured for the occasion, even if we know almost nothing about their provenance (or that of the chains). Indeed, it would be hard for the originals to have survived the health measures, which were very strict in the Italian ports of Venice, Ancona and Leghorn.[32] Yet, in Bologna, some things become clear in connection with a slave freed in 1683, a certain Giovanni Maria Ghiselli. Despite payment of a ransom, he was handed over naked to the Venetian ambassador in Istanbul. In fact his owner had been obliged to free him following political pressure, but was not pleased. In consequence, 'angry at having to leave him, he took away even his shirt' and 'although begged to' did not even wish to 'give him his irons'. Despite this attack on the future return ceremony, later in Bologna Ghiselli displayed 'the signs of his captivity'.[33] In the church of San Gerolamo della Certosa one can still see the chains associated with him; these are clearly false chains, since they cannot be the ones he had worn in Istanbul. Nor does one need the competence of a smith to assume that the chains hanging up there are not authentic, since they all have the same shape and the same weight irrespective of origin and date, from the Barbary Coast to Istanbul, from the mid seventeenth till the late eighteenth century.

The Disguises of Giuseppe Rovere

One intrigue complicated by disguise surrounds the history of a 20 year-old young man who became a slave of the Turks in 1767. This is a classical case worthy of further analysis, since it opens up a window onto more general questions. He was called Giuseppe Rovere, and his story is told by those who freed him, namely the officers of the Ferrara brotherhood for the ransom of slaves. This brings us back to the town whose signore had been Alfonso d'Este, the organizer of the fake corsair attack. It was not a frontline town in the clash of civilizations. The fact that the theme of disguise re-emerges here shows how far the Turkish obsession marked not just the lands and seas exposed to contact, but also more sheltered, inland places.[34] As regards the source, we cannot trust its informative value too much, since it is shot through with narrative clichés and ethnic and religious stereotypes: the Turks are violent, false and lascivious,[35] the renegades are tempters, and Islam is a deviant Christian sect. Be that as it may, here is the story.

'Rich in many miseries', Giuseppe wandered from town to town looking for opportunities to survive: in short, he was a representative of that floating population against which the authorities used to thunder. One day on the shore near Ancona he saw landing 'a fine Tartan he thought was Christian'. Unemployed and naive, with five companions like himself, he visited the vessel, which however proved to be Turkish. The captain immediately sailed off and sold those unfortunates as slaves in Albania, at Dulcigno (Ulcinij). From there Giuseppe ended up in Tunis and began a curriculum of hard labour, blows, and sexual and religious abuse, until his liberation three years later. The 'triumphal entry' to Ferrara took place on 17 April 1770, in the traditional Turkish disguise of the ransomed.[36]

But his story does not end there. The circumstances of his capture did not convince everyone: how could one mistake a Turkish ship for a Christian one? The gossip did not please his liberators, who had bet on the spectacular return of the young man; they accordingly moved to counter-attack. The opportunity came with the ransom of the next slave. Alongside the new freedman, who, also, wore 'barbarous clothing', Giuseppe, 'ransomed five years earlier', was made to parade a second time. He was shown 'dressed in his Barbary garment, which he had himself conserved so as to refute the calumnies of the crowd who were accusing him of being a rogue fleeing or escaped from justice'; on the contrary, he was now devoting himself 'to the hard labour suited to his condition'.[37] That is what the plebs suspected: it was not thoughtlessness that had made the young man board a Turkish ship, but the desire to escape that drove many under pursuit to flee; perhaps the Turkish ship did not even exist and the young man had quite simply fled. Then things had turned bad, and for some reason or other he had become a slave, but that was another story.

To stop these rumours, recourse was had to renewed display of the Turkish garments, which can have been false and in no way disputed what was suspected. The proof is not convincing to us, but what about to contemporaries? Unfortunately, we know nothing else about the gossip regarding Giuseppe. It is possible that the young man really fell into a trap. The tartan he had boarded was a single-masted coastal trampship,[38] which could easily have been camouflaged. But it is a fact that the early modern Mediterranean was criss-crossed by a great traffic in clothing belonging to the enemy: authentic garments and false garments, garments for war and garments for feast. A meeting with people disguised as Turks or as Christians was quite within the bounds of possibility.

Jews or the Cultural Exception

And what about people disguised as Jews? In fact only a few of the elements just considered apply to Jews, a minority without a territorial base or military support. In this case the disguises are one-directional: Jews disguise themselves as something else, but there is no advantage to disguising oneself as a Jew. Absent by definition from the military confrontation, Jews were widely used in the game of espionage. The reasons (familiarity with languages, widespread family and commercial links, vulnerability to blackmail) are also recognized by undoubtedly non-anti-Semitic historians;[39] ideological constructions around the subject are quite another matter, not worth wasting time over. During the months preceding Lepanto, on 2 June 1571, a Portuguese Jew who had turned Turk and was dressed as a Christian pilgrim was arrested in Venice:[40] in short, a Turk rather than a Jew. But cases of real Jews disguised as something else seem to be missing from the rich dossier of Venetian espionage. Despite the possible utility of such disguise, it might well be that *commettants politiques* had difficulty in breaking the recognition taboos that anti-Jewish legislation imposed.

On the other hand, in the literature on roguery the Jewish theme is parallel to the Muslim one: only in this context was passing as a Jew – or in fact as an ex-Jew - advantageous. For the sake of symmetry, let us take up the *Vagabondo* by Rafaele Frianoro: 'A few pretend to have once been rich Jewish usurers, and relate how they were aroused by dreadful visions to leave their goods and to follow poverty ... In all the towns where they have themselves been baptized again, they go once again asking alms from the true believers'.[41] As was the case for the false ransomed slaves, the interrogation of a Roman beggar in 1595 might seem to confirm the reality of the phenomenon (the conditional is obligatory): 'those passing through villages and pretending to be Jews who have turned Christian say they have come to the holy faith with their families, and receive great alms'.[42] But perhaps more convincing are the false bulls of indulgence discovered by the Holy Office in Udine in 1558 in the names of individuals claiming to be converted Jews.[43] Additionally, one has to cite a few legal texts in which it is hard to assess the degree of dependency on current stereotypes. In the mid seventeenth century Antonio Maria Cospi, secretary to Ferdinand II of Tuscany, had no doubt of the existence of false converts. 'If they pretend to be baptized Jews the corpus delicti will be immediate, namely if there is circumcision. And for women, if they can give an account of the Mosaic Law and the Hebrew language. They are to be found at the exits of churches, and often have themselves recommended from the pulpit'. The method for unmasking the women is not very certain, but at least one does what one can. A little later Marc'Antonio Savelli, auditor in the Florence criminal court, confirmed that certain rascals liked to 'pretend to be Lutherans, Calvinists or Jews who had come to the Faith' and go begging 'particularly in the countryside, making simple people believe all sorts of things, to extract money from them'.[44] Defending simple people is a recurrent theme in these learned writings.

The obligatory badge of recognition and infamy opens up a new, entirely Jewish front. We shall not here take up the question of the origins of the stigma, its form and its function. We know that in general a pointed hat was required north of the Alps, an O on the clothing or conspicuous earrings in Italy, while the preferred colour was yellow.[45] All this from our viewpoint technically represents a variant of disguise; in other words, Jews were obliged to disguise themselves according to a visual model developed by the majority and reinforced by substantial iconography.[46] Immediately, exceptions appeared for travellers or privileged professional groups. By comparison with an official and artificial model of Jewish appearance, these exceptions may be interpreted as legal 'return' disguises. Thus, when Hercules I d'Este renewed the requirement for the badge in 1496, he exempted, following payment, the bankers, while in Rome, Bologna and Venice it was particularly doctors who enjoyed this dispensation.[47] Alongside the legal exceptions, abuses and swindles developed: all of them illegal disguises by comparison with the constraint of legal disguise.

The fluctuation of constraints, prohibitions and exemptions ended up deceiving even those who had to execute the orders. On 18 April 1559 the Venetian Council of Ten revoked the exemption from the yellow hat traditionally given by the rectors of Padua to Jewish students; though undoubtedly a coincidence, those were precisely the days of the peace of Cateau-Cambrésis, that is of the Spanish victory in Italy. The rectors hesitated to apply the order, fearing the flight of all the Jewish students, but the Ten brusquely confirmed their wish. Thereupon the rectors, inflamed, displayed zeal and arrested certain Jewish students travelling with black hats. But they were once again mistaken and were given a reprimand, since in this case there was a dispensation, which had been awarded by none other than the Ten.[48] One cannot without consequences liberate the forces of refusal and repulsion; meddling with forced disguise unleashes mechanisms dangerous to all. In fact the theme of Jewish disguises persisted dramatically: imposition of the yellow star, by the Nazis, attempts to flee the deadly identification ... The spasmodic desire to fix identity with outside signs perpetuated the dynamics of disguise even when these had become exhausted elsewhere.

Mimicry and Social Pressures

Three examples only, going backwards in time and rather haphazardly, can show other variants of the phenomenon of putting on others' garments. The Tabarka affair is well known. A small island off the Tunisian coast governed by the Genoese, Tabarka was for centuries a sort of neutral point between Christianity and Islam. In 1741 the Bey of Tunis occupied it, reducing to slavery 800 people. Their tragedy aroused great emotion, but solution took long to come, and it was not until 1768 that a collective ransom for the survivors was paid.[49] In the account of a monk born in Tabarka, Stefano Vallacca, we can read an illuminating episode. During captivity, one day a mother saw her daughter Sinforosa [Pretty] 'dressed in Turkish style'. Then she shouted 'Ah! My daughter, you are a Turk'[50] after which she fainted and died. Yet the signal was false, since the girl had not apostatized, indifferent to the love of 'Mahemed, an attractive, very white young Turk' – and thus at the apex of the colour hierarchy. But the mother thought she had understood everything from the clothing; she had read it not as a mere functional necessity but as a declaration of belonging.

The same was true (without romantic or apologetic mediation) when in 1694 the Venetian army occupied Chios, and 300 Latin Christian women were found dressed in Turkish style. Subjected to religious verification, they were recognized not to have apostatized; they had merely adapted themselves to the local atmosphere and to the inevitable marriages, often in agreement with their Jesuit confessors, who had authorized them to act 'Nicodemically'. A furious anti-Jesuit dispute accompanied this affair.[51]

And let us go back to medieval Spain, where considerable importance was allotted to the question of the Mozarabs of Toledo. These were Arabic-speaking Christians, who, for ancient social or cultural reasons, were dressed as Moors. After the reconquista their troubling presence was tolerated for some time – until the obsession with *limpieza de sangre* brought their extinction in the fourteenth century.[52] It would seem that none of the cases cited, Tabarka, Chios or Toledo, can be confused with the phenomenon of apostasy, even though they have in common the manipulation of clothing.

From Crypto-identities to Interior Identities

In our varied material, disguises, though bound up with fundamental religious themes, do not imply inward transformation: it is either instrumental, or imposed, or even forced. Our main interlocutors are the civil or military authorities, not theologians or inquisitors. But why were disguises so widespread? Let us first consider that we become aware of them only if they are revealed. The infinite numbers of successful cases remain protected by the silence of the sources. It has to be said that in the centuries covered by our study, disguise was particularly favoured by a remarkable exteriorization of identities, expressed through the distinctive force of personal attributes. Indeed clothing, equipment, and customs of human groups differing in origin, legal status, religion or occupation were differentiated, and typified in the same geografical space. Official discourse appreciated this transparency, this full legibility, in societies meant to be immobile and controllable in their formalized inequality. The literature on the *Habitus mundi* seemed to supply an excellent tool with a view to establishing a rigid taxonomy, within which hairstyles and dress attracted much more attention than strictly morphological features.[53] (This priority was particularly justified if related to the anthropological reality of the Ottoman Empire, where a mosaic of peoples and a multitude of renegades lived; the charming whiteness of the young Mahemed in love with Sinforosa is noticed around 1770, which is precisely the beginning of another age, the age of physical racism.)

In principle, all this made recognition easy, but at the same time facilitated deceit in the event of low visibility, or surprise, or lack of information: the apparent evidence of perception was de facto translated into potential ambiguity; official expectations favoured falsifications that ended up by denying the expectation itself. This is more or less the case with the sumptuary laws promulgated by European cities between the Middle Ages and early modern times; created to fix everyone's appearance within their social and legal station, they gave rise to usurpation of the signs of belonging.[54] It was also the case for the outside privileges given the shame faced or hidden poor, privileges bound to produce a picaresque sample of simulations of dissimulation.[55] The history of make-up and of the theatre would certainly have something to add in all these realms. Yet there were forces operating in the opposite direction to disguises and obstructed them: curiosity towards strangers; the absence before the bourgeois age of the notion of anonymity and privacy; the impossibility of passing unseen in a non-'globalized' and barely urbanized world, which kept all its particularities. The reasons for the success of disguise were also those for its frequent failure.

Here we come to the central point. In early modern Europe we see the progressive affirmation of individual, internal, immaterial identities, independent of collective judgement, not necessarily in harmony with the values of the surrounding milieu.[56] Machiavelli was already speaking of Europe as the space of numerous personal 'virtues'.[57] These virtues were the fruit of a polycentric political organization that differed from the oriental despotisms that Montesquieu was to conceptualize in depth.[58] Although it is sometimes reduced to stereotype and has to be reconsidered from decentralized standpoints,[59] individualism, with all the nuances that accompany this concept, remains a strong component of the European identity. Thus, if we shift to the language of historical anthropology, modern Europe moved from a 'shame culture' to a 'guilt culture',[60] without having reached – here it is sociology that is talking – our own 'liquid modernity', where identities become light, fluid and multiple.[61] It is very likely that initially the immersion of this identity into the ego was limited to restricted intellectual or moral elites; indeed, today such liquid identity is reserved to the fortunate inhabitants of the First World, whereas the wretched of the Earth are prisoners of unambiguous, stigmatizing identities. In the centuries at the centre of our attention, most people continued to assess their neighbours on the basis of a visually stereotyped culture, in turn coming from elementary corporeal and vestimentary symbolism.[62] But the automatic recognition of identity, of which disguise was both cause and consequence, produced a paradoxical secondary effect, namely the widespread diffusion of a sense of insecurity. Additionally, in all fields of theology, politics and social description, there developed an outright obsession with simulation.[63]

My argument seeks to be indicative rather than probative, as the standards of proof required of the judge and the historian notoriously differ.[64] Even so, in the worst cases, the obsession with simulation degenerated into an aberrant discursive tradition of a universal conspiracy, which is the transposition of an individual paranoid pathology to the collective level: a plot organized by Jews and/or Muslims, in tandem with lepers, heretics, witches and all sorts of plague spreaders, all of them being mistrusted and persecuted human groups.[65] It may be that the climate of insecurity contributed to introducing among wider circles the salutary suspicion that human reality cannot be reduced only to its visible exterior. Without any doubt, the construction of modern individual identity rests on 'high' historical processes such as the breaking of religious unity, the secularization of societies, and the separation of ethics from law. In conclusion, however, I wonder if one ought not also to take into consideration another, 'lower' phenomenon: the abuse of the practice of disguise, that ultimately led to mistrust of over-easy and immediate criteria of identification. The implicit revolt against the excesses associated with exteriorization finally reveals that all identity is only a product of invention, a fact of revocable decision. Here, then, the celebratory teleology of individualism is replaced by a fine example of heterogenesis of ends. This outcome does not frighten the historian, accustomed to meeting many apparent paradoxes: to give only one, the notion of tolerance, born in light of the practical impossibility of exterminating those of a different religion.[66]

In short, if we come back to our case, we seem to pass from crypto-identities in the literal sense of 'hidden' (thus invented and rather dishonest) to 'crypto'-identities, in the literal sense too of invisible (thus private, and often sincere) ones.

Translated by Iain L. Fraser

Notes

1. Ossola (2001); Pagden (2002).
2. Pertusi (1976), pp. 20–21.
3. Babinger (1953), pp. 430–5; Schwoebel (1967), pp. 131–4.
4. Antonaci (1955), p. 118; Moro (1986), pp. 106–22.
5. Gualdo Rosa (1982), pp. 86–7.
6. Boulenger (1933), pp. 28–9.
7. *Vocabolario degli Accademici della Crusca* (1691), p. 1736.
8. Sallmann (2003), pp. 68–97.
9. Braudel (1976), p. 201.
10. Sebag (1989), p. 111.
11. Molho (2003).
12. Infelise (2002), pp. 3–35.
13. Preto (1994), pp. 98–108; Preto (2003), p. 126.
14. Brotton (2002).
15. Roscioni (1992).
16. In P. Camporesi (1973), pp. 115–6, 163.
17. Camporesi (1973), p. 352.

18. Ginzburg (1984), p. 7.
19. Prosperi (2000), p. 54.
20. Solerti (1891), pp. 35–7; Ceccarelli, (1998), pp. 139–41.
21. Foucard (1881), p. 81 (1 July 1480).
22. Schwoebel (1967), pp. 82–115.
23. Lazzari (1952), p. 42 and p. 44.
24. Papalas (2002), pp. 315–21; de Bondt (2002).
25. Rodi (n.d.), cc. 705r–706r.
26. Davis (2003), pp. 179–87.
27. Ricci (2002), pp. 140–2, 148–9 and 157–92.
28. Dan (1649), p. 60, 199 and 224; Lovarini (1931), pp. 172–3; Bono (1964), pp. 283–309 and 470–4; Buonafalce (2000), pp. 141–3.
29. Scaraffia (1999), pp. 25–6; Moroni (2000), pp. 24–6 and 30–1.
30. Deslandres (1903), p. 400.
31. Deslandres (1903), pp. 395–6; Lenci (1994), pp. 45–8.
32. Cipolla (1992), pp. 67–75.
33. *Nel riscatto di Gio. Maria Ghiselli bolognese fatto in Costantinopoli* (1683), p. 14.
34. Ricci (2002), pp. 7–17.
35. Wheatcroft (1995), pp. 208–30; Merle (2003), pp. 168–77.
36. Badia (1770).
37. Cittadella (1775), p. XIII.
38. Marzari (1998), p. 32.
39. Roth (1933), p. 210; a particular case: Tollet (1998).
40. Preto (1994), p. 103 and pp. 481–5.
41. Camporesi (1973), pp. 140–1, 358.
42. Del Col (1998), pp. CVII–CVIII and p. CCXII.
43. Camporesi (1973), pp.2. 44–5, 140–1, 358, 367, 402–3.
44. Owen Hughes (1986); Sansy (1992).
45. Blumenkranz (1966).
46. Toaff (1989), pp. 214–9 and 333; Muzzarelli (1999a), pp. 287–98.
47. Del Col (1998), p. CLXII.
48. Bitossi (1990), pp. 167–88.
49. Bitossi (1997), pp. 271–2.
50. Preto (1975), pp. 189–90.
51. Hernández (1995).
52. Merle (2003), pp. 146–8.
53. Calvi (2002).
54. Ricci (1998), pp. 109–36.
55. Prodi and Reinhard (2002). There is an admirable bibliography in Prodi and Marchetti (2001), pp. 179–319.
56. Chabod (1965), pp. 48–52.
57. Carile (1995), pp. 29–32; Woolf (2000), p. 61.
58. Herzfeld (2002).
59. Peristiany (1965); Fiume (1989). The distinction between shame culture and guilt culture (due to Dodds, 1951) is discussed in Egmond and Mason, (1997) pp. 39–40 and 59–65.
60. Bauman (2000); Bauman (2003), pp. 55–86.
61. *Le vêtement. Histoire, archéologie et symbolique vestimentaires au Moyen Âge* (1989).

62. Villari (1987), pp. 3–48. Many case studies in *Fälschungen im Mittelalter* (1988); Zarri (1991).
63. Ginzburg (1991), pp. 109–11; Ginzburg (1999), pp. 13–49. See also Conconi (2000), pp. 38–54.
64. Preto (1987), pp. 5–76; Ginzburg (1989), pp. 5–61.
65. Remotti (1996), pp. 3–10.
66. Prosperi (1986).

References

Antonaci, A. (1955), *Otranto. Testi e monumenti* (Galatina).

Babinger, F. (1953), *Mehmed der Eroberer und seine Zeit. Weltenstürmer einer Zeitenwende* (München).

Badia, G. (1770), *Istorico discorso ... per la redenzione di Giuseppe Rovere già schiavo in Tunesi* (Ferrara).

Bauman, Z. (2000), *Liquid Modernity* (Cambridge).

_____. (2003), *Intervista sull'identità*, by B. Vecchi (Rome and Bari).

Bitossi, C. (1990), *Il governo dei Magnifici. Patriziato e politica a Genova fra Cinque e Seicento* (Genova).

_____. (1997), 'Per una storia dell'insediamento genovese di Tabarca. Fonti inedite (1540–1770)', in *Atti della Società ligure di Storia patria*.

Blumenkranz, B. (1966), *Le Juif médiéval au miroir de l'art chrétien* (Paris).

Bondt, C. de (2002), 'The Court of the Estes, Cradle of the Game of Tennis', *Schifanoia*, 22/23, 81–102.

Bono, S. (1964), *I corsari barbareschi* (Turin).

Boulenger, J. (1933), *Les aventures du capitan Alonso de Contreras (1582–1633)* (Paris).

Braudel, F. (1976), *La Méditerranée et le monde méditerranéen à l'époque de Philippe II* (Paris).

Brotton, J. (2002), *The Renaissance Bazaar. From the Silk Road to Michelangelo* (Oxford).

Buonafalce, I. (2000), 'I Trinitari a Livorno: la forza dell'esempio, l'impatto delle immagini', *Nuovi studi livornesi*, VIII, pp. 141–8.

Calvi, G. (2002), 'Abito, genere, cittadinanza nella Toscana moderna (secc. XVI–XVII)', *Quaderni storici*, 110, 477–503.

Camporesi, P. (ed.) (1973), *Il libro dei vagabondi* (Turin).

Carile, P. (1995), Introduction to Montesquieu, *Lettres persanes* (Paris).

Ceccarelli, F. (1998), *La città di Alcina. Architettura e politica alle foci del Po nel tardo Cinquecento* (Bologna).

Chabod, F. (1965), *Storia dell'idea d'Europa* (Bari).

Cipolla, C.M. (1992), *Il burocrate e il marinaio. La 'sanità' toscana e le tribolazioni degli inglesi a Livorno nel XVII secolo* (Bologna).

Cittadella, C. (1775), *Discorso ... in occasione del solenne incontro fatto al già schiavo in Algeri Luigi Fioretti* (Ferrara).

Conconi, B. (2000), *Le prove del testimone. Scrivere di storia, fare letteratura nella seconda metà del Cinquecento: l'Histoire mémorable di Jean de Léry* (Bologna).

Dan, P. (1649), *Histoire de Barbarie et de ses corsaires* (Paris).

Davis, R.C. (2003), *Christian Slaves, Muslim Masters. White Slavery in the Mediterranean, the Barbary Coast, and Italy, 1500–1800* (Basingstoke and New York).

Del Col, A. (1998), *L'Inquisizione nel patriarcato e diocesi di Aquileia, 1557–1559* (Trieste).

Deslandres, P. (1903), *L'ordre des Trinitaires pour le rachat des captifs* (Toulouse and Paris).

Dodds, E.R. (1951), *The Greeks and the Irrational* (Berkley).

Egmond, F. and P. Mason (1997), *The Mammoth and the Mouse. Microhistory and Morphology* (Baltimore and London).

Fälschungen im Mittelalter: Internationaler Kongress der Monumenta Gemaniae Historica, München, 16–19 September 1986 (1988) (Hannover).

Fiume, G.(ed.) (1989), *Onore e storia nelle società mediterranee* (Palermo).

Foucarde, C. (1881), 'Fonti di storia napoletana nell'Archivio di Stato in Modena', in *Archivio storico per le province napoletane*, VI.

Ginzburg, C. (1984), *Prefazione* in R. Chartier, *Figure della furfanteria. Marginalità e cultura popolare in Francia tra Cinque e Seicento*, tr. it. (Rome).

_____ . (1989), *Storia notturna. Una decifrazione del sabba* (Torino).

_____ . (1991), *Il giudice e lo storico. Considerazioni in margine al processo Sofri* (Torino).

_____ . (1999), *Rapporti di forza. Storia, retorica, prova* (Milano).

Gualdo Rosa, L., I. Nuovo and D. Defilippis, (eds) (1982), *Gli umanisti e la guerra otrantina. Testi dei secoli XV e XVI* (Bari).

Hernandez, F.J. (1995), 'Language and Cultural Identity: the Mozarabs of Toledo', in A. García y García, P. Weimar, *Miscellanea Domenico Maffei dicata. Historia-Ius-Studium*, pp. 71–90.

Herzfeld, M. (2002), 'The European Self: Rethinking an Attitude', in A. Pagden, *The Idea of Europe. From Antiquity to the European Union* (Cambridge and Washington), pp. 138–70.

Infelise, M. (2002), *Prima dei giornali. Alle origini della pubblica informazione* (Rome and Bari).

Lazzari, A. (1952), *Le ultime tre duchesse di Ferrara* (Rovigo).

Lenci, M. (1994), *Lucchesi nel Maghreb. Storie di schiavi, mercanti e missionari* (Lucca).

Le vêtement. Histoire, archéologie et symbolique vestimentaires au Moyen Âge (1989) (Paris).

Lovarini, E. (ed.) (1931), *La schiavitù del generale Marsigli sotto i tartari e i turchi da lui stesso narrata* (Bologna).

Marzari, M. (1998), 'Galere, fuste, galeazze, sciabecchi: le navi dei corsari', in S. Anselmi (ed.), *Pirati e corsari in Adriatico* (Milan), pp. 23–35.

Merle, A. (2003), *Le miroir ottoman. Une image politique des hommes dans la littérature géographique espagnole et française (XVIe–XVIIe siècles)* (Paris).

Molho, A. (2003), 'Il Mediterraneo', in M. Tangheroni, (ed.), *Pisa e il Mediterraneo. Uomini, merci, idee dagli Etruschi ai Medici* (Milan), pp. 273–79.

Moro, D. (1986), 'La tradizione storiografico-documentaria otrantina nel corso del '500', in C.D. Fonseca (ed.), *Otranto 1480*, II (Galatina).

Moroni, M. (2000), *L'economia di un grande santuario europeo. La Santa Casa di Loreto tra basso Medioevo e Novecento* (Milan).

Muzzarelli, M.G. (1999a), *Guardaroba medievale. Vesti e società dal XIII al XVI secolo* (Bologna).

Nel riscatto di Gio. Maria Ghiselli bolognese fatto in Constantinopoli (1683), (Bologna).

Ossola, C. (ed.) (2001), *Europa: miti di identità* (Venice).

Owen Hughes, D. (1986), 'Distinguishing Signs. Ear-Rings, Jews and Franciscan Rhetoric in Italian Renaissance City', *Past and Present*, 112, 32–59.

Pagden, A. (ed.) (2002), *The Idea of Europe. From Antiquity to the European Union* (Cambridge and .Washington)

Papalas, A.J. (2002), 'The "Trattato del giuoco della palla di messer Antonio Scaino da Salò" and Ferrarese cultural Ideology in the Time of Alfonso II ', in P. Castelli (ed.), *Francesco Patrizi filosofo platonico nel crepuscolo del Rinascimento* (Florence), pp. 315–21.

Peristiany, J.C. (1965), *Honour and Shame. The Values of Mediterranean Society* (London).

Pertusi, A. (ed.) (1976), *La caduta di Costantinopoli. Le testimonianze dei contemporanei* (Milan).

Preto, P. (1975), *Venezia e i turchi* (Florence).

_____ . (1987), *Epidemia, paura e politica nell'Italia moderna* (Rome and Bari).

_____ . (1994), *I servizi segreti di Venezia* (Milan).

_____ . (2003), *Persona per hora secreta. Accusa e delazione nella Repubblica di Venezia* (Milan).

Prodi, P. and V. Marchetti (eds.) (2001), *Problemi di identità tra Medioevo ed Età Moderna* (Bologna).

Prodi, P. and W. Reinhard (eds.) (2002) *Identità collettive tra Medioevo ed Età Moderna* (Bologna).

Prosperi, A. (1986), 'Il grano e la zizzania: l'eresia nella cittadella cristiana', in P.C. Bori, *L'intolleranza: uguali e diversi nella storia* (Bologna), pp. 51–86.

_____ . (2000), 'Parrocchie tridentine e schiavi da riscattare. Schede di ricerca', in *Nuovi studi livornesi*, VIII, pp. 45–68.

Remotti, F. (1996), *Contro l'identità* (Rome and Bari).

Ricci, G. (1998), *Povertà, vergogna, superbia. I declassati fra Medioevo e Età moderna* (Bologna).

_____ . (2002), *Ossessione turca. In una retrovia cristiana dell'Europa moderna* (Bologna).

Rodi, F. (n.d.), *Annali di Ferrara*, Biblioteca Comunale Ariostea of Ferrara, MS I 645.

Roscioni, G.C. (1992), *Sulle trace dell'Esploratore turco* (Milan).

Roth, C. (1933), *Gli Ebrei in Venezia* (Rome).

Sallmann, J.-M. (2003), *Géopolitique du XVIe siècle, 1490–1618* (Paris).

Sansy, D. (1992), 'Chapeau juif ou chapeau pointu? Esquisse d'un signe d'infamie', in G. Blaschitz, H. Hundsbichler and G. Jaritz (eds), *Symbole des Alltags, Alltag der Symbole* (Graz), pp. 349–75.

Scaraffia, L. (1999), *Loreto* (Bologna).

Scchwoebel, R. (1967), *The Shadow of the Crescent: The Renaissance Image of the Turk, 1453–1517* (Nieuwkoop).

Sebag, P. (1989), *Tunis au XVIIIe siècle. Une cité barbaresque au temps de la course* (Paris).

Solerti, A. (1891), *Ferrara e la corte estense nella seconda metà del secolo decimosesto. I 'Discorsi' di Annibale Romei* (Città di Castello).

Toaff, A. (1989), *Il vino e la carne. Una comunità ebraica nel medioevo* (Bologna).

Tollet, D. (1998), 'Les Juifs furent-ils, dans la Confédération polono-lituanienne, les agents des Turcs?', in G. Motta, *I Turchi il Mediterraneo e l'Europa* (Milan), pp. 152–68.

Villari, R. (1987), *Elogio della dissimulazione* (Rome and Bari).

Vocabolario degli Accademici della Crusca (1691) (Florence).

Wheatcroft, A. (1995), *The Ottomans. Dissolving Images* (Harmondsworth).

Woolf, S. (2000), 'Knowledge of others and self-perceptions of European identity', in *Historein. A Review of the Past and Other Stories*, 2, pp. 55–64.

Zarri, G. (ed.) (1991), *Finzione e santità tra Medioevo ed Età moderna* (Turin).

Chapter 2

Segregation, Migration and Recuperation of the Orient in Mediterranean Europe during the First Modernity
The Case of Semitic Spain

André Stoll

For María Soledad Carrasco Urgoiti

In the Europe of the First Modernity, who were the prototypical foreigners, migrants, marginalized? What path was threaded by these paradigmatic Others through the invading discourses of political, religious, media and other powers during this era of major territorial, scientific and anthropological discovery? And what space was reserved for them in the imaginary museum of models of collective identification by their 'sympathizers', these historians, writers and thinkers, these inventors of alternatives, still obliged to function within the realm of these very same powers?

Let us suggest some brief answers by focusing on the area of cultural discourses produced by the Spanish monarchy, foremost among European, indeed among world powers during its imperial expansion in the sixteenth century. The fact that this Spain was ruled by laws reflecting an absolutist policy of repression of alterities, lived under the omnipresent Inquisition, and was flooded by religious propaganda embodied in baroque affective imagery suggests a first hypothesis.[1] The rejected, the migrants, the marginalized peoples of the time were the descendants of the Iberian peninsula's 'interior orientals'. Because of their centuries-old civilization of diversity, after the fall of Granada, they were condemned to embody in the story of the Spanish monarchy's foundation the concept of an Evil to be either extirpated or assimilated.

This first hypothesis, however, implies another one, which far transcends its geographical and historical dimensions. On the European level the Hispanic community's 'interior orientality' is of course unique, because of its long duration (as much as eight centuries) and because of the more or less peaceful coexistence of three ethnic groups, cultures and religions. But this uniqueness will also be revealed, paradoxically, by the sort of relations maintained by Christian Spain during the time of the imperial monarchy with the descendants of those very same interior orientals. These relations include dimensions of rejection, of fascination and of usurpation that have also determined the attitude of the other European societies throughout their history towards the Orient.

Cultural Transcendence of the Iberian Orient

The existential space of what we have here defined as the Spanish society's internal orient spreads over two fields of very unequal historical extension and discursive importance. The first coincides with the time of political and civilizing domination of the Arabs (Moors) over more or less extensive territories in the Iberian Peninsula (al-Andalus). Historically, it starts with the Arab invasion of the Visigoth Empire in 711 and ends on 2 January 1492 with the triumphal entrance of the Catholic Monarchs Ferdinand and Isabella in Granada, capital of the last of the Moorish kingdoms to fall before the onslaught of the Reconquest. The second – on which we intend to focus – covers the increasingly more violent and efficient efforts of the imperial monarchy to obliterate the religious and cultural heritage of the descendants of that interior orient whose political existence it had just annihilated. The first of these acts of severance was the royal decree of 31 March 1492, which ordered the expulsion of all Spanish Jews unwilling to accept baptism within three months, thus launching the most massive and dramatic exodus of Jewish people in modern history before the Final Solution. The final stage of this procedure of eliminating the 'internal orient' occured in 1609, when an ordinance of Philip III unleashed the definitive and equally monstrous expulsion of all Moriscos, the last of whom left their Iberian homeland a few years later, in 1613.

This Spanish interior orient is Semitic in the original meaning of the term:[2] Jewish (Sephardic) as well as Islamic (Moorish) in the cultural area of al-Andalus, Judeoconvert and Morisco in 'post-Granada'[3] Spain. The civilization that the Arabs introduced and spread in Iberian territories was characterized generally by a remarkable intercultural transcendence. Within this climate of cooperation, their Oriental cousins the Sephardim even enjoyed particular rights and privileges that put them above the Christian common people of al-Andalus (the Mozarabs). Additionally, Moors and Sephardim are conjoined in the same negative area within the genetic concept of Hispano-Christian identity, which inspired the Reconquest knights, as well as the 'post-Granada' propagandists of casticism.[4] Contrary to the tenets of this concept of identity (which also contributes to give legitimacy to the imperial monarchy), the origins of the internal orient go back to long before the very arrival of Christianity and the Visigoth kings' assumption of power in the Iberian

Peninsula. According to their foundation myths, some Jewish communities traced their origins to the diaspora that followed the destruction of the First Jerusalem Temple (587 BC), and others to those descendents of Semitic tribes who, following the destruction of their Second Temple by the Roman general Titus in AD 70, had found refuge in far-away Iberia, where they had met such favourable living conditions that Sepharad,[5] the ancient biblical name for Spain, eventually became for them synonymous with 'Promised Land'.

The Arabs who, a few years after invading through Gibraltar in 711, extended their domination, and especially that imposed in Cordoba by the Umayyad 'Abd al-Rahman I in 756, over nearly the whole of the Iberian peninsula enjoyed from the start the Sephardim's active cooperation. To avenge the harassment and persecutions suffered under their Visigoth tyrants, they willingly extended their liberators' unconditional support in all military, administrative and urban initiatives destined to lay the foundations of a modern multi-ethnic state. In the time of the Cordoban Caliph 'Abd al-Rahman III (912–961), Jewish culture was thus able to achieve its highest flowering in medieval Europe, along with that of the Arab rulers. However, this golden age of Jewish culture was brutally interrupted during the twelfth century by the arrival of the Almoravides and Almohades and the ensuing change it caused as far as the Arab masters' attitude towards the non-Muslim populations, who were henceforth subjected indiscriminately to forced conversion campaigns, waves of persecutions, and massacres. The fate of the great philosopher Maimonides (born in Cordoba in 1135) is a typical example of the ill treatment that the Sephardim suffered at the hands of the Almohades. He managed to escape the anti-Semitic persecutions by fleeing first to Palestine and then to Egypt. His correspondence from exile is full of lamentations about the humiliating treatment of his compatriots at the hands of the Arab authorities. They illustrate the highly conflictual climate that had spread in contemporary al-Andalus where, towards the end of the twelfth century, no synagogue or church remained active. On the other hand, the Christian knights who, starting from the Cantabrian mountains had managed to push the Reconquest as far as Andalusia (fall of Cordoba: 1236; of Seville: 1246) generally felt powerfully drawn to the cultural achievements and artistic refinement of the Muslims whom they had subjected (to wit the *mudéjar* style of architecture)… which did not prevent them from continuing, to the sound of their war-cry 'Santiago!', their military and religious struggle against the domination of the 'Infidels' over the remainder of al-Andalus territory.[6]

Even though perturbed by periods of ethnic and economic conflict, the cohabitation of three monotheistic ethnic groups and religions led to the formation of combinatory ways of life and cultures which, in their intriguing polyphony, were to remain unique in the whole of medieval Europe. In this context two literary works among the most important to be produced by this model bilingual (and sometimes trilingual) intercultural 'laboratory' are Ibn Hazm of Cordoba's 1022 *The Dove's Necklace* (*Tauq al-hamama*), a nostalgic initiation to the Umayyad' court's precepts of oriental courtship, and the autobiographical *Libro de Buen Amor* (circa 1340) of Juan Ruiz, the Archpriest of Hita, in which the refined eroticism of Arab poetry coincides with fervent litanies to the glory of the Virgin Mary and the satirical imagination of popular story-tellers with the verbal alchemy of the cabbalistic tradition.

The benefits to be drawn from this cultural crossbreeding for the Europe of the future is clearly illustrated by the famous Toledo 'Academy of the Interpreters' founded and encouraged in the thirteenth century by the philosopher-king Alphonse X. It gathered together Arab, Jewish and Christian scholars for the grandiose purpose of translating into vernacular languages the acquisitions of Oriental sciences, medicine and philosophy. It also intended to transmit the knowledge and wisdom of ancient Greek philosophy (particularly Aristotle and Plato) to Western thinkers who, until then, had only vague notions about it.[7] During the interminable *Guerra fronteriza* (Frontier War) of the fourteenth and fifteenth centuries for the Reconquest of what remained of al-Andalus, frequent skirmishes opposed the Castilian knights to the alcaides of the Arab forts along a meandering front north of Malaga. That in no way prevented the people on both sides from meeting and celebrating their aspirations to common life and loves. The poetic treasure of the *romances fronterizos* and the charming sequence of 'Moorophile' tales, which, in the second half of the sixteenth century, contain lessons of conviviality, aimed at the people in power, bear witness to this fact.

Another example of extraordinary trans-cultural creativity contrasting with the growing anti-Semitic mob fanaticism is the famous *Alba Bible*, which the Grand Master of the Chivalric Order of Calatrava, Don Luis de Guzman enjoined rabbi Moses of Arragel to compose, in the hope that, thanks to the translation into Castilian of the original Hebrew, the reconciliation of the Christian and rabbinic exegeses be facilitated. Thus was born one of the most marvellous and original examples of the art of manuscript illumination in Europe.[8]

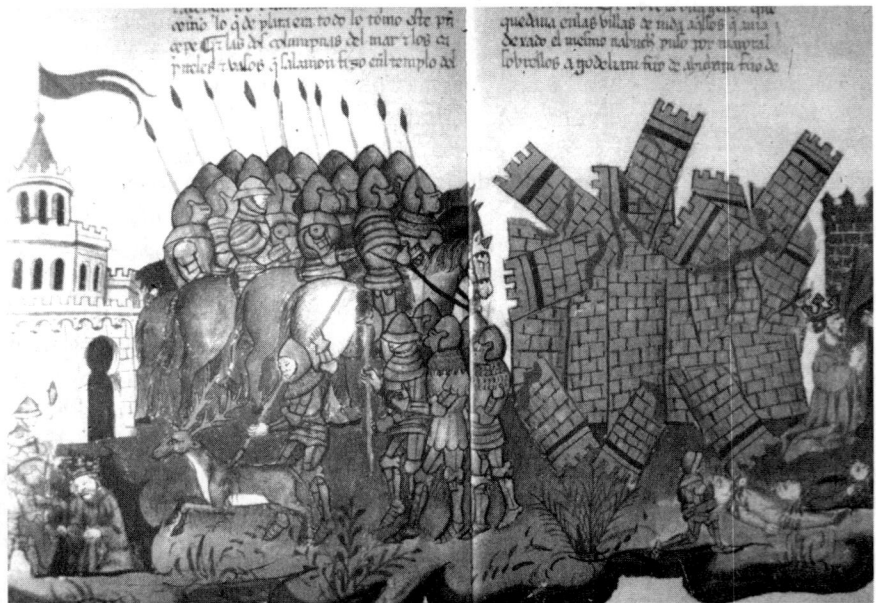

Figure 2.1 'The Fall of Jerusalem'. *Biblia de Alba* (1430). (*FMR*, Edition française, n. 38, June 1992). © Franco Maria Ricci, 1998.

The results of linguistic crossbreeding are just as diversified. Thus, even more than the Bible, the sermons of the rabbis in the synagogues, the Haggadah narrative, the Rosh Hashana and a good number of other Jewish prayers were uttered almost exclusively in Castilian. However, for the publication of these prayers, the Castilian of the Judeo-Spaniards is usually transcribed in Hebraic letters and composed right to left.[9]

Despite these various projects which had great cultural importance, the pattern of relations between the Christian populations and their Sephardic compatriots had begun to deteriorate from the fourteenth century. Collective acts of violence were committed, sporadically at first but with increasing regularity almost everywhere in the 're-conquered' areas against the *aljamías* of the Jewish folk, who were envied the allegedly excessive privileges accorded them by the royal financial administration. Pogroms fuelled, at least since the events in Saragossa in 1250, by rumours concerning ritual murders attributed to the Jewish communities in conjunction with the Pessah celebrations, first occurred in Seville in 1391. They soon spread to the whole region and led, one century later, to the famous trial of a group of Sephardim burned at the stake after being accused of having murdered the Santo Niño de la Guardia.[10] The same climate saw the promulgation of the dreadful 1380 decree of the Toledo Cortes ordering the Jewish communities to gather in neighbourhoods separate from the rest of the cities. Not satisfied with the creation of these ghettos, the ecclesiastical authorities of Seville went one step further in their anti-Jewish zeal by ordering the

Figure 2.2 'We were Slaves of the Egyptian Pharaoh'. *The Haggadah of Barcelona*, foglio 30 *verso*. (*FMR*, Mensile di Franco Maria Ricci, n. 32, April 1985). © Franco Maria Ricci, 1998.

Figure 2.3 'These are the Matzot of Affliction'. *The Haggadah of Barcelona* (Middle of the Fourteenth Century), foglio 28 verso. (*FMR*, Mensile di Franco Maria Ricci, n. 32, April 1985). © Franco Maria Ricci, 1998.

expulsion of all Sephardim from the territory of the Andalusian capital's archbishopric and charging the Inquisition with purely and simply appropriating the whole of their belongings.[11] Even though municipalities with important Jewish commerce and trade activity, such as Jerez de la Frontera, Teruel or Valencia managed for a time to prevent the Inquisition's tribunal from entering their jurisdiction, their opposition was not sufficient to spare their compatriots the fate which would befall a few years later all the Spaniards who remained loyal to the Mosaic law.[12]

The Tearing: Expulsion and Migration

The victorious completion in 1492 of the last stage of the military Reconquest by the Catholic Monarchs Ferdinand and Isabella put a definitive end (which could be foreseen for some time) to the century-long coexistence between Muslim, Jewish and Christian Spaniards. At the same time, the 'legitimate' basis was laid for the progressive erasure from the future generations' collective memory of the civilizing advantages acquired during that long period of shared power in the Peninsula. In fact, the fall of the capital city of the last bastion of Moorish civilization on Iberian lands signalled nothing less than the start of a progressive step-by-step ideological denigration of the Moors and Sephardim, those 'internal orientals' with the doubtful if not fatal status of new Christians, which could probably never fully achieve the honourable condition of those who had been born *cristiano viejo* (old Christian).[13]

However, the Muslim inhabitants of al-Andalus' last Arab kingdom were not the first to bear the consequences of the Catholic monarchy's triumph over what remained of the body politic of Semitic Spain. By the peace accords which specified the conditions of the peaceful surrender of Granada, reached at the end of 1491 in Santa Fe between the victorious monarchs and the Moorish king Boabdil 'el Chico', they were guaranteed the right of residence and the safeguard of their religious, cultural and linguistic traditions such as the Arab tongue and books composed in it, as well as their specific ancestral attire and hygiene (especially bathing). This peace treaty is thus an unheard-of model of modernity, of harmonious inter- and pluri-cultural cohabitation in Europe. To be sure, family members of king Boabdil 'el Chico' took advantage of the right of emigration granted by the Santa Fe accords, and a significant number of the Nasride regime's senior government officials immediately went into exile, first for a short time in the Alpujarras, then to Morocco and the neighbouring North African countries under Ottoman rule. But the political elite's choice did not entail a massive wave of emigration on the part of Grenadine Moslems. Only ten years later, following the unilateral revocation of the Santa Fe guarantees by the monarchy, intensive onslaughts were unleashed against their cultural and religious identity (collective baptisms, evangelization campaigns, confiscation of their books in Arabic, etc.) and spread with increasing violence all throughout the sixteenth century,[14] culminating in their complete expulsion during the first years of the next.

In fact, the first victims of the draconian repressive measures were the kingdom of Granada's Jewish citizens. A royal ordinance of 31 March 1492 forced them either to accept baptism within three months after the promulgation of the decree (at the end of April) or to be expelled from Spain and have their belongings confiscated. In the face of this fatal dilemma, numerous Sephardim faithful to Mosaic law sadly opted to tear themselves away from their ancestral life and prosperity rather than betray their deepest convictions in exchange for a fractured, borrowed identity, forever exposed to inquisitorial and racist prosecution.[15] They were obliged to sell their movable goods and real estate properties for nominal sums and forbidden to bring out anything but letters of credit, which would only enrich foreign bankers. So that the refugees (or rather those among them who did not lose their lives during the perilous trek through the Iberian homeland or during the sea crossing) landed totally destitute in their new country, steeped with their families in poverty and despair by the cupidity of ecclesiastical Inquisitors and civil prosecutors.[16]

Despite the disastrous conditions under which they had been expelled, the refugees themselves or their descendants shortly succeeded in transmitting their courageous entrepreneurial dynamism to the citizens of their new homelands. They thus contributed significantly to the economic and commercial prosperity of those realms that would shortly emerge as dangerous rivals to the Spanish monarchy on international markets. A wave of immigrants from Portugal, a country who tolerated them for a few years, until the Inquisition arrived and set up shop, stretched along the maritime ports of Western Europe (Bordeaux, Rouen, Antwerp, Amsterdam, Hamburg, etc.). Numerous Sephardim found refuge in such prosperous Italian cities as Leghorn, Pisa, Venice, Naples, Ferrara and mostly in the capital of Christendom. But by far the greatest number of émigrés ended up in the large cities of the vast Ottoman Empire and of its North African political and religious dependencies. Istanbul and Salonika thus became the most populous and culturally flourishing urban entities of the Spanish Oriental diaspora, where it only ceased to prosper when destroyed by the Nazi occupants of Greece in 1941.[17]

Wherever these refugees settled, they soon distinguished themselves by their dynamism and the effectiveness of their many economic, financial and cultural activities. After the decline of Antwerp, Amsterdam won at the beginning of the seventeenth century the honorific title of 'Jerusalem of the North'; its important 'Portuguese' community (as all bilingual Jews of Iberian origins who had transited through Portugal were known) not only played a preponderant role in the trade with the Indies, but through academies and discussion groups, fervently fostered the linguistic, literary and intellectual traditions inherited from the distant homeland from beyond the Pyrenees.[18] To have found refuge in one of the tolerant large cities of Europe did not automatically entail for those outcasts from Spain the end of their itinerant life. On the contrary, it sometimes marked the start of new wanderings, as illustrated by one of the most impressive feminine personalities of sixteenth century Europe, the 'Portuguese' Doña Beatriz de Luna, alias Gracia Nassi Mendes. In Antwerp, the first longer stop of her exile (1536), this widow of an important and powerful merchant in the colonial trade, Francisco Mendes, had succeeded, by the middle of the sixteenth century, in directing the most powerful banking dynasty in Europe, which controlled the whole of the spice trade with the East and West Indies. But as the climate of repression became more and more insufferable for the newly converted Christians in the Flemish capital, Doña Gracia was forced to flee, first to Venice (until 1550) and finally to transfer the administration of her commercial empire to Ferrara, under the aegis of the Dukes of Este, at that time (in 1530–1570) devoted patrons of the liberal arts and letters. There, for several years, she was the brilliant muse of an elite circle of philosophers, artists and men of letters. At the same time, she was promoting the publication, by the firm of Abraham Usque, of trilingual editions of the Bible and the translation into vernaculars of such Hebrew liturgical texts as the Haggadah and one of the best known works of Jewish vernacular literature, *Consolaçam ás Tribulaçoes de Israel*. Faced, however, with a worsening political climate, which favoured an anti-Semitism until then unknown in Ferrara, Doña Gracia fled once more and this time left Christian Europe forever and, having changed her Christian name Beatriz de Luna into Doña Gracia Nassi, settled for the rest of her life in the capital of the Ottoman Empire, Istanbul. There she and her

Figure 2.4 'Flogging a Spanish Female Criminal', *Das Trachtenbuch des Christoph Weiditz von seinen Reisen nach Spanien (1529) und den Niederlanden (1531/32).* (Berlin und Leipzig: Walter de Gruyter & Co., 1927), Plates 44 and 45.

family managed once more to win the favour of the Sultan and to place themselves high in the state hierarchy as an important financial, political and intellectual power. She died in Istanbul (very probably around 1569), without having seen the Jewish city of Tiberias, recently revitalized with the support of her own family.[19]

Oppressed Cultural Crossbreeding

The humiliations and prosecutions imposed by the Inquisition upon the converted Jews who had remained in their ancestral fatherland (*judeoconversos* or simply *conversos*) are generally well known and do not need to be detailed here. Let us simply recall the stifling climate of ubiquitous surveillance exercised by the Inquisition agents – pleasantly called familiars in Spanish – on the everyday life of these new Christians (*cristianos nuevos*). The Inquisition was on the lookout for the slightest deviation from the habitual outward expression of their old Christian (*cristianos viejos*) compatriots' religious faith. For a converso to be arraigned, it was sufficient to be suspected of having attended clandestine Hebrew rites in one of the miserable backyard synagogues which seem to have survived for a time to serve the small number of crypto-Jews who had escaped being burned at the stake or, grotesquely, simply to dislike pork meat, to fry with olive oil rather than with lard or to avoid conducting business on a Saturday. The penalties incurred by the conversos for such 'crimes' against the Catholic faith ranged from the donkey-back 'ride of shame' inflicted on a culprit wearing the *sanbenito* (rough flax sack cloth bearing satanic symbols) and the *coroza* (pointed cowl) and escorted by some henchmen (alguaciles) who flogged them, to execution at the stake as the apotheosis of a spectacular auto-da-fé. At any rate, the simple fact of being brought before an Inquisition tribunal was sufficient to bring about the automatic confiscation of the accused's possessions and the dishonour of all the members of his family, including the descendants, in other words destitution and *condemnatio memoriae* which also affected his children's and grandchildren's generation.[20] Among the repressive measures inflicted upon the Spanish conversos one is generally less known and yet one of the most pernicious, because of its ties with Inquisition justice: the racist 'blood purity statutes' (*estatutos de pureza de sangre*) that the monarchic authorities established in order to prevent the descendents of the Sephardim from accessing 'honourable' professional positions in the service of the State, the Church or the Army. These 'social hygiene' statutes were enforced even before 1492 against the Jews of Castile; starting in the 1520s, they began to be systematically applied throughout the country, excluding from public positions all applicants unable to prove three generations of 'old Christian' descent. That effectively excluded all Judeoconverts, unless the venality of the judges entrusted with verifying the authenticity of the genealogic documents submitted proved stronger than their anti-Semitism (which seems to have been frequent, judging from the important place of the *letrados*'s corruption in contemporary satire).[21] The true sociological impact of these repressive measures can only be fully understood in the light of their function as an efficient juridical and administrative vehicle of the casticist discourse of mono-cultural absolutism's propagandizers. That, more than any other of the governing power's ideological constructs, proved responsible for the division of contemporary Spanish society into two allegedly antagonistic fractions: that of the 'good' and noble Christians of ancient stock (*cristianos viejos*) and that of the *cristianos nuevos*, genetically devoid of honour and suspected of anti-patriotic subversive actions.

The difficulties facing Granada's Moriscos after the Catholic Monarchs' unilateral breach of the Santa Fe peace accords constitute a 'dramatic construct' on the part of the civil authorities, which differs from the Inquisitorial harassment that their Judeoconvert compatriots were subjected to in their everyday life.[22] If Arabic speakers still partially enjoyed, under emperor Charles V, the privilege of leading the kind of life to which they had been used for centuries, it is thanks to important sums of money that their spokesmen paid the civil authorities as bribes in exchange for these officially abolished rights.

Yet the general quality of their social and cultural life kept worsening year by year. The most spectacular signal sent by the victorious monarchy towards whatever bore witness to the grandeur of the past Arabic civilization was Charles V's decision to erect, within the walls of the residential capital of Granada's Moorish kings, a classical palace of monumental dimensions which was to 'correspond to the grandeur of his heroic soul'[23] and overshadow, by its majesty, all comparable edifices of the European Renaissance. The Emperor's purpose was obvious: the size of this palace and its architectural and iconographic references to the grandeur of its ancient roman model, Rome's Pantheon ('La Rotonda'), were designed to replace the paradigm of the high yet decadent Arab European civilization, symbolized henceforth by the filigreed architecture of the Alhambra's exotic Moorish palaces. In fact, this long unfinished imposing 'Casa Real Nueva' was never, despite the Emperor's intentions, to be converted into the centre of the new Hispanic Empire's capital: that distinction would be achieved by the Escorial monastery palace built by Philip II after the victory of Saint-Quentin to be the arcanum of the known civilized world.[24]

Faced with the draconian restrictions that young Philip II imposed, as soon as he ascended his father's throne, on the life and culture of Grenadine Moriscos, some of their intellectuals had recourse to a curious cultural crossbreeding: the clandestine circulation among their brethrens of 'aljamiado' manuscripts composed in Spanish and transcribed in Arabic script. An example recently discovered and highlighted by modern scholarship is the manuscript of the Mancebo de Arévalo's *la Tafçira*: its chapter entitled 'La Kaída del Andaluzziyya' proves the complete familiarity of the author with the three languages and traditions: the Arabic, the Hebrew and the Castilian. Its content is all the more revealing of the spirit of solidarity which reigned among the different marginalized groups that it identifies the suffering of the Sephardim and converts as that of a 'Nuevo Israel', and associate it with the destiny of the Jews since Egyptian exile, the repeated destruction of their temple and its ensuing dispersion through the world.[25]

Facing such harmonization efforts, the vestiges of a true crypto-Islamism or crypto-Judaism become rather rare.[26] Other Morisco intellectuals preferred to choose another literary genre dear to Renaissance humanists and reformers. They entrust

Straßentracht der Morisken-Frauen in Granada

Street-dress of Morisco women in Granada   Vestido de paseo de las mujeres moriscas en Granada

Figure 2.5 'Street Dress of Morisca in the Kingdom of Granada'. *Das Trachtenbuch des Christoph Weiditz ...* , Plate 84.

their intercultural migrants' erudition to 'mirrors of princes' through which they dared to confront the hegemonic discourse of the absolute monarchy with their own vision of a pacified Hispanic society reconciled with the living – Semitic – forces of the past. Thus in his 1566 Memorial, prince Francisco Núñez Muley, a descendant of the last Merini sultan of Morocco[27] attempts to dissuade King Philip II from eradicating all the remains of the Moriscos' Arab culture, by demonstrating the legitimacy of their religion as part and parcel of their cultural heritage and a guarantee of their complete fidelity to the Crown. In vain: in the very same year of 1566, the King's Pragmatic decrees the total eradication of Arab culture in Spain. It rigorously forbids the Granada Moriscos the use of Arabic and Arabic names, and the possession of books written in Arabic – which will lead to the first *autos-da-fé* of printed publications in Spain – the wearing of traditional dress, festive celebrations (with their *zambras, leilas,* etc.) the use of makeup and, last but not least, all religious practices including the existence of Koranic schools. Only works of medicine and philosophy in Arabic were exempted, since the authorities strictly controlled their possession and circulation.[28] The rebellion provoked by the *Pragmática* among the inhabitants of the Alpujarras was brutally suppressed in 1570 by Don Juan of Austria, the King's young half-brother, after which the survivors of the massacre were evicted and dispersed in small groups in the other provinces of the Peninsula. Even before the Duke of Lerma's expulsion decree triggered the Moriscos' final exodus from their Iberian homeland in 1609, the descendants of the Granada Moors had for several decades been successively deprived of their former identity and reduced if not to actual servitude, at least to social marginality, and to the hazards of the wanderer's life.[29]

Mediterranean Excursions: Foundation Myths of Europe's Civilizations

As specific as the process of segregation may appear, indeed of exclusion of its own 'Oriental' components by the Spanish society of the First Modernity, it will, at second glance, prove just as characteristic of the common history and theory of the civilization of Europe itself. Under particular conditions, the founding of the Spanish Catholic monarchy reproduces the same 'scandalous' relation to the Orient which, in a disguised manner at the level of mythological recounting, had already presided at the founding of the brilliant civilization, which, for the first time, came to bear the name Europe. And not only of that particular one: for the genesis of European civilization unfolds by successive stages during which, under the term emancipation, is reproduced every time the paradox of repudiation of the very Orient to which the nascent civilization is indebted for its birth and early development, and above which it claims to rise as its sublime and modern 'purified' transmutation.

A Few Examples

According to the classic ancient mythological stories (Homer, Hesiod, Moschos, Ovid and others), the Near East, in this case the Edenic Phoenician region, was the birthplace of young princess Europa, carried off over the Mediterranean by the supreme god of the Hellenic pantheon, disguised as a white bull, to the island of Crete. There she gave birth to her sons Minos and Radamantes. From this 'supernatural' alliance of Zeus and the aristocratic Phoenician maiden arose, under the aegis of the Creto-Minoic culture, that brilliant Mediterranean civilization named Europe, after its mother.[30] Therefore, we are not dealing here with the displacement of the fascinating daughter of the Orient to an 'island of love' situated in her homeland's closest neighbour to the West, but rather with the elevation of this exquisite incarnation of the Orient above her genetic identity to divine status. It is her own ecstatic abduction which transforms her into the genetrix of a civilization 'divinely' superior to the one of her birth: thanks to her election by the Greek pantheon's supreme God, the daughter will henceforth rise immeasurably above her mother. The violence of the abduction from which this elevation after all proceeded, as well as the pain of separation, are softened, even covered up at the level of mythological narrative (to wit in Ovid) by the evocation of an anxious homesickness for her Phoenician shores that the king's daughter felt as she was carried off by the white bull over the waves of the Mediterranean: '...pavet haec litusque ablata relictum respirat'.[31]

The foundation myth of Europe is thus revealed not only as a pleasant historiographic fiction about the succession of civilizations, but also, and this will have far more serious consequences, as discursive performance, as the euphoric disguising of an hegemonic ideological construct. The ancient fable attempts to hide the superiority complex which underlies it by having the delights of a divine amorous union cover up the process of assimilation by Greece of the scientific, cultural, political and other achievements of the Near-Eastern civilization of Babylon, Egypt and Phoenicia among others. That superiority complex will manifest itself more clearly in the foundation stories of the future civilizations of the Mediterranean. One after the other will deem itself fundamentally (and therefore also morally) superior to the Oriental civilization which gave it birth and nurtured it up to the ecstatic moment of its own emancipation.[32] The relationship of the European civilizations to the Orient will henceforth be determined by a permanent oscillation between fascination before a beauty that harks back to their youth (in the time frame of human existence) and their contempt for a civilizational and moral 'primitivism' which they claim to have outgrown at the very moment their identity was constituted. Even before the appearance of the name Europe to designate the successive Western and in particular Mediterranean civilizations – Herodotus seems to have been the first to distinguish between Europe, Asia and Africa and to speak of the Europeans as members of an homogenous culture – is thus established this opposition between a 'primitive' or 'decadent' – according to the period considered – Orient and a series of invariably constantly young, modern and educated Europes.

Carthage, or Renounced Phoenicia

One of the most striking examples of the radicalization of this discursive stratagem of degradation of the Orient of the origins is the mythological foundation of the flourishing maritime Republic of Carthage story as entrusted by Virgil to the goddess Venus in Book I of his *Aeneid*. Here it is the kingdom of Tyre – once more Phoenicia! – that has become the paradigm of barbarism and corrupted morals, even though it is the homeland of the queen of Carthage, Elissa-Dido. For, according to Aeneas' divine mother, Elissa's husband Sychaeus, the richest landowner in Phoenicia was murdered in Tyre by her own brother, Pygmalion the tyrant. This caused the victim's young widow and a few companions to seek refuge on the shores of Libya where she courageously undertook to found a new Phoenician city. Rather than as an example of criminal cupidity, Elissa's own brother Pygmalion 'scelere ante alios immanior omnia', appears here as the supreme representative of a corrupted and sacrilegious régime ('A long series of crimes, a long series of peripeteia') – the murder of Sychaeus was committed 'in front of the altars'.[33] The illustrious refugee will replace this corrupt realm with a vigorous and modern (as indicated by its name 'qart hadasht') Phoenician polis.[34]

In a barely veiled fashion, the mythogenic story spread by the Roman epic poet situates this alternate Phoenician republic within a 'European' origin, an origin similar to that of Crete, founded by the Phoenician princess Europa, and functioning poles apart from a genetic homeland rejected for its moral decay. Compared to the Greek version of the myth, Virgil's has nevertheless profoundly debased its relationship of dependency to the Oriental 'generating homeland' by depicting it as a society infected by corruption and criminal passions. This does not prevent another Europa arising from the emancipating figure of Elissa-Dido; her foundation act will be to create a vast Mediterranean Empire with hybrid and even dialectic characteristics: a 'European' civilization construct rises henceforth on an 'Oriental' substratum.[35] Through her civilizing and cultural achievements, Carthage will in turn bequeath this 'mixed-blood' identity to many nations from which modern Europe will arise: Cyprus, Malta, Sicily, Sardinia, Spain.[36]

Now, the Virgilian epic as a partisan mythography of Imperial Rome simultaneously contains a contrary vision of an independent 'Oriental' (from the Roman point of view) Carthage. While implicitly acknowledging the maritime Republic of Carthage's new status as a grandiose civilization, because of her moral antagonism with the Orient from which it originated, Virgil recounts its relationship with her Roman rival. Consequently, he is compelled to regard her as an evil power also, in other words as an 'Oriental' one, in the same sense that ancient Phoenicia was evil in its relation to Queen Dido. The Roman poet's tale thus plays on two opposing semantic registers. More than a century after the annihilation of the Carthaginian Mediterranean Empire, the only way the glorifier of Augustus could justify its eradication by the Romans was to make Dido, the founder of this flourishing commercial power, play the role of the 'Oriental' seductress of 'pious' Aeneas, assimilating her to Circe, the Homeric epic's 'magician'. And, in the eyes of the Roman poet, just as bewitching Circe by the virtuous and faithful Ulysses, Dido the 'Oriental' deserves to be forsaken ('repulsed') by Aeneas, because of her emotional 'deviance' from the 'superior' *logothète*[37] (founder of the *urbs*) mission entrusted Aeneas by his mother, Venus.

The encounter with the Queen of Carthage will therefore remain one among so many other 'tests' that the future founder of Rome will have to pass victoriously along the road that will lead him to heroic status. Imperial Rome will henceforth take upon herself (implicitly, of course) the title of primary Mediterranean power in 'Europe', by contrast with the 'Oriental' Carthage, which she has just eliminated from history.

Let us list one other revealing semiotic substitution. For the founder of the new Phoenician city, her native criminal Orient is fittingly embodied in the masculine figure of Pygmalion the tyrant. For Virgil, on the other hand, 'Oriental' Carthage requires representation by the ambivalent image of a powerful and seductive woman, that is to say by a particularly intriguing metamorphosis of that pernicious breed of 'conjurers', 'witches' and such-like lascivious paramours hailing from the Orient who succeed for a time in diverting the heroes from their mission of founding a new and virtuous civilization. Without exception they will, however, end up condemned to everlasting damnation in the memory and moral judgment of future generations. For the European logothesis, the 'Orient' will forever be represented, if at all, by that bewitching femme fatale named *bayadère, odalisque*, etc.

The 'European' Excellence of al-Andalus

One can also observe strong tendencies toward the 'Westernization' of the civilization of the Andalucí past's 'interior orient' in the interpretation of history by the Morisco intellectual elites in 'post-Granadine' Spain. These intellectuals do not, however, insist on foundation myths that claim the superiority of al-Andalus' Arabic civilization over that from which it originated. Their main endeavour is rather to prove the 'Western' (or 'European') excellence of that civilization, whose most direct heirs they claim to be, by arguing that it was in perfect harmony with the system of values affirmed by the contemporary imperial monarchy. The favourite 'media' vehicle of their claim is the launching of a popular 'Moorophile' fiction whose protagonists are equally virtuous Muslim and Christian nobles operating in the conflictive context characteristic of the final stage of the Reconquest. It is not fortuitous that this 'Moorophile' literature, invested with the political function of 'mirror of Princes', bloomed forth at the start of the 1560s. At that time the Moriscos and their Judeoconvert, humanist and reformer allies still nurtured the hope of obtaining from young King Philip II an abatement of the coercive policy to which they were subjected and that had been intensifying since the beginning of the century.

Their earliest 'Moorophile' text, and one of the most influential, is a charming anonymous little story generally known as by the title *El Abencerraje*. This tale is derived from an anthology of popular romances going back to the last stage of the frontier wars in Andalusia. It recounts the capture one night between the battle lines of Abindarráez, of a young and valiant knight of the Grenadine Abencerraje dynasty by Rodrigo de Narváez, a Reconquest officer belonging to the military order of Calatrava. Abindarráez had dared to cross the enemy lines in search of his betrothed, the beautiful Jarifa, who awaited him in her father's fortress. Thanks to the chivalrous fidelity of the Moor, the military confrontation of the Castilian knight and the noble Granadine does not end in death, but soon turns into mutual affirmations of esteem and a veritable contest between those representatives of two political systems, to determine who prevails over the other in generosity, courtesy (in the service of ladies) and nobility of heart. An *exemplum virtutis* of extraordinary moral transcendence results from this rivalry. It tends to demonstrate not only the possibility of a deep friendship between the representatives of two opposing political and military groups, but more importantly the perfect equality of the honour codes of Christian knighthood and Muslim nobility. This implicitly makes it into a 'mirror of princes', as evidenced by the address of its new 1565 edition to King Philip II in person. It is designed to remind the royal authorities of the exemplary treatment by the Catholic Kings of the Arab population once their capital of Granada had fallen. Therefore it was morally incumbent upon the royal authorities, as heirs to this exemplary system of virtues, to grant the contemporary Moriscos (as well as the Judeoconverts who shared their fate) the same moral and honourable status as the old Christians enjoyed by the simple virtue of their birth.[38]

But it was mostly in the last decade of the sixteenth century, a phase of decline in King Philip II's reign which saw a dramatic deterioration of Spain's economic and social situation, that the model of the moral and cultural excellence of the civilization of al-Andalus grew in importance among the partisans of a reactivation of the country's productive resources. During those years, the Morisco intellectuals had every reason to raise their voices also in favour of the Judeoconverts who were exposed to a new upsurge of popular hostility. One of the principal causes of this resurgence of anti-Semitism was the arrival of a large number of Portuguese Jews. The 1580 incorporation of Portugal into the Habsburg domain had opened the Spanish market to them, even though the 'statutes of blood purity' as well as the ingrained prejudices of popular casticism wanted to exclude them or at least to confine them into a veritable 'moral ghetto'.[39] To demand the abrogation of these racist laws and to denounce the climate of daily persecution in which the new Christians of Jewish descent lived thus became a foremost humanistic obligation. The romantic tales and historical chronicles implicitly do so by celebrating the virtues and splendours of the al-Andalus civilization.

Cordoba, or the New Carthage

While the intentions of the 'Moorophile' writers did not seem to have changed, to wit the insistence on the Moriscos' social and economic integration by dint of their cultural assimilation, their strategies had meanwhile become more radical. Not content with following the *mudéjar* model, they now started to subvert the very bases of the neogothic myth, which justified the monarchy's claim to absolute power as well as the racism of the 'statutes of blood purity' and the ubiquitous Inquisitorial suspicion of Judeoconverts.

The first, and the most courageous writer to engage in this enterprise of demolition of the dominant legitimist discourse's foundations is, curiously enough, Miguel de Luna, the Morisco doctor from Granada who was King Philip II's Arabic interpreter; in 1592 he published the First Part of an historical chronicle entitled *Historia verdadera del rey Don Rodrigo* (*The True History of King Rodrigo*).

In this historical account, which harks back to the circumstances of the 711 Arab invasion of the Peninsula, Luna paints a grandiose fresco of the rise and glory of the Caliphate of Corboba, the most powerful Arab state to have existed in the land of Iberia. Through his novelistic idealization of this imperial civilization, the author seems to pursue a double goal. By glorifying the valour of the troops under the command of Tariq and their behaviour towards the Iberian subject populations, Luna, who claims to be only the translator of 'the wise Alcayde Abulcasim Abentarique, of the Arab nation and native of Arabia Petrea', forges the paradigm of

Figure 2.6 'The Great Mosque of Córdoba. The Villaviciosa Chapel with the Mihrab in the Background'. (*FMR*, English Edition n. 33, July/August 1988). © Franco Maria Ricci, 1990.

a 'just' conquest, poles apart from that of the last Visigoth king, Don Rodrigo, who acts as an usurper and the people's enemy.

In the Second Part of his imaginative *True History*, published in 1600, two years after the accession to the throne of Philip III (whose Arabic translator Miguel de Luna will remain), he finally raises the civilization of the Cordovan caliphate to the paradigmatic heights of a civilization unsurpassable in virtue, heroism and cultural splendour. The majesty of imperial Cordoba is embodied for him in the second successor of Caliph 'Abd al-Rahman III, Miramolín Jacob Almansor, whose name echoes in fact that of the all-powerful Emir Abu 'Amir Muhammed, known as al-Mansur, that is to say 'the Victorious'.[40] On the head of that intrepid conqueror, he heaps all imaginable military, political, moral and aesthetical perfections: Almansor is a brilliant strategist, magnanimous and generous towards the vanquished, a skilful negotiator, the equitable protector of all his subjects, be they Jews, Christians or Muslims, charitable to the poor, a courteous servant of the ladies, lover of literature, polyglot. He is the Arabic incarnation of these very same ideals of virtue that the Renaissance manuals of Princes' education, Machiavelli's *Prince* (1513), Castiglione's *Book of the Courtier* – which was published in 1534 in the poet Boscán's famous Castilian translation in 1534[41] – and the *Mirror of Princes* by Guevara (1529) give as the appanage of that 'uomo universale', the hero of 'arms and letters'.[42] It is therefore obvious that the political import of this portrait goes beyond the historical trajectory of al-Andalus and the dream of a saviour that contemporary Moriscos might be tempted to cherish to escape their modern bondage. In many ways, Almansor actually corresponds to the idealized image composed by a nostalgic contemporary hagiography of Emperor Charles V who, in turn, shows through in his role for young Philip III of just and good sovereign, acting like the father of all his subjects, to whatever 'nation' they may belong.[43]

In order to show the providential role of the Muslim conquest of Spain and thus to upend the dignity of the Reconquest's official historiography, Miguel de Luna must have had at his disposal a variety of Arab (or Arabophile) sources which suggested his own enthusiastic vision of al-Andalus' evolution.[44] He no doubt found certain elements of his portrait of Don Rodrigo in compilations of popular romances which recount that this last of the Visigoth kings dishonoured la Caba, daughter of count Julián, the legitimate heir to the crown of Toledo who had sought refuge in Ceuta. The maiden wreaked revenge by helping the Arab troops to land on her Iberian homeland at Gibraltar.[45] But it is rather in Arabic documents circulating among Morisco erudites, and in their translations into Spanish,[46] that most of the sources of his subversive inspiration can be found.

One of his most significant models among these chronicles of Hispano-Arabic origin is surely the *Historia sarracina* of Pedro del Corral which, as indicated by its subtitle, comprises a 'Crónica del rey don Rodrigo con la destruyción de España y cómo los moros la ganaron. Crónica caballeresca del rey Don Rodrigo'. The Arab origin of this Saracen story, which circulated as early as 1430 and was published in Seville in 1499 is by the Moor Ahmad al-Razi, who set this Don Rodrigo legend down towards the end of the tenth century, after which it spread among the Spanish speakers of al-Andalus under the title *Crónica del moro Rasis*.[47] As an apologetic view of andalusí civilization, al-Razi's chronicle[48] is representative of a literary and historiographic current widespread among Hispano-Roman as well as Arab cultured circles, and not only among them. It is significant that under the Visigoth kings foreshadowing of this view can already be found in the opposite camp, as is proven by the famous *Laus Hispaniae* which Isidore of Seville (560?–636) had celebrated in his treaty *De origine Gothorum* for the glory of the sovereigns who had converted to Catholicism.[49] In contrast to this apology of militant (and anti-Semitic) Catholicism, the writings of such eminent Hispano-Arab poets as the two epistles of Ibn Hazm of Cordoba and of 'al-Shaqundi[50] later contributed effectively to make their evocation of the civilizing and cultural excellence of al-Andalus into a powerful mythological cliché that even the most stubborn defender of the neo-gothic and casticist discourse was hard put to root out from the collective memory of their 'post-Granada' contemporaries. So that, albeit implicitly, the grandeur of Muslim civilization shows through in the first history of the Moors written in Latin by a Christian, the *Historia Arabum* of Rodrigo Ximénez de Rada, whose first edition was published in Toledo in 1583 but which, in Spanish translation, had already appeared in the context of the *Primera Crónica General* of King Alphonse X, the Wise.[51]

That Miguel de Luna attributed the first version of his chronicle to an Arab author named 'the wise Alcayde Abulcasim Abentarique' whom he had merely translated may seem bizarre to today's reader. Yet he sticks quite closely to literary and historiographic reality when he claims in his 'Proemio al Christiano Lector' to have put down 'a truth widely known and respected among the Arabs, but which is lacking in our historians'. And he adds that this truth not only concerns 'the defeat of King Rodrigo and the conquest of Spain', but also 'the wars of the Arab kingdoms and of all Africa … in which just desserts will be given him according to the valour and the honour of each [combatant]'.[52] The notion of claiming a fictitious Arab historian as the original author of their own text written in Spanish had already been used by chivalric romance writers as early as the first 'post-Granada' years, for example the *Crónica de Lepolemo, llamado el Caballero de la Cruz, hijo del emperador de Alemania* (Valencia, 1521) who, as indicated by the title, was 'composed in Arabic by Xartón, and put into Spanish by Alsonso de Salazar'.[53] Against the regime's political rhetoric there had arisen a tradition of literary fabrications of 'alternative' or 'dissident' works like Luna's, practised by certain Morisco, Judeoconvert and other authors. Without a doubt, a few years later, the most grandiose such work and at the same time the most irritating because of its ironic implications is *El Ingenioso Hidalgo Don Quijote de la Mancha*, which Cervantes insistently claims throughout its two Parts (1605 and 1615) to have translated from 'Cide Hamete Benengeli, historiador arábigo'.[54]

One of the most significant episodes narrated by Hispano-Arabic historiography in the fashion of al-Razi's chronicle, on which, however, de Luna does not explicitly insist, concerns the antecedents and circumstances of the Umayyads' assumption of power in Cordoba. According to that tradition, 'Abd al-Rahmán I ben Muauia, nephew of the Tenth Caliph of the Orient Hichém (724–743), was born in a monastery near Damascus in March AD 731. The new Abbasid dynasty settled in Damascus after the 750 overthrow and execution of Caliph Marúan II in Egypt, and proceeded to hunt down and assassinate their rivals the Omeya princes. Young 'Abd al-Rahman was the only survivor of his family's murder. Along with his faithful vassal Bade, he managed to flee and reach the shores of North Africa; after a long journey along the Mediterranean coast, he landed in Almuñécar in 756. In Archidona, he succeeded in having himself proclaimed as Emir; he took advantage of the dissentions within the political class in Cordoba, and soon succeeded in overthrowing Emir Iussuf al-Fikri and in becoming the founder of the powerful Umayyad (Western) dynasty, which will lead the Cordoba Caliphate to the summit of its imperial glory.[55]

The analogies of this tale with the foundation myth of Carthage in its Virgilian version are striking. Here again, a crime committed by a Near Eastern ruling class and the wanderings and subsequent elevation to heroic stature of the only survivor of the slaughter of his family are called upon to determine a new and glorious Arab civilization which *ipso facto* reproduces the great mythical paradigm of the Oriental civilization of the West (eventually of Europe) 'divinely' rising above its own origins.

A distinction should, however, be made. The crime committed in Damascus by the Abbasids is meant to underscore the heroic grandeur of their only survivor, but will not thereby serve to denigrate *per se* the Arab civilization dominant in the Near East; and this notwithstanding the profound rivalry that continues to oppose the Umayyad to the Abbasid régime. A clear rupture by the rulers of al-Andalus will only occur when illustrious Abd al-Rahman III, having defeated Omar ben Hafsun, decides in 929 to assume the title of Caliph and Emir of the Faithful and to separate politically the caliphate of Cordoba which he founded from the up to then all-powerful caliphate ruled from its capital of Damascus. An even more clear-cut rupture, from the point of view of the competition between Muslim civilizations, will occur in the relations of the Cordoban Emirs with the Fatimid dynasty on the other side of the Straight of Gibraltar. These rulers of North Africa refused to recognize the legitimacy of the Cordoban Umayyads, which rests on their claim to be descended from the Caliph of Damascus Hicham and from prince Muauia, who died prematurely. On their part, the rulers of Cordoba, in their desire to equal and even to surpass the fame of the Oriental caliphs, ceaselessly boast of the oriental splendours of their urban and architectural creations, such as the palaces of their ephemeral capital-residence Medina Azahara, for example, or the magnificent Cordoba mosque, the most grandiose edifice in the known world.[56]

Oriental Granada, or Paradise Recovered

The Cordoban paradigm of the excellence of al-Andalus promoted by Miguel de Luna was joined in 1595 by that of the brilliant civilization of Nasride Granada articulated by another Morisco, Ginés Perez de Hita in the First Part of his *Guerras civiles de Granada*, entitled *Historia de los bandos de Zegríes y Abencerrajes, caballeros moros de Granada*.[57]

This work is composed in both prose and verse. It combines the informative richness of an historical chronicle inspired by the 'classic' one that Hernando del Pulgar composed at the beginning of the century at the request of Queen Isabella with the melancholic charm of the romances which arose during the *guerras fronterizas* (border wars) and the almost inexhaustible imaginative resources of the folk legends. It constitutes a veritable summa of the plurisecular al-Andalus Arab civilization at the peak of its glory. The author excels in evoking with colourful emotion the magnificence of the court of Boabdil 'El Chico', the last Moorish king of Granada just before it was swept away by the military might and the moral stringency of the victorious Catholic monarchy.[58] Before the reader's admiring eyes unfolds the dazzling spectacle of the stately reign of courtesy, of the joust and sumptuous entertainments and amorous intrigues that transform the Alhambra palace and the Generalife gardens in the settings of an exotic dream.[59] But this display of aesthetic refinement also includes signs of decadence: crimes of passion, moral corruption, bloody infighting for power among the aristocratic clans, the most spectacular of those crimes being the murder in the famous fountain of the Patio de los Leones by the Zegris faction (and possibly King Boabdil also) of almost all the members of the Abencerraje dynasty, whose survivors then entered the collective memory of succeeding generations as examples of righteousness.

In this paradise on the brink of disaster, however, corruption was not prevalent enough to impede the capacity of certain members of its chivalric elites for outstanding political and moral integrity sufficient to elevate them to the status of role models, and not only for their Muslim compatriots. Thus noble Muza and his companion Albayaldos give proof of such military valour, generosity, courtesy and political acumen that after the fall of Granada the Catholic Kings warmly receive these new converts[60] among the elites of their own realm.

The lessons to be drawn from this transition epic are clear. Having been eliminated as the cultural underpinning of a decadent régime, the Muslim civilization of Granada did not thereby lose its status as a model of excellence for future generations, much to the contrary. That was achieved because the flower of her chivalric elite managed to keep its moral, cultural and political dignity by linking it to the code of Christian values of the new masters of Spain. The acknowledgment on the part of the Catholic monarch themselves of the virtues and the outstanding civic integrity of these refugees from the fallen Nasride régime had repercussions for the very Muslim civilization to which they belonged. It proved its Western (and thus European) worthiness to the same degree as that claimed by the founders of the 'post-Granadine' monarchy. Together with the magnanimity of King Ferdinand and Queen Isabella as shown by their exemplary attitude towards the Muslim population in the treaty of Santa Fé, the outstanding merits of the Moorish knights of Granada was designed to serve as a 'Mirror of Princes' for King Philip II, who was considering the expulsion of the Moriscos from their Iberian homeland, after having already torn their ancestral cultural and religious identity from them.

The Other of this paradigmatic 'western' version of Arabic civilization could henceforth only be its North African counterpart, from which it had issued and which still aspired in vain to be its rival in Oriental pomp: the splendours of the Alhambra had already long overshadowed the cultural achievements of the Fatimide régime. Therefore, for the historian of civilizations Pérez de Hita, the primitivism of the Arabic civilization beyond the Strait of Gibraltar was the only alternative to the decadent Granadine display.

With the 'Moorophile' enthusiasm of the European Romantics the gulf deepens even more, in the collective memory of modern societies, between the Arab civilization with 'European' connections and that which, being rooted in North Africa, is fundamentally characteristic of 'Oriental barbarity'. A.M. Sané, the French translator of Ginés Pérez de Hita's chronicle, attests the radicalization of that antagonism eloquently. Its publication in Paris in 1809 unleashed an unprecedented surge of literary and artistic imaginary depictions of the Oriental marvels of Granada and her Alhambra.[61]

In an important preface entitled 'Quelques réflexions sur les Musulmans d'Espagne, les anciens Espagnols, et sur cet ouvrage' ('Some Remarks on the Muslims of Spain, the ancient Spanish and the Present Work'), Sané provides a clearly differentiated panoramic comparative review of the Arab contributions to the everyday life of the inhabitants of Spain. The preface ends with a lucid theory of the causes of the decadence to which the 'generous and valiant nation' of the Moors of Granada finally succumbed. Sané's historical overview, punctuated with expressions of admiration, starts with the first Arab warriors whose 'virile experience of overcoming reverses … taught the Spanish how to win' (p. X); then goes on to the 'Corboban poets' for whom 'the reign of the great Abderames … were like the centuries of Augustus or the Medici' (p. XXXIV) and ends up in the far reaches of the 'Paradise' of industrious Granada which 'was a diligent hive whose bees never rested' (p. XXXIX). In the Frenchman's mind, there is no doubt that the wonders of the 'famous empire' of the last Moors of Granada are an integral part of European civilization: as far as he is concerned, Granada in fact represents 'the last sigh of European chivalry' (p. III). His admiration for the achievements of the Moors' civilization did not, however, prevent him from offering his readers a disillusioned diagnosis of the fatal disease of that Granadine society 'intoxicated with delights on the edge of the tomb' (p. III). He lists various pathologies: 'relaxation of the religious spirit' (p. XIX), 'civil dissensions' (p. II), the permanent threat from foreign enemies, and finally the flaw represented by a curious mixing of bloods ('The Moors of Spain perished because they ceased to be pure Moors, to become half-breeds, half African, half European', p. XIX) – all that, in his eyes, fatally contributes to 'the singular spectacle of a nation which perishes in the midst of amusements' (p. II). The greatest Evil that afflicts the Spanish Muslims does not, however, result from their interior disorders, but from the North African 'barbarity' from which they originated and to which the road to exile leads them back '…we see the Muslims come out of their scorching Africa as barbarians, becoming in Spain the most courtly, the most civilized of nations, and fall back into profound barbarity upon their return' (p. XXXI).[62]

The effects of this vision of two opposed Muslim civilizations soon manifested themselves in the whole of Europe. Let us consider as an example a youthful work by the German Jewish poet Heinrich Heine: his 1823 drama *Almansor*. The eponymous hero, son of a Moorish Granadine nobleman who moved to Morocco after the fall of his city, returns to his native Andalusia in search of his childhood beloved, Zuleima, who was given the name Doña Clara when she was baptized. It is obvious that the author projects upon the character of the young Moor back in a country that has become foreign to him, his own existential condition as a Rhenish Jew in a Germany that, after the Napoleonic occupation, has fallen back into its traditional absolutism and anti-Semitism. From this point of view, evil is obviously embodied first and foremost in the moving forces of that triumphant Spain that the Enlightenment intellectuals had ceaselessly denounced through their 'leyenda negra' (black legend): the vulgar materialism and racist arrogance of pícaros replacing 'old Christian' nobles in positions of honour, the horrors of the Inquisition, the missionaries' sadism, the ambiguous identities deriving from the blood purity statutes.

Now, in a historical retrospective which the author, following the model of Greek tragedy, entrusts to the objective voice of a Chorus, another opposite extreme of the Arab civilization of Spain emerges, and it is no less hated by the Moriscos than the militancy of the Inquisitors and agents of casticist ideology. It is the 'barbarity' in which are steeped the Muslim societies of the Near East and their North African equivalents, from which the founders of the high Arab culture of Spain are descended. Before it could reach its incomparable flowering, its Golden Age, the civilization of the Moors had (according to the Chorus) to cut the umbilical cord, which kept it tied to that 'Barbary', to 'the throne of the Caliphs of Damascus'. Only after the separation of the Spanish Muslim from his 'Oriental brother in religion' that 'A breath of life, purer than in the harems of the Orient, wafted through the sumptuous buildings of Cordoba'.[63] Now, from Cordoba to Granada science and beauty, the melancholic romances sung to guitar music, the chivalric service of love and of ladies reign amidst a heavenly nature. But in Damascus and her 'African' dependencies can be found only despotism, the enslavement of women, the roughness of its graphic signs, and general obscurantism, and these iniquities go, in the eyes of the Moriscos, beyond the evils that they themselves have to suffer at the hands of their country's new masters. Significantly, Zuleima/Doña Clara's adoptive father, a noble Granadine lord who, having converted to Christianity, has been able to keep part of his fortune, claims to have chosen the constraints of submission to militant Catholicism's laws, and even to the fury of 'fearsome Ximenes' over emigration to Muslim North Africa, which many members of Granada's former ruling class ('the best among our people') had chosen.[64]

Here once more, in the mythic image of the emancipating break, was revealed the historic act of the founding of an Oriental civilization 'of the West' or 'of Europe', opposed to that of its origins by the very existence of its splendour and by the 'modernity' of its code of political and moral values. But at the same time, in the area of diffusion of Heine's *Almansor*, was heralded a revealing semantic displacement within the negative affective field that concerned the Muslim Orient. For it is surely not by chance that in 1865 the play's French translator substitutes for 'the dark harems of the Orient' as the literal translation of verse 1182 in the German original should have read, with 'les mornes harems asiatiques' (the dismal Asiatic harems).[65] In view of the negative connotations that in Nineteenth Century France were attached to the term *asiatique* – and in particular to China, which embodied despotism, obscurantism and bloodthirsty justice[66] – it can be readily imagined what the real place reserved for the Muslim Orient in the collective imagination of the contemporary colonizing nations must have been.

Translation from the French by Léon-François Hoffmann

Notes

1. The works of F. Rodríguez de la Flor, in particular (1999), are excellent introductions to the profusion of symbolic codes spread by Counter-Reformation Spain.

2. In the present study, and in accordance with its etymology and traditional use in medieval Europe, the term Semitic refers to the Arab (Muslim) population of Spain as well as to the Jewish (Sephardic) one. According to Scriptures, both Jews and Arabs are descended from Noah's son Sem. In the special case of Spain the numerous interdependencies between Sephardis and Moors during the entire history of al-Andalus justify the use of this common denominator, all the more so in view of the many discriminatory measures to which the descendants of both were subjected equally after the fall of Granada. See Pulido Serrano (2003), p. 175.

3. We have substituted the term 'post-Granada' for those expressions which generally characterize the Spanish sixteenth century as a 'Golden Century' or which, because of supposed points of resemblance with other nations of contemporary Europe, include it into such concepts of artistic or religious periodisation as 'Late Renaissance', 'Counter-Reformation', 'Baroque', etc. Since my intention was to elucidate the consequences of the fall of Granada on civilizations and cultures of Semitic origin during the sixteenth century imperial Monarchy, the historic term 'post-Granada' seemed the most adequate because of its discursive neutrality.

4. By the noun casticism (adjective: casticist) we mean, following Américo Castro (1963, 1974) the discourse of the militant defenders of a hostile separation between Spanish *cristianos viejos* (old Christians) and *cristianos nuevos* (new Christians of Jewish or Muslim descent), according to which the latter can be excluded from all the material and spiritual privileges that the genetic (!) possession of honour assures the former.

5. On the biblical reference to Sepharad and its diffusion in Medieval Spain, see Besso (1981). Besso (p. 649) points out that the distinction between the terms Ashkenasim and Sephardim (Sp: '*sefardíes*') was not made and did not begin to enter into general European usage before the expulsion of the Jews from Spain.

6. The following exemplify the numerous publications that have focused on the civilization of al-Andalus and on the Sephardim's contribution to it in the context of the *Quinto Centenario* of the year 1492: Solà-Solé et al. (1984); Vallvé Bermejo (1986, 1989); Lacave (1987); *Las tres culturas de la Corona de Castilla y los sefardíes* (1990); Dodds et al. (1992); Beinart (1992); Rubiera Mata (1992); Harvey (1992); Vernet (1993). The by now classic study by Caro Baroja (1986) remains of fundamental interest. For the most complete and diversified information currently available on the history of al-Andalus see Lévi-Provençal

(1999), Arié (1997) and the *Historia de España Menéndez Pidal* (2000), vols IV–V and VIII.

7. See Márquez Villanueva (1994, 1996), pp. 23–34; Cardaillac (1992).

8. See Schonfield, J. (ed.) (1992). For the intellectual context, see Sáenz-Badillos (2005).

9. See Besso (1981), pp. 658–9, and, for a more general view Septimus (1982).

10. See Baldeón Baruque (2000), in particular pp. 81–97.

11. According to Saraiva (1950–1962), who stressed the eminently economic character of the concept of 'New Christian', the activities of the Inquisition, at least in Portugal, reveal fairly specific strategies, if not finalities. I.S. Révah (1959–1960, pp. 47–48) wrote: 'La fonction du tribunal du Saint-Office n'était pas de détruire les judaïsants, mais de les fabriquer; elle n'était pas non plus d'assimiler les Nouveaux-Chrétiens, mais de les séquestrer et de les multiplier. Le nom de Nouveaux-Chrétiens était la désignation démagogique par laquelle le groupe dominant au Portugal depuis le milieu du XVIe siècle s'efforça d'écarter la bourgeoisie de la direction politique de l'État et de l'hégémonie économique'.

12. For an overall survey of this evolution, see Cohen (1996) and Pérez (2005).

13. See Stoll (2005a). In his analysis of the ambiguous condition of converted Jews 'de conversion renovada', P.-A. Fabre (1999, pp. 882, 887) insists on the dialectic fact of the 'fatal assignment' of that category of new Christians to their status, which consists in 'allegorical instrumentalisation … as a sign of renewal'.

14. For an overview of these repressive measures, see Cruz and Perry (1992).

15. A few months later, in October of the same year, another paradigm of mistrusted alterity submitted to the constraint of an unavoidable cross-breeding, that of the Amerindians, was projected into the Hispanic community's imagination. Their fate will be reminiscent of that of the Orientals of the Iberian interior.

16. See Alcalá (1995).

17. Méchoulan (1992) provides a complete overview of Sephardic emigration. See also Díaz Esteban (1994), Bernal, J. (1992) and the economic point of view provided by Israel (1985). On Sephardim in Amsterdam: Kaplan (1996). On the evolution of the Sephardim Ottoman exile, see for example Bernal (1992); Saperta y Beja (1979).

18. For more details about the literary production of the Sephardic diaspora, see Stoll (1995), Bosse, Potthast and Stoll (eds) (1999), especially López Estrada, Díaz Esteban (2001, too) and Brown. On one of the most exciting literary documents generated by 'Andalusian' exiles (in the present case: in Italy), see Stoll (2001).

19. According to her biographer Cecil Roth (1990, p. 31) she was 'maybe the most brilliant Jewish woman of all history'. This novel can be considered as an illustration of an important chapter on the Sephardic diaspora exposed in Roth's book *A History of the Marranos* (1932). See also *Donna Grasya Nasi*, a two-act play composed in Turkish by Beki L. Bahar, translated into French by Eli Elkabes as *Doña Gracia Nasi* and published by ISIS in Istanbul in 2001.

20. Among the many studies concerning the Inquisition should be mentioned the recent ones by Kamen (1997) and García Cárcel and Moreno Martínez (2000). See also Révah (1959–1960), p. 43; Carrete Parrondo (1992), and Yerushalmi (1998).

21. The best source of information on this subject remains Sicroff (1960).

22. For an overall view, see Vincent (1987).

23. According to the biographer of the Mendoza dynasty, Gaspar Ibáñez de Segovia, quoted after Galera Andreu (2004), p. 102.

24. See the general description of Charles V's Alhambra palace in Galera Andreu (2001); also *Imágenes en el tiempo. Un siglo de fotografía en la Alhambra 1840–1940* (2003), photographs of the palace and its frescoes, pp. 71–74.

25. See Rubiera Mata (1995), pp. 315–23; the preliminary study by Vincent (1996); Bernabé Pons (2001a), pp. 91–101. The place of this apology of the Moriscos' natural rights within the frame of the acculturating measures taken against the Moriscos of Granada is the focus of Vincent (2002).

26. See Márquez Villanueva (2000), pp. 527–9. Márquez Villanueva rightly keeps cautioning certain modern scholars who tend to summarily confuse *cristianos nuevos* with *judaïzantes* (judeoconverts accused by the Inquisition to refuse to submit to Catholic dogma) or crypto-muslim suspected by the civil authorities of collaboration with the Ottoman Empire, the exterior enemy, and thereby of criminal disregard of their duty as Spanish patriots. See Doron (2000), pp. 13–24.

27. On the genealogy and the activities of this convert, see Rubiera Mata (1996), pp. 159–67. See the preliminary study by Vincent (1996), p. XXXI. Vincent (2002) situates this apology of the Moriscos' natural rights in the framework of its author's biography and in that of the acculturating measures directed at the Moriscos of Granada.

28. The discrimination and exclusion measures generally directed at medicine and astrology exercised by Moriscos have been amply described in García Ballester (1984). On the other hand, Vincent (1999, p. 47) mentions 'a certain number of Morisco physicians or surgeons, apothecaries and barbers who practiced without interference and sometimes even amassed considerable fortunes'.

29. A detailed account of the living conditions of the Moriscos before 1609–1613 can be found in de Epalza (1992). On the contemporary stereotypic view of the Granada Morisco as interior enemy, see the pertinent anthropological introspection of the collective imagination being carried out by González Alcantud (2002), in particular Chapters I–III, pp. 13–78.

30. The artistic and literary elaboration of the Europe myth has recently been traced in the exhibition catalogue *Il Mito di Europa* (2002), see in particular Romualdi (2002).

31. Ovid, *Metamorphoses*, II, vv. 833–75, citation vv. 873–4.

32. It is obvious that the consequences of this original discursive disposition coincide largely with the attitude of modern European societies, particularly the French and the Anglophone, vis-à-vis the Orient, as Saïd demonstrated in his fundamental book *Orientalism* (1978).

33. 'Longa est iniuria, longae / ambages' (I, vv. 341–2); 'ante aras' (I, v. 349). Quoted and translated after Virgil (1981), p. 18. Venus' story is in verses I, 335–69.

34. On the literary and iconographic representation of the myth of the foundation of Carthage, see the contributions of Ladjimi, Balmelle and Rebourg's to the catalogue of the exhibition *Carthage. L'histoire, la trace et son écho* (1995: esp. pp. 50–67). See also the contributions of Bondi and Moscati. On the impact of this myth on the cultural imaginations in Europe and especially in the Mediterranean world, see Martin (1990). On the personality of the founder of Carthage, see, in particular, Ducos (1990).

35. In what follows, I will use the term 'Europe' and its derivatives 'unwarrantedly', taking into account the fact that the concept of Europe as a distinct civilization only appeared later – in the sixteenth (the Discoveries) century and, even more forcefully, in the nineteenth (the Romantic) century (see Victor Hugo among others) – as an allegorical-utopic (and not yet historical) representation of a cultural landscape, homogeneous in the diversity/plurality of its components. According to the traditional codes of iconographic representation, the figure of Europe represents the most ancient of the continents, endowed by distinctive emblematic signs (symbols) different from the three other known continents of Africa, Asia and America, and complementary to them. (See for example Tiepolo's frescoes in the residence of the Wurtzburg Bishop-Princes.) In their opposition

to the Ottoman Empire's Islam, for example (the Crusades), the Western 'Republics' concur and act as members of a spiritual body named Christianity, leaving the concept of Europe to the mythologues of Antiquity.

36. See the relevant contributions in *I Fenici* (1998), 'Parte Seconda', pp. 140–242.

37. It seems legitimate to apply to Aeneas the term *logothète*, in the sense of 'founder of a political and social system', just as it is fitting for his bard Virgil, a 'founder of discourse' as Roland Barthes calls the three at first sight so dissimilar writers that he joins together in his brilliant essay *Sade, Fourier, Loyola* (1971).

38. See Carrasco Urgoiti (1956, 1976, 2001 and 2005), López Estrada (1993), pp. 13–126, and Stoll (1998).

39. See Révah (1959–1960), p. 40.

40. On the point of view of contemporary research on that Hispano-Arabic civilization's period of glory, see Dozy (2001); Vallvé Bermejo (1992).

41. See Castiglione (1994), Mario Pozzi's recent edition of that translation of *Il Cortigiano*.

42. The distribution and considerable success of Luna's book abroad seems to have profited from its 'exotic' invention characteristics. See on this question Bernabé Pons (2001b).

43. See Márquez Villanueva (1981, 1997).

44. See Hernández (1996), in particular the 'La conquista de al-Andalus' chapter, pp. 163–248.

45. This perspective is also the starting point for Goytisolo's experimental novel *La reivindicación del Conde Don Julián* (1970).

46. For the modern editor of de Luna's *Historia verdadera*, the knowledge of scientific and historiographic works in Arabic belonging to the rich cultural heritage of al-Andalus and their spread among the erudite Morisco readership seems undeniable. Yet for today's scholars the extent to which these works were read as well as details concerning them, including their titles and the names of their authors, remain enigmatic. As a collaborator in the court of Kings Philip II and Philip III, Luna probably had free access to the Escorial library, where erudite books in Arabic which had escaped the pyres in 1566 were stored and communicated to a few selected scholars. (See Bernabé Pons, 2001b, pp. LXV–LXVIII.)

47. Could the latter be that Arabic book about which (without naming it) the historian Marmol Carvajal says that Luna (who he doesn't name) put it into Spanish so as to use it as a source for his own Historia verídica? See the presentation and the extracts of Pedro del Corral's *Crónica sarracina* in Viña Liste (2000), pp. 564–82.

48. See Lévi-Provençal (1953).

49. On the texts of Isidore of Seville, 'al-Razi and other authors of the laus Hispaniae, see Rodríguez Alonso (ed.) (1975) and Vallvé Bermejo (1999), pp. 25–30.

50. The translation of the famous *Risála fi fadl al-Andalus* of al-Shaqundi has been reproduced by García Gómez in his book *Andalucía contra Berbería* (1974), pp. 43–141. For other sources of 'aljamiado-morisque' origin, see Bernabé Pons (1993–1994).

51. In the prologue to his *Historia Arabum*, Ximénez de Rada (1999) actually expresses the hope that, despite the events reported in his preceding *Historia Ostrogothorum*, the calamities that befall Spain since the arrival of the Arabs in the Peninsula will soon come to an end: 'Que calamitatum aceruis Hispania dispendia sit perpessa in superioribus, ut licuit, explicavi; nunc de excidiis Arabum, que utinam sint postrema, a quibus nichil fuit in Hispaniis intemptatum, finem imponere dignum duxi...'. On the conflictive process of constructing Spanish historiography, see García Cárcel (2004).

52. Paraphrase of an affirmation found in Luna's 'Proemio al Christiano Lector'.

53. See Carrasco Urgoiti, López Estrada and Carrasco (2001), pp. 37–8.

54. On the significance of this transcultural operation by Cervantes, see Stoll (2005b) (forthcoming in 2006a and b).
55. A very eloquent example of this sort of legendary evocation of Emir 'Abd al-Rahman's flight is extensively quoted by Rubiera Mata (1992, pp. 221–3) after an anonymous work entitled *Ajbar maymun'a*, i.e. 'Collection de jábar'.
56. See Vallvé Bermejo (2003), especially the Summary in the Introduction, pp. 7–15.
57. This work was first presented by Carrasco Urgoiti (1956) and (1976), in part. pp. 72–136. The current state of research on it has been reported by Correa Rodríguez in Pérez de Hita (1998) and Carrasco Urgoiti, López Estrada and Carrasco (2001). Because in the Second Part of his chronicle, which only appeared in 1619, is treated the cruel Alpujarras War (1568–1570), this book never attained the extraordinary international success accorded the First Part thanks to its subject matter and poetic charms. See Gil Sanjuan in Pérez de Hita (1998).
58. On the Kingdom of Granada in the light of present historiographic, sociological and cultural research, see Arié (1990, 1997, 2004) and Arié's contribution to the *Historia de España Menéndez Pidal* (2000), vol. VIII.
59. In the case of poetry, how little this idealized image of Granadine culture corresponded to the actual intellectual mediocrity of the Nasride regime can be deduced from Rubiera Mata (1992), pp. 129–48.
60. On the eminently cultural rather than religious character of these knights' conversion to Christianity, their goal being total assimilation, see Stoll (2005a), in particular pp. 646–8. See also Foa and Scaraffia (1996) and Attias (1997).
61. The fact that the rebirth of 'Moorophile' literature took place in (pre)revolutionary France rather than in Spain is less surprising that might appear at first sight. For in Spain the public's appreciation of 'Moorophile' fiction rapidly lessened, if it didn't disappear altogether, after the expulsion of the Moriscos in 1609–1613. In Ancien Régime France, on the other hand, fascination for the Moors' Oriental exoticism remained permanently fuelled by a number of female novelists (from Mlle de la Roche-Guilhem and Mlle de Scudéry to Mme de Gomez and Mme de La Fayette). Its recrudescence at the end of the eighteenth century (owing in particular to Florian's popular novel *Don Gonzalve de Cordoue*, 1791) can thus be explained as the revelation of a Spain different from that elaborated in the 'black legend' of the Enlightenment Philosophes, and also as the answer of romantic imagination to the ascetic rigour of revolutionary classicism. For this evolution, see Carrasco Urgoiti (1956), Segunda Parte, 'Época neoclásica y prerromántica', pp. 121 et seq. For the repercussions of the Nasric Granadian civilization on European memory and imagination, see the fundamental González Alcantud and Zabbal (2003).
62. Sané (1809). The Roman numerals following the above quotations refer to this edition.
63. Heine (1994), p. 47, verses 1175–1182, 239 and 229 of the *Almansor*, translated and paraphrased by the author.
64. On the historical importance of this emigration, see Bernabé Pons (2006). For a more detailed analysis of the play, see Stoll (2003).
65. Heine (1865), p. 128.
66. This fusion of imagery concerning Asia and China in colonial Europe can be documented by the highly popular illustrated voyage account of Marquis de Forgues (1844), or that by Marquis d'Hervey Saint-Denys (1859). For Daumier's witty satire on the contemporary stereotypes of Chinese barbarity, see Stoll (1987), pp. 319–59.

References

Alcalá, Á. (ed.) (1995), *Judíos, Sefarditas, Conversos. La expulsión de 1492 y sus consecuencias* (Valladolid).

Arié, R. (1990), *L'Espagne musulmane au temps des Nasrides (1232–1492)* (Paris).

_____. (1997), *Aspects de l'Espagne musulmane: histoire et culture* (Paris).

_____. (2004), *Historia y cultura de la Granada nazarí* (Granada).

Attias, J-C. (ed.) (1997), *De la conversion* (Paris).

Bahar, B.L. (2001), *Donna Grasya Nasi* (Istanbul).

Baldeón Baruque, J. (2000), E*l chivo expiatorio. Judíos, revueltas y vida cotidiana en la Edad Media* (Valladolid).

Barthes, R. (1971), *Sade, Fourier, Loyola* (Paris).

Beinard, H. (1992), *Los Judíos en España* (Madrid).

Bernabé Pons, L.F. (1993–1994), 'Laus Al-Andalus en la literatura morisca', *Revista del Instituto Egipcio de Estudios Islámicos en Madrid* (Madrid), pp. 149–60.

_____. (2001a), 'Un tiempo para los moriscos: el calendario islámico del Mancebo de Arévalo', in M.J. Rubiera Mata (ed.), *Carlos V, los moriscos y el Islam* (Madrid), pp. 91–112.

_____. (ed.) (2001b), *Miguel de Luna, Historia verdadera del Rey Don Rodrigo* (Granada). Introduction pp. VII–LXX.

_____. (2006), 'Las emigraciones moriscas al Maghreb: balance bibliográfico y perspectivas', in A.I. Planet and F. Ramos (eds), *Relaciones hispano – marroquíes: una vecindad en construcción* (Madrid), pp. 63–100.

Bernal, J. (1992), 'Los Sefardíes en el Imperio Otomano (Siglos XV–XIX)', in M.A. Bel Bravo et al. (eds), *Diáspora sefardí* (Madrid), pp. 93–160.

Besso, H.V. (1981), 'Los sefardíes: españoles sin patria y su lengua', *NRFH*, XXX, 648–65.

Bondi, S.F. (1988), 'Le origini in Oriente', 'L'andamento della storia', in *I Fenici*, pp. 28–45.

Bosse, M., B. Potthast and A. Stoll (eds) (1999), *La creatividad femenina en el mundo barroco hispánico. María de Zayas – Isabel Rebeca Correa – Sor Juana Inés de la Cruz* (Kassel), 2 vols.

Brown, K. (1999), 'La poetisa es la luna que con las de Apolo viene: Nuevos datos sobre y textos de varias poeticas sefardíes de los siglos XVII y XVIII', in Bosse, Potthast and Stoll (eds), vol. II, pp. 439–80.

Cardaillac, L. (ed.) (1992), *Toledo, siglos XII–XIII. Musulmanes, cristianos y judíos: la sabiduría y la tolerancia* (Madrid).

Caro Baroja, J. (1986), *Los judíos en la España moderna y contemporánea* (Madrid).

Carrasco Urgoiti, Ma.S. (1956), *El moro de Granada en la literatura* (Del siglo XV al XIX) (Granada).

_____. (1976), *The Moorish Novel: 'El Abencerraje' and Pérez de Hita* (Boston).

_____. (2001), F. López Estrada and F. Carrasco, *La novela española en el siglo XVI* (Madrid and Frankfurt on Main).

_____. (2005), *Vidas fronterizas en las letras españolas* (Barcelona).

Carthage. L'histoire, la trace et son echo (1995), exhibition catalogue, Musée du Petit Palais, 9 March – 2 July 1995 (Paris).

Carrete Parrondo, C. (1992), *El judaísmo español y la Inquisición* (Madrid).

Castiglione, B. (1994), *El cortesano, Mario Pozzi* (ed.) (Madrid).

Castro, A. (1963), *De la edad conflictiva* (Madrid).

_____. (1974), *Cervantes y los casticismos españoles* (Madrid).

Cervantes, M. de (1988), *Don Quijote de la Mancha*, J.J. Allen (ed.) (Madrid).

Cohen, M.R. (1996), *Under Crescent and Cross. The Jews in the Middle Ages* (Princeton).

Cruz, A.J. and M.E. Perry (ed.) (1992), *Culture and Control in Counter-Reformation Spain* (Minneapolis).

Díaz Esteban, F. (ed.) (1994), *Los judaizantes en Europa y la literatura castellana del Siglo de Oro* (Madrid).

———. (1999), 'La poetisa entre los literatos. El ejemplo de Isabel Enríquez entre los judaizantes del siglo XVII', in Bosse, Potthast and Stoll (eds), vol. II, pp. 419–37.

———. (2001), 'Pensamiento judío en Amsterdam en el siglo XVII', in J. Targarona, A. Sáez-Badillos, R. Izquierdo (eds), *Pensamiento y mística hispano-judía y sefardí* (Cuenca), pp. 237–76.

Dodds, J.D., T.F. Glick and V.B. Mann (eds) (1992), *Convivencia. Jews, Muslims and Christians in Medieval Spain* (New York).

Dozy, R. (ed.) (2001), *El esplendor de los Omeyas de Córdoba. La civilización musulmana de Europa occidental.* Catalogue of the Medina Azahara exhibition.

Ducos, M. (1990), 'Passion et politique dans les tragédies de Didon', in *Énée et Didon. Naissance, fonctionnement et survie d'un mythe, Interdisciplinary Colloquium*, ed. by R. Martin (Paris), pp. 97–106.

Epalza, M. de (1992), *Los Moriscos antes y después de la Expulsión* (Madrid).

Fabre, P.-A. (1999), 'La conversion infinie des conversos. Des "nouveaux-chrétiens" dans la Compagnie de Jésus au XVIe siècle', in *Annales*, vol. 54, no. 4, July–August, 1999, 875–93.

Foa, A. and L. Scaraffia (eds) (1996), *Dimensioni e problemi della ricerca storica, 2* (Rome).

Galera Andreu, P. A. (2001), 'La "Casa Real Vieja" y la "Casa Real Nueva". Concepto y visión de la Alhambra por los reyes cristianos en la Edad Moderna', in J.A. González Alcantud and A. Malpica Cuello (eds), *Pensar la Alhambra* (Barcelona), pp. 98–108.

García Ballester, L. (1984), *Los moriscos y la medicina. Un capítulo de la medicina y la ciencia marginadas en la España del siglo XVI* (Barcelona).

———. (2004), *La construcción de las historias de España* (Madrid).

García-Cárcel, R. and D. Moreno Martínez (2000), *Inquisición: historia crítica* (Madrid).

García Gomez, E. (1974), *Andalucía contra Berbería* (Barcelona).

González Alcantud, J.A. (2002), *Lo moro. Las lógicas de la derrota y la formación del estereotipo islámico* (Barcelona).

González Alcantud, J.A. and F. Zabbal (eds) (2003), *Histoire de l'Andalousie. Mémoire et enjeux* (Montpellier).

Goytisolo, J. (1970), *La reivindicación del Conde Don Julián* (Barcelona).

Harvey, L. P. (1992), *Islamic Spain. 1250–1500* (Chicago).

Heine, H. (1865), *Drames et Fantaisies,* Introduction by Saint-René Taillandier (Paris).

———. (1994), *Historisch-kritische Gesamtausgabe der Werke,* Manfred Windfuhr (ed.) (Hamburg).

Hernández Juberías, J. (1996), *La península imaginaria. Mitos y leyendas sobre al-Andalus* (Madrid).

Historia de España Menéndez Pidal (2000), directed by J.M. Jover Zamora, vols IV, V and VIII (Madrid).

I Fenici (1988), exhibition catalogue, Palazzo Grassi, Venice, dir. by S. Moscati (Milan).

Il Mito di Europa. Da fanciulla rapita a continente (2002), exhibition catalogue, Galleria degli Uffizi, Firenze, 11 June 2002 – 6 January 2003 (Florence).

Imágenes en el tiempo. Un siglo de fotografía en la Alhambra 1840–1940, exhibition catalogue (2003), Sala de Exposiciones del Palacio de Carlos V (15.1.–15.6.2003) (Granada).

Israel, J. (1985), *European Jewry in the Age of Mercantilism, 1550–1700* (Oxford).

Kamen, H. (1997), *The Spanish Inquisition: An Historical Revision* (London).

Kaplan, J. (1996), *Judíos nuevos en Amsterdam. Estudios sobre la historia social e intelectual del judaísmo sefardí en el siglo XVII* (Barcelona).

Lacave, J.L. (1987), *Sefarad, Sefarad, La España judía* (Barcelona).

Las tres culturas de la Corona de Castilla y los sefardíes (1990), Junta de Castilla y León (ed.) (Salamanca).

Lévi-Provençal, E. (1953), 'La Description de l'Espagne d'Ahmad al-Razi. Essai de reconstitution de l'original arabe et traduction française', *Al-Andalus*, VIII, 51–108.

_____. (1999) *Histoire de l'Espagne musulmane* (Paris).

López Estrada, F. (ed.) (1993), *El Abencerraje (Novela y romancero)* (Madrid).

_____. (1999), 'Una voz de la Holanda hispánica sefardí: Isabel Rebecca Correa', in M. Bosse, B. Potthast and A. Stoll (eds), vol. II, pp. 395–418.

Márquez Villanueva, F. (1981), 'La voluntad de leyenda de Miguel de Luna', NRFH, XXX, pp. 359–95.

_____. (1994), *El concepto cultural alfonsí* (Madrid).

_____. (1996), 'In lingua Tholetana', in *La Escuela de Traductores de Toledo* (Toledo), pp. 23–34.

_____. (1997), *El problema morisco (Desde otras laderas)* (Madrid).

_____. (2000), 'Sobre el concepto de judaizante', in Aviva Doron (ed.), *'Encuentros' and 'Desencuentros'. Spanish Jewish Cultural Interactions Through History* (Tel Aviv).

Marquis de Forgues (pseudonym Old Nick) (1844), *La Chine ouverte* (Paris).

Marquis d'Hervey Saint-Denys (1859), *La Chine devant l'Europe* (Paris).

Martin, R. (ed.) (1990), *Énée et Didon. Naissance, fonctionnement et survie d'un mythe*, Interdisciplinary Colloquium (Paris).

Méchoulan, H. (ed.) (1992), *Les Juifs d'Espagne. Histoire d'une diaspora. 1492–1992* (Paris).

Moscati, S. (1988), 'L'impero di Cartagine', in *I Fenici*, pp. 54–61.

Ovid, *Metamorphoses*, II, vv. 833–75, citation vv. 873–4.

Pérez, J. (2005), *Los judíos en España* (Madrid).

Pérez de Hita, G. (1998), *La guerra de los moriscos (Segunda Parte de las Guerras civiles de Granada)*, P. Blanchard-Demouge (ed.) (Granada). Preliminary study by J. Gil Sanjuán, pp. IX–XC.

_____. (1999), *Historia de los bandos de Zegríes y Abencerrajes (Primera Parte de las Guerras civiles de Granada)*, P. Blanchard-Demouge (ed.) (Granada). Preliminary study by P. Correa Rodríguez, pp. VII–CLXXXI.

Pulido Serrano, J.I. (2003), '¿Sacrilegios judíos? Análisis de un modelo antisemita', in P. Joan i Tous and H. Nottebaum (eds), *El olivo y la espada. Estudios sobre el antisemitismo en España* (siglos XVI–XX) (Tübingen).

Révah, I.S. (1959–1960), 'Les Marranes', *Revue des Études juives*, vol. I (CXVIII).

Rodriguez Alonso, C. (ed.) (1975), *La historia de los godos, vándalos y suevos de Isidoro de Sevilla* (León).

Rodriguez de la Flor, F. (1999), *La Península metafísica. Arte, literatura y pensamiento en la España de la Contrarreforma* (Madrid).

Romualdi, A. (2002), 'Il mito di Europa nell'antichità', in *Il Mito di Europa*, pp. 39–50.

Roth, C. (1932), *A History of the Marranos*, French translation *(1990): Histoire des Marranes* (Paris).

_____. (1990), *Doña Gracia Nasi* (French translation of *Doña Gracia of the House of Nasi*, New York, 1946) (Paris).

Rubiera Mata, M.J. (1992), *Literatura hispanoárabe* (Madrid).

_____. (1995), 'Nueva hipótesis sobre el Mancebo de Arévalo', *Sharq Al-Andalus. Estudios Mudéjares y Moriscos*, 12 (Teruel, Alicante), pp. 313–33.

_____ . (1996), 'La familia morisca de los Muley-Fez, príncipes meriníes e infantes de Granada', *Sharq Al-Andalus. Estudios Mudéjares y Moriscos*, 13 (Alicante, Teruel), pp. 159–67.

Sáenz-Badillos, A. (2005), 'Intelectuales judíos y conversos en el siglo XV', in Piñero Ramírez, P. M. (ed.), *Dejar hablar a los textos. Homenaje a Francisco Márquez Villanueva* (Seville), vol. I, pp. 261–77.

Said, E.W. (1978), *Orientalism* (London).

Sané, A.M. (1809), 'Quelques réflexions sur les Musulmans d'Espagne, les anciens Espagnols, et sur cet ouvrage'. Preliminary study in *Histoire chevaleresque des Maures de Grenade, traduite de l'espagnol de Ginès Pérez de Hita, ... par A. M. Sané* (Paris), vol. I, pp. I–LVII.

Saperta y Beja, E. (1979), *Salonique et ses judéo-espagnols* (Paris).

Saraiva, A.J. (1950–1962), *História da cultura em Portugal*, vol. III (Lisbon).

Schonfield, J. (ed.) (1992), Moshe Arragel, *La Biblia de Alba: An Illuminated Manuscript in Castillan* (Madrid and London).

Septimus, B. (1982), *Hispano-Jewish Culture in Transition* (Cambridge).

Sicroff, A.A. (1960), *Les Controverses des status de 'pureté de sang' en Espagne du XVe au XVIIe siècle* (Paris).

Solà-Solé, J.M., S. Armistead and J.H. Silverman (1984), *Hispania Judaica: Studies in the History, Language and Literature of the Jews in the Hispanic World* (Barcelona).

Stoll, A. (1987), 'L'astuzia degli assediati. Ovvero come Daumier tratta la "civiltà" ' in A. Stoll, (ed.), *Honoré Daumier – Il ritorno dei barbari. Europei e 'selvaggi' nella caricatura*, exhibition catalogue (Milan) (German orig.: Hamburg 1985).

_____ . (1995), 'Sepharads Widerstand. Zur poetischen Produktivität der jüdischen Kultur Spaniens nach dem Vertreibungsedikt', in A. Stoll, (ed.), *Sepharden, Morisken, Indianerinnen und ihresgleichen. Die andere Seite der hispanischen Kulturen* (Bielefeld), pp. 15–46.

_____ . (1998), 'Abindarráez y Narváez. El último de los Abencerrajes, un cristiano noble y la persecución de los judíos conversos. Un cuento del Renacimiento español', in A. Stoll (ed.), *Averroes dialogado y otros momentos literarios y sociales de la interacción cristiano – musulmana en España e Italia* (Kassel), pp. 141–85.

_____ . (2001), 'El Saco de Roma o la caída de la cultura medieval española. Acerca del destino del escandaloso *Retrato de la Lozana andaluza* de Francisco Delicado', in J.L. Castellano and F. Sánchez-Montes (eds), *Carlos V. Europeísmo y Universalidad* (Madrid), vol. V, pp. 609–42.

_____ . (2003), 'Paul et Virginie à Grenade. Perspectives interculturelles sur la maurophilie du poète Henri Heine dans sa tragédie *Almansor*', in J.A. González Alcantud and F. Zabbal (eds), pp. 29–68.

_____ . (2005a), 'Conversiones/Inversiones. Modelos de asimilación para Moros/Moriscos y Judeoconversos en la literatura española del siglo XVI', in P. Piñero Ramírez (ed.), *Dejar hablar a los textos. Homenaje a Francisco Márquez Villanueva* (Seville), vol. II, pp. 775–810.

_____ . (2005b), 'Wer ist Dulcinea, und was schreibt Cide Hamete Benengeli? Cervantes' Erkundung der semitischen Zwischenwelten Kastiliens', in C. Strosetzki (ed.), *Miguel de Cervantes', Don Quijote'. Explizite und implizite Diskurse im 'Don Quijote'* (Berlin), pp. 99–135.

_____ . (forthcoming in 2006a), 'Aldonza/Dulcinea en el manuscrito iluminado de Cide Hamete Benengeli. Hacia una arqueología cultural de los fundamentos aljamiados del *Quijote*', in Martínez de Castilla Muñoz N. and Rodolfo Gil Benumeya Grimau (eds), *Cervantes en lo morisco Sociedad Estatal de Conmemoraciones Culturals* (Seville, 19–21/5/2005) (Madrid).

_____ . (forthcoming in 2006b), 'Felices encuentros con el manuscrito árabe de Cide Hamete Benengeli o Momentos fundacionales de una escritura 'mestiza'', in M.J. Rubiera Mata (ed.), *Cervantes entre las dos orillas* (Alicante, 14–16/11/2005) (Alicante).

Vallvé Bermejo, J. (1986), *La divisón territorial de la España musulmana* (Madrid).

_____ . (1989), *Nuevas ideas sobre la conquista árabe de España, Toponimia y onomástica* (Madrid).

_____ . (1992), *El califato de Córdoba* (Madrid).

_____ . (1999), *Al-Andalus: Sociedad e instituciones* (Madrid).

_____ . (2003), *Abderamán III. Califa de España y Occidente* (912–961) (Barcelona).

Vernet, J. (1993), *El Islam en España* (Madrid).

Viña Liste, J.M. (ed.) (2000), *Textos medievales de caballerías* (Madrid).

Vincent, B. (1987), *Minorías y marginados en la España del siglo XVI* (Granada).

_____ . (1996), Preliminary study to A. Gallego Burín and A. Gámir Sandoval (eds), *Los moriscos del reino de Granada según el Sínodo de Guádix de 1554* (Granada).

_____ . (1999), 'Morisques, médecins et culture', in *Aulas y saberes.* VI Congreso Internacional de Historia de las Universidades hispanas (Valencia, december 1999) (Valencia), vol. I, pp. 41–49.

_____ . (2002), 'Histoire d'une déchéance: La famille des Fez Muley à Grenade au XVIe siècle', *Cahiers du C.R.I.A.R.*, 21, 69–79.

Virgil, (1981), (Virgile), *Énéide. Livre I – IV,* Jacques Perret (transl. and ed.), (Paris).

Ximénez de Rada, R. (1999), *Historia Arabum, in Roderici Ximenii de Rada Opera omnia Pars III,* J. Fernández Valverde and J.A. Estévez Sola (eds) (Turnhout).

Yerushalmi, Y.H. (1998), *Essais sur l'histoire des Juifs, des marranes et des nouveaux-chrétiens d'origine hispano-portugaise* (Paris).

Chapter 3

Gender and the Body

Giulia Calvi

This chapter identifies some of the places and ways in which male-female relations, together with the symbolic representations of the masculine and feminine, contribute to the construction of an image of Europe. Unlike scholarship on the production of high culture and the circulation in literary circles of the *querelle des femmes*,[1] this analysis turns to the writings of historical anthropology for its material. The construction of identities is thus examined by reference to certain visible markers, namely the body and dress, as well as through the primary and constitutive relations of the heterosexual couple, as reflected in marriage customs and family behaviour.[2] Male and female bodies are thus located at the nexus of a double trajectory: on the one hand they are the sites on which the cultural and bodily strategies of appearance are written; on the other hand they are both the subjects and objects of ritual manipulation, social practices and exchange.[3] These spheres of inquiry allow us to trace a human geography that both describes and delimits regions, and more circumscribed zones within them. The ethnographic culture of sixteenth century Europe defines, uses and appropriates a range of configurations of masculine and feminine to cast them into themes and reinforce awareness of a distinct dimension of its own culture. Gender relations, in the historical forms in which they were expressed, thus become one of the identifying discourses that, albeit in a discontinuous, fragmentary and irregular manner, distinguish and delineate borders as well as long-term continuities. Bodies, clothing, exchanges and rituals differentiate the regions of Northwest Europe, the Mediterranean, Northern Scandinavia and the East. These partitions are by no means rigid and unmoving, however: within them one notes tensions, contradictions and transformations set in motion by the spread of Christianity, the caesura of the Reformation, and the broadening of cultural and mental horizons brought about by conquest and expansion beyond Europe.

I chose to examine a sixteenth-century production that transmits a gaze that is both astonished yet free of the sense of a consolidated western superiority. It is a gaze shaped by classical sources – Herodotus, Livy, Strabo, Tacitus, Pliny – and by those of late antiquity; by travel diaries and missionary accounts, scientific writings, and the images of clothing and costumes portrayed in drawings, engravings and books that proliferated throughout Europe. Structured on synthesis, repetition and accumulation, this body of sources develops a discursive model grounded in analogy: the texts and images highlight the continuities and similarities between the peoples of classical antiquity and the modern inhabitants of some European and extra-European territories, over the centuries. The observations of these sixteenth-century writers were thus constructed through an oscillating movement that, departing from their present, swung back in time towards classicism and its sources, embracing a universalizing narrative of development. The risk of study by analogy, as already highlighted by Foucault, is that 'by virtue of this game, the world remains the same'.[4] There is no doubt that the teleological structure of the narrative, and the use that these texts make of chronology, sources and citations, raise many problems. Nevertheless, the figure of analogy is not the only one used to explain the nexus between images from the past and those of the present, between European and extra-European territories, and between continuity and change within human cultures and groups. One also perceives a strong sensitivity and attention to differences and how they are expressed and physically and socially represented. The curiosity about and study of such elements produce a tension that interrupts the dependence on analogy and its self-referential circle. The 'similar' co-exists with and slowly gives way to that which is 'different'; that in turn motivates reflection, often dense with projections regarding one's own identity and that of others.[5]

The sources for this analysis consist of European costume books printed in the sixteenth century,[6] as well as some of the most widely-diffused tracts published on the habits and customs of world peoples. These are texts in which the focus on differences, and, by contrast, on the construction of a clearly articulated, cross-cutting European identity among them, are grounded not only in the physical characteristics of the body and dress, but also in the social behaviour, rituals, customs and traditions that accompany human groups and mark the life course as they journey from birth to death.

A deeply engrained gender perspective permeates these tracts. Clothes and bodies not only distinguish Europeans from the others, but, in all examples, men from women. Human groups are examined with attention to the sexual division of social roles and to the core of the traditions, habits and shared experiences that give rise to these divisions: the construction of the conjugal couple through marriage and the creation of the nuclear family. Indeed, wedding costumes are at the heart of these collections, and the construction of the marital couple occupies a consistent iconic and narrative space in the two sets of sources.

Defined in this way, one can also interpret gender relations in terms of the degree of christianization of an area that, over the course of centuries, became European, and, above all, Western, though the gradual extension of the Greek, Roman, and Mediterranean culture of the dowry. Yet, while the degree of sexual discipline and social constraint brought about by the Christian form of marriage constitutes a powerful watershed in the gender relationship/image of Europe, the texts and iconography also reveal indigenous traditions external to it. This difference is most acute in the extreme northern regions of Scandinavia and in the areas that extend between the Aegean Sea and the Black Sea, and between the Black Sea and the Baltic Sea.[7] Unsystematically quoting sources from the classical era and late antiquity, the sixteenth-century texts and images persistently reproduce a tension between the 'civilizing' figure of the Christian wife and mother and the mythological woman warrior, who reached from the Caucuses to the still unknown regions of Scandinavia. Patterns of non-dotal marital exchange continued to characterize vast areas of Central and Eastern Europe, and sixteenth-century observers refer to the persistence of family forms which were neither monogamous nor nuclear, but rather characterized by polygamy and the buying and selling of wives and children as slaves.

Though well within the confines of Europe, the extreme north of Scandinavia and the area located between the Aegean and Black Seas, and the region between the Black and the Baltic Seas constitute the borderlands in which Western ways of life eroded and became lost. In these areas, relations between men and women constitute a break from the traditions of Mediterranean classicism and their identification with a nuclear family organized around a married couple. From the regions of the extreme North and the East, the armed bodies of Amazons continued to intrude and nurture a pre-Christian gendered imaginary well into the sixteenth century.

Costume Books

Since the Renaissance, printed 'collections of clothing' have provided a series of representations of local, civic, national and religious identities. One particular element of their literary, editorial and visual value is located in their dual elaboration of gender. To define and distinguish oneself and others by that which one wears (or does not wear) means placing the body on the stage of an ordered theatre of the world in which the subjects are systematically represented at the polar ends of masculine and feminine. The collections, which oscillated between representations of the flexible meaning of *habitus* and the more traditional one of costume, were a considerable success for publishers and booksellers. Volumes containing engravings of various sizes were often taken apart and sold by the page; these soon became objects of curiosity, decoration, amusement and collection. While 216 different collections circulated in Europe between 1520 and 1610, production intensified[8] most perceptibly after 1550, principally in the cities of Paris and Venice, the two most prominent centres for publishing.

Beyond the above-mentioned characteristics and the captivating and exotic tone that the collections transmitted to their audiences, the repetition of the images, their wide circulation, and the reiteration of the models diminished, so to speak, each author's originality. The discursive and self-referential structure of the texts and images themselves was reinforced, making them a precious resource for anthropological analysis, or, more precisely, for an anthropology of the representation of gender in early modern Europe. The overlapping and interweaving of citations and copies gave rise to a palpable consensus that, over time, took on the weight of an iconographic hegemony.

This process contributed first to the definition of European men and women with respect to peoples elsewhere, and then to the elaboration of more circumscribed similarities and qualities particular to their more local 'position': north or south; east or west; urban or rural; and across social classes, religious affiliations and the life course. Costume books can thus be analysed for their capacity to gather and distribute the most visibly evident components of belonging that is constructed alongside the production of otherness. The most important quality of these collections, which varied in their internal organization, the coherence of their iconographic contents, and the presence or absence of written text, lies in their unilateral undertaking – and their capacity to do so – to represent the 'other' non-western peoples in a broad sense, who became, *de facto*, the 'represented'. For centuries it would be the western gaze, via images, literature, and geographical, anthropological and clinical investigation, to define and fix the representation of world peoples.[9]

Due to these books' diffusion and versatility of use, one notes a certain convergence in their contents, whereby original plates produced by one author might be set alongside copies reproduced from works by other authors or anonymous sources circulating in the market. Next to cosmographies, these texts offer descriptions of peoples and cities, and travel narratives, a more or less ordered overview not only of Italian and European fashions and manners, but also those of some regions of Africa, the Far East, and, less frequently, some islands and territories of Scandinavia and the New World. Nevertheless, to deduce that the multiple identities represented by these texts suggest a simple binary opposition between us – European, Western – and them would be overly reductionist and simplistic. In reality, beyond the traditional reiterations derived from classical writers, no conscious or coherent discourse on the superiority of Europe was developed before the eighteenth century. Instead, these texts transmitted a pre-colonial, pre-imperialist discourse which outlined a vision in which knowledge and power are not mutually constructed. Sixteenth-century Europe viewed the 'other' with fear and trepidation: it constructed mythologies, analogies and metaphors from within a weak and shaky perspective. In order to define themselves, Europeans needed to construct the other – an other from whom they could take distance, in which they could examine their own reflection, against whom they could compete, or on whom they could project their desires, anxieties and feelings of nostalgia. This continuous manipulation of identities, borders, and distinctions varies from one text to the other, and maps a flexible geography of inclusion and exclusion. It is a geography delineated by the points of view and positions proposed by each text, and through which the gaze of the reader is oriented. Thus, Spanish, Venetian or German texts provided different definitions of the borders of Europe, and, above all, different cultural characterizations of what was meant by European or non-European. These collections located the outer reaches of the European continent in the territorial sense, but above all in the cultural sense, in the semi-known lands of the northern extremes of Scandinavia, the East and the shifting border that is European Turkey (including Constantinople, which, rooted in West, signalled the passage to the East).

In 1520, the German Johann Boemus published a compendium, in Latin, on the habits and costumes of world peoples. This work enjoyed great popular success, and was printed in numerous editions and translations. Boemus interpreted the diversity of cultures with the image of the mirrors in which readers were instructed to concentrate their gaze so as to 'fashion their body and soul' and 'organize their life'.[10] Differences among world peoples make sense within a process of self-awareness, of the self-fashioning of Europeans. The author identified western man (and thus also the reader) with Ulysses, who had to stop the ears of his companions with the 'wax of good judgement' in order to elude the songs of the sirens, that is, of the non-Europeans, the 'barbarians', the 'other'. Ulysses saved himself from their seductive calls by countering them with the bulwarks of European identity: rationality, Christianity, 'politics', national and ethnic belonging, monogamous marriage and the norms that regulate patrilineal succession.[11]

I have selected two points of view that correspond to the extreme margins of Europe, as it was represented and imagined: the extreme north of Scandinavia, and the Mediterranean area that includes European Turkey. In these two areas, sixteenth-century Europe had constructed images of two societies which, though they contained significant imaginary and projective components, for the most part were not cast as superior or inferior to Western Europe. These societies were instead contrasted through much more complex operations that problematized not only differences and similarities, but also elements in which gender relations represented a defining tension. The religious split brought about by the Reformation definitively separated Mediterranean Europe from that of the Northwest, especially from an anthropological point of view. The culture of honour that distinguished the Mediterranean countries, European Turkey included, underwent a deep transformation in the reformed area. With regard to social manners and behaviour between men and women, this transformation appeared as the site where pre-marriage practices and the forms of socialization between the sexes were modernized within a different organization of the private and public spheres. For that reason, both sixteenth-century books on manners and contemporary treatises trace a line which clearly demarks a Europe of 'traditional powers', comprising the Mediterranean area (including the south of France and European Turkey) in which common elements of social organization are intentionally accentuated, from a 'new or modern' Europe that comprises the area of the Reformation, but nevertheless maintains an indigenous mythology extending from the northern extremes of Scandinavia to Moscow and some areas of Eastern Europe. This mythology, largely unknown in Renaissance Italy and Europe, was first introduced by Olaus Magnus in his history of the Northern Peoples printed in Rome in 1554. It fed into an image of gender identities and relations that allowed an indigenous component of otherness – irreducible to that of Christianity – to flower.[12]

In all of these sources and texts, the masculine and feminine body represent the symbolic intersection of appearance, transformation and manipulation. It is also the site on which one bases reflections on the differences or similarities among peoples within a shuffling of scientific paradigms. To the Aristotelian lesson of genetic differences deriving from the 'various imaginings of fathers' during conception, one can contrast that of Hippocrates and of the experience according to which 'the varying figures' in which human beings are born are due to the fact that 'they eat the same foods and drink the same waters, they dress in identical fashion and observe the same customs'. In sixteenth-century Europe, difference and similarity were not elaborated in terms of essentialisms such as race, skin colour, or biological superiority. Instead, they were discussed along non-linear and heterogeneous itineraries.

Points of View: Venice and Vecellio

The two collections of Cesare Vecellio, *Degli habiti antichi e moderni di diverse parti del mondo* (Ancient and Modern Costumes from Different Regions of the World), published in Venice in 1590, and then expanded in 1598 under the title *Degli habiti antichi e moderni di tutto il mondo* (Ancient and Modern Costumes of the World) are illustrated with 415 and 503 plates, respectively.[14] Compared to prior collections, including those by Italians (Bertelli, Vico, Grassi) French (Boissard), Flemish (De Bruyn) and German (Weiditz, Amman) authors, those of Vecellio represent a point of arrival for their breadth, completeness, coherence and refinement. While the others, all published before 1580, were considerably thinner and without any written commentary, those of Vecellio instead constituted a genuinely synthetic work that offered readers a wide panorama of the varieties of people and cultures that populated the sixteenth-century world. Vecellio drew liberally from his predecessors, often including previously published images that were already well known among readers, and thus authoritative in the emerging field. Each illustration appears alone, and is flanked by a page providing a detailed description of the image, from the top of the engraving down. Vecellio began with the hairstyle or headdress, and worked his way down over the shoulders, the bust, arms and hands, and ended with the feet. He then explained how the particular costume was used, on what occasions and by whom it would be worn, and to what extent the particular fashion was diffuse among a people. Another characteristic element of each illustration was the uniqueness of each subject, and his or her isolation from any narrative context. While to some extent this demonstrates the renaissance tradition of portraiture, it also exemplifies the culture of self-fashioning and the use of models. These illustrations can be compared to emblem books, or to the collections of botanical engravings in which each plant species is presented singly, divided by genus on distinct plates set one next to the other.[15] This iconographic approach, oriented towards analogy, was useful in representing the masculine and the feminine in both the natural and human worlds. Vecellio's explicit intent was to delineate a history of clothing, and thus, to provide a reasoned history of the images engraved on the plates – their origins, historical roots and diffusion. In this sense, the figures in his books do not appear as abstract models, but as objects defined by tradition, usage and behaviour, and by place, ritual and power. In sum, Vecellio's models appear related to the complex functions required and imposed by a society in the process of transformation.

Most of the Vecellian genealogy of ancient and modern clothing deals with women's fashion, and the female body played the greatest role in giving shape to the world theatre. In the first edition of his book, the commentary accompanying each plate is in Italian, and often occupies more than one page. The author indulges in a certain amount of digression on etymologies, myths about the origins of each place, its landscape, noble lineages and anecdotes. The text was drastically reduced in the 1598 edition, and specific references were discarded in favour of greater emphasis on synthetic and general models. Furthermore, the descriptions in this second edition were printed in both Italian and Latin, suggesting the desire to export the Italian image abroad, which would guarantee a broader international circulation than the preceding volume. The 1590 edition was directed towards a predominantly Italian readership, and provided a more individualizing and fragmentary discourse which tied the grammar of appearance to the diversity of local situations, tastes, trends, lifestyles and landscapes. Divided into two books, the first presented and defined European costumes, while the second concentrated on Asia and Africa. Unlike Amman and Boissard, Vecellio specifically mentions Europe, defining it as an autonomous, inclusive organizational category (in his definition, Turks, Greeks, Dalmatians, Croats and Russians are all part of Europe). In the first edition, Nordic peoples are left out as a collective identity. This changing definition of what constitutes Europe, evident in the most noted costume books (Amman, Boissard, Vecellio), highlights the unstable and precarious character of the European continent's location within a certain shared geopolitical and cultural space, the points of reference being essentially the cities. Indeed both Boissard and Amman limit themselves to presenting, on the frontispiece of their work, the allegory-myth of Europe without transforming it into a category of geographical space.[16] Nevertheless, it is interesting to note that, despite the repetition of the model (the feminization of the four continents, the dominant position of Europe with attributes of sovereignty or else the mythological figure of the capture of Europe), Amman overturns this representation, introducing a male version of the continents in which European man is depicted nude with a bolt of fabric and scissors in hand. Rooted in the Bible, it is an eloquent image of the self-fashioning of European man, an emblem of his modernity, of his transformative and performative capacity, in contrast to the static representations of the other three male continents depicted in their native costumes.

The discourse on appearance found in these texts was a dawning field, and Vecellio noted the uncertainties, lack of information, and experimental nature of the exercise from the very outset of his books, which he dedicated to his readers:

No one can understand the degree to which I laboured to compile the costumes within, many of which we have only barely learned of, given the distance to these far-off lands and our ignorance of these countries, some of which have no trade, and thus do not present the opportunity to develop relations that provide such certainty. To this I add, if you like, that many parts of the world are still beyond our knowledge, are still being discovered, and that of many of those which have been discovered within our memory and the memory of our fathers, we know just barely their name, let alone the clothing or costumes that they wear.[17]

Nevertheless, in the internal structure of his book Vecellio pushes himself further, and defines a European territory that comprises the Western monarchies; Flanders and Holland; the cities of Germany and Italy; and the dukedoms and kingdoms of western Europe including Moscovy and Russia; Greece, Turkey, Hungary, Croatia, and Dalmatia. The extreme north of Europe appears as a territory fragmented by uncertain borders running from Sweden to the Baltic territories, to Poland and then as far as Moscovy and Russia. Its indeterminateness of the last Thule is evident in the void of images produced by European draughtsmen and engravers: it indicates the lack of information about the northern world, submerged in darkness and ice.[18] Cities define spaces and mark borders – in the cities, marriage costumes, decorations and rituals distinguish the local identities. Bridal clothing and women's clothing in general make visible, in the traditional organization of the lifecycle, ethnic and religious minorities, border areas where jurisdictions are often confused or contested as was the case with the Christian women of Pera and Adrianopole in Turkey, the Jewish women of Salonica, the Venetian women in Dalmatia and the Aegean islands, Polish women in Germany, and women gypsies in Hungary.

Vecellio structured the second edition of his book (1598) in a completely different way. The work is divided into 12 books, of which the last is entirely dedicated to the costumes of the New World. Europe as an autonomous category of geographical space disappears, and each book is dedicated to a single people and its costumes.

The New World Within

Book V of Vecellio's second edition introduces something new: northern costumes from the three kingdoms of the extreme north of Scandinavia, Finland, and Moscow. None of the European authors from whom Vecellio had copied many images had gone so far as to include the hyperborean regions or the inhabitants of Thule (only the Venetian Pietro Bertelli had designed a Finnish costume); on the whole, Italian culture continued to depend on what it could glean from the work of the 'auctores', who, in Medieval times, had dominated in the field of geographical and encyclopaedic studies. In Venice, Ramusio had printed the travels of Pietro Querini, who had been shipwrecked near the Lofoten islands in 1432. The reports of envoys from the Holy See, at the forefront those of Antonio Possevino written between 1577 and 1580, however, remained inaccessible and locked within the archives of the Curia, and then the *Compagnia di Gesù*. Scandinavia remained *terra incognita* until the publication (1554) in Rome of the Latin edition of the Great History of the Northern Peoples, written by the Bishop of Uppsala Olaus Magnus, and later translated into the vernacular. Torquato Tasso, who read Olaus, was the only Italian scholar interested in the myths of the North. Vecellio himself relied on Olaus as his source for information on these peoples. He copied the images, and had them engraved and reproduced in a handful of tables. Without having to cross the Atlantic, the North represented the new world in the heart of Europe.

In 1596, two years before the second edition of Vecellio's *Costumes*, Giovanni Botero published the first complete edition of his *Relazioni Universali*.[19] In the traditional preamble and in the geopolitical explanation, the description of Europe that appears in Book I is identical, to that which appeared two years later in Vecellio's book, which included the peoples of the North and the 'European Turks'.

Botero relaunched the image of the 'new world' of the North, constructing a text that oscillates between attempting to integrate the Scandinavians, who by then had assimilated the social and religious models of the rest of Europe, yet suggesting rejection and suspicion towards an indigenous population still tied to its pagan heritage. Thus, while the Swedes' knack for making 'bread from the bark of pines and firs' seemed to indicate a certain level of domestication, the Lapps' habit of covering themselves in animal skins confirmed the absolute opposite: 'in the winter they wear the skins of sea cows, or entire bearskins. They tie them to their heads, leaving only an opening for their eyes – this has given some writers cause to report that they are as hairy as animals'.[20] The legends of sorcerers and the shaman culture also provoked fears: 'They are very good at spells, they call the winds and the clouds and the storms and practise other frightful arts'; 'The Biarmi live like the Lapps: they adore fire, they revere magic and they fill the air with spells, stirring up storms, and transfixing men'. While Botero ignored the women of these populations, Olaus Magnus and Vecellio both gave them ample space. In Vecellio's volume, of the 24 plates that portray the northern costumes, 12 are dedicated to women and 12 to men. Indeed, the way to integrate these 'healthy and robust' northern peoples into Europe, with their great physical strength and simple clothing designed to protect them from the ice and long frigid nights, and their near total lack of cities and recognizable forms of government, was via their women and the depictions of their bridal costumes, and hence, Christian marriage. Vecellio designed the 'Bride of *Livelandia*', who wears on her head 'a crown of gold … veiled with a cloth similar to the head coverings worn by nuns. It is usually made of silk or satin or other delicate cloth, and it symbolises the woman's chastity. Until she is married, a girl never looks a man in his face without the permission of her mother'.[21]

In the text by Olaus Magnus, the section devoted to the Northern peoples' marriage customs is extremely detailed, providing a close description, for each class and ethnicity, of the norms regulating how spouses were selected, the marriage rituals, the payment of the dowry and the exchange of gifts. In this way the Catholic wedding, rooted in Roman law, in princely government, and laws, marked a turning point for the area's transformation into Christian society. Nevertheless, the christianization of Scandinavian society was not uniform, and the Bishop Olaus Magnus observed with great attention the syncretistic practices, as well as the resistance to the adoption of the Catholic wedding. In the case of the abduction of the bride, that was still in practice, these resistances ensure the violent relationship between the future bride and groom. As one moves north and east, the areas in which christianization, and thus the civilization and pacification of customs did not occur, became greater. From this perspective, the Latin rite of Catholic marriage defines western Europe both with respect to bordering orthodox countries, and to those areas in which indigenous marriage customs endured. The Lapps, for example, perform weddings with the fire produced by striking a stone with iron, because they believe that 'the happiest marriages are those made by this fire and in the rock that ignites it – they must be as joined and united as the couple.'[22] Fire remained at the heart of Scandinavian ritual – the sacredness of light infused the Christian ceremonies: baptisms and funerals were conducted by the light of torches that were borne into the church and blessed.

Only marriages between the nobles were celebrated 'with the customs and rituals used in Christian weddings, with the benediction of the priest, the giving of a ring and the gift of the dowry (from the husband to the wife), the contents of which are constituted by the laws of the land ... the size and quality of the dowry is fixed by law, whether for a king, private gentlemen, noblemen, or commoners'. The bride and bridegroom promise to live together forever, 'and with the holy Church as their witness, they take the ring and kiss' and are blessed by the priest.[23] After other solemnities the ceremony ends with

all of the relatives forming two lines, the men carefully led by a man on one side, and the women by a woman on the other, on a day organized with great pomp, all on horseback, on both sides, ... they go to the parish church. There, with great torches alight, the bride, with a crown on her head, is blessed by the priest. She proceeds through the middle to the main altar, where she moves next to the groom. Both are solemnly asked if they agree to live together through adversity and prosperity ... exchanging the ring and being blessed, they declare and confirm all of the preceding ceremony ... But the Muscovites, the Ruthenians, the Lithuanians, the Livonians, and especially the Curati, peoples who are at the borders of these northern men, we shall show what customs they, especially the lower classes, observe for their weddings ... because their marriages are made by capturing virgins, without other ceremony. Just as Roman Law and the princely constitutions instruct that the only legitimate marriages are those celebrated with a wedding ceremony, with the participation of a priest, it is the custom of these people to consider the kidnapping of a virgin from her father as a legitimate marriage, ... as recounted by Livy, the Romans did the same, for lack of women, by abducting their brides from neighbouring peoples with whom they were otherwise denied marriage. Any peasant who wished that his son take a wife would call together all of his kin and neighbours and suggest that in this or that castle there was a young marriageable girl whom they could capture and bring to his son for a wife. These ... armed and on horseback ... would band together to kidnap the girl, who, as regards marriage, is free to contract one. Thanks to their spies who have watched over her and her whereabouts, she is abducted. The girl protests, shrieking for help from her family and friends. And if they respond to these cries, they quickly arm themselves and race to free her from her kidnappers. A fight ensues, and the winners of the battle become owners of the girl.[24]

Despite the Germanic custom of the groom providing a dowry for his wife, it was mainly the élites who assimilated the Catholic wedding ceremony into their customs. The lower classes and other ethnic groups not belonging to the Scandinavian

Figure 3.1 *Cesare Vecellio*, The National Library of Norway, Picture Collection.

Figure 3.2 *Cesare Vecellio*, The National Library of Norway, Picture Collection.

peninsula remained faithful to the custom of bride stealing. Next to the ethnography of the nuptial traditions that define the rules and limits of European civility, Magnus's text takes up the tradition of classical writers, among whom is Procopius of Cesarea, who emphasized the lack of assimilation among the Nordic peoples, most clearly evident in their women, 'monstrous' witches, and huntresses [Fig. 3.1].

As one moved towards the north of Lapland, the contrast became ever more clear, with no sign at all of *civillé* and in the progressive obliteration of gender differences.[25] Women, especially the Christian mothers of the North, who 'don't go to church more than once or twice a year, only doing so to baptize their children' would be the intermediaries in the civilizing process of these savage peoples.[26] [Figs. 3.2 and 3.3] Nevertheless this acculturation was fragile, historically anchored in the Christianization and transformation of civil society through the institution of marriage and the formation of a Christian family.

In the years in which Vecellio designed his plates, the fracture imposed by the introduction of the Lutheran faith by Gustavo Vâsa was already beyond repair, and the Catholic faith had been abandoned. Olaus Magnus, in exile in Rome from protestant Sweden, interpreted the schism forced by the Lutheran reform as of an irreversible return to barbarity and corruption. Nordic women, the heroic warriors, the Amazons of their mythical and timeless past, became the misguided protagonists of this perversion of custom. For Olaus Magnus, the transformation of dress, its fashions and colours were a sign of this new illegitimate behaviour. Simplicity and honesty in dress belonged to a prehistoric past when 'clothing was very different from what one sees today, especially in the internal and external decoration of women'. Magnus compared the modest tunic of the past with the 'ragged outfit' of the present which barely covered the 'corrupted mind' of the Lutheran reform.[27] The caesura of the Reformation fed the nostalgia for a mythical and uncorrupted past that itself was tied to origin myths. In these, a complicated saga of chivalry, punctuated by virgin warriors and female pirates at battle on the seas and lakes of ice, transmitted to late renaissance Europe the narration of female heroism. In time, tamed by 'honest feminine dress' and marriage, the virgin warriors laid down their arms and gave birth to the pacific kingdoms of the north. Aluilda, Stiche, Rufila and Rusla, Nordic Amazons, having abandoned the war for sea and land and masculine courage, gave life to the royal races of Sweden, Norway, and Holland.[28]

Olaus Magnus took the genealogical tradition of the Germanic Amazons from Enea Silvio Piccolomini's *Historie di Boemia* (History of Bohemia), who repeated it from Paolo Orosio. Magnus emphasized its common roots in the Caucuses, the territory that classical authors called Scythia.[29]

In Olaus Magnus's writings, it was the men, the princes, who succeeded in taming the virgin warriors, in compelling them to put down their arms and found, within marriage, the royal dynasties of the North.

In contrast, in Vecellio's text and illustrations, northern Europe after the Reformation was the site of the emancipation of female behaviour in particular. From Saxony to Sweden, and also in England and Holland, the dress of women, their unveiled faces, their familiarity with urban space and the market, the courting rituals in which they engaged and the relations between men and women were radically different from those of women in Catholic Europe. In Silesia, 'maidens are openly embraced and kissed by their lovers, and they exercise great familiarity with them, dancing and conversing with them; they are not mistrusted by their fathers or mothers, perhaps because of the strict laws against adultery, but in those countries there are no prostitutes'. In the work of Johann Boemus, Germany, split by the Reformation, was shown to be open to the aesthetic tastes and behaviours that arrived from Italy and France.[30] How people dressed brought the themes of change, consumption, and modernity to the forefront. In general, the reformed areas coincided with greater sexual liberty for young women. Furthermore, more flexible pre-marital rules of behaviour, and less female segregation also seemed to be related to the absence of prostitution, which was also due to the strict laws against adultery. The feminine identity that resulted in these countries was thus more visible and certain, far from the games of masquerade, artifice and ambiguity so diffuse in Rome and Venice, where a courtesan might hide her identity dressed as a noble or married woman. England followed northern Europe's lead in the general emancipation of female customs.

The Mediterranean

In sixteenth-century costume books, the organizing principle for material, which spun out from Italy and Europe towards the Orient, Africa, and finally the New World, was accompanied by a thinning out of sources and a simplification of images that often coincided with single national examples. The known map of the world was discontinuous, and, with regard to the extreme regions of the North and Africa, fraught with myths and stereotypes and based on a cartography still in flux and dependent on travel diaries and reports. However, for the more temperate zones of the Mediterranean, architectural and iconographic sources, and some printed texts allowed Vecellio to identify ancient fashions and their transformation. Fashions disappear, fall into disuse and are born anew: the criteria that determine this trajectory of ascent, acceptance and decline are those of the style's functionality and the strength of the social, professional or generational groups that adopted them.

From the middle of the sixteenth century everything began to change, to multiply, and become more expensive. This whirling sense of uncontrollable and uncontrolled change was the starting point from which Vecellio turned his gaze from the present to the past, and began his work of systematically cataloguing attire. The change was not neutral; it belonged to the sphere of private consumption activated by noblewomen, especially those in Venice. As protagonist of modern luxury, and therefore of a transformation in consumption begun forty years before, the Venetian noblewoman changed styles in unpredictable ways.[31] Starting from this awareness of a fleeting modernity that would become ungovernable unless it was analysed – and disciplined – Vecellio inserted the theme of fashion within the more traditional theme of the transformation of all things. In his text, he insinuates an analogy between the permanence of male fashion and the stability of the (Republican) political regimes. Francesco Sansovino had confirmed this hypothesis for Venice, opposing it to the other major Italian cities for its conservatism.[32] It was also true for Florence where enduring fashions, especially for men, republicanism, and the stability of the government were part of the discourse on clothes, the consumption of fashion and the relations between the sexes in Italy and late renaissance Europe.[33]

Of the 339 plates that represent Europe, 202 of them portray female fashions (59.5%) and 137 portray male dress. The numeric proportion between Italy and Europe is practically identical. Book VIII, however, is in net contrast with this vision of a 'feminized' Europe. In this book, 25 of the 32 plates portraying Turkish dress feature male costumes, most of which are for military or religious functions. The European observers' lack of access to Turkish women is reflected in the low number of illustrations dedicated to them (7), but those which are included hint at a sensuality and eroticism (women seated with their legs crossed, bare footed, or wearing trousers) unseen in the rigid postures assumed and illustrated in the plates on western women.[34] Vecellio's source for most of these plates was the French geographer Nicolas de Nicolay, author of the extremely well-received *Les navigations, pérégrinations et voyages en la Turquie*, printed in Lyon in 1568.[35] Here, too, the vision projected of Europe ran in two directions, defined both by the construction of an irreducible diversity, and assimilation. With the exception of the Orient, which was once again feminized in the iconography of Vecellio's books, the continents of Africa and the New World were both represented by men, for the most part nude and armed.

In Europe, and especially in Italy, processes of social integration blurring local differences are visible. The protagonists of modernization in Italian society came from the private nobility of gentlemen through a style that was repeated plate after plate and that the text extends to 'nearly all Italian gentlemen' who 'wear the same outfit, consisting of a silk hat, long cloaks with short busts and tight sleeves, wide trousers fastened at the knee, and silk tights tied with wide laces and decorated with bows.'

The appearance of the merchant also ceased to be defined according to any one locality: modern gentlemen and merchants, portrayed in the same clothing, and accompanied by the same text, felt at home in Rome, Venice, Milan, Naples and Florence, attracted by life at court or at the centres in which the liveliness of exchange represented an opportunity for investment, trade and mobility. A comparison of the two editions of Vecellio's books demonstrates a significant difference in this regard: while the two modern masculine figures are completely missing from the first edition, they appear systematically in the second. Vecellio brings to the forefront, even if through image and allusion, the loci of transformation and tension, the areas arousing anxiety that, to paraphrase Norbert Elias, become socio-genetic points of social tension:[36] the blood nobility in crisis, menaced by the rise and mobility of other social classes; the new nobility, of offices and courtrooms, who aspire to assume a class identity. The clothing of the period sheds light on these processes of integration and distinction, of strategies of attack and defence.

The imperfect location of women within the patrilineal social systems was another area which, in ancien régime societies, fed a social and cultural unrest that was difficult to contain.[37] In Vecellio's work, the grand theme of family and female honour was expressed in an extensive series of plates that cut across European and

Figure 3.3 *Olaus Magnus*, The National Library of Norway, Picture Collection.

extra-European societies. We thus observe the delineation of geopolitical areas internal to legal and religious systems that have differing interpretations of control over female sexuality and male and familial honour. The texts and illustrations break down the theme through a traditional tri- or four-part typology that defines the civil state of the woman (maiden, bride, wife or widow) and thus her position in the hierarchy and the rules that regulate her appearance – the colours, the styles, the fabrics and the complicated limits of visibility. A woman's social status introduced some variation in the level of control and the liberties conceded. The typology was systematically applied to all of the world's societies, and the European patrilineal perspective was exported and used as an interpretative code which could be universally applied to define the status of women.

The observation of women moved from Italy and Venice and focused most closely on the maiden – the young woman waiting for marriage – and, to a minor extent, the bride. The image of the young unmarried Venetian noblewoman, hidden from the view of even her closest relatives, veiled and 'without any ornament' was a genuine topos reproduced by all of the costume books and even copied in the *libri amicorum*, travel albums, that, embellished by drawings, symbols, and short texts, were carried by students – especially Germans – in their travels to Italy.[38]

Family honour, above all visible in the clothing of the maiden, nevertheless constitutes a part of a local, mobile and relational language that distinguished the women of the urban elite. While in Venice the threshold of modesty grew ever higher, in Mantova it was lower, and maidens of the noble classes were free to circulate with their faces unveiled. In Ferrara, the threshold of invisibility ascended once more, and the 'young women of the town wear a veil with which, if they feel watched, they cover their faces'. Freedom and control were also related to the maiden's social rank, and visibility while segregation varied depending on whether one lived in the city or the countryside.[39]

Vecellio also studied and reproduced the clothing of women elsewhere in Europe. In Paris, women 'covered their faces outside of the home, wearing, in the manner of a mask, a piece of black silk or satin with two holes'.[40] In Spain, young veiled maidens 'expertly arrange an opening in their cloaks with their hands at their eyes so that they can see'.[41] Spain was no exception, however, in that the geography of honour was discontinuous.[42]

The image of the maiden and the woman of Granada constitute a true *topos* in the sixteenth-century collections of costumes. Used and copied over and over again by the main European authors, the original comes from the *Trachtenbuch* designed by the German Christoph Weiditz in 1529 during his travels to Spain in the court of Charles V. These images hint at a quality of exoticism within Catholic and Mediterranean Europe. In the engravings, the dark-skinned 'Moors of Barbary' with their Muslim origins, evoke a culture that is both 'other' and assimilated. This unique quality appears in the texts, images, fashions, and dress. Other sources from that same period confirm that the Ottoman Turks were considered part of Europe. Indeed this 'Italian intimacy with the Islamic other'[43] established a mutually respectful relationship with many aspects of Ottoman society, within a broader and commonly shared Mediterranean culture. Gender relations and women in Ottoman Islamic culture have hardly been studied, but the few existing monographs appear to suggest a convergence in the transformation processes that swept across the Eastern Mediterranean towards broad and internally intersecting cultural contexts. Contributions from Latin, Greek Orthodox and Islamic cultures shaped forms of cultural exchange, borrowing and fusion.[44]

Vecellio's plates on the clothing of the Turks for the most part are taken from the French geographer Nicolas de Nicolay, who, sent by Henry II of France, arrived in Istanbul in 1551 as part of Ambassador Gabriel d'Aramon's retinue. Nicolay published the most detailed book of middle eastern costumes of the age. In his work, the author describes how he was assisted with the selection of models, costumes and styles by Zafer Aga, a Ragusan eunuch who had been raised in the court of a local pasha. Nicolay's *Navigations, pérégrinations et voyages* were published in Turkish and later translated into many languages, and they enjoyed long success. The engravings in these books projected not only the gaze of the royal geographer, but also the internal and complicit gaze of Zafer Aga. Along with Nicolay's illustrations, Vecellio probably also consulted one of the first reports on the Istanbul of Suleiman the Magnificent. This text, by Luigi Bassano, 'protégé and servant' of Cardinal Rodolfo Pio di Carpi[45] was written and printed in Rome in 1545. Bassano, a Croatian raised in court as a page, tended to emphasize common features in the Ottoman society in which he had lived, drawing many similarities between it and that of the western Mediterranean. Reared among different idioms and cultures, he was a cultural mediator with an eye turned more to similarities than differences. He skilfully identified a series of parallelisms between the function of sexually segregated spaces in the Mediterranean area, drawing connections between the seraglio, the court and the monastery. Indeed, in his eyes, the Sultan's harem, usually impenetrable to the masculine gaze and composed of 'one hundred damsels who would later marry the pages', functioned exactly like the European courts governed by women,[46] who prepared and concluded marriage agreements between the young women of the local aristocracy and the gentlemen at the service of the court. Furthermore, the seraglios, as implied by the word itself, were 'like our monasteries, ringed by high windowless walls'.[47]

Vecellio depicted the costume of the pages, and also here identified similar functions: 'One finds a great number of young men in the seraglio inhabited by the Sultana, boys taken, donated, and given in tribute to the great Sultan. They call these boys "pages", just as we do'.[48] Compared to the Venetian one, Turkish society appears to be archaic yet orderly and the difference between male and female dress is less pronounced.[49]

The segregation of noblewomen constitutes a code that unites the Mediterranean, patrilineal societies in which sons are the only inheritors (even if the first amount 'taken from the inheritance is the dowry promised to the wife').[50] The difference with the Ottoman culture is found in the latter's social mobility and in the universal practice of slavery connected to it. The Grand Turk would 'never take a royal as his wife, or give his daughters to a king or to another high prince, but ... marries his daughters and sisters to slaves ... it is absolutely true that he makes them noble, and immediately gives them the dignity of the pascià'.[51] Finally, indifference to the legitimacy of birth and widespread homosexuality mark the insurmountable threshold that divides Christian culture from Islam.

In the same years in which Vecellio outlined his *Costumes*, Giovanni Botero published his *Relazioni universali*. This is another instance where the European Turks are compared to Mediterranean Christians 'because of the continuous conversation with the Christians, they have the highest opinion of Christ ... in fact, many consider him God and Redeemer, and it was not long ago that some Christians were put to death in Constantinople and they showed great courage: it was held that many from the Porte felt the same.'[52]

The Bride Price, Polygamy, Slavery

Prior to the eighteenth century, of the Europeans who had spent time in the Balkans during the early centuries of Ottoman rule, only Venetian diplomats and German travellers had left detailed observations on ethnic differences among Slavs, unbiased by anti-Turkish propaganda.[53] In the 1520s, the German writer Johann Boemus's landmark compendium on the customs and costumes of the world was published in Latin, and then subsequently translated into the principal European languages.[54] He began his work with a study of Africa, then proceeded to the Orient and finally Europe. As in the work of Olaus Magnus, the drama of the Reformation and the religious diaspora runs through the text, marking an irreparable break from the equilibrium of the past. In the preface, Boemus lays out a linear vision of history, understood as the progressive disciplining of savage traits and the civilization of customs, starting with the acceptance and diffusion of the incest taboo. The prohibition on 'sexual coupling, without distinction, with one's own mothers and daughters' regulates, so to speak, the relationship between the sexes and culminates in the idealization of the nuclear family, where men are 'content to stay under their own roof, with their own wife and children, all happy together.'[55] In addition, a third norm was added to the incest taboo and the monogamous nuclear family: the custom of wives bringing a dowry to their husbands.

Boemus's examination of Europe starts from Greece and proceeds towards the north-east. Working in a counter-clockwise direction, the author dwelt at length on Germany and then moved through the north and north-west regions to Italy (and thus to Rome) and the Mediterranean regions. Interestingly, in contrast to observations made in the texts already mentioned here, and to other costume books, Boemus argued that it was Greece – not Rome – to be the first to shape a European identity. This identity, according to the author, was based on a 'new' model of marriage and a set of rules that excluded women from the public sphere and rights of citizenship. The reforms of Solon changed the rules of matrimony, introducing a dowry system whereby 'only women would bring, from their fathers' houses, a few garments and some pots of little value'. In addition, Solon abolished the archaic custom by which the new husband was required to advance a 'price' to the father of the bride,[56] and he prohibited 'the sale of daughters and sisters, unless they had been found to have fornicated with others'.[57] We will see below how the bride price and the selling into slavery of wives and daughters are tightly interwoven features of the systems of marital exchange that characterized the 'barbaric' cultures north east of Greece. According to Boemus, in the long period spanning from classical antiquity to the sixteenth century, Europe applied the three 'Greek' rules according to which political identity was based on gender – that is, the exclusion of women from political life (from the Senate) and from citizenship, as well as the exclusion of mother's name and line from descent.[58]

Shifting his analysis towards the north east, and thus the broad and ill-defined territory of ancient Thrace – which he calls Romania – Boemus notes that the Greek marriage rules tend to disappear. However, within the oft-repeated clichés found in the ancient literature about 'barbaric' peoples – polygamy, promiscuity, a lack of control over virgins – one identifies, starting with Herodotus, a system of family formation quite distinct from the western regime of the dowry, that tends to characterize eastern Europe all the way to Russia. In the area spanning from Germany and extending towards Russia and the Caucasus, two features in particular appeared either on their own, or together. Both the 'bride price,' that is, the purchase of wives, and 'voluntary slavery', or the selling of wives, daughters, and at times even the head of the family himself, are distinct traits of this model. Described first by Herodotus, this system was also noted by authors of late antiquity, compendium writers, sixteenth-century travellers, and even folklorists of the nineteenth-century.[59]

Recent anthropological work comparing marriage customs between ancient societies and contemporary non-European populations suggest that the price of the bride is at the heart of the economy of primitive societies. In order to put together the necessary sum, a poor man may even indebt himself for life, in other words accept the condition of servitude'[60] or, having paid a high price for his wife, to sell her, together with some of his children. These studies thus posit a causal relationship between bride price and voluntary slavery, both being features found not just in historical written sources, but still today among the African and Asian populations that accept this marital regime. With regard to populations in Eastern Europe, folklore, literary sources, and anthropological studies trace an albeit flexible line, between the Western and Mediterranean areas in which the dowry was observed, and southern Slavs and the peoples of the Caucuses, who, until the twentieth century still observed the bride price.[61] Nineteenth-century sources attest to the continued vitality and persistence of these nuptial practices throughout vast areas of Central Europe. These marriage rituals began with the festive auctioning off of young women in a context that recalls the descriptions of Herodotus.[62] On another note, it is not coincidental that in sixteenth-century texts the expression *Schiavonia*, referred to some of the Balkan territories, or that the '*schiavon*', i.e. slavic (from slave) language was spoken by the Livonians, Prussians, Polacks, Dalmatians and Croats.

Boemus attributes to his contemporary Romanians the notes Herodotus made on Thrace, and writes that these peoples would mark, with a tattoo, the foreheads of the most valued young women, indicating that they were to be sold at the highest price, while 'the ugly girls must offer a dowry in exchange for a husband'.[63] This last statement probably goes back to Pomponio Mela who, writing in the first century AD, noted the practice among elites of selling young noblewomen at auction, sometimes for great sums. In contrast, less socially attractive women were provided dowries to encourage potential husbands.[64] The ambiguous terminology used by the Greco-Roman writers to illustrate the ritual complexity of these 'barbaric' customs, the meaning of which escaped the understanding of western colonizers, leads us to take the conclusions of the sixteenth-century authors with a grain of salt, as they base their arguments partly on these sources, and partly on later sources and reports of their contemporaries. Of course, Boemus does collect information, though probably confusing it, and he dwells in detail on many other ways in which the ritual interdependence between men and women not only demarcates areas of cultural difference, but also provides a site at which some Asian customs are received and transmitted to Europe. While Boemus does often refer to polygamy in only a very vague way, attributing it to undisciplined habits and using it to distinguish the non-Christian territories of Eastern and Northern Europe, at times his discussion of the practice is accompanied by more careful observations. Thus, in his descriptions of Romania, Boemus refers to the persistence of some forms of female 'heroism', which he suggests is Asiatic in origin and probably connected to polygamy. In particular, he elaborates on the ritual suicide of a chosen wife next to the body of her dead husband. This practice intensifies competition among wives, as it is seen as a sign of election.[65] While this suicide ritual, which recalls the self-immolation of Indian widows that Montaigne described with admiration,[66] only appears in Boemus' writings on Romania, he attributes the practice of voluntary slavery to a much vaster area. It was practised in Russia by nobles who sold 'themselves, their wives, and children'[67]; in Livonia, Prussia, and Poland where all speak the 'Slavic' tongue and where voluntary slavery is common even among the poorer classes. Moving from the east towards the centre of Europe, Boemus arrived in his native Germany, and it is to this country and its regions that the author devoted the most substantial part of his work. Here, as is well documented by the abundant literature,[68] the system of matrimonial exchange involves the purchase of the bride by the groom, who pays, in kind, with 'two oxen, a horse, a pick, a shovel, and a shield'. There were well-defined rules on inter-marriage, and the law prohibited 'taking for one's wife one's mother-in-law, one's daughter-in-law, one's step-daughter, one's step-mother, the daughter of a brother or sister, the wife of one's brother, or the sister of one's wife; neither may siblings form relations among themselves.' Violation of this law would result in the confiscation of property.[69]

In early modern Europe, the rules and rituals of marital exchange traced the border between an area where the dowry was the most practised form of exchange, and another, where the bride price tended to prevail. These two systems give rise to a series of questions that cannot be addressed here. Over time, the relationship between men and women, like that between parents and children, was intersected by processes that reified the female sex in particular, making of it an object of public and ritualized buying and selling. The secular persistence of these traditions raises many questions on the different ways that social and family interdependence is articulated, on the status of personal liberties, on rights and on the very concept of personhood and property in the various regions of Europe. The importance of all of these elements cannot but influence our current arrangements in the relations between men and women.

Our early modern European texts emphasize a historical representation of the bodies of men and women, as the changing of fashions and ornaments erases all reference to nakedness or nature. Thus, together with kin, couple, family and household, clothed bodies are classified among the basic components of the space and human landscape of Europe throughout the centuries. Nevertheless, the discursive strategies underlying the hegemonic position of the nuclear family based on monogamic marriage in the western area of Europe reveal that processes of couple, family and household formation were also cultural, imaginative and emotional constructions as well as morally charged projections aimed at defining historical identities. However, it would be naïve to conceive of this in terms of a simplistic binary opposition: indeed the subject position of the western European observer was fashioned out of a multiple set of gendered viewpoints which distinguished Mediterranean and reformed European men and women; western and orthodox Christians; the Islamic and Jewish peoples of large parts of Central, South and South Eastern Europe, as well as the dwellers of the extreme areas of Scandinavia.

In all of these texts the Protestant Reformation inaugurates 'contemporary' history and interrupts the hazy *longue durée* narrative implied by the systematic use of classical sources. The Reformation changed the doctrinal and ritual basis of marriage which, as we have seen, is both a key iconographic feature of costume books and one of the main elements of social classification in ethnographic tracts. All the early modern authors we have discussed witnessed, albeit from different confessional standings, the dramatic social changes brought about by the Reformation accompanied by a refashioning of gender relations. In this changing perspective marriage was a distinguishing, yet highly mobile feature of early modern European societies. In the light of marriage, gender relations could become a measure of the progressive Christianization of broad areas of Europe which were in time assimilated to classical and Mediterranean culture owing to the introduction of the dowry. However, this representation of the control of sexuality and of social pacification through the ritual of Christian marriage coexisted with the recording of indigenous practices mainly located in the Scandinavian peninsula and in the vast regions stretching between the Aegean and Black Seas and between the latter and the Baltic Sea. Armed bride stealing, non dowry exchange, polygamy, different practices of endogamy, rituals varying according to ethnicity, social standing and place, the selling of wives and children as slaves, turned the process of couple, family and household formation into a complex and contested domain.

Defined in terms of otherness *vis-à-vis* extra-European territories and the recently conquered New World, early modern representations of gender identities and relations do not offer us a coherent and one-dimensional image of Europe, but rather a heterogeneous and at times conflicting set of discourses, tensions and visual strategies within an interpretive framework lacking a unified perception of historical time and space.

Notes

1. Bok (2001); Anderson and Zinsser (1988).
2. For good overviews on the history of the family in Europe, see Goody (2000); Barbagli and Kertzer (2001, 2003).
3. Jones and Stallybrass (2000); Kopytoff (2001).
4. Foucault (1966), p. 35.
5. Foucault (1966), p. 69.
6. Weiditz (1994); Weigel and Amman (1577); Boissard, (1581); de Bruyn, (1581); Vecellio (1590, 1598).
7. Hartman (2004); Todorova (1990, 1997).
8. Tuffal (1955); Vico (1558); Bertelli (1563, 1589); Grassi (1585); Vecellio (1590, 1598).
9. One cannot but refer to Said (1978); Clifford (1988), pp. 215–51.
10. Boemo (1543), Proemio; Thamara (1556); Boemus (1555); for a discussion of Boemus see Hodgen (1964), pp. 131–43.
11. Boemo (1543), p .5.
12. Magnus (1565). On Olaus Magnus see Johannesson (1982).
13. Rosaccio (1600), p. 48.
14. There is little information on Cesare Vecellio: born at Pieve di Cadore in 1521, he was the son of Ettore Vecellio. He studied first under his paternal uncle Francesco, and then for a time under Tiziano, his second cousin. He worked in the latter's workshop, and became one of his most faithful followers. He followed Tiziano to Augusta in 1548 and stayed with him at his home in Venice. Only after the death of Tiziano (1576) was

Vecellio recognized in his own right as a skilled painter, engraver, and book miniaturist. Cesare left many works of art in the area around Belluno and drew the figures of his book for *Habiti* (1590). He died at an advanced age, in Venice, in 1601: at age 69 his first collection of clothing was printed and at age 78, two years before his death, he published the second, expanded and definitive edition. See Ticozzi (1817).

15. Wilson (2005); Hillman and Mazio (1997).
16. Prosperi (1993).
17. Vecellio (1598), c.3v.
18. De Anna (1993).
19. Botero (1894).
20. Botero (1894), Part III, Book III, p. 97.
21. Vecellio (1598), c. 289.
22. Magnus (1565), p. 51v.
23. Magnus (1565), p. 171v.
24. Magnus (1565), p. 173.
25. Magnus (1565), p. 298.
26. Magnus (1565), p. 301.
27. Magnus (1565), p. 169.
28. Magnus (1565), p. 70v. Giritha then gave birth to a son, who peacefully reigned over Denmark for the next 50 years. Alff battled two other virgin warriors – Sticha and Rufila – who, with a powerful armada wanted to conquer the kingdom of the Fronds. The kingdome of Norway was also endangered by a courageous virgin, Rusla, who fought against her brother and was eventually killed by him. The King of Holland battled and won against a Norwegian virgin warrior, Pusila.
29. Magnus (1565), pp. 70v–71.
30. Magnus (1565), pp. 120–120v.
31. Vecellio (1598), p. 109.
32. Sansovino (1581), cc. 150v–151.
33. Calvi (2002).
34. Guérin-Dalle Mese (1998); Levi Pisetzky (1973); Albanese (1996).
35. de Nicolay (1568).
36. Elias (1976).
37. Cazzetta (1999); Wiesner-Hanks (2000); Eden et al. (1999).
38. Vecellio (1590), c.123; Vecellio (1598), c. 95.
39. Vecellio (1598), c. 176.
40. Vecellio (1598), c .232.
41. Vecellio (1598), c .255.
42. Vecellio (1598), c. 267.
43. Kahf (2002), p. 59.
44. Kahf (2002); Ahmed (1992); Davis (1986); El Guindi (2003).
45. Bassano (1545).
46. Bassano (1545), p. 12v.
47. Bassano (1545).
48. Vecellio (1598), p. 379.
49. Vecellio (1598), p. 386 and p. 374.
50. Vecellio (1598), p. 13v.
51. Bassano (1545), p. 21.
52. Botero (1894), Part III, Book III, p. 100.

53. Todorova (1997), p. 65ff.
54. Boemo (1543).
55. Boemo (1543), Proemio.
56. Boemo (1543), p. 87.
57. Boemo (1543), p. 87v.
58. Boemo (1543), p. 88v.
59. Stahl (1974).
60. Testart and Brunaux (2004), p. 621.
61. Testart and Brunaux (2004), p. 630; Stahl (1974).
62. Testart and Brunaux (2004), p. 627.
63. Boemo (1543), pp. 98v–99.
64. Testart and Brunaux (2004), pp. 624–5.
65. Boemo (1545), p. 98v; Loomba (1993); Mani (1998).
66. de Montagne (1986), pp. 404–5.
67. Boemo (1543), p. 108.
68. Owen Hughes (1978); Petot (1992); Kuehn (1991).
69. Boemo (1543), p. 137.

References

Ahmed, L. (1992), *Women and Gender in Islam* (New Haven and London).

Albanese, D. (1996), 'Making it new: humanism, colonialism and the gendered body in early modern culture', in V. Traub, M.L. Kaplan, D. Callaghan (eds), *Feminist Readings of early modern culture* (Cambridge), pp. 16–43.

Anderson, B.S. and J.P. Zinsser (1988), *A History of Their Own: Women in Europe from Prehistory to the Present*, 2 volumes (New York).

Barbagli, M. and D.I. Kertzer (eds) (2001), *Storia della famiglia in Europa. Dal Cinquecento alla Rivoluzione Francese* (Rome-Bari).

———. (2003), *Il lungo Ottocento* (Rome-Bari).

Bassano, L. (1545), *I costumi e modo di viver de' Turchi minutamente descritto* (Rome).

Bertelli, F. (1563), *Omnium fere gentium nostrae aetatis habitus,* which partly reproduces the anonymous text printed in Paris in 1562, *Recueil de la divérsité des habits qui sont de present en usaige tantes pays d'Europe, Asie, Affrique et illes sauvages, le tous fait après le naturel,* (unknown engraver) (Venice).

Bertelli, P. (1589), *Diversarum nationum habitus* (Padua).

Boemo, G. (1543), *Gli costumi, le leggi et l'usanze di tutte le genti racolte qui insieme da molti illustri scrittori* (Venice).

Boemus, J. (1555), *The Fardle of Factions,* trans. William Waterman (London).

Boissard, J-J. (1581), *Habitus variarum orbis gentium.* Habitz de nations etranges. Trachten mancherley Volker des Erdskreysz (Mechlin).

Bok, G. (2001), *Le donne nella storia europea* (Rome-Bari).

Botero, G. (1894), *La vita e le opere di G. Botero con la quinta parte delle Relazioni universali e altri inediti,* C. Gioda (ed.) (Milan).

Calvi, G. (2002), 'Abito, genere cittadinanza nella Toscana moderna (secoli XVI–XVII)', *Quaderni Storici,* 110, pp. 477–503.

Cazzetta, G. (1999), *Onestà e consenso femminile nella cultura giuridica moderna* (Milan).

Clifford, J. (1988), 'On Collecting Art and Culture', in J. Clifford (ed.), *The Predicament of Culture* (Cambridge and London).

Davis, F. (1986), *The Ottoman Lady. A Social History from 1718 to 1918* (New York).

De Anna, L. (1993), *Il Settentrione d'Europa nella coscienza italiana fra il XIV e il XVI secolo*, in S. Gensini (ed.), *Europa e Mediterraneo tra Medioevo e prima Età moderna: l'osservatorio italiano* (Pisa), pp. 141–70.

de, Bruyn, A. (1581), *Omnium pene Europae, Asiae, Aphricae atque Americae gentium habitus* (Antwerp).

de, Montagne, M. (1986), *Saggi, Della virtù*, Book II, XXIX (Milan).

de, Nicolay, N. (1568), *Les navigations, pérégrinations et voyages faites en la Turquie, 1567–1568*. Présenté et annoté par Marie-Christine Gomez-Géraud et Stéphane Yérasimos (Paris, Presses du CNRS 1989).

Eden, F., L. Hall and G. Hekma (eds.) (1999), *Sexual Cultures in European National Histories* (Manchester).

El Guindi, F. (2003), *Veil* (Oxford and New York) (originally published in 1999).

Elias, N. (1976), *Über den Prozess der Zivilisation* (Baden-Baden).

Foucault, M. (1966), *Le mots et le choses* (Paris).

Goody, J. (2000), *The European Family* (Oxford).

Grassi, B. (1585), *De veri ritratti degli abiti di tutte le parti del mondo* (Rome).

Guerin, J. –Dalle Mese (1998), *L'occhio di Cesare Vecellio: abiti e costumi esotici del '500* (Alessandria).

Hartman, M.S. (2004), *The Household and the Making of History. A Subversive View of the Western Past* (Cambridge).

Hillman, D. and C. Mazio (eds.) (1997), *The Body in Parts: Fantasies of Corporeality in Early Modern Europe* (New York).

Hodgen, M.T. (1964), *Early Anthropology in the Sixteenth and Seventeenth Centuries* (Philadelphia).

Johannesson, K. (1982), *The Renaissance of the Goths in Sixteenth Century Sweden. Johannes and Olaus Magnus as Politicians and Historians* (Berkeley).

Jones, A.R. and P. Stallybrass (2000), *Renaissance Clothing and the Materials of Memory* (Cambridge).

Kahf, Ma (2002), *Western Representations of the Muslim Woman* (Austin).

Kopytoff, I. (2001), 'The Cultural Biography of Things: Commodization as Process', in A. Appadurai (ed.), *The Social Life of Things. Commodities in Cultural Perspective* (Cambridge), pp. 64–91.

Kuehn, T. (1991), *Law, Family and Women. Toward an Anthropology of Renaissance Italy* (Chicago).

Levi Pisetzky, R. (1973), *Moda e costume, in Storia d'Italia*, v.5, 'I Documenti' (Turin).

Loomba, A. (1993), 'Dead Women Tell No Tales: Issues of Female Subjectivity, Subaltern Agency and Tradition in Colonial and Post Colonial Writings on Widow Immolation in India', *History Workshop Journal*, 36, pp. 209–27.

Magnus, O. (1565), *Historia delle genti et della natura delle cose settentrionali* (Venice).

Mani, L. (1998), *Contentious Traditions. The Debate on Sati in Colonial India* (Berkeley, Los Angeles and London).

Owen Hughes, D. (1978), 'From Brideprice to Dowry in Mediterranean Europe', *Journal of Family History*, 3, pp. 262–96.

Petot, P. (1992), *Histoire du droit privé francais*, I, La famille (Paris).

Prosperi, A. (1993), 'Europa "in forma virginis": aspetti della propaganda asburgica del '500', *Annali dell'Istituto storico italo-germanico di Trento*, XIX, pp. 127–52.

Rosaccio, G. (1600), *Il Microcosmo* (Florence).

Said, E. (1978), *Orientalism* (New York).

Sansovino, F. (1581), *Venezia città Mobilissima* (Venice).

Stahl, P.H. (1974), *Ethnologie de l'Europe du sud-est* (Paris and La Haye).

Testart, A. and J-L. Brunaux (2004), 'Esclavage et prix de la fiancée. La société thrace au risque de l'Ethnographie comparée', *Annales*, 59, 3.

Thamara, F. (1556), *Libro de las costumbres* (Anvers).

Ticozzi, S. (1817), *Vite dei pittori Vecelli di Cadore: libri quattro* (Milan).

Todorova, M. (1990), 'Myth-Making in European Family History: The Zadruga Revisited' *East European Politics and Societies*, 4, pp. 30–76.

_____ . (1997), *Imaginning the Balkans* (New York and Oxford)

Tuffal, J. (1955), 'Les recueils de costumes gravés au XVI siècle', *Actes du I Congres international d'histoire du costume, Venise 31 aout-7 septembre 1952*, Centro internazionale delle Arti e del Costume (Venice), pp. 262–9.

Vecellio, C. (1590), *Degli habiti antichi et moderni di diverse parti del mondo* (Venice).

_____ . (1598), *Habiti antichi et moderni di tutto il mondo* (Venice).

Vico, E. (1558), *Diversarum gentium nostrae aetatis habitus* (Venetiis).

Weiditz, C. (1994), *Das Trachtenbuch von seinen Reisen nach Spanien und den Niederlanden*, Theoder Hampe (ed.) (also: Berlin, Verlag von Walter de Gruyter & Co., 1927) (New York).

Weigel, H. and J. Amman (1577), *Habitus praecipuorum populorum, tam virorum quam foeminarum singolari arte depicta* (Nuremberg).

Wiesner- Hanks, M. (2000), *Women and Gender in Early Modern Europe* (Cambridge).

Wilson, B. (2005), *The World in Venice: Print, The City, and Early Modern Identity* (Toronto).

Chapter 4

Magic and Witchcraft

Stuart Clark

Magic and witchcraft were topics of very wide dispersion in pre-modern Europe, extending not just to what we recognize today as the 'occult' but across broad areas of religion, politics, philosophy and historical thought. Among the developments in which they played an influential part were the reformations of the European churches, the consolidation of styles of charismatic rulership in states and judiciaries, the spread of apocalyptic eschatology, and the rethinking of scientific theories and practices. As a discursive tradition, the demonology that underpinned debates in these many areas was therefore of major significance in the cultural and intellectual life of the period.[1] Did this in itself contribute to any sort of collective European consciousness? Demonology was certainly pan-European in its character and cultural space. It illustrated traits of mind and language, forms of explanation and understanding, and concepts, symbols and motifs that were common to educated men in universities and professions throughout the continent. Contributors to the subject were educated in similar ways, read and cited the same books, including each others, appealed to the same scholarly authorities, and cycled and recycled the same assumptions and arguments, wherever they were located. This intellectual community undoubtedly shared a common experience and culture across Europe, such that magic and witchcraft were talked about in Edinburgh much as they were in Erfurt, and in Copenhagen much as in Coimbra. This was not, however, a feature of pre-modern European high culture that was subject-specific or unique to magic and witchcraft; it applied to most topics of international debate at the time. In this respect, Europe had few internal borders in any intellectual field. Opportunities for self-conscious reflections on Europe specific to magic and witchcraft based solely on the sharing of a demonological discourse itself therefore seem limited. The most we can do is to plot these common discursive patterns, seeing them as a kind of European intellectual patrimony that was implicitly recognized by those who followed them.

If we turn from the manner in which they were discussed to the content of beliefs in magic and witchcraft and their application to situations, the possibilities are much more promising – despite the complete absence of these topics from recent studies of 'the idea of Europe'.[2] Of course, the terms 'magic' and 'witchcraft' are of no value at all in *our* historical vocabulary since, compared to (say) 'war' or 'literacy', they simply fail to predicate. It is not, therefore a question of identifying anything that we could agree to label in this way. But the two terms (together with their allies 'paganism', 'superstition', and, above all, 'idolatry') were used all the time in pre-modern Europe, and why, how, by whom, and (above all) against whom they were used are matters of critical historical importance. The concept of 'witchcraft', the more dramatic and sensational of the two, was deployed within Europe (not without opposition, of course) for a variety of reasons, not least because witches and demons were sincerely believed to pose a real threat to the values and institutions of civilized life. While these values and institutions may not have been explicitly defended as 'European', they were definitely associated with 'Christendom', and to the diminishing extent that these two identities were assimilated, demonism could be imagined as an anti-European conspiracy. Certainly, Christendom and Satandom were mutually entailed contraries. Much more important, witch-hating was a cultural weapon, useful for demonizing enemy faiths and religious deviance, and here it could be deployed not just within European evangelical and confessional campaigns but outside the continent as well. As religion ceased to define common enquiries and the idea that 'Christendom' defined Europe became more and more untenable, so the relationship with non-Europeans took over as a main source of European self-awareness. For as long as Christendom and diabolism survived in partnership, therefore, the diabolizing of non-European cultures was necessarily a form of Europeanizing too.

'Magic' was of much broader application, adopted mostly as a term of refusal and exclusion by those representing orthodoxies – mainly religious, but scientific and medical too – who were anxious to repudiate beliefs and practices they found to be deviant. This accounts for the huge attention paid to magic in the general literature and institutions of religious reform – in sermons, catechisms, guides to the Commandments, confessors' manuals, and casuistry, and in the church courts and inquisitions of Europe. What were condemned most often were the resources and techniques adopted by ordinary Europeans to protect themselves from sickness and other misfortunes – popular forms of divination, astrology and folk healing, for example – especially whenever the times, places, persons, and things of 'official' religion were subject to creative adaptation by the laity for material ends. A particular target was the widespread assumption of a power in the pronunciation of words. Additionally, the adherents of one religion might call the practices of another 'magical', as in the Protestant condemnation of many Catholic sacramental practices, including the Mass itself, and the Catholic equating of heresy with sorcery. These various uses gave magic an extraordinary diffusion in the era of confessionalism and reform; this, again, is a pan-European cultural phenomenon. But however generalized the use of the word 'magic' to create boundaries and identify taboos, we should not forget its sinister implications too. For magic, just as much as witchcraft, was regarded as demonic, largely because those who condemned it thought of it as without intrinsic efficacy – a practice that only delivered the ends it aimed at because the devil stepped in to provide them. 'Magic', like 'superstition', was a label with lethal connotations in sixteenth- and seventeenth-century Europe.

As an indication in symbol of the way issues of demonic deviance served to identify and marginalize those beyond the pale of European religious purity – whether they lived within or without its geographical boundaries – we may take the emblem of 'Europa' published in Cesare Ripa's immensely popular *Iconologia*. First published in Rome in 1593 without images, the book was illustrated for the 1603 edition and then repeatedly edited, adapted, and translated down to the end of the eighteenth century, becoming the single most influential iconographical source book of the pre-modern period. Predictably, 'Europa' is depicted, alongside her three rival continents, with all the attributes of queenly superiority – symbols denoting greater power, arms, authority, riches, arts, learning, beauty, and abundance. In addition, in her right hand she holds a temple, 'per dinotare', wrote Ripa, 'ch'in lei al presente ci è la perfetta, e verissima religione, e superiore a tutte l'altre'.[3] By this simple equivalence, false and imperfect religion became anti-European as well as ungodly, and its eradication, in the name of whatever faith (Ripa's is a Catholic Europe, of course), became an affirmation of European as well as Christian values. Falseness and imperfection could take multiple forms, but the categories of 'magic', 'superstition', and 'idolatry' embraced many of them, and witchcraft might even be considered the quintessence of religious deviance – in its own way, an emblem of all that was excluded from Europa's temple.

What happened outside Europe's boundaries is the best known and most clear cut example of how images of religious purity and deviance served to reinforce a sense of European identity. As many recent studies have shown, the entire language of witchcraft, together with the concepts of 'magic', 'superstition' and 'idolatry', were brought to bear on the religions of non-European cultures, notably in the newly conquered and colonized 'New World' of America, as a form of conceptual and linguistic – and physically violent – acculturation. A cultural form, imagined in Europe, was thus instrumental in the 'othering' of European values and institutions and the creation of a continental ideology. That pre-modern Europe defined itself, and claimed superiority, in opposition to supposedly backward and primitive 'other' cultures, has, of course, long been understood. In 1980, for example, Peter Burke argued that the 'subjective reality' of sixteenth- and seventeenth-century Europe as a form of collective consciousness was 'defined by contrast not only to the Ottoman Empire but also to India, China, Peru, and Brazil'. This idea has been confirmed by countless other studies and is now taken for granted, even in fields like the development of early modern cartography. The 'cannibal' was one outcome of the process described by Burke, and the Mercator projection was evidently another.[4]

But the New World 'witch' was a third. By the late sixteenth century, the Dutch artist Crispin de Passe was able to engrave and publish a print designed by his Antwerp colleague Martin de Vos depicting the earthly 'children' of the god Saturn, in which magicians and witches engaged in the wild revelries of the 'sabbat' were represented alongside native Americans working in mines, serving their ruler, and preparing and devouring human flesh. In an essay on this print Charles Zika comments: 'As miner and cannibal, the Amerindian is transported to Europe; the Amerindian is incorporated into the sociological, psychological, religious and cosmological schemas of the old world by being made a sibling of the witch, both of them progeny of the same father Saturn'.[5] In 1627 the English parish priest Richard Bernard remarked casually but typically that among the most authentic witches were the populations of the 'savage nations' of the world, 'amongst whome, by travellers relations, witchcraft is rife'.[6] In modern scholarship, applications of European witchcraft beliefs to Amerindian religions have been identified – to take just the most recent research – in Brazil, New Spain (Mexico), Peru, and Venezuela at every level of the extirpation campaigns.[7] In Portuguese America, the work of Laura de Mello e Souza has shown how the struggle to possess and convert 'new' lands was inserted into a very old European Christian demonomachy. The devil of the new world was evidently the devil of the old. The occupants of these lands were seen as devils themselves or followers of devils, either – in the most positive light – innocently seduced by demonic illusions, or – in the most negative – fully complicit in pacts and witches' sabbats via their religious leaders, the *pajés*. In addition, the Inquisition punished the 'witchcraft' and 'magic' that it found in many indigenous techniques for healing, such as the Afro-Brazilian religious ritual, the *calundus*, just as it did when faced with forbidden therapies in the popular culture of metropolitan Portugal.[8]

In New Spain the positive and negative readings of native errors were repeated and given equal weight down to about 1530. But thereafter the situation deteriorated. By the middle of the sixteenth century, according to Fernando Cervantes, 'a negative, demonic view of Amerindian cultures had triumphed and its influence was seen to descend like a thick fog upon every statement officially and unofficially made on the subject'.[9] Thereafter direct demonic intervention had to be blamed for the idolatry and superstition that continued after initial conversion and baptism, with the result that the optimism of the Franciscans who had arrived in Mexico in the 1520s was replaced by pessimism among their Dominican successors. Inquisitorial methods again emerged, directed against failings that were now interpreted much more ominously as apostasy secured by pacts, rather than as simple misguidedness.

Perhaps the most ruthless and sustained attempt to demonize Amerindian religion took place in Peru, particularly once initial feelings of success gave way to the realization that salvation would be slow and, as in New Spain, other reasons for continued idolatry would have to be found. The Spanish reinterpretation of Andean religions tells a rich and complex story of how European demonology was applied to visions, apparitions, and dreams to yield a catalogue of demonic illusions, how false cults in Peru were seen in a tradition of demonically inspired error reaching back to pagan antiquity, and how the demonizing of native religions turned conversion into exorcism. As Kenneth Mills writes: 'The demonological system that had been inherited from early Christian commentators and the friars and inquisitors of medieval Europe, and refined by their Renaissance and early modern successors, could be used to incorporate the "idolatry" of America'. Eventually, the Indians came to be seen as voluntary devil-worshippers and their devils as not just unseen influences but real presences – 'audible advisers, participatory familiars, and even physical objects of worship'.[10] It was thus in the 1570s that the Viceroy Francisco de Toledo initiated a policy of *reducción*, aimed repressively at the 'extirpation of idolatry' and inaugurated by instructions, like those of 1571, that spoke of 'sorcery' as a main obstacle to evangelical teaching.[11]

Actual trials for magic and witchcraft – or at least investigations concerning them – were naturally one outcome of these various collisions between Europeans and the cultures they demonized. In colonial Venezuela, for example, within the remit of the third Inquisition tribunal to be set up in the Americas, at Cartagena in 1610, a number of witchcraft cases were tried by the central officials, but several hundreds of accusations of sorcery and magic were left to be dealt with by regional commissioners. One of the *visitadores de idolatría* in the Archdiocese of Lima in Peru, Sarmiento de Vivero told a woman he was interrogating in 1662 that she and others were 'sorceresses' deceived by the devil.[12] A virtual witches' sabbat is described in the investigation conducted in 1598 by the Mexican Inquisition into the relationship between a Spanish woman and an Indian woman named Catalina, both of whom had supposedly attended nocturnal meetings where there was dancing, demon-worship, and mock religion.[13]

But there are many textual indications of what happened as well. The Jesuit Pablo José de Arriaga, in his *La extirpación de la idolatría en el Perú* (1621), 'freely borrowed from the tradition of the witches' sabbat presided over by the Devil and involving followers who attended and worshiped him'.[14] The first work written in Mexico on the subject of the diabolism inherent in its native religion, Fray Andrés de Olmos's *Tratado de hechicerías y sortilegios*, written in Nahuatl, was modelled on an influential European text by Martín de Castañega, entitled *Tratado muy sotil y bien fundado de las supersticiones y hechicerías y vanos conjuros y abusiones* (1529), and virtually paraphrased it.[15] The themes of demonic imitation and trickery are naturally uppermost in the Jesuit José de Acosta's *Historia natural y moral de las Indias* (1590), of which book 5 is simply a European demonology transposed into an ethnography of the 'religion, or superstition and rites, and idolatries and sacrifices' of 'Indians'. 'In Peru', De Acosta typically writes, dealing with the subject of demonic forms of unction, 'the sorcerers and ministers of the devil also used to anoint themselves freely, and there was an infinite number of seers, practitioners of witchcraft, sorcerers, soothsayers, and a thousand other kinds of false prophets; and even today a large part of this plague still persists, though in secret, for they dare not employ their devilish and sacrilegious ceremonies and superstitions openly.'[16] Similarly, the *Apologética Historia* of the Dominican Fray Bartolomé de las Casas is 'filled with devils deemed constantly to be transporting men and women through the air, tempting witches to obtain unbaptized infants for their cannibalistic rites, turning men into beasts, faking miracles and appearing in human and animal forms'.[17] In 1585, in a book on the revival of idolatry in Chiapas, Fray Pedro de Feria typically reported that a confraternity of Indians, calling themselves the 'Twelve Apostles', was in fact a coven of witches; 'they go out at night and travel from mountain to mountain and from cave to cave, and they hold meetings and consultations where, under the guise and appearance of religion, they perform their own rites, giving cult to the Devil and plotting against our Christian religion'. In much the same way, half a century later, Jacinto de la Serna could assimilate the Indian *titzil* (medicine man or healer) to the European sorcerer – just as the healers of the European countryside were assimilated to witches – via the concept of the demonic pact.[18]

What exercised these writers most, and led them to the assimilations they made, was an initial perception that the rites they and their predecessors encountered in the New World were indeed strikingly similar to Christian ones. This is something that we might plausibly attribute to their incapacity to make sense of them in any other way – a product of European 'recognitions' when confronted by definitionally non-European practices. But for those concerned, the objective explanation could only be demonic. The Christian devil was 'God's ape', constantly seeking to be honoured in ways that corresponded exactly but inversely with those of the true religion. This fundamental idea structured the entire history of pre-modern witchcraft beliefs and made the witches' sabbat as believable as the rites it parodied. In the New World it was put to use in exactly the same way to account for the local religions and condemn them as idolatrous. It allowed Fray Olmos, for example, in his *Tratado*, to cast Indians as active devil-worshippers and members of a counter-church, just like the witches of Castañega's *Tratado*. Satan had set up a mimetic inversion of the Catholic Church: 'It had its "exacraments"', remarks Cervantes, 'to counter the Church's sacraments; it had its ministers, who were mostly women, as opposed to the predominance of male ministers in the Church; and it had its human sacrifices which sought to imitate the supreme sacrifice of Christ in the Eucharist'.[19] The argument was self-fulfilling in the sense that the more elaborate the rites, the more convincing they became as exact replicas and deliberate idolatries, as opposed to haphazard errors; just as the domestic witches of Europe became more and more credible, and not less, as demonological depictions of their replica religion became more and more detailed as well. In both cases alike, what seemed like sanctity was but perfect dissembling.[20]

Easily the best known single example of the textual assimilation of a new world religious ceremony to old world witchcraft occurs in the Huguenot Jean de Léry's *Histoire d'un voyage fait en la terre du Bresil*.[21] In the first edition, published in Calvinist Geneva in 1578, Léry had already applied the model of demonic possession to female Brazilians whom he claimed to have seen in trance states whilst living among the Tupinamba in the Bay of Rio during 1557. They were, he said 'visibly and actually tormented by evil spirits'. But by the time of the third edition in 1585, Léry had had the benefit of consulting Jean Bodin's *De la démonomanie des sorciers* (1580), and could now turn to the much more elaborate and powerful narrative of the witches' 'sabbat' as a way of categorizing the rites he had seen (the *Histoire* also appeared in 1580, 1599 and 1611). Having summarized Bodin's own account of the sabbat he added:

> *I have concluded that the master of the one was the master of the others: that is, the Brazilian women and the witches over here were guided by the same spirit of Satan; neither the distance between the places nor the long passage over the sea prevents the father of lies from operating in both places on those who are bound to him, by the just judgement of God.*

This enabled Léry actually to refer to 'this witches sabbath' when recounting Tupinamba ceremonies. As Stephen Greenblatt comments: 'Léry evidently felt he had found in Bodin's account the European ritual that most resembled the astonishing scene he had witnessed more than twenty years earlier, a resemblance that transcended the immense cultural and geographical distance he himself continually remarks [on]'.[22] What was hidden in Europe was being openly practised in the New World – and, from this perspective, no doubt in other continents too.

However, there is in many ways a more interesting example of this ideological incorporation in a much less well-known work by another Frenchman, the *L'Antidemon historial* of a canon regular of the minor order of St Ruff, Jude Serclier, published at Lyon in 1609. Two things make this treatise more significant to us than Léry's travel journal. One is that it offers a complete demonology, well within the conventions of that genre of writing as it was practised throughout Europe between the mid-fifteenth and late-seventeenth centuries. It therefore discusses all the usual aspects of diabolical witchcraft – the pact, the sabbat, human sacrifice, shape-changing, the sexuality of demons, and so on – all the while borrowing extensively from other authorities in the field like Paulo Grillando and Martín Del Río. The theme on which the whole argument rests, moreover, is also central to demonology – that of witchcraft as a mocking, dissembling mimicry ('singerie') of the true faith. Serclier traces this particular kind of idolatry backwards in time to the pagan religions of the pre-Christian world, but he also identifies it geographically in the contemporary societies of the 'new lands' ('terres neuves'). He is quite explicit about moving beyond the Satanism in the festivals of 'Europe, Asia, and Africa' to consider 'the Indies and new lands discovered in our age', to see how the devil has usurped 'our' Christian festivals and ceremonies among their inhabitants too. The result – and this is the second important feature of this text – is that deeply embedded in his demonology is a detailed survey of the religious festivals of the Mexicans ('Mexiquains'), identifying in every one a deliberate and meticulous, and thus demonic, 'singerie' of European Christianity. This occurs in book 11 of the treatise, entitled 'Des festes et solennitez tant des anciens Hebrieux que des Chrestiens, sur lesquelles Satan a moulé celles du Paganisme, et autres'. Among the 'others' are the new world Mexicans and the old world witches.[23]

There is no doubt that Serclier was indebted to De Acosta's *Historia Natural y Moral* for his information, which he virtually plagiarizes (and geographically misplaces); this is not original ethnography. What is noteworthy, rather, is the contextualizing of individual rituals in the 'Mexican' festive calendar in a demonology focusing on religious parodies. For Serclier (as for De Acosta, who was actually talking about Andean religion as well), both the December festival of *capacraymi*, when sheep and lambs were sacrificed and royal nobles brought before the three statues of the sun God, and also the adoration of the idol Tangatanga as one in three and three in one, were obvious appropriations and mockeries of the Trinity. In the festival of *citua*, sacrifices and other ceremonies in honour of the new moon and for banishing evil were Satanic copies of the rites of the Old Testament Jews at each renewal of the moon, when they too sacrificed and observed the Sabbath by divine command. During the month and festival of *raymicantará rayquis*, the Indians made processions – 'notez la singerie', exclaimed Serclier – against the plague, floods, and drought, while their adoration of the deity Tezcatlipoca on 19 May included an 'aperte singerie tirée sur la saincte cérémonie de Pains'. Serclier (again, following De Acosta) saw many parodic parallels not just in the content of ritual processions but in their intent to secure goods and satisfaction for sins. Faced with reports of processional censing before relics or statues of the gods, he could only resort to Psalm 141, 2: 'Let my prayer be set forth before thee as incense'.

Worse still, Indian rites celebrated counterfeit miracles – indeed, counterfeits of particular miracles like the exodus of the Jews from Egypt, copied in the departure of the Mexicans from the province of Aztlán led by their guiding devil, the deity Huitzilopochtli, whose 'idol', carried in a 'coffre de iouc' and worshipped in a tabernacle at each pause in the journey, promised them success and riches and gave them their laws, ceremonies and institutions. 'Que représente tout cela autre chose', asked Serclier, citing Exodus 25, 'que la saincte Arche d'Alliance ainsi reverée des Israélites, recevans tout secours et aide de Dieu par son moyen?' During their wanderings, the Mexicans were menaced by enemies and punished for their murmurings by attacks from serpents (Numbers, 21), and consulted their god who instructed one of his priests to number and divide them into tribes (Numbers, 1, 2, 3). When, eventually, the Spanish armies arrived, Moctezuma sent his priests to consult the idol about the outcome of the conflict, whereupon Tezcatlipoca rejected the king in precisely the terms used by God in rejected Saul, when the prophet Samuel mourned for him: 'How long wilt thou mourne for Saul, seeing I have rejected him from reigning over Israel' (1 Samuel, 16, 1).

Finally, and perhaps worst of all in the age of the Catholic Reformation and the battle for the Tridentine Mass, Indian religion abused and counterfeited the sacraments. Under the devil's guidance 'Mexicans' (Andeans in De Acosta) ordained their priests and anointed them with suitably black concoctions, as well as parodying penitence and extreme unction. During the December festival of *capacraymi*, and again during *coyaraymi*, the female religious made bread from maize flour mixed with sheep's blood for priests to give to the people 'arranged in order', which they received reverently in hope of union with the Sun and the Inca, promising always to serve them. Two days before celebrating the main festival of Huitzilopochtli, in May, an idol of honey and maize was made in his likeness and, after being carried in procession and worshipped, was broken into fragments and fed to all the people as the 'flesh and bones' of their god. Acosta had seen in this an exact parody of Corpus Christi and claimed to be astonished by it. Even Serclier felt uncomfortable in speaking of 'Communians' and said so, but there was possibly an even greater risk in his description of the idol itself as 'l'idole de paste [pâte]', precisely the terms used by Protestants throughout Europe to ridicule the eucharist of their Catholic enemies.

The texts of Jean de Léry and Jude Serclier, as well as the deeds of colonizers and extirpators throughout the New World itself, illustrate both the 'othering' of Europe as an idea and also the general principle (stated by Michel de Certeau) that early modern travel literature and early modern demonology were structurally identical, the first 'a great complement and displacement' of the second.[24] As if to confirm this by way of a negative, there is the counter-instance of Montaigne, with his fierce hostility to Eurocentrism, his complete scepticism concerning witchcraft, and his sceptic's indifference to the supposed certainties that turned cultural disparities into 'superstitions'. The patterns discernible in the New World were also repeated elsewhere – indeed, wherever Europeans observed and represented other cultures across the known globe. The first Portuguese explorers in West Africa, for example, applied the same conceptual categories of idolatry and witchcraft to the religions they encountered, bequeathing an ethnographic legacy that lasted into the twentieth century.[25] 'They are all idolaters and sorcerers', wrote Duarte Pacheco Pereira of native West Africans early in the sixteenth century, 'and are ruled by witchcraft, placing implicit faith in oracles and omens'. The very categories of 'Fetish' and 'fetishism' were themselves derived from a Portuguese term for witchcraft (*feitiçaria*): 'In consequence', writes Wyatt MacGaffey, '*feitiçaria*, a term that had obscurely designated certain marginal practices in Christian Europe, was appropriated to characterize the entirety of African religion and the kind of social order it was believed to support'.[26]

What happened *inside* Europe when labels like 'witchcraft' and 'magic' were deployed to marginalize, exclude, or extirpate has not always been thought of in the same way, even if the concept of 'acculturation' entered frequently into the historiography of this subject from the 1970s onwards. Yet Europe had its own internal missionaries, especially those sent into the remotest of its Catholic regions and what English Calvinists called 'the dark corners of the land'. Writing of those undertaken in Portugal, José Pedro Paiva, concludes that they were 'one of the privileged strategies used by the church to "christianize" the populations'.[27] What was discovered by them was also condemned in the same way as non-European religions were demonized by their 'external' colleagues. Indeed, those sent to places like the French maritime provinces or southern Italy often complained that things were no better there than in the New World or in Japan. 'Whether they were in Mexico, Poland or Castile, the missionaries' primary concern was to make sure of the masses' belief', suggests their foremost historian, Louis Châtellier.[28] The enemy was obviously the same, and so were the sins; identifying both was therefore integral to each mission. If an image of Europe arose at the edges of overseas colonization, the very same image was invoked whenever the churches – Catholic and Protestant alike – encountered the marginally religious at home. Both frontiers were constitutive of the relationship between Christianization and Europeanization.

'Vos Indes sont ici!' 'We have Indians at home!' 'Otras Indias!' Everywhere in Europe, the lament was the same. In 1624, the Capuchins entered the Cévennes, calling the region 'les Indes et le Japon de l'hérésie de la France'.[29] In 1627 it was said that people in the mountainous regions of the diocese of Gap knew so little religion that they worshipped the sun, a report similar to that by a chronicler of the Capuchins in Provence: 'On voyoit dans les vallées du Chansaur, du Devoluy, du Gaudemar et autres de ce diocese comme dans des nouvelles Indes des personnes qui ignoroint s'il y avait un Dieu, et comme il le fallout adorer et server'. Missions to the

French countryside by the religious orders, wrote the Capuchin Yves de Paris in his *Les Heureux success de la piété*, were 'les essais de celles qu'ils entreprennent dans les nouveaux mondes avec un plus grand peril de leurs personnes, et non pas quelquefois avèc plus de fruict, et avec un plus grand gain des ames.' It comes as no surprise that a copy of José de Acosta's *Historia natural y moral de las Indias* was kept in the library of the Capuchins in Gap.[30] In 1628, the English MP Sir Benjamin Rudyerd told the English Parliament that 'there were some places in England which were scarce in Christendom, where God was little better known than amongst the Indians [and] where the prayers of the common people are more like spells and charms than devotions.' Later in the century, in the context of conversion of American 'Indians', it was again said in England that there were 'Indians in Cornwall, Indians in Wales, Indians in Ireland'.[31] In Italy, the idea seems to have been even more common – almost a cliché of evangelism. Jesuits described Sicily as a 'vera India' in 1568 and the Abruzzo as 'India italiana' in 1571, and in 1553 the Counter-Reformation preacher Silvestro Landini called Corsica 'la mia India'. Adriano Prosperi, who cites many other examples, reminds us that such sentiments could be comforting as well as disillusioning to Jesuits, offering them the prospect of a plentiful harvest of souls. What is important here is the way the New World reacted on the Old, crudely and simplistically providing a category for what were seen as their parallel failings.[32]

The internal colonizations, like the external, were thus locked in a battle with the same enemies: pagans, idolaters, and demons; and everywhere, the missionary carried with him the same vocabulary of magic and witchcraft. What could result is graphically illustrated by the case of the Jesuit Julien Maunoir's mission at Douarnenez in Brittany during the 1640s. Maunoir had followed another famous missionary to this area, Michel Le Nobletz, whose reports of magic and witchcraft among the Breton peasants inspired the historian Jean Delumeau to talk likewise about the 'christianizing' of Europe after the Council of Trent. Significantly, Le Nobletz had sent Maunoir a copy of the famous Dominican witchcraft manual, the *Malleus maleficarum*, warning him that he would need to use it to save Breton souls, 'a prediction that came true in the event'. Maunoir himself (who incidentally described seventeenth-century Ushant as more like Canada than France in its level of piety) decided that the best way to combat the vices he found and their demonic inspiration was to write his own treatise to help his colleagues interrogate suspected witches during confession. Questions would be asked about the devil and his meetings, and to help with these Maunoir provided a full description of the witches' sabbat and the demonic pact. But he also listed the signs that indicated that someone might be a witch, which included 'not to know the catechism, or to know it badly, though capable of learning it. ... to have the cross on one's chaplet broken or not to have it at all. ... to have a chaplet of many colours. ... to have some agnuses or medallions in which there is something absurd or which are not like those that the Church normally uses. To be familiar with persons whom one knows to be of the Cabbala'. Maunoir himself used this sort of questionnaire at the general confessions that were held at the end of his missions, and Châtellier comments that he seems to have seen the sabbat as the 'crystallization of the world's sins' and disorders. But what is most noticeable is the exact coinciding of the evangelical agenda of a Tridentine missionary with the fundamentals of diabolical witchcraft. Maunoir's advice about how penitents might protect themselves from the devil and avoid any relapses into witchcraft covered all the features of Counter-Reformation piety including frequent confession and prayer, membership of a confraternity, the keeping and drinking of holy water, and the possession of an Agnus Dei (or other consecrated object) which was to be kissed often. Consecrated objects (lamb or bread) hung around the neck should replace magical talismans and amulets and offer further protection. Against the temptations of witchcraft, Maunoir recommended this to ordinary Bretons: 'cross yourself, say your Pater and your Ave, and utter the names of Jesus, Mary and Joseph ... close your eyes, think that you have God in your heart, with the crucifix, and imagine that you are kissing its feet, without ever stopping to talk to the demon or listen to him, and without fearing or fighting him otherwise than by saying "My God, I renounce this temptation and give myself totally to you"'. Precisely these spiritual therapies against witchcraft were commonly included in the demonology of the Catholic Reformation too – in the writings across Europe of men like Juan Maldonado, Jodocus Lorichius, Francisco Torreblanca, Francesco de Osuna, Friedrich Forner, Pierre Crespet, and Adam Tanner. But it is important in the present context to find such 'textbook' formulations working themselves out on the ground in the form of questions asked of sinners by internal missionaries like Maunoir.[33]

'Magic', however, had a further place in early modern culture as an intellectual construct, in the form of the 'high' magic that, with its promise of universal wisdom and technical marvels, attracted so many European thinkers and their mostly courtly patrons during the sixteenth and seventeenth centuries. This kind of intellectual practice focused on the studies of natural magic (scarcely distinguishable from natural philosophy), astrology and alchemy, and aimed at the uncovering of natural secrets and the production of wonderful effects. Rulership in particular seems to have established affinities with magic, turning princes into magi and the practice of government – portrayed in works like Francis Bacon's *New Atlantis* – into a kind of political thaumaturgy, built on its own kinds of secrets – *accana imperii*, indeed. Here too, implications for some form of European consciousness may not seem initially forthcoming, setting aside the once again strongly pan-European appeal of high magic and the international manner in which the same magical ideas, texts and practices were shared across the continent. One looks in vain for 'Europa' (though not 'Atalanta') in the extensive and complicated symbolism of the alchemists.

Nevertheless, Colette Beaune has written about the idea of Europe in fifteenth-century books of astrology and this might be worth following up for the later centuries, during which astrology's appeal remained strong.[34] Various aspects of intellectual magic also appealed to particular men with strong views about political and religious union across Europe, notably Guillaume Postel, Michael Maier, Johann Amos Komensky (Comenius), and Samuel Hartlib. This connection may well have been conceptual, not accidental, aimed at a non-particularism secured by magic's pretensions as a universal form of wisdom. Above all, perhaps, the politics of intellectual magic meant that it was promoted most often in relation to ideas of

European empire – by Philip II at the Escorial, by Rudolf II in Prague, and by John Dee and Giordano Bruno in relation to the 'British' empire of Elizabeth I.[35] Imperial pretensions were not identical to 'European' ones, often extending beyond them to statements about 'world monarchy', but they were close enough in the early modern centuries to suggest that magic was conceptually linked to a certain kind of pan-European politics – in the way that (as William Eamon has recently shown) the hunting of alchemical secrets provided not just metaphors but patterns for the pursuit and manipulation of political ones.[36] The researches of the intellectual historian Frances Yates certainly support this possibility.[37]

There is, for example, the symbolism of the scene depicted in a 'British Hieroglyphic' on the titlepage of John Dee's *General and rare memorials pertayning to the perfect arte of navigation* (1577). Navigation does not seem like a magical art (even if magnetism was always cited as a classic instance of an 'occult' quality), although in Dee's mental world it is never wise to separate out anything we might call 'technology' or 'science' from his all-embracing magical interests. The titlepage implies this, without having much to do with the contents of the text that follows; a book aimed at persuading Elizabeth I to establish a coastal naval force to protect her realm from pirates is presented as a contribution to the knowledge of secrets. At the top of the scene is the motto: 'Plura latent quam patent' ('More things are concealed than are revealed'), the classic slogan of intellectual magic; the scene itself is lit by rays shed by the Tetragrammaton, the equally classic foundation of cabalistic inquiry; and another figure included in it is the Archangel Michael, with whom Dee later tried to converse in order to learn the secrets and, indeed, the very language of the Creation. The European dimension is provided by the depiction of Elizabeth, sitting enthroned on a ship named 'EUROPA', with the mythological figure of Europa on her bull swimming alongside. Elizabeth, the ruler of 'Britain' and guardian of its seas, is also the helmswoman of Europe, sitting (as Dee explained in his text) 'at the Helm of this Imperiall Monarchy: or, rather, at the Helm of the Imperiall Ship, of the most parte of Christendome'.[38]

Notes

1. Clark (1997).
2. For example, from Schmitt (1990); Perrin (1994); Pagden (2002).
3. Ripa (1970), pp.332–4, quotation p. 333. The 1970 edition is a facsimile of the 1603 edition. On the visual tradition of 'Europe, Queen of the continents', see Wintle (1996), pp. 80–6.
4. Burke (1980), p. 25; Wintle (1999), esp. pp. 145–6, 150–3; Wintle (2001). Cf. Margolin (1982).
5. Zika (2003), quotation p. 416. See also Zika's forthcoming book, *Appearances of Witchcraft*.
6. Bernard (1627), p. 94.
7. In addition to the recent studies cited below, see MacCormack (1995); Del Pino Díaz (2002), esp. the essays by the editor and by B. Vitar and H. Sáinz Ollero. Older accounts include Duviols (1972) and Delumeau (c.1978), pp. 254–62.

8. De Mello e Souza (1990); See also De Mello e Souza (1986).
9. Cervantes (1994), p. 8.
10. Mills (1997), pp. 216 and 220, and chapter 7. Cf. MacCormack (1991).
11. Gose (2003), p. 150.
12. Mills (1997), p. 220.
13. Details in Lewis (2003), pp. 127–9, and passim for many other examples of the application of European demonological categories to colonial people's daily lives.
14. Mills (1997), p. 223, note 39, citing other uses of the sabbat analogy.
15. Cervantes (1994), p. 25.
16. De Acosta (2002), bk 5, pp. 250–328, quotations at pp. 250 and 310.
17. Cervantes (1994), pp. 32–3; cf. De las Casas (1958), pp. 299–345.
18. Cervantes (1994), p. 35 (Feria) and pp. 35–6 (Serna).
19. Cervantes (1994), p. 25.
20. The argument only worked up to a point, however; see Clark (1997), pp. 134–47, for the occasions when it collapsed under the weight of largely linguistic instabilities.
21. For this whole subject in the context of French literature, see Closson (2000), pp. 231–8; Lestringant (1996), esp. pp. 77–91.
22. De Léry (1585), pp. 280–1; Greenblatt (1991), p. 15, cf. pp. 14–19; De Certeau (1988), pp. 209–43; Grafton et al. (1992), pp. 108–9.
23. Serclier (1609), p. 339; all quotations from pp. 339–46, 512–4, 528–34; cf. for Serclier's derivations, De Acosta (2002), pp. 314–28 (bk 5, chs 28–31).
24. De Certeau (1988), p. 242, n. 52.
25. Here I follow MacGaffey (1994), pp. 261–4.
26. MacGaffey (1994) p. 264, following W. Pietz's (1987) fascinating essay on the relationship of the fetish to medieval and early modern Christian ideas of idolatry.
27. Paiva (1997), pp. 21–22, citing Fr. A. das Chagas (1957), p. 42.
28. Châtellier (1997a), p. 93.
29. Citation from Venard (1984), p. 86.
30. All citations from Dompnier (1984).
31. All citations from Hill (1963), pp. 96–7.
32. Prosperi (1999), esp. pp. 66–72. (I am grateful to Diogo Curto for recommending this essay.) See also Selwyn (2004).
33. For Maunoir, see Châtellier (1997a), pp. 163–4 and p. 174, and Châtellier (1997b), esp p. 42 on the *Malleus maleficarum*. For the demonology of the Catholic Reformation, see Clark (1997), pp. 530–2.
34. Beaune (1982).
35. Goodman (1988), pp. 1–49; Evans (1973), pp. 196–242; Clulee (1988).
36. Eamon (1994), pp. 269–300.
37. Yates (1972, 1975).
38. Corbett and Lightbown (1979), pp. 34–37, 49–56. Sherman, (1995), pp. 152–71, argues that the titlepage generates interpretations 'that the rest of the text cannot support', although, presumably, even unfulfilled expectations have to be interpreted.

References

Beaune, C. (1982), 'La notion d'Europe dans les livres d'astrologie du xve siècle', in *La Conscience Européenne au xve et au xvie siècle (Actes du Colloque Internationale organisé à l'Ecole Normale Superieure de Jeunes Filles), 30 Sept–3 Oct, 1980*, (Paris), pp. 1–7.

Bernard, R. (1627), *A Guide to Grand-jury Men* (London).

Burke, P. (1980), 'Did Europe Exist before 1700?', in *History of European Ideas*, 1.

Cervantes, F. (1994), *The Devil in the New World: The Impact of Diabolism in New Spain* (London).

Châtellier, L. (1997a), *The Religion of the Poor: Rural Missions in Europe and the Formation of Modern Catholicism, c.1500–c.1800* (Cambridge) (first pub. as *La religion des pauvres: les missions rurales en Europe et la formation du catholicisme moderne xvième-xixième siècles*, Paris 1993).

_____. (1997b), *Miracles et sabbats: Journal du Père Maunoir: Missions en Bretagne, 1631–1650* (Paris).

Clark, S. (1997), *Thinking with Demons: The Idea of Witchcraft in Early Modern Europe* (Oxford).

Closson, M. (2000), *L'Imaginaire démoniaque en France (1550–1650)* (Geneva).

Clulee, N.H. (1988), *John Dee's Natural Philosophy: Between Science and Religion* (London).

Corbett, M. and R. Lightbown (1979), *The Comely Frontispiece: The Emblematic Title-Page in England 1550–1600* (London).

Das Chagas, F.A. (1957), *Cartas espirituais* (Lisbon).

De Acosta, J. (2002), *Natural and Moral History of the Indies*, J.E. Mangan (ed.), intro. by W.D. Mignolo (Durham and London).

De Certeau, M. (1988), *The Writing of History* (New York).

De las Casas, F.B. (1958), *Apologética Historia*, J. Pérez de Tudela Bueso (ed.) (Madrid).

De Lery, J. (1585), *Histoire d'un voyage fait en la terre du Bresil* (3rd edn, Geneva).

De Mello e Souza, L. (1986), *O Diabo e a Terra de Santa Cruz: Feiticaria e Religiosidade Popular no Brasil Colonia* (São Paulo). Now trans. as *The Devil and the Land of the Holy Cross: Witchcraft, Slavery, and Popular Religion in Colonial Brazil* (Austin, 2003).

_____. (1990), 'The Devil in Brazilian History', *Portuguese Studies*, 6, 85–93.

Del Pino Diaz, F. (ed.) (2002), *Demonio, Religión y Sociedad entre España y América* (Madrid).

Delumeau, J. (c. 1978), *La Peur en Occident, xive-xviiie: une cité assiégée* (Paris).

Dompnier, B. (1984), 'Mission lointaine et mission de l'intérieur chez les Capucins français de la première moitié du xviie siècle', in Duboscq and Latreille (eds), *Réveils missionaries*, pp. 91–106.

Duviols, P. (1972), *La Lutte contre les religions autochtones dans le Pérou colonial* (Lima and Paris).

Eamon, W. (1994), *Science and the Secrets of Nature: Books of Secrets in Medieval and Early Modern Culture* (Princeton).

Evans, R.J.W. (1973), *Rudolf II and his World: A Study in Intellectual History* (Oxford).

Goodman, D.C. (1988), *Power and Penury: Government, Technology and Science in Philip II's Spain* (Cambridge).

Gose, P. (2003), 'Converting the Ancestors: Indirect Rule, Settlement Consolidation, and the Struggle over Burial in Colonial Peru, 1532–1614', in K. Mills and A. Grafton (eds), *Conversion: Old Worlds and New* (Rochester), pp. 140–74.

Grafton, A., A. Shelford and N. Siraisi (1992), *New Worlds, Ancient Texts: The Power of Tradition and the Shock of Discovery* (Cambridge and London).

Greenblatt, S. (1991), *Marvelous Possessions: The Wonder of the New World* (Chicago).

Hellinga, L. et al. (eds) (2001), *The Bookshop of the World: The Role of the Low Countries in the Book-Trade, 1473–1941* (Houten).

Hill, C. (1963), 'Puritans and "The Dark Corners of the Land"', *Transactions of the Royal Historical Society*, 5th series, 13.

Lestringant, F. (1996), *L'Expérience Huguenote au nouveau monde (xvie siècle)* (Geneva).

Lewis, L.A. (2003), *Hall of Mirrors: Power, Witchcraft, and Caste in Colonial Mexico* (Durham and London).

MacCormack, S. (1995), 'Limits of Understanding: Perceptions of Greco-Roman and Amerindian Paganism in Early Modern Europe', in K.O. Kupperman (ed.), *America in European Consciousness, 1493–1750* (Chapel Hill), pp. 79–129.

———. (1991), *Religion in the Andes: Vision and Imagination in Early Colonial Peru* (Princeton).

MacGaffey, W. (1994), 'Dialogues of the Deaf: Europeans on the Atlantic Coast of Africa', in S.B. Schwartz (ed.), *Implicit Understandings: Observing, Reporting, and Reflecting on the Encounters between Europeans and other Peoples in the Early Modern Era* (Cambridge).

Margolin, J-C., (1982), 'L'Europe dans le miroir du Nouveau Monde', in *La Conscience Européenne au xve et au xvie siècle (Actes du Colloque Internationale organisé à l'Ecole Normale Superieure de Jeunes Filles, 30 Sept–3 Oct 1980* (Paris), pp. 235–64.

Mills, K. (1997), *Idolatry and its Enemies: Colonial Andean Religion and Extirpation, 1640–1750* (Princeton).

Pagden, A. (ed.) (2002), *The Idea of Europe from Antiquity to the European Union* (Cambridge).

Paiva, J.P. (1997), *Bruxaria e superstiçã num país sem 'caça às bruxas' 1600–1774* (Lisbon).

Perrin, M. (ed.) (1994), *L'Idée de l'Europe au fil de deux millénaires* (Paris).

Pietz, W. (1987), 'The Problem of the Fetish II', *Res*, 13, 23–45.

Prosperi, A. (1999), '"Otras Indias": Missionari della Controriforma tra Contadini e Selvaggi', in A. Prosperi, *America e Apocalisse e altri Saggi* (Pisa and Rome), pp. 65–87.

Ripa, C. (1970), *Iconologia overo descrittione di diverse imagini cavate dall' antichità, e di propria inventione*, intro. by Erna Mandowsky (Hildesheim).

Schmitt, J-C. (1990), *Europe: mémoire et emblèmes* (Paris).

Selwyn, J.D. (2004), *A Paradise Inhabited by Devils : The Jesuits' Civilizing Mission in Early Modern Naples* (Aldershot).

Serclier, J. (1609), *L'Antidemon historial, où les sacrileges, larcins, ruses, et frauds du Prince des tenebres, pour usurper la divinité, sont amplement traictez* (Lyons).

Sherman, W.H. (1995), *John Dee: The Politics of Reading and Writing in the English Renaissance* (Amherst).

Venard, M. (1984), '"Vos Indes sont ici": Missions lointaines ou/et missions intérieures dans le catholicisme français de la première moitié du xviie siècle', in G. Duboscq and A. Latreille (eds), *Les Réveils missionaires en France du moyen-âge à nos jours (xiie–xxe siècles)* (Paris).

Wintle, M. (1996), 'Europe's Image: Visual Representations of Europe from the Earliest Times to the Twentieth Century', in M. Wintle (ed.), *Culture and Identity in Europe: Perceptions of Divergence and Unity in Past and Present* (Aldershot).

———. (1999), 'Renaissance Maps and the Construction of the Idea of Europe', *Journal of Historical Geography*, 25, 137–65.

_____ . (2001), 'Representations of Europe in Cartography and Iconography from the Low Countries', in L. Hellinga et al. (eds), *The Bookshop of the World: The Role of the Low Countries in the Book-Trade, 1473–1941* ('t Goy-Houten), pp. 191–205.

Yates, F.A. (1972), *The Rosicrucian Enlightenment* (London).

_____ . (1975), *Astraea: The Imperial Theme in the Sixteenth Century* (London).

Zika, C. (2003), *Exorcising our Demons: Magic, Witchcraft and Visual Culture in Early Modern Europe* (Leiden and Boston), pp. 411–44. Orginal edition: 'Fashioning New Worlds from Old Fathers: Reflections on Saturn, Amerindians and Witches in a Sixteenth-Century Print', in D. Merwick (ed.), *Dangerous Liaisons: Essays in Honour of Greg Dening* (Melbourne, 1994), pp. 249–81.

_____ . (forthcoming) *Appearances of Witchcraft*.

Part II: Communities

Discussions on communities in the European past have traditionally been cast along two conceptual axes: one focuses on the emergence of the state and on the birth and triumph of national sentiment; the other, often in contrast with the first, has been inspired by Marxist thought and concentrated on the emergence first of socio-economic and then of cultural bonds of solidarity, especially among workers and artisans. More recently, mostly since the middle of the twentieth century, historians have also cast their attention on the history of the family (and all its attendant institutions) in an attempt to tease out of the records of the past forms of discipline, and of collective sentiments associated neither with the state, nor with the emerging consciousness of class solidarities. In an attempt to 'relativize' the role of the state as the main promoter of social organization, we have cast our own attention on different forms of communities, and of varying ways of imagining them. Many years ago, Marcel Mauss suggested that there exists a 'cohésion sociale dans les sociétés polysegmentaires'. Our intention is to capture some aspects of such social cohesion, especially in dimensions of the past which document the existence of European-wide discursive traditions about different sorts of communities.

The fashioning and contemporary weight of such communities can be illustrated through a variety of perspectives. In some cases, the correspondence between scholars generated a sense of community based on European-wide networks of exchanging information. In other cases, different sorts of networks – some of which, based initially though they were in Europe, came to encompass groups working in nearly every part of the world then known to Europeans – bound merchants in a universe defined by the practices and values of exchange, trust and reputation. Discipline was not always enforced by the same means, nor did its violation produce the same consequences. What emerges below does, nonetheless, suggest ways in which civil society came into being: disciplinary forms ascribed to the family, the church, the school, or even intellectual institutions and merchant networks all point towards the existence of different levels of power aimed at circumscribing the behaviour of different segments of society. To explore these social organizations is not to impute the existence of idyllic anticipations of civic society, but to identify the ties (not necessarily those prescribed and enforced by the state's power) that nevertheless bound groups of people into different sorts of communities.

Different ways of imagining communities in Europe also had an important bearing on contemporary political and legal discursive traditions: from Christianity as political discourse to the languages of Roman law; from the metaphors of resistance to the courtier's behaviour; and alongside these, one also finds local and personal systems of justice which were never effectively undermined nor completely appropriated by the state.

One final, somewhat specific point. In the chapters that follow there emerges a picture of a wide variety of doctrines and political languages. One wonders if this picture of diverse discursive traditions about power, the state, and society could not be used to fruitfully challenge the current, distinguished tradition which at least for three scholarly generations – from the fundamental work of Hans Baron and Eugenio Garin, to that of John Pocock, Quentin Skinner and several others – has insisted upon the centrality of republican thought in early modern European political discource.

Chapter 5

A Republic of Merchants?

Francesca Trivellato

According to the *Oxford English Dictionary*, the noun 'cosmopolite' – a rendering of the Greek term for 'a citizen of the world' (*kosmos* = world, *polites* = citizen) – was first employed in English by Richard Hakluyt in his *Principal navigations* in 1598, and was commonly used during the seventeenth century.[1] In its modern English usage, cosmopolitanism is thus inextricably linked to the transoceanic voyages of European ships and the adventurous merchants and travellers who boarded them. Building on this view, various Enlightenment thinkers, including Montesquieu and Voltaire, fashioned the enduring image of a European entrepreneurial mercantile society, in which economic prosperity goes hand in hand with political liberty, religious toleration and open-mindedness.[2] This association between 'freedom' and 'commerce' undergirds the Enlightenment concept of cosmopolitanism, according to which the self-interested pursuit of profit leads to the erosion of ethnic and religious identity, the creation of a freer and more diverse society, and ultimately to the dissolution of group constraints on individuals. The rise of western individualism, following this reasoning, is first and foremost a by-product of the expansion of market relations. If today the term 'cosmopolitanism' still evokes progressive notions of liberal pluralism and universalism, it is largely because of the lasting legacy of this Enlightenment discourse. This legacy has surely left a mark among historians of European trade in the early modern period, some of whom have presented us with quasi-heroic portraits of cosmopolitan European merchants who subordinated all social and religious considerations to the quest for lavish material gains.[3]

Such celebratory portrayals of cosmopolitan European merchants have not gone uncontested. A large body of literature has challenged on both a micro and a macro level standard neo-Marxist and neo-liberal accounts that conceive the transformation from a feudal to a commercial society as a solely (western) European phenomenon.[4] There remains the question of how merchants enlarged the scope of their transactions, in Europe and elsewhere: was it by disregarding communitarian affiliations and acting as atomized actors in more and more anonymous and secure markets, and thereby giving rise to what we might call a cosmopolitan 'republic of merchants'? If so, then cosmopolitanism defines a harmonious (or at least non-conflictual) interaction among a diversity of actors, especially in busy commercial centres (many but not all, located along the sea). But cosmopolitanism as commonly understood cannot account for the glue that allowed merchants to extend cooperation beyond the closed boundaries of their communities. In other words, we need to ask exactly how merchants belonging to different ethnic and religious groups not only interacted with each other, but actually found the means to sustain long-lasting business relations.

In this essay, I will focus on how merchants, particularly those involved in trade over distant regions and continents and in international finance, secured their operations when dealing with agents to whom they had no 'natural' affiliation.[5] I begin by unravelling some fundamental theoretical premises about market relations that shape the image of cosmopolitanism bequeathed by the Enlightenment and embraced by Weberian sociology. I then examine the main features of the early modern European commercial organization to highlight institutional, practical and discursive resources that facilitated exchanges across vast geographical and cultural divides. Here I insist on the importance of business correspondence in the making of a cross-cultural 'republic of merchants,' both because it was an essential tool of information transfer and because, by means of rhetorical and legal conventions, it made economic obligations intelligible and enforceable among a surprising multiplicity of traders. Throughout the essay, and especially in the third and fourth sections, I call attention to Sephardic Jewish merchants as a minority group whose participation in the 'republic of merchants' is revelatory of the forms of inclusion and exclusion in the cosmopolitan commercial society of early modern Europe. Sephardic merchants were the most successful trading diaspora of the early modern period: they exerted particular influence on Atlantic commerce between 1650 and 1750,[6] and continued to be vital players in the Mediterranean throughout the eighteenth century. Their accomplishments in long-distance trade derived primarily from the assistance that they received from co-religionists scattered around the globe; and yet, we should not forget that they routinely worked together with non-Jews. It is those relations that we need to investigate in order to understand fully the nature of cosmopolitanism in the commercial world, and the role of social networks in market expansion. Moreover, their identity as well as the ways in which they were perceived by outsiders transcended predictable geographical and cultural divisions between North and South, East and West.

Images of Cosmopolitanism

'The market,' wrote Weber, 'is fundamentally alien to any type of fraternal relationship'.[7] The progressive de-personalization of market relations was, according to the German sociologist, a uniquely European phenomenon, and had its origins in Italian medieval cities.[8] In keeping with this account, European traders, especially those involved in dealings with faraway regions and financial speculations, increasingly saw themselves as part of a 'republic of merchants', which transcended the confining borders of their families, neighbourhoods and ethnic or religious communities. In their pursuit of profit, they could count on impersonal capitalist institutions to protect their contracts and create opportunities for lucrative exchanges with other merchants with little or no regard for their national, ethnic or religious background.

The Weberian paradigm informs a variety of historical interpretations, which differ in chronology and in the emphasis they place on the importance of cultural norms or institutional elements, but all trace an evolutionary trajectory toward increasingly anonymous and undifferentiated market relations.[9] In line with the concept of a medieval 'commercial revolution' put forth by Robert Lopez and others, economic historian Avner Greif dates the emergence of an 'individualistic' society to the twelfth century, when Italian maritime republics like Genoa and Venice established new institutions (including partnership contracts and specialized courts) that allowed members of diverse communities to cooperate economically. Today's modern western world, in this view, was born at that time, and superseded a Mediterranean 'collectivist' society in which informal mechanisms of reciprocity favoured intra-group exchanges but seriously obstructed inter-group relations.[10] Another interpretation, perhaps more widely accepted, dates this transformation to the seventeenth and eighteenth centuries, and locates it in northern rather than southern Europe.[11]

Market relations are commonly seen as constitutive of modernity at large. Intellectual historian Thomas Haskell explores the connection between the rise of capitalism and humanitarianism, and stresses the changes that capitalist development brought to the forms of promise keeping. Haskell recognizes that trust also exists outside capitalist structures, as a cultural practice that is 'deeply embedded in a fabric of social relationships and dependent in part on an effectively institutionalized threat of force in the event of non-compliance',[12] but argues that only in the eighteenth century did an economic system appear in Western Europe and North America which depended on the expectation that most people keep their promises. When this system was elevated to the predominant social norm, contractual relations replaced those based on social status, customs and traditional authority, and allowed for people who shared no ties of blood, faith or community to engage in market transactions. Haskell's goal here is to link humanitarianism (of which the abolition of slavery and the construction a 'man of principles' are emblematic) to an exclusively Western, capitalist calculating mentality.[13]

We can trace the origins of the connection between market relations and notions of egalitarianism, if not humanitarianism, to the high and low Enlightenment. More specifically, glimpses of this narrative surface in several representations of the Royal Exchange of London as the site where profit and tolerance met to dissolve all prejudicial differences. In 1711, in one of the very first numbers of his *The Spectator*, which became one of the most imitated European periodicals of the eighteenth century, Joseph Addison described enthusiastically his visits to the Royal Exchange as follows:

Sometimes I am justled among a Body of Americans; sometimes I am lost in a Crowd of Jews, and sometimes in a group of Dutch-men. I am a Dane, a Swede, or a Frenchman at different times, or rather fancy myself like the old Philosopher [Socrates], who upon being asked what country-man he was, replied that he was a Citizen of the World.[14]

In his *Lettres philosophiques* (1734), Voltaire claimed to have been equally impressed by the diversity of people that animated the Royal Exchange upon his visit to London. With greater intellectual acuity than Addison, he pushed the argument further to fully articulate the interdependence of commerce and religious toleration:

Enter into the London Stock Exchange ... and you will see representatives of all nations gathered for the utility of mankind; there, the Jew, the Mohammedan and the Christian behave towards each other as if they were the same religion, and reserve the word 'infidel' for those who go bankrupt.[15]

Later in life, in the article on 'Tolerance' in his *Philosophical Dictionary* (1764), a summa of his thought, Voltaire again resorted to the image of the marketplace as the site where profit and tolerance meet to dissolve all prejudicial differences:

In the stock-exchanges of Amsterdam, London, Surat, or Basra, the Gherber, the Banian, the Jew, the Mohametan, the Chinese Deist, the Brahmin, the Greek Christian, the Roman Christian, the Protestant Christian, the Quaker Christian, trade with one another; they don't raise their dagger against each other to gain souls for their religions.[16]

There is some truth and a lot of idealization in these vignettes. Merchants of all backgrounds undoubtedly strolled together down the docks of many ports all over Europe, the Mediterranean, and the Indian Ocean. They also, cautiously but opportunistically, did business with whomever could deliver good deals and acceptable guarantees. However, disproving Addison and Voltaire, historian David Hancock describes the merchant community of mid-eighteenth-century London as one 'markedly hostile to foreigners and strangers'. His figures for the non-English members of London commercial society (5% Scots, 5% Jews, 4% Huguenots, and less than 1% Irish) are a striking corrective to romanticized images of cosmopolitanism.[17] Others have put forth more optimistic figures, arguing that up to one-third of the merchants of the City of London was of 'foreign origin or descent'[18] (although most of them were Dutch Calvinists and Huguenots, who integrated more easily than other foreign minorities in England). The number of Jewish brokers in the London Stock Exchange from 1687 to 1830 was capped at twelve (over a total of 124 licensed brokers);[19] and Muslim traders in the English capital were few and far between. It is also curious to notice that a 1761 engraving of the London Royal Exchange depicts the different physical locations in which various foreign merchants were supposedly located.[20] Such a corporatist representation of the London marketplace contrasts with the idealized images of its cosmopolitan community.

In addition, Voltaire was a notorious anti-Semitic polemicist, who launched a vicious assault on Jews, whom he accused of sectarianism and barbarism, in spite of (or, because of) his commitment to universal tolerance.[21] The most aggressive rebuttal to Voltaire's claims came in 1762 from the Portuguese Jewish economic thinker and intellectual Isaac Pinto, who accused Voltaire not of being offensive and anti-Semitic, but of being inaccurate. Voltaire, Pinto remarked, improperly equated the poor Ashkenazim (namely those underprivileged who were arriving in Amsterdam from Germany and Poland) with the Jewish people *tout court*, and thus failed to distinguish 'the Spanish and Portuguese Jews from the rest,' although the latter 'never mingled or joined with the masses of the other sons of Jacob...'[22] Himself a member of the wealthy elite of the Dutch Sephardic community, Pinto could not contain his pride and sense of superiority, and took advantage of the more positive image that his fellow Sephardim enjoyed.[23]

How receptive was Christian commercial society to Pinto's claims? While the European savants continued to struggle to be inclusive of Jewish minorities, did the 'republic of merchants' put profit above communitarian identity? As late as 1790, only a few months before the emancipation of the Jews proclaimed by the French Revolution, a correspondent of the wealthy Roux of Marseille wrote them from Lyon that as an exception he would consider their recommendation for the rich Jewish merchant Chaim Aghib, who in turn had been recommended to the Roux by other prosperous Jewish traders. Normally, the Lyon correspondent wrote in a letter to Marseille, he would not do any business with members of the Jewish 'nation' because they denied Christ's revelation. But given that the Roux themselves had recommended Aghib, he would trade with him.[24] Aghib was an affluent Sephardic merchant of Livorno, then one of the most thriving and diverse port-cities of Mediterranean Europe. Pinto had Jews like him in mind when he responded to Voltaire. His religious convictions, however, made Roux's correspondent insensitive to Aghib's social standing. One way to interpret this episode is to conceive it as one in which economic interest trumped religious animosity. As we look at this episode of inter-cultural business cooperation more closely, however, it appears less as the result of an anonymous quest for profit than as a specific set of personal relations. The market that triumphed was one embedded in social networks, and business correspondence was the vehicle through which the logic of social networks was communicated and put to work. This example indicates that the 'republic of merchants' was not universally inclusive in the late eighteenth century and continued to recognize corporatist, communitarian affiliations even when it subordinated them to economic interest.

In this and many more cases, 'fraternal relationships' were a precondition rather than an enemy of the market. Studies of early modern England, the most commercialized economy together with the Netherlands at the time, persuasively show that social credit and economic credit were inseparably intertwined.[25] Evidence of this nexus is abundant in the contemporary mercantile discourse. The most imitated merchant manual of early modern Europe, Jacques Savary's *Le parfait negociant* (1675), pronounced with no hesitation that a merchant's foremost quality was to be a man of good reputation, to be considered an honest and trustworthy person.[26] A century later, in his classic of 1776, Adam Smith maintained that the credit that someone 'may get from other people, depends ... upon their opinion of his fortune, probity, and prudence'.[27]

As self-evident as such statements may appear, they nonetheless leave us wondering: What 'other people'? To whom should a merchant prove 'his fortune, probity, and prudence'? Most historical and anthropological literature that insists on the role of personal reputation and credibility, whether it emphasizes cultural norms or rational calculation, generally looks at the ways in which they worked in one locality (a village, a region, or even a big city) or among one ethno-religious group living in dispersal. Even the cross-cultural function performed by diasporic communities is normally attributed to their internal cohesion, with little attention paid to the character of their relations with outsiders.[28] This approach easily leads to essentialized notions of ethnic and religious solidarity, and neglects frequent instances of rivalry and mistrust among members of the same community.[29] When economic historians point to the advantages of ethnic and religious networks in lowering transaction costs and mobilizing capital over long distances, or stress the self-enforcing mechanisms created by the market itself, they focus on patterns of informal cooperation within a closed community. According to this view, institutional innovation alone can be the engine for the expansion of a 'republic of merchants'.

Institutional development certainly had important effects, but did not alter altogether the corporatist nature of early modern European society and the extent to which deep-seated religious divisions influenced business organization. The position of Sephardic merchants was unusual in some respects, but hardly unique. Legal discrimination was often coupled with self-exclusion. Forbidden by their religion from taking oaths, the Quakers were barred from both common law and equity courts in England until the 1689 Act of Toleration granted them permission to use a special form of affirmation in place of the oath.[30] In Amsterdam as in Catholic Europe, Jews were prohibited from entering guilds. Foreign merchants too did not always obtain the same legal and diplomatic protection as other subjects. At the same time, various European states competed to secure the services of religious minorities who were able to connect distant parts of the globe, especially in areas where they could not aspire to military or economic supremacy. While European vessels and merchants increasingly penetrated remote regions and key sectors of colonial trade, the commercial world of the early modern period was nothing like today's globalizing economy. With feeble standardization and homogenization of international markets, trading diasporas and religious and ethnic networks played a major role in favouring market integration. In turn, their success was not simply the result of their internal interdependence, but also a measure of their ability to cooperate with outsiders.

Sources of Integration in the 'Republic of Merchants'

In 1764 on the Ionian island of Zacynthus, which was under Venetian domination from 1485 to 1797, a Greek captain, Dario Costopulo, drafted his testament in Greek and Italian. Among his bequests, he listed some properties and commercial interests in Livorno: Joseph and Raphael Franco, the richest Sephardic firm in town, owed him 203 gold florins for the sale of a grain and silk cargo, and held in custody a trunk full of his silver and gold objects and other miscellaneous items. More of Costopulo's belongings were in the hands of another Jew of Livorno, Isaac Calvo.[31] We do not know what relationship Costopulo entertained with these Sephardim in Tuscany, and for how long they had been doing business together; they certainly were neither kin nor co-religionists. We also know that the Greek community, although it became more established in Livorno in the late eighteenth century, could not compete with the Jews when it came to economic influence in the Tuscan port and in Mediterranean commerce. We may be tempted to read this episode in light of the cosmopolitan flavour that historians and literary critics alike, from Fernand Braudel to Predrag Matvejevic, have attributed to Mediterranean societies.[32] We may even construct a universal category out of the 'littoral society' that, writing about the Indian Ocean, Michael Pearson describes as 'much more cosmopolitan than are parochial inland people for, at the great ports which constitute the notes of the littoral, traders and travellers from all over the ocean, and far beyond, were to be found'.[33] But going beyond such invocations of cosmopolitanism, how can we explain satisfactorily why Costopulo chose to entrust some of his affairs to the Francos and Isaac Calvo, and how he conducted his affairs with them over prolonged periods of time (as the bequests lead us to believe) although they were members of two separated communities, living apart, sharing no common heritage, and both deprived of their own state authorities? In the absence of their court records and business letters, we can only speculate about the nature of their business association. For sure it rested on a variety of structural and customary elements that were common to European long-distance trade and fostered market integration.

Like the republic of letters and the scientific community of the seventeenth and eighteenth centuries, the 'republic of merchants' had its own institutions and discursive practices.[34] Communication was vital to both communities, that of savants and that of merchants and bankers. Geographical and cultural distances put obstacles between buyers and sellers, lenders and borrowers. Well after Magellan first crossed the Pacific in 1521, and even after Spanish galleons began to sail regularly between Acapulco and Manila in the 1560s, thus linking the entire globe together, the infrastructure of overseas and overland transportation remained fragile. Some progress, however, was made in the speed and safety with which goods, people, and information travelled during the early modern period. Across most of Europe, private and public postal services improved in reliability, regularity and coverage.[35] Navigation times, maritime insurance and freight costs in the Mediterranean as a whole decreased only modestly during the sixteenth century.[36] In contrast, the number of European vessels that sailed to Asia increased steadily between 1500 and

1800, and over 70 per cent of those ships that left also returned to Europe.[37] Navigation time between Europe and Asia, though, was not curtailed. It normally took 180 days to sail from Lisbon to Goa, and 200 days to come back, unless unexpected winds, shipwrecks, piracy attacks or crew mismanagement caused delays. From northern Europe to India the outward voyage usually lasted six to eight months and the homebound journey seven to nine months in the seventeenth century.[38] Perhaps the most impressive advances in the integration of inter-continental markets occurred in the English Atlantic from the late seventeenth to the mid-eighteenth century, when new regular courier services carrying packages, personal and business letters, as well as a growing number of newspapers, came into existence.[39] All in all, however, no revolution took place in inter-continental transportation before the advent of steamships and the telegraph, and structural uncertainties loomed large over long-distance trade.[40]

Logistical improvements were only part of the story. Equally important was the ability of actors to understand each other, and ensure that their contracts and obligations were enforced. Most merchants, certainly most of those regularly involved in overseas trade, were polyglot. In his *England's Treasure by Forraign Trade* (1664), Thomas Mun urged merchants 'to attain to the speaking of divers Languages'.[41] A mid-eighteenth-century compilation of the best European commercial treatises identified four main languages adopted by European merchants in different areas: Spanish ('in Usage in almost all the East, particularly on the Coasts of Afrik'), Italian ('understood on all the Coasts of the Mediterranean'), German (good in 'almost all the northern Countries', meaning northern Europe), and French ('which is now become almost universally current, fashionable and useful').[42] Indeed, Italian and Spanish remained widely spoken throughout the early modern Mediterranean next to an array of languages, including Greek, Ladino, Armenian, Arabic and Persian, employed in specific pockets of land and sea and by certain groups. After the arrival of Portuguese traders, soldiers and missionaries in the Indian Ocean, 'a sort of nautical Portuguese' achieved a 'quasi-universal status' there.[43] As late as 1757, at the battle of Plassey, which marked the beginning of British colonial rule over India, Robert Clives addressed the indigenous contingents of his troops in Portuguese.[44] Needless to say, the Portuguese spoken in India was a hybrid language. Similarly, countless pidgin idioms developed in many parts of the globe, especially in coastal areas.[45] One wonders to what extent the *lingua franca* used by Christian slaves and their Muslim wardens in North Africa was also employed among traders. In the words of one of the captives who, after his release, composed a popular account of his days in Algiers, this *lingua franca* was 'the common Language between the slaves and the *Turks*, as also among the slaves of several Nations, it being a mixt Language consisting of *Italian, Spanish, French and Portuguese...*'. Born to fulfil utilitarian purposes, this *lingua franca* nevertheless generated some misunderstandings: the word 'forti', for example, meant 'gently' rather than (as one would expect) 'strongly'.[46]

To surmount the cultural and linguistic barriers they encountered when travelling or dealing abroad, European merchants often employed translators and brokers. In the most isolated localities these translators and middlemen acted alone;

in larger centres, they were often organized in guilds or family clans and hired by local courts, commercial institutions and diplomatic offices. Upon their arrival at the tip of Africa in 1652, Dutch settlers relied on a native young woman, whom they called Eva, as their interpreter and informer. For some years, Eva proved invaluable. She was even able to manipulate the exploitative sexual relations she engaged in with top-ranking Dutch men in order to enhance her position; but as the colonizers imposed their rule, they needed her less and less, and in the end she died an outcast of both the colonial community and her own.[47] In most colonial settings, intelligence gathering and cultural mediation were as crucial as plunder and military force in paving the way of empires. To enter the intensively competitive world of the Indian Ocean in the sixteenth century, the Portuguese crown trained renegades, captives, converts and native adventurers, and employed them as both interpreters and spies (*linguas*).[48] Two centuries later, the British in India relied heavily on cultural and commercial intermediaries, *banians* and *dubashs*, whose names meant 'men of two tongues'.[49] As C.A. Bayly put it, 'The expansion of knowledge was not so much the by-product of empire as a condition for it'.[50]

Imperial structures served both state representatives and private merchants with protection and channels of information. Often seen as antagonistic to mercantile ventures, the Ottoman Empire offered its high officials and numerous Ottoman-Muslim traders opportunities and security in their personal commerce with Venice in the late sixteenth and early seventeenth centuries.[51] Moreover, Ottoman courts accepted legal documents drafted in various towns and regions of the empire, and thus facilitated the job of travelling merchants and their commissioners.[52] Much scholarship has investigated the synergy between private networks and European state-sponsored commercial institutions. The English East India Company, which held exclusive rights over Anglo-Asian trade, is the best example of a European chartered company that both acted as a state monopoly and regulated the extent to which its officials and certain merchant groups could use its infrastructures to boost their private affairs. The Company devised, for example, special policies allowing Sephardic merchants to export coral to and import diamonds from India.[53] When they needed to procure their precious stones, Jean Chardin, Thomas Pitt and other notable connoisseurs and dealers consistently relied on Sephardim who had moved to Madras under the aegis of the East India Company.[54]

Credit was the measure of trust, especially for distant agents who needed to raise capital and make sums available overseas. Many economic historians take the history of credit as emblematic of the evolution from informal to impersonal institutions. Beginning in the thirteenth century, European merchants resorted to bills of exchange as credit instruments that allowed them to make monetary conversions, defer payments, and transfer money abroad. During the sixteenth century, bills of exchange became more and more international, and regularly rolled over third parties, both at specialized fairs and outside them.[55] Later, the English and Dutch East India Companies, founded in 1600 and 1602 respectively, gave birth to the modern stock market. In this respect, they represent a significant step forward in the formation of more integrated and anonymous financial markets.[56] Tradable shares, combined with the creation of financial institutions such as the Bank of Amsterdam and the Bank of England, attracted enormous capital to Amsterdam and London from local as well as foreign investors. This afflux of capital was facilitated by the regular publication of stock prices in a variety of periodicals. A fundamental asymmetry of information, however, existed between investors and the Companies' boards of trustees in seventeenth- and eighteenth-century Europe. The private and corporate interests of Companies' directors, in addition, did not always go hand in hand.[57] Catastrophic episodes such as the South Sea Bubble of 1720 only confirmed the larger public's preference for investment in the public debt.[58]

Considering the structure of northern European stock markets and long-distance trade more generally, the rise of anonymous financial institutions did not render personal ties irrelevant. Throughout the eighteenth century, Parisian notaries played a key role in transmitting information about and among lenders and borrowers.[59] Stock market speculation, moreover, did not improve merchants' ability to transfer money overseas. In the sixteenth century, bills of exchange circulated in Latin Christendom alone. Only in the eighteenth century and infrequently did bills of exchange begin to travel between the Ottoman Empire and Europe (mostly via Marseille).[60] A common way of transferring sums between England and India, the so-called 'respondentia' or 'bottomary' loans were a mixture of insurance contracts on a ship's cargo and a tool to raise capital, and had fairly high interest rates. For these reasons, personalized credit lines remained necessary to borrow and lend capital overseas, especially for those family firms, trading diasporas and informal cross-cultural networks that contributed to the European commercial expansion in so many ways.

Instrumental to the functioning of the 'republic of merchants' was the ability to enforce contracts and obligations among actors who were scattered in distant regions, where different legal cultures and institutions existed. The *Consulate of the Sea*, first printed in Barcelona in 1494, incorporated a variety of legal codes and customary norms in use in the medieval Mediterranean and constituted the basis for future developments of an international mercantile law. In mid-sixteenth-century Italy, legislative and jurisprudential compilations on this subject appeared.[61] After the French monarchy issued the *Ordonnances du commerce* in 1673–81, several European states began to codify merchant law, which maintained a corporate nature: it was law delivered by merchants for merchants. Commercial courts adopted a summary procedure that did not admit lawyers or other legally trained professionals, witnesses, appraisals or written evidence, and issued sentences (which were the only written records released by such courts) solely on the basis of the so-called 'nature of things,' that is, the patent truth according to shared notions of equity. In addition, to speed up the course of trials, these sentences could not, in principle, be appealed to higher courts. These procedures were meant to provide merchants with a rapid and effective legal system.

Proponents of the new institutional economic history have insist that starting in the Middle Ages merchant courts were decisive in enforcing contracts among parties that did not know each other, and thus in expanding the geographical and social borders of market transactions. This view may give the erroneous impression that all disputes adjudicated by a merchant court were easily resolved. Thick piles of court records kept in present-day archives, however, are overwhelming evidence of the tortuous paths taken by most lawsuits initiated by merchants. Before Napoleon, the *lex mercatoria* remained a heterogeneous and highly localized combination of merchant guilds' statutes, customary norms (both written and oral), and collections of previous sentences or summary legislation; additionally, specialized courts did not exist everywhere. Personal and corporate clienteles (which often worked to the detriment of foreign merchants) influenced the outcome of a lawsuit time and again.[63] Furthermore, although in theory sentences issued by mercantile tribunals could not be appealed, merchants routinely obtained permission to appeal, and dragged lawsuits from one civil court to another. The result was a frequent journey from commercial to ordinary and then high tribunals, if not the coexistence of all three levels of adjudication, which threatened to leave one or both parties impoverished and exhausted. At the end of the seventeenth century, the Italian legal scholar Ansaldo Ansaldi blamed merchants who abandoned old-time simplicity in order to bring their cases to court.[64] Ansaldi was right to be sceptical of the tribunals' ability to restore a merchant's reputation or secure his property rights, although merchants could not function outside legal norms and customs.

Business Letters and the 'Republic of Merchants'

In 1622, in one of the earliest English treatises that incorporated merchant law in the literature of *ars mercatoria*, Gerard Malynes also expressed scepticism toward legal formalities. 'Faith or trust,' he asserted, 'is to be kept betweene merchants, and that also must be done without quillets or titles of the law, to avoid interruption of trafficke, wherein his [i.e., a merchant's] Suretiship is to be considered according to the promise...'[65] Letter-writing, Malynes added, was the key tool to enforcing agreements between a merchant and his agents.[66] Fredric Lane makes the same arguments in his work on the fifteenth-century Venetian merchant Barbarigo.[67] Throughout the early modern period commission trade remained indeed inseparable from the practical and legal functions fulfilled by business correspondence. Letters allowed merchants to acquire information that helped them minimize their risks, venture into new markets, and monitor the conduct of distant agents. They accomplished these crucial tasks by means of forging a common discourse, grounded in rhetorical and legal conventions, which transcended linguistic, cultural, and legal barriers, and thus proved indispensable to building networks of communication across the 'republic of merchants'.

Under the pressure of growing market relations in medieval Italy, merchant papers (including letters and in contrast to all other privately drafted papers) were admitted as proof in court.[68] This was not a uniquely European phenomenon. After the ninth century, as Chinese society became increasingly commercialized, contracts drawn up by interested parties began to replace government registers of land tenure.[69] In Europe, the legal validity of business letters did not eliminate the need for notarized documents (powers of attorney, maritime insurance and other contracts filled notarial registers), but facilitated commission trade. It also had an impact on the language of letter-writing, whose style and terminology became more and more standardized. Little changed in the formulas used in business letters in the course of the early modern period (although the style became more gallant and verbose), and little variation existed from one location to the other: this consistency made letters more rather than less effective, and enhanced their ability to reach a diversity of actors. In the late fourteenth and early fifteenth centuries, the intense correspondence between the Tuscan merchant Francesco Datini and the Florentine notary Lapo Mazzei shows that expressions of friendship responded to the rhetorical conventions necessary for contractual agreements.[70] Three centuries later, Savary reiterated that friendship (*amitié*) was the bond of business association.[71] Obligations, promises, rewards, threats, and complaints were all articulated in merchants' letters according to rhetorical conventions that incorporated legal and customary norms and at the same time served to enact actual relations of power. On the basis of information about the successes and failures of various agents, for example, correspondents could enforce collective sanctions. Business correspondence thus helped lay a bridge between mercantile communities who shared a common search for profit but lacked powerful institutional deterrents against dishonesty. More than the letters' legal validity *per se*, it was their capacity to transmit information about merchants' reputation and aptitude combined with their highly codified language that made them essential to the working of the 'republic of merchants'.

The correspondence of a Sephardic partnership of Livorno in the early eighteenth century provides us with many examples of the helpfulness of private letters in the conduct of commission trade that traversed profound cultural and geographical barriers.[72] Between 1704 and 1746 Ergas & Silvera wrote 13,670 letters to Christian and Jewish merchants across western Europe and the southern shores of the Mediterranean as well as to Hindu agents in Goa, the capital of Portuguese India. Writing either in Italian or in Portuguese, they were able to weave tight networks of reciprocity and credibility with both co-religionists and non-Jews. The language and content of their letters reveal the process of cultural mediation in which they were involved. The Italian and Portuguese in their letters are syntactically and grammatically impure (their Portuguese is Italianized in its verbal forms and terminology as well as influenced by Spanish). With intriguing frequency, God's protection is invoked or greetings for religious festivities are expressed in letters addressed to non-Jews both in Europe and outside Europe. Linguistic and cultural comprehension, however, was not enough to forge alliances among actors who were linked by neither kin, ethnic nor religious affinities. Deterrents and enforcement mechanisms were necessary. Even among members of the same community trust was never a given; it had to be supported by marriage alliances and other social ties as well as constantly monitored and reinforced by tangible and satisfactory deeds. Business correspondence provided merchants with the best means of keeping trust alive. It did so by channelling information that served as both an incentive to develop cooperative relations and a threat against fraudulent or disappointing performances.

For historians, business correspondence offers the best evidence of how trust in mercantile affairs was the result of a dynamic process of interaction as well as shared discursive practices.

The same letter was generally shipped via different routes to reduce the risks of loss, and its contents were reported to various correspondents, often present in the same locality. This scheme stirred competition among agents as well as multiplied the venues of information gathering, thus tightening the mechanisms of reputation control. When the dialogue between senders and addressees became a polyphonic choir because of the number and interconnectiveness of those involved, the effectiveness of commercial letters in enforcing good conduct also increased. What matters here is that information flow created informal and yet solid systems of obligations even within networks that were not internally homogeneous. Like all Jews, Ergas & Silvera were banned from trading in Portugal and its overseas empire. They could therefore count on little help from the law. But business letters permitted them to build close alliances with Christian and Hindu agents who served them in Lisbon and Goa for over three decades. Their Christian agents in Lisbon were nearly all Italians (Genoese and Florentine for the most part), and had been apprenticed in the same customary norms about mercantile affairs and business writing as Ergas & Silvera. Their Hindu agents in Goa were among the wealthiest merchants in town and all members of a caste, the Saraswat, who served the Portuguese administration in the area. They were tax collectors, custom house farmers, diplomats and translators of the *Estado da Índia*, ship suppliers and brokers for Europeans in the region. Their various functions required that they learn not only various European languages, but also the legal formulas and rhetorical conventions necessary to conduct business with Western merchants.

When they wished to convey their satisfaction with the most fulfilling business relations they entertained with their addressees, Ergas & Silvera congratulated them for their 'good correspondence' (*boa correspondencia* in Portuguese or *buona corrispondenza* in Italian); and they used this expression regardless of the religious affiliation of their addressees.[73] Hindu merchants of Goa adopted analogous formulas in their letters to various European correspondents in the last quarter of the eighteenth century, in which they spoke, for example, of 'mutual and familiar correspondence' ('mutual e familiar correspondencia').[74] Naturally, 'correspondence' also meant the letter-exchange itself. This semantic overlap is indicative of the importance of private letters in creating and maintaining relations of dependency and reciprocity among culturally and geographically distant actors in long-distance trade. Business correspondence could play this role because the expansion of European colonial powers imposed European legal customs. Stateless diasporas such as the Sephardim gained from and helped generate this uniformity in discursive practices, which equipped them with an important weapon with which to spread their influence in cross-cultural trade at the fringes of mercantile empires. At the same time, Sephardim, as most trading diasporas, belonged to discriminated groups in Christian Europe and their place in the European commercial society of the time was determined by other than strictly economic factors.

The Boundaries of the 'Republic of Merchants'

Membership in all political and social bodies in early modern Europe was not only *de facto* but also *de iure* unequal. So was membership in the 'republic of merchants'. Assets and capital availability constituted an important but not the sole criterion in determining one's position in the commercial society of the time. Ethnic and religious affiliations were also determinant. A number of religious and ethnic minorities played an important role in the economic development of early modern Europe – notably the Jews, the Huguenots, the Armenians, the Quakers, and later the Greeks. They did so because their minority and diasporic status rendered them privileged agents in cross-cultural trade.[75] Rulers interested in their services made special provisions to ensure their safety, and the elite members of these communities were often highly respected merchants. Economic exchange, however, was not an abstract equalizer, and they continued to suffer social stigmatization as much as legal discrimination.

Beginning in the late sixteenth century, several western European states, large and small, all inspired by what Jonathan Israel has called 'philosemitic mercantilism', competed to attract Jewish merchants and their families particularly to northern and central Italy, the Holy Roman Empire, the Netherlands, isolated parts of France, and later England. Sephardic Jews had useful connections with mainland and overseas Iberian territories as well as the Balkans, the Levant and North Africa. The privileges granted to Jews in different parts of Europe were limited in time and in the range of benefits they included, though the general trend during the seventeenth century was toward a more stable and favourable set of rules regulating the Jewish presence in Christian Europe (outside Iberia, of course).[76] While legal and political arrangements varied greatly from place to place, and nowhere did Sephardic Jews and Iberian New Christians acquire full civic and political rights, the most affluent embraced the social codes of the upper echelons of the Christian majority. They shaved their beards, dressed like local elites, attended the opera and theatre, decorated their houses to host respectable Gentile guests, and stood out as refined and cultivated in contrast to their Ashkenazi co-religionists.[77] In Amsterdam and the Dutch Caribbean, Christian and Sephardic attitudes towards African slaves were virtually indistinguishable: acculturated Sephardic Jews acquired Black slaves and strove to be identified as unmistakably 'White' as a way to break with a long European tradition that perceived Jews ambivalently as either 'Black' or 'White'.[78] The incorporation of Christian cultural and social norms was especially fast and deep in England, where numerous conversions also occurred.[79] So pronounced was this tendency among prosperous Sephardic families of western Europe, and Atlantic port-cities in particular, that some scholars have identified it with a distinctive form of precocious Jewish acculturation in contrast to the later transformation of Berlin Jews.[80]

To insist on this pattern of change is not to depict a rosy picture. Anti-Semitic sentiments and incidents were pervasive in the European commercial world. On more than one occasion, Sephardic financiers of Amsterdam took advantage of their widespread connections to acquire political and military news before diplomats did, and made use of this news to influence the fluctuations of the Amsterdam stock exchange. In 1688, one of these speculations precipitated a financial crisis and provoked a major wave of anti-Semitism.[81] Wealthy Sephardim were thus reminded of their precarious inclusion in the Christian 'republic of merchants'.

Sephardic Jews also challenged the unity and character of European commercial society because their lives, economic activities and self-representations traversed predictable geo-political and cultural lines. To begin with, the kinship structure of the Sephardic elite was strictly endogamic (with a preference for marriages between patrilinear first cousins and between uncles and nieces), and included levirate unions (that is, bigamy), which stood in contrast to the accepted practices of the Christian majority.[82] In many other ways, the prosperous Sephardim of western Europe unsettled accepted normative frameworks by occupying an unstable space between modernity and traditionalism, and by keeping one foot on the north-western bank of the Mediterranean and one on its south-eastern shore. Beginning in the 1670s, a new contingent of Sephardic families moved from Italy and western Europe to Ottoman ports in the Levant and North Africa. There, the newly arrived western Sephardim, fewer in number than the indigenous Jews but more heavily involved in international trade, kept their distance from pre-existing Jewish and even Sephardic residents.[83] In Tunis, they formed their own congregation between 1685 and 1710, and everywhere they constituted a small, close-knit elite of 'European Jews' or 'Franks', as they were known in the Ottoman lands.[84] These European Jews in the Levant and North Africa were for the most part subjects of the Grand Duchy of Tuscany and trafficked under French diplomatic protection. They demanded, not always successfully, to be treated as peers by the French, English, Venetians, and Dutch with whom they traded, and at the same time lived back to back with Ottoman subjects.

When the European commercial society of the eighteenth century reached its peak, western Sephardic merchants were also the most acculturated among the Jewish population of the old continent. At the same time, they had relatives and close ties to co-religionists on the south-eastern bank of the Mediterranean and family structures unlike those prevalent in Europe. This position was not without paradoxes. The prosperous and well-integrated Sephardim of Amsterdam, London, Bordeaux, Hamburg, Venice and Livorno saw themselves as part of a diaspora that was anchored to geographical locations and social practices that modern sociologists and critics would see as incompatible with a western process of modernization. European Christian elites resisted treating them as equals, and some of the most vigorous proponents of Enlightenment toleration continued to demonize them for their alleged separatism and traditionalism. A diverse and proactive 'republic of merchants' developed in early modern Europe, but not one that was blind to ethnic and religious identities to the extent that some modern critics and scholars would like us to believe.

Conclusion

Trade, and long-distance trade in particular, brought people into contact; it often erupted in cultural and military confrontations, but just as frequently prompted individuals and groups who had little or nothing in common to create new opportunities and to assess new sources of revenue (which did not necessarily have the same meaning or returns for all actors involved, as the European trade in African slaves testifies). The growth of European intercontinental commerce in the sixteenth century inaugurated a new era not only because it laid the basis of imperial colonialism, but also because it multiplied the situations in which agents belonging to different cultural, economic and political milieux found themselves doing business together. One of the striking outcomes of the European expansion was, in the words of a comparative historian of pre-modern legal systems, the creation of 'an uneasy trust' that made cross-cultural exchange possible. The interaction between European and non-European agents produced what she calls 'routines that generated, if not trust, at least firm expectations about behaviour'.[85] These routines, as I have tried to show, were determined largely by the institutional and customary organization as well as by the discursive practices of European long-distance trade.

Fundamental to the creation of these routines was business correspondence. All forms of cross-cultural trade required a certain degree of mutual understanding (both literal and conceptual) of the terms of the exchange at the very least. As we saw in the case of Ergas & Silvera, private letters furnished merchants the discursive and practical tool to forge alliances with remote agents towards whom they felt no 'natural' loyalty, even in places where they lacked access to military and legal protection. While improved communication and transportation networks, innovations in partnership and credit contracts, and business organization more generally eased market integration during the European commercial expansion, these institutional developments alone are not sufficient to explain how merchants cooperated across geographical and cultural lines. The English trade with the North American continent, the fastest growing European commercial sector in the eighteenth century, remained the province of private, often family-run partnerships until the mid-eighteenth century and even after.[86] These private networks were all but closed and stable. Their ability to open and penetrate new markets depended on the creation of an ongoing 'conversation' among the actors involved in the exchange, and this 'conversation' relied on all available sources – letters, newspapers, and personal scrutiny.[87] In some areas, including the southern Mediterranean and the Indian Ocean, where periodical publications of prices, stock and exchange rates or gazettes were rarely available, business correspondence was often the only means through which distant and diverse agents could carry on this 'conversation' – a 'conversation' that was multilingual and cross-cultural, but employed legal conventions imposed by the Europeans. These conventions, which rendered the language of business correspondence more and more uniform, bred a discourse of obligations and reputation control whose borders expanded across linguistic and cultural lines. In the practice of letter-writing we thus find the most vivid evidence of a trans-national, cross-cultural 'republic of merchants' in the making.

The cosmopolitan nature of this 'republic of merchants' as we have examined it here was not the spin-off of individualism. A shift in the European idea of cosmopolitanism, which linked it to the rise of individualism, is more easily identifiable than a shift in commercial and political practices. During the sixteenth and seventeenth centuries, Jewish entrepreneurs and scholars who championed the cause of their people with various European governments repeatedly emphasized the economic contribution that Jewish merchants would bring to the general public and the treasury.[88] Never did these pleas, however, imply anything but the separate, and legally inferior, place of Jews in Christian society. The Enlightenment idea of cosmopolitanism introduced a new conception of religious tolerance that was linked to the creation of a universal subject; in this intellectual construction, the expansion of market relations was inseparable from the progressive dissolution of restrictive social bonds of corporate societies, including ethno-religious distinctions. This intellectual construction, however, was not an authentic mirror of the practices of cross-cultural trade in eighteenth-century Europe. Cosmopolitanism in the world of business remained very much tied to forms of communication and the social interaction between discrete communities.

In conclusion, European commercial society expanded its borders and increased its cohesion during the early modern period, but by the time of the Enlightenment it had hardly become an undifferentiated entity in which economic interest erased other forms of identification and discrimination. Secondly, while institutional innovations in business organization contributed strongly to this expansion, and changes in European policies and thought also sustained it, we should not underestimate the importance of informal inter-communitarian alliances and the extent to which these alliances rested on shared discursive practices as much as on the infrastructures and legal institutions of trade. The position, activities and outside perception of prominent Sephardic merchants in western Europe are symptomatic of the complexities that need to be explored in order to comprehend the making of a 'republic of merchants'.

Notes

1. 'To finde himselfe [a] *Cosmopolite*, a citizen ... of ... one citie vniuersall, and so consequently to meditate on the Cosmopoliticall gouernment thereof.' This passage is also quoted in Schlereth (1977): xxi–xxii.
2. Chabod (1961): 95–124. The French term 'cosmopolitan' was first used in the mid-sixteenth century by the heterodox humanist Guillaume Postel to invoke the unity of all Christians; Recuperati (1983): 265. Alchemists also soon adopted it. In the eighteenth century it become fairly common and had a generally (though not universally) positive value in the milieu of the *philosophes*. In 1762 "cosmopolite" made its way into the *Dictionnaire de l'Académie* with a rather negative meaning – '*Un cosmopolite n'est pas un bon citoyen*'; Recuperati (1983): 268. In this essay, I necessarily disregard important ethical, political and cultural theories of cosmopolitanism. The historical and philosophical literature on the subject is vast. In addition to Schlereth (1977), see Pomeau (1966); Nussbaum (1997); Frijhoff (1999); Kleingeld (1999); Breckenridge et al. (2002); Scuccimarra (2006). When I proofread this essay, Jacob (2006), which promises to be an important study of cosmopolitanism in early modern Europe, was not yet available.
3. Particularly heroic depictions in Nerlich (1987) and Landes (1998).
4. Remarkable studies of the sophisticated credit and market organization of non-western merchants and their relation to political power in the Ottoman Empire and the Indian Ocean include Kafadar (1986); Hanna (1988); Lombard (1990), III; Das Gupta (2001). Today's globalization has shaken up Eurocentrism in many ways, and the Chinese diaspora in South-East Asia has been described as made of 'cosmopolitan capitalists' (Hamilton 1999).
5. In this essay, I use the term 'merchant' in the meaning that it had acquired for some time when Beawes equated it to 'him who *buys* and *sells* any *Commodities in Gross*, or *deals in Exchanges*; that *trafficks* in the way of *Commerce*, either by *Importation or Exportation*; or that carries on business by way of *Emption, Vendition, Barter, Permutation, or Exchange*; and that makes a continued Assiduity or frequent Negociation in the Mystery of merchandizing his sole business.' Beawes (1751): 31.
6. Israel (2002).
7. Weber (1968): II, 637.
8. See, in particular, the discussion devoted to 'the rise of the calculative spirit' and 'the Occidental city' in Weber (1968): I, 375–80 and III, 1212–372, respectively. It is beyond the scope of this essay to discuss the relationship between the two strings of Weber's theory of modern capitalism, the one that emphasizes ethical and cultural norms and the one that stresses the role of institutional development.
9. Recently, Seabright (2004).
10. Greif (1994, 2001, 2006): 278–81.
11. An original formulation in North and Thomas (1973).
12. Haskell (1998): 265.
13. Haskell (1998): 267–73.
14. Quoted in Schlereth (1977): 101.
15. Quoted in Sutcliffe (2003): 242.
16. Quoted in Schlereth (1977): 102. Here 'stock-exchanges' stand for market places in general.
17. Hancock (1995): 45. The title of Hancock's book may appear in contradiction with these statements. The expression 'citizens of the world', he claims, was a current description of eighteenth-century London merchants; Hancock (1995): 20n17. But he stresses the

obstacles that the Scottish merchants about whom he writes had to overcome to insert themselves into the upper echelons of London business milieux.

18. Chapman (1992): 30. For Morgan (2000): 92, 'The merchant community of London [in the eighteenth century] was cosmopolitan; the financial hub of the metropolis attracted continental traders including Dutch, Huguenots, Germans and Jews, who all participated in the capital's commerce with its American hinterlands'.
19. Pollins (1982): 56.
20. 'An Elevation, Plan and History of the Royal Exchange of London' (1761) drawn by John Donowell (fl. 1753–86) and engraved by Anthony Walker (1726–1765). Copy owned by the author and reproduced in McCusker (2005): 302.
21. Sutcliffe (2003): 19, 231–46. See also Hertzberg (1968).
22. Quoted in Kaplan (1997): 140. Pinto's *Apologie pour la nation juive* was published anonymously. Similar negative descriptions of Ashkenazi Jews were common in England as well; Katz (1994): 258.
23. Werner Sombart's identification of these Sephardic merchants with the modern cosmopolitan spirit of capitalism in the early twentieth century is a telling reminder of the coexistence of prejudice and admiration; Sombart (1997). For a critical assessment of Sombart's anti-Semitism, see Zemon Davis (1997).
24. 'Votre recommandation pour Vita Aghib, juif très riche, qui vous a été recommandé par une autre maison juive ... Il faut qu'il vienne de votre part pour que nous en fassions le cas. La prophétie s'accomplit bien chez nous, car c'est une natione que nous n'aimons pas, n'ayant pas voulu traiter ni faire aucun commerce avec eux.' Quoted in Carrière (1973): 283.
25. Muldrew (1998); Finn (2003).
26. 'La première qualité que doit avoir un Marchand à la vente de sa marchandise, c'est d'estre homme de bien ... L'homme de bien consiste à être de bonne foy, à ne tromper personne...'; Savary (1675): livre I, chap. 7, p. 70. See also livre II, chap. 47, p. 33.
27. Smith (1976): 122.
28. Thus in Curtin (1984).
29. Greif (1994, 1998, 2001, 2006); Landa (1994): esp. 101–14.
30. Price (1996): IV, 64–5.
31. Molho (2003): 277–8.
32. Braudel (1972–1973); Matvejevic (1999).
33. Pearson (2003): 39.
34. See, among a vast literature, Goodman (1994), and Goldgar (1995) on the republic of letters, and Shapin and Schaffer (1985), and Biagioli (1993) on what I anachronistically referred to as 'the scientific community'.
35. Headrick (2000): 184–6; Jeannin (2001); Benaiteau (2002); Bottin (2002).
36. Braudel (1972–1973): I, 355–71.
37. de Vries (2003).
38. Pearson (2003): 186–7.
39. Steele (1986). The French were less effective than the English in establishing reliable communication networks across the Atlantic in the eighteenth century; Banks (2002).
40. Braudel (1981–1984): I, 415–30; Menard (1991). Headrick (2000): 182 dates such revolution to the invention of the visual telegraph by Claude Chappe in 1793.
41. Reprinted in McCulloch (1954): 53.
42. Beawes (1751): 33. It is possible that by Spanish Beawes meant Portuguese as well. Others had commented before on the spread of French (see *Britannia Languens, or A Discourse of Trade...* (London 1680), reprinted in McCulloch (1954): 436). Russian

merchants were accustomed to learning German and Dutch to communicate with foreign traders; Bushkovitch (1980): 15.

43. Pearson (2003): 39.
44. Pearson (2003): 156.
45. Useful references in Hymes (1971), and Byrne and Holm (1993). I thank Linda Rupert for helping me navigate the oceans of the literature on pidgin and creole languages.
46. d'Aranda (1666): 14.
47. Wells (1998).
48. Couto (2003).
49. Bayly (1996): 45.
50. Bayly (1996): 56.
51. Dursteler (2002).
52. Hanna (1988): 49–50.
53. Yogev (1978).
54. Sir John Chardin and his brother Daniel entered into partnership with the brothers Rodrigues in India in 1682. The association failed after about 20 years when the two brothers accumulated enough capital to trade on their own. Beinecke Library (New Haven, CT), *John Chardin correspondence and documents, 1671–1719*, Box 1, Folders 1–5. See also Samuel (2000): 354–60.
55. De Roover (1953); Boyer-Xambeu et al. (1994); De Maddalena and Kellenbenz (1986).
56. Neal (1990) and (2000); Gelderblom and Jonker (2004).
57. To be elected in the Court of Directors of the English East India Company one needed to hold at least £2000 in the Company's stocks. Directors had a corporate interest in maximizing the Company's imports, but this could sometimes conflict with their primary private interest as exporters; Chaudhuri (1978): 132.
58. Barron Baskin (1988): 201.
59. Hoffman et al. (2000).
60. Eldem (1999).
61. The first systematic treatise on merchant law was published in 1553 by Benvenuto Stracca (1509–1578). For a survey of the history of commercial law, see Hilaire (1986).
62. Milgrom et al. (1990).
63. Lane (1944): 99.
64. 'Mercatores male agunt qui relicta veteri simplicitate subtilizant in Foro'. Ansaldi (1689): 622.
65. Malynes (1622): 93.
66. '… a Factor is created by Merchant Letters'. Malynes (1622): 111. Here 'factor' means a merchant's agent overseas, who traded in his own name and was legally responsible for any malfeasance, rather than a salaried employee. On the difference between 'factor' and 'agent,' see Hancock (1995): 124. The terminology in this matter was not always so clear-cut.
67. Lane (1944): 97–8.
68. Fortunati (1996).
69. Hansen (1995).
70. Trexler (1980): 136.
71. 'La premiere chose que doivent avoir deux Associez est l'amitié & la deference l'un pour l'autre …' Savary (1675), livre 2, chap. 43, p. 2.
72. For more on what follows, see Trivellato (2003) and (2006).
73. Examples in letters addressed to the Sephardic family Belilios in Aleppo, in September 1725, as well as the Hindu family Kamat in Goa, in Janaury 1727. Archivio di Stato, Florence, *Libri di commercio e di famiglia*, 1939.

74. Xavier Center of Historical Research, Goa (India), *Mhamai Correspondence/ Portuguese,* 14001. No letters by the correspondents of Ergas & Silvera survive, but there is no reason to suspect that those written by other Saraswats a few decades later differed in any significant way. On the Saraswat of Goa in the seventeenth and eighteenth centuries and their archival records, see Pearson (1972 and 1981), De Souza (1985), and Pinto (1994).
75. Curtin (1984).
76. Israel (1998): 46–7 and *passim.*
77. Israel (1998): 116. Numerous restrictions and exceptions existed, but did not reverse the overall direction of this pattern. In Venice Jews never acquired full real estate property rights, while in Livorno they did. In Bordeaux they were not allowed to attend the theatre (Nahon (2003): 90). Only in 1725 were restrictions eased on dress codes and theatre and opera attendance in Hamburg, Altona and Wandsbek (Israel (1998): 209).
78. Schorsch (2004): 180. It was in the late eighteenth century that Jews began to be attributed with fixed 'racial' traits of their own; Wahrman (2004): 90–4.
79. Endelman (1979): 118–65; Endelman (1990): 9–33.
80. Dubin (1999); Sorkin (1999).
81. Israel (2002): 453–4.
82. On levirate and bigamy among the Sephardim of Livorno, see Galasso (2002): 9, 28–39. For Bordeaux, see Nahon (2003): 114.
83. On the Western Sephardim in Aleppo, see Milano (1949); Schwarzfuchs (1984); Masters (1987); Philipp (1994). An earlier and larger Sephardic culture had set root in the Balkans and the Ottoman Empire in the sixteenth century. See Lewis (1984); Benbassa and Rodrigue (2000).
84. Lévy (1999).
85. Benton (2002): 26.
86. Price (1991); Hancock (1995).
87. Hancock (1998).
88. Notable examples are Rabbi Simone Luzzatto's *Discorso circa il stato de gl'Hebrei* printed in Venice in 1638 and Rabbi Menasseh Ben Israel's mission to Oliver Cromwell in 1655. See Ravid (1982).

References

Ansaldi, A.(1689), *De commercio et mercatura discursus legales* (Rome).
Banks, K.J. (2002), *Chasing Empire Across the Sea: Communication and the State in the French Atlantic, 1713–1763* (Montreal and Ithaca).
Barron Baskin, J. (1988), 'The Development of Corporate Financial Markets in Britain and the United States, 1600–1914: Overcoming Asymmetric Information', *Business History Review,* LXII, 2.
Bayly, C.A. (1996), *Empire and Information: Intelligence Gathering and Social Communication in India, 1780–1870* (Cambridge).
Beawes, W. (1751), *Lex Mercatoria Rediviva, or, The Merchant's Directory* (London).
Benaiteau, M. (2002), 'Communication postale et cosmopolitisme au XVIIIe siècle', in L. Bianchi (ed.), *L'idea di cosmopolitismo: circolazione e metamorfosi* (Naples).
Benbassa, E. and A. Rodrigue (2000), *Sephardi Jewry: A History of the Judeo-Spanish Community, 14th-20th Centuries* (Berkeley, Los Angeles and London).
Benton, L. (2002), *Law and Colonial Cultures: Legal Regimes in World History, 1400–1900*

(Cambridge).

Biagioli, M. (1993), *Galileo, Courtier: The Practice of Science in the Culture of Absolutism* (Chicago).

Bottin, J. (2002), 'Négoce et circulation de l'information au début de l'époque moderne', in M. Le Roux (ed.), *Histoire de la poste: de l'administration à l'entreprise* (Paris).

Boyer-Xambeu, M-T., G. Deleplace and L. Gillard (1994), *Private Money and Public Currencies: The 16th Century Challenge* (Armonk, NY).

Braudel, F. (1972–1973), *The Mediterranean and the Mediterranean World in the Age of Philip II*, 2 vols (New York).

_____. (1981–1984), *Civilization and Capitalism, 15th–18th Century*, 3 vols (New York).

Britannia Languens, or A Discourse of Trade... (1680), reprinted in J.R. McCulloch, (ed.), *Early English Tracts on Commerce*, (Cambridge, 1954).

Breckenridge, C.A., H.K. Bhabha and D. Chakrabarty (eds) (2002), *Cosmopolitanism* (Durham, NC).

Bushkovitch, P. (1980), *The Merchants of Moscow, 1580–1650* (Cambridge).

Byrne, F. and J. Holm (eds) (1993), *Atlantic Meets Pacific: A Global View of Pidginization and Creolization (Selected Papers from the Society for Pidgin and Creole Linguistics)* (Amsterdam and Philadelphia).

Carrière, C. (1973), *Négociants marseillais au XVIIIe siècle: Contribution à l'étude des économies maritimes* (Marseilles).

Chabod, F. (1961), *Storia dell'idea d'Europa* (Bari).

Chapman, S. (1992), *Merchant Enterprise in Britain: From the Industrial Revolution to World War I* (Cambridge).

Chaudhuri, K.N. (1978), *The Trading World of Asia and the English East India Company 1660–1760* (Cambridge).

Couto, D. (2003), 'The Role of Interpreters, or *linguas*, in the Portuguese Empire during the 16th Century', *E-Journal of Portuguese History*, I/2, accessible online at http://www.brown.edu/Departments/Portuguese_Brazilian_Studies/ejph/.

Curtin, P.D. (1984), *Cross-Cultural Trade in World History* (Cambridge).

D'Aranda, E. (1666), *The History of Algiers and its Slavery: with many remarkable particularities of Africa...* (London).

De Vries, J. (2003), 'Connecting Europe and Asia: a Quantitative Analysis of the Cape-route Trade, 1497–1795', in D.O. Flynn, A. Giráldez and R. von Glahn (eds), *Global Connections and Monetary Hisotry, 1470–1800* (Aldershot and Burlington, VT), pp. 35–106.

Das Gupta, A. (2001), *The World of the Indian Ocean Merchant, 1500–1800* (New Delhi).

De Maddalena, A. and H. Kellenbenz (eds) (1986), *La repubblica internazionale del denaro* (Bologna).

De Roover, R. (1953), *L'evolution de la lettre de change XIVe–XVIIIe siècles* (Paris).

De Souza, T. (1985), 'Mhamai House Records: Indigenous Sources for Indo-Portuguese Historiography', in *II Seminário Internacional de História Indo-Portuguesa. Actas* (Lisbon), pp. 931–941.

Dubin, L.C. (1999), *The Port Jews of Habsburg Trieste: Absolutist Politics and Enlightenment Culture* (Stanford).

Dursteler, E. (2002), 'Commerce and Coexistence: Veneto-Ottoman Trade in the Early Modern Era', *Turcica*, 34.

Eldem, E. (1999), *French Trade in Istanbul in the Eighteenth Century* (Leiden, Boston and Cologne).

Endelman, T.M. (1979), *The Jews of Georgian England, 1714–1830: Tradition and Change in* a Liberal Society (Philadelphia).

_____ . (1990), Radical Assimilation in English Jewish History, 1656–1945 (Bloomington).

Finn, M.C. (2003), The Character of Credit: Personal Debt in English Culture, 1740–1914 (Cambridge).

Fortunati, M. (1996), Scrittura e prova: I libri di commercio nel diritto medievale e moderno (Rome).

Frijhoff, W. (1999), 'Cosmopolitisme', in V. Ferrone and D. Roche (eds), Le monde des Lumières (Paris), pp. 31–40.

Galasso, C. (2002), Alle origini di una comunità: Ebree ed ebrei a Livorno nel Seicento (Florence).

Gelderblom, O. and J. Jonker (2004), 'Completing a Financial Revolution: The Finance of the Dutch East India Trade and the Rise of Amsterdam Capital Market, 1595–1612', Journal of Economic History, 64, 3.

Goldgar, A. (1995), Impolite Learning: Conduct and Community in the Republic of Letters 1680–1750 (New Haven).

Goodman, D. (1994), The Republic of Letters: A Cultural History of the French Enlightenment (Ithaca and London).

Greif, A. (1994), 'Cultural Beliefs and the Organization of Society: A Historical and Theoretical Reflection on Collectivist and Individualist Societies', Journal of Political Economy, 102, 5.

_____ . (1998), 'Historical and Comparative Institutional Analysis', American Economic Review, 88, 2.

_____ . (2001), 'Impersonal Exchange and the Origins of Markets: From the Community Responsibility System to Individual Legal Responsibility in Pre-modern Europe', in M. Aoki and Y. Hayami (eds), Communities and Markets in Economic Development (Oxford).

_____ . (2006), Institutions and the Path to the Modern Economy: Lessons from Medieval Trade (Cambridge).

Hakluyt, R. (1598), The Principal Navigations Voyages, Traffiques and Discoueries of the English Nation (London).

Hamilton, G.G. (ed.) (1999), Cosmopolitan Capitalists: Hong Kong and the Chinese Diaspora at the End of the Twentieth Century (Seattle and London).

Hancock, D. (1995), Citizens of the World: London Merchants and the Integration of the British Atlantic Community, 1735–1785 (Cambridge).

_____ . (1998), 'Commerce and Conversation in the Eighteenth-Century Atlantic: The Invention of Madeira Wine', Journal of Interdisciplinary History, 29, 2.

Hanna, N. (1988), Making Big Money in 1600: The Life and Time of Isma'il Abu Taqiyya, Egyptian Merchant (Syracuse, NY).

Hansen, V. (1995), Negotiating Daily Life in Traditional China: How Ordinary People Used Contracts, 600–1400 (New Haven and London).

Haskell, T.L. (1998), Objectivity is not Neutrality: Explanatory Schemes in History (Baltimore and London).

Headrick, D.R. (2000), When Information Came of Age: Technologies of Knowledge in the Age of Reason and Revolution, 1700–1850 (Oxford).

Hertzberg, A. (1968), The French Enlightenment and the Jews (New York).

Hilaire, J. (1986), Introduction historique au droit commercial (Paris).

Hoffman, P.T., G. Postel-Vinay and J.-L. Rosenthal (2000), Priceless Markets: The Political Economy of Credit in Paris, 1660–1870 (Chicago).

Hymes, D. (ed.) (1971), Pidginization and Creolization of Languages (Proceedings of a

Conference held at the University of the West Indies, Mona, Jamaica, April 1968) (Cambridge).

Israel, J.I. (1998), *European Jewry in the Age of Mercantilism 1550–1750* (London and Portland).

———. (2002), *Diasporas within a Diaspora: Jews, Crypto-Jews and the World Maritime Empires, 1540–1740* (Leiden, Boston and Cologne).

Jacob, M.C. (2006), *Strangers Nowhere in the World: The Rise of Cosmopolitanism in Early Modern Europe* (Philadelphia).

Jeannin, P. (2001), 'La diffusion de l'information', in S. Cavaciocchi (ed.), *Fiere e mercati nella integrazione delle economie europee, secc. XIII-XVIII* (Florence).

Kafadar, C. (1986), 'A Death in Venice (1575): Anatolian Muslim Merchants Trading in the Serenissima', *Journal of Turkish Studies*, 10.

Kaplan, Y. (1997), 'The Self-Definition of the Sephardic Jews of Western Europe and Their Relation to the Alien and the Stranger', in B.R. Gampel (ed.), *Crisis and Creativity in the Sephardic World, 1391–1648* (New York).

Katz, D.S. (1994), *The Jews in the History of England 1485–1850* (Oxford).

Kleingeld, P. (1999), 'Six Varieties of Cosmopolitanism in Late Eighteenth Century Germany', *Journal of the History of Ideas*, 60, 3.

Landa, J.T. (1994), *Trust, Ethnicity and Identity: Beyond the Institutional Economics of Ethnic Trading Networks, Contract Law, and Gift Exchange* (Ann Arbor).

Landes, D. (1998), *The Wealth and Poverty of Nations: Why Some are So Rich and Some So Poor* (New York).

Lane, F.C. (1944), *Andrea Barbarigo, Merchant of Venice (1418–1449)* (Baltimore).

Lévy, L. (1999), *La nation juive portugaise: Livourne, Amsterdam, Tunis, 1591–1951* (Paris).

Lewis, B. (1984), *The Jews of Islam* (Princeton, NJ).

Lombard, D. (1990), *Le carrefour javanais: essai d'histoire globale*, 3 vols (Paris).

Luzzato, Rabbi S. (1638), *Discorso circa il stato de gl'Hebrei* (Venice).

Malynes, G. (1622), *Consuetudo, vel, Lex Mercatoria, or, The Ancient Law-Merchant...* (London).

Masters, B. (1987), '"Trading Diasporas" and "Nations": The Genesis of National Identity in Ottoman Aleppo', *International History Review*, 9.

Matvejevic, P. (1999), *Mediterranean: A Cultural Landscape* (Berkeley).

McCulloch, J.R. (ed.) (1954), *Early English Tracts on Commerce* (Cambridge).

McCusker, J.J., (2005), 'The Demise of Distance: The Business Press and the Origins of the Information Revolution in the Early Modern Atlantic World', *American Historical Review*, 110, 2.

Menard, R.R. (1991), 'Transport Costs and Long-range Trade, 1300–1800: Was there a European "Transport Revolution" in the Early Modern Era?', in J.D. Tracy (ed.) *The Political Economy of Merchant Empires* (Cambridge), pp. 228–75.

Milano, A. (1949), *Storia degli ebrei italiani nel Levante* (Florence).

Milgrom, P.R., D.C. North and B.R. Weingast (1990), 'The Role of Institutions in the Revival of Trade: The Law Merchants, Private Judges, and the Champagne Fairs', *Economics and Politics*, 2, 1.

Molho, A. (2003), 'Il Mediterraneo', in M. Tangheroni (ed.), *Pisa e il Mediterraneo: Uomini, merci, idee dagli Etruschi ai Medici* (Milan).

Morgan, K. (2000), *Slavery, Atlantic Trade and the British Economy, 1660–1800* (Cambridge).

Muldrew, C. (1998), *The Economy of Obligation: The Culture of Credit and Social Relations in Early Modern England* (New York).

Nahon, G. (2003), *Juifs et Judaïsm à Bordeaux* (Bordeaux).

Neal, L. (1990), *The Rise of Financial Capitalism: International Capital Markets in the Age of Reason* (Cambridge).

_____. (2000), 'How it all Began: The Monetary and Fiscal Architecture of Europe during the First Global Capital Markets, 1648–1815', *Financial History Review*, 7, 2.

Nerlich, M. (1987), *Ideology of Adventure: Studies in Modern Consciousness, 1100–1750*, 2 vols (Minneapolis).

North, D.C. and R.P. Thomas (1973), *The Rise of the Western World: A New Economic History* (Cambridge).

Nussbaum, M. (1997), 'Kant and Cosmopolitanism', in J. Bohman and M. Lutz-Bachmann (eds) *Perpetual Peace: Essays on Kant's Cosmopolitan Ideal* (Cambridge, MA and London), pp. 25–57.

Pagden, A. (2000), 'Europe: Conceptualizing a Continent', in A. Pagden (ed.), *The Idea of Europe from Antiquity to the European Union* (Cambridge).

Pearson, M.N. (1972), 'Indigenous Dominance in a Colonial Economy: The Goa *Rendas*, 1600–1670', *Mare Luso-Indicum*, 2.

_____. (1981), 'Banyas and Brahmins: Their Role in the Portuguese Indian Economy', in N.N. Pearson, *Coastal Western India: Studies from the Portuguese Records* (New Delhi), pp. 93–115.

_____. (2003), *The Indian Ocean* (New York).

Philipp, T. (1994), 'French Merchants and Jews in the Ottoman Empire during the Eighteenth Century', in A. Levy (ed.), *The Jews of the Ottoman Empire* (Princeton), pp. 315–25.

Pinto, C. (1994), *Trade and Finance in Portuguese India: A Study of the Portuguese Country Trade, 1770–1840* (New Delhi).

Pollins, H. (1982), *Economic History of the Jews in England* (London and Toronto).

Pomeau, R. (1966), *L'Europe des Lumieres: Cosmopolitisme et Unité Européenne au Dix-Huitième Siecle* (Paris).

Price, J.M. (1991), 'Transaction Costs: A Note on Merchant Credit and the Organization of Private Trade', in J.D. Tracy (ed.), *The Political Economy of Merchant Empires* (Cambridge), pp. 276–97.

Price, J. (1996), 'English Quaker Merchants and War at Sea, 1689–1783', in J. Price, *Overseas Trade and Traders: Essays on Some Commercial, Financial and Political Challenges Facing British Atlantic Merchants* (Aldershot and Brookfiled, VT).

Ravid, B. (1982), '"How Profitable the Nation of the Jewes are": The "Humble Addresses" of Menasseh ben Israel and the "Discorso" of Simone Luzzatto', in J. Reinharz and D. Swetschinski (eds) *Mystics, Philosophers, and Politicians: Essays in Jewish Intellectual History in Honor of Alexander Altmann* (Durham, NC), pp. 159–80.

Recuperati, G. (1983), "Cosmopolitismo", in N. Bobbio, N. Matteucci and G. Pasquino (eds), *Dizionario di politica*, 2nd edn (Turin), pp. 262–70.

Samuel, E. (2000), 'Gems from the Orient: The Activities of Sir John Chardin (1643–1713) as a Diamond Importer and East India Merchant', *Proceedings of the Huguenot Society*, XXVII, 3.

Savary, J. (1675), *Le parfait négociant, ou, Instructon générale pour ce qui regarde le commerce de toute sortes de marchandises, tant de France que des pays étrangers* (Paris).

Schlereth, T.J. (1977), *The Cosmopolitan Ideal in Enlightenment Thought: Its Form and Function in the Ideas of Franklin, Hume and Voltaire, 1694–1790* (Notre Dame, Ind.).

Schorsch, J. (2004), *Jews and Blacks in the Early Modern World* (Cambridge).

Schwarzfuchs, S. (1984), 'La "nazione ebrea" livournaise au Levant', *La rassegna mensile di Israel*, 50.

Scuccimarra, L. (2006), *I confini del mondo: storia del cosmopolitismo dall' antichità al*

Settecento, (Bologna).

Seabright, P. (2004), *The Company of Strangers: A Natural History of Economic Life* (Princeton, NJ).

Shapin, S. and S. Schaffer (1985), *Leviathan and the Air-pump: Hobbes, Boyle, and the Experimental Life* (Princeton, NJ).

Smith, A. (1976), *An Inquiry into the Nature and Causes of the Wealth of Nations*, R.H. Campbell and A.S. Skinner (eds), 2 vols (Oxford).

Sombart, W. (1997), *The Jews and Modern Capitalism* (New Brunswick and London).

Sorkin, D. (1999), 'The Port Jew: Notes Towards a Social Type', *Journal of Jewish Studies*, 50, 1.

Steele, I.K. (1986), *The English Atlantic 1675–1740: An Exploration of Communication and Community* (New York and Oxford).

Sutcliffe, A. (2003), *Judaism and Enlightenment* (Cambridge).

Trexler, R. (1980), *Public Life in Renaissance Florence* (New York).

Trivellato, F. (2003), 'Juifs de Livourne, Italiens de Lisbonne et hindous de Goa: réseaux marchands et échanges interculturels à l'époque moderne', *Annales HSS*, 58, 3 .

———. (2006), 'Merchants' Letters across Geographical and Social Boundaries', in F. Bethencourt and F. Egmond (eds), *Correspondence and Cultural Exchange in Europe, 1400–1700* (Cambridge).

Wahrman, D. (2004), *The Making of the Modern Self: Identity and Culture in Eighteenth-Century England* (New Haven and London).

Weber, M. (1968), *Economy and Society: An Outline of Interpretative Sociology*, 3 vols (New York).

Wells, J.C. (1998), 'Eva's Men: Gender and Power in the Establishment of the Cape of Good Hope, 1652–1674', *Journal of African History*, 39, 3.

Yogev, G. (1978), *Diamonds and Coral: Anglo-Dutch Jews and Eighteenth-Century Trade* (Leicester).

Zemon Davis, N. (1997), 'Religion and Capitalism Once Again? Jewish Merchant Culture in the Seventeenth Century', *Representations*, 59.

Chapter 6

A European Community of Scholars
Exchange and Friendship among Early Modern Natural Historians

Florike Egmond

Introduction

Intellectual traditions and fields of expert knowledge are not among the easiest phenomena to pin down to a particular geographical area. In the early modern period ideas and (re)presentations travelled via persons, manuscripts, correspondence, publications, pictures, maps and various types of objects. As Stuart Clark has argued, there were no geographical boundaries in most intellectual debates in Europe.[1] Science itself, moreover, was certainly no exclusively European phenomenon. In terms of its intellectual tradition early modern European medicine (to name but one of its branches) was unthinkable without the influx of ideas and practices from the Middle East.

In this essay I hope to show, however, that a closer look at the formation of a new field of scientific expertise in early modern Europe may be revealing with respect to the questions of how science in Europe obtained a specifically European character, how it contributed to the growth of a European identity, and how it may even have contributed to a phenomenon known as particularly European: the scientific revolution. The emphasis here will not be on the history of (scientific) ideas, but on practices, the construction of a new field of knowledge, and the consequences of such practices with respect to the formation of a European community of scholars. That is why this chapter focuses on one particular field of scientific expertise rather than dealing with a broad range of the sciences, while yet hoping to contribute to the more general discussion about the phenomenon of European scientific development. The approach is cultural and social, starting from the assumption of a non-teleological course of history. The perspective is close to a 'constructivist' view of history, without, however, assuming intentionality, which could threaten to take us straight back into teleology. In other words, I regard the process of the formation of a new field of scientific expertise as the result of the varied (and sometimes contradictory) intentions and wishes of many individuals and groups – which themselves were deeply influenced by long discursive traditions. This process itself was, moreover, influenced by many other developments over which the persons directly concerned had no control, as well as by chance. And there was nothing inevitable about either effects or consequences.

The focus here is on a particular, albeit wide category of knowledge – expertise about living nature (plants and animals), or natural history as it is often called – and the persons who specialized in this field during the sixteenth century. Natural history became a new field of *specialist* expertise in the course of this century, but expertise of nature was, of course, nothing new in itself and by no means a specifically European phenomenon. Throughout history and prehistory and all over the world fishermen, hunters, farmers, healers and many others have always possessed considerable practical expertise about living nature.[2] Yet, during the period between, roughly, 1520 and 1620, a particularly strong fascination with nature spread throughout Europe, while the available information about animals and especially plants multiplied and was systematized in various ways. At the beginning of the sixteenth century there was no European community of expert natural historians; by the end of that century such a community did exist. Large numbers of naturalists all over the continent exchanged a vast amount of information by various means.[3]

It is not so much *what* the experts (whatever their background or training) knew about nature, but the ways in which that knowledge was presented and organized, shared, exchanged and represented, that concern us here. From the 1550s onwards – if not earlier – men and women involved in this domain recognized each other as experts in a common field and as members of a 'virtual' and extremely heterogeneous community which shared a specialized interest. The growth of this community of experts and the development of certain modes of exchange (of information and gifts) formed a crucial part of the construction of this new field of expertise. Exchanging information, keeping in touch, developing informal rules of exchange and establishing a community were no 'mere' social aspects of the intellectual formation of a new discipline. Without the process of defining certain types of knowledge as expert knowledge, establishing a common fund of expertise, a language and terminology in which to write about it and developing a special mode of depicting this information (in the form of 'scientific illustration', which answers at least up to a point to different rules from 'artistic representation'), there would have been no field of knowledge called natural history. That is why it is crucial to look closely at concepts that played a key role in this developing community of naturalists, such as exchange and friendship. To learn more about these notions and what they meant in practice may help us understand how certain types of expert knowledge (out of a much larger range of knowledge) were demarcated, (re)presented and recognized as 'science', or in other words how a scientific discipline was formed – processes that still go on today and demand critical reflection.

One of Europe's greatest botanists, Carolus Clusius (1526 Arras – 1609 Leiden), played a central part in all of the abovementioned developments, as author, translator, explorer and writer of the first Spanish flora, director of a botanical garden, illustrator, advisor of aristocratic collectors, protégé of aristocrats and himself patron of younger scholars and illustrators, and correspondent with hundreds of fellow experts and informants.[4] That is the reason why this contribution focuses on his network and correspondence. The latter not only reflects the development of a renowned scholar's practices, exchanges and ideas; it also shows how his network snowballed, and how new styles of exchange were moulded in the interaction of European experts from different countries, thus creating 'European' styles of scientific exchange and a 'European' community of naturalists.

Fashionable Nature: the Botanical Renaissance of the Sixteenth Century

From the early decades of the sixteenth century, a wave of interest in nature swept through Europe: nature became fashionable. As yet I know of no really satisfactory survey of the various factors that contributed to the sudden upsurge of this interest among a wide range of Europeans. There is no doubt, however, that the discovery of the New World and the transportation of exotic naturalia to Europe from all over the world stimulated this fascination. The Middle East (especially Persia) was already famous for its sophisticated garden culture in medieval times. It is not generally known, however, that the New World formed an example as well. Spanish conquerors were amazed and impressed by the Aztec gardens and menageries in and around Tenochtitlán which they encountered upon their first arrival in 1521. In these gardens plants were grown for pleasure as well as for medicinal and ritual use.[5] The great voyages of discovery to the New World and Far East and explorations in the Middle East led to the introduction of exotic plants or drugs based on them (such as potatoes, tomatoes, tulips, quinine) in Europe, which in the long run would have enormous effects on food, medicine and Europe's physical appearance. Clusius was personally involved in the introduction and scientific description of both the potato and various types of tulips in the Low Countries. As a more short-term effect, the very existence of the strange plants and animals discovered in newly explored regions demonstrated the incompleteness of the knowledge of natural historians from antiquity. It triggered new investigations both in and outside Europe.[6]

The interest in nature focused mainly on plants and gardens, and to a somewhat lesser extent on animals, which were much more difficult and expensive to transport and keep. Three major manifestations were the creation of numerous private gardens all over Europe, the proliferation of botanical and zoological motifs in decorative art (such as tapestries, frescoes) and the collection of naturalia (such as plants, shells, and parts of animals) and of their visual representations in drawings, watercolours, woodcuts, engravings or illustrations from printed works. In the rich aristocratic and princely collections of the period, naturalia were often part of much larger *Kunst- und Wunderkammern*. Almost every self-respecting nobleman owned a garden and showed off exotic flowers to his visitors.[7] Some even owned a maze or a private menagerie. It is among·members of the elite who owned parks or gardens and had a passion for growing exotics that we should look for a particular category of experts in natural history. Quite a few of them took gardening and botany very seriously indeed and read as widely as possible on the subject. The fact that they were rich and sometimes acted as patrons to scholars and scientists as well as artists should not obscure the fact that they could also become real experts in their own right who conversed and corresponded about plants on a more or less equal footing with scholarly experts such as Clusius. Princess Marie de Brimeu and the Count of Aremberg in the Low Countries and the English Lord Zouche are good examples among Clusius' correspondents. An aristocrat with a particularly varied collection was Charles de Saint Omer, Lord of Moerkercke and Dranoutre, who lived near Bruges in the Southern Netherlands. His collection comprised books, tapestries, a menagerie, gardens, a maze, prints, paintings and coins, naturalia and other curiosa. He commissioned the famous botanical and zoological watercolours of the *Libri Picturati* collection now held in Krakow and was one of Clusius' first patrons.[8]

Cultural interests and the fashion of collecting and display often coincided or overlapped with scientific and commercial ones. The Spanish king Philip II, for instance, who sent out the Spanish physician Francisco Hernandez to investigate, describe and depict the flora of Mexico, was very much alive to the possibility of creating plantations in the New World to grow medicinal plants for commercial purposes.[9] Economic motives were even more prominent in the early explorations of the Dutch in the East Indies. The instruction to the commanders of the first Dutch ships sent out to the East Indies to explore and bring back herbs, fruits and spices was certainly of help to botanists, but had been inspired mainly by the expectation of enormous profits in the spice trade. Nor were academic institutions interested in nature for exclusively scientific reasons. Many European universities claimed prestige and status by creating botanical gardens during this period. All of the oldest such gardens in Europe (e.g. Pisa, Padua, Bologna, Leipzig, Leiden) originated between 1520 and 1610.[10] They formed the visual proof that these universities took their teaching of medicine and medicinal herbs seriously, while at the same time demonstrating how these universities vied with each other and with aristocratic garden owners by growing rare exotic plants whose medicinal value was often irrelevant.[11]

From its earliest phase (roughly the second quarter of the sixteenth century) the fascination with nature and curiosities by no means affected only the rich or the learned. The origins of many smaller and more specialized collections comprising naturalia and their pictures can be traced to the decades between 1540 and 1590 and to men (and a few women) who belonged to the professional middle classes. They too could own a garden and grow new plants from seeds or cuttings obtained by barter.[12] The most important non-elite collectors and aficionados of natural history all over Europe were apothecaries, perfumers and druggists.[13] As such they have not been taken seriously enough by historians of science. Some well documented examples show that their interest in nature could go far beyond mere professional (medicinal) requirements and manifest itself in ways that equalled or came close to scholarly or elite forms of expertise. Some owned experimental gardens, grew exotics, compiled encyclopaedic surveys of information about nature, and had portraits of plants or animals painted. Apothecaries such as Hugh Morgan, James Garet Jr and

Thomas Penny in England, or their Continental counterparts Peeter van Coudenberghe, Thomas de la Fosse, Jean Mouton and Christiaan Porret (in the Low Countries) – all of them correspondents of Clusius – were famous for being the first to grow certain exotic plants in Europe and to experiment with highly prized new varieties of non-indigenous flowers. The gardens owned by these men and their upper-class counterparts were visited both by foreign travellers, aristocratic collectors (such as Sir Philip Sidney or Lodovico Guicciardini), scholars (like Lipsius or Lobelius), and by many anonymous friends and relatives who all shared an interest in plants, animals, exotic naturalia, or 'curious simples' as they were often called at the time.[14] The comparatively democratic openness of these gardens to visitors of various classes and backgrounds (though they were certainly not public domains) should perhaps be contrasted with the relatively closed character of most *Kunst- und Wunderkammern*, which seem to have been visited mainly by members of the elite.

During the sixteenth century natural history thus formed an increasingly varied field of practice which was inextricably connected with collecting, gardening, the universities, and the great voyages of discovery as well as with the more mundane worlds of apothecaries and folk healers. Consequently, expertise in this domain belonged to men and women who came from enormously different backgrounds. Precisely because there was neither a demarcated discipline nor a formal training in natural history yet, all forms of expertise (whether based on medicinal practice, book learning, collecting, growing plants, voyages, or attempts at describing and classifying) were relevant. Moreover, all 'experts' – including those with a university training (which inevitably was *not* in natural history) – were to a large extent amateurs. The value and status of their respective types of expertise still had to be compared, weighed and established. This process would take a large part of the sixteenth century and was even then by no means concluded, although by the late sixteenth century the hierarchy of the various types of naturalist expertise was fairly clear. In this sense natural history was unlike law or medicine. In those fields the distinctions between university trained physicians (or lawyers) of high status and other practitioners (such as surgeons or notaries) dated back to much earlier periods.

Medicine as taught at the universities was, however, highly relevant to the development of natural history as a field of expertise. Plants and to a somewhat lesser extent animals were of crucial importance to all types of medicine since many contemporary drugs were plant based. Expertise in the medicinal qualities of plants belonged, however, to apothecaries, who generally did not go to university but learned their trade in practice. Yet, a large majority of the men who have become known as the principal experts in natural history of the sixteenth century in Europe north of the Alps – the most famous are Leonhart Fuchs, Otto Brunfels, and Hieronymus Bock during the 1530s–1540s; Pierre Belon, Guillaume Rondelet, Conrad Gessner, Carolus Clusius, Rembertus Dodonaeus, and Kaspar Bauhin during the 1550s–1610s – had studied medicine. Some of them were actually employed as general practitioners, or acted as private physicians to aristocrats or princes. In the latter case they were probably appointed to such posts partly because they could also offer advice on matters of botany, gardening and collecting naturalia.

By the late sixteenth century some men with this type of expertise obtained chairs at universities, which had by then created (generally combined) chairs in anatomy and botany within the medical faculty. And a very few, like Clusius, managed to make a living as experts in natural history thanks to the patronage of princes, aristocrats and (later) universities.

These scholars, many of whom spent a large part of their working life outside university circles, developed special expertise in this field and were recognized by their contemporaries as specialists. They did so by drawing upon a vast range of different forms of expertise, which comprised both learned (written and to a large extent classical) knowledge, the everyday practical expertise of those who were in daily touch with nature and *naturalia*, their own observations and research, information deriving from rich collectors, folklore and many other sources. They constructed surveys of all available information about nature and attempted to classify and systematize it. From the mid-1530s and especially during the 1560s–1590s new illustrated botanical surveys (by Fuchs, Brunfels, Dodonaeus and Clusius) were published. Each of them experimented with new ways of ordering and presenting nature.[15] Thousands of watercolours and woodcuts of plants and animals were produced during the 1530s–1600s, some of them made 'after nature', while printed works experimented with new forms of scientific illustration. Even though the use of such illustrations could be haphazard and their quality was by no means always good, this relatively new visual means directly contributed to the spread of information about nature, new forms of standardization, and the identification of plants and animals throughout Europe. Knowledge of nature changed dramatically during the sixteenth century.

It would be a mistake, however, to imagine that only the men whom we now regard as the great botanists of the sixteenth century were involved in this practice of ordering, classifying, describing and depicting nature. Aristocrats such as Saint Omer and apothecaries such as James Garet Jr (about whom more will be said below) shared these interests and were involved in the same process of discovery. Their assistance, information and ideas were, moreover, indispensable to the scholars who further selected, channelled, organized and translated some of this knowledge and elevated it to the level of specialist expertise. The main difference between these three categories of experts – aristocrats with collections, gardens and varying degrees of erudition; apothecaries with great practical expertise, better access to folk knowledge and often considerable erudition; and the scholars themselves – seems not to have been their type of interest or even their range of knowledge, but its results. The rich collectors created gardens and collections, only a few of which still remain. Most apothecaries generally did not write books and typically, those who did are usually classified as scholars rather than as apothecaries. But scholars published.

Naturally, the success of naturalists to proclaim themselves as experts depended not only on their ability to develop their own traditions, expand and define their expertise and community, but also upon their recognition as experts by others. Conditions were right at the time. Various institutions (such as universities and courts) and groups (rich collectors, aristocrats) needed experts in natural history, or thought they did given the fashion of nature. The growth of this new field of expertise may well in fact have been as much an effect of this demand as of the activities on the part of the experts themselves to widen their expertise and promote it. In good Renaissance fashion the fact that people of quality (i.e. high status) were interested in being seen as patrons of naturalists, owners of exotic gardens and collectors of naturalia in itself raised the status of this field of knowledge. Within little more than half a century (between circa 1530 and 1590) natural history established itself as a respected scholarly and elite activity and a recognized field of expertise.

Botany in particular also gained a place as a specialization within the academic domain of medicine.[16] Given the medical background of most of the scholars who subsequently became specialists in botany this might seem natural, but as indicated above, the knowledge of medicinal plants had up till this period been regarded as belonging much more to the domain of the practical experts – the apothecaries – than to that of the learned physicians. The process by which university-based medicine appropriated botany and established it as a respectable form of scientific knowledge resembles in some respects the similar appropriation of anatomy and dissection, which in earlier times had belonged largely to the domain of the (non-university trained) surgeons.[17] These are, in fact, by no means unique examples in which the formation of a field of specialized knowledge went hand in hand with the increase in status of that particular type of knowledge, the development of jargon, and the exclusion of others from (continued) access to specialized knowledge. Precisely in the latter respect there was a crucial difference between dissection/anatomy and botany, however. Medical faculties all over Western Europe could and did impose a monopoly on dissection by means of closing off access to dead bodies to all others. There was no way of doing the same with nature, and the contribution of practical (non-university-based) expertise to botany, zoology and plant-based medicine continues to be important up to this day.

Even by the end of the sixteenth century natural history as a whole had not yet become a clearly demarcated domain of knowledge. In fact, precisely because of the continuous influx of practical expertise and the continued involvement of people with diverse backgrounds and types of knowledge, it continued to overlap with alchemy, collecting, art, and medicine during the whole of the early modern period. In consequence it suffered to some extent from boundary problems in defining its identity as a serious field of study. Interestingly, natural history may prove to be an example of an initially successful 'attempt' to become a serious field of knowledge – a discipline – which in the very long run has turned out to be less than completely successful. Unlike medicine, natural history has always remained part of the 'soft' section of the sciences. Until the present it has remained relatively open to amateurs who can still today reach a very high level of expertise without advanced technology or formal training.[18]

In terms of contents and approach natural history changed drastically in the course of the sixteenth century. The attempts of various scholars to invent new systems of organization and classification were cause for debate, which triggered new research concerning the best criteria for classification and systems of naming.[19] Both the practical uses (as food and medicine) and the symbolic or religious relevance of plants and animals continued to be important throughout the sixteenth and seventeenth centuries. Yet, nature was increasingly studied for its own sake, in non-emblematic and matter of fact ways.[20] Observation, practical experience, experiment, standardized description, classification and a non-emblematic approach to the object of study – all characteristic of a scientific attitude often labelled as 'modern' and 'rational' – dramatically gained in importance during the sixteenth century. Clusius both embodied these developments and was a key figure in them. His many publications and letters demonstrate his life-long emphasis on precise observation and description, interest in field observation and ecology, and attempts to expand the knowledge of 'exotic' nature.

In spite of the fact that the term 'scientific revolution of the seventeenth century' originated as part of a whiggish and evolutionist style of historiography and has given rise to much unfortunate reification, it is tempting to describe these changes in the approach to natural history during the sixteenth century as a first phase of the scientific revolution or even as an earlier revolution in the life sciences. It is intriguing to note that the term 'botanical *renaissance* of the sixteenth century' (which has, to my knowledge, been invented during the twentieth century) couches the important changes in this field in cultural rather than scientific terms. We may well ask whether this could not itself be a result of the eventually unsuccessful attempt of the 'soft' (i.e. non-mathematical and non-mechanistic) life sciences to raise their status. If the botanical renaissance should indeed be regarded as an early scientific revolution in the life sciences – and the topic certainly deserves much more research and extensive discussion – that would open up a new range of questions with respect to the life sciences themselves, to changing early modern attitudes to nature, and to the issue of Europe. After all, the scientific revolution has been described as a uniquely European phenomenon and regarded as indelibly connected with modernization and the growth of a rational mindset.

A European Community of Experts: Clusius' Network

One of the reasons why Carolus Clusius is now known as possibly *the* foremost botanist of the sixteenth century was his European stature, which rested on three pillars: his travel and investigations in several European countries, his publications, and his wide-flung network of correspondents. Clusius was born in the Southern Netherlands. He trained as a physician, studied both in the Southern Netherlands and in Germany and France, travelled and did botanical research in Spain, Portugal, the Southern Netherlands, Hungary, Germany and England, lived and worked in the Southern Netherlands, at the Habsburg court in Vienna, on an aristocratic estate in Hungary, at Frankfurt and at the university of Leiden. At least from the mid-1560s (after his return from Spain to the Southern Netherlands) until his death in Leiden in 1609 he maintained friendly exchanges by letter with a very large network of friends, collectors, fellow experts and others.

Some 1500 letters remain, of which the bulk of more than 1300 (most of them written to Clusius) are kept in Leiden University Library, the town where he spent his last years as honoured professor and director of the newly created *hortus botanicus*, while about 200 (mainly by Clusius) are held by the library at Erlangen in Germany.[21] Next to the correspondence of Conrad Gessner, the Clusius correspondence may well be the most valuable collection of correspondence in the field of early European natural history. This is partly because of the stature of Clusius himself, but perhaps even more so because the Clusius correspondence predominantly consists of letters sent *to* him from all over Europe. It thus allows us to study a whole community of European naturalists, while opening up research possibilities concerning differences in regional or national styles of natural history throughout Europe.[22] The reasons why so many more letters *to* Clusius than *by* him have been preserved are simple. While the letters sent by Clusius were dispersed all over Europe, the letters sent *to* him centred on one person. Clearly Clusius must have taken very good care of them. Just like later botanists such as Linnaeus and Darwin, Clusius used correspondence as a research instrument. The letters which he preserved formed a permanent and rich source of information. But there was more to it. They were also the manifestation of important friendships and the material evidence of the growth of a European community of naturalists and of his own central position in that community. In their letters to Clusius, some of its members explicitly designated it as a growing community of 'friends' and a *republic of letters*.

Between circa 1560 and 1609 Clusius corresponded with at least 300 different persons throughout Europe. Given the fact that a considerable number of them were expert botanists, collectors, and garden owners who in their turn commanded large and partly overlapping networks of friends, acquaintances and fellow experts, the range of Clusius' network of information and exchange is amazing. Even the limited preliminary research which has been done so far shows that nearly every one of Clusius' 300 correspondents had access – via either correspondence or personal contact – to many more local and other informants, with whom they in their turn maintained relations of exchange. Clusius' correspondents lived all over Europe, from England to Hungary and Austria, from Greece and Italy to Poland, and from Spain and Portugal to the Northern Netherlands, France, Germany and Norway. In a geographical sense his network was truly European. If we try to imagine the range of information and informants to which he must have had access – by adding the networks which his correspondents commanded to Clusius' own – it is no exaggeration to claim that he directly or indirectly had access to all of the then relevant persons in Europe, as well as in some other parts of the world.

The range of Clusius' correspondence network was wide in a social sense as well. He exchanged information with social equals, but also with people of a higher and lower social position. Among Clusius' correspondents are aristocratic collectors, princes, courtiers and rich patrons (some of whom have been mentioned above), such as the Count of Aremberg, Lamoraal van Egmont, and Charles de Saint Omer in the Southern Netherlands, Sir Philip Sydney and Lord Zouche in England, Ludwig I Duke of Wurttemberg and Ludwig VI Elector of the Palatinate in

Germany, the Hungarian Count Batthiany, Princess Marie de Brimeu, famous humanists such as Benito Arias Montano and Justus Lipsius, fellow botanical physicians or experts such as Felix Platter, Joachim Camerarius, Matteo Caccini, Ulisse Aldrovandi and Simon de Tovar, printer-publishers and artists such as Christoph Plantin, Franciscus Raphelengius and Anselmus de Boodt, diplomats such as Ogier de Busbeq, and apothecaries such as the Garet family, Jean Mouton, Christian Porret and Hugh Morgan. But this list also includes relatives and many others. The better known Clusius became as a leading botanical expert, the more his epistolary contacts proliferated. His network snowballed.

A point of special interest with respect to the growth of a community of experts in natural history and the development of a new discipline concerns the role of women. Clusius never married, and we know of no affairs, lovers or children. He did have many friends, however, and kept up friendly exchanges of letters with some for decades. Among them were several women. For instance, ten letters from Anna von Aicholtz Starzerin to Clusius survive (for the years 1588–1592): she was Clusius' landlady for most of his long stay in Vienna, and the wife of one of the professors at the University of Vienna. The 25 letters from the rich Viennese garden owner Anna Maria von Heusenstain to Clusius likewise testify to a long-standing friendship spanning the years 1588–1606. His best known and almost lifelong female friend, however, was the notorious Netherlandish princess Marie de Brimeu. Twenty-seven of her letters to Clusius have been preserved from the period 1571–1607. She was the owner of a superb garden and an enthusiastic amateur grower of tulips and other exotic flowers and shrubs.

None of Clusius' correspondence with women friends has been published or even described or analysed, but even a quick perusal of the letters written to him by Marie de Brimeu and Anna Maria von Heusenstain makes clear that Clusius did not discuss only household or family matters with them. In fact, a large part of their letters to him concern plants, the best ways of growing them in their gardens, and exchanges of seeds, cuttings, bulbs, and fruits. By such means both garden owners and botanical experts increased their knowledge and experience in this field. Nor did they discuss only common garden flowers or plants for kitchen gardens. Like the male garden owners in Clusius' network, these women grew precious exotica such as white oleanders, tulips and Spanish lilies, and took pleasure in showing these (plus their close connection with Clusius as expert) to their neighbours. Clusius discussed plants and gardening with them on the same footing as with some of his male correspondents. With respect to the formation of disciplines and expert knowledge it is extremely interesting that botany, plants and gardens were one of the few (semi-) public domains in which women could gain particular forms of expertise and be addressed as such in these relatively private exchanges.[23]

Modes of Exchange

It is equally fascinating that none of the undoubtedly learned and well educated women of generally high social position who corresponded with Clusius did so in Latin. They used either French, German or Dutch/Flemish, while Clusius probably responded in the same language. It is not enough in this respect to point out that women at the time did not have access to universities or other forms of higher education, since many of Clusius' male correspondents likewise preferred the vernacular. Their choice of language seems to have been only partly related to their social or educational status. For instance, the fact that Polish or Hungarian correspondents wrote in Latin is simple enough to explain. Most of the humanists (such as Lipsius, or the Laurin brothers, who were core members of the Bruges humanist circle) as well as several German, French, Dutch and English physicians wrote in Latin, although they could have used their respective vernacular languages if they had wanted to. Some of the learned Italians (such as Ferrante Imperato, Hieronimo Calzeolari, Giacomo Cortuso and Giuseppe Benincasa/Casabona) did indeed prefer Italian, while quite a few other men who must have known Latin preferred French. Dutch, German and possibly Spanish seem to have been used mainly by correspondents who did not know Latin. A few correspondents used more than one language, either in one and the same letter or successively, changing back and forth. This was the case with the rich bourgeois garden owner Johannes van Hoghelande from Leiden, who mixed French and Latin, the German or Austrian Christian von Ecgk, who wrote in French for some years, then changed to German and later turned back to French, and the German Joannes Lewenklau, who alternated between Latin and Italian.

Judging from the information available at the present time about the bulk of the letters sent to Clusius, about half of them were written in Latin, a third in French, while the others were in Italian, German, Spanish or Dutch (in that descending order). Clusius himself was a polyglot. He read and wrote an impressive number of languages: besides Latin, Dutch and French, he was fluent in German, Italian and Spanish. He could probably read and understand Portuguese, read (classical) Greek, and may have understood some Hungarian. One of the few languages he did not manage to master well was the present day lingua franca, English. We may infer that Clusius' correspondents could generally write to him in the language of their choice because he was at home in so many of these languages. Clusius himself did not invariably adapt to his correspondents' choice of language, however. In the correspondence (1550–1578) with Hubertus Languetus, a friend from his student days in Paris, Languetus always used Latin, while Clusius consistently wrote back in French – perhaps for nostalgic reasons.

The multiple language use in this correspondence should make us wonder. Latin was perhaps slightly less of a lingua franca in early modern Europe than we might have thought. Should we interpret the possibility offered by Clusius to his correspondents to use the language of their choice as part of a code of civility? It may certainly have had this effect on some of his less educated correspondents, who obviously felt at home writing to Clusius in their vernacular (or dialect) and in handwriting that had very little to do with the beautiful and legible hand in which humanists were supposed to write. But could there be more to it than civility? Could the fact that Clusius learned so many different languages (whatever practical reasons may have existed) imply that Latin was not enough for his purposes, and that communication in the vernacular with informants from other countries was essential to his type of research? Did this apply to other natural historians too? In a more general sense, could this point to a difference in styles of communication between naturalists and other scholars of the early modern age?[24]

These are issues that cannot be answered without further investigation of the languages used in correspondence by other European naturalists and of their correspondents' backgrounds. It certainly looks, however, as if the fact that natural history was (as yet) less closed off by scientific disciplinary boundary markers than some other branches of the sciences had its effects on the use of language. In comparison with the mathematical sciences or even the medical sector, a specialized jargon developed relatively late and only slowly in natural history. This may have happened precisely because botanical expertise was based to a considerable extent on local knowledge and first-hand observation. Communication with non-elite practical experts and other non-university-trained persons could not be conducted in Latin. Yet they possessed important information, as Clusius and others well realized. From both his printed works and his correspondence, it is evident that Clusius was seriously interested in 'folk' nomenclature of plants, its possible relevance to their classification, and in local information about the natural 'habitat' of plants. His own multilingualism and the fact that he conducted correspondence in so many different languages may therefore well be clues to his innovative research methods and, vice versa, to the way in which the vernacular languages and 'practical expertise' were making their way into and contributing to the new discipline of botany.

The topic of language clearly demonstrates why the Clusius correspondence forms such a crucially important source for the study of the formation of a new field of knowledge. It certainly deserves to be compared in depth with the correspondence of his even more famous counterpart, the Swiss humanist, physician and naturalist Conrad Gessner, with those of other well-known botanists from Northern Europe such as Mathias de l'Obel (Lobelius) and Rembertus Dodoens (Dodonaeus), and with the correspondence of famous naturalists in Italy and France.[25] Naturally, correspondence formed only one of the means of information exchange among early modern experts in natural history: there were face-to-face meetings, travel, social gatherings, and – for quite a few of the European experts in botany – the participation in a court or aristocratic setting as either patron or protégé. Information was likewise exchanged by means of printed books and treatises, objects (such as plants, seeds, fruits or pictures of them), and via herbalizing expeditions, diplomatic missions, voyages of discovery, meetings of academies or university gatherings. Yet, correspondence has the unique advantage of being a means of conveying information *about* all of these other aspects of exchange as well as a means of information exchange itself and an instrument in the creation of a community of scholars by the very means of exchanging information.

The considerable number of Clusius' correspondents who did not belong to the range of university-trained scholars or even the social elite do not quite fit the usual image of members of the republic of letters (which has, however, mainly been studied in its seventeenth-century manifestations). Nor do the styles of exchange characteristic of the letters written to Clusius conform to the stereotypic image of humanist letters. In fact, quite a few of the letters written to Clusius look as if no very particular care had been taken about composition, layout, or handwriting. The contents usually match their appearance. Clusius was clearly held in great respect and affection by most of his correspondents, but they rarely go out of their way to address him in a formally deferential way. Clusius must either have been a very easy person to approach, even in his later years when his reputation had reached its peak, or the rules of deference in the circles of naturalists appear to have been less strict than among humanists. Moreover, anarchy appears to reign in the correspondence concerning the topics that could be discussed and the order in which to do so. Apart from the fact that information about previous letters and sent packages can nearly always be found in the first few lines, while greetings to and from family members, friends and other naturalists are usually reserved for the last ones, no order seems to have been prescribed. Requests for seeds, information about new plants and bad growing seasons, new publications, complaints about servants, information about political events, gossip about affairs, illness, marital problems, or financial misfortunes of acquaintances, a request for some new shoes to be sent, news about the great voyages to the East and West Indies, hints at religious controversy and so on are mentioned indiscriminately. Ciceronian models of written eloquence are a long way off.

Such elementary characteristics are revealing. Most of these exchanges were largely informal and matter of fact. They belonged to an ongoing exchange between people who shared the same interests, so that many things did not need to be explained. Clusius was neither a prince nor an apothecary, but he corresponded with members of both social groups about nature, recognizing a shared interest in nature, special expertise and a real pleasure in it which could suspend (if not obliterate) social differences that would probably have been very hard to ignore under any other circumstances in this age.

Among the most interesting general characteristics of these letters are their liveliness, practical orientation, and above all, the fact that they were obviously *not* meant for publication or even circulation on a larger scale.[26] They neither look nor read like the semi-public type of correspondence which was written to be passed on or read aloud, and which belongs rather to the circles of Grotius, Lipsius, Mersenne or Erasmus.[27]

Friendship and Exchange

The theme of friendship is explicitly mentioned in almost every single letter in the Clusius correspondence. Could there be a link between the informal character of the exchanges between these naturalists, the frequent use of the vernacular, the apparent ease by which significant status differences were set temporarily aside, on the one hand, and the formation of a European community of scholars and the establishment of a new field of expertise, on the other hand? While exploring these issues, it should be kept in mind that the concept of friendship had a much wider meaning during the early modern period than it does now and could include the notion of mutual assistance and kinship. It played an important part in humanist correspondence of the seventeenth century as well as in the more mundane exchanges of, for instance, early modern merchant families, while it implicitly or explicitly carried overtones of the classical rhetorical concept of friendship.[28]

In the Clusius correspondence the notion of friendship is closely linked with the idea of disinterested services to a friend and of gift exchange.[29] The letter which the Flemish merchant Hendrik Bloeme sent in 1601 from Frankfurt to Clusius (in Leiden) is typical in this respect:

> *I send you in this box three leaves of my Indian fig[30] and two of my aloë americana plants. If I had had any larger ones I would have sent them to you, but I have shared all of them with friends who also desired them and don't have any more at the moment ... I thank you very warmly for the gift that it has pleased you to make to me of your Historia plantarum and of the book by monsieur de St. Aldegonde and consider it a great favour. I have always regarded myself as very much obliged to you for the many courtesies that I have received from you over such a long period and have often wished for an occasion that would enable me to do just something in return, but continuing to burden myself with new favours (without using any ceremony) I ask you affectionately whether there is anything with which I can serve you, or whether there is anything here that would be pleasant to you; please ask me directly. ...[31]*

In fact, all of the letters – as well as the objects they accompanied – formed part of an ongoing gift exchange which comprised not only material gifts (such as plants, seeds, pictures of plants, books, etc.), but also non-material ones such as pleasure, assistance, knowledge, respect and time. Perhaps the most valuable gift of all expressed and made via these letters was the feeling of belonging to a virtual but very real and wide-flung community of friends and naturalists. Even now, these letters help us to reconstruct that community of exchanges. At the time they both embodied and helped to constitute it. Sharing was seen as a virtue, as a means of giving pleasure, and as a sign of friendship. Liberality and generosity – to share and be seen to share – were very important in the virtual community of sixteenth-century naturalists, for both men and women.

Clusius' own career is illuminating in this respect. He started out as a young physician from the Southern Netherlandish nobility whose passionate interest in plants and animals may well have been fed by a wish to escape from the contemporary world of religious persecution and warfare. Not only Clusius himself but many of his friends and relatives had suffered losses on those accounts.[32] In the course of his professional life he built up an extensive knowledge of European botany by personal observation and field trips (in France, Spain, Portugal, Hungary, Austria, Germany and England). For various reasons he did not travel to Italy himself, however, nor did he ever leave Europe. For information about plants and animals from Asia and the New World as well as for expertise concerning plants grown in

Italy, the Balkans, Greece, Poland, and the Middle East he was thus completely dependent on his correspondents. Moreover, his many friends who owned gardens all over Europe continued to provide him during the whole of his life with information about the best ways to grow certain types of plants – especially those imported from different climates – how to multiply them, sow or prune them, and how to develop new varieties.

Clusius was generally regarded as a man who shared plants, roots, bulbs, seeds and (probably to a lesser extent) ideas. There are very few letters from his correspondents in which he is not thanked by them for the latest box of seeds and cuttings and offered new ones in return. To Anna Maria von Heusenstain and many others, Clusius was first and foremost a generous benefactor, provider of plants, exotica, botanical knowledge and friendship:[33]

> I ask you, Sir, … In return let Sir ask from me whatever he wants. When I obtain some rarity which according to my opinion Sir does not have, then I will send it to Sir. But since Sir has been gone from here, nobody will give me anything. They just say to me, ask Sir Clusius, let him give it to me.

Until shortly before his death Clusius maintained his complex pattern of give and take, keeping up friendships and gift exchange relations via correspondence. The amount of time and effort it must have taken him to do so is a direct reflection of the importance of such exchanges to Clusius, in terms of both friendship and the maintenance of his position as leading European expert. If Clusius could not become a leading figure in this new field of expertise without relying strongly on a large network of informants (as well as on important patrons), we may conclude that no naturalist could gain prestige or even become a real expert without the help of others.

The emphasis on disinterested friendship and a 'free' exchange of gifts may have been especially strong in the European ('virtual') community of naturalists which had, after all, only started to develop from the 1530s onwards. This was very much a new community of experts that tried to carve out its own niche in a social and cultural domain in which many different parties operated – such as university academics, physicians, surgeons, aristocratic garden owners, apothecaries, explorers, peasants and local healers – and where different economies overlapped and clashed. Not only did their domain lack clear boundaries, but the status of their expertise was uncertain as well. 'Free' gift exchange was in everyone's interest because it helped raise the general quality of the available expertise and thus the status and honour of the discipline (and by extension those of its members). Thus the idiom of friendship both expressed and underpinned the value of free exchange, which itself helped to create a 'virtual' community of natural history experts throughout Europe.

We should not be naïve, however, about how 'free' such exchanges actually were. The Clusius correspondence contains many clues to the informal but very important rules of behaviour governing these apparently liberal exchanges. Once a person was recognized as 'a friend' – that is, a fellow member of the network of naturalists – it was not done to withhold information or lie about it, refuse to give counter gifts, be stingy, steal bulbs (or have them stolen by servants), publish someone else's results or discoveries without any form of recognition, bribe agents or brokers in order to obtain rare naturalia that were destined for someone else, plagiarize (although the definition and the notion of authorship were not identical with modern ones), etc. For instance, the apothecary James Garet Sr wrote to Clusius about the rich bourgeois garden owner Johannes van Hoghelande in whose garden he had seen some beautiful flowers that were a present from Clusius himself: 'he is so possessive and I could not get any out of his hands, patience'.[34] A remark by James' son Pieter in a letter to Clusius also reveals that sharing was certainly not done indiscriminately:[35]

> *Paludanus[36] begged me to give it* [i.e. a special type of gum used by Indians to waterproof their canoes] *to him or at least part of it, but I refused, hearing that he wanted to describe it, and I told him that if you wanted him to have part of it you would make a present of some to him.*

In other words, when Pieter Garet discovered that Paludanus wanted to 'steal' the honour from Clusius of being the first to describe or publish a special gum, he protected Clusius – and thereby his own good relationship with him, also leaving the option open for Clusius to show his generosity and give some of the gum to Paludanus. Transgressions of these rules of civility and courtesy resulted in conflict, broken friendships, denial of access to further information, or loss of reputation and status in the virtual community of scholars.[37] Ultimately, an offending person could be informally ostracized from this virtual community. Thus the rules governing interaction in this new field were deeply rooted in European (non-national) discursive practices that went back at least to classical antiquity: gift exchange, friendship, and honour.

Introducing Exotic Naturalia

Naturalia – especially exotic ones – were not only relevant, however, to a scholarly community in the making. European society was by this time geared to merchant enterprise, the market and commodities.[38] If the famous tulip craze and the fortunes made in the spice trade (nutmeg, pepper, ginger and cinnamon) were seventeenth-century phenomena, already during Clusius' life-time Philip II had demonstrated an interest in creating plantations in the New World to grow medicinal plants for commercial purposes, and agents who bought or collected naturalia for scholars came up against rivals who bought naturalia for commercial purposes or on behalf of rich(er) collectors. Thus, an economy of free exchange and barter among experts overlapped and sometimes clashed with a market economy.

The introduction of exotic naturalia is particularly interesting with respect to the formation of a new field of expertise and a European community of scholars. As indicated above, sixteenth-century Europeans were fascinated by exotica, while exotic naturalia were among the most prized and expensive items in collections.[39] Clusius was one of the first naturalists to devote a special publication to exotic plants and animals, describing and depicting many of them for the first time in print.[40] He himself never travelled outside Europe, however, and relied for this information upon correspondence with a number of men who either themselves visited Africa, the Middle East or Asia, or maintained close personal contacts with those who did.[41] Most of these 'information brokers' belonged to the world of trade, shipping, exploring and medicine. Members of the Garet family, whom we have already encountered briefly, are among the most interesting ones. In their persons they united both a commercial and a scholarly interest in exotic naturalia, the world of medicine and that of trade, while connecting the community of European experts with that of the great explorers of the New World and Asia.

James Sr and his sons James Jr and Pieter worked as apothecaries and spice traders.[42] They originated in Antwerp, fled the Southern Netherlands in 1569–1570, no doubt for religious as well as economic reasons, and moved to London, where they joined the Dutch Reformed Church at Austin Friars. In the course of the 1590s Pieter moved to Amsterdam, which by then was no longer part of the Netherlands under Habsburg rule but belonged to the newly formed and predominantly Protestant Dutch Republic. In London the Garets grew European and exotic plants in their gardens, experimented with them, and exchanged information with fellow botanists, druggists, perfumers, and spice traders. Besides receiving and corresponding with many learned guests from the European continent, they formed part of a highly specialized London circle of botanists, physicians and apothecaries which included Hugh Morgan, Thomas Penny, John Gerard, Thomas Moffet, Jacob Cole (Ortelianus), Richard Garth, Mathias de L'Obel, and John Rich, many of whom likewise corresponded with Clusius. Both the younger Garets developed a regular passion for exotic naturalia. James Jr was especially interested in new varieties of tulips and lilies. In 1589–1590 he also grew potatoes in his garden, a most exotic plant that had just been imported from Peru. He was closely in touch with the famous overseas adventurers of this period, such as Sir Francis Drake and Thomas Cavendish – the latter visited Garet at home in London and discussed his voyages and discoveries at Garet's kitchen table. It was through James Garet Jr, for instance, that Clusius gained access to some of the newly discovered drugs and plants brought from Roanoke and Virginia, while the first volumes of the *Great Voyages* dealing with the expeditions to those regions were being published by the De Bry family, who moved in the same circles, from 1590 on.[43] Together with his fellow London apothecary Hugh Morgan, 'royal druggist' and likewise correspondent of Clusius, James Garet Jr pioneered the importation of drugs and the cultivation of plants from the New World in Britain.[44]

In Amsterdam Pieter Garet likewise owned a garden where he grew exotica. In his turn he maintained close contacts with the first Dutch who explored the East Indies, such as Wybrant van Warwijck and Jacob van Neck. He may even have had a contract with the East Indies Company to provide the outward-bound ships with drugs for the medicine chests. Although he was a merchant himself, Pieter complained bitterly in a letter to Clusius when he discovered that upon the return of several ships from the East Indies, buyers from the emperor's court in Vienna or

Prague were ready to board the ships in the harbour of Amsterdam, in the middle of the night if necessary, and pay enormous sums for exotica, thereby preventing him from obtaining anything special for Clusius or for himself.[45]

The correspondence between the three Garets and Clusius spanned many years. Their relationship with Clusius was one of mutual respect, friendship and exchange, and was certainly not the much more one-sided contact between commercial suppliers and a scholar. The Garets were well aware (as the above quotations concerning Paludanus show) of the rules of etiquette and civility in the community of expert naturalists. Their interest in naturalia started as a commercial one in drugs and spices, but soon expanded and came to include a scholarly one as well. They combined knowledge of published scholarly works and a practical interest in growing exotic plants with an awareness of the importance of (indigenous) nomenclature and of accurate description and depiction of the original habitat (and use) of plants and animals. It is hard to find better examples of combined practical and scholarly expert knowledge and the way such expertise contributed to natural history. Clusius duly acknowledged the role of the Garets in his publications – another example of his scrupulous adherence to a code of scholarly behaviour with respect to naming sources that was developing during this period.

The very introduction of exotic, non-European naturalia, their special commercial and scholarly value, and the prestige to be gained by a naturalist by being the first to identify, describe and depict an exotic plant or animal, may all have concurred to strengthen the European identity of the community of scholars who studied such naturalia.

A European Community?

The Clusius correspondence thus shows us a community of experts and a field of expertise in the making. A wide-flung network was purposely constructed all over Europe (and to some extent beyond) during the second half of the sixteenth century, while various types of knowledge and practices were demarcated and adapted in order to distinguish them as specialist expertise. In terms of status, practical expertise was slowly elevated to a discipline – a process that was certainly in the interest of the men who tried to profile themselves as scholars and experts in this domain. Judging from the many references to friendship and the informal rules that governed gift exchange, these experts recognized each other as members of a virtual community that shared an interest in naturalia. Ignoring those rules of exchange could entail informal social sanctions and even the (partial) exclusion from shared expert knowledge and information. The frequent use of the idiom of friendship pervades these exchanges, which furthermore attest to the practices of friendly (though not necessarily 'free' or 'disinterested') gift exchange. The fact that a few of Clusius' correspondents explicitly used the term *republic of letters* reflects their self-awareness as a community.

Was there anything specifically European about this? And can it tell us something about the development of a European identity or image? The answers to such questions can only be tentative, given the fact that this essay explores a specific branch of the early modern sciences and is not comparative in nature. While the connection between the 'botanical renaissance of the sixteenth century' and the 'scientific revolution of the seventeenth century' (known as an eminent feature of European science) remains to be seriously investigated, we can already isolate two of the specifically European aspects of this community of exchange. First, Clusius exchanged information with men and women living in European countries as far apart as Norway and Portugal, England and Hungary or Italy and Holland, in all of the major European languages of his time. Many of his fellow naturalists had similar, if smaller, networks of correspondence, and many of their correspondents themselves were in touch with each other. We may argue, therefore, that this 'virtual' community of natural historians in itself helped to give body to Europe – both by its very existence and the frequent exchanges, and by its contacts with parts of the world outside Europe. The importance of exotic naturalia – which were valuable in scientific terms as well as in terms of trade and collecting – and the very use of the term 'exotic' in Clusius' correspondence and publications, may indeed have heightened the awareness among European naturalists of distance and difference between Europe and far off, exotic places.[46] In all of these exchanges the *concept* of Europe seems to have remained completely implicit. Yet, the long-standing European *styles* of honour, friendship and gift exchange that are reflected in the Clusius correspondence deeply influenced the practices of this community of scholars. In that indirect way they confirmed and strengthened its European character and probably contributed to the formation of Europe as a concept and mental community.

Ideals of free and disinterested communication and information exchange among scholars and scientists have not disappeared and continue to play some part down to the present. Yet, the situation described in this essay – even if it fits more general patterns of discipline formation in some respects – did not persist. In the course of the seventeenth and eighteenth centuries specialization within and between disciplines increased and concurred with the growth of national institutions and discourses. Even though natural history remained more open to the influx of practical expertise than many other scientific disciplines, the distinctions between amateurs and professionals increased. Could that perhaps explain why Charles Darwin operated in a much more one-sided manner with respect to exchanges than Clusius had done some 300 years earlier? According to one of Darwin's most important biographers, Janet Browne, Darwin used his vast correspondence network just like Clusius – in order to obtain information from a wide geographic and social range of informants – but he usually did not reciprocate, either with ideas or gifts.[48] Should we conclude that the sixteenth-century community of naturalists was more European, and somewhat less divided by boundaries of state and status than its successors?

Notes

1. In his paper on magic and witchcraft for the conference on which this volume is based.

2. This type of expertise has been called savoir prolétaire by Frank Lestringant. See Lestringant (1991), p. 34. Cf. Ginzburg (1990); Egmond and Mason (1997, 1999).

3. Reeds (1991); Mirek and Zemanek (1998); de Koning (1995).

4. The old biography by Hunger (although it is written in Dutch and German) still provides the best overview of his life and work. See Hunger (1927 and 1942).

5. Heyden (2000); Velsaco Lozano (2000).

6. On the connections between the voyages of discovery, the New World and natural history, see Olmi (1992), esp. pp. 211–55; Lowood (1995).

7. For gardens of this period see, for instance, the excellent Strong (1979); and Härting (2000). For science at court (in Mantua) see Franchini et al. (1979); Biagioli (1995).

8. On Charles de Saint Omer and the Libri Picturati (A. 16–30) botanical and zoological watercolours in Krakow, see Egmond (2005).

9. See Kamen (1997), p. 91; and for Hernández: Pardo Tomás (1996).

10. Zemanek (1998).

11. That lines distinguishing 'scientific' academic gardens and the private ones of rich collectors should not be drawn too sharply is also clear from Brunon (1999), esp. p. 71.

12. Whether this holds true as much for Mediterranean as for north-western Europe has to be investigated further.

13. There is a quantity of extremely fragmented information on apothecaries and their interest in nature, but (to my knowledge) no monograph or synthetic essay. See Dilg (1994). For Jesuits as apothecaries in America, see Anagnostou (2000).

14. See, for example, for short descriptions of Guicciardini's visits to the gardens of Charles de Saint Omer and Peeter van Coudenberghe (respectively near Bruges and Antwerp) Guicciardini (1994).

15. On new classifications of nature see, for instance, Atran (1989).

16. For the creation of a field of expertise see especially Findlen (1999). See also Findlen (1994). Cf. Reeds (1991).

17. See Park (1994); French (1990); Pouchelle (1983), pp. 23–37; Pelling and Webster (1979), esp. pp. 174–78; and a major study which addresses the issue of the relations between surgeons and physicians specifically: Huizenga (2003).

18. See the extremely interesting essay concerning hierarchies of scientific disciplines by Secord (1996).

19. Two centuries before Linnaeus, Clusius and some of his contemporaries were, for instance, experimenting with binomial (Latin) nomenclature. Some of the plant names used by Clusius are, in fact, still in use in more or less the same form.

20. For the notion of an emblematic worldview see Ashworth Jr. (1990), pp. 303–32. Cf. Thomas (1983), and pace Foucault (1966).

21. Far more letters to Clusius (some 1200) than letters written by him to others (some 300) have been preserved. An as yet unknown number, which probably will run to dozens rather than hundreds, is scattered throughout libraries and archives all over Europe.

22. These are some of the topics of the European Clusius project (2005–2009), which is organized from the University of Leiden. As one of the first results of this project a volume will appear in 2006–7 bringing together a number of essays by international scholars from various countries and disciplines about Clusius' work, network, correspondence and role: Egmond et al.(eds) (forthcoming).

23. Bots and Waquet (1997), pp. 96–8, discuss women as absent from the republic of letters with a few exceptions and do not mention their role in botany. Cf. *Les Correspondances* (1976). Although the longstanding connection between women and botany seemed such an obvious one (but perhaps is not), the literature I have been able to find as yet concentrates almost completely on the eighteenth and nineteenth centuries, with the exception of a small number of seventeenth-century Dutch and German female artists (such as Maria Sybilla Meriam, Alida and Maria Withoos, and Rachel Ruysch, the daughter of a well-known Dutch collector) who depicted naturalia.

24. Biagioli's work has inspired many of the topics raised in this essay. See especially: Biagioli (1989, 1990, 1992, 1995, 1996).

25. Relevant publications about the correspondence of Renaissance naturalists north of the Alps are usually old, if they exist at all, and their correspondence has usually been studied from a limited perspective, focusing either on biographical aspects or on elements which could be used to write a history of 'progress in science'. On Gessner see, for instance, Rath (1950, 1951, 1980); Durling (1965); Wellisch (1975); Longeon and Sabot (1976). For a more general study on early modern correspondence, see Bethencourt and Egmond (eds) (forthcoming).

26. The fact that these sixteenth-century letters were definitely not meant for publication (unlike some letters among humanists from the seventeenth century) undermines the often implicit assumption in discussions of early modern correspondence that earlier examples of correspondence were often meant for 'public' use while later ones had a more 'private' character. That assumption seems to based on evolutionist or teleological models of historical development and the idea that 'the private' and 'privacy' (much like 'the individual') were niches carved out of a larger public domain only during the Renaissance.

27. See Bots and Waquet (1997); and cf. *Les Correspondances* (1976). See also Berkvens-Stevelinck et al. (2005), which I have not been able to consult, however, for this essay.

28. See also Trivellato's essay in this volume.

29. Present day discussions about gift exchange by historians generally go back to issues raised in Mauss (1990); see also Zemon Davis (2000).

30. An opuntia cactus.

31. Hendrik Bloeme (original in French; my translation), dated 13/23 April 1601 from Frankfurt to Clusius in Leiden, University Library Leiden, VUL 101.

32. See Hunger (1927/1942). For the example of Aldrovandi as a scholar who sought refuge from religious disputes in the study of nature, see Olmi (1976).

33. Von Heusenstain (original in German; my translation), 9 January 1589 from Starhemberg to Clusius in Frankfurt, University Library Leiden, VUL 101.

34. James Garet Sr (original in Dutch; my translation), 4 April 1592 from London to Clusius in Frankfurt, University Library Leiden, VUL 101.

35. Pieter Garet (original in Dutch; my translation), 30 January 1602, from Amsterdam to Clusius in Leiden, University Library Leiden, VUL 101.

36. Bernardus Paludanus (1550–1633), a physician and collector, lived in the town of Enkhuizen in North Holland. He had a private botanical garden and his collection of curiosities was famous throughout Europe north of the Alps. Many foreign guests of high rank visited him. He travelled widely, but from his international correspondence very few letters survive, while he published very little (botanical entries for the *Itinerario* by his friend and fellow townsman Jan Huygen van Linschoten, many of which were based on Garcia de Orta's *Colóquios dos simples*). There is no monograph on him. See Schepelern (1985); Drees (n.d.).

37. Cf. Bots and Waquet (1997), pp. 124–26; and for a much later period cf. Goldgar (1995). For a comparison and differences between northern Europe and Italy in this respect see Findlen (1999), esp. pp. 383–89.
38. Smith and Findlen (2002).
39. See e.g. Schnapper (1988).
40. Clusius (1605).
41. For example, the letters sent to Clusius by Esaia Le Gillon from Prague cover topics about Hungary, Turkey and Persia, while a request from Clusius to bring back seeds and cuttings was handed to all captains of Dutch vessels bound for the East Indies.
42. I am preparing an essay specifically dealing with the Garets, their letters and biographies, based on extensive archival research. They also figure in Harkness (2002) whose study of this London community is forthcoming.
43. See: Matthews (1967) and Sauer (1971).
44. See Pelling and Webster (1979), p. 178. Cf. Roberts (1965).
45. Pieter Garet in Dutch, 9 February 1605 from Amsterdam to Clusius in Leiden, Leiden, University Library, VUL 101.
46. See especially Mason (1998), and its extensive bibliography on the exotic.
47. See Huppert (1999).
48. Browne (2002), pp. 9–14.

References

Anagnostou, S. (2000), *Jesuiten in Spanisch-Amerika als Übermittler von heilkundlichem Wissen* (Stuttgart).

Ashworth, Jr, W.B. (1990), 'Natural History and the Emblematic Worldview', in D.C. Lindberg and R.S. Westman (eds), *Reappraisals of the Scientific Revolution* (Cambridge), pp. 303–32.

Atran, S. (1989), *Cognitive Foundations of Natural History: Towards an Anthropology of Science* (Paris and Cambridge).

Bethencourt, F. and F. Egmond (eds) (forthcoming 2006–7), *Correspondence and Cultural Exchange in Early Modern Europe* (Cambridge).

Berkvens-Stevelinck, C., H. Bots and J. Häseler (eds) (2005), *Les grands intermédiaires culturels de la République des Lettres. Etudes de réseaux de correspondance du XVIe au XVIII siècles* (Paris).

Biagioli, M. (1989), 'The Social Status of Italian Renaissance Mathematicians, 1450–1600', *History of Science* 27, pp. 105–147.

_____. (1990), 'The Anthropology of Incommensurability', *Studies in the History and Philosophy of Science* 21, pp. 183–209.

_____. (1992), 'Scientific Revolution, Social Bricolage, and Etiquette' in R. Porter and M. Teich (eds), *The Scientific Revolution in National Context* (Cambridge), pp. 11–54.

_____. (1995), 'Le Prince et les savants. La civilité scientifique au 17me-siècle', *Annales*, 6, 1417–53.

_____. (1996), 'Etiquette, Interdependence, and Sociability in Seventeenth-Century Science', *Critical Inquiry* 22, pp.193–238.

Bots, H. and F. Waquet (1997), *La République des Lettres* (Paris).

Browne, J. (2002), *Charles Darwin. The Power of Place. Volume II of a biography* (London).

Brunon, H. (1999), 'Il bell' ordine della natura: spazio e collezioni nel giardino di villa Medici', in M. Hochmann (ed.), *Villa Medici. Il sogno di un cardinale* (Rome), pp. 67–73.

Clusius, C. (1605), *Exoticorum libri decem* (Leiden).

Les Correspondances. Leur importance pour l'historien des Sciences et de la Philosophie. Problèmes de leur édition (1976), in *Revue de Synthèse*, Série Générale Tome XCVII, Troisième Série 81–82 (Paris).

Davis, N. Zemon (2000), *The Gift in Sixteenth-century France* (Oxford).

Dilg, P. (1994), 'Apotheker als Sammler', in A. Grote (ed.), *Macrocosmos in Microcosmo. Die Welt in der Stube. Zur Geschichte des Sammelns 1450 bis 1800* (Berliner Schriften zur Museumskunde, 10) (Opladen), pp. 453–74.

Drees, J. (n.d), 'Die "Gottorfische Kunst-Kammer". Anmerkungen zu ihrer Geschichte nach historischen Textzeugnissen', in U. Kuhl (ed.), *Gottorf im Glanz des Barock. Kunst und Kultur am Schleswiger Hof 1544–1713* (4 vols., Schleswig-Holsteinisches Landesmuseum), vol. II, pp. 11–28.

Durling, R.J. (1965), 'Conrad Gesner's Liber Amicorum, 1555–1565', *Gesnerus* 22, pp. 134–59.

Egmond, F. (2005), 'Clusius, Cluyt, Saint Omer. The Origins of the Sixteenth-century Botanical and Zoological Watercolours in Libri Picturati A. 16–30', *Nuncius* 20, pp. 11–67.

Egmond, F. and P. Mason (1997), *The Mammoth and the Mouse. Microhistory and Morphology* (Baltimore and London).

_____. (1999), 'A horse called Belisarius', *History Workshop Journal* 47, pp. 240–52.

Egmond, F., P. Hoftijzer and R.Visser (eds), (forthcoming 2006–7), *Carolus Clusius. Towards a Cultural History of a Renaissance Naturalist* (Amsterdam).

Findlen, P. (1994), *Possessing Nature: Museums, Collecting and Scientific Culture in Early Modern Italy* (Berkeley).

_____. (1999), 'The Formation of a Scientific Community: Natural History in Sixteenth-century Italy', in A. Grafton and N. Siraisi (eds), *Natural Particulars* (Cambridge, MA), pp. 369–400.

Foucault, M. (1966), *Les mots et les choses* (Paris).

_____. (1980), *Power/Knowledge. Selected Interviews and Other Writings, 1972–1977* (New York).

Franchini, D.A., R. Margonari, G. Olmi, R. Signorini, A. Zanca and C. Tellini Perina (1979), *La scienza a corte. Collezionismo eclettico natura e immagine a Mantova fra Rinascimento e Manierismo* (Rome).

French, R.K. (1990), 'Natural Philosophy and Anatomy', in: J. Céard, M. M. Fontaine and J-C. Margolin (eds), *Le corps à la Renaissance. Actes du XXXe du XXXe Colloque de Tours 1987* (Paris), pp. 447–60.

Ginzburg, C. (1990), 'Clues: Roots of an Evidential Paradigm', in C. Ginzburg, *Myths, Emblems, Clues* (London), pp. 96–125.

Goldgar, A. (1995), *Impolite Learning. Conduct and Community in the Republic of Letters, 1680–1750* (New Haven and London)

Guicciardini, L. (1994), *Descrittione di tutti i paesi bassi*. A cura di D. Aristodemo (Amsterdam).

Harkness, D.E. (2002), '"Strange" Ideas and "English" Knowledge. Natural Science Exchange in Elizabethan London', in P.H. Smith and P. Findlen (eds), *Merchants and Marvels*, (New York and London), pp. 137–60.

Härting, U. (ed.) (2000), *Gärten und Höfe der Rubenszeit. Im Spiegel der Malerfamilie Brueghel und der Künstler um Peter Paul Rubens* (Exhibition catalogue Gustav-Lübcke-Museum Hamm and Landesmuseum Mainz) (Munich).

Heyden, D. (2000), 'Jardines botánicos prehispánicos', *Arqueología Mexicana* 57, pp. 18–23.

Huizenga, E. (2003), *Tussen autoriteit en empirie. De Middelnederlandse chirurgieën in de veertiende en vijftiende eeuw en hun maatschappelijke context* (Hilversum).

Hunger, F.W.T. (1927 and 1942), *Charles de l'Escluse (Carolus Clusius) Nederlandsch Kruidkundige, 1526–1609* (2 vols, The Hague).

Huppert, G. (1999), *The Style of Paris. Renaissance Origins of the French Enlightenment* (Indianapolis).

Jardine, N., J.A. Secord and E.C. Spary (eds) (1996), *Cultures of Natural History* (Cambridge).

Kamen, H. (1997), *Philip of Spain* (New Haven and London).

Koning, J. de (1995), 'The Development of Botany in the Sixteenth Century', in A. Minelli (ed.), *The Botanical Garden of Padua 1545–1995* (Padua).

Lestringant, F. (1991), *L'atelier du cosmographe ou l'image du monde à la Renaissance* (Paris).

Longeon, C. and A. Sabot (comments and transl.) (1976), *Conrad Gesner. Vingt lettres à Jean Bauhin fils (1563–1565)* (Saint Étienne).

Lowood, H. (1995), 'The New World and the European Catalog of Nature', in K. Ordahl Kupperman (ed.), *America in European Consciousness, 1493–1750* (Chapel Hill and London), pp. 295–323.

Mason, P. (1998), *Infelicities. Representations of the Exotic* (Baltimore and London).

Matthews, L.G. (1967), *The Royal Apothecaries* (London).

Mauss, M. (1990), *The Gift. The Form and Reason for Exchange in Archaic Societies* (London). Originally published as 'Essai sur le don. Forme et raison de l'échange dans les sociétés archaïques', *L'Année Sociologique*, Series 2, (1923–24), vol. 1.

Mirek, Z. and A. Zemanek (eds) (1998), *Studies in Renaissance Botany* (Polish Botanical Studies 20) (Krakow).

Olmi, G. (1976), *Scienza e natura del secondo cinquecento* (Trento).

_____. (1992), *L'Inventario del mondo. Catalogazione della natura e luoghi del sapere nella prima età moderna* (Bologna).

Pardo Tomàs, J. (with J.M. Lopez Piñero) (1996), *La influencia de Francisco Hernández (1515–1587) en la constitución de la botánica y de la materia médica modernas* (Valencia).

Park, K. (1994), 'The Criminal and the Saintly Body: Autopsy and Dissection in Renaissance Italy', *Renaissance Quarterly* 47, pp. 1–33.

Pelling, M. and C. Webster (1979), 'Medical Practitioners', in C. Webster (ed.), *Health, Medicine and Mortality in the Sixteenth Century* (Cambridge), pp. 165–235.

Pouchelle, M.C. (1983), *Corps et chirurgie a l'apogée du Moyen Age. Savoir et imaginaire du corps chez Henri de Mondeville chirurgien de Philippe le Bel* (Paris).

Rath, G. (1950), 'Die Briefe Conrad Gessners aus der Trewschen Sammlung', *Gesnerus* 7, pp. 140–70.

_____. (1951), 'Die Briefe Conrad Gessners aus der Trewschen Sammlung', *Gesnerus* 8, pp. 195–215.

_____. (1980), 'Konrad Gessner's Briefwechsel', in R. Schmitz and F. Krafft, *Humanismus und Naturwissenschaften* (Boppard), pp. 101–12.

Reeds, K. (1991) *Botany in Medieval and Renaissance Universities* (New York and London).

Roberts, R.S. (1965), 'The Early History of the Import of Drugs into England', in F.N.L. Poynter (ed.), *The Evolution of Pharmacy in Britain* (London), pp. 165–86.

Sauer, C.O. (1971), *Sixteenth-Century North America* (Berkeley, Los Angeles and London).

Schepelern, H.D. (1985), 'Natural Philosophers and Princely Collectors: Worm, Paludanus and the Gottorp and Copenhagen Collections', in O. Impey and A. MacGregor, *The Origins of Museums: the Cabinets of Curiosities in Sixteenth and Seventeenth-Century Europe* (Oxford), pp. 121–27.

Schnapper, A. (1988), *Le Géant, La Licorne, La Tulipe. Collections françaises au XVIIe siècle* (Paris).

Secord, J.A. (1996), 'The Crisis of Nature', in N. Jardine, J.A. Secord and E.C. Spary (eds), *Cultures of Natural History* (Cambridge), pp. 447–59.

Smith, P.H. and P. Findlen (eds) (2002), *Merchants and Marvels. Commerce, Science and Art in Early Modern Europe* (New York and London).

Strong, R. (1979), *The Renaissance Garden in England* (London).

Thomas, K. (1983), *Man and the Natural World* (Harmondsworth).

Velsaco Lozano, A.M. (2000), 'El jardín de Itztapalapa', *Arqueología Mexicana* 57, pp. 26–35.

Wellisch, H. (1975), 'Conrad Gessner: a Bio-bibliography', *Journal of the Society for the Bibliography of Natural History* 7, part 2, pp. 151–247.

Zemanek, A. (1998), 'Renaissance Botany and Modern Science', in Z. Mirek and A. Zemanek (eds), *Studies in Renaissance Botany* (Polish Botanical Studies 20) (Krakow), pp. 9–47.

Chapter 7

The Court Galaxy

Rita Costa Gomes

Societies in Europe before the eighteenth century were characterized by the existence of very narrow elites that lived in particular environments, and in special material, physical and cultural conditions. To live at court, or to share the values and forms of life that flourished there was a well-known aspect of such differences. In an attempt to understand the emergence of common languages across the continent, I explore common European discursive traditions that emerge from the world of the courts, of what can be called a 'courtly idiom' with a defining set of themes and arguments. In what follows the reader will not find a detailed account of a series of European courts that would be remarkable for their cultural or artistic brilliance, nor a comparative portrait of the internal hierarchies of historical courts. The first section of the essay, inevitably more abstract in approach, aims to replace the consideration of single historical courts, even if studied comparatively, with a larger, more complex vision. At any single time, there were in pre-modern Europe, a multiplicity of courts large and small, irregularly distributed in space, and these appear to our observation clustered in a certain design. In other words, they appear as a galaxy composed of many types of bodies. For the onset of this vision the sociological theory of Norbert Elias provides a solid base because it proposes conceptual tools to tackle such complexity, and illuminates the common structures and forms of the court galaxy. The second and third sections of this essay examine the constitution of some themes and arguments of the 'courtly idiom' relating them to the changing human environments of specific historical courts. I will discuss how human physical proximity to the ruler in court environments came to be conceived and named since medieval times, how it generated notions of 'secrecy' and practices of distinction, and how these contribute to explain emerging concepts of a clear and trenchant opposition between individual and society in early modern Europe.

Is there a generally accepted definition of what a court was? The search for a historical definition of the court in pre-modern European authors, in fact, reveals a striking resemblance in the content of the available texts, indicating elements of a core concept that remained fundamentally valid in thirteenth-century Iberia,[1] as in Renaissance Italy,[2] as well as in French and German dictionaries from the late seventeenth century.[3] Those elements comprise the *presence* of a monarch or prince, the collection of *people* of varied origins, status and occupation surrounding the ruler, and the *place* itself (or, to be more precise, the space-time complex) in which that presence occurs. However, in our present state of knowledge it is possible to go beyond the historical pictures of single royal or princely courts.[4] Norbert Elias aimed to present such a picture in his study of Louis XIV's court in France, even though his was intended to be a casestudy aimed at broader generalization. Despite such limitations, Elias inaugurated a sociological explanation of the position of kings in pre-modern societies, one that proposed a new object for historical research.[5] Monarchical power, as much as it claimed a mysterious nature outside or above society, was in fact socially constructed. Therefore, historians should explain how monarchical regimes in the past required not only a juridical and institutional setting, but equally the maintenance of a characteristic social form surrounding the rulers. Courts were products of social figurations, defined by Elias as the objective result of how people actually behave, and of how they express their motivations in their actions. In successive generations, the same patern or overall form in their human relationships (such as, in this case, the court figuration) will be reproduced, most of the time unknowingly and unintentionally.[6]

In this essay I maintain a distinction between the concept of pre-modern courts, and that of 'court society', in the sense proposed by Elias in his theory of figurations. The notion of 'court society' does not entirely coincide, in fact, with any specific court or set of courts as they are generally studied by historians. The concept refers to a field of relations in which social forms of varied profile, institutional definition and duration might exist, a field that is associated with the social reproduction of medieval and early modern kingship. This association is indirectly referred to by medieval and early modern *topoi* found in some texts, as in 'there are no courts without kings' (and the obverse formulation), or 'monarchy makes the nobility, and the nobility makes monarchy', a formula rendered famous by Montesquieu. Useful notions of 'court' and 'court society', however, are correlative. That is, the latter is not an entirely separate entity that can be perceived *per se*, nor abstractly constructed as an *ideal typus*.[7] It is an empirical or 'real-type' concept which can only be explored through the study of individual royal, princely and ecclesiastical courts. Following Elias' proposal, we shall not look to isolated organisms, to each court as an *unicum*; rather we shall search for interrelations and equilibriums of forces in a wider and differently conceived area of observation. Our object is indeed closer to what sociological theory defined, for instance, in the seminal work of Pierre Bourdieu, as a social field. Inside the field that Elias named 'court society' we observe a certain difficulty in establishing clear dichotomies between 'public' and 'private', 'political' and 'domestic', an aspect discussed later in this essay.

The adoption of Elias' concept of 'court society' allows for the study of regularities observed through historical analysis across different areas of Europe, as well as for the comparison of several courts separated in time and/or space. By considering the social field as a whole, we are able to more easily understand how national historiographical traditions appropriated royal and dynastic claims to distinction and singularity regarding each monarchical court, underlining its supposed uniqueness. Noticing common traits in several royal courts, historians have provided general explanations based on a succession of 'models' for court organization and practice in the several political centres of early modern Europe. Those 'models' could be found, for instance, in Burgundy, Spain or France, courts that were simply 'imitated' elsewhere, as Rome or Byzantium were 'imitated' in previous centuries. In this paper we consider instead the simultaneous existence at any single time of a multiplicity of such centres in medieval and early modern Europe, that is, a galaxy of courts. Mutual influences and attraction of the single entities or bodies that constitute this 'galaxy' contribute to explain that social types and roles in court can be recognized in different cultural and linguistic contexts, a fact that deserves to be examined in more detail than through the rough lens of 'diffusionist' theories of explanation. The metaphor of the 'galaxy', being associated with a paradigm of complexity, seems useful because it equally refers to the repetition of the same pattern on different scales. The courts of the past present a large degree of 'self-similarity' in their structure, that is, they often contained smaller parts that replicate the whole. Such was the case with monarchical courts that included several households (the queen's *familia*, and that of heirs to the throne), or with the papal court which attracted the households of cardinals. The 'galaxy' can be observed and studied this way in the intricacy of its different levels or structural scales. Each cluster of courts, on the other hand, can be observed and studied in relation to the overall design.

Problems of linguistic transmission are just one aspect of the ways of sharing and communicating cultural values in the court galaxy, through the circulation and reception of texts, both printed and in manuscript form. In Europe, the world of courts was multilingual and was connected, from late medieval times, not only to Latin but also to the expansion of vernaculars. The predominance of vernacular forms of textual transmission in 'court society' since the high Middle Ages demands that particular attention be given to translation, without neglecting the important role played by the Latin language in the culture of pre-modern elites. Other questionnaires and other sources have been constructed recently by historians, regarding for instance artistic and material culture, or ritual practices, domains which also reveal the constitution of other common 'languages' in the galaxy of courts. Besides, the 'language' trope can also be fruitfully used in our analysis of 'court society' and the discursive traditions that developed in it. A common 'idiom of courtliness' emerged from the galaxy of European courts, an 'idiom' that should be considered alongside other 'languages' enumerated by Pocock as being central to the construction of European political traditions, such as 'medieval scholastic, Renaissance emblematic, biblical exegesis, common law, classical republicanism, or commonwealth radicalism'.[8]

In order to explore some characteristic assumptions and arguments of the 'idiom of courtliness', different bodies in this galaxy, that is, different types of courts should be considered – princely courts, royal courts, even ecclesiastical and papal ones – and an exclusive attention to the Renaissance, or to the courts of absolutist kings, proves to be misleading. As Malcolm Vale clearly states, 'the distinction often made between medieval household and early modern, or Renaissance court is an inherently false and artificial one'.[9] Vale's study of a defined cluster of courts in the thirteenth and fourteenth centuries is an excellent example of new problems raised by historical comparison of several contemporary courts. As is often the case in court studies, none of the courts he compares, associated with 'three sovereign powers (the kings of England and France, and the German emperor)' and six other smaller principalities – Flanders, Brabant, Hainault, Artois, Holland and Zeeland – actually corresponds to the political geography of modern nations. This cluster of north European medieval courts was subject to historical processes of mutual fashioning, and smaller courts gravitated into the sphere of others. To give an example, that of Artois was successively attracted to France in the thirteenth, and then to Burgundy in the fourteenth century. Cultural forms emerged and were transformed in this cluster of courts which presented a basic similarity in the structure of offices and internal departments, and shared the same linguistic predominance. Both of these historical realities, the institutional similarity and the predominance of French as a courtly language, were obscured by the history of late medieval monarchical states, and in the case of England, according to Vale, by the prevailing analysis of centralizing tendencies of the late medieval royal government.

One example of those shared cultural forms is important to our argument. The institutional analysis made of this cluster of courts allows us to conclude that in the late thirteenth century a fundamental mutation occurred in them. This major change had a bearing on the structural separation between the hall (*aula*), the chapel (*capella*) and the chamber (*camera*), and gave rise to what Vale calls a 'chamber system', that is, a new prominence given to the mechanisms of proximity and control of the access to the king's person. The new importance of the *camera* since the 1200s can be set against the complexity of the status classifications and processes of '*rangmanifestation*' that this author otherwise reconstructs, in a minute decipherment of the regime of remunerations of courtiers through cloth and other materials. There is a distinctive character to those forms of consumption, opposing the courts where such luxury consumption took place to the rest of the society. As Malcolm Vale claims, 'hierarchical structures – which were difficult (or indeed impossible) to maintain or enforce outside – were more effectively kept in place' at court, and he shows precisely how those forms of consumption were directly connected to the building of courtly hierarchies.

From the point of view of the internal organization of medieval courts, such hierarchical complexity also required a better grasp of classification ranks, now more easily brought about by the use of a scale of fixed sums of money corresponding to the different hierarchical positions ascribed to each individual (regardless of the effective payments to the courtiers being made in money, or in any other form). The complexity in the processes of *rangmanifestation* in late medieval courts can be equally related, as suggested above, to the need for a 'chamber system', since such a system could more effectively prevent conflicting claims of rank and precedence. The possibility of these conflicts multiplied whenever kings or princes ate with the whole court in solemn banquets or made appearances in prescribed moments of the year, activities that were related to the mechanisms and institutions emerging from the *aula* (hall). The 'withdrawal' of the monarch was thus obtained through a systematic regulation of his daily presence, leading to clearer distinctions between types of distance (intimate, personal, domestic, etc.) towards his person. Those different distances, in a way, also materialized in the 'chamber system' as an architectural program. This general tendency towards a stricter regulation seems to have occurred, in fact, concurrently with a particular ordering of physical spaces evident in many royal and ecclesiastical residences, that is since the thirteenth century. In most western European courts, the so-called 'chambers of state' then became distinct from the 'retirement' chambers ('retraite'), a usage that was spread across the continent, in both secular and ecclesiastical contexts, by the 1350s. This was a structural trait of courtly spaces that was to last well into the early modern age.[10] Both in its physical, spatial reality and as a set of practices regarding human interaction at court, the 'chamber system' as evident in northern European 'court society' represents a distinct cultural form emerging after 1200.

This form seems to be related to some aspects of the 'idiom' of courtliness, namely the central role that arguments and notions of 'secrecy' have in it. In order to explore this relation, let us look at another set of historical courts. Our second example of a cluster of courts brings us to the Iberian Peninsula from the mid-thirteenth and fourteenth centuries, and it includes several royal courts – Castile, Mallorca and Aragon, Portugal and Navarre. A historical process of cultural transmission of a set of specific texts occurred in those royal courts, texts originally compiled or composed in Arabic and then translated into Latin or Hebrew and the vernaculars Castilian, Catalan and Portuguese. These texts propose a circulation of arguments and concepts related to the figures of kings, as well as to the human relations implicating those surrounding the monarchs. Our analytical perspective is not, however, comparative. We do not aim to compare texts to discover 'similarities' or 'proximities' between political cultures in distinct areas of the late medieval Mediterranean world. These texts, both in their Arabic as in their non-Arabic versions, in fact represent a diversified 'crystallization of common-places', as proposed by Jocelyn Dakhlia. This author suggestively reminds us that 'the problem is not that of looking for a filiation, for an index or trace of the transmission of textual matter – but from the identification of a *topos*, from the study of its elaboration, to attempt a search of its meanings in a precise cultural and political context'.[11]

Such was the well-known case of the pseudo-Aristotelian *Sirr-al-Asrâr* or 'Secret of Secrets', some of whose texts were also translated in other parts of medieval Europe, by relying on other linguistic chains of transmission, Latin, Greek or Hebrew. Their circulation and their presence in the royal and princely libraries of late medieval Europe are well established, as this text appear not only in Iberia.[12] Due to the impressive quantity[13] and quality of the Iberian translations,[14] their characteristics have been explored mostly by philologists and literary historians. Their role in the emergence of an 'idiom of courtliness' in specific Iberian contexts nevertheless demands further attention, and the multiplication of the texts has yet to be related to the study of the royal courts themselves.[15]

Suffice is to remember, among other aspects, the contribution of these translations to the transformation of the political vocabulary of medieval Castilian and medieval Catalan, particularly by creating a set of new words – generally cultisms borrowed directly from Latin. In fact, a whole semantic area emerges in these texts for the first time in the vernaculars, an area which was to become central to the debates of the so-called 'didactic literature' of the 1300s, that is, to the development of a literature of precepts and *institutio* of both monarchs and courtiers. These semantic fields are organized around concepts of 'counsel' and 'secrecy', and include words related to courtly practices and to the hierarchical value of proximity to the monarch's person. Some of the arguments developed by the thirteenth-century Iberian texts are centred in the dyadic relations of the king and the courtier. At the same time, there is a clear presence in some of these texts of theories regarding 'correspondences' between the individual and the natural world, as well as philosophical notions of cosmic hierarchy, and beliefs in restricted forms of knowledge which attributed great importance to the decipherment of 'occult' meanings hidden in the physical world. In other words, that dyadic relation between ruler and courtier, in these texts, was not conceived as autonomous, nor purely influenced by human behaviour.

Particularly revealing, in several of these Iberian texts, is a theorization concerning the value of 'secrecy' ('*poridad*', '*poridat*', '*puridade*') in interpersonal relations, both for maintaining the favour of the king and for preventing the dangers arising from the loss of his trust. The word comes from the Latin *purus* and it covers a semantic area that is, according to Corominas, 'similar to the family of the German words *treu* and *trauen*, or the English true, associating notions of "fidelity", "truth" and "trust"'.[17] At the same time, proximity to the ruler is mentioned in these texts as the main formal principle of courtly hierarchies, expressed in a variety of typical figures that can be found in them, including those of governor, secretary, ambassador or messenger, military leader, and so on.

Under what conditions were these textual traditions received in Iberia? We should relate that reception to the fact that the 'system of the chamber' could also be found there, as in the northern courts referred to above. By the early 1300s it had clearly emerged both in the normative sources and in bureaucratic practice in the Christian courts we are considering. For example, in all of them chamber scribes intervened in a growing number of governmental mechanisms, and a 'small' or 'chamber seal' (*sello de la puridad*) was used as a parallel means of authenticating royal mandates. As the cases of Mallorca and Aragon clearly show, the chamber had acquired undisputed autonomy among the institutional and ceremonial features of the court.[18] Thus, the transformations of contemporary realities in the expansion of 'court society' in Iberia, and especially the importance of the 'chamber system' in Iberian courts must be taken into account in the textual reception referred to above. Those were the realities that the courtly public of Iberian courts was facing, and they were framed and discussed with the help of the '*topoi*' from the 'adab' literature – to use this relatively imprecise term[19] – as new words were also appearing to name them, words first used in textual translations of that literature into the Iberian vernaculars.

These texts represent, as it were, a recognizable thread inside the multicoloured fabric of the medieval transmission in Europe of practical norms to be taught and learned regarding behaviour appropriate to life at court. Equally important to our analysis is the claim made by Grunebaum, followed by others, that the texts of the *adab* represent 'above all, an approach ... so to speak, a principle of form, not an array of materials', since this principle of form or 'way of approach' can also be detected in the contemporary movement towards the writing and compilation of specialized works on related subjects emerging in Iberia in the same period that these translations were made. These subjects were to be codified independently, in the context of the late medieval Christian world, under the disciplinary order of the 'mechanical arts', and these originated a growing field of 'practical' texts with their own methodological claims and assumptions.[20] The textual universe of the 'adab' and the technical literature, separated in content but often close in form and similar in their reception, proposed a composite figure of the competences of the Iberian medieval 'courtier', competences that go well beyond the usual motif of the *probitates* associated with the ideals of knighthood. Among these were *opificium* which included the arts of building and projecting order in urban space, *armatura* and the arts of war, *navigatio* including what we would call geography and trade, *venatio* or hunting and falconry, the courtly arts or *theatrica* such as jousting, wrestling, dancing and making music, horse-riding, all of these requiring a certain proficiency in distinct symbolic codes such as, for instance, heraldry. That this corpus of 'technical' precepts could be transmitted in an autonomous way, but alongside the ethical frame, occasionally 'penetrated of religious intertext',[21] of the 'adab' in its abundant variations and precepts (made of accumulations of anecdotes, examples and proverbs) is one of the clearest signs of an expanding 'court society' in the late medieval Iberian world.

All of this defies the simplified picture of an alternative between 'clerical' or 'knightly' origins of the courtliness idiom, an opposition that the studies of Jaeger and Scaglione, followed by others, have nuanced in a fundamental way.[22] In the context of western Christian Europe, 'court society' in the late medieval period should be seen as a differentiated area of society, where models of behaviour and specific figures of hierarchical order emerged, and these implicated both ecclesiastical and secular aristocracies. The forms of 'practical' knowledge mentioned above flourished there, and carved their own sphere side by side with the theoretical distinctions between human virtues and values necessarily reflected in external conduct that were also proposed by the textual traditions circulating mostly in the clerical and Latin world. Courtliness can be viewed, as Jaeger convincingly argued, as a form of 'medieval Europe's memory of the Roman statesman, of his humanity and urbane skilfulness in guiding the state and facing the trials of public life', a memory cultivated with success in the ecclesiastical Episcopal courts and debated in the clerical world of the schools.[23] But the corpus of Iberian texts we are considering equally shows that late medieval courtliness joined to this remembrance, among other aspects, new assumptions about voluntary subordination of oneself to the authority and person of a ruler in order to gain his trust. The cultivation of a set of practical disciplines, not only intellectual competences, was proposed as a condition to adhere to a distinctive way of life practised at court. The late medieval 'idiom of courtliness' detectable in this Iberian corpus of translated texts remained solidly grounded in practical reason, even as it articulated practice with judgments about human values. It proposed the existence of secular hierarchies in which individuals could progress, and it pointed to the value of personal subordination and close interaction with the ruler in such a progress. It was nevertheless an idiom limited to a world of signs to be deciphered, of opinions to be weighed according to authority, of forms of knowledge more humble (or in the clerical view, 'servile' or ancillary) than the world of speculative reasoning proper to 'higher' disciplines. If it implied careful consideration of men's actions, late medieval 'courtliness' in the Iberian context was nevertheless practised as an 'art', and it remained connected to discourses pertaining to the cultivation of virtues.

The awareness of a continuity between the courtliness of the medieval period and the portrait made of the Renaissance courtier by authors such as Castiglione cannot elude, however, the important changes represented by the latter, changes that are detectable in the notions of 'secrecy' and the arguments of subordination we are considering.[24] The Renaissance courtier, both in its male and female incarnations, was described with unparalleled success by Castiglione in a book which had, as shown by Peter Burke's research, around 150 editions in many languages and probably counted more than 300,000 readers in the two centuries following its first publication in 1528.[25] The forms of distinction that are described in the ideal put forward by Castiglione diverge in many interesting ways from the composite figure of the late medieval Iberian courtier. This is a vast question in itself, which will remain in the background as I explore the problems that currently interest me. In regard to the role of the technical and practical universe of the 'mechanical' arts, for instance, it should be noted that these were themselves newly subjected by Castiglione's courtier to a general strategy of concealment, but one that wanted to make of naturalness or ease in every talent a universal rule, for both men and women. Although Castiglione portrays a courtier who was entirely devoted to his courtly existence, almost a 'profession' of a new sort, the practical competences required for court life are marked by an ideal of grace and modesty that implies a distance from any technical specialization. To this difference we should add at least two other main contrasts with the late medieval arguments that concerns us in this essay. The aim of Castiglione's courtier, remembers Vasoli, is to guide and mentor the prince as a new demiurgic figure, as a participant or interpreter of the 'secrecy' of power.[26] Although some figures of the medieval 'counsellor' could be close to such a high concept of the courtier's role – we think, for instance, of some Platonian accents of the 'Secret of Secrets' – his autonomy in action, and the participatory ideal envisioned by Castiglione announce new arguments. Finally, the book conveys an acute perception of the courtier as a social being, and of the importance of the 'ethos' of dependence at court.[27] This latter aspect is of crucial importance to our discussion.

Beyond the dyadic relation of the courtier to the ruler that, as we saw, was a central argument regarding subordination to the monarch in late medieval texts, we find in Castiglione a cultural assumption that the courtier equally depended on the judgment of his audience, that is, of the court as a whole. Depending on the reputation and image carefully built in his pairs was a necessary condition to the fulfilment of a 'perfect form' of the courtier. Many authors have analysed the importance of this argument for the awareness of personal identity detectable in early modern European texts. This concern with projecting an image of the person and trying to fashion that image according to specific models or figures is at the heart of the debates about court life in the 1500s. Again, separating the medieval experience from the later debates about this subject can be misleading. The issue has recently been revisited by Caroline Bynum, who restated the medievalists' conclusions that the discovery of models and roles was not only a 'concurrent development', but presented an 'intimate and dialectical relationship' with a sense of the individual emerging in twelfth-century texts, just as it did in the numerous books of *institutio* in the 1500s. This is an aspect that can be distinguished from what would be a 'theory of the person', and especially of the inner self or *interior homo*.[28] That this latter sphere was the object, in the 1500s, of more sophisticated debates regarding notions of transparency and secrecy was a crucial contribution of the 'idiom of courtliness' to the discursive traditions regarding a theory of the person. Congruence between inner and outer self had been a major argument of medieval spiritual literature, a proposed ideal according to which secrecy of the inner sphere was devalued, since it precluded the manifestation of the intention to sin, and therefore, says Bynum, 'that sin could be measured, punished and remitted'. In the figure of Castiglione's courtier, we find the different proposal of disciplining oneself not to live outside of 'human commerce', and at the same time of finding a way to self-preservation and self-expression through concealment of inner dispositions and choices.[29] Realities external to the self, and specifically the human universe of the courts, appeared not only clearly separated from that self, but ultimately threatening or worthy of appeasement.

In no other author can we find a clearer expression of this courtly notion of secrecy of the self, associated with ideas of subordination to outside conditions, than in Baltasar Gracián. The diffusion of Gracián's ideas is certainly related to the expansion of 'court society' in European contexts, where his books found their public. There were more than 15 editions in at least 10 different European languages of the 'Oráculo Manual' (1647), both made directly from the original and from the French version of Amelot de la Houssaye under the title of 'L'homme de cour'.[30] The cultural assumptions that are a point of departure for Gracián are also those of the Jesuit scholarly world, that is, of the 'subjunctive mental mode', as Nancy Struever calls it, brought about by the predominance of rhetorical theory and practice. Rhetorical detachment, she observes, 'results in a sense of the layered and indirect quality of experience … the subjunctive mode emphasizes the "real" world as entirely mediated, indeed, distorted by symbol'.[31] This 'mental mode' can be detected in the importance of the concept of *aparencia* (appearance or semblance) in Gracián's works: *'las cosas no pasan por lo que son, sino por lo que parecen'* (things do not exist for what they are, but for what they appear to be) and, conversely, 'that which is not seen appears not to exist'.[32] Gracián points in this collection of aphorisms to the careful consideration of 'occasions' and 'appearences', that is, he advises the courtier to take the world as it appears, for what surrounds him is but a sum of appearances. The same methods would apply to the consideration of how the person could become 'credible' in one's involvement with others – through the controlled projection of semblances, the transformation of spontaneous tendencies into good reflexes of defence and display, and through cultivated caution regarding any form of human interaction.[33]

In his 'Oráculo Manual', Gracián assumes that concealing from others the inner self is liberating, as long as there is a simultaneous transparency of the subject to himself. The latter is not, however, a transparency that would be obtained by unveiling obscure inner depths of the person, as occurs with the modern Freudian paradigm; it is a pragmatically oriented knowledge of less commendable traits or defects, obtainable by simple self-observation of one own's actions. Instead, what the Jesuit proposed was a universal value of dissimulation, an art most useful to the courtier but ultimately allowing all men (although, with more difficulty, women) the construction of the 'person' – since for Gracián an essential contrast exists between the *'sujeto'*, or so to speak the mere human animal, and the *'persona'* or moral subject.[34] This universal (but gendered) value of dissimulation is based, observed Villari, in a fusion of two different discourses, the one that proposed 'prudence' as the main precept recommended to princes, and the one that exalted 'patience' as the virtue of the subjects, by discovering what both had in common – precisely, to dissimulate. The Aragonese author looks from the point of view of the court into society at large, and takes the value of dissimulation as a principle that could be applied even beyond the field of political action.[35] Gracián's most diffused works, like the 'Oráculo Manual', represent some of the earliest formulations of the modern concept of the *'homo clausus'*, as Norbert Elias observed. The individual appears here as an autarchic entity, sealed or imprisoned 'under lock and key' in his or her 'inside', isolated and autonomous as it faces society, whereas society is seen as an outside reality, merely exterior to the individual, and a threatening order to the 'person'.[36]

These visions proposed by the idiom of courtliness of the 1600s, therefore, appear more radical and complex than a simple opposition of 'private' to 'public' selves, for 'court society', as we saw, defies those same distinctions in past societies as an extreme example of a social field in which they could not be defined with clarity.[37] The authority of the ruler over the person of the courtier was conceived in similar terms to that of the head of the house (*Hausherr*), blurring the distinction between 'domestic' or 'politic' forms of subordination. Conversely, it might be said that only 'public' persons existed at court, if we follow the suggestive proposal of Habermas that absolutism created something similar to a 'public sphere' through the reverberation or the projection of the image of the king into society, as the embodiment of monarchical power. There was, nevertheless, a discursive tradition which expressed such hybrid realities. Gracián's sources also demonstrate an acute awareness of the continuity of discursive traditions in the Iberian world regarding the court and the arguments of courtly interaction as a source of knowledge about human relations marked by such blurred distinctions. He not only refers to major authors of the Castilian 'didactic literature' in his works, especially Don Juan Manuel, but praises the original form of the 'Conde Lucanor', with his short narratives, as a successful example of *'agudeza fingida'*.[38] The affinity is not superficial, nor connected exclusively with formal aspects of the texts. The use of medieval sources by Gracián denotes a revival of a debate based on common cultural assumptions about what was 'counsel' and 'prudence', and it shows an underlying dialogue taking place in his work with those authors from the past.

Together with this theory of the person, the other theme of the idiom of courtliness we are considering revolves around subordination, as a fundamental category of experience in 'court society'. We shall conclude with a few remarks about it. Subordination, as we saw, has a central role in Gracián's vision of courtliness. It had a personal dimension, since the 'person' accepts and takes the sum of appearances that the world is, as a reality to which he must submit, and it was also in relation to a proposed concept of *'ocasión'*, the 'occasion'. But some important distinctions can be made between the 'subordination to the ruler', for instance as it was conceived in the language of republicanism, and the one these texts refer to, in the case of the courtier. If both can be seen as 'voluntary', the differences go well beyond a simple opposition between 'unconditional' or limited forms of subordination. As suggested by Simmel, there are distinct social forms in which 'the subordination under an individual power is not the consequence or the expression of an already existing group'.[39] We should consider the courtier in such a position towards the ruler.

In other words, it was not primarily as 'subjects' or 'naturals' of a prince, it was not as members of a political community or any form of consociation that courtiers voluntarily subordinated themselves to a monarch. The latter relation was not predetermined by other relations, of the previous type. In fact, the relation of subordination of the courtier to a ruler can even be in total contradiction with those mentioned above. This happened in the case of the courtier who was a stranger or a foreigner, who was not part of the community of the 'natural subjects'. Or in the case of the 'favourite' or *'parvenu'*, who stepped outside his or her ascribed status or expected social position, acquiring a new one inside the social field of 'court society'. As Angela de Benedictis shows in her essay in this volume, the possibility of revoking or contesting one's subordination to the ruler, for instance in the case of the 'right of resistance', was always simultaneously an expression of belonging to the community, and this occurred beyond the conditional or unconditional characteristic of that subordination. It is in this fundamental aspect that the latter relation substantially differs from the subordination of the courtier that, as such, does not depend on appurtenance to a previously existent group. The distinction is not used, significantly, by a constellation of European authors of the 1600s and 1700s who criticize the figure of the courtier and discuss the validity of the discourse of *'politesse'* based on the ideals of republicanism. In England in the 1600s, according to Hampsher-Monk, 'the artificiality of courtly culture was retrospectively stigmatised as a culture of deceit, linking an aesthetic preoccupation with style and moral deviousness', and the 'polite arts' were seen as having a defined role in 'the loss of republican liberty' in the archetypical example of Rome.[40] Some well-known Dutch tracts from the 1660s equally resuscitated arguments and *topoi* of the anti-courtier literature, in a polemic against monarchical regimes of power.[41] Yet, these texts do not build their arguments against subordination to the monarchs outside the cultural assumptions regarding self and society that we have been analysing, and equally revolve around notions of sincerity and autonomy of the self that were intrinsic to the idiom of courtliness.

Again, we can see how a productive and coherent argument about subordination is combined with those assumptions regarding a theory of the person in a different way, for instance, in Gracián's theory of 'occasions'. The court was a social and political universe in which it was not the common and equal bond linking the individuals to the ruler that was prevalent. Rather, it was precisely the personal and unequal relation of each subordinate to the ruler that gave solidity to the social form characterized by subordination under one sole individual. A theory of '*ocasión*' oriented the search for the uniqueness of events susceptible of exalting one's position at court, a search that revealed the person through his actions. That is not to say, of course, that courts were necessarily devoid of communitarian dynamics. The forms of communal experience that could develop in court are, in fact, a much less known aspect of 'court society' than the individualization and self-restraint required by courtly behaviour. Sahlins referred to a concept of 'hierarchical solidarity' as a useful complement, to be adopted alongside the canonical distinction between 'organic' and 'mechanical' forms of solidarity made by Durkheim. The proposal is most useful in the analysis of subordination in the courtly universe of close relations to the ruler. As Sahlins observes, the coherence of the members of such subgroups would be 'not so much due to their similarity (mechanical) or to their complementarity (organic), as to their common submission to the ruling power'.[42] Such forms of 'hierarchical solidarity' did in fact develop in court society, most visibly for instance in specialized bodies of service like the royal and princely chapels, or the royal or ecclesiastical chambers. But at court, it was the varying closeness or distance to the monarch which created the differentiation necessary to maintain that particular design of human relations or, if you want, that characteristic hierarchical pattern. Gracián referred to this reality developing heliocentric metaphors of explanation of the power of monarchs, and insisted upon a 'radiating' presence of the 'prudent' courtier as both an aesthetic ideal and a way of finding one's position in the world.

Both in Castiglione and in Gracián's works, the discourse of courtliness claims the subordination to the ruler as a basis for a certain sense of the self. An awareness of the effect of a projection of a semblance of that self upon others extends the argumentation, which we detected in late medieval texts, of gaining the ruler's trust through that subordination. But, contrary to its Roman predecessors, we do not see in Gracián's Stoicism, for instance, any orientation or concern towards the good of the community. That is, in these early modern texts we see how this relation of subordination implicates in the first place the person as a person and only secondarily – and even consequently, as it occurs with the individual's position in courtly hierarchies, always depending on the king's will and discretion – as a member of a group. Subordination is conceived in this field, not according to 'a cardinal assumption that subjection to unchecked power is equivalent to servitude' and intrinsically demeaning,[43] but as a means of creating another reality, or as Gracián would say, another '*artificio*'. This was an artifice which, as we saw, protected the individual from his hostile social condition. But 'without artifice', Gracián also claims, 'nature itself is perverted', and the 'person' could not emerge in the unavoidable interaction with others. Beyond the recognition of the personal forms of subordination required of the courtier laid a creative tension between inner freedom and dissimulation, the latter seen both by Castiglione and by Gracián as a form of empowerment stemming from the very old practices and discursive traditions of 'secrecy' and its precepts.

To conclude, I have suggested in this essay that some of the arguments and ideas expressed through the 'idiom of courtliness' challenge and refine our understanding of discursive traditions of pre-modern Europe regarding politics and society. They illuminate other forms of subordination than the ones that bound men living together in territories, cities or communities to the authority of monarchs and princes, either secular or ecclesiastical. Certain aspects of the early modern notions of the self cannot be fully conceptualized within the language of republicanism because they stem from different perspectives and experiences. The emergence of such arguments, on the other hand, appears to be related to the transformations of 'court society' detectable at the level of the internal organization and the social practices of different clusters of historical courts after the 1200s. The world of the courts in Europe resembles the design of a galaxy, with numerous and diverse centres irregularly distributed throughout the continent. The complexity of this world defies explanations based solely on the obvious uniqueness of each single body, of each single court.

Notes

1. Costa Gomes (1995), pp. 3–4
2. Bertelli (1986).
3. Duindam (2003), p. 3.
4. Compare for instance Dickens (1977) and Adamson (1999).
5. See critical arguments and discussion of Elias' theories by historians LeRoy Ladurie (1983), Bertelli and Grifò (1985), Asch (1991), Knox (1991), Bucholz (1993), Dean (1994), Gordon (1994), Duindam (1995), Farge (1997), LeRoy Ladurie and Fitou (1997), Winterling (1997).
6. Elias (1982, 1983).
7. Elias (1983), pp. 21–2.
8. Pocock (1987).
9. Vale (2001), p. 18.
10. Kerscher (2000); Costa Gomes (forthcoming).
11. Dakhlia (1995), pp. 50–1. See also Dakhlia (1998), pp. 11–22.
12. Manzalaoui (1974); Ryan and Schmitt (1982).
13. A complete description of the Castilian corpus: Haro Cortés (1995), pp. 23–75. See in particular the sections devoted to the following texts: *Bocados de Oro, Libro de los buenos proverbios, Poridat de las Poridades* and *Secreto de los Secretos, Libro de los Doce Sabios* or *Tractado de la Nobleza y Lealtad, Flores de Filosofia, Libro de los Cien Capitulos,* and also the sections on *Libro del Consejo y de los Consejeros* and *Castigos de Sancho IV,* although the latter were not, strictly speaking, translations from the Arabic. For the Catalan: Lloyd A. Kasten (1934) pp. 70–3, Llabrès y Quintana (1898). For the Portuguese case: Ackerlind (1990), pp. 25–7; Moreira de Sá (1960).
14. For example, the Castilian version of the maxims of Ibn Fâtik, an author from the eleventh century, is considered the closest to the Arabic text: 'a splendid example of the art of translation. ... if it continues to be very popular for centuries, this was due as much to the quality of the translation as to the intrinsic interest of Al-Mubashshir's work': Rosenthal (1961), p. 155.
15. Some suggestions regarding the case of Castile: Menéndez Pidal (1972); Maravall (1983); Kinkade (1972); Deyermond (1985), pp. 158–67.
16. Such is the case of the Castilian '*oficio*', '*príncipe*', or the verb '*publicar*', among other words. See Bustos Tovar (1974).
17. Corominas and Pascual (1981), s.v. '*Puro*'.
18. '*Ordenacions fets per lo molt Alt Senyor en Pere Terç Rey Darago sobra lo Regiment de tots los officials de la sua cort*', in de Bofarull y Mascaró (1850), vol 5, p. 175. This text compiled in 1344 circulated in Castile, but also in France and Burgundy in the 1300s and 1400s. The edition cited above refers to the Catalan text, which is a translation and adaptation of the Leges Palatinae of the King of Mallorca, dating from 1337. The Catalan text was translated into Castilian by order of Prince Carlos, the son of Philip II of Spain, in 1562. It was also published in Spanish by Manuel Lasala in 1853, and again in a major collection of sources in 1866. It was the object of a series of studies by German scholars, published between 1908 and 1920 (namely by Fincke and Klüpfel). More recently, see Schena (1983); Schena and Trenchs (1990); Palacios Martin (1995). The text of this ceremonial has been extensively used in an important study by Kerscher (2000).
19. The term 'adab literature' includes a vast array of texts that transmitted knowledge pertinent to 'good education' or 'good manners' in medieval Islam, as opposed to

specialized or in-depth forms of knowledge. A critical discussion of the generality of the term can be found in Malti-Douglas (1985), pp. 7–15.
20. Eis (1967); Allard (1982). For a discussion of the importance of 'secrecy' in the technical literature, see Ong (2001).
21. Malti-Douglas (1997).
22. Jaeger (1985); Scaglione (1991).
23. Jaeger (1985), p. 257; Jaeger (1994), pp. 292–324.
24. On the relations of these texts and their Italian context, see one of the sources of the current debate in the essay (first published in 1937) by Battaglia (1991). For an overview of the Italian sources, see in Prosperi (1980).
25. Burke (1995).
26. Vasoli (1980).
27. Quondam (1980). For a discusssion of the continuities and innovations in the figure of the courtier, see Scaglione (1991), pp. 229–47 and also Quondam (2000).
28. Kramer and Bynum (2002).
29. The problem can be observed also from the point of view of anti-courtier sensibilities of the 1500s, such as they are expressed in the work of Luther, Calvin or Montaigne in their new ideals of 'sincerity': Martin (1997).
30. On the translations see Gambin (1992); Mansau (1993). See also the general introduction of del Hoyo (1967).
31. Struever (1970), pp. 155–6. On the importance of the *ratio studiorum* in the intellectual universe of Gracián, see among others Battlori (1958), p.108 ff.
32. '*Oráculo Manual*' in Gracián (2001), p. 236 and p. 247 (# 99, 130).
33. Forcione (1997), pp. 41–7. See also Maravall (1975).
34. Gambin (1990).
35. Villari (1987), pp. 28–9.
36. Elias (1991).
37. Our analysis differs in this point from that proposed by Comparato (1996).
38. Pelegrin (1988); Hinz (1999).
39. Simmel (1971), p. 102.
40. See, for instance, Klein (1990); Hampsher-Monk (2002).
41. Velema (2002). For the anti-courtier literature, see Smith (1966); Uhlig (1973); Kiesel (1979).
42. Sahlins (1985), pp. 45–6.
43. Skinner (2002).

References

Ackerlind, S.R. (1990), *King Dinis of Portugal and the Alphonsine Heritage* (New York).
Adamson, J. (ed.) (1999), *The Princely Courts of Europe, 1500–1700* (London).
Allard, G. (ed.) (1982) *Les Arts Mécaniques au Moyen Âge* (Montréal and Paris).
Asch, R. (1991), 'Court and Household from the Fifteenth to the Seventeenth Centuries', in R. Asch and A. Birke (eds), *Princes, Patronage and the Nobility. The Court at the Beginning of the Modern Age, c. 1450–1650* (Oxford).
Battaglia, S. (1991), 'La letteratura del comportamento e l'idea del cortigiano', (original edition 1937), in *La Mitografia del Personaggio* (Napoli), pp. 81–92.
Battlori, M. (1958), *Gracián y el Barroco* (Rome).

Bertelli, S. (1986), 'Il concetto di Corte', in J.C. Margolin, D. Bigalli, A. Tenenti (eds), *Ragione e Civilitas. Figure del vivere associato nella cultura del Cinquecento Europeo* (Milan).

Bertelli, S. and G. Crifò (eds.) (1985), *Rituale. Cerimoniale. Etichetta* (Milan).

Bofarull, y Mascaró P. (ed.) (1850), *Colleción de Documentos Inéditos del Archivo General de la Corona de Aragón* (Barcelona).

Bucholz, R. (1993), *The Augustan Court. Queen Anne and the Decline of Court Culture* (Stanford).

Burke, P. (1995), *The Fortunes of the Courtier. The European Reception of Castiglione's 'Cortegiano'* (Oxford).

Bustos Tovar, J. (1974), 'Notas para el léxico de la prosa didáctica del siglo XIII', *Studia in honorem Rafael Lapesa*, vol. 2, (Madrid), pp. 149–55.

Comparato, V.I. (1996), 'A Case of Modern Individualism: Politics and the Uneasiness of Intellectuals in the Baroque Age', in J. Coleman (ed.), *The Individual in Political Theory and Practice* (Oxford), pp. 149–70.

Corominas, J. and J.A. Pascual (1981), *Diccionario Crítico Etimológico Castellano e Hispánico* (Madrid).

Costa Gomes, R. (1995), 'Usages de cour et cérémonial dans la péninsule Ibérique au Moyen Âge', in *Traités de savoir-vivre en Espagne et au Portugal du Moyen Âge à nos jours* (Clermont-Ferrand).

_____ . (2003), *The Making of a Court Society. Kings and Nobles in Late Medieval Portugal* (Cambridge).

_____ . (forthcoming), 'The inner quarters of the king's heart: the language of proxemics in late medieval European courts'.

Dakhlia, J. (1995), 'La question des lieux-communs. Des modèles de souveraineté dans l'Islam méditerranéen', in B. Lepetit (ed.), *Les Formes de l'Expérience* (Paris).

_____ . (1998), *Le Divan des Rois. Le politique et le religieux dans l'Islam* (Paris).

Dean, T. (1994), 'Le corti. Un problema storiografico', in G. Chittolini, A. Molho and P. Schiera (eds), *Origini dello Stato. Processi di formazione statale in Italia fra Medioevo ed Età Moderna* (Bologna).

Deyermond, A. (1985), 'The Libro de los engaños: its Social and Literary Context', in G. Burgess and R. Taylor (eds), *The Spirit of the Court. Proceedings of the Fourth Congress of the International Courtly Literature Society* (Cambridge), pp. 158–67.

Dickens, A.G. (ed) (1977), *The Courts of Europe. Politics, Patronage and Royalty, 1400–1800* (London).

Duindam, J. (1995), *Myths of Power: Norbert Elias and the Early Modern European Court* (Amsterdam).

Duindam, J. (2003), *Vienna and Versailles. The Courts of Europe's Dynastic Rivals, 1550–1780* (Cambridge).

Eis, G. (1967), *Mittelalterliche Fachliteratur* (Stuttgart).

Elias, N. (1982), *State Formation and Civilization* (Oxford).

_____ . (1983), *The Court Society* (Oxford).

_____ . (1991), *The Society of Individuals* (Oxford).

Farge, A. (1997), *Des Lieux pour l'Histoire* (Paris).

Forcione, A.K. (1997), 'At the threshold of modernity: Gracián's El Criticón', in N. Spadaccini and J. Talens (eds), *Rhetoric and Politics. Baltasar Gracián and the New World Order* (Minneapolis), pp. 3–70.

Gambin, F. (1990), 'Saber y supervivencia. Anotaciones sobre el concepto de persona en Baltasar Gracián', in A. Heredia Soriano (ed.), *Actas del VII Seminario de Historia de la Filosofía Española y Iberoamericana* (Salamanca), pp. 369–80.

_____ . (1992), 'Las traducciones al italiano del Oráculo Manual y Arte de Prudencia de Baltasar Gracián', *Actas del VII Seminario de Historia de la Filosofía Española e Iberoamericana* (Salamanca), pp. 287–303.

Gordon, D. (1994), *Citizens without Sovereignty. Equality and Sociability in French Thought, 1670–1789* (Princeton).

Gracián, B. (2001), *Obras Completas*, L. Sánchez Laílla (ed.) (Madrid).

Hampsher-Monk, I. (2002), 'From Virtue to Politeness' in Q. Skinner and M. Van Gelderen (eds), *Republicanism. A Shared European Heritage* (Cambridge), vol. 2, pp. 85–106.

Haro Cortès, M. (1995), *Los Compendios de Castigos del siglo XIII: técnicas narrativas y contenido ético* (Valencia).

Hinz, M. (1999), 'Mentire con la verità. Baltasar Gracián e Juan Manuel', *Annali di Storia Moderna e Contemporanea*, 5, pp. 43–64.

Hoyo, A. del (1967), *Obras Completas de Baltasar Gracián* (Madrid).

Jaeger, C.S. (1985), *The Origins of Courtliness. Civilizing Trends and the Formation of Courtly Ideals, 939–1210* (Philadelphia).

_____ . (1994), *The Envy of Angels. Cathedral Schools and Social Ideals in Medieval Europe, 950–1200* (Philadelphia).

Kasten, L.A. (1934), 'Several Observations Concerning *Lo libre de saviesa* Attributed to James I of Aragon', *Hispanic Review*, 2, pp. 70–73.

Kerscher, G. (2000), *Architektur als Repräsentation. Spätmittelalterliche Palastbaukunst swischen Pracht und zeremoniellen Voraussetzungen: Avignon-Mallorca-Kirchenstaat* (Tübingen).

Kiesel, H. (1979), *'Bei Hof, bei Höll'. Untersuchungen zur literarischen Hofkritik von Sebastian Brant bis Friedrich Schiller* (Tübingen).

Kinkade, R.P. (1972), 'Sancho IV: puente literario entre Alfonso el Sabio y Juan Manuel', *Publications of the Modern Language Association*, 87, pp. 1039–51.

Klein, L. (1990), 'Politeness in Seventeenth-century England and France' in *Cahiers du Dix-Septième Siècle*, 4, pp. 97–100.

Knox, D. (1991), ' "*Disciplina*": the Monastic and Clerical Origins of European Civility', in J. Monfasani and R.G. Musto (eds), *Renaissance Society and Culture. Essays in honour of Eugene Rice Jr* (New York).

Kramer, S.R. and C.W. Bynum (2002), 'Revisiting the Twelfth-century Individual. The Inner Self and the Christian Community', in G. Melville and M. Schuerer (eds), *Das Eigene und das Ganze: zum Individuellen im mittelalterlichen Religiosentum* (Münster), pp. 57–85.

LeRoy Ladurie, E. (1983), 'Auprès du Roi, la Cour', *Annales. Économies, Sociétés. Civilisations*, 38, 1 pp. 21–41.

LeRoy Ladurie, E. and J-F. Fitou (1997), *Saint-Simon ou le Système de la Cour* (Paris).

Llabres y Quintana, G. (1898), *Libre de paraules e dits dels savis e filòsofs* (Palma de Mallorca).

Malti-Douglas, F. (1985), *Structures of Avarice: the Bukhalâ in Medieval Arabic Literature* (Leiden).

_____ . (1997), 'Playing with the Sacred: Religious Intertext in Adab Discourse', in *Humanism, Culture and Language in the Near East. Studies in Honour of Georg Krotkoff* (Winona Lake), pp. 51–9.

Mansau, A. (1993), 'Recepción/traducción de Gracián en Francia', in J. Ayala (ed.), *Baltasar Gracián. Selección de estudios, investigación actual y documentación* (Barcelona), pp. 87–93.

Manzalaoui, M. (1974), 'The Pseudo-Aristotelian *Kitâb Sirr al'asrâr*', *Oriens*, 23–24, pp. 174–257.

Maravall, J.A. (1975), 'Antropología y política en el pensamiento de Gracián', (first published in 1958), in *Estudios de Historia del Pensamiento Español, III – Siglo XVII* (Madrid), pp. 197–241.

_____. (1983), 'La cortesia como saber en la Edad Media', in *Estudios de Historia del Pensamiento Español, I – Edad Media* (Madrid), pp. 255–67.

Martin, J. (1997), 'Inventing Sincerity, Refashioning Prudence: the Discovery of the Individual in Renaissance Europe', *The American Historical Review*, 102, pp. 1309–42.

Menéndez Pidal, R. (1972), 'De Alfonso a los dos Juanes. Auge y culminación del didactismo (1252–1370)', in *Studia Hispanica in honorem Rafael Lapesa*, vol. 1, (Madrid), pp. 63–83.

Moreira de Sá, A. (ed.) (1960), *Segredos dos Segredos. Tradução portuguesa segundo um manuscrito inédito do século XV* (Lisbon).

Ong, P. (2001), *Openness, Secrecy, Authorship: Technical Arts and the Culture of Knowledge from Antiquity to Renaissance* (Baltimore).

Palacios Martin, B. (1995), Sobre la redacción y difusión de las 'Ordinacions' de Pedro IV de Aragón y sus primeros códices, *Anuario de Estudios Medievales*, 25, pp. 659–81.

Pelegrin, B. (1988), 'Gracián, admirateur pirate de Don Juan Manuel', *Bulletin Hispanique*, 90, pp. 197–214.

Pocock, J.G.A. (1987), 'The Concept of a Language and the *métier d'historien*: Some Considerations on Practice', in A. Pagden (ed.), *The Languages of Political Theory in Early Modern Europe* (Cambridge), pp. 19–38.

Prosperi, A. (1980), 'Libri sulla corte ed experienze curiali nel primo '500 italiano', in A. Prosperi (ed.), *La Corte e il Cortegiano*. Vol II – *Un modello europeo* (Rome), pp. 69–91.

Quondam, A. (1980), 'La "forma del vivere". Schede per l'analisi del discorso cortigiano', in A. Prosperi (ed.), *La Corte e il Cortegiano* (Rome), pp. 15–68.

_____. (2000), 'Tipologie culturali del Gentiluomo di Antico Regime. Polemichette e Notarelle a proposito di una nuova edizione del *Libro del Cortegiano*', in *Questo povero Cortegiano. Castiglione, il Libro, la Storia* (Rome), pp. 545–602.

Rosenthal, F. (1961), 'Al-Mubashshir ibn Fâtik: Prolegomena to an Abortive Edition', *Oriens*, pp. 13–14.

Ryan, W.F. and Ch. B. Schmitt (eds.) (1982), *Pseudo-Aristotle The Secret of Secrets. Sources and Influences* (London).

Sahlins, M., (1985), *Islands of History,* University of Chicago Press.

Scaglione, A. (1991), *Knights at Court. Courtliness, Chivalry and Courtesy from Ottonian Germany to the Italian Renaissance* (Berkeley, Los Angeles and Oxford).

Schena, O. (1983), *Le Leggi Palatine di Pietro IV di Aragona* (Cagliari).

Schena, O. and J. Trenchs (1990), 'Le leggi palatine di Giacomo III di Maiorca nella corte di Pietro IV d'Aragona', *XIII Congreso de Historia de la Corona de Aragón. Comunicaciones – III* (Palma de Mallorca) pp. 111–119.

Simmel, G. (1971), *On Individuality and Social Forms* (Chicago).

Skinner, Q. (2002), 'Introduction', in Q. Skinner and M. Van Gelderen (eds), *Republicanism. A Shared European Heritage* (Cambridge) vol. 1, pp. 1–8.

Smith, P. (1966), *The Anti-Courtier Trend in Sixteenth-Century French Literature* (Genève).

Struever, N. (1970), *The Language of History in the Renaissance* (Princeton).

Uhlig, C. (1973), *Hofkritik im England des Mittelalters und der Renaissance. Studien zu einem Gemeinplatz der europäischen Moralistik* (Berlin and New York).

Vale, M. (2001), *The Princely Court. Medieval Courts and Culture in North-West Europe* (Oxford).

Vasoli, C. (1980), 'Il cortegiano, il diplomatico, il principe (riflessioni su "Il Libro del Cortegiano")', in *La Cultura delle Corti* (Bologna), pp. 64–87.

Velema, W. (2002), 'That a Republic is Better than a Monarchy: Anti-monarchism in Early Modern Dutch Political Thought', in Skinner and Van Gelderen, *Republicanism*, vol. 1, pp. 9–25.

Villari, R. (1987), *Elogio della dissimulazione. La lotta politica nel Seicento* (Bari).

Winterling, A. (1997), 'Hof. Versuch einer idealtypischen Bestimmung anhand der mittelalterlichen und fruhneuzeitlichen Geschichte', in A. Winterling (ed.), *Zwischen 'Haus' und 'Staat'. Antike Höfe im Vergleich, Historische Zeitschrift. Beihefte-Band 23* (München).

Chapter 8

Rites of Passage and the Grand Tour
Discovering, Imagining and Inventing European Civilization in the Age of Enlightenment

Robert Wokler

In the Middle Ages the diverse peoples of Europe could have imagined themselves drawn together, both theologically and politically, by their shared Christian faith and the vestiges of an imperial polity marked by the absence of internal frontiers. While their multiple allegiances were often in conflict, at least the appearance of an overarching framework that united them could be articulated in the common language of their diplomats, priests and professors. But with the Reformation and its attendant wars of religion, together with the dynasties whose authority was consolidated in the sixteenth and seventeenth centuries, that European community, defined by Western Christendom, collapsed and was throughout this period progressively replaced by institutions heralding the advent of the modern nation-state and its philosophies of *ragione di stato*. The Treaty of Westphalia of 1648 which ended the Thirty Years' War consecrated the territorial sovereignty and independence of the states and empires of which fragmented Europe had come to be comprised, putting paid to papal claims of transnational supremacy. The Treaty of Utrecht of 1713 likewise brought to an end the ambitions of universal empire that might have been entertained by Louis XIV of France. Thereafter Europe seemed destined, politically, to be no more than a confederation of states, wherein peace might be negotiated only through alliances formed by its separate members, such as were envisaged in the Age of Enlightenment by the abbé de Saint-Pierre, Rousseau and Kant and which, after the Second World War, came to be enshrined in the European Community.[1]

In the course of the eighteenth century these political developments were nevertheless accompanied by economic and cultural changes which helped to foster an image of European integration such as had been unknown in its early modern history connected with the establishment and evolution of separate states, religions and languages. With the advent and triumph of commercial society in Western and Northern Europe, the infrastructure of traffic within the continent, including the network of roads, rivers and canals that lubricated both internal and external trade, was improved on a scale not witnessed since the age of the Antonine emperors. Relative peace and prosperity and the absence of epidemic disease spurred substantial growth of the populations of European cities, where vastly improved rates of literacy nurtured scientific and humanistic academies and through a burgeoning book trade extended the influence as never before of Europe's international republic of letters. In the mid-eighteenth century the term *civilization* came for the first time to acquire its modern meaning as a progressive force in opposition to barbarism, which in the Age of Enlightenment was also associated with Christendom's legacy – the Crusades, the Inquisition, the St Bartholomew's Day Massacre and the Revocation of the Edict of Nantes- whose fundamentalist spirit of fanaticism could now be regarded as Europe's middle-aged immaturity or retrogression from its Greek and Roman ideals.[2]

In opposing the Augustinian doctrine of original sin and the mysteries of revealed religions, writers and philosophers of the eighteenth century joined a conception of mankind's reason and perfectibility to a veneration of Europe's ancient cultures, whose fresh efflorescence in the Renaissance was deemed to have marked a new dawn of human history after a thousand benighted years of obscurantist priestcraft and feudal oppression. That dawn had proved shortlived, however, largely because its achievements in recovering the arts and philosophy of ancient Rome, and in paying tribute to and attempting to revitalize the political institutions and values of the Roman Republic in particular, had been obscured by forces generated quite independently of the Renaissance and in a different part of Europe but which came to be felt at the same time and were marked by an attachment to an altogether different Rome, that is, of Pauline and Augustinian Christianity. The Reformation and the Counter-Reformation together turned the culture of Europe away from classicism and instead towards the theology of an otherworldly pilgrimage unsuited, in both the Renaissance and the Enlightenment, to recover the tangible treasures of ancient Rome before they had been tarnished by Christianity.

Europe's religious wars of the sixteenth and seventeenth centuries seemed to cosmopolitan tourists of the eighteenth century to be sectarian reversions to the dark ages of medievalism which the Renaissance had confronted but not overcome. Worse still for such tourists, the principal universities of Europe had, in the course of the previous two centuries, by and large abandoned many of their earlier functions as progressive seats of learning in order, rather, to consolidate the strictures of the orthodox theologies of their day. By the mid-eighteenth century their role as institutions for the ordination and instruction of clerics, especially in Italy, France and England, made them appear conservative bastions within closed ideological borders, in need of lifting in an age of grand tourism that provided an alternative map of the more expansive and engaging mind of Europe as a whole, designed to complete the education of young gentlemen once released from the clutches of their university tutors. In many respects, the itinerary of the Grand Tour offered a programme of postgraduate studies which aimed to lift the veil of ignorance of an undergraduate curriculum that embraced classical languages but not the civilizations that had produced them. To the benighted theologies of the universities of Oxford, Cambridge and Paris, it provided both liberation and the promise of a countercultural experience, substituting travel, a comparative anthropology of modern Europe's inhabitants and curiosity in the relics of Europe's achievements before the advent of Christianity in its most sectarian forms, to the interpretation of Scripture and doctrines. Already in the seventeenth century the scholar James Howell had portrayed foreign travel as 'a *moving* Academy, or the true *Perpatetic Schoole*',[3] and by the eighteenth century tourism formed a central part of the education of inquisitive thinkers and writers, for which 'a restless curiosity' in pursuit of even 'the most doubtful promise of entertainment or instruction', was essential to a traveller, remarked Edward Gibbon, adding that 'the arts of common life are not studied in the closet'.[4] In cultivating their minds, freed from the trappings of both ignorance and barbarism, tourists of the Age of Enlightenment sought to retrace what they took to be European civilization's roots, sources and tributaries. In inspecting the monuments of both classical architecture and Renaissance art, they were not only modernity's amateur archaeologists determined to preserve Europe's ancient relics and treasures. They were also modernity's secular pilgrims, embarked on journeys to civilization's holy land to pay it their devotion at its most genuinely as opposed to obscurantist sacred sites.[5]

Tourists of one denomination or another had been in great abundance in European history before the eighteenth century, and many of the motives that had inspired travellers in medieval and early modern Europe – diplomacy, commerce, adventure and, especially outside Europe, missionary zeal and anthropological curiosity – remained widely prevalent. If the practice of inviting predominantly French philosophers to grace the court or tutor the children of enlightened monarchs in Europe's hinterland became almost commonplace in the late eighteenth century, this convergence of philosophy with kingship along lines promoted in Plato's Republic was not unprecedented. However much we might associate that practice with enlightened despotism – a term employed by Diderot himself in his *Mémoires pour Catherine II*[6] – his own presence at the court of Catherine, or Voltaire's at Frederick's, or Condillac's in Parma, had been prefigured in the seventeenth century by Descartes's and Pufendorf's invitations to Stockholm. In the Age of Enlightenment, travellers' tales, either of real or imaginary journeys, became an established literary form, not only of exoticism but above all as a means of self-inspection, whereby fictitious foreigners drawn from beyond Europe's borders might be granted insights into the character of Europeans themselves, as in Marana's *Espion turc* or Montesquieu's *Lettres persanes*.[7] But perhaps the most striking differences between grand tourism in the eighteenth century and journeys undertaken by earlier travellers revolve around the conceptions of civilization which inspired eighteenth-century voyagers to retrace Europe's origins and partake of its most glorious antiquity.[8]

Most if not all of them came from the Protestant north and west of Europe, already identified in the eighteenth century, not least by Montesquieu himself, with the spirit of both modern liberty and enterprise. The great majority journeyed south to Catholic France and Italy, occasionally embracing Switzerland as well. In embarking on the Grand Tour they sought to complete their education by retracing the lineage of their own world, whose ancient and Renaissance ideals and standards of taste inspired what they regarded as the best of contemporary culture. 'The noblest prospect which a Scotchman ever sees', Dr Johnson famously remarked, 'is the high road that leads him to London', but he supposed London and England more generally to be just the modern executors of civilization's literary and philosophical inheritance. 'A man who has not been in Italy, is always conscious of an inferiority', Johnson added, for 'the grand object of travelling is to see the shores of the Mediterranean'.[9] Although other tourists, like the splenetic Tobias Smollett, might prefer to report on the nature of France's and Italy's contemporary inhabitants than to savour their monuments,[10] most shared Johnson's awe as first-hand witnesses of Continental Europe's achievements. For much of the mid- to late-seventeenth century and throughout the eighteenth century, the Grand Tour was largely conceived, by those who embarked on it, as a peripatetic *cours de civilisation européenne*. While in some instances French, the pre-eminent grand tourists were above all Englishmen, Germans and Scandinavians, and their principal urban destinations were, in the north of France, Paris, and in the south, Nice, Montpellier, Aix and Arles, followed by, in Italy, Genoa, Turin, Venice, Florence, Naples and Rome. If they travelled eastwards from England or south from Scandinavia, for the most part on separate journeys often though not always undertaken by different tourists, they were drawn as well as to the imperial capitals of Berlin and Vienna, perhaps even more to the splendours of Prague, Leipzig and Dresden, or to the smaller and architecturally more compact university towns of Göttingen or Jena. From all directions they were drawn as well to Amsterdam, Rotterdam and The Hague in the United Provinces and to Antwerp, Brussels and Louvain in the Austrian Netherlands. In central Europe grand tourists frequently journeyed by pleasure boats down both the Rhine and the Danube, whose attractions included not only the fashionable spas sprinkled on the shores of the region's two most illustrious rivers but also, particularly along the Rhine, some of Europe's most visually agreeable landscapes. Tourists for whom the rugged delights of nature surpassed those of culture at its best, occasionally travelled by way of Lyon and Grenoble across the Alps into Switzerland on expeditions to the glaciers of Chamonix, but even the hardiest among them, if they had the right connections, were characteristically pleased still more by the domestic charms, comforts and conversation they might be invited to enjoy at Voltaire's house at Ferney near Geneva.

En route to Paris, if they embarked from the south of England and travelled across the Channel by way of Dover and Calais, they might pause to visit the castle of the Prince de Condé at Chantilly, not so much to admire its Gothic splendour as to inspect its elegant formal gardens, festooned with fountains and waterfalls and decorated with aviaries filled with ornamental birds. At the Benedictine abbey of

Figure 8.1 Genoa, Palazzo Ducale, facade. (Archivio Alinari, Florence).

Saint-Denis, they could behold the crown of Charlemagne, Virgil's mirror, the shoulder bone of St. John the Baptist, a box containing some of the Blessed Virgin's hair and 'other sacred toys', including a crucifix carved by Pope Clement III from Christ's original cross and a reliquary which the friar who conducted them would have tourists 'believe was stained by the natural blood of our Saviour', remarked a sceptical John Evelyn in his diary.[11] At the great Palais de Versailles, they might be disappointed at the small rooms which hardly failed to conceal its overall 'pompous appearance' as reported by Horace Walpole, who initially travelled there in 1739 in the company of the poet Thomas Gray, an assessment echoed by Arthur Young not long before the outbreak of the Revolution.[12] If they judged some of its waterworks childish they could still admire the grandeur of Versailles' formal gardens designed by André Le Nôtre, however, and if they travelled down the Seine to Saint-Cloud or up to Fontainebleau they were almost invariably dazzled by graceful buildings and cultivated landscapes of a quality and character that Versailles lacked. Perhaps their favourite among the royal chateaux in the vicinity of Paris, however, was that of Marly-le-roi, where Louis XIV and Madame de Maintenon had built a palatial retreat called l'Ermitage and there entertained King James II of England after his enforced abdication. As reported by the Duc de Saint-Simon in his *Mémoires*, Marly's lakes had once been stocked with pedigree carp, and for much of the eighteenth century classics of the French theatre like Molière's *Le Bourgeois gentilhomme* were staged in its gardens in the presence of the king's courtiers and foreign tourists alike.

Marly was destroyed in the course of the French Revolution, although some of its treasures, and particularly its sculptures, survived and are still on display in the Louvre and elsewhere in Paris.

In Paris, once ensconced at the Hôtel Anjou in the Faubourg St Germain or perhaps in a furnished room or apartment nearby such as Edward Gibbon rented in 1763, the tourist would relish the glorious gardens of the Luxembourg, the Palais Royal and the Tuileries. He or indeed she would delight in the air among the windmills of Montmartre and, above all, bask in wonder at the spires, domes, turrets and friezes of that city's grandest monuments – Notre Dame, the Invalides, the Sorbonne and the Louvre. Already in the eighteenth century the Seine wended its sinuous path through Paris between banks which displayed its architectural glories to greater dramatic effect than the Thames flowing through London, and to visitors also acquainted with the rivers of Central Europe its bridges seemed as elegant as those that crossed Prague. It was also in Paris, above all other destinations on the Grand Tour, that European travellers endeavoured to perfect their command of the French language, which in the Age of Enlightenment serviced the interests of diplomacy and even successfully competed with Latin as the international republic of letters' principal medium of exchange, and it was in Paris as well that they cultivated the standards of taste – in dress, dining, comportment and conversation – that had come to be deemed most appropriate to polite society. Nowhere else in Europe were civilization's refinements more conspicuously displayed in *bonnes manières*. Not every tourist, however, was captivated by the sights or fragrance of France's capital, and virtually none were impressed by the integrity of the tailors, hatters and tradesmen who fitted them with the silk, velvet and stockings required to make the right impression within fashionable society, so sharply contrasted with the ragged bustle outside. 'The charms of Paris have not the least attraction for me', remarked Walpole on a much later visit to France. 'It is the ugliest, beastly town in the universe,' he added,[13] forever complaining of its filthy river, devilish inhabitants, narrow streets with virtually identical houses and barbarous cold worse than London's. On no other matter apart from their shared contempt for Paris would Walpole and Rousseau ever agree, but at least Walpole was spared Rousseau's ignominious fate in being buried there.

From Paris they would journey south along the Rhône, either by carriage or boat on the lengthiest and most arduous stage of their journey only pausing briefly to rest or shop in Lyon, until they reached the elegant and flourishing resort of Nice or the more vulgar attractions of the port of Marseilles. The Côte d'Azur, however, was not yet the haven for rich foreigners which it would become in the nineteenth and twentieth centuries, and tourists who travelled to the Mediterranean coast to escape the cold winters of England or Germany preferred the Provençal air of Aix, with its fountains around which they could stroll in greater comfort than those of Paris, and even more of Arles, whose ruins and antiquities offered them a French foretaste of Rome. The climate and waters of Montpellier, too, were deemed salubrious, and tourists who sought other distractions might be drawn there even more by the conviviality of students who flocked to the most progressive university in eighteenth-century France, where they could engage in wider pursuits less circumscribed by

Figure 8.2 Marly, air view of the chateau and gardens. This painting is in the museum (chateau) at Versailles. (Bridgeman Art Library, London).

theologians than was so often the case in Paris. From Nice tourists would proceed to Genoa in Italy, either by boat from Marseilles hugging a shoreline often foraged by pirates, or along the still sometimes treacherous coastal road where they might instead be at the mercy of bandits.

In Genoa eighteenth-century tourists could, together with the Président Charles de Brosses or Mrs Piozzi, the former Helen Thrale, admire that city's glorious harbour and the fine palaces surrounding it, among them the Palazzo Ducale designed in the late eighteenth century by Simone Cantone. Some, however, who had learnt a refined Italian described by Howell as a *lingua Toscana in boca Romana*,[14] found the native Genoese less receptive to their skills than they hoped or might even, like the diminutive Mrs. Piozzi herself, be agitated by street urchins who would clasp her knees and rummage for her purse even while she was carried aloft in a chair. That mode of transport, as well as coaches and carriages, seemed in abundance in the principal Italian cities of the north, unlike the south where even the rich perambulated on foot. In Turin, in particular, a distinguished citizen's reputation

Figure 8.3 Turin, Palazzo Reale, Chinese Room. (Bridgeman Art Library, London).

might be ruined if he were seen strolling without a chair through its elegant public squares, and the etiquette which there required that even sightseers' feet be firmly planted in the air led tourists like the botanist James Edward Smith to lament the haughtiness and ceremonious dress of the inhabitants of this capital of Piedmont who would not make social visits to their superiors without wearing a sword or clutching a *chapeau de bras*.[15] However precious and dull its natives, Turin's wide avenues and grand buildings, many built in the early eighteenth century after the French siege of 1706, were regarded by most tourists as impressive, none more perhaps than the Palazzo Reale whose rococo interiors seemed even more extravagant than the splendours of the palace of Marly.

Turin was definitely worth a visit for the grand tourist, but a long stay there was thought ill-advised. After Genoa it was a detour and comfortable stopover on the leisurely route to Italy's jewel in the crown on the Adriatic coast, that is, Venice – the most admired and most often painted of all European cities in the eighteenth century, as it remains the most frequently visited in the world today. In Venice, tourists could luxuriate in appreciation of the Ponte di Rialto and the Palladian fronts to the churches of Santa Lucia, San Giorgio Maggiore and San Francesco della Vigna, all the while in awe at the sight not only of the Grand Canal and the Doge's Palace but also the glories of Veronese, Titian and Tintoretto lodged within the great monuments of a modern republic whose constitution had already survived longer than that of ancient Rome. Few paintings better display the political pageantry that this republic could still mount in the mid-eighteenth century after three hundred

Figure 8.4 Canaletto, 'Reception of the French Ambassador in Venice'. This painting is in the Hermitage in St.Petersburg. (Bridgeman Art Library, London).

Figure 8.5 Johann Zoffany, 'The Tribuna of the Uffizi'. The painting belongs to H.M. Queen Elizabeth II.

years of decay than the portrayal, by Canaletto, of the reception of the French Ambassador in 1742, later acquired by Catherine II of Russia and now lodged at the Hermitage in St Petersburg. Absent from this picture, because he would only be appointed a year later, is the Ambassador's secretary, one Jean-Jacques Rousseau.

In Florence, which enchanted Walpole as much as Paris had disgusted him, visitors could appreciate the treasures of the Pitti Palace and the Uffizi Gallery, including pictures or sculptures of Raphael, Rubens or Michelangeo such as are depicted by Zoffany, himself an eighteenth-century grand tourist, in his painting of the Tribuna of the Uffizi. If they wished to admire the marbles of Florence they could choose between Donatello's David in the Bargello and Michelangelo's now in the Accademia, not forgetting Michelangelo's equally celebrated Pietà Palestrina nearby. If they felt disinclined to linger too long in the mausoleum of the Medici they could behold the glistening villas, vineyards and olive groves on the surrounding hills or steal a glimpse of the Duomo round a bend of the via Boccaccio as students attending the European University Institute in San Domenico di Fiesole may still do today if they stroll to the city after their classes. With the other major towns of Tuscany so much relished by visitors today – Pistoia, Sienna, even Pisa -grand tourists of the seventeenth and eighteenth century were relatively unimpressed. Such towns were considered too conspicuously medieval, their narrow streets, broken pavements and grated windows cramped by a gloomy insularity that contrasted with the lush expansiveness of the hills outside. Of my own favourite small Italian city, Lucca, they might well have thought the same as Hobbes, who in the twenty-first chapter of his *Leviathan* had remarked that from 'the word LIBERTAS' inscribed on that republic's turrets no man can infer that there is more liberty there than in Constantinople.[16]

Naples, in the eighteenth century the largest town in Italy and by common consent the most beguiling, dazzled tourists not only on account of its vast monuments, castles, colonnades and magnificent outlook on the sea, but perhaps above all because of the exuberance and vitality of its people, then and now forever in the streets, engaged in virtually endless dramas even more captivating than those on the stage of the San Carlo and other Neapolitan theatres. While Florentine Italians often portrayed Naples as a paradise inhabited by devils, visitors from abroad, like Goethe as he recounts in his *Italienische Reise*, were besotted and intoxicated by its charms, of an openness such as to make the capital of the world at the base of the Tiber, which he had visited earlier, seem instead like a cloister built on a poor site.[17] To these delights, for those who did not wish to forget the history of civilization that had drawn them there, a certain gravitas was added in the Age of Enlightenment by the excavations begun at Pompeii and Herculaneum or by Virgil's tomb.

As distinct from Naples but more like Paris, Rome was often judged a mixed blessing by tourists, struck as they were by the contrast between the magnificence of St Peter's or the Vatican Museum on the one hand, and on the other the narrow streets of crowded houses, suffused with the smell of garlic, which gave eighteenth-century Rome the appearance of an unworthy offspring of its imperial past. To foreign observers its natives were not remotely so entrancing as the Neapolitans, and as de

Brosses records, uncharitably, a quarter of the figures one might see in its streets were statues, another quarter were priests and yet another did virtually nothing at all.[18] But if modern Rome lacked civilization's delights, its antiquities – even in the eighteenth century when the Coliseum had come to be filled by warrens and sheds for domestic animals and the Forum was divided into stalls for a twice-weekly market – surpassed in splendour those which survived anywhere else in the world. There could have been no more enthusiastic or better-informed guide to Rome's ancient treasures than Winckelmann, who in 1763 was appointed superintendent of Roman antiquities and for the next five years until his untimely death in Trieste guided Wilkes, Boswell and other notable visitors to Rome on their tours. Chief among the men inspired by his learning and the awe he felt himself for the civilization that had been Rome's was Gibbon, who after a sleepless night in 1764, as he reports, hastened to the ruins of the Forum and, noting every spot where Romulus had stood, Cicero had spoken or Caesar fell, embarked on his history of the *Decline and Fall of the Roman Empire*.[19] With Winckelmann and Gibbon together in Rome, the Grand Tour – conceived as bearing witness, through its ancient monuments, to the history of Western civilization itself – achieved its eighteenth-century apotheosis.

The journey south from Protestant England and Germany to Catholic France and then Italy and thereby to Europe's pagan and pre-Christian roots was not, however, conceived as embracing European civilization in all its rich diversity; seldom did grand tourists for whom a first-hand grasp of at least the remnants of that history could be described as their chief objective stray far in their pilgrimage from the paths pursued by Evelyn, Gibbon, Johnson or Goethe. Although agents of Lord Arundel, the Duke of Buckingham and, later, William Petty scavenged Greek antiquities in the seventeenth century, and while the classicists Jacob Spon and George Wheler journeyed there to investigate ancient inscriptions, until the end of the eighteenth century travellers to Greece rarely included tourists, who would instead arrive in great numbers only after they had been stirred by the imagery of poets such as Byron in *Don Juan* and, following Byron's death, of romantic enthusiasts of Greek nationalism in the nineteenth century. Ancient Athens might have been the school of Hellas and, thus, when it was absorbed by the Roman Republic in the course of the Macedonian Wars, the fount that inspired Rome as well and, through Rome, gave birth to Western civilization's literature, philosophy and some of its civic ideals. By way of Pope's translations of both the *Iliad* and *Odyssey* tourists of the Age of Enlightenment could draw inspiration from not only classical but even pre-classical Greece, and through the Society of Dilettanti which a number of aristocratic tourists had formed in London in 1734 and which would eventually inspire the foundation of the Royal Academy, their interest in ancient art and antiquities eventually turned from Italian to Greek culture.[20] A two-year archaeological and architectural expedition to Greece came to be launched in 1751 by the Society, which thereby established itself as the principal sponsor of Stuart's and Revett's (ultimately) five-volume *Antiquities of Athens* of 1762–1830,[21] and from 1764 to 1766 the Oxford don and historian of Troy, Richard Chandler, set out to tour both Greece and Asia Minor under the aegis of the Society.[22]

But while perhaps moved by the same ambitions as had stirred so many travellers to Italy throughout the Age of Enlightenment, this venture in the domain of scholarship and erudition provided no spur to grand tourism in Greece. Unless they also happened to be professional archaeologists, architects or historians, eighteenth-century enthusiasts of Homer, Thucydides, Plato and democracy by and large sought only to recover that Greek legacy in their imagination and did not set out to cross the Balkans or discover, in the Levant, the remains of a world that had for centuries belonged to the Ottoman Turks. In the early nineteenth century, when the British ambassador to Constantinople took it upon himself to rescue fragments of the Parthenon frieze, he forsook the example of Winckelmann, Gibbon and other tourists of the Age of Enlightenment, looting it instead and transporting it to Scotland in the manner of Napoleon's imperialist theft from Egypt of the Rosetta Stone. That relic of an even more ancient civilization than the Parthenon frieze, in turn, was surrendered to the British for whom it became a trophy and, together with the Elgin Marbles plundered from Athens, is now lodged in the British Museum.

Nor did grand tourists of the eighteenth century cross the Pyrenees to Spain. The frontiers of European civilization which they breached had already drawn Western European travellers to Russia by the 1720s and would by the 1770s prompt them to travel to Scandinavia, still later inspiring the great project of Edward Daniel Clarke, beginning in 1799 when he was initially accompanied by Robert Malthus and others, to open the vista of civilization to Nordic and Oriental no less than to mainstream Occidental readings.[23] The history of late eighteenth-century anthropology (when the term first acquired its modern meaning as the science of human nature) owes perhaps as much to such literature as, in a somewhat earlier period, to Jesuit and other commentaries on the peoples of China and New World Amerindians. But comparative and synchronic studies of the diverse populations and races which comprise our species did not, and perhaps could not, take the same form as diachronic accounts of the roots of Western civilization, from which point of view it might have been thoughtlessly supposed, by northern Europe's grand tourists, that the glories of Spanish culture, at their height in the fifteenth and sixteenth centuries, had come to be superseded by the achievements of other European peoples. For the same reason that eighteenth-century (and indeed later) philosophers judged that there was no Spanish Enlightenment, travellers of the period setting out on the Grand Tour displayed hardly any enthusiasm for the attractions of Spain or for Spanish thinkers or writers apart from Cervantes, even though their precursors in the seventeenth century, sometimes guided by Howell,[24] had been drawn there when it was still one of the jewels in the firmament of European Christendom.

They did, however, travel to Switzerland, often on the same journeys as they made to France and Italy, but not for the same reasons. Most tourists to Switzerland had scant interest in tracing civilization's trajectory, still less in uncovering its classical roots. Switzerland appealed to them instead because it was, by and large, civilization's opposite, the uncouth state of nature most accessible to Europeans, such as Rousseau – cultivated society's fiercest enemy in the Age of Enlightenment – had so romantically portrayed. It was from Chamonix in 1760 that the philosopher Horace

Bénédict de Saussure resolved to scale Mont Blanc, while from the inns soon afterwards established not only at Chamonix but also Grindelwald and Lauterbrunnen leisurely tourists were enabled to study alpine plants, and more adventurous hikers, like Wordsworth, could manage to negotiate mountain passes without having to camp overnight in the snow. Since it had come to be widely supposed by persons who reflected on such matters that mankind had not sinfully stumbled in his original state but had on the contrary risen from it, scaling mountainous heights might indeed be deemed compatible with human progress, requiring as it did so many of civilization's artefacts, including barometers, quadrants, compasses, ropes and heavy shoes, none of which, however, managed to save Walpole's spaniel, which he had ill-advisedly brought to the Alps for company, when it was consumed by a wolf.

The Low Countries and the Hapsburg and Prussian territories of Central Europe attracted tourists' interest as well, offering, by contrast with the antiquities of the south and the wilderness of the Alps, glimpses of the efflorescence of European culture in its most golden age of modernity before the rise of both England and France. They were filled with awe at the sight not only of Amsterdam's magnificent Guildhall, the mansions of the Keizersgracht, the Noorderkerk and other Protestant churches and the Sephardic Synagogue, but also at the bustle of traffic along and beside its glorious canals. Here they found a city, luxuriating in its commerce, still virtually in its prime, relishing a period of ascendancy of far closer historical proximity than Rome's, seeming more even than the port of London in the eighteenth century to form the gateway to the world. In Rotterdam they were enchanted not only by buildings scarcely less opulent but by the splendid panorama of its waterfront, the Boompjes, and by the humanist spirit of the northern Renaissance which Erasmus had bequeathed to it, destined in each case to be ground into dust by the Luftwaffe in May 1940. In The Hague they could relish the Mauritshuis and especially the Ridderzaal, one of the glories of medieval European architecture, as well as gawk at the cabinet of curiosities in the collection of the Prince of Orange. If they sought further evidence of Holland's contribution to the civilization of modern Europe, they would not fail to visit the sumptuous royal palace and baroque gardens of Het Loo, the charming harbour of Dordrecht or the university towns of Utrecht and especially Leiden, in the eighteenth century perhaps the most progressive seat of higher education anywhere in the world, to which scholars and students from all corners of Europe flocked. Nor would they forget to inspect the collections of the Holbeins, van Dyck, Rubens, Rembrandt and Vermeer which formed the supreme treasures of Dutch art. Proceeding south to the Austrian Netherlands they would be drawn to the quieter civility of Antwerp, the exquisite Grand'Place and Théâtre Royal de la Monnaie of Brussels and the Gothic Hôtel de Ville of Louvain, in the eighteenth century also a vibrant and flourishing centre of learning.

Berlin's and Vienna's architectural delights were more manifestly imperial than most of the fine buildings in the principal cities of the Low Countries, while for many tourists of the Age of Enlightenment who visited it the glistening monuments, mansions, palaces, squares and bridges of Prague made its architecture seem the most elegant and refined in the whole of Europe. Frederick the Great's Palace of Sans Souci at Potsdam near Berlin and the Schloss Schönbrunn in Vienna were deemed to rival the Palace of Versailles in scale, grandeur or pretentiousness, but tourists who wished to spend less time indoors than was required for excursions through the rooms of these vast edifices could instead enjoy strolls through Berlin's Tiergarten and along Unter den Linden or, in Vienna, in the gardens of the Belvedere Palace, in the already famous woods outside the city or, in winter, even across the Danube when it froze. For tourists who might also imagine themselves cultivated sportsmen, Vienna in particular, with its riding and fencing schools was unrivalled by any other city in Europe. From Vienna or Prague they might journey to Dresden, the Elector of Saxony's official seat elegantly tucked along the banks of the Elbe, which at the hands of the Allies was to suffer a fate similar to that of Rotterdam in the Second World War but has since been more lovingly restored. From either Dresden or Berlin they would often visit Leipzig to inspect its Romanushaus or the Alte Rathaus in the Marktplatz, and while these buildings struck them as less imposing than those of Berlin or Dresden, tourists to Leipzig generally found the city's inhabitants livelier and more companionable. Such attractions as distinct from those of urban architecture also drew them to some of Germany's smaller university towns in other regions, such as Göttingen or Jena.

If European tourists of the eighteenth century were largely determined to bear witness to their civilization's origins and inheritance, they relied heavily in their travels upon its modern technology – the vastly improved infrastructure of its roads and its networks of post horses and carriages which transported them, and the inns and taverns through which they passed, often assisted by such modern luxuries as an inflatable bath and modern necessities like latch keys that could ensure their safety and secure their purses in hostel rooms while they slept. Above all, to make their journeys both possible and tolerable, tourists of the eighteenth century required the facility of two essential aids which substantially defined their way of life – leisure and wealth – not widely available in any earlier periods of European history. Civilization had by the eighteenth century come to mean more than just the refinements of the arts, sciences and culture; it had come as well to mean commercial society, or capitalism as it would be called in the nineteenth century, denoting civilization's highest stage – the German term *bürgerliche Gesellschaft* standing at once for commercial as well as civil society. With leisure and wealth tourists could contemplate its visceral no less than spiritual delights, conceiving rites of passage across Europe's frontiers through images of freedom or sex, to be realized or fulfilled by valets, grooms, prostitutes and other professional servants provisioned at the staging posts of their journeys or at their destinations by a fresh market catering for their acquired tastes.

European civilization was not only uncovered and retraced in the Grand Tours of eighteenth-century travellers. It was in crucial respects invented by those who set out in search of it, no less than were contemporaneous or subsequent ideas of national identity inspired by notions of a community imagined through similarly creative leaps of faith and pilgrimages of another sort. To subscribe to the idea of

Europe internally *sans frontières* and defined instead by its common history it was not even necessary to embark on the Grand Tour. Kant's conception of perpetual peace within a continent politically shaped by the Treaties of Westphalia and Utrecht required the crossing of borders only in his mind, since as he recounts in his *Anthropologie* he became so violently sick on a short sea journey which he took as a young man[25] that he never again departed from Königsberg.

Together with other cosmopolitan thinkers of his day Kant envisaged the future of Europe as populated by citizens of the world, spiritually united by ties more durable than their separate political allegiances, languages and religions. In identifying the rights of man to be exactly the same as those of the citizen, however, the French Revolutionary *Déclaration des droits de l'homme et du citoyen* of 1789 established both the philosophical and practical framework not for European civilization but rather the modern ethos of the nation-state, initially conceived as civilization's instrument or vehicle, although in time, however, it would instead become its negation. For in promoting the liberation of distinct peoples by way of their acquisition of territorial sovereignty, the nation-states established in Europe in the wake of the French Revolution were in the early twentieth century to drive them towards the Treaty of Versailles, out of which was to arise the fractious disintegration of European polities along the fissures of geographical, linguistic and cultural boundaries exploded in the Second World War. A flicker of the world that had been lost with the age of the Grand Tour could be witnessed in 1989 with the fresh and overwhelmingly peaceful dissolution of some of those boundaries on account of the collapse of Europe's communist regimes, but by then and shortly afterwards, in the Balkans and for many of its own disillusioned citizens as well as other peoples throughout the world whose history was no longer cast in its shadow, the exemplary role once ascribed to Europe as the bearer of the whole of Western civilization had come to seem grievously tarnished if not fatally flawed.[26]

Notes

1. Commentaries on the themes just intimated in this paragraph can be found in Pagden (2002); Hay, (1968); Chabod (1959); Delanty (1995); Gowan and Anderson (1997); Milward (1992).

2. See Starobinski (1989).

3. Howell (1642), sect. 1, p. 8.

4. Gibbon (1966), p. 135. For just that reason Howell had encouraged travellers to seek only the company of natives of the countries they visited, since 'the greatest bane of English Gentlemen abroad', he remarked (sect. 3, p. 32), 'is too much frequency and communication with their own Countrey-men'.

5. Among the best treatments of the history and itineraries of the Grand Tour known to me are Batten, (1978); Black (1985); Cohen, (1992); Dolan, (2000, 2001); Frantz (1968). On the history of travel and tourism in general, see especially Hulm and Youngs, *The Cambridge Companion to Travel Writing* (2002), and Roche (2003). My greatest debt is to Hibbert (1969).

6. See Diderot (1966), p. 118.

7. Among the most classic treatments of this subject remain Chinard (1913) and Atkinson (1969).

8. In contrasting the objectives of grand tourists from those of earlier voyagers and travellers, I of course do not mean to obscure the distinctions made by other commentators – for instance Buzard (2002) – between tourism in the Age of Enlightenment and more widespread forms of tourism that developed later, still less mass tourism such as came to be possible, and prevalent, in the twentieth century. But to my mind the ideological roots of modern tourism, however much more popular, democratic and vulgar it may appear, ought properly to be traced to the Grand Tour. Karl Baedeker's much appreciated nineteenth-century guidebooks for travellers were direct descendants of the classic treatment of the subject in the Age of the Enlightenment, Thomas Nugent's, *The Grand Tour*, first published in 1749.

9. Boswell (1934–50), 3.10 and 5.121.

10. See Smollett (1760).

11. See de Beer (1955), c. 17 November 1643, 2.85–90.

12. See Walpole (1937–83), 13.167–8, letter to Richard West, c.15 May 1739; Young (1794), 1.10.

13. Walpole (1937–83), 14.143, letter to Gray, 19 November 1765.

14. See Howell (1642), sect. 11, p. 139. Gibbon, by contrast, found himself at a disadvantage throughout his tour of Italy on account of his having scant mastery of Italian despite his perfect command of French.

15. See de Brosses (1995), pref. H. Juin de Brosses to M. de Neuilly, 24 November 1739, p. 148; Lynch Piozzi (1967), 1 November 1784, pp. 30–2; and Smith (1793), 3.124.

16. See Hobbes (1660), ch. 21, para. 8.

17. See Goethe (1957), remarks of 3 March, 13 March and 19 March 1787, pp. 189–90, 204–6 and 213–14.

18. de Brosses (1995), de Brosses to M. de Neuilly, undated, pp. 167–8.

19. See Gibbon (1966), p. 134.

20. See Cust and Coluin (1898).

21. On the subject of seventeenth-, eighteenth- and early nineteenth-century travel to Greece by scholars as distinct from tourists – that is, by professionals rather than amateurs – see

especially Constantine (1984), and Dolan (2000), ch. 4: 'Greece and the Levant – the Archaeological Appropriation of the Historical Frontier', pp. 113–49.

22. See Chandler (1817).
23. See Clarke (1810–23).
24. See Howell (1642), sect. 7, pp. 86–101.
25. See Kant (1980), Bk. I, § 29, p. 69n.
26. For another point of view with regard to these developments, informed by an outsider's grasp of European history at least as deep and rich as that of anyone I know or have read whose outlook is embraced by it alone, see Pocock (1997). For their forbearance and advice on particular themes I am grateful to Diogo Curto and Anthony Molho. For providing images of each of the plates illustrated here I am much indebted to Helen Chillman, Librarian of the Visual Resources Collection of Yale University's Art and Architecture Library, and I am also grateful to the Lord Chamberlain for his permission to reproduce Zoffany's Tribuna of the Uffizi.

References

Atkinson, G. (1969), *The Extraordinary Voyage in French Literature* (New York).

Batten, C. (1978), *Pleasurable Instruction: Form and Instruction in Eighteenth-Century Travel Literature* (Berkeley).

Beer, E.S. de (ed.) (1955), *The Diary of John Evelyn*, 6 vols (Oxford).

Black, J. (1985), *The British and the Grand Tour* (London).

Boswell, J. (1934–50), *The Life of Samuel Johnson*, eds. G.B. Hill and L.F. Powell, 6 vols (Oxford).

Brosses, Président de (1995), *Lettres familières d'Italie* (1740), pref. H. Juin de Brosses to M. de Neuilly, 24 November 1739 (Brussels).

Chabod, F. (1959), *Storia dell'idea d'Europa* (Rome).

Chandler, R. (1817), *Travels in Asia Minor, and Greece: or, an Account of a Tour made at the Expense of the Society of Dilettanti*, 2 vols (London).

Chinard, G. (1913), *L'Amérique et le rêve exotique dans la littérature française au XVIIIe siècle* (Paris).

Clarke, E.D. (1810–23), *Travels in Various Countries of Europe, Asia and Africa*, 6 vols (London).

Cohen, M. (1992), 'The Grand Tour: Constructing the English Gentleman in Eighteenth-Century France', *History of Education*, 21.

Constantine, D. (1984), *Early Greek Travellers and the Hellenic Ideal* (Cambridge).

Cust, L.C. and S. Coluin (1898), *History of the Society of Dilettanti* (London).

Delanty, G. (1995), *Inventing Europe: Idea, Identity, Reality* (London).

Diderot, D. (1966), *Mémoires pour Catherine II*, ed. P. Vernière (Paris).

Dolan, B. (2000), *Exploring European Frontiers: British Travellers in the Age of Enlightenment* (London).

Dolan, B. (2001), *Ladies of the Grand Tour* (London).

Frantz, R.W. (1968), *The English Traveller and the Movement of Ideas* (New York).

Gibbon, E. (1966), *Memoirs of My Life* (1796), ed. G.A. Bonnard (London).

Goethe, J.W. von (1957), *Italienische Reise*, eds. H. von Einem and E. Trunz (Hamburg).

Gowan, P. and P. Anderson (eds) (1997), *The Question of Europe* (London).

Hay, D. (1968), *Europe, the Emergence of an Idea*, 2nd edn (Edinburgh).

Hibbert, C. (1969), *The Grand Tour* (London).

Hobbes, T. *Leviathan*, ch. 21, para. 8.

Howell, J. (1642), *Instructions for Forreine Travell* (London).

Hulm, P. and T. Youngs (2002), *The Cambridge Companion to Travel Writing* (Cambridge).

Kant, I. (1980), *Anthropologie in pragmatischer Hinsicht* (1798), eds. K. Vörlander, S. Kopper and R. Malter (Hamburg).

Lynch Piozzi, H. (1967), *Observations and Reflections made in the Course of a Journey through France, Italy, and Germany* (1789), ed. H. Barrows, 1 November 1784 (Ann Arbor).

Milward, A. (1992), *The European Rescue of the Nation-State* (London).

Pagden, A. (ed.) (2002), *The Idea of Europe: From Antiquity to the European Union* (Cambridge).

Pocock, J.G.A. (1997), 'Deconstructing Europe', in P. Gowan and P. Anderson (eds) *The Question of Europe* (London).

Smith, J.E. (1793), *A Sketch of a Tour on the Continent, in the Years 1786 and 1787*, 3 vols. (London).

Smollett, T. (1760), *Travels through France and Italy* (London).

Starobinski, J. (1989), 'Le mot civilisation', originally published in *Le Temps de la réflexion* in 1983, reprinted in his collection of essays, *Le remède dans le mal* (Paris).

Walpole, to Gray, 19 November 1765, in W.S. Lewis, (ed.), *Horace Walpole's Correspondence*, 48 vols (New Haven).

Walpole, to Richard West, c. 15 May 1739, (1937–83) in W.S. Lewis, (ed.), *Horace Walpole's Correspondence*, 48 vols (New Haven).

Young, A. (1794), *Travels During the Years 1787, 1788, & 1789*, 2nd edn (London).

Chapter 9

Citizenship and the Language of Statecraft

Janet Coleman

Introductory Methodological Considerations

This contribution focuses its investigation on a necessarily limited selection of discourses and practices that illustrate the construction of an image, or rather, several images of 'Europe'. It concerns itself specifically with the question: how was citizenship variously defined from the period of Christian Roman imperial statecraft as experienced and described by St. Augustine to its much later realizations during the seventeenth and eighteenth centuries? We are examining the chronological period retrospectively called 'pre-modern': the legacy of Christian Rome to 'the Middle Ages' and its later trajectory towards 'the Enlightenment'. The discourses have been isolated mainly from juristic and theologico-philosophical texts of this period. They reveal shifting but related traditions and practices that were themselves directed and channelled by already inherited, and established, long-standing formulations, well before the term 'Europe' came to be applied in its 'modern', eighteenth-century sense. The presumed univocal 'modern' sense of 'Europe' will itself be contested, not least because it implies an historical inaccuracy: we have become accustomed to drawing a strict line to divide off the pre-modern from the modern. What follows, however, is a 'problematizing' of the constructs: pre-modern, 'early modern' and modern, in order to reveal continuities in the image of European citizenship and its corollary, statecraft, with the latter's distinct power to define citizen membership in the social whole.

Below, we shall observe a late medieval/Renaissance/Reformation shared range of languages: in law, in theology, in socio-political theorizations and practices. The shared languages must, however, be understood as using *and abusing* a classical Greek and Roman inheritance of specialized ways of speaking about what politics is for and how the socio-political domain is best to be arranged for the kinds of beings humans were presumed to be. It is the answers to these questions: what were humans presumed to be and what were their potentials capable of actualization? that were to be taken as foundational for whatever else could be said about citizenship and the state. The answers, as we shall see, were various.

Within Catholic scholasticism itself, assumed to be quintessentially 'medieval', there were debates over the extent and quality of human capacities for self-governance. These debates gave rise to an array of socio-political theories about citizenship which entailed different perspectives on what the state was for. Furthermore, scholastic Catholicism did not end with the sixteenth- century Reformation. It was, however, transformed by the socio-political and theological debates of reformers and in conflict with them. Undoubtedly, the confessional divide, from the Reformation onwards, altered the mental categories in which citizen allegiance to the state would come to be discussed. This divide affected talk about duties/obligations, rights, and the purposes of the 'state' and its constitutional configuration. The alterations were in those directions that we can, ultimately and retrospectively, discern as being the source(s) of modern discourse on citizenship and statecraft. But these developments were not in themselves motivated by a dominant teleology. Rather, the investigation provided below highlights that citizenship and statecraft were variously imagined, conceptualized and realized during the late medieval to early modern and modern periods across Europe, where 'Europe' was imagined not only as a geographical area but as a conceptual space. The conceptual shifts that occurred, and what was required for such shifts to occur, came about interstitially, unpredictably, depending on local as well as centralizing tendencies in conflict with one another. The observed 'shifts' are, in part, dependent on our retrospective ability to recognize them, but without at the same time obscuring the remaining continuities. Hence, charting the languages of citizenship and statecraft requires that we do two things: observe diachronic alterations across time and also synchronic similarities and differences occurring at a given time. That there are indeed, distinct characteristics of the European 'modern' state and its citizens depends on these characteristics being defined by their origins and opposites in the 'pre-modern' period so that aspects of the latter can be seen to be still with us, sometimes *in absentia,* and sometimes in reconfigured form.

No matter whose language we investigate during this *longue durée,* we will not be able to divorce religious from political and juridical enunciations as though they were mutually exclusive. They were not: they were complementary. The shift away from a unified Catholic Christendom was not, during the sixteenth-century Renaissance or Reformation and their aftermath, to some secular characterization of Europe. The shift was rather to confessional divides as discrete objects of loyalty wherever one found religiously identifiable, local communities of practice within defined but shifting geographical borders. All such were Christian of one kind or another. Each came to think of itself as 'the chosen people', drawing on a Pauline language of evangelization and conversion, of Gentiles first and Jews thereafter. The forging of Europe as a set of shifting concepts over time was undertaken *sub specie aeternitatis* and in socio-legal languages that were penetrated by doctrinal Christianity, variously interpreted and applied. The inheritance of the languages of ancient Greek philosophy as translated into Latin, of Justinian's Roman law, of what was called the *ius commune,* of civil and canon (church) law along with the more specific and evolving *ius proprium* of different cities and 'states' were not simply in constant conflict; they were all penetrated by a variety of inharmonious perspectives gleaned from the Bible. This varied and inharmonious inheritance was used, differentially, by authors seeking a kind of harmony in discordance in order to serve their own competing agendas and patrons. But the primary issue of contention would become which Christian doctrine and its attendant concepts of state and citizenship was to be held legitimate? Therefore, who was to be seen as 'one of us' or outside, other and unacceptably different? The problem of configuring 'Europe' is well revealed in the enduring debates concerning the theory and practice of procedures and justifications for inclusion and exclusion from the community. Over the centuries such skirmishes raised issues of intolerance and toleration that were centrally defining of whatever 'Europe' and 'Europeans' were understood by themselves to be in our period.

Not Greece, but Rome and Christian Imperial Rome

It is common to speak of cultural revivals in both late antiquity and during the Renaissance as renewed engagements with themes that had been on the philosophical, practical and political agendas of ancient Greek and Roman authors. My aim here is to highlight how the ancient Greeks had far less influence than the Romans, both on the Latin Christian world of late antiquity and on the Italian Renaissance and thereafter, notably concerning what each later period constructed as their image of the city and its citizens.[1] Although the discourses of the ancient Greeks on the city and its citizens educated and helped to give rise to what Romans said about the *civitas,* it was the distinctive Roman transformations of Greek theory and practice, to suit their own times, needs and temperaments, that set the parameters for later Latin western discussions of the 'state' and its purpose. Furthermore, Christian doctrine had been harnessed by the late fourth-century North African Roman St Augustine to a set of distinctly imperial Roman discourses and realities in order to present an image of the earthly and heavenly cities and their respective citizens that was to endure and inspire into the sixteenth century and beyond in the Latin west. Augustine's Christian understanding of Cicero's republican Rome, its virtues, vices and institutions, was read through his experiences of imperial Rome's emphasis on law and order, on state authority, and on politics as the utilitarian means to achieve minimum disorder through political authority as imposition, especially but not uniquely in times of crisis and cultural disruption. In Augustine's own lifetime when the *Theodosian Code* of Roman law was in preparation, and during the sixth century (534 AD) when Justinian had codified Rome's legal inheritance, the resultant *Corpus Iuris Civilis* that was the staple of later civil lawyers' commentaries, was already Christian. Europe, as it came to be conceived by self-nominated 'Europeans' was not an ancient concept for them. It was what they took to be 'Roman', improved by Christian doctrine. Their engagement with the pagan writings of Aristotle and Cicero, indeed with the whole antique heritage and especially Roman historians, was skewed to their own purposes and circumstances in what they conceived as the Christian *saeculum.*

There are no triumphalist claims being made here in arguing that Christian theological and political discourses penetrated concepts of the state and citizenship into the 'modern' period. One may, like Rousseau, see this as a liability.[2] But it is the view taken here that this is what was conceived as distinctly 'European', for better or worse.

The Language of Citizenship and Statecraft, Inherited and Evolved

What the High Middle Ages, the Renaissance and the ensuing early-modern European world inherited of Roman law was the Christian Emperor Justinian's sixth-century compilations: The *Codex, Institutes, Digest* and *Novellae.* It is important to grasp, even generally, what Roman law intended if we are to see what Europeans later made of it in their attempts to deal with their own circumstances and times. Justinian's *Institutes,* drawing on Gaius (I.8), divides Roman private law into categories dealing with persons, things and actions.[3] The *Institutes* deal with persons in terms of *status.* What surprises anyone familiar with modern state law is that in contrast to it we are not given *per se* a law of persons or a conception of rights but rather, a detailed set of taken-for-granted, legally material, *status* distinctions between freemen and slaves. There is *no* discussion of Roman citizenship *per se.*[4] The freeborn Roman citizen is presumed male, of age, and of sound mind who is head of a family. Everyone else is legally inferior, so that everyone has a legally appointed and legally defined place.

The *Institutes* (I.1.4), furthermore, distinguish between public and private law. Public law pertains to the organization of the state/empire; private law to the well-being of individual citizens. *The content of public law is not further explained.*[5] Private law is what we would today think of as family law. The three-fold origin of private law is said to be collected from the precepts of nature, from those of the law of nations or from the civil law of Rome. [*Institutes* I.1.4].[6] *Ius civile* is that part of private law which the Roman state had specifically developed for the well-being of its citizens.

Such free citizens are divided into two classes: those who are independent (*sui iuris*) and those dependent on another (*alieni iuris*). [*Institutes* I.4–5]. The central object of definition is the free male citizen *sui iuris.* This was the Roman *paterfamilias* with paternal power, *patria potestas,* a lifelong 'obligation' to his familial dependants, children and slaves.[7] His *libertas* was not the freedom of an individual against the authority of the community but was, rather, a duty to respect what is due to others as well as a capacity to claim what is due to himself. The law further distinguishes between the rich (*assidui*) and the poor (*proletarii*) to maintain a differential distinction in dues dependent on status. Citizens were, therefore, equally subject to the law but this was no egalitarian claim. Romans were equal before the law but not to equal things, insisting as they did on proportional fairness or equity. Furthermore, all Roman citizens had a 'right' to participate in public life but not to participate equally, only according to *status*, or what later became rank.[8]

It is significant that Justinian's *Institutes* discuss the *duties* created by the legal relation,[9] and this will be important to us in what follows. So too will be the observation that instead of a specified definition of citizenship, there are elaborate discussions of how those without it may acquire it, procedurally. Roman law is concerned with legally acquired and acknowledged *status* comprising *libertas*, *civitas* and *familia*. Thereafter, the concern is with those of lesser legal status who, like slaves and through manumission, are future sources of *cives* recruitment.

This tells us that Roman citizenship was attributive. It was not an innate natural right but a 'right' acquired in law. This civic freedom was an enduring legacy to our period. A free man, in Roman law, was free only because he was acknowledged to be a member of the civic body. Roman *libertas* was an acquired civic capacity, resting on positive laws and hence, Romans identified their liberty with their 'constitution', be it republican or imperial. Their freedom was the sum of civic capacities granted objectively (not subjectively to an individual) by the laws of Rome. The evolving laws of Rome were conceived as positive restraints in order to distinguish the unqualified power to do whatever one likes (license) from the restraining moderation of liberty. What must be observed is the central role of legal and thereby civic 'incorporation' into a community. Where Roman history shows Romans to have increasingly expanded this legal 'invitation' to all free men living in the Empire, the European future would be curiously as much concerned with those who could not be invited in, indeed, who could and should be excluded.

Because Justinian's *Institutes* (I.3.1–2) referred to *libertas* as man's natural power to do what he pleases so far as he is not prevented by force or law, there was much subsequent discussion of whether this *libertas* referred to some natural instinct peculiar to man, and even animals, a range of pre-regulated natural habits governed by a law of nature. Later, we shall see how Thomas Aquinas, a medieval Dominican, would interpret this from within a Christian perspective. There are also confusing selections from the classical jurists Gaius and Ulpian on whether the *ius naturale* should be fused, or not, with the *ius gentium* which gave rise to enormous debates in medieval and later centuries' legal commentaries. The crux was the statement at *Institutes* I.2 pr.: that the law of nature is that which she has taught all animals; a law not peculiar to the human race, and Gaius I.1: that the law which natural reason makes for all mankind is applied the same everywhere and is called the *ius gentium*. That rule-following is rational and universally human because humans alone may be considered endowed with reason was to become central to the discussions of the ubiquity of politics, statecraft and citizenship in later periods. Following Ulpian [D.47.10.3] legal capacity implies recognition of an agent's intentionality. This is why madmen and infants are not considered capable in law. The *ius civile*, the law of the state, is that law which each people had established for itself and peculiar to it, and in Rome, it was originally thought to be derived from custom and applied only to Roman citizens. The rest of humanity, foreigners (*peregrini*), were held to be subject to the *ius gentium*. But with expansion and the increasing complexity of the legal system, law came to be derived from a variety of sources including edicts of both 'foreign' and urban praetors. After 212 AD the *Constitutio Antonina* conferred Roman citizenship on all free men living in the Empire so that the *ius civile* was 'universalized', not separating Roman citizens and their law from the *ius gentium* which applied to all others. Justinian, following Constantine, especially refers to the significance of local and regional customs that are not uniform across the Empire. But he says [C.8.52.2] that regional customs may not prevail against reason nor against legislation. By Justinian's day every freeman was held to be a *civis*.

That regional custom may not prevail against reason or legislation is of some importance to us in what follows in our period. After Constantine, the *Theodosian Code* 16.2.25[10] had already expressed a view on what had become the Roman state's religion in the 380s. True *religio* claims that the heretic commits sacrilege not merely in the bureaucratic sense of refusing imperial orders but also in the religious sense of challenging the true faith which issues from the emperor. It is not clear if Constantinian, Theodosian or subsequent Justinian declarations of true religion were to be interpreted as imperial whim or rather, as reflections of the decisions of a network of by then established episcopal politics and Church councils. Conclusions of Church councils had come to be incorporated into imperial legal responses and by 421 AD already reflected the recognition of the institutional Church's privileged place in the eyes of the 'state'.[11] This meant that there was a legal distinction between a 'state's' *religio* and everything else as pagan, heretical or Jewish *superstitio*. Increasingly what was taken to be traditional *religio* became a defined set of beliefs authorized by descent from the apostles and the Council of Nicaea, 'spoken' by imperial lips. Those deemed heretics, pagans, Jews and not, therefore, holding to Christian Roman *religio* were, in principle if not always in practice, excluded from legal capacities and therefore, from the attribution of *civis*. This would come to penetrate a variety of 'European' self-definitions not least when they came to define the heretic in their midst.

Where Justinian defines *libertas* [Institutes I.3.1–2; D.1.5.4 pr. Florentinus] he refers to a power of doing what one pleases except so far as prevented by force or law. This means that even slaves were in some sense 'free' under this definition. In distinguishing between slaves and freemen, Justinian speaks of slavery as by *ius gentium*, whereby a man is subjected to the dominion of another, and he adds something that is not in Gaius, that this is against nature. [Gaius I.52; *Institutes* 1.3.2; D.1.5.4.1; 12.6.64].[12] In Roman law slavery was not an absolute *status* independent of relations to others. It is not quite a condition of rightlessness or dutilessness (in our language) but rather the opposite of the legal personality inhering in a freeman presumed to have legal capacities.[13] Justinian indeed provides a range of causes of enslavement: under *iure gentium*, the result of birth, traced from the descent of the mother even if the father is free, or from capture in warfare; under *iure civili*, the result of a thief caught in an act, if a freeman. The grounds for enslavement under Justinian, altering certain earlier modes, included a penalty imposed for serious misconduct, or a penalty on a freeman fraudulently allowing him/herself to be sold as a slave and sharing the price of the sale. The consequences of this kind of enslavement were that all public and private relations were ended, one was treated as though dead, no wills were operative, one's property went not to heirs but to the slave owner, although a slave's liability for committing delicts remained and the slave owner could be sued for what his slave undertook. This penalty of enslavement and its civic liabilities would also be important for our period in excommunication procedures. Slavery in Roman law was not, therefore, some judgment of permanent natural faculties because if it were it could not be ended by a juristic act (manumission). What was transferred in the release by an owner and the creation of a *civis* was not ownership, since a man was not thought to own himself,[14] but rather, transfer from a class of things which can, in law, be owned into a class of persons who, in law, are members of the civil body. The citizen capacities that are thereby inferred from the legal disabilities discussed in Roman law are, for instance, that the *civis* could be a witness, could give evidence in litigation, make a will, and convey property in civil form. Certain later Europeans, on the contrary, would argue that enslavement was some recognition of permanent incapacity in natural faculties that could not be ended by any juristic act.

Justinian added a third definition of *ius naturale* in the *Institutes* I.2.11 where he claimed that it is observed uniformly by all peoples and is sanctioned by divine providence and lasts forever, being immune from change. Indeed, in Justinian's Constitution *Deo Auctore*, he had asserted 'that we govern under the authority of God; our Empire is delivered to us by His Divine Majesty; and we rest all of our faith, not in arms, soldiers or our own skill but in our hopes in the providence of the supreme trinity and in Him alone'.[15] The double objective of Christian imperial majesty is highlighted: military might and law, achieved through divine guidance. The emperor aims to govern the state with justice in times of peace and war.[16] This understanding of the purpose of statecraft supplemented what Augustus had previously instituted when he became sole ruler. He had insisted on a return to republican constitutional forms and restored to the popular assembly the legislative powers that had been lately vested in the Triumvirate. But his intentions were made clear concerning law-making: he did not intend to restore any effective power to the people, but rather, designed a means of giving him a way of making his will effective. The people had conferred imperial power on him by the *Lex de Imperio*, giving him absolute discretion in a number of administrative matters. Subsequent emperors emphasized the *Principum Placita*. By the third century AD the emperor was openly acknowledged to be above the law and the sole legislator. Ulpian had written: *Quod principi placuit legis habet vigorem* and by the third century even the Senate's *consulta* were no more than rubberstampings of the emperor's proposals. Late Roman law, notably during St Augustine's own lifetime, was thereafter presented in the form of the emperor speaking to his people, often in the corporate 'we' form of address or sometimes '*iuxta statutum legis meae*', the emperor as a severe but loving *paterfamilias* responding to questions, threatening penalties, explaining why changes in the law are necessary, most notably in family law.

The *Theodosian Code* (incomplete), published in 438 AD and compiled by emperor Theodosius II and his advisers rationalized inherited legislation and legal opinions, assembling imperial constitutions from Constantine, after 312, on. Not only does the *Code* give us a view of the last expression of Roman imperial unity as St Augustine himself would have known it; it reveals that from Constantine onwards, Christian bishops had become one increasingly influential section of the community and they now could approach the emperor without fear. Although internal Church discipline was regulated by canons of Church councils, bishops found it convenient to request the backing of the secular arm to enforce ecclesiastical rule. This is one major tradition of discourse that our later period would know, inherit, and use when they discussed the various ways in which the citizen was 'made' and the purposes of statecraft in the governance of Christian peoples. But it was only one, undoubtedly powerful, tradition that would be vigorously contested.

Augustine, the Pre-eminent Church Father, on Citizenship and Statecraft

Those 'pre-moderns' from the fifteenth to the eighteenth centuries who were not experts in the traditions of Roman law could, nonetheless, abstract its message from many of the writings of Augustine and they did so. Theologians and preachers epitomized his views to a wider public. Augustine's views derived from, but crucially broke with, the ancient philosophical tradition of Plato, Aristotle, Cicero and the Stoics. His vision implies a power of ordinary citizens as almost non-existent, that of passive membership of the Roman *urbs*. Neither Plato, Aristotle nor Cicero had held to such an empty notion of citizenship, nor to such strong views on maintaining an uncritical faith in, and obedience to, the authority of a *princeps* as did Augustine. But Augustine's late imperial North African and Roman world was not theirs.[18] On his view 'the people' were not to be seen as active deliberators engaged in self-governance but rather, as often irrational consensus-seekers needing to be led to that consensus, most efficiently by one or a few men of authority and uncommon insight with supreme coercive command at their disposal. Augustine, like his later followers, had accepted the late imperial Roman conditions of dominance and subservience as the very framework of all authority, even if he was also aware of abuses of power. Likewise, he argued that the Church on earth is a mixed community of the predestined saved and damned, but nonetheless, he believed that as an authority, backed by its interpretation of scripture, which is never wrong, it still had a certain ability to discern when to take severe measures even against those who might be innocent. This paralleled his view of the role of the Roman magistrate and judge whose knowledge was not infallible but whose duty was the same. His argument was that humans always do, indeed must, operate within and under even inscrutable authority, and authority is necessarily of a certain kind in this life precisely because of what he thought human nature now to be, 'fallen', with consequences to be observed in our discussion below. Hence, fallen human nature itself determines what politics necessarily is for. His focus on our need to have faith in authority was a consequence not only of his 'reading' of human nature through pagan philosophy, in history, and through scripture, but also of his having been a late imperial Roman expressing widely shared views on state authority, coercion and the utility of paternalistic government for the good of its citizens even against their wills. On to a Roman imperial argument concerning what law was for and how it operated in citizens' lives, Augustine grafted his version of why Christians should hold it permissible to do good to a man against his will, the very purpose of statecraft being the securing of a temporary peace and concord in society.

Where Roman positive civil law held to the principle that no law-abiding freeman should be violated against his will, Augustine in his dialogue with his friend Evodius, *De libero arbitrio*, a text of supreme importance during the Middle Ages, Renaissance and early-modern periods, modified this. Indeed, he thought that Roman imperial law instantiated his own beliefs on the matter. He agrees that the state's guiding mandate from God's eternal justice is to protect the people and therefore requires that it enact law for the people's protection. *Ius civile* deals with crimes that need to be punished if peace is to be maintained among ignorant humans. The law does this to the extent that such matters can be regulated by men. But Augustine insists that humans are changeable and subject to time. From this there follow two possible scenarios. 1) If a people is moderate and serious and a diligent guardian of the common utility, thinking less of private good than public good, then it is right to enact a law *permitting* this people to choose for itself the magistrates through whom its affairs are to be administered. 2) But if this same people, having become depraved little by little, preferring private to public good, sells its votes, is corrupted by those who covet honours and turns the regime over to shameful and villainous people, then it is right that if some good and most capable man is to be found, he might *remove* from the people the power to bestow honours and hand it over to a few good men or even one. These two scenarios would be invoked time and again in later European discussions of citizenship and the purposes of statecraft.[19] Hence, Augustine insists that the *ius civile* can and must change depending on the character of a people. With an iniquitous people the law suited to them must suit their depraved character. Roman law principles, where civic capacities, 'rights', are attributed, civic acquisitions are, for Augustine, changeable. Depraved wills can and must, therefore, be violated for their own good so that the peace and security of the social whole is maintained.

Scholastic Debates over the Extent and Quality of Human Capacities for Self-governance

In what follows, I shall present in brief a particular, vociferous argument, already prevalent in university circles of theologians in the thirteenth century. This argument will give us some insight into the parameters of a debate that extended down the centuries, helping to craft those views on citizenship and statecraft which battled it out in the construction of pre-modern and then modern European positions on both these concepts. The debate was between those whom I call neo-Augustinians on the one hand (e.g. Henry of Ghent, Giles of Rome, James of Viterbo) and neo-Aristotelian intellectualists on the other (e.g. Albertus Magnus, Thomas Aquinas, Godfrey of Fontaines, John of Paris). The theme under discussion was one that was treated by theologians, political theorists, rhetoricians, lawyers and other professionals. A definition of the common good was sought and then the debate ensued as to how it may be achieved.[20]

Neo-Augustinians during the thirteenth and fourteenth centuries, despite their increasingly intense engagement with the newly translated *Ethics* and *Politics* of Aristotle, were more influenced by Augustine's understanding of the category: 'post-lapsarian man', the imperfect, fallen individual. Neo-Augustinians included certain secular university masters and Franciscan theologians. They held to the view that fallen human nature shows itself in each and every individual: everyone is first and foremost a self-lover. Their love of the community is only secondary and in consequence of self-lovers' perception of the *utilitas* of the community for themselves.

Neo-Aristotelian intellectualists, on the other hand, including university secular masters as well as Dominican theologians, argued that naturally we love the community and neighbours before the love of self, so that the common good always and naturally takes priority over the good of the individual which, in fact, derives from it. Most notable in the Dominican discursive tradition was a distinctive perspective on the consequences of the Fall: they held that humans nonetheless maintained the capacity, as individuals and collectively, to will and act according to right reason and perform what natural law commands. It is this Dominican tradition that led to talk of rights as claims, whereas neo-Augustinians submerged rights into prior, known duties.[21]

Here we are choosing to look at synchronic antitheses in different medieval traditions of discourses on human nature, the common and individual good, citizenship and the purposes of statecraft. The scholastic question addressed by all of these authors was: if the life of perfect virtue is the goal of the imperfect individual, and God is the goal of the life of perfect virtue, then was it possible to conclude that the individual can secure his union with God only by means of incorporation into the common good of society? If this were the case, then was the individual in some sense subordinated to the common good of the political community as a necessary precondition to his participation in eternal beatitude? In the more narrow, political sense, the issue being addressed was whether our natural inclination to live in society somehow made the constitution, regulation of, and participation in, a law-governed political regime a necessary precursor to an individual's salvation. Were citizenship and statecraft necessary to salvation in the next life?

Those theologians more knowledgeable about, and influenced by, Aristotle's explanations of how the *polis* was capable of being discussed as a self-contained ethical environment for moral agents, tended to spend a good deal of their time elucidating the virtues of good governance and good citizenship prior to anything else they might say about man's final salvific end. The common good or common utility as the aims of action were contrasted with the aim of private advantage which they equated with tyranny.[22] Each person was therefore to be ordered to what is common. And it was thought impossible for the good of the community to be neglected without the individual's good thereby, and in consequence, being damaged and dishonoured. Hence, the common good was to be sought before the individual good and this was possible for each and every *civis* no matter what his actual *status* or rank in the community. This was his adherence to natural law principles. It is for this reason that it was held that law by its very definition not only commands those actions which contribute to the common good but also serves as a rule or plan as to how members of the political community ought to live, law being able to educate men to live the best life in concert. On this view, law is not simply instituted to prevent men from committing evil acts; it is capable of instilling goodness in people. Hence, every prudent legislator intends to make his citizens just, not simply obedient. Law is therefore, instituted not simply to ensure that there will be no injustice but to ensure that people will act through reason.

This neo-Aristotelian Dominican view was exemplified in the writings of Albertus Magnus and his student, Thomas Aquinas. For Aquinas, there was a *natural object* of both the human intellect and human will and this natural object was the common good.[23] For Aquinas, therefore, there is one standard of truth or rightness for everyone and it is equally known by everyone. All people realize that it is right and true to act according to reason, and each and everyone is capable of doing this naturally and without supernatural grace added to his natural capacities. Aquinas observes that it is imperfect things that tend towards their own good, that of the individual. More perfect things tend towards the good of a species. The even more perfect tend towards the good of a genus. The most perfect, God, secures the good of all being and the good of the universe. By analogy he argues that since the good of the human community, that is the species, is the ultimate goal of human life, the *bonum humanum*, then not only is the common good more divine than any individual or less common good, but so too are those humans who are responsible for the community or *respublica*, whatever its constitution, be it a city-state republic or a monarchy. Every human accordingly can come to the conclusion that the whole community of the universe is governed by divine reason, that there is a rational guidance of created things, and this is called eternal law. The eternal law is conceived of as the plan of government in the supreme governor, God, so that all schemes of government of those who direct as subordinates must derive from this eternal law. In consequence, all laws in civil societies, so far as they accord with right reason, derive from the eternal law. Hence, the good of the just and well-organized community is one which, in being sought through good statecraft and good citizenship, establishes the necessary, if not sufficient, setting for the achievement of the individual's ultimate good. The best political society, on Aquinas's view, is one in which the moral underpinnings of civil law are taught by the Church following divine positive law, notably the Ten Commandments. Citizens are virtuous not only through reasonable acts as enshrined in civil positive law, thereby securing their external goal: the common good of the community. They are also Christians seeking an internal goal, salvation. For Aquinas, because the goodness of God is the common good for all mankind, humans retain, after the Fall, their natural inclination to love God more than themselves and a natural inclination to seek the common good before their individual good, which will only follow in consequence.

Neo-Augustinians however, provided a different perspective on the same issues. For them, the life of perfect virtue could only be achieved through incorporation, not into any particular historical, political community but rather, into the Church community.

Without incorporation in the Church, the perfect virtue of salvation was impossible no matter how law-abiding and morally responsible one might be in whatever political community in which one might find oneself. Despite their appeal to Aristotle, they resisted the view that it was open to human reason to devote oneself or indeed, sacrifice oneself, for the well-being of one's earthly *respublica*. Instead, they adopted Augustine's thesis that the love of anything beyond oneself is not natural to humans. It requires the additional grace that comes from baptism and membership in Christ's Church. They agreed with Augustine that fallen man now only had the capacity to love himself first and to seek his own benefit *before* that of others. They could not love God first and their neighbours through God in consequence. For an individual to be able to act in ways expressive of loving God and community before self required the iniquity of the human will to be reorientated by grace. Nature, society and politics could not achieve this. Membership in the Church alone could ensure a supernatural help added to natural inclinations which they regarded as either powerless, imperfect or corrupted. Contrary to the views of Aquinas, neo-Augustinians did not accept that our natural inclinations alone could ensure that any good act be performed with the right intentions in this post-lapsarian world. And therefore, unlike neo-Aristotelians who held to law being intelligible to human rationality, neo-Augustinians insisted that religious, rather than political, communities were the correct model for the context of human acts undertaken upon command of a superior so that obedience to a superior is the rule.

What runs through most of the arguments put forward by neo-Augustinians is the view that human beings may indeed be integral parts of political communities in these fallen times; but what ultimately defines their participation in the *respublica* is their own perceived need to be protected from the worst consequences of self-lovers' behaviour. For this reason humans owe duties of obedience to authorities, charged with the public duty of securing peace and concord amongst self-lovers. Political authority, statecraft, is ultimately, and by papal concession, a *remedium peccati*. Hence, strictly speaking, there are no 'rights' of resistance; there are only duties to secure the best means to self-benefit in post-lapsarian times when self-lovers only have the capacities to seek their own good first before any common good. *Recta ratio*, right reason, for them is primarily an authoritative communication to Christ's vicars and thereafter, from the pope by concession, to secular public authorities, and not to all men.

In short, one view held that the common good was a natural object of human desire and could be achieved through the natural deployment of right reason on the part of each and every individual as master of himself, while the other insisted that the common good had to be imposed, coercively if need be, on recalcitrant and disorderly, self-focused, human nature.

Validated Membership in European Communities

Now this debate itself was played out in both theory and in the practical procedures which justified the inclusion or exclusion of individuals or groups within communities in Christian Europe. Processes of excommunication and inquisitorial trials were mirrored in 'state' and city courts, taking this debate from the fourteenth into the later sixteenth centuries. Tracing these debates one observes a range of pre-modern social mentalities and attitudes to the changing criteria that determined social inclusion and exclusion and the means to achieve social unity. During these centuries it raised issues of intolerance and toleration concerning perceived external behaviour in the *foro externo*. By the sixteenth century it can be shown that interior dispositions in the *foro interno* were increasingly thought to be 'read off' of people's external behaviour. As a consequence, the respective roles of Church and public authorities in maintaining communal discipline, peace and order, became high priorities not only in discourses but in legal stipulation and enforcement, in Catholic as well as Protestant regions. The attributive qualities of citizenship and the purposes of statecraft can be seen to alter as we examine the procedures of excommunication from the community. Here I believe we can reveal a tradition of distinctly European discourses on the ways in which, depending on one's status in a hierarchy of citizenship, one was held to be responsible before the community for maintaining one's *fama*, one's reputation, in good order. This took the form of procedures, such as defamation by public rumour of individuals judged contumacious by communities or authorities in their name. It highlights the rites of passage that were variously established if one were to achieve validated membership in community. The aim was for individuals to correct their private sins, in public, for the public good and procedures became increasingly vicious.

Communal Discourses and Citizenship

Before we track what eventually happened during the sixteenth century to conceptions of citizen inclusion and exclusion, we need first to observe a range of practices on the ground in 'Europe', from city-state Italian communes to cities with their own borough laws in monarchies like that of England. There is no doubt that the political structures which evolved from at least the thirteenth century onwards to foster new economic activities and civic self-governing independence owed little to ancient or late imperial Rome. Instead we confront indigenous solutions to medieval and later problems, accretions of customs and dilutions of classic Roman law. Urban cultures across Europe from at least the thirteenth century established their own rules to deal with disruptive circumstances, traditions and interests. Without written constitutions, communes operated under local customs, laws, regulations or statutes that established the functions and duties of magistrates and the composition of councils that were different from those of neighbouring communes. Into the fifteenth century the idea persisted that each city had its own laws, be it within a monarchy like that of England, or self-governing and only notionally under the aegis of the Holy Roman Emperor in the *regnum italicum*, and therefore, each was unique. Where no superior authority was recognized in the daily governance of the community, the city was *de facto* deemed its own 'prince'. This produced characteristic civic outlooks and local patriotisms.

It has often been observed that their debt to an inheritance of ancient Rome and especially to Justinian's *Corpus* was in fact, restricted. Unlike what we observed in

Roman private law where there was no definition of the citizen offered, medieval and later jurists sought technical definitions of citizenship and thereby validated their own city, wherever it was located.[24] The concern to seek definitions, of the good ruler or magistrate, or of citizenship, was characteristic of medieval schools in general and of law faculties and practising lawyers in particular. Learned men had come to think and operate within corporatist or conciliar paradigms that had come to suit a European society with numerous collective and consensual practices. Cities across Europe were engaged in 'making citizens', nominating men to a kind of nobility in order to create a larger class of men who would owe the commune not only military service but public engagement in the maintenance of concordant rule.[25] In practice, city codes did not speak of the nature of citizenship or its modes of acquisition. Instead, different cities and communes across Europe evolved varied practices for making their citizens, dividing them into numerous legal and social categories. Citizens were categorized into *maiores* and *minores* with numerous finer distinctions, largely in terms of wealth, sometimes of birth, indicating a general acceptance of social inequality and hierarchy comprising fine distinctions in rank and *status*. What was always emphasized, however, was the active adherence to the communal contract, taken on oath, which designated the act of acquiring citizenship everywhere. But only those recognized as full citizens, that is, those who in practice were party to the contract, had the right to participate fully in its political life and to hold office, taking an active role in assemblies and approving laws, swearing in magistrates, electing others or being elected in turn. Contemporary Italian jurists had come to speak about the various *de facto* means of acquiring and losing citizenship. They distinguished between native citizenship – granted by being a son of a citizen or by having been born within the territory of the city, and naturalized citizenship – a grant by the city to a 'foreigner' and made on petition of individuals or groups of people.

We can only here allude to an astonishing historical fact about citizenship from the thirteenth to sixteenth centuries: not only in Italy but across Europe, the distinction between the category of citizen and that citizen with eligibility to civic office narrowed, everywhere. Participatory citizenship in the sense of participating in collective corporate politics, through membership in guilds, for instance, narrowed to near vanishing point. A confidence in public right reason declined so that collective politics came to be understood as finding the right leaders to govern the led in those communities constitutionally organized as either republics or monarchies. In Italy as elsewhere by the turn of the sixteenth century, government even in republics like Venice and Florence came to be respectively narrow or extended oligarchies if they were not already taken over by *signori* or princes increasingly claiming an access to an exclusive rationality or to a divine right to govern.[26] Across Europe and not simply in Italy, the great merchants and bankers, the landed and entrepreneurial interests of local oligarchies, rejected the idea of corporate guild equality. Instead, a hierarchy of guilds was either confirmed or eliminated outright, to be replaced by international merchants and bankers comprising an elite. They came to see themselves, with the help of humanist education, as a class apart, united by business, patronage and family ties. Renaissance civic humanism fostered an ethic of civic nobility among wealthy patricians with a distinctive set of values. Most notable was their explicit view that the people, once thought capable of reason, were now the irrational multitude, judging inaccurately by superficial appearances and only interested in making certain that they were not oppressed, their property not taken and their wives and daughters not dishonoured.[27]

During the fourteenth century Marsilius of Padua in the *Defensor Pacis* had sketched in detail another image: he established that the whole people as a rational multitude was to be considered the infallible Human Legislator and that those who were thereafter elected to public office were regulators, doing the will of the corporate people. He defended this vision by proclaiming the earlier corporatist view: 'that most citizens are neither vicious nor undiscerning most of the time; all or most of them are of sound mind and reason and have a right desire for the polity and for the things necessary for it to endure, like laws and other statutes or customs. For although not every citizen nor the greater number of them be discoverers of the laws, yet every citizen can judge of what has been discovered and proposed by someone else and can discern what must be added, subtracted or changed' [*DP* I, xiii.3]. In contrast, fifteenth-century humanist literature emphasized how 'most of humankind neglects to cultivate virtues which is no more than right reason'. Therefore, they must look to those who are more noble, those with more intelligence and virtue than themselves.[28]

Communal Excommunication as European Discourse

If we now remind ourselves of that little local scholastic debate between neo-Augustinians and neo-Aristotelians at the turn of the thirteenth into the fourteenth centuries, we recall a range of arguments concerning the common good that would come to be decisive in later theory and practice of citizenship and statecraft. Conceptions of personality and personal responsibility were integral aspects of what the good citizen could be taken to mean. From where did such conceptions of personal responsibility derive? Much important work dealing with our 'pre-modern' period has highlighted the ways in which people tended to define themselves largely in collective and corporate terms.[29] In trying to explain what individuality and autonomy meant for people who lived during the pre-modern *longue durée*, historians have highlighted how individual self-consciousness was usually discussed by contemporaries in relation to groups to which people belonged. Individuals had multiple identities that derived from membership in families, in craft guilds, in corporations, in estates, in parish residences, in cities where they were citizens and might hold public office, and from their participation in devotional societies and other sodalities. Contemporary narratives that concerned the self-fashioning of individuals always took into account local collective behavioural regulations, what today sociologists call 'social control mechanisms'. Within these were developed recognized strategies to retain or preserve one's *fama*, one's good name and reputation.

Fama

Fama and *infama* were concepts much discussed. But one's *fama* was always an attributed quality, attributed by others who judged you from the outside and according to your *status* and the actions you displayed. To claim to have a recognized, good reputation was related to a simultaneous duty on the part of all members of the group to reveal their neighbours' private sins in the interests of the peaceful order within the community. It was necessary to keep one's *curriculum vitae* of expressed passions and their disciplining in good order as well as open to public scrutiny, especially if one expected to be offered citizenship or to hold public office. Various qualities were demanded from and ascribed to the pre-modern citizen. Here, I believe, we see an especially European discourse on the acceptable self.

Some medieval and early modern towns only granted citizenship after a thorough investigation into the moral record of the candidate. Adulterers, bankrupts, bastards were all refused citizenship *status* in many European cities.[30] People who had gained citizenship were supposedly of ostensibly irreproachable *fama* and conduct. A hierarchy that ran from the common men and ignorant peasants, to merchants, craftsmen, lawyers, to the higher public notables of the community differentiated men in terms of the virtues that were expected to be displayed by each *status* category. Each had validated ways of revealing their respective commitment to the community in their public actions and deportment. The requirement that there be validation by public authority was never in question, although debates between heretics and the orthodox concerned which legitimating public authority to accept. The concept of legitimate authority was the *sine qua non* for the control and sanction of young and old and guarantor of one's proof of being a responsible member, a part of the public and its collective judgment. It brings to our notice the extent to which even the humblest in *status* were encouraged and ready to pursue and punish neighbours and outsiders who failed to control their conduct by the prevailing, current, local and therefore 'orthodox' norms. It was essential that each individual be engaged in crafting, disciplining and then revealing a certain kind of public *persona*, open to scrutiny by all, familial intimates and communal neighbours. The concern was to ensure that people conformed to validated *types* and if they did not do so, they would be ridiculed, punished, exiled or even killed.[31]

Heresy

There is now a well-known view that religious heresy was regarded, like leprosy, as a disease of the communal body. It needed to be cut off like a diseased limb, if the rest of the body was to flourish.[32] On this view, the public good was always and invariably to come before the private good of any individual. Excommunication was the spiritual and legal remedy, analogous to the surgeon's knife. The twelfth-century English jurist Bracton compared the legal *status* of the leper to that of the excommunicated: he could not sue in court, make gifts of land or inherit property. The royal court in England saw leprosy as depriving someone of his honour and *fama* through the process of segregating him from the community. A similar attitude to, and procedure for, heretics, treated as diseased, came to be developed systematically. Heretics were not only those considered as religious deviants but also were seen as those who constituted factions and disrupted, often with violence, the peace, security and well-being of the social whole. Heresy was the general term used to indicate some permanent opposition or conflict internal to the unified community. When it specifically referred to Christians, it referred to matters of doctrine and the moral behaviour of the baptised members of the body of Christ. Although there were some who attempted to use the word heresy only in terms of adherents to Christian doctrine and not to refer to those outside the Church, increasingly those regarded as infidels, Jews and others who were not committed to Catholic practices were deemed heretics and a danger to the community. Into the late sixteenth century and thereafter, it became increasingly difficult to express toleration for those who lived in the midst of Christian communities, Protestant or Catholic, and who held to their own beliefs and practices.

Numerous texts with titles such as *de forma vitae* or *de amicitia*, which mixed observations of ancient moralists like Cicero and Seneca with Christian ethical teaching were written over the centuries, not so much for private moral instruction of the individual young person or even the king, but rather, as instructions for realizing the social aspirations of the communal society, seen as a group of citizens freely sworn to uphold a body of rules in pursuit of their vision of communal well-being.[33] The swearing of an oath to community was central to this pre-modern mentality. So too was the expectation that the punishment of those who defaulted on their sworn oaths was a public issue under law. Ritual confession of those judged to have done wrong, in the presence of witnesses and other oath-takers, was also a central practice of this social togetherness, just as were the penalties of corporal punishment, public humiliation, even death. The voluntary acceptance of collective rules of behaviour was thought to express the underlying consensus on which the positive law of the community was founded. Such voluntary acceptance of rules of behaviour in turn depended on the belief that every person of whatever *status* was capable of governing his own emotions and actions by reason and indeed, was obliged to discipline his behaviour by what was called *public right reason*. If in some way he showed himself not to be governed by the public norms of reason, he showed himself to act against accepted norms and thereby removed *himself* from the community so that it was expected that legitimate public authorities would acknowledge this removal, isolate him, ensure that no one had contact with him and even kill him so that he did not pollute the community and what it took to be its common good.[34]

Heresy and Oaths

Heretics were often distinguished by their refusal to swear oaths. In this they revealed themselves not only as religious deviants but as treasonous if not simply irrationally indifferent to the common good. Furthermore, an oath-taker calls God to witness that he is swearing a commitment to some future act. As a consequence he invokes God as a judge and avenger and in the case where he swears an untruth, for example in a case of perjury, a curse is always implied. While an oath cannot be lawful if it obliges the swearer to commit an unlawful act, it was held that a rash or coerced oath, taken before God, is still binding because the oath binds one to God. A promissory oath binds the swearer even if it is to his disadvantage, discomfort or inconvenience, but not if it leads to his self-destruction. This was still the case at the end of the seventeenth century in Protestant England. Indeed, Protestant legal casuists prided themselves on the strictness of their teaching compared to Catholic casuists. And during the sixteenth and seventeenth centuries oaths became a favoured tool of secular authorities, Paolo Prodi having argued that the early modern state came to monopolize oaths, thereby sacralizing state power by means of a secular oath which bound the individual to an absolute community.[35] It is noteworthy that medieval and early modern Catholic casuistry developed in directions which seemed to exploit the ambiguity in cases where there was reason to believe that the oathswearer had mental reservations at the time that he swore, or that he had been forced to swear through fear and therefore, could claim that his oath was not binding.[36] In general, however, oaths were tests of political trustworthiness and ideological commitment to the community and its good, in France, in German lands as well as in England from the Middle Ages onwards.

The complex issue of voluntary and forced conversion or baptisms from the Middle Ages onwards, especially regarding Jews, continued to be part of the much larger debates on the legitimacy of conversion through fear of violence and this in itself incorporated the debate between civil and canon lawyers over the issue of *iustus metis*, sufficient and constant fear, which might cause an oath to be invalidated. This dealt not with Jews but with oaths of allegiance to different popes during the Great Schism within Christendom, lasting into the middle of the fifteenth century. It was the civil lawyers who tended to think that a coerced oath was rescindable. They looked at agreements men made from the point of view of contract. Violence or its threat within a contract provided a potential *exceptio* for future non-performance. Violence or fear of violence (*actio quod metus causa*) may not immediately annul a contract one has entered into, but it could legitimately be used in a future court case to decide whether or not the contract could be enforced if it had been entered into out of fear of violence. Civil lawyers, therefore, held that it was the job of civil courts to judge whether or not to annul certain contracts.

But canon lawyers, especially those dealing with *res spirituales*, held that agreements must be based on voluntary and true consent for them to be valid. If canon law prohibited certain actions then a coerced oath concerning such actions would be invalid. But if canon law did not insist on free consent, say of women or minors, then an oath which bound an individual to performance, because it was performed before God, even if coerced, was not to be annulled. The argument was that Church courts only seek the completion of a promise, and an oath was a promise made before, indeed, to God. To contravene even a coerced oath therefore required absolution for it not to be seen as a *sin* of perjury before God. Some canon lawyers like Hostiensis thought a coerced oath was ultimately invalid, but as an oath, before one might be absolved from performing what one had promised, it was a venial sin. For the Church, the oath, even if coerced, remained valid until the person received absolution. It was held to be a valid oath, even if coerced, not because the person who had sworn had intended it, but because the Church required it to be so until the Church, through the mercy of its own judges, offered absolution. Before absolution was offered, if it was, they followed the principle: *ex vi precepti non ex vi iuramenti*. And certain theologians were even harsher than canon lawyers. Aquinas, in fact, held that the contravention of a coerced oath was a mortal, not venial sin (ST IIa88; 89 and 98 on oaths, *iuramenta*). The coerced oath still remained valid before God although from Church leniency or mercy the contravenor was not punished as having mortally sinned *if* his oath was judged to have been induced through fear (*metus causa*). But for Aquinas, no amount of coercion is sufficient to sanction the breaking of an oath to God, even if such an oath is extracted from minors. The release from the performance is, for Aquinas, only through Church authority and he argues that it is not possible for any civil authority to annul an oath even if it was found that such an oath was contrary to the needs of the community as a whole.

Let us recall that for Aquinas, men are said to be masters of their own affairs through acts of reason whose norm is species specific and not individually and subjectively specific. Men often fail in acting reasonably or justly but they have the capacities to guide their lives, their passions and their wills, by reason. It is the exercise of right reason, which is prudence, that enables those in public office to judge whether acts are ordered to the common good of the community. Legitimate public authority, whether it is vested in one man or many, has as its aim the seeking and securing of the common good of the multitude first, and only in consequence, also the good of the individual. Right reason in the public forum is applied to judgments of human action that either foster or threaten the well-being of the communal whole. This is what statecraft does. In doing wrong, men depart from the order laid down by reason. Hence, where punishment is imposed by public justice, Aquinas insists that its purpose is the public good and its maintenance.

The Common Good, Accusation and Denunciation, Heresy

There is also, according to Aquinas, a certain kind of private reproof that may be offered from love for the private good of a sinner. But in communities, that of the Church and in society, correction is concerned with those wrongs that have been committed by individuals which are harmful to others or the general good. An act of justice, that is, a positive law remedy, is brought in to maintain law and order between people (ST IIa IIae 68.1 f.). Aquinas discusses two acts in the process of correction: they are accusation and denunciation.[37] The act of accusation seeks punishment of a sinner along with the common good. The act of denunciation seeks the reform of the sinner and his individual good. Private denunciation should always precede public accusation. A denunciation depends on the improvement which can be expected both in the character of a sinner and in the repercussions his sins have on the community. If there is no improvement that can be hoped for, then one considers whether the sin infects others. Aquinas gives the example of heresy. If the sin infects others then for the sake of the whole community and at the expense of the reputation, *fama*, of the sinner, the sin must be laid before those in authority. For Aquinas, the good of the many is always preferred to the good of one person (IV Sent. 19.2 3a ad 2). Public accusation is necessary whenever the common good, be it spiritual or corporeal, is directly endangered. He says that *anyone* is bound to lay a public complaint in cases where a crime tends to harm society. But there must be evidence. If we are required to give evidence by a person with authority, then we must give such evidence, whenever the law says we must, namely when the crimes are public and notorious.[38]

What, we may ask, constitutes acts that put a community in danger? It is significant that much emphasis is placed on injurious words, defamation.[39] Aquinas speaks of defamation as the taking away of a person's character by drawing attention to anything that detracts from that character's good name or *fama*, his public *persona* and standing. If defamation is justified, then the consequences are dire, leading to excommunication, loss of both property and the capacity to have any communication, verbal or commercial, with those in the community, or exile. It can even lead to death. Furthermore, Aquinas makes clear that accusation and denunciation are not only the duties of public authority but of fellow neighbours, citizens, brethren, since sins against the public good must be subject to public correction and at the expense of the individual.[40] When the sin is so extreme and incurable and the harm caused to others outweighs the possibility of the sinner's reform, then Aquinas says that both human and divine law require that the sinner be killed. If a crime has threatened to destroy a community or its good moral standing, its *fama*, then the perpetrator should be prevented from corrupting the whole community. The most repellent of such forms of corruption and pollution is, for Aquinas, the obstinate maintenance of heretical beliefs. Incorrigibility does not seem to be inferred from people's expression of false or perverse opinions so much as from the stubborn resistance to change those opinions once authorities have instructed them about authoritative decisions and interpretations. The obstinate resistance to authoritative decisions, after two formal warnings, is the sign of a heretic (ST IIa IIae 11.1). This obduracy, he says, deserves banishment not only from the Church by excommunication but also from the world by death (11.3). Obduracy is the key. In Latin the term is *contumacia*. It is not so much an error in belief than a voluntary, chosen unwillingness to accept the prevalent norms of behaviour, determined by whatever public authority that is respected at the time, be it Church or state.

Communal Prevalent Knowledge and Contumacy into the Seventeenth century

This says something much broader about how pre-modern European communities were thought to be held together and what threatened them. It is not a view unique to medieval Catholic scholasticism. Indeed it was sustained in post-Reformation communities and states. In fact, the 'absolute' state described by Hobbes in the seventeenth century, and often taken as the prototype of our modern state, provides a rational choice version of the consequences for any individual unwilling to obey the sovereign's law and accept the sovereign's definitions. He is thrown out of the community and his life mirrors the hypothetical state of nature in being nasty, brutish and short. He is excommunicated. Hobbes thought it would be irrational for anyone not to see it as essential that he obey the positive laws and behavioural norms of the community, whatever these were. And it is noteworthy that Hobbes's sovereign has authority within the limits of orthodox Christianity, i.e., Protestant Christianity, but the sovereign also controls those limits, dictating what Christianity is.[41] Insofar as law, in general, for Hobbes, is not counsel but command of the sovereign, be the sovereign an assembly or one man, and the sovereign is not itself subject to the civil laws, Hobbes insists that the New Testament is not law or command but only counsel. It becomes command, that is law, only where the sovereign makes it so.[42] And since the commonwealth is but one (legal) person Hobbes insists that it ought also to exhibit to God a single worship: 'which then it doth, when it commandeth it to be exhibited by private men, publicly. And this is public worship, the property whereof, is to be uniform' (*Lev.* part II, ch. xxxi).

European early-modern states and their courts, where states in the Protestant world had established national churches, maintained precisely the arguments we found in scholastic authors who were concerned with the maintenance of the common good through law. But where the neo-Aristotelian intellectualist discursive tradition insisted that law was itself rational and known by each and every man as master of himself, the neo-Augustinian position insisted that law was simply authoritative command and was to be obeyed. Hobbes most vociferously complained about those who appeal to *recta ratio*, right reason, which, he insisted was none other than their own reason. This, in effect, was nothing but their own passions imposed on others (*Lev.* part I, ch.v). This kind of reason could not be obeyed, was not obliging, unless it had been established as command by one overriding sovereign power, a vision of statecraft whose absolute power consisted in defining what justice was to be, and threatened, through force, the consequences of excommunication, even death to the non-compliant. This vision of statecraft and 'citizenship' turned every individual into a potential heretic were he not sufficiently rational to realize that his very survival depended on compliance with positive law and the authorised representative actor's, the sovereign's, determination of what was to be acceptable prevalent knowledge within the commonwealth.

Nor did Hobbes' final vision of statecraft emerge as a logical conceptualization in his own mind alone. It was a result of what had already occurred in European history as communities sought stabilization, even survival, especially during the post-Reformation religious wars. We can trace this by observing that when Aquinas had been writing at the end of the thirteenth century, he had been careful to distinguish heretics from other non-believers, infidels such as Jews, Muslims or pagans. The heretic was defined as one who, in having been baptised as a Christian, or as a Jew who had undergone conversion to Christianity, had been incorporated into the Christian community, but who thereafter had developed their own erroneous interpretations and practices to which they thereafter obdurately clung. Aquinas's Dominican Order was itself founded as a preaching order, especially to religious deviants and heretics and the Inquisition was largely in their hands. If we look at the *Manual for Inquisitors*[43] published in 1376 by the Dominican Nicolau Eymerich from Gerona in the Catalan-Aragon kingdom, we see how he constructed questions which he thought inquisitors needed if they were to interpret the varieties of 'mental turpitude' of which the heretical mind was capable. In the sixteenth century his *Directorium* was printed and re-edited, the most important edition and commentary having been made in 1578 by the canonist Francisco Peña in the name of the Senate of the Roman Inquisition. For both the fourteenth-century Eymerich, and even more vigorously for Peña at the end of the sixteenth century, heresy came to be the name given to all those who reject the Church's authoritative interpretation of Christ's teaching as true. This meant that Jews who had never been baptised or converted and therefore who had never been members of the faith community, were to be excommunicated, forcibly removed from communication with Christians in civil society to what sounds to modern ears like ghettoes.[44]

By the end of the fourteenth century heresy had come to be defined as whatever is opposed to the faith in whatever way. All those who, no matter in what manner, are found opposed to Christian doctrine meant in its largest acceptance, that is, as dogma, as customary usage, as conventional juridical codes and their intentions, are heretics. Now heretics are not only apostate or erroneous former Christians but also Jews, Saracens, all infidels and all delinquents in matters of faith. The heretic is he who chooses error, who is obstinate and therefore withdraws himself from the community by choosing to rebel against what is deemed the common good. The focus is on the perceived danger to the prevalent beliefs of a community by those judged pertinacious, contumacious and obdurate in their unwillingness to correct what are considered errors by those charged with the public authority to establish what the community holds to be its truth and therefore its common good. Eymerich casts the Christian community of the faithful as the victim of those who trouble public peace and order by their depravity. He writes that any nation that does not root out these seditious elements allows itself to be perverted and subverted and is engaged in its own eventual disappearance (*Directorium*, 29–30; 48–53). This in itself is against both natural and divine law, both of which oblige us to fulfil our duties to self-preservation. And because Eymerich recognizes that Jews and Christians share the Old Testament, he insists that they cannot be distinguished from Christians and Christians cannot consider them Jews. But where Jews differ in their interpretation of the Old Testament from what Christian theologians and preachers teach about it, they are directly attacking Christian law and in denying it must be forced by judges of the Christian faith, 'our bishops and inquisitors', to respect these truths (75). Eymerich insists that Jewish misinterpretation of the shared Old Testament is, in effect, their throwing away not only their own belief but 'our' belief (76). The rooting out of heresy had become an argument approaching 'raison d'état'. Emergent states, whatever their confessional allegiance after the Reformation, would adopt this argument with speed.[45]

A major section of the *Directorium* deals explicitly with what was called 'the defamed of heresy' and the defamation originates in what public rumour, notably amongst simple people in a community hold to be heretical behaviour or speech. The Inquisitor takes into account informants who give testimony, making a judgment on their decency and honesty, but also takes into account rumours emanating from the vile and infamous as well, even from other heretics or perjurers and criminals. All testimony is accepted. By the time we read Peña's late sixteenth century re-edition and commentary we see that now defamation, from whatever source, is to be followed by a procedure where the accusation or testimonies of only two witnesses suffice for a condemnation. He refers specifically to problems in his own time and especially to the defamation of those suspected of the Protestant heresy. He refers to the Council of Toulouse forbidding all those defamed of heresy from sitting amongst counsellors or magistrates or from assuming any public role whatever (96). And Peña, uniquely, makes clear that if false testimony has been given in a defamation, he and other Inquisitors will *not* punish the false defamer, as was previously done, by delivering him to the secular arm for punishment. Peña thinks that such malicious defamation of an innocent man is far less dangerous to the *res publica* than is the possible existence of heretics who infest the community. Far more than Eymerich, Peña is absolutely certain that the mental commitment to heresy is completely revealed by bodily gestures, general conduct and speech.

There is no need to list the terrible punishments that were inflicted even on what turned out to be the innocent in defamation proceedings. What is meant to be observed is an attitude to social wholeness and fears about social dissolution which lasted well into the seventeenth century and beyond in Protestant regions as much as in Catholic ones. Peña made it clear, as did many others, that the Inquisitor must remember, as the Hobbesian sovereign must remember, what is his first priority when he holds trials to condemn someone to death. This first priority is not the saving of the soul of the accused. It is to procure the public good and to terrorize the people. The public good must be placed very much higher than any charitable consideration of the individual (130). The exterior signs of heresy are all those actions and words which are witnessed, even by the most humble or malicious and envious, to be in disaccord with the common habits of the people (135). The pre-modern denunciation of private sins so that they might be corrected for the public good therefore placed the maintenance of one's own *fama*, one's reputation and good name, in constant jeopardy. Hobbes's sovereign statecraft ensures this even more absolutely than any previously imagined, or realized, statecraft across Christian Europe.

Conclusion

When Agnes Heller argued that 'Europe' was a uniquely modern Enlightenment notion of a recognizable, collective identity, the historical response to this should be sceptical. The *historical* response to Reinhart Koselleck's view, that modernity is itself a conceptual closing off of the pre-modern from the modern in what he called the eighteenth- century *Sattelzeit* in Germany, following on from the French Revolution, should also be sceptical.[46] Crucial aspects of the pre-modern are still with us, for better or worse. Not only did the shared, systematic, legal inheritance of Roman jurisprudence and *ius commune* law, civil and canon, continue either in coordination with or in debate and conflict with, the *ius proprium* of principalities and city republics into the nineteenth century. It continued into the project to construct a new European common law. There was a constant refinement of the frames of legal and other kinds of thinking from the past without ever 'starting again' because this itself would be a conceptual impossibility.

The contested concept 'Europe' is indeed not simply a geographical entity. Insofar as Europe is an *historical experience*, it has been suggested here that its historicity is in the *fact* of the on-going internecine spiritual and political warfare, the emergent conflict between Catholics and Protestants, their mutual post-Tridentine absorption of the positions of their opposites, while nonetheless maintaining their different perspectives on man's rationality and capacity for disciplined self-governance. Where different views emerged to highlight the different presumed roles of the will, the desires, the reason in human activity, a two-fold argument that was already evident in medieval scholasticism itself produced different attitudes to the individual's good and to the means to secure the common good. From these we get an array of conflicting views on citizenship and statecraft. The modern European, indeed Euro-American debate over whether right is prior to the good or good is prior to right emerges, still ongoing, in the modern debates between liberals and communitarians. These refer directly or indirectly to what I have referred to as the ongoing internecine spiritual and political conflict in Europe down the centuries.

If we had traced specifically the languages of rights used in the pre-modern period studied, we would have discovered that such rights were always understood within community (community of the species or that of political society) where individual rights were seen as not opposing community values. What one might call the European pre-modern conception of the self was a normative self. It was not self-defining or unique. It was attributive. The self's normativity had already been defined by God in whose image man was made and the self's responsibility for discipline or governance was through the deployment of right reason, available to all humans, *either* through rational self-reflection on natural law principles, *or* through authoritative imposition by rational authorities doing God's will in history. In both discursive scenarios there were held to be moral rules that were *a priori* binding, obliging men to their duties. During the seventeenth and eighteenth centuries both Catholic and Protestant natural law theorists reveal that there still remained a confrontation between protagonists of a variety of recognizably scholastic and ancient ideas of morality and values as naturally *a priori* inherent, a *lex* already inherent, in the structure of the world and of God's providential ordering, accessible in some way or other to human reason.

But there were also a few who came to argue that morality was entirely a conventional emergence, a response of no more than reasoned utility to individual acts of will. Morality, therefore, was now to be conceived as an historically contingent set of rules created by men alone in their respective responses to experienced contingencies. For such moral sceptics, God's wishes may not be inferred, nor is it presumed that humans are sent into the world upon God's business, performing God's commands. In other words, there appeared a strange discourse that insisted that morality was not to be found in naturally motivated agreement amongst men, but rather, right and wrong were to be defined by a sovereign, created by unsocial, fearful beings whose only end is to find the most secure means of achieving self-preservation. Such fearful beings set up an artificial contractual society to secure precisely what they most love: themselves and their survival. Here, rights are really civil permissions, telling contractees what the conventionally-established rights-bearer is at liberty to do and not what he must or must not do. Technically, there is no sovereign law that is unjust and no subject or citizen can claim against sovereign injustice by right, because on this view, there is no prior objective justice, either to which men may have access, or which they may rationally presume can be realized before they contract with one another and set up a sovereign third party to keep them in awe. There is no *lex* prior to the sovereign's justice. The European medieval and Renaissance discourses on rights and obligations therefore took a particular turn especially in the eighteenth-century theories of moral sceptics and modern subjective right was born.[47] The new moral scepticism had come to redefine citizenship and statecraft on the basis of a reconfigured model of human nature, a voluntarist, desirous model where reason instrumentally serves the individual's passions. The person as citizen or subject, newly defined, is in need of an artificial social contract which will eliminate, through coercive positive law, the threats to peace and order that non-social, self-interested selves pose to one another and the social whole. Such a citizen or subject is no longer said to have any knowledge of overall ends to structure his means-ends deliberations to acquire what he simply desires. His ends are privately attained from intensely individualized experiences and the most dominant end is simply to stay alive. The individual who then covenants with others to establish the sovereign state gives up his natural liberty or right to use his power as he wills, his right of governing himself, in order to secure his primary end: self-protection. A recognizably European liberal self emerges from this for whom right is always prior to the good. It is this citizen, created by a particular understanding of 'the state' and its power, that is itself an emergence from one, earlier, recognizably European Christian discourse on the purpose of politics and coercive law: the neo-Augustinian conceptualization of man.

Today, it is often amongst elites that one finds a shared lack of faith or unbelief in precisely that cosmology of the past and the constitutional arrangements to which such Christian cosmologies gave rise. What I hope to have demonstrated is that what is no longer believed in, indeed modern unbelief and the politics that results from doubt and unbelief, is framed *in absentia* by what Europeans once did believe. Modern unbelief itself cannot be understood, nor the citizenship and statecraft that result from it, without unbelief's opposite and origin. This is the peculiarly European tradition.

Notes

1. Coleman, (2000a, 2000b, 2003).
2. Rousseau, Book II, ch. 3 and Book IV, ch. 8 dealing with the problem of attachments to sectional interest groups, corporate wills, and citizens' orientation to the common good, the general civil will.
3. Buckland (1975); *The Institutes of Justinian* (1967); *The Institutes of Gaius,* part I (1969).
4. Gardner (1993).
5. Stein (1995), pp. 499–504. When Justinian distinguishes between the law of nature (*ius naturale*), the law of peoples (*ius gentium*), and the law of the state (*ius civile*) the distinction is with respect to private law alone. Buckland (1975), p.x, observes that *ius naturale* was borrowed from Greek philosophy but only appears amongst lawyers around the time of Augustus; *ius civile* meant in republican terms, unwritten law, common law – as opposed to enactments; *ius gentium* was as old as Cicero. The contrast between *ius civile, ius gentium* and *ius naturale* belongs to the Empire.
6. Unlike *ius civile* the laws of nature and peoples are not really divisions of varieties of private law but rather are the sources from which the rules of private law are derived.
7. Johnston (1999).
8. On the difference between Roman *libertas* and Athenian *eleutheria*, see Coleman (2000a), ch. 1 and p. 240. Hence, there were specially privileged classes of freemen citizens (*ingenuus*) and also *cives* whose 'rights' were more or less restricted. The classes with more restricted legal capacities included freedmen, *cives liberti, libertini cives*, with specified relations to their respective *patronus*.
9. Gaius says nothing of legal capacities and duties involved in ownership or usufruct or servitudes, nor, in the law of contract does Gaius say anything about the duties of the parties.
10. *Codex Theodosiani libri XVI* (1954).
11. Hunt (1993).
12. What did 'contrary to nature' mean? This too would open up huge debates in our period as to whether or not the precepts of natural law prohibited the enslavement of other men, but allowed it under *ius gentium* as the result of capture, some natural disability, or conventional expediency. What is known as the 'second scholastic' interpreted this confusion in dealing with New World native peoples.
13. Wirszubski (1950), pp. 30–1.
14. Buckland (1975), p. 72.
15. *The Institutes* (1967), prooemium, confirm this conception of Christian Roman statecraft by opening with the following address: 'In the name of our Lord Jesus Christ, the Emperor Caesar Flavius Justinianus, conqueror of the Alamanni, Goths, Franks, Germans, Antes, Alani, Vandals and Africans, pious, happy and glorious conqueror and vanquisher, to young men serious of learning the law, greeting'.
16. *Institutes* (1967), prooemium.
17. From within his own late imperial Roman context, Augustine recapitulated the then standard and unquestioned view about hierarchies of power from the emperor, the army, government, oligarchies, families, masters and servants.
18. Where Augustine was perhaps the most outspoken in his times about the degree to which no person escapes in this world, that kind of verbal and social conditioning to which he is subjected by authorities, his insight would be revived and seen as relevant to one particular medieval and later Renaissance and Reformation mentality, shared by some political theorists, lawyers and theologians alike who wrote not only for princes but who also favoured aristocratic/oligarchic republics and disseminated a view of the

authoritative Church conceived as a monarchy. Coleman (2000b), pp. 193–8; p. 198 on papal monarchists.

19. Most notably in Machiavelli (1532), *Il principe*.

20. Kempshall (1999); Coleman (2006).

21. Coleman (1987, 1991).

22. They discussed how justice was concerned with what is both common and particular so that the human community depends on just communication or exchange, notably but not exclusively, of individual possessions to ensure the self-sufficiency of the whole. The principle behind this just communication or exchange was seen as concerned with what is common, determining equity according to a hierarchy of worth of associated individuals exemplified in the just ordering of their interpersonal relations.

23. For Aquinas, the order of the precepts of the natural law corresponds to the order of our natural inclinations which are neither perverse nor powerless. The natural inclination to the good in rational man is twofold and interrelated: it is to know the truth about God and to live in society. Therefore, all man's actions connected with such inclinations come under the natural law. We see here a much more detailed specification of natural law than could ever have been elicited from Roman law itself. Instead it derives from a Christian re-interpretation of Cicero's Stoicism and Aristotle's emphasis on directive reason as found in his *De Anima* and in his ethical and political writings. It is also imbued with the various views of commentators on canon law.

24. Hence, when Bruno Latini spoke of the city as a gathering of people formed to live justly, the city not being defined geographically simply because its inhabitants happen to live together inside the same walls, his message was extracted with approval into the *Liber customarum* of London, the administrative heart of the English monarchy. Nor was it communal Italians alone who were called citizens even by Italians themselves. Bartolus, the distinguished fourteenth-century civilian spoke of the kings of France and England as Roman citizens, *cives Romani*.

25. Bartolus observed what was *de facto* practice: that citizenship was a convention of civil law based on the *ius gentium* rather than on natural law. Citizenship was the conventional law of a *civitas*. And he observed that a foreign merchant could be made a citizen of a city by law and would henceforth be considered a *civis verus* as much as would be a native inhabitant. Later in the fourteenth century Baldus observed that membership of the *populus* imbues a social individual with active political characteristics which he would lack were he not incorporated and attributed public personality. These were descriptions by professional jurists of the status of citizen with optimum capacity. See Canning (1987).

26. Najemy (1982); Rubinstein (1966, 1968, 1979); Pullan (1999).

27. Coleman (2000b), c. 6 with reference to Machiavelli, *Discorsi* and Guicciardini.

28. Poggio Bracciolini (1997), pp. 22–3; Rucellai (1960), pp. 85ff.

29. Zemon Davis (1986), p. 53.

30. Boone and Prak (1966).

31. Should 'pre-modern' Europeans have sought recourse to Roman law guidance in these matters they would have found it in Justinian's *Digest* 47.10. The difference is that Roman law sought to prevent people from intentionally composing and publishing anything that might bring someone into hatred, ridicule or contempt [D.47.10.3 and 5]. However, see D.47.10.15–18. Anyone who brings an action of insult on false evidence will be condemned in special proceedings, that is to say, he will suffer exile, deportation or expulsion from his order [D.47.10.43]; some of what follows here draws on the author's recent publication: Coleman (2005).

32. Moore (1976).
33. Albertanus of Brescia (1980).
34. Compare Locke (1690), paras.7–8.
35. Spurr (2001); Prodi (1992).
36. Schüssler (2003).
37. The distinction between accusation and denunciation was clarified earlier in the thirteenth century by Pope Gregory IX, Dec. Greg. IX,v.1.16 in *Corpus iuris...*, (1879–81) vol. II, pp. 737–8 and Decretum II.2.7 in *Corpus iuris...*, vol. I, pp. 483–504.
38. *Summa Theologiae*, IIa IIae 64.2.
39. Compare Justinian's *Digest* and n. 31 above.
40. For a similar argument, Marsilius of Padua, *Defensor Pacis*, II, chs 8.3; 8.8; 9.7; 9.12; 10.3; 12.7; 19.1– 2; 19.3; Coleman (2000b), ch. 4, esp. pp. 158–60.
41. In part III of *Leviathan*, 'Of a Christian Commonwealth', he frequently calls the civil sovereign the chief pastor. He spends much time discussing excommunication, historically. In chapter xliii he observes that what is necessary to salvation is contained in two virtues: faith in Christ and obedience to laws. He insists that the laws of God are none other than the laws of nature, 'whereof the principal is that we should not violate our faith, that is, a commandment to obey our civil sovereigns which we constitute over us by mutual pact one with another'. He insists, ch. xxxix, that there are Christians in the dominions of several princes and states but that they are each subject to that commonwealth of which each is a member, and hence, their particular kind of Christianity is stipulated by the community to which they belong and over whom they have established a sovereign authority.
42. Hobbes, *Leviathan*, part iii, ch. xlii: the acts of council of the apostles were not coercive laws but counsel only, and therefore, the books of the New Testament, though most perfect rules of Christian doctrine, could not be made laws by any other authority than that of kings or sovereign assemblies.
43. *Directorium ...* (1973); Ererra (2000); Prosperi (1998), pp. 6–12.
44. Eymerich had explicitly said that the pope as vicar of Christ not only has absolute power over all Christians but also over all infidels and all men. *Directorium ...* (1973), 76–77.
45. Eymerich derives the meaning of heresy philologically and shows the heretic to be one who voluntarily withdraws from the common life (47–48). He provides some extraordinary insights into the social conditions at the end of the fourteenth century especially regarding Jewish converts to Christianity. The Jewish convert must follow the law of Philip II [*Leyes de Castilla* (1973), 1.2.c.8 Judios y moros, p. 74.] and change his name and he is advised enthusiastically to choose a name from the Christian martyrology, otherwise he will arouse suspicions as to his origins. A Jew who converts to Christianity and changes his name is actively being encouraged to change his identity by becoming incorporated into the membership of the faith community through which all others derive their identity. The Dominican Inquisitor, Eymerich, furthermore insists that Jewish children or Jewish adults, baptised under threat of confiscation of their goods or from fear of corporeal punishment or by whatever force, (*metus causa*), even unto death, are obliged to observe what they promise since their baptism (76).
46. Heller (1992) is referred to in Molho (unpublished); Koselleck (1985).
47. Modern subjective right had to do something drastic to the discourse of both Catholic and Protestant casuists of the seventeenth and eighteenth centuries for whom there still remained *precepta certa*. They had to replace the precepts of natural law completely with convention. Nation-states, therefore, had their own laws relative to them, their own

circumstances and their own histories. Whatever rights citizens of such nation-states could legitimately claim were positive, state-defined liberties rather than universal, species specific normative rights. Such positive rights were thereafter to be taken as foundational.

References

Albertanus of Brescia (1980), *De amore et dilectione Dei et proximii et aliarum rerum et de forma vitae*, in S. Hiltz, 'De amore et dilectione dei et proximii et aliarum rerum et de forma vita: an Edition', Ph.D dissertation, transcription based on the manuscript in the University of Pennsylvania library (University of Pennsylvania).

Aquinas, T. ab., *Summa Theologiae*.

Boone, M. and M. Prak (eds) (1966), *Statuts individuels, statuts corporatifs et statuts judiciaires dans les villes européennes (moyen âge et temps modernes)* (Leuven).

Buckland, W.W. (1975), *Textbook of Roman Law from Augustus to Justinian*, 3rd rev. edn. P. Stein (Cambridge).

Canning, J. (1987), *The Political Thought of Baldus de Ubaldis* (Cambridge).

Codex Theodosiani libri XVI (1954) 3 vols, Th. Mommsen and P. Meyer (eds) (Berlin).

Coleman, J. (1987), 'The Two Jurisdictions: Theological and Legal Justifications of Church Property in the Thirteenth Century', in *Studies in Church History*, 23, 75–110.

Coleman, J. (1991), 'The Dominican Political Theory of John of Paris in its Context', in *Studies in Church History, subsidia 9: The Church and Sovereignty* (Oxford), pp. 187–224.

Coleman, J. (2000a), *A History of Political Thought from Ancient Greece to Early Christianity* (Oxford).

_____ . 2000b), *A History of Political Thought from the Middle Ages to the Renaissance* (Oxford).

_____ . (2003), 'Images of the City and its Citizens in Late Antiquity and the Renaissance', in Z. von Martels and V.M. Schmidt (eds), *Antiquity Renewed: Late Classical and Early Modern Themes* (Leuven/Paris), pp. 35–62.

_____ . (2005), 'Scholastic Treatments of Maintaining one's *Fama* (reputation/good name) and the Correction of Private "Passions" for the Public Good and Public Legitimacy', *Cultural and Social History*, 2, 23–48.

_____ . (2006), 'Are there any Individual Rights or only Duties? On the Limits of Obedience in the Avoidance of Sin According to Late Medieval and Early Modern Scholars', in V. Makinen and P. Korkman (eds), *Transformations in Medieval and Early Modern Rights Discourse* (Dordrecht), pp. 3–36.

Corpus iuris canonici (1879–81), ed. E. Friedberg (Leipzig).

Directorium inquisitorum, Le manuel des inquisiteurs (1973), trans., intro. and notes, L. Sala-Molins (Paris).

Ererra, A. (2000), *Processus in causa fidei: L'evoluzione dei manuali inquisitoriali nei secoli XVI–XVIII e il manuale inedito di un inquisitore perugino* (Bologna).

Gardner, G.F. (1993), *Being a Roman Citizen* (London).

Heller, A. (1992), in B. Nelson (ed.), *The Idea of Europe. Problems of National and Transnational Identity* (New York).

Hobbes, T. (1660), *Leviathan*.

Hunt, D. (1993), 'Christianising the Roman Empire: the Evidence of the Code', in J. Harries and I. Wood (eds), *The Theodosian Code: Studies in the Imperial Law of Late Antiquity* (London), pp. 143–60.

The Institutes of Gaius (1969), text with translation, ed. F. de Zulueta (Oxford).

The Institutes of Justinian (1967), trans. J.B. Moyle (Oxford).

Johnston, D. (1999), *Roman Law in Context* (Cambridge).

Kempshall, M. (1999), *The Common Good in Late Medieval Political Thought* (Oxford).

Koselleck, R. (1985), *Vergangene Zukunft. Zur Semantik geschichtlicher Zeiten* (Frankfurt, 1979), translated as *Futures Past, on the Semantics of Historical Time* (Massachusetts and London).

Leyes de Castilla, (1973), in L. Sala-Molins, *Le Manuel des Inquisiteurs* (Paris).

Locke, J. (1690), *Second Treatise of Government.*

Machiavelli, N.(1532), *Il principe.*

Molho, A. (unpublished), 'Images of Europe, 5–6 March 2004, introduction'.

Moore, R.I. (1976), 'Heresy as Disease' in W. Lourdaux and D. Verhelst (eds), *The Concept of Heresy in the Middle Ages (11th–13th c), Proceedings of the International Conference, Louvain, 1973* (Leuven), pp.1–11.

Najemy, J. (1982), *Corporatism and Consensus in Florentine Electoral Politics, 1280–1400* (Chapel Hill, NC).

Poggio Bracciolini, G. F. (1997), 'On the Misery of the Human Condition', (1455) trans. in J. Kraye (ed.), *Cambridge Translations of Renaissance Philosophical Texts,* vol. 1 (Cambridge).

Prodi, P. (1992), *Il Sacramento del Potere* (Bologna).

Prosperi, A. (1998), 'L'arsenale degli inquisitori', intro. to A.A. Cavarra (ed.), *Inquisizione e indice nei secoli XVI–XVIII. Controversie teologiche dalle racolte casanatensi* (Rome).

Pullan, B. (1999), ' "Three Orders of Inhabitants": Social Hierarchies in the Republic of Venice', in J. Denton (ed.), *Orders and Hierarchies in late Medieval and Renaissance Europe* (London), pp. 147–68.

Rousseau, J-J., *The Social Contract.*

Rubinstein, N. (1966), *The Government of Florence under the Medici (1434–94)* (Oxford).

———. (1968), 'Florentine Constitutionalism and Medici Ascendancy in the Fifteenth Century' in N. Rubinstein (ed.), *Florentine Studies: Politics and Society in Renaissance Florence* (London), pp. 442–62.

———. (1979), 'Oligarchy and Democracy in Fifteenth-century Florence', in S. Bertelli, N. Rubinstein and C.H. Smyth (eds), *Florence and Venice: Comparisons and Relations* (Florence), pp. 99–112.

Rucellai, G. (1960), *Il Zibaldone (1464),* A. Perosa (ed.) (London).

Schüssler, R. (2003), *Moral im Zweifel, Die Scholastische Theorie des Entscheidens unter moralischer Unsicherheit* (Paderborn).

Spurr, J. (2001), 'A Profane History of Early Modern Oaths', *TRHS,* 6th ser., pp. 37–64.

Stein, P. (1995), 'Ulpian and the Distinction Between *Ius Publicum* and *Ius Privatum*' in R. Feenstra et al. (eds), *Collatio iuris romani: études dédiées à H. Ankum* (Amsterdam).

Wirszubski, C. (1950), *Libertas as a Political Idea at Rome During the Late Republic and Early Principate* (Cambridge).

Zemon Davis, N. (1986), 'Boundaries and the Sense of Self in 16th Century France', in T.C. Heller, M. Sosna and D.E. Wellbery (eds), *Reconstructing Individualism: Autonomy, Individuality and the Self in Western Thought* (Stanford).

Chapter 10

Images of Law in Europe
In Search of Shared Traditions

Pietro Costa

European Common Law: a Point of Departure

It is difficult today to conceive of law in Europe without considering Europe as something much more binding than a mere geographical reference. Over the course of many decades, a new juridical system has been taking shape, distinct from the nation-states that up until the Second World War entirely coincided with Europe, as a political and legal entity. Indeed the last great European civil war marked the beginning of the construction of a transnational order whose juridical shape appears to be both original and problematic. This system has not manifested itself in the form of a federal super-state, capable of surpassing national sovereignties in a single bound, nor has it been reduced to a sort of updated and extended *Zollverein*. Instead it gives rise to an original and complex political and normative configuration.

On the other hand, we are not faced with an experiment in legal engineering, promoted by a self-referential bureau-technocratic elite: the juridical area that has taken shape is the effect of profound socio-economic processes whose frame of reference differs from the system of nineteenth-century nation-states. This does not attenuate, however, but in a certain sense aggravates, the problems inherent in the current process, which, given its global importance, demands a strong cultural legitimation and a precise sense of destination. In short, it demands that a common normative system be combined with shared values, finalities, mentalities and 'forms of life'. In relation to this fundamental demand, the theme that has found expression in two, fortunate and ambiguous formulas, 'identity' and 'roots', has served as catalyst for discussions among scholars and lay people.

Sharing an identity and cultivating the memory of its very origins are mutually reinforcing elements. It follows that the urgency to define 'Europe' as a collective entity, to which to attribute the norms and institutions that make up the new transnational order, gives rise to a stronger 'demand for history': the necessity to find the 'objective' proof of a shared destiny, in some moment in the recent or remote past.

In short, it is understandable that the tendency to make a 'political' or, if you will, 'civil' use of history is on the rise. This attitude had already manifested itself in nineteenth-century nation-building processes (in Germany as much as in Italy) and it would be rather peculiar for today's Europe-building to totally disregard it. One should ask oneself, however, to what degree 'professional' historiography is called upon to respond to this widespread demand.

Obviously, the historian is not a disinterested observer, removed from his historical context: it is his present (the society and culture to which he belongs) that prompts and provides him with the tools for his inquiry. At the same time, however, one can suggest that the very sense of the historiographic operation lies in the difficult undertaking of prizing distance, grasping difference and respecting ('historicizing') the 'otherness' of the past.

In this perspective, Europe's present (the existence of a common European juridical area) is a reality that prompts study and stimulates questions, but does not predetermine the answers. I shall therefore not pose myself the goal of searching for recent or remote precedents of the present European juridical order. I shall also be wary of possibly drawing, from one past experience or another, models that can be applied to apparently analogous phenomena, but situated in radically different historical contexts. A phenomenon of our present (the existence of a European order characterized by a plurality of sovereign states belonging to a shared juridical space) can only serve as stimulus to formulate two closely related questions. The first is to ask ourselves whether, beyond the relevant political and juridical differences between medieval and modern Europe, there has ever been a common connective tissue between them. Second, we must inquire into the nature of this fabric: whether it coincided with the creation of a veritable 'common juridical space', or if it comprised only the sharing of argumentative styles, theories, images, if, in short, it simply resorted to a shared paradigm within a specific 'discursive tradition'.

The Recovered Tradition: The Neo-Pandectist Approach

Whatever the disciplinary ambit considered, it is reasonable to suggest that, in medieval and modern Europe, there existed cultural traditions endowed with an intrinsic expansive force, with a capacity to be proposed in different contexts, distant in both time and space. When we turn to the juridical discourse, the hypothesis risks holding little interest, precisely because it is too easily verifiable, and so evident as to appear obvious, given the impressive *longue durée* of Roman law in the juridical culture of Western Europe.

Yet the evidence of the datum paradoxically transforms itself into quite a complex historiographic problem. It is a fact that the Justinian *Corpus iuris* is a text that has been studied and valued by jurists, from its 'rediscovery' in the lower Middle Ages to nineteenth-century German pandectism, right up to its latest transfiguration. One may nonetheless ask: is it sufficient to recognize that European juridical culture has continuously confronted the *Corpus iuris* in order to affirm the existence, in the most disparate countries and times, of a tradition that draws its basic unity from this foundational text and proceeds from one context to another, connecting them like the water of a single river?

This question may seem rhetorical only if we neglect to consider the peculiar modalities whereby law has been 'historicized', i.e. has been made the object of historical study. Suffice it to recall the jurist who had a determining influence on the historic study of law and made the connection between history and law his own programmatic manifesto: Friedrich Carl von Savigny. According to Savigny, law is history. Roman law, however, is not identical with and does not dissolve in the histories, contexts and cultures that use it: Roman law traverses contexts and epochs, in some way remaining unscathed and uncontaminated, indeed to the point of proposing itself as the link between a remote past and the present. More than history as such, Roman law is *in* history: it is no coincidence that Savigny masterfully reconstructed the history of medieval juridical culture in a work that bears the most appropriate title of *Geschichte des römischen Rechts im Mittelalter*.[1]

Law is history, and because Roman law is the unbroken thread that unwinds through history and joins past and present, history is never 'only' history and the present is never separated from tradition: history and theory, historical reconstruction and juridical construction, comprehension of the past (of Roman law) and response to the practical and theoretical problems of the present (by means of Roman law) are closely related.

In this perspective, our problem – as to whether shared argumentations, images and theories in the juridical culture of the past continue to exist and how they function – is solved, so to speak, even before we articulate it. Roman law guarantees continuity (in time) and sharing (in space) of tradition and these can be conceived as a waterway where Roman law (more or less fluidly) flows right up to the present.

This approach cannot be separated from the conviction that the historian is strongly 'responsible' towards the present: historical reconstruction (the history of Roman law in its long journey) is an important operation because it is not 'disinterested' or gratuitous; it is related to building theories and models for our age. The function of historiography is therefore not only cognitive but also practical and constructive.

Is it legitimate today to be a Savignian (explicitly or implicitly)? Far from being academic, the question is unavoidable because recent years have witnessed the forceful assertion of a perspective that can be called Savignian or, if we prefer, neo-pandectist. In this regard, read the programmatic declarations of the imposing work that Reinhard Zimmermann devoted to the *Law of Obligation*.[2] Zimmermann is in search of something that initially may look like the theme of our study: he is in search of a shared tradition (in particular, a 'civilian tradition' in his case) that can be found in Europe's past legal culture. Zimmerman does not doubt that this tradition exists and he indicates with precision the parameters that enable its identification, characterization and use.

In his opinion, the Roman law tradition enables us to work out legal categories which, thanks to their general nature and flexibility, are suitable to the new European (and, more generally, transnational) juridical environment. Neo-pandectism accomplishes this task on the basis of a few fundamental assumptions: first, Roman law is presented as an insuperable point of reference for a rational solution of conflicts; second, Roman law is the engine of an intact tradition that cuts across the medieval and modern ages and comes right up to our times. Precisely this tradition places this 'treasure', the precious inheritance of the Roman law, in our hands. Tradition (to put it like Savigny) is the channel of transmission of a knowledge we take possession of in order to solve the problems of the present: the comprehension of the past does not find its own legitimacy in itself (Zimmermann declares that he does not cultivate 'antiquarian' interests). The present is the criterion for evaluating the past, the parameter on the basis of which one judges the relevance or irrelevance of historical data.[3]

One wonders if it is appropriate to be 'Savignians' today. Surely, there must be different answers, depending on the 'linguistic game', i.e. the discursive undertaking, one intends to address. In this regard, an illuminating distinction, formulated by Umberto Eco, comes into play, between 'use' and 'interpretation' (of a text or, more generally, of the past).[4] Nothing prevents me from freely *using* the 'materials' offered by cultures near or far, breaking and recomposing them (without worrying about their original significance), in order to form schemas, models and arguments functional to the cognitive and practical needs of my present. One must be aware, however, that such a use of the past has little to do with its history and that, for methods and ends, it is an operation which differs from the historical-hermeneutic activity employed in the difficult undertaking of giving sense to a text in the context (discursive and situational) in which it effectively functioned.[5]

The methodological legitimacy of a 'neo-pandectist' approach is therefore indisputable, provided that it does not present itself as a historical-hermeneutic operation, but instead as a juridical-constructive one. Contrarily, one would incur a serious misunderstanding if one claimed that the tradition 'invented' by neo-pandectism in function of the present were to occupy the entire area of a historiographic reconstruction.

In fact, the neo-pandectist approach takes for granted and assumes as a point of departure an element that for the historian is a problem and a (hypothetical) point of arrival, and conversely presents a datum (that for the historian is unavoidable) as a secondary incident: the datum is the extraordinary multiplicity and variety, in early-modern and modern Europe, of norms, institutions, juridical systems, discursive styles and cultures; and the problem (difficult for the historian, not only to solve, but even to formulate) is the existence of forms of communication and sharing that are capable, if not of surpassing, at least of 'traversing' the fragmentation and differentiation of contexts.

In Search of Shared Traditions: The *Ius Commune* and Natural Law Theory

The principal feature in the polycentric medieval society is perhaps the multiplicity of political institutions. Their autonomy tends to lessen in the territories where the unifying action of the sovereign is more successful, but consequently the distance is accentuated between the political orders that embraced the principle of *superiorem non recognoscentes*.

Taking this datum as a premise, our problem can be formulated in the following terms: was there in medieval and early-modern Europe a connective tissue capable of joining differentiated political institutions, a structure capable of expressing an underlying unity beyond multiplicity?

We may attempt to reply to this question by referring to very diverse profiles of the politico-juridical experience and doctrine. In my case, I shall reason by evoking two scenarios apparently without any significant connections: the *ius commune*, on one hand, and the natural law discourse, on the other. My goal is not to provide the solution to the problem, but instead only to delineate a possible approach to it.

The Ius Commune and Its Interpretatio: An Ancient 'European Juridical Space'?

If we are in search of a connective tissue that underlies the multiplicity of politico-juridical institutions, the *ius commune* seems to offer us the solution to our problem, for it seems to perfectly correspond to this possibility. We must proceed with caution, however, to avoid that the 'de-historicizing' attitude reproached in pandectism (old and new) should not otherwise ensnare our comprehension of *ius commune*.

Ius commune is not an 'invented' tradition, constructed around Roman law in order to guarantee its passage from one generation to another. *Ius commune* includes Roman law as much as it includes canon law or the *libri feudorum*. Even in cases where the *Corpus iuris* is the principal reference text, this text does not exist as such, and does not by itself produce sense: it functions concretely in the historical context (in medieval Europe and then again in early-modern and modern Europe), inasmuch as it is 'rediscovered' by interpreters who study and use it in function of their practical and cognitive necessities. The *ius commune* is not (pace Savigny) Roman law in the Middle Ages: it is a new and original phenomenon, inseparable from the societies and cultures in which it develops, produced by the incessant (I might say 'interminable') and creative *interpretatio* brought into being by a specialized (and socially privileged) body of *doctores*.

Recognizing the precise historical nature of *ius commune* protects us from neo-pandectist temptations. The problem, however, is to evaluate whether referring to the phenomenon of *ius commune* is sufficient to find a solution to our problem, i.e. the indisputable proof of the connective tissue (of the unity underlying the multiplicity of politico-juridical institutions) that we are searching for.

That this connective tissue may exist, once again seems to be demonstrated by the very notion of *ius commune*. The *ius commune* can be conceived solely in as much as it is constituently connected to the *ius proprium*: while, on one hand, the medieval jurist contemplates an open multiplicity of differentiated institutions, on the other, he is also convinced that it is possible to trace them all back to a unitary principle. In the system of the *ius commune* that Francesco Calasso termed 'classical', multiplicity and unity imply one another: far from being self-sufficient monads, the *iura propria*, the multiple and autonomous normative systems, exist inasmuch as they are rooted in the connective tissue of the *ius commune*.

Today, such a clear and harmonious solution holds yet another attraction that is more evident than it was in the years in which Calasso was writing his *Introduzione al diritto commune*:[6] it is the attraction that in general, thanks to the insidious but tempting reasoning by analogy, the Middle Ages exerts with regard to our present 'trans-statal' and 'trans-national' condition. It is no coincidence that there has been talk of a new medievalism:[7] an approach that views the Middle Ages as a sort of gigantic workshop, an open-air laboratory where an extraordinarily current experiment was conducted, i.e. the construction of a juridical system that was either totally or partially free from the state's premises. In this perspective, what lies *before* the (modern) state is ideally connected to what comes *after* the (modern) State and makes it possible to affirm that the path of a 'stateless juridical system' has been interrupted by the advent of the modern state, but nonetheless can be tried, given that it was already tried in the past.[8] It is from this perspective that a recent, renewed interest for Althusius depends: an Althusius assumed as a sort of 'anti-Bodin', an Althusius as the theorist of a system rescued from the straits of 'modern' sovereignty.[9]

Is it appropriate to give in to the discreet appeal of *ius commune* after having resisted the indiscreet charm of neo-pandectism? In this case too, we should appeal as historians to a good dose of critical awareness. First, there is a risk to applying a rhetorically efficient but analytically weak reasoning (as is the case with all arguments from analogy) if we draw on the 'classical' *ius commune* as a term of reference for constructing, for our use, a trans-statal political space. This risk arises because of the enormous difference between the contexts we want to compare. Second, and this is the profile that directly concerns our problem – we risk assuming the *thema probandum* as already proven: that is to say that the 'classical' *ius commune* was a system capable of attracting to its orbit the very numerous planets, i.e. the multiple institutions that made up medieval and early-modern society.

Is it possible to support such a thesis, and what specific sense should be imputed to it? I feel that in order to support, in all of its rigour and significance, the thesis that the *ius commune* was the connective tissue underlying the plurality of juridical systems, it is necessary to go back to Francesco Calasso's argumentations of more than fifty years ago. The entire book revolves around the need to grasp the unity underlying the plurality of juridical systems that characterized medieval society. While, on one hand, Calasso is open to the institutionalist vision of law and thus acutely aware of the multiplicity of political bodies and their complex socio-political and juridical configurations, on the other hand his philosophy of history urges him to search for the logic of unity in the unfolding of multiplicity.

The unity Calasso is thinking of is not an evanescent symbol: it is a juridical system, an effective ordering of social relations within which (and in dialectical relation to which) the numerous politico-juridical bodies are placed. The soul, the propulsive force of the *ius commune* is, of course, also for Calasso, the *interpretatio* that jurists perform around the norms (the *Corpus iuris*, firstly) which they themselves assume ('construct', legitimate) as authoritative sources. For Calasso, however, mindful of idealism and Croce's philosophy, *ius commune* is 'thought', in its deepest meaning, and for this very reason it is not an unproductive, passive, academic contemplation of reality. It is, on the contrary, action that moulds and forges the world to which it refers. Common law is therefore a system in which a sophisticated juridical doctrine, interpreting a precise and refined complex of norms, creates a 'shared' juridical system to which (following the unending dialectic of many and one) all the politico-juridical institutions refer. Calasso gives a clear and rigorous answer to our question: particular juridical systems presuppose a unity that is, on the one hand, symbol and doctrine, but, on the other, serves to order or shape experience.

Can we content ourselves today with such a clear-cut answer? It is my impression that, in Calasso's perspective, the juridical efficacy of the *ius commune* is more postulated than demonstrated. If the focus of our research is the analysis of the concrete functioning of a specific politico-juridical institution (the analysis, I would say, of its juridical everyday existence), it is necessary to seriously consider the historical morphology of the body analysed, without imagining 'generalizing' shortcuts: it is necessary, in short, to hypothesize (without this sounding like an oxymoron) as many juridical micro-histories as there are existing politico-juridical bodies.[10]

Of course, in order to understand the juridical life of specific political institutions, the *interpretatio doctorum* (therefore the *ius commune* which is both its product and foundation) is indispensable. Suffice it to consider that these institutions disregard the (modern) principle of hierarchy of normative sources, dispose of often rudimentary *iura propria* and must resort to the specialist knowledge of jurists in order to regulate social relations. It is therefore a true but elliptical expression to state that the *ius commune* has a normative effectiveness: for it to be fully effective, we must say that a certain political body regulates the social relations that unfold within its sphere employing different tools; that one of these (certainly not the least important) has precisely to do with the *ius commune* and coincides with the set of argumentations, principles and theoretical schemas that a professional class of *doctores* has produced by creatively interpreting prescriptive texts.

It is within the confines of a given politico-juridical institution (an institution that can only be 'particular' and different from other institutions from which it is separated in time and space) that social relations find their daily regulation and juridical form; and common law performs an effective regulatory action inasmuch as it is applied (adapted, transformed) by one politico-juridical body or another. For this very reason, it is pertinent to mention the difficulty of conceiving of common law as a unitary and undifferentiated entity and notice that, even only in Italy (without referring to more strongly differentiated contexts), the common law practised in Venice or the one practised at the same time in Naples or Rome or Tuscany, were not the same, even though there were many common features in the diverse experiences and all of them relevant.[11]

If this is true, the unity of the common law cannot be made to coincide with its alleged capacity to order: there is no 'shared' juridical system, distinct from the 'particular' politico-juridical institutions. In short, medieval *ius commune* is not an anticipated version (a sort of dress rehearsal) of the present 'European juridical space', that concerts its competences with those of the national states that make it up.

Instead, it is advisable to shift our attention from the normative system to the discourses, insisting on the close implication (if not the identity) between *ius commune* and *interpretatio doctorum*. Despite the differences between the 'particular' political institutions, a shared tradition thus emerges: i.e. the set of argumentations, principles, definitions and theoretical schemes which formed the specialist knowledge of a professional class; a knowledge that presents itself as an uninterrupted exegesis of the authoritative Great Texts (the *Corpus iuris*, first and foremost).

The *ius commune* substantially coincides with the specialist knowledge of a professional class of *doctores iuris*: it is in the realm of knowledge and not in that of the normative system that we must seek forms of sharing that largely surpass the different 'local' realities. It is true that the differentiations, even within juridical knowledge, are accentuated the more we draw away from the medieval *koiné*, but not so much as to make the hypothesis of a lasting sharing of methods and definitions of object inadmissible.

Of course, the 'shared' juridical knowledge was not merely a contemplative knowledge: it produced significant effects, etched into the practice and deeply influenced the life of the politico-juridical institutions, precisely because for a very long time (in substance until modern codifications) the fulcrum of the legal system was the *dicere ius*. The protagonist was the judge and the tools he employed, the schemas, argumentations and principles that supported his decision-making process, were taken from the *ius commune*, which thus took on the form of a veritable condition of possibility of the system's functioning.

If this is true, Calasso's idea of the direct normative efficacy of the *ius commune* could be restated in the name of the 'jurisprudential' nature of the early modern juridical system, by pointing out the strong relationship between juridical knowledge and practice.[12]

In this perspective we can refer to the pioneering studies that Gino Gorla undertook and promoted on the theme of the 'Great Courts of law' (such as the Roman *Rota*, the *Sacro Real Consiglio* of Naples, the *Kammergericht* and so on). The Great Courts (inasmuch as courts of appeal and, in any event, for their authoritativeness) objectively contributed to forming the modern centralized states, strengthening their internal juridical unity. According to Gorla, however, the Great Court did not exhaust its function within the bounds of a specific political institution. On the contrary, thanks to the authoritativeness of its sentences, it strengthened the sense of a common juridical area: the collections of *decisiones* by the main courts proliferated and were widely circulated among European states; in making their decisions, judges were often inspired by the sentences of law courts in other states; they looked toward the *lex alii loci* and the uniform jurisprudence of foreign jurisdictions and supported their argumentations resorting to the *opinio communis doctorum*. In short, they presupposed the existence of a shared juridical space within which the different normative systems were inscribed; and the load-bearing beam of this space was the *ius commune*, 'put in action' by the jurisprudence of the Great Courts of justice.[13]

Such studies have attained innovative results on a terrain that until relatively recently was long neglected.[14] We must, however, question whether it is legitimate to resort to them in order to demonstrate the existence of a common juridical space that underlies the growing diversification of sovereignties. In this case too, the most prudent hypothesis appears to be the most persuasive. The circulation of *decisiones* and the recourse to foreign jurisprudence do not suffice to give sentences a normative value that goes beyond the ambit of the politico-juridical institutions to which the courts belong.[15] Reference to the *lex alii loci* is not so much the evidence of the existence of a juridical-normative space as it is of a discursive space, of a shared tradition and knowledge. The *lex* or foreign sentence do not have a different value from the one attributed to the opinion of an authoritative *doctor* or to an *opinio* considered *communis*, and they serve the same purpose: that of enriching the repertory of argumentations the judge can resort to in administering justice.

Even from Gorla's 'realistic' approach it is no longer possible to assume the existence of a shared juridical space in early-modern Europe as proven. Only this hypothesis is still convincing (and draws further confirmation from the studies devoted to the jurisprudence of the Great Courts of law): the hypothesis (which has been widely verified by historiography) of a strongly coherent juridical knowledge, relatively continuous in time, and homogeneous beneath the surface of non-negligible 'local' differentiations.

The *Ius Commune* as Shared Knowledge: The Representation of the Necessary Order

The discourses created by a professional group of *doctores iuris* are the phenomenon to which we should turn our attention in order to answer our question: that is to say, in order to describe the features of a shared tradition underlying the multiplicity of political bodies. It is not possible, however, in this instance, to go searching for analytical answers. I shall therefore limit myself to indicating a possible direction of investigation.

Of course, the search for a unitary tradition, underlying the multiplicity and variety of the protagonists that concretely build it, presents a non-negligible risk: that of emphasizing the circulation and sharing of argumentations, images and theories, underestimating the differences (of time, places, authors, interests, conflicts and powers) which cannot but deeply influence even a homogeneous and coherent knowledge like juridical knowledge.

Nonetheless, the risk, though existent, must not dissuade us from attempting to grasp the characteristic aspects of a discursive tradition. Towards this end, it could be productive to resort to Kuhn's concept of paradigm,[16] practised with the necessary prudence and flexibility: it would in substance be a question of focusing on the elements that enable knowledge to become 'science', i.e. specialist and authoritative knowledge, and then to understand how medieval and early-modern legal knowledge formed itself, developed its own *method* and determined its own *object*. I shall limit myself to drawing attention to several general characteristics involving both the method and object of the *interpretatio* of the *ius commune*.

It is necessary to pay attention to the peculiarity of this *interpretatio*. Our modern term of interpretation does not do it justice. For the contemporary jurist, interpretation presupposes the existence of the text on which the interpretation is performed: it presupposes that a set of parameters are given that make it possible to consider a certain text as a *juridical* text. For our contemporary jurist, the constitution, the law and administrative regulations 'exist': they are 'already-given' texts and, as such, must be deciphered; it is from these texts that the jurist departs, though he often sees in the exegesis of the normative text only the point of departure for a more or less markedly systematic construction.

The stance of the medieval jurist differs in many ways. First, the main method is the direct relation between the jurist and the text: juridical knowledge is essentially a hermeneutic practice and coincides with the task of deciphering authoritative texts. A more decisively 'systematic' approach takes root only very slowly.

Second, if, on one hand, prescriptive and authoritative texts dominate the scene and knowledge is essentially interpretation, on the other hand the interpretation appears (to the eyes of us 'moderns') unrestrainedly 'creative' and substantially indifferent to understanding the text's 'original' meaning: the ancient text is a pre-text, a very rich and sophisticated lexical repertory that the interpreter takes possession of with the same freedom with which workmen used the marble of pagan temples to erect new cathedrals. The re-reading of an ancient text is in reality its continuous re-writing, a sort of still perfectly 'innocent' deconstructionist practice. Of course, the waters of the tranquil 'actualization' of ancient wisdom will be stirred by the humanists, but the *mos gallicus* will not at all decree the end of the paradigm: in fact, the *usus modernus Pandectarum* will prevail and the *ius commune* and its *interpretatio* will support the jurisprudence of the Great Courts of Law.

Third, and this is the determining aspect, the medieval jurist does not have an 'already given' prescriptive legal text: he is not the interpreter of the edicts of some sovereign or another, he does not move in the constrictive but reassuring orbit of the sovereign state. He performs, so to speak, a twofold motion: he constructs the *Corpus iuris* as a prescriptive and authoritative text, at the same time presenting his own knowledge as the faithful interpretation of a text which he himself (culturally and socially) has 'invented'.

The *interpretatio* thus poses itself at the centre of the paradigm precisely because it proposes itself as an instrument of method and definition of object.[17] It is a method that assumes Roman law as the primary point of reference for legal knowledge, though it rests this thesis on arguments that change each time: Roman law appears as an indispensable point of reference inasmuch as the manifestation of supreme imperial authority or the expression of human reason (as Baldus sustains introducing a thesis destined to enjoy great popularity), or because founded on a widespread custom or because received *iussu principis* within a given political institution.[18]

In the *De Usu et Authoritate Juris Civilis Romanorum per dominia principum Christianorum*, by Oxonian jurist Arthur Duck,[19] which was widely translated throughout Europe at the time, we find a didactic listing of the reasons that enjoin jurists, though operating in the most diverse European countries (from Sicily to Iceland, from Portugal to Poland), to act in the ambit of the *interpretatio* of the *ius commune*. This is a *ius commune* that does not coincide with Roman law but which in any event finds its crux in Roman law,[20] not owing to the ancient and illegitimate Roman imperial expansion, but because the most diverse peoples, by now free and sovereign, assume it as '*rationem scriptam*' and feel it must be valid '*pro jure naturali et gentium*'.[21] It is indeed by the will of Providence that '*leges romanorum apud Gentes Europaeas ut veram justitiae et Prudentiae Civilis Normam conservari, quas una cum Fidei Christianae lumine et literarum omnium scientiam solis Europaeis concessit*'.[22]

Roman law as positive law, clearly distinct from natural law, draws its universal validity from the emperor's *absoluta potestas*; Roman law is now seen as the *ratio scripta* and, as such, capable of being proposed as the inevitable point of reference for all 'European' peoples (as Duck writes); finally, Roman law is turned into 'natural law theory', Roman law is the very essence of order, its 'natural' configuration – as Duck again declares, though this thesis is widely diffused in seventeenth-century treatises.[23] For this very reason it is destined to gather the *consensus omnium*. Arguments and images change in the course of time (and these are certainly not negligible or secondary changes), but a definition of object continues to be used (even in very different contexts) which presents Roman law (and, more generally, the *ius commune*) as a set of principles and theories capable of representing the fundamentals of order: of order as such, before the specific layout of a particular politico-juridical institution.

The conceptual frame the jurist delineates, creatively interpreting the authoritative texts, does not serve to describe a specific political institution (and therefore can be easily adopted by jurists operating in differentiated historical contexts), nor is the expression of an academic or 'antiquarian' attitude towards the ancient Roman vestiges: it is the description of a system of forms and rules that does not necessarily coincide with the positive order of a specific *regnum* or of a specific *civitas*, but instead presents itself as the very structure of human society.

The implicit and shared definition of object is precisely the representation of the order underlying human intercourse as such: an order that the jurist delineates by means of interpreting the *ius commune* and, in particular, that Roman law whose authority, though diversely founded through time, is always reconfirmed and strengthened. It is easy therefore to understand that in this perspective Roman law appeared as the very incarnation of reason, indeed to the point of being assumed as identical in content with natural law; and even when the *ius commune* was presented as distinct from natural law, the former was presented as a faithful application of the latter. The validation of Roman law as '*ratio scripta*' and the representation of the order as a necessary structure of human society are strictly connected statements.

The (often implicit) conviction of describing, by means of the *interpretatio*, not so much *an* order as *the* order is perhaps one of the most recurrent features of medieval and early-modern juridical discourse. The order appears as the immanent structure of reality: it is an order removed from the dimension of temporality and impervious to all hypotheses of change. It is the representation of the necessary order (of the order as such) that forms both the overall object of the jurist's discourse and the strongest tool of his self-legitimation.

The Natural Law Theory and Enlightenment: Planning an Alternative Regime

Roman law is not a historical relic: it is a *ratio scripta* that solicits an *usus modernus* of the Pandects that were 'rediscovered' in the twelfth century. The *usus modernus Pandectarum* (attributing the widest possible meaning to this term[24]) becomes a shared knowledge, a tradition capable of bridging very diverse times and contexts because it is supported by a shared paradigm: the observance of a common method (by a 'deconstructionist' hermeneutical practice that rewrites ancient texts in function of the present) and by a common definition of the object (order as the intimate and necessary structure of society).

Supported by a specific paradigm, the *interpretatio* of the *ius commune* therefore appears as a widely shared discursive tradition. Can we assert that this is the only phenomenon of this kind in the juridical culture of the *ancien régime?* It is my opinion that we can find at least one other example of 'shared tradition': a discourse characterized by premises, argumentative styles and finalities completely different from the *ius commune* tradition; a discourse that instead draws strength from an often sharp criticism of it but that, in its own way, presents the features that we wish to underline: considerable homogeneity, widely shared argumentative style and definition of object (in short, a paradigm), and thus a capacity to propose itself as a common idiom, as a theoretical *lingua franca*.

We should grasp the point when it emerges and sketch the profile of this discursive tradition moving from the concept of order implied by the *usus modernus Pandectarum*: order as a structure of reality. Jurists are not the only ones to trace order back to *natura rei*; the whole medieval and early-modern culture represents reality as an ordered cosmos and conceives order as a hierarchy. For both the jurist and the medieval theologian, reality itself is given as an ordered whole, composed of ontologically differentiated and hierarchically arranged bodies. God, the angels, men, animate beings and (from a different point of view) the emperor, the vassal, the servant are distinct steps of a pyramid: both the cosmos and human society subsist inasmuch as they are arranged according to an unequal and hierarchical structure, culminating in a peak. An 'ontological' difference distinguishes the different steps of the hierarchy: command and obedience are articulations of a whole that dictates the rules to each composing part.

It is by these coordinates that jurists conceive the relation between the universal empire and the *civitates*; it is in full acknowledgement of society's unequal structure and the juridical differentiation of individuals that jurists elaborate the doctrine of *status* and describe the different obligations and prerogatives of each class of subjects, whose concrete legal condition depends on their belonging to one or another politico-social body and the position they occupy in the network of dominations and subordinations that constitutes the essential fabric of order.

When and how does an alternative appear? We necessarily refer to Hobbes, in particular, and in general to the assertion of a new paradigm, the natural law theory, with its characteristic manner of conceiving order, individual rights and their reciprocal connections.

For Hobbes, order is not already given; it is not a profile of human nature: order is natural only for social animals, for the society of ants and bees, but not for human society for which conflict and not order is natural. The spontaneous political, civil vocation attributed to the human being by Aristotle's *Politica* (one of the Great Texts, an *auctoritas*, on a level with the *Corpus iuris*, to which politico-juridical culture refers at least until the eighteenth century) makes room for the drive of human beings who exist in the 'state of nature' to conserve themselves and to destroy the other. Thus if the human condition is naturally dis-ordered and condemned to conflicts, order ceases to be a datum, a reality that has always existed, and becomes a problem, *the* problem to solve. And whatever be the specific solution recommended by this or that natural law theorist (absolute sovereignty, mixed government, radical democracy or what have you), order is, in any event, uprooted from its former 'naturalness' and placed into the sphere of a brand-new and problematic artificiality: order does not exist *in rerum natura*; it is the product of a decision, of an invention.

With the representation of order, the vision of individuals and rights also changes. By means of the 'state of nature' (a sort of mental experiment), the individual becomes conceivable 'as such': while the individual was placed in relation to bodies and hierarchies by medieval and early-modern culture and was attributed privileges and obligations according to his position in the network of subjections and powers, now the individual is represented in his 'naked' existence, in his state of original equality, in his condition of holder of rights immediately connected to his person.

We are faced with the emersion of a veritable paradigm (in the Kuhnian sense of the term): a new way of looking at reality, a theory that adopts (as always occurs) antecedent materials, but bends them to a different use, manipulates them to compose a new lens, a new instrument for representing the world.

Of course, tracing the multiplicity and variety of natural law approaches to the unity of the 'paradigm' is fruit of a schematization and we must be aware of its limits. Let us bear in mind at least the following profile: that the discontinuity provoked by the natural law theory paradigm, in the phase of its founding, is in some manner limited by the very argumentative schema that it itself uses, characterized by the distinction between 'state of nature' and 'civil order'.

It is in the 'state of nature' that men are free and equal. The concept of the 'state of nature' is indeed a precious tool to grasp the very essence of the human condition, reducing belonging and obedience to mere incidents; but precisely for this reason it offers an abstract, simplified and bare representation of human existence. This representation, therefore, will have to be enriched and completed by further determinations, in the course of analysis. Advancing along the line that, from the representation of the 'original' foundation of order, leads to the description of the social and political reality in all its variety and complexity, the natural law theorist will be able to make up for the inequalities and subjections of which the individual in his essence is free.[25] For a quick reference, consider Grotius' *Introduction* to Dutch law,[26] that returns to distinguish between legally differentiated individuals,[27] between *mondigen* and *onmondigen*, between the one who is fully capable and master of his own actions and the other who enjoys a more limited juridical capacity and remains subjected to tutelage.[28]

Let us also bear in mind, from another viewpoint, the flexibility of the natural law schema, that can be used to legitimate the most diverse political formulas (from the rigorous absolutism of Hobbes to the more compromising absolutism of Pufendorf, from the limited sovereignty of Locke to the 'moi commun' of Rousseau) and we shall have yet another argument to avoid exasperating the internal unity of natural law theory.[28]

With all the necessary caution we can nonetheless single out some parameters that make it possible to speak of natural law theory as a shared theoretical idiom within markedly different contexts: suffice it to consider some recurrent *tòpoi* such as the concept of 'state of nature' and its constitutive distinction from 'civil society'. These *tòpoi* are anything but harmless and academic argumentative passages. Rather, they transmit an original vision of the individual and order and enable the formation of a new paradigm, which is exactly antithetical to the dominant paradigm in the practice of the *usus modernus Pandectarum*. Consider, first, the method: while for the *ius commune* jurist, knowledge coincided with the creative interpretation of authoritative, prescriptive texts, for the natural law theorist the discourse develops departing from philosophical-anthropological axioms on which the foundation and representation of the order depends. Second, consider the object: while the jurist saw, in duly interpreted Roman law, the tool by which to grasp the fundamentals of an existent and necessary order, the natural law theorist drew from the analysis of human nature the conviction that order, far from being already given, had to be invented as an 'artificial' construct.

Of course, the new theoretical idiom was weakened by its use for different ideological-political goals. A particular significance is therefore acquired (in the direction of strengthening an effectively unitary and shared argumentative schema) by a peculiar use of the inherited theory of natural law which, in the course of the eighteenth century, spread in France, Italy and Germany.

If we look to eighteenth-century Europe, natural law theory cannot be termed the exclusive theoretical matrix of political and juridical Enlightenment, since this composite movement of opinion (perhaps the first, modern 'movement of opinion') drew on different theoretical lexicons and philosophical orientations. The inheritance of natural law theory, however, played a key role and favoured a vision of order on which the very possibility of the Enlightenment's political rhetoric depended.

For natural law theory, the 'state of nature' was a tool functional to launching a new anthropology: it focused on the individual 'as such', represented his essence and declared his original attributes (equality, liberty, rights). Situated in the hypothetical moment of origins, the state of nature was presented as the collector of original and thus fundamental aspects of the human being, before the complications introduced by the inevitable exigencies of the juridical-social order. What comes first in time, situating itself 'at the origin', is the founding element; what comes after is the derived or founded reality. The connection between the two levels of existence, however, is conceived more as one of contiguity and adaptation than as a relation of contradiction or tension.

Politico-juridical enlightenment holds (even beyond a doctrinaire adhesion to one seventeenth-century *auctoritas* or another) the central message of the 'state of nature' – the image of a human being definable in his essential qualities and original and inalienable prerogatives – but it introduces a specific tension between 'before' and 'after', between the 'moment of foundation' and what is founded, rejecting the hypothesis of a substantial compatibility between the human being's natural (essential) status and his 'acquired' (let us say, historically determined) condition.

The image of what the human being is, originally and in essence, becomes the parameter by which to evaluate the human condition in its concrete and current state of existence. The hypothesis of a pre-established harmony between 'essence' and 'existence' ceases: concrete existence does not correspond to what human nature demands. A human being is by nature what he must, always and in any event, be able to be. The anthropological assumptions of the natural law theory tradition are transformed into a deontological paradigm that questions everything that does not correspond to it: what *must be* collides with what *is*; the essential features of human nature demonstrate the illegitimacy of historically consolidated forms of human society. Present-day civilization, far from enabling the development of the human being's essential prerogatives, is limited to tossing 'garlands of flowers onto chains of iron' that in the individual suffocate 'the sentiment of the original liberty they seemed to be born unto'.[29]

Such a use of the inherited theory of natural law supports the rhetoric of reforms: it can successfully develop in very diverse historical contexts; it denounces the illegitimacy of the existing order in the name of the liberty, equality, fundamental and original rights of the human being and inaugurates that 'age of rights'[30] (and that culture of rights) usually presented as one of the tokens of modernity.

It is necessary, however, to avoid raising possible misunderstandings, born, as often occurs, of an excessively simplified representation of historical change, that is incapable of considering seriously the complex web between historical fractures and continuities.

Eighteenth-century reformers (and the theoreticians of natural law theory before them) do not suddenly discover the unknown terrain of rights. On the contrary, the *ancien régime* was characterized, at most, by a legal hypertrophy and a very complicated geography of prerogatives and obligations. The very notion of liberty (emblem in some manner of politico-juridical modernity), and the Grotian (and Lockeian) celebration of the individual's *proprium*, and of his intangible and inalienable sphere, are difficult to conceive without evoking the old medieval connection between *libertas* and *immunitas*, the idea of a liberty-immunity as an ambit free from the pressure of a superior power.

Such a subtle network of continuities prevents us from attributing the monopoly of the 'discourse of rights' to modernity (unless we choose to remain tributaries to a dated and ideological vision of modernity itself). We must not be intimidated, however, by the acknowledgement of the underlying continuities to the point that we are prevented from grasping the points of rupture and the change in perspective, ending up by refusing the *Legimität der Neuzeit* and seeing in modernity a sort of pale or deforming (in any event 'illegitimate') repetition of forms and theories already acquired in previous centuries.

The point of rupture is not provided by the discourse of rights as such; it is given, first, by the new connection between rights, the individual and the order, and then by a perspective that becomes the very condition of possibility for the rhetoric of reforms: the tension between essence and existence, between what must be and what is. It is in this new and unexpected gap that the discourse of rights enters forcefully: liberty and property (a feature that circulates throughout eighteenth-century literature and will become the crux of the future juridical civilization) acquire a new value as an instance of a rhetoric that delegitimates the existing order, while, concurrently, attempting to imagine an alternative. The novelty of the discourse of rights and the possibility it offers to become the nucleus of a different paradigm is born from it being used to place what exists in default and claim its transformation. The discourse of rights becomes an obligatory passage for the two essential components of the enlightened rhetoric: *criticism*[31] and *reform*, the delegitimation of what is and the imagining or planning what can and must be, what does not yet exist but can come into being.

Placed at the centre of a rhetoric that criticizes the existent and plans reforms, that is transformation, the discourse of rights introduces the horizon of temporality into the representation of order. The order that ancient juridical knowledge represented as necessary and immobile, an intimate form of a reality free from becoming, is now assumed to be the result of a construction, an invention, a transformation for which rights appear to be the main lever. The polemic of many reformers against Roman law and its *interpretatio* is not a parochial and superficial polemic: it is the ultimate expression of a conflict between paradigms (between visions of the individual, rights and order) whose stakes were a marked transformation of the existing politico-social order.

The Variety of Traditions and the 'Lesson' of History

I have attempted to draw attention to two shared traditions in pre-revolutionary Europe: two traditions that assumed order as their object, but offered representations which, more than being different, were in conflict with each other.

What type of relationship is it possible to establish between these by-now temporally distant traditions and our present, which is dominated by the phenomenon of constructing a European juridical area?

The effort to establish adventurous analogies between today's European common law and the ancient *ius commune* has failed (at least for those who share the preceding argumentations), precisely because the latter seems to possess the features of a shared discursive tradition,[32] more than of a veritable legal system. Of course, our intellectual lexicon, as well as our juridical lexicon, would not exist without the contributions of the different cultures that preceded us. Is this observation sufficient, however, to present the relationship between several traditions of the past and the culture of our present by resorting to the metaphor of 'roots'?

At the end of this analysis, I can confirm the 'preventive' suspicion I expressed earlier. Seeing in some tradition of the past *the* 'root' of an identity that unfolds in the present means using an image that presupposes a teleological and, in some way, 'providentialist' vision of history: only within such a philosophy of history is it possible to assume a moment of the past, one of its 'traditions', as the seed that already virtually contains the tree.

For those who do not share such a philosophy, none of the traditions I mentioned can be assumed to be the root of our present. If nothing else, the multiplicity and reciprocal incompatibility of the 'shared traditions', intervene to ward off this risk. It is not from history that an obligatory identity for the present is spontaneously generated, just because history (and therefore also European history) is a magma where the most diverse orientations, values, interests and projects clash and transform themselves in a process characterized by the contingency and indeterminacy of its outcomes.

This does not imply, however, that the *Historie*, the scholarly reconstruction of the past, is irrelevant or gratuitous, extraneous to understanding our present and planning our future. The 'lesson' of history, the contribution of historiography to the comprehension of our present, on the contrary, will be efficient all the more it remains immune to continuity and teleology and pays attention to rejections, differences, interrupted paths and unexpected openings.

Going back over the itinerary of our 'shared traditions' (the *interpretatio* of the *ius commune*, the discourse of rights of the eighteenth-century reformers) makes us aware, on one hand, of the great variety of juridical devices and, on the other hand, of the universalistic vocation of a discourse of rights that, in certain respects, has been implemented, but for many other aspects has been interrupted by the nineteenth-century nation-state. Reflecting on the contradictory multiplicity of traditions, in short, can contribute to extend the spectrum of possibilities: it can help us contain the tyranny of the present, attribute greater value to differences and, for this reason, expand the domain of the conceivable.

Notes

1. Savigny (1986).
2. Zimmermann (1992, 1998).
3. Cf. Crifò (1999).
4. Eco (1979), pp. 59–60; Eco (1990), pp. 32–3.
5. Bretone (1997), quotation p. 198, effectually writes: 'neo-pandectism forces text content inside the interpreter's schemas and paradigms. These paradigms act as essences, lasting truths, or external categories rather than as heuristic tools of a historic-hermeneutic operation with an outcome that is (by definition) unforeseeable. The objective neo-pandectism pursues, if we look closely, is not historic comprehension but instead, to keep or recover a tradition, acknowledge its millenarian continuity, whether real or unreal'.
6. Calasso (1951).
7. Bull (1977); D'Andrea (2002).
8. According to Bellamy (2003), the pre-modern tradition is heuristically interesting in order to understand the present European order.
9. Duso (2002).
10. Costa (1995).

11. Sbriccoli (2000); Mazzacane (2001).
12. Lombardi (1967).
13. Gorla (1981).
14. This is also the direction of important works by Mario Ascheri (1989) and the rich volume edited by Sbriccoli and Bettoni (1993). Also interesting are the contributions by Vallone (1988), Petronio (1997) and Miletti (1998).
15. Birocchi (2002), p. 85 ff.
16. For an example of a historiographical application of the concept of paradigm, see Costa (1986).
17. For the doctores legum, 'common law is not only the work tool that enables juridical reasoning to create tension between law and itself, it is also the result of this tool's application'. See Renoux-Zagamé (1990), quotation p. 143.
18. Luig (1977).
19. Wijffels (1990).
20. Considering that it includes 'jus Feudorum et jus canonicum; et jam sunt connexa et involuta cum jure Civili Romanorum, et cum eo juris vim habent apud omnes fere populos Christianos': Duck (1689), p. 72.
21. Duck (1689), pp. 24–7.
22. Duck (1689), pp. 405–6. 'Roman laws, as the very deposit of justice and juridical wisdom, are preserved by European peoples, inasmuch as only Europeans have been invested with them together with the light of Christian faith and the mastery of culture'.
23. Thieme (1977).
24. As to the 'narrow' or 'broad' sense of the term, see observations by Luig (1991).
25. Cappellini (1987).
26. Grotius (1953).
27. Grotius (1953), pp. 14–5.
28. Grotius (1953), pp. 20–1.
29. Rousseau (1750).
30. The reference is to Bobbio (1990).
31. In the sense of Foucault (1997).
32. Convincing argumentations in this direction in Lacché (2003).

References

Aacheri, M. (1989), *Tribunali, giuristi e istituzioni dal medioevo all'età moderna* (Bologna).
Bellamy, R. (2003), 'Sovereignty, Post-Sovereignty and Pre-Sovereignty: Three Models of the State, Democracy and Rights within the EU', in N. Walker (ed.), *Sovereignty in Transition* (Oxford and Portland), pp. 167–89.
Birocchi, I. (2002), *Alla ricerca dell'ordine. Fonti e cultura giuridica nell'età moderna* (Turin).
Bobbio, N. (1990), *L'età dei diritti* (Turin).
Bretone, M. (1997), 'La "coscienza ironica" della romanistica', in *Labeo*, 43, pp. 187–201.
Bull, H. (1977), *The Anarchical Society* (Basingstoke).
Calasso, F. (1951), *Introduzione al diritto comune* (Milan).
Cappellini, P. (1987), ' "Status" accipitur tripliciter. Postilla breve per un'anamnesi di "capacità giuridica" e "sistema del diritto romano attuale" ', *Annali dell'Università di Ferrara*, Nuova Serie, Sez. V, I, pp. 29–97.
Costa, P. (1986), *Lo Stato immaginario. Metafore e paradigmi nella cultura giuridica italiana fra Ottocento e Novecento* (Milan).

_____ . (1995), 'Ius commune, ius proprium, interpretatio doctorum: ipotesi per una discussione', in A.Iglesia Ferreiorós (ed.), *El dret común i Catalunya* (Barcelona), pp. 29–42.

Crifò, G. (1999), 'Pandettisti e storicisti nel diritto romano oggi', in *Diritto romano attuale. Storia, metodo, cultura nella scienza giuridica*, 1, 11–28.

D'Andrea, D. (2002), 'Oltre la sovranità. Lo spazio politico europeo tra post-modernità e nuovo medioevo', *Quaderni Fiorentini*, 31, 77–108.

Duck, A. (1689/1971), *De Usu et Authoritate Juris Civilis Romanorum per dominia principum Christianorum* (London and Bologna).

Duso, G. (2002), 'L'Europa e la fine della sovranità', *Quaderni Fiorentini*, 31, 109–39.

Eco, U. (1979), *Lector in fabula* (Milan).

Eco, U. (1990), *I limiti dell'interpretazione* (Milan).

Foucault, M. (1997), *Illuminismo e critica* (Rome).

Gorla, G. (1981), *Diritto comparato e diritto comune europeo* (Milan).

Grotius, H. (1953), *The jurisprudence of Holland* (Oxford).

Lacché, L. (2003), 'Europa una et diversa: a proposito di ius commune europaeum e tradizioni costituzionali comuni', *Teoria del diritto e dello Stato. Rivista europea di cultura e scienza giuridica*, 1–2, 40–71.

Lombardi, L. (1967), *Saggio sul diritto giurisprudenziale* (Milan).

Luig, K. (1977), 'Der Geltungsgrund des römischen Rechts im 18. Jahrhundert in Italien, Frankreich und Deutschland', in *La formazione storica del diritto moderno in Europa* (Florence), pp. 819–45.

_____ . (1991), 'Samuel Stryk (1640–1710) und der Usus modernus pandectarum', in M. Stolleis (ed.), *Die Bedeutung der Wörter. Studien zur europäischen Rechtsgeschichte. Festschrift für Sten Gagnér zum 70. Geburtstag* (München), pp.219–35.

Mazzacane, A. (2001), ' "Il leone fuggito dal circo": pandettistica e diritto comune europeo', *Index*, 29, 97–111.

Miletti, M. (1998), *Stylus judicandi. Le raccolte di 'decisiones' del Regno di Napoli in età moderna* (Naples).

Petronio, U. (1997), *I Senati giudiziari, in Il senato nella storia. Il senato nel medioevo e nella prima età moderna* (Rome).

Renoux-Zagamé, M.-F. (1990), 'La méthode du droit commun: réflexions sur la logique des droits non codifiés', *Revue d'histoire des Facultés de droit et de la science juridique*, 10–11, 133–52.

Rousseau, J.-J. (1750), *Discours qui a remporté le prix à l'Académie de Dijon, en l'année 1750 ...* (Genève).

Savigny, F.C. von (1986), *Geschichte des römischen Rechts im Mittelalter* (Aalen).

Sbriccoli, M. (2000), 'Intervento', in *Alberico Gentili nel quarto centenario del De Jure Belli* (Milan), 207–17.

Sbriccoli, M. and A. Bettoni (1993), *Grandi Tribunali e Rote nell'Italia di antico regime* (Milan).

Thieme, H. (1977), *Naturrecht und römisches Recht*, in *La formazione storica del diritto moderno in Europa*, I (Firenze), pp. 95–111.

Vallone, G. (1988), *Le decisiones di Matteo d'Afflitto* (Lecce).

Wijffels, A. (1990), 'Arthur Duck et le Ius commune européen', *Revue d'histoire des Facultés de droit et de la science juridique*, 10–11, 193–214.

Zimmermann, R. (1992), *The Law of Obligations. Roman Foundations of the Civilian Tradition* (Cape Town).

_____. (1998), 'Savignys Vermächtnis. Rechtsgeschichte, Rechtsvergleichung und die Begründung einer Europäischen Rechtswissenschaft', in P. Caroni and G. Dilcher (eds.), *Norm und Tradition. Welche Geschichtlichkeit für Rechtsgeschichte?* (Köln, Weimar and Wien), pp. 281–320.

Chapter 11

Resisting Public Violence
Actions, Law, and Emotions

Angela De Benedictis

The history of late medieval and early modern Europe (and the historiography on Europe) abound with images of rebellion and profiles of rebels.[1] These images gradually acquired importance, starting in the beginning of the fourteenth century, when an imperial law of Henry VII of Luxembourg defined *crimen rebellionis* in new and broader terms for the centuries to come. The long process in whose course the state (the prince, its officials, and its governing agencies) was to acquire the monopoly of the legitimate use of physical force began then, and it was evident both in the power of government institutions, and in juridical and political knowledge. Those images – of criminal acts and of disobedient subjects – have prevailed over and eclipsed other images, which presented the very same actions as legitimate and just by aiming to protect the subjects from the violence committed against them by the princely state. I wish to dedicate my essay to these other images, which for the moment are no more than a colourful collage.

Resisting 'Public' Violence: Images and Voices of (Almost) Daily Conflicts (Fourteenth Century)

In 1360, the court of the podestà of Florence accused eight men and one woman from San Niccolò della Pila (in the hills of the Mugello) of 'sedition and rebellion', of disturbing the peace and quiet of the parish of San Niccolò, and of acting against the sovereignty and the people of Florence. They had illegally joined forces and had conspired to prepare the liberation of one of their neighbours – a certain Migliore – from the hands of the podestà's police, who held him captive for debts not paid to citizens of Florence. The eight men and the woman had attacked the police shouting, 'to arms, to arms, let's kill them!' They were found guilty of rebellion and condemned to decapitation.

In the Florentine state of the second half of the fourteenth and the first half of the fifteenth centuries, this was a widespread practice: the inhabitants of communities attacked the podestà's men in order to free their neighbours who were about to be arrested. They were not always accused of rebellion, however. Indeed, the conviction of the 'rebels' from San Niccolò della Pila turns out to be an exception. The criminal sources analysed for this[2] and other cases of rural insurrections provide strong evidence for the images and voices of those who resisted 'public violence' in the conviction that they were doing the right thing.[3]

In 1399/1400, again in the Mugello, in San Niccolò a Montecarelli, another rural insurrection against the Florentine authorities was triggered, so it seems, by the heavy tax load imposed on the inhabitants of those mountainous territories. A father, his wife, and two of their children attacked the officials and a notary of the podestà while they were arresting a neighbour who had not paid his taxes in Florence. During the attack, the woman cried 'Run, run men! That we should have lost our feudal lords only to end up with so cruel a tyranny'.[4] In the summer of 1402 (according to the podestà's sentence) a number of 'traitors and rebels' from the Florentine Alps went to Bologna to plan the assault of Fiorenzuola. The project envisaged that, at the toll of the bells, their armed men were to enter the castle, where their armed friends would have been waiting with offensive and defensive weaponry.[5]

In spite of the differences in these situations, each of these three cases of rural revolt in the Florentine state shows groups of people that intervene in defence of those who refuse to obey the injunction of the podestà's officials. In all cases the group's action begins or is sustained by voices calling for collective defence: human voices ('run, run men', 'acuromo, acuromo') and voices that are associated with the life of the people in their respective communities (hammering of the bells). In real life, the actions and voices appear as moments that were inseparable from a political routine. What is particularly interesting is that those actions and those voices can be 'seen' and 'heard' not only in criminal doings, but also in some texts, which were fundamental for the juridical culture (and, consequently, the political jargon) of the late Middle Ages and the early modern period. This dual presence suggests that, inevitably, one must address the problem of the relationship between historical 'reality', political-juridical discourse and language.[6]

Juridical Texts for Almost Daily Use and Other Scenes from Almost Daily Conflicts (Fourteenth to Fifteenth Centuries)

The texts that offer images of 'lived reality' include Bartolo da Sassoferrato's commentary upon Henry VII's imperial constitution *Qui sint rebelles* dated 1312,[7] Bartolo's *Commentaria* of the *Tres Libri Codicis*, and Lucas da Penne's commentary of the same *Tres Libri*; all of them were elaborations of the juridical knowledge and culture[8] that originated around the middle of the fourteenth century (more or less contemporary with the 'rebellions' in the Florentine state referred to above). These texts are all fundamental for the criminal legal doctrine of the following centuries, up until the ninenteenth century.

Two of the most important passages of Bartolo's commentary upon *Qui sint rebelles*,[9] contained the affirmation that resistance was legitimate. Although this might seem contradictory, this was the very same doctrinal text which provided a gloss of an imperial constitution where resisting was defined as *crimen laesae maiestatis*. Of course, resistance could be legitimate only in specific circumstances and under certain conditions, as was made clear from reference to two passages, respectively, the tenth and the twelfth book of the *Codex* (C. 10, 1, 5 and C. 12, 40, 5). Bartolo's commentary of the *Tres Libri Codici* [10] explicitly listed the different circumstances that legitimated resistance. They related to problems of revenue (*De iure fisci*) and to the housing of soldiers (*De metatis et epidemiticis*).

We begin with issues relating to taxes, and the commentary of l. *Prohibitum*. The prince's envoys, when they perform a formally illegitimate or unjust deed, may be resisted by anyone with interests in the matter. In order to resist more efficiently, anyone may call relatives, friends and neighbours, who can take action even without being sent for. So that the helpers might reach the oppressed more quickly, for some time now – writes Bartolo – it is practice *per consuetudinem* that the oppressed cry out for help at the top of their lungs 'succurrite, succurrite', with the aim of rallying all those who can hear. In the case of soldiers' lodging and the commentary of l. *Devotum*, defence is possible – even the use of physical force – against soldiers who exact more than agreed upon for their lodging and who violate somebody's property. Moreover, if the soldiers want to expel someone from his property, the victim's friends and neighbours can strike them with the intent of impeding this.

A short time after Bartolo's commentary, the jurist Lucas da Penne interpreted the *Tres Libri* in a publication that proved a great success.[11] What da Penne wrote on the two laws *Prohibitum* and *Devotum* considerably amplified Bartolo's arguments. In the commentary of l. *Devotum*, not only the oppressed and their friends and neighbours could jointly resist to defend an oppressed person. It was the *populus* (the '*ipsa plebs*' referred to in the law) who could resist and rebel, since, given the fact that justice was neglected, the law was poorly observed. It was possible for a private person and the *populus* to resist an abuse, defend, against defamation such as *lex virtutis*, even kill someone who committed sacrilege. And – according to da Penne, basing himself on the authority of the Old Testament: *Maccabees* 2.4 – the *populus* could also rebel against a usurer, or kill a sacrilegist and an idolater. To resist actions committed *contra iura* and against justice, it was necessary to remember the difference between *iustitia* and *neglectus iustitiae*. If the prince neglected justice, one could pose resistance also to the prince.

Not much later, basing himself on a classification of the types of war considered by Luca da Penne, the canonist Giovanni da Legnano considered the possibility of particular body-to-body war performed in self-defence. The question posed in *De bello et de duello* was explicit: against whom could this particular war be declared? Was it legitimate against a superior?[12] The following extensive quotation conveys a sense of his position:

> And the first question is, whether a man may declare this war against his own superior. The gloss on ff. De iustit. et iure, l. ut vim, says not; it is based on ff.

De rei vindic., l. qui restituere; *and ff. De iniuriis, l.* iniuriarum, *§ i. The text of xi, q. iii, ch.* qui resistit, *supports this. I think that the gloss, as it stands, is not quite accurate, but that a distinction must be drawn. Either it is clear that the superior is acting unlawfully, or it is clear that he is acting lawfully, or there is a doubt. In the first case, I think resistance should be offered; C. De iure fisci, l.* prohibitum; *and C. De metatis, l.* devotum. *And this is especially so when what he does is something outside his office, not concerning himself. In the second case, resistance should not be offered; ff. De rei vindic., l.* qui restituere; *and ff. De iniuriis, l.* qui iniuriarum, *§ i. In the third case, it should only be offered if what has been done is something that cannot later be repaired. For such things, when once done, cannot be regarded as undone; ff. De captivis, l.* in bello, *§ facti. For in such cases the law, which forbids an appeal before final judgment allows an appeal, as is noted in C. Quor. app.* non recipiuntur, *l.* ante sententiae tempus.[13]

An already known question was part of the argument: 'Whether one may summon one's friends to help in the defence of one's property'.[14] Da Legnano's answer was the following:

> *… friends may help their neighbours in this, as I said above, because to do so proceeds from the root of charity; De Poenit., dist. ii, ch.* proximos. *And if this is allowed, the question is at once solved which might ask whether a man incurs excommunication laying hands on a clerk, while defending the goods of a neighbour against violence. Because he does not incur it, since this is not one of the things that are punished by the canon, but rather permitted'.[15]

Any act of violence eventually committed must however only be defensive and not vengeful, and considered in relation with the people's condition.[16]

The preceding texts, which we know were widely known, allow us to have a closer look at other popular insurrections, apart from those of the Florentine state. The *populus* that rebelled against neglectus iustitiae, or more specifically against unjust tax collections, could also be found in other mountains. This was the case, for example, in 1407, in the Episcopal Principality of Trent, in the town of Trent. Here, however, accusing the people of rebellion led to excommunication and interdict since the state's prince was a bishop. The *consilium* of a famous *canonist*, Francesco Zabarella, stood in defence of the *populus* against this serious accusation. For Zabarella, the people of Trent had rebelled against tax collections unjustly carried out by the bishop's officials. They had occupied the town gates and the castles, strategic positions in the town and territory. They had destroyed the houses of some officials. They had manifested the intention of submitting themselves to another lord, seeing that the bishop already had not respected certain preceding agreements. They were afraid the bishop wanted to subjugate the town and even kill some of his citizens. For this reason, they had him arrested. Zabarella's juridical argument was that the citizens had been provoked and could therefore legitimately defend themselves. The citizens were justified insofar as they were moved ('*commoti*') by the improper extortion of the bishop's officials. On the other hand, the bishop had not put an end to the extortions, but had rather allowed them, thus further burdening the citizens, something he was not allowed to do by law. The bishop had in this way acted like a private person, one was thus allowed to resist *de facto* and, if necessary, with violence. There was a law that explicitly allowed it: '*C De iure fiscil Prohibitum*'.[17]

Resisting to Defend a Common Good, or Unjust Violence against the Prince?

In the treatise *De Guelphis et Gebellinis (Quaestio III)*, Bartolo had written that if it was legitimate to summon one's friends to defend personal property, it was even more so to defend a public good.[18]

Two centuries later, the followers of Luther could not agree on how to defend a 'public' good such as the new religion of the German nation was not a question upon which the followers of Luther had a unanimous opinion.[19] As is well known, in 1530, Melanchthon was against the opinions that upheld the necessity of resisting Charles V, but in a *consilium* he presented their line of reasoning (the Emperor gave orders on questions that went beyond his competence, he did not act according to justice) and their sources (the gloss; Bartolo and his commentary of l. *Prohibitum*). However, these opinions were accepted and expounded in the *consilium* on the problem 'Quod liceat inferiori magistratui in certis casibus se contra superiorem defendere', drawn up by the jurists of Wittenberg in October 1532.

I cannot here enter into the debate on (individual and/or collective) 'legitimate resistance' in the Lutheran and Calvinist Protestant Reformations.[20] But one can say that both the material known for some time,[21] as well as the recently renewed interest in the topic,[22] can offer significant elements with which to evaluate the grounds on which the defence of a public good such as religion was reserved to those who held public authority. The question persisted elsewhere. This is very well proven by a discourse that denied as absolutely unjustifiable the use of any form of violence against the prince by the citizens, who could not enjoy public authority.

In 1605 Alberico Gentili, the jurist who had fled from Italy for religious reasons and who had become famous in Elizabethan England, wrote a slim treatise entitled *De vi civium in regem sempre iniusta*.[23] Alberico's position was unambiguous: no form of violence by the citizens was admissible against a legitimate prince, not even if the prince should govern tyrannically, that is to say, by offending the *res publica*. One had to honour the prince and not speak badly of him, because his *potestas* derived from divine and natural law. There could be no prince who harmed the homeland; nor could one uphold the notion that one was to honour the homeland more than the prince. An injury to the prince would result in grave harm for the mass of his subjects, much greater harm than that perpetrated by any tyrannical government. On the other hand, only God could correct a bad government: no citizen could be an adequate doctor for a sick government, even less so could the multitude of citizens altogether. This would have been totally absurd.

Gentili's arguments traced most of the debate on legitimate resistance and on the use of violence as legitimate means of defence that had developed especially among jurists and theologians beginning with the Lutheran Reformation. This debate had distinguished the Calvinist Reformation from the religious wars, and it had been central in the Second Scholastic period. Luther, Peter Martyr Vermigli, Sleidanus, Calvin, Beza, Michel de l'Hospital, Bodin, Franciscus Junius Brutus, de la Noue, Vasquez and Covarruvias were among Alberico's preferred interlocutors. Naturally, among them one also finds Thomas Aquinas, as well as jurists such as Alciato and Deciani, and philosophers and historians such as Cardano and Sigonio. In order to refute the well-known positions of the Catholic theologian Roberto Bellarmino, who was hostile towards the Anglican monarchy, Gentili had to sustain the absolute nature of regal power. For this reason, the *regius professor* of Oxford mostly addressed authors who had only one goal: to demonstrate that one could in no way resist the prince, not even by doubting the perfection of his laws. The prince could not be a tyrant; he was to be obeyed and revered always and anyhow. The only possible form of defence from the prince was flight.

Since there could never be a just cause for rebellion or for resisting the prince, Gentili (repeatedly) quoted Bartolo in relation only to the parts of the commentary of the imperial law *Qui sint rebelles*, where the fourteenth century jurist glossed the imperial definition of rebel as infidel and disobedient and therefore as guilty of *crimen laesae maiestatis*. Someone like Bartolo, who acknowledged some possibility of resistance, could not represent an acceptable image. Scipione Ammirato, interpreted according to the then prevalent Tacitism, could conclude the *regalis disputatio* with dignity: rebellions did not produce any effect because they almost always arose only from ambitions for power, not from love of freedom; for this reason tyranny followed upon tyranny.[24]

Legitimate Resistance and War, 1: Catalonia 1640

In spite of Gentili (and many others who were of his opinion), during the Thirty Years' War the problem of legitimate resistance was on the daily agenda of every individual and every people who experienced the war – because of its dimension of 'religious war' and because it gave rise to those conflicts that were to become the 'revolts' of the seventeenth century. And given that it was a real war, the behaviour of the soldiers, who lodged in territories and communities, concretely demonstrated – even more so than the behaviour of the tax collectors – the sort of violence to which one could, indeed should, resist: *vim vi repellere licet*. Some sources are particularly eloquent on this score, as they are in the case of the well-known Catalan uprising.

In 1640, the Catalan people rose up also against the 'unlawful' billeting of soldiers, considered to contradict the statutes of common law, and therefore the Catalan Constitution. Accused of rebellion and infidelity by the 'tyrant' Olivares, the Catalan population found scores of defenders among jurists and theologians. The jurist Martì Viladamor attributed the immediate cause of the 'movements' and 'alterations' – in short, of the events that had transpired – to the injustices perpetrated by Olivares, by his ministers, and by his officials. In defence of those injustices, the 'law' allowed for private people and the *plebs* to reprimand those who had acted against justice and to punish them without being accused of committing a crime. According to Viladamor, this was meant to give license to the oppressed, who, as Bartolo states, 'in order to resist may call their friends and neighbours to help them resist, and that they may help without being summoned'.[25] Whatever action was committed under the authority of a just law was not sinful. 'What can we say about the oppressed Catalans who resisted not only in order to thwart forbidden forms of lodging, but also to defend themselves against the horrors caused by this lodging, the offences against honour, the lives, the properties against God himself, to defend themselves against the imminent damages?'. According to the law, 'not resisting would have been a fault, and not reacting a shortcoming'.[26]

The 'law' Viladamor had in mind – even before referring to the statutes of common law and the Catalan Constitution – was the l. *Devotum*, which he read in the commentary of Lucas da Penne. On the other hand, the l. *Prohibitum*, in both Bartolo's and da Penne's commentary, was useful to his claim that a people was allowed to move together in order to resist. In the 'external forum', therefore, the Catalan people were no rebels. But for Viladamor they were not rebels even by the laws of the 'internal forum'.

> *In defence of the neighbour whose honour, life or goods are in apparent danger, both the rules of justice and those of charity can oblige; with the difference that the rules of justice oblige in both of the forums ..., whereas the rules of charity oblige only in the internal one, for which someone normally commits a very serious sin who does not defend his neighbour when he is in a condition to do so, or possesses such an authority that he is obliged to do so by the rules of justice, or not having such authority is obliged to do so solely by the rules of charity. The rules of justice bind public persons, ministers and superiors, and also prelates and public magistrates, such as the Catalan deputies and governors and aldermen of municipalities because the law gives them this authority. The rules of charity, on the other hand, oblige all in extreme need without exception, when no one of those obliged by law proceeds to defend an oppressed person.*[27]

This latter case had come about in Catalonia. Nobody among those who should have had defended the oppressed with efficient means of resistance. For this reason, desperate to find a solution, the Catalans had had no choice but feel agitated, upset, and irritated for so many vexations. Nothing else could have happened, therefore: 'the people united and with aggrieved souls they arose, guided by the divine spirit – as is written in Maccabees 2. 4. 39 –'.[28] In this case, the Catalans were not the sum of the Catalan 'individuals' but, once again, the Catalan people (also in the sense of the *plebs*), which for Viladamor was a public and not a private subject. In addition, that people (as other disconcerted, upset, and irritated peoples in Europe) found the inspiration and the courage to resist injustices in the images contained in 1 and 2 *Maccabees*, in the story of the Jews who wanted to fight for love of the law of Moses, for their allegiance to God and for their Temple in Jerusalem.

The Maccabees: The Archetype of Resistance

The Maccabees had resisted King Antiochus, who had required all the inhabitants of his kingdom to become one sole people, even at the cost of having everyone forego their own laws. Antiochus had sent his couriers to Jerusalem and into the towns of Judea with letters containing the orders to obey the foreign laws. The inhabitants of these towns were asked to forget their own laws and to abandon their traditions. Whoever did not obey the king's command would be condemned to death.[29] When it had become evident to Judas Maccabaeus and his brothers that the danger was growing and that the enemy's army had set up camp in their territory, when they found out that the king had ordered the destruction and the annihilation of their people, they reacted by saying: 'Let us repair the destruction of our people, and fight for our people and the sanctuary'. They had united the council to prepare for war and to pray and implore pity and mercy from the Lord.[30] Judas Maccabaeus had then told the Jews united in Masfra: 'Take your arms and prove that you are worthy men. From the first morning hours onward, be ready to fight against these pagans. They have joined forces against us to destroy us and our temple. It is better to die in battle than to see the ruin of our people and the temple. May God's will be done'.[31] This was the way to react to fear and dismay.[32] The Jews had also rebelled against Lysimachus because of the raids committed by the three thousand armed men at his command. Excited and furious, the people had thrown themselves against Lysimachus' men: some had used stones, others sticks, still others handfuls of soil. Many of Lysimachus' men had been wounded, some killed, and all the others forced to run. Lysimachus, who had been the first to profane the Temple, was killed close to the treasure chamber.[33]

The example of the people of Israel, in the images of its actions, served as an antidote to the Catalan people for the immobilizing fear and the dismay into which the public violence of the king's soldiers could have reduced it. Alberico Gentili had understood that stories (sacred and profane) could have this function. In his *De vi civium in regem semper iniusta* he had repeatedly sustained that the examples did not serve in any way to comprehend and resolve the problem at issue. The reason for this was clear and simple: in the examples from sacred and profane stories, the princes – the princes the people could resist – had much less power than present day princes. According to Gentili, this power was and had to be irresistible anyhow. In seventeenth-century Europe, Gentili's opinion was for many people the basis of a certain and indisputable political-juridical doctrine. For others, though, such as the Catalan Viladamor, it was to be refuted in those cases, that could arise and that did arise, where a prince acted unjustly against his subjects – as with prince Philip IV, who thought to impose one law alone onto his subjects, just as Antiochus had done with the Jewish people.

Resisting a regal right that was perceived as violent (and as such within the purview of tyrant's right) led the Catalan people to insist on the validity of the law to which they felt bound, the divine and natural law that was an irremovable component of their own laws. More than a nostalgic and unrealistic reference to the past, this meant wanting to imagine the future all the while keeping in mind the past. It meant wanting to imagine the triumph of their normative universe over the concrete experience of fear, pain and death dealt to the bodies of individuals and to the body of the community by the violence of the king's law. It was this type of experience that generally could bring individuals and peoples both to personal sacrifice (martyrdom) in order to reconstruct, regenerate, or recreate a normative universe, and to resistance in order to actively act towards the definition of a normative universe different from the one of the preponderant dominant power. The two books of *Maccabees* contain the archetype of martyrdom as well as the passage from martyrdom to resistance.

The problem of the use of violence (by the subjects against the prince or by the prince against the subjects) was not resolved once and for all on the basis of a 'political thought' or a 'juridical doctrine' that, nonetheless, was starting to become prevalent. The problem *vim vi repellere licet* continued to be considered also by those who thought that rebellions were to be condemned, but wondered about their (potential) causes.

Legitimate Resistance and War, 2: Switzerland 1653

In 1653, this question was particularly pertinent in Switzerland. Between January and September of that year, a 'peasant war' radically questioned the authority's claims to detain the monopoly on law and violence, i.e., the central and most important foundations of political power and stately sovereignty, be these foundations impersonated by the emperor or a king, by territorial princes, or by governing agencies of the *res publica* such as a council of citizens. Many images of this war (as they are brought down to us by sources and by historians who have used them) sketch a complex economic and political crisis and the peasant experience of this crisis. They show that the peasants felt physically and materially threatened. They show how, in order not to be annihilated in their existence as individuals and communities, these peasants felt the necessity to help one another, and therefore rallied friends and neighbours by ringing the bells. They show that the peasants classified as tyrants those who tried to annihilate their individual and collective existence. They show that, when necessary, they used violence to defend themselves, and how in these cases they appealed to the argument of a 'just war'.[35]

A few months after the 'peasant war' had ended with the peasant's defeat, the son of one of the protagonists in these events (on the side of the authorities) defended his doctoral thesis at the University of Basel. Johann Friedrich Burckhardt presented a commentary of the imperial constitution *Qui sint rebelles* from 1312,[36] and in the preface he justified his choice of topic: the topic 'rebellions' was quite common in that century, especially and above all in the territories of the Swiss Cantons.

Burckhardt's dissertation was divided into twelve theses. The first five addressed the definition and identification of the rebel and the rebellion. Following the constitution of Henry VII, Burckhardt sustained that rebels were all those who did not preserve the loyalty they had assumed towards the prince or the *res publica*, in short those who did not obey orders, thus generating a state of war. Rebels were those who nullified the bonds of obedience and loyalty, posed resistance to their superiors and their jurisdiction, and tried to cast off the yoke and set themselves free. Rebellion was a movement of contumacious subjects who resisted the law and that was lawful. One could be a rebel by doing something against the prince, or by not doing and not obeying, or also by resisting in both ways. Against whom did rebels rebel? In the time of Henry VII, author of the imperial constitution, only against the emperor. Today – Burckhardt specified – they also rebelled against the princes electors, the princes, the *res publicae*, in other words against everyone who did not acknowledge to have a superior.

The sixth to the twelfth theses dealt with the causes of rebellion, and remedies for avoiding them. The first and most important cause of every rebellion was seen in the excessive 'tyranny of the magistrates', or in the 'unusual taxation and oppression [of the subjects] above all through excessive taxes and tributes'. Offences against the two pillars of every society, namely religion and justice, were also cause for rebellion. Those who offended justice today, commented Burckhardt, were also the court bureaucrats who interpreted the laws and consequently acted not according to justice but according to the prince's will. The subjects' rebellion could also be caused by some form of 'pain' deriving from the prince, by the fear that the prince would present a serious threat or commit an act of oppression: in order to prevent fear and oppression the subjects often rebelled. On the other hand, princes who ruled their subjects in a reign of terror were real tyrants and not princes. Here Burckhardt's thesis was sustained by a quotation from Scipione Ammirato (the same *Italus* adopted by Alberico Gentili for motivating the futility of any rebellion): 'From desperation immediately arises the strict proposal to commit anything sacrilegious & horrible. And the prince can never have a more ferocious enemy than the desperate citizens. Scipione Ammirato lib. I. disc. 8'.[37] Among the causes for rebellion there was also the situation deriving from the fact that the poor could see others living in conditions of excessive luxury and idleness.

The identification and condemnation of some of the causes of rebellion did not prevent Burckhardt from drastically stating his point of view in the last three theses. In order to circumvent rebellions, one had to find solutions to avoid them, or else they had to be put down with opportune methods. If the remedies initially found did not work, it was appropriate to try other and better ones; otherwise, one could resort to war against the rebels. Once the rebels had been overcome with weapons, they would need to be punished according to the situation at hand: from the loss of everything pertaining to civil law to capital punishment, banishment, or other forms of punishment.

To Resist is to Exist

By definition, the seventeenth century was the century of revolts and rebellions. In those days, it was common for the 'people' of Europe to construct the social reality of the crises they experienced by feeling that life was threatened and endangered, and wanting, instead, to preserve it. 'The shape of the crowd's actions and their choice of targets were informed by their construction of the crisis of the early 1640s, a crisis simultaneously experienced as a threat to both livelihoods and liberties'. It becomes clear that 'popular violence was neither simply reactive nor narrowly instrumental'.[38]

The more it manifested itself, beyond concrete repression, the more theoretical attempts increased in number aimed at neutralizing it. The first to come to mind is obviously Thomas Hobbes: not only because of the fear wilfully inspired by the image of *Leviathan*,[39] but also because of the safety *Leviathan* promised to the subjects/citizens for the preservation of their lives. With this 'classic of politics', published in 1651, Hobbes was the first to blend a scientific political theory with an anthropology grounded in the canons of the new science of the seventeenth century, i.e., a general theory of human nature constructed on a psychological conception based on an inquiry concerning physiological mechanisms.

The new general scientific theory of human nature was, however, also used to claim that the subjects/citizens could react to the king's violence with their own violence, in cases where royal violence led to the destruction, and not the preservation of their lives. Resistance became necessary for affirming existence. It was this reasoning that was so radically reflected in Baruch Spinoza's *Political Treatise* (on the basis of the *Ethics*), notwithstanding the profound and strong condemnation (*Ultimi barbarorum!*) of the popular fury, which in 1672 had afflicted the free Republic of the United Provinces. Everybody had the innate inclination to concatenate the emotions (*conatus*) and in this way – through the power of affirmation – to actively resist the more powerful external forces trying to destroy it. People everywhere established common habits (*consuetudines*) and acted to help their neighbours, driven by an ethics of resistance and love.[40]

When the sovereign, stimulated by the logic of ambition to dominate, oppressed the subjects beyond the physical limits of what they could bear, he became a tyrant, so that the subjects were induced by their *conatus* to preserve their lives. Then the subjects created a state of war according to a 'right to war'[41] that consisted exclusively in the actual power to resist and defend oneself, with all possible means, against tyrannical violence. The state of war was always latent in civil society; it became explicit when the exercise of sovereignty was lived by the multitudes as true aggression. At this point the king could be deprived of the power by which he dominated, not so much on the basis of civil law, but rather by right of war. Speaking of right of war was the same as saying that the subjects could react to his violence only with violence.[42]

A situation that had physically and/or emotionally become unbearable, intolerable for the subjects/citizens, would lead to indignation, wrath and rebellion. In this case, the act of resisting regarded all those individuals for whom the tyrant's actions had transformed the subjects' habitual feelings of fearfulness and respect into 'indignation'. Although indignation was apparently one of the most negative emotions,[43] being a hateful emotion, there was nevertheless something positive at the root of this hate. The relationship of identification, of similarity, of love that every person had for his/her kin necessarily meant taking action to free them from their ills, for which all suffered. 'This imitation of the emotions, when it is related to pain, is called "compassion"', Spinoza had written in the *Ethics*.[44] This emotion led everyone to feel pity for every man who was unhappy and to free him from unhappiness.[45] Compassion, and benevolence born out of pity, induced people to move together to resist against pain.[46]

Resistance and 'Moral Economy'

Tax increases on countless food items that characterized the fiscal politics of many large and small governments in that part of the seventeenth century dominated by the 'winds of war' provoked by Louis XIV were certainly felt to be an evil to be done away with, something that provoked individual and collective indignation.

In the years from 1686 to 1699, a real peasant movement developed in the *Kleinstaaten*, the *Miniaturherrschaften* of the Rhine-Maas-Land, the 'land without borders' between the Rhine and the Netherlands, against the attempt to raise the tax on the unit of measure of beer on behalf of the territorial lord Kornelimüster (an abbot).[47] Part of the movement wanted a judicial solution (which was considered the result of legitimate resistance conducted by way of the courts), while others spoke out in favour of a direct right of self defence. When, in 1698, the abbot did not respect the judicial solution obtained five years earlier, and once again raised the tax on beer without the population's consent, the subjects of the 'political microcosm' of Kornelimünster decided unanimously to take action. They came together in the parish church to assure themselves of the divine benediction for the punitive actions planned against the hosts who had obeyed the abbot's orders. The protest was reinforced by rivers of beer, in a territory where – as in other territories of the Holy Roman Empire of the German Nation – raising the price of beer was tantamount to raising the price of bread in other parts of Europe. But the question was not simply an economic or fiscal one. The territorial lord had tried to fiscally exploit the daily needs regarding a foodstuff as necessary as beer without the subjects' prior consent. From the moral point of view, this was considered unacceptable behaviour: and as such, it authorized the subjects to resist, even by violence. In 1699, the subjects' procurator denied the abbot's *ius superioritatis*. Some time later, the abbot accused the subjects at the *Reichshofrat* in Vienna, deeming them guilty of sedition and rebellion. Shortly afterwards, the abbot, judged to be a tyrant, was killed in an ambush. Yet the conflict between the subjects of Kornelimüster and the subsequent territorial lords continued for another century amid highs and lows: it was not always about beer but also, at the end of the 1780s, about the so-called 'wheat monopoly', which was in the hands of a society of mill leaseholders. Be it beer or wheat, the fundamental problem was that taxes and monopoly were considered unjust, a blow against the principles of justice, common good, sufficiency, tradition. For the subjects all of this went beyond the acceptable limits.

The conflict in question could also pertain to a community's pasture rights, as in Bibersbach in 1735. In order to defend these rights against the claims or abuses of the territorial lord, the community's lawyers drew upon the expert opinion of the Italian jurist Baldo degli Ubaldi, in the passage where Bartolo da Sassoferrato's student held that, according to natural and people's law, and according to civil and canon law, one could meet violence with violence: '*vim vi repellere licet*'. It was therefore legitimate to resist the private person and to resist the prince who unjustly used violence: in this latter case, this prince need not be considered a prince, but simply a person.

The actions of the subjects of the imperial *Miniaturherrschaften* were informed by those principles that Edward P. Thompson recognized in the bread and butter riots of eighteenth century England, and which he defined as the poor man's 'moral economy'.[48] In all the immediate popular actions, clear 'notions of legitimacy' were detectable. The behaviour of the men and women in the crowd was therefore guided by the conviction that they were defending rights and traditions, and they were so sure of the community's approval that fear and deference toward the authority were completely annulled. An offence against the moral principles of the community could habitually constitute the incentive for immediate popular action, as much as an effective state of deprivation of a good of daily sustenance.

Final Considerations

Baruch Spinoza, the 'theoretician' of resistance as the affirmation for the existence of individuals, multitudes and communities, explicitly addressed the problem of *vim vi repellere licet* in a part of his *Tractatus politicus* where the central point was the discussion of the defence of the Aragonese peoples' liberty and the ensuing resistance against any kind of king or prince who would exercise public violence by depriving them of that liberty.[49] His deliberations contained no trace of a qualitative difference between an individual's or a people's indignation and the indignation of those, among the people, who had to protect that good. In both cases, resistance derived from the attitude everybody had towards connecting the emotions. This is what the inhabitants of the Mugello had done in the second half of the fourteenth century, the citizens of Trent at the beginning of the fifteenth, … and in all the other cases considered here up until the eighteenth century.

In different places and times and in different political and social contexts, bodies composed of individuals, groups and communities, showed the same capacity to recognize the various material, institutional and symbolic ways in which public violence was exercised.

Today, to the degree for which it is possible for us historians to observe the practices and the discourses used to react to public violence (that is, to the violence of the prince's law and of his officials), it is equally possible to observe that the prince's public violence was not necessarily considered legitimate by those at whose expense it was exercised. Individuals, groups, bodies and communities defined as rebels by the prince's law and by its interpreters, showed by their behaviour to have been entirely aware that they lived in a normative world[50] which consented to them the right to resist legitimately to the law, to its applications and to the discourses of its interpreters.[51] The practices and discourses as well as the knowledge accumulated over time, of those who resisted were expressed, depending on time and circumstances, as the needs of individuals, or, more frequently of groups, bodies and communities.[52] Only in recent decades have the forms of this resistance been identified, in their specificity, by historians. For this reason, today, we begin to recognize images of Europe which, for a long time, were obscured by the long shadows of a history of the state's power, and of the state's right – a history constructed 'teleologically' and defined by the 'irresistible' process of constructing an exclusive monopoly of the legitimate use of power.

Translated by Friederike Oursin

Notes

1. I am making the deliberate, even if slightly risky, choice of not giving a general bibliography on the topic of revolts, rebellions and revolutions. The limitations of the present essay do not allow for it. I do, however, feel the need to mention that the problem has also been of interest for another historian who is part of the same section of this book; namely Coleman (1990).
2. Cohn (1999), p. 145.
3. That Cohn did not emphasize this evidence can be ascribed to the fact that resistance was not part of his 'set' of problems.
4. Cohn (1999), p. 154: 'Acuromo, acuromo, che noy perdiamo el nostro Signore et noi aviamo si crudel tiranno'.
5. Cohn (1999), pp. 162–63.
6. On this aspect, see the recent methodological proposals by Schorn-Schütte (2004).
7. The constitution *Qui sint rebelles* – or, from its incipit, *Quoniam nuper* – was published in Pisa in 1312 by emperor Henry VII to punish the 'rebel' Robert of Anjou. Henry's constitution and Bartolo's gloss were then inserted into the *Volumen legum* of the *Corpus iuris civilis*, as collatio undecima, after the nine collationes of *Novellae* by Justinian and immediately after the tenth collatio containing the *Libri feudorum*. Sbriccoli (1974), pp. 141 ff.; Quaglioni (1994, 1999).
8. On juridical knowledge and culture, see the papers presented by Coleman and Costa in this volume.
9. The gloss to *Tenore* and the gloss to *Rebellando*.
10. Bartolus (1574), (consulted edition).
11. Luca da Penne (1582). The importance of Luca da Penne's writings (see the classic study by Ullmann (1946)) and his use also in later centuries in relation to the topic at hand, was brought to attention by D'Addio (1954); Maffei (1956); Calasso (1965).
12. Giovanni da Legnano (1964), Ch. LXVII, LXXXIX, pp. 276–7.
13. Giovanni da Legnano (1964), p. 209.
14. Giovanni da Legnano (1964), Ch. CVIII.
15. Giovanni da Legnano (1964), p. 301.
16. Giovanni da Legnano (1964), Ch. CXIV: 'Of equivalence in the act of violence itself. How should the act be done?', p. 304.
17. Girgensohn (2001), the consilium is edited on pp. 374–83.
18. '... sicut enim ad tuitionem rerum liceat congregare amicos, ita multo magis ad tuitionem publicam, ut ff. de vi et vi armata, l. iii, § cum igitur [D. 43, 16, 3, 9]'. The treatise was edited by Quaglioni (1983). Quotation on p. 137. The government of a city was also considered a public good: this passage was, in fact, used also in case the prince of a territorial state wanted to change the government of a city in that state, to defend the

town from the prince's violence. A particular case, in the relationship between Pope Julius II and Bologna, De Benedictis (2004).

19. Some were for Nicodemism: Ginzburg (1970).
20. See now, the new results by von Friedeburg (1999, 2001, 2002). For the Netherlands, van Gelderen (1992).
21. Many of them, as is well known, in Skinner (1978).
22. Among them also some papers contained in De Benedictis and Lingens (2003) (especially Scattola, Strohm, von Friedeburg and Stock), that are mentioned in De Benedictis [2002a].
23. One of the three *Regales Disputationes*, dedicated to James I, the new king of England; see also Panizza (1981), pp. 160–3.
24. Ammirato (1599), L. XIX, Discorso X.
25. Martì Viladamor (1995), p. 107 (the translation from the Castilian is mine).
26. Martì Viladamor (1995), p. 108.
27. 'Alla difesa del prossimo che si trova in manifesto pericolo dell'onore, vita o beni, possono obbligare sia i precetti della giustizia, sia quelli della carità, con la differenza che mentre i precetti della giustizia obbligano nell'uno e nell'altro foro ..., i precetti della carità obbligano solo nel foro interiore, per il quale generalmente commette peccato molto grave chiunque non difenda il prossimo pur potendo farlo, o abbia autorità tale per cui vi è obbligato dai precetti di giustizia, oppure non avendo tale autorità sia obbligato solamente dai precetti di carità. I precetti di giustizia obbligano le persone pubbliche, ministri e superiori, e anche prelati e magistrati pubblici, come i deputati di Catalogna e consiglieri e giurati delle università, perché il diritto dà loro questa autorità. I precetti della carità obbligano invece senza eccezione tutti nel bisogno estremo, quando nessuno di coloro che sono obbligati per giustizia va a difendere l'oppresso'. Martì Viladamor (1995), p. 109. I have already worked with this text in De Benedictis (2002b).
28. Martì Viladamor (1995).
29. Mc 1, 1, 41–53, quoted from the original edition Martì Viladamor (n.d.), cap. XIII, p. 105.
30. Mc 1, 3, 42, in Martì Viladamor (n.d.), cap. XIX, p. 157.
31. Mc 1, 3, 59, in Martì Viladamor (n.d), cap. XXII, p. 178.
32. As also in Mc 1, 13, 1–7 (Simon assumes command of the Jews), in Martì Viladamor (n.d), cap. XIV, p. 117.
33. Mc 2, 4, 39–42, in the original edition Martì Viladamor (n.d).
34. These reflections on the text and on the Catalan experience (which of course can also be of more general value) are suggested to me by the reading of Cover (1992), especially Chapter 5: 'Violence and the Word', pp. 206–8. For other aspects of the question, see Assmann (1999).
35. Suter (1997).
36. Burckardus (1654). Quoted indirectly by Suter (1997), p. 563 ff., I was able to consult a copy of the thesis at the Max-Planck-Institut für Europäische Rechtsgeschichte, Frankfurt am Main.
37. Burckardus (1654).
38. According to the analysis by Walter, (1999) p. 8.
39. Bredekamp (1999). I limit the literature on Hobbes to this monograph of the art historian from Berlin.
40. For this interpretation of Spinoza I follow Bove (1996). However, I explicitly refer to the Italian translation, Bove (2002), especially pp. 24–28, 149–54, 305–23. New, and very

interesting, the book by the same translator of Bove: Del Lucchese (2004). From the literature on Spinoza, regarding the questions tackled here, I only quote Balibar (1996), and Costa (1999), especially pp. 220–46.

41. It is impossible not to think back, for example, to the 'just war' invoked by the Swiss peasants in 1653!

42. I have paraphrased, in these last lines, the Italian translation of Spinoza (1999): VII, 30, p. 147. In the Latin original is the following: 'Nam ut Art. 5 et 6. Cap. 4. ostendimus, Rex non iure civili, sed jure belli dominandi potentia privari potest, vel ipsius vim vi solummodo repellere subditis licet' (Spinoza [1999], p. 146). This quotation very succinctly stresses the importance of the role of Latin which Françoise Waquet presents in her contribution to this volume.

43. '… hatred towards a person who has done harm to another we shall call "indignation" ', Spinoza, (2000), Part Three: On the Origin and Nature of the Emotions, Proposition 22, Scholium, p. 181.

44. Spinoza (2000), Proposition 27, Scholium, p. 184.

45. Spinoza (2000), Proposition 27, Corollary 3, Demonstration, p. 185.

46. The 'commozioni' mentioned in Martì Viladamor's Catalan text come to mind regarding this proposition of Spinoza's.

47. Gabel (1995). This line of research is part of the Widerstandsforschungen developed as part of a wide-ranging project promoted above all by Peter Blickle and Reinhard Schulze in the 1980s and 1990s. For an overview, I only quote Blickle (1997).

48. Thompson (1971), reprinted in Thompson (1991).

49. Spinoza (1999), pp. 143–9.

50. In the sense used by Cover (1992), p. 206.

51. Schorn-Schütte (2004); Quaglioni (2003), pp. 369–76.

52. As von Friedeburg (1999) and (2002) has very well explained; von Friedeburg (2001). Such variety of situation and practices is, in my estimation, only partially and insufficiently understandable by distinguishing practices and discourses that are typical of a class-based 'right to resist' from practices and discourses that characterize a popular 'right to resist'. This point also emerges from Reinhard (1999), pp. 226–39.

References

Ammirato, S. (1599), *Discorsi sopra Cornelio Tacito* (Venice).

Assmann, J. (1999), *Das kulturelle Gedächtnis. Schrift, Erinnerung und politische Identität in frühen Hochkulturen* (Berlin).

Balibar, E. (1996), 'What is "Man" in Seventeenth-Century Philosophy? Subject, Individuals, Citizen', in J. Coleman (ed.), *The Individual in Political Theory and Practice* (Oxford), pp. 215–41.

Bartolus a Saxoferrato (1574), *In Tres Codicis Libros Commentaria* (Augustae Taurinorum).

Blickle, P. (ed.) (1997), *Resistance, Representation and Community* (Oxford).

Bove, L. (1996), *La stratégie du conatus: affirmation et résistance chez Spinoza* (Paris).

_____ . (2002), *La strategia del conatus. Affermazione e resistenza in Spinoza* (Milan).

Bredekamp, H. (1999), *Thomas Hobbes Visuelle Strategien. Der Leviathan: Das Urbild des modernen Staates. Werkillustrationen und Portraits* (Berlin).

Burckardus, J.F. (1654), (Johann Friedrich Buckhardt), *Dissertatio inauguralis juridico politica ad Constitutionem Henrici VII. Imperator. Rom. c. unic. Qui sint rebelles in Extravag. maxime accomodata …* (Basileae).

Calasso, F. (1965), 'Luca da Penne', in *Annali di storia del diritto*, IX, pp. 313–69.

Cohn, S.K. Jr (1999), *Creating the Florentine State. Peasants and Rebellion, 1348–1434* (Cambridge).

Coleman, J. (1990), *Against the State. Studies in Sedition and Rebellion* (London).

Costa, P. (1999), *Civitas. Storia della cittadinanza in Europa. 1. Dalla civiltà comunale al Settecento* (Rome and Bari).

Cover, R.M. (1992), *Narrative, Violence and the Law. The Essays of Robert Cover*, Martha Minow, Michael Ryan and Austin Sarat (eds.) (Ann Arbor).

D'Addio, M. (1954), *L'idea del contratto sociale dai sofisti alla riforma e il 'De Principatu' di Mario Salamonio* (Milan).

De Benedictis, A. (2002a), 'Resistere: nello Stato di diritto, secondo il diritto "antico", nell'Europa del "diritto al presente" ', *Quaderni fiorentini per la storia del pensiero giuridico moderno*, XXXI, 273–321.

_____. (2002b), 'Identità comunitarie e diritto di resistere', in P. Prodi and W. Reinhard (eds), *Identità collettive tra Medioevo ed Età moderna. Atti del Convegno internazionale Bologna 28–30 settembre 2000* (Bologna), pp. 265–94.

_____. (2004), *Una guerra d'Italia, una resistenza di popolo. Bologna 1506* (Bologna).

De Benedictis, A. and K.H. Lingens (eds) (2003), *Sapere, coscienza e scienza nel diritto di resistenza (XVI–XVIII sec.) – Wissen, Gewissen und Wissenschaft im Widerstandsrecht (16.–18. Jahrhundert)* (Frankfurt am Main).

Del Lucchese, F. (2004), *Tumulti e indignatio. Conflitto, diritto e moltitudine in Machiavelli e in Spinoza* (Milan).

Friedeburg, R. von (1999), *Widerstandsrecht und Konfessionskonflikt. Notwehr und Gemeiner Mann im deutsch-britischen Vergleich 1530 bis 1669* (Berlin).

_____. (ed.) (2001), *Widerstandsrecht in der frühen Neuzeit. Erträge und Perspektiven der Forschung im deutsch-britischen Vergleich* (Berlin).

_____. (2002), *Self-defence and Religious Strife in Early Modern Europe: England and Germany, 1530–1680* (Aldershot).

Gabel, H. (1995), *Widerstand und Kooperation. Studien zur politischen Kultur rheinischer und maasländischer Kleinterritorien (1648–1794)* (Tübingen).

Gelderen, M. van (1992) *The Political Thought of the Dutch Revolt* (Cambridge).

Ginzburg, C. (1970), *Il nicodemismo. Simulazione e dissimulazione religiosa nell'Europa del '500* (Turin).

Giovanni da Legnano (1962), *De bello, De represaliis et De duello*, edited by Thomas Erskine Holland, Washington, 1902 (New York).

Girgensohn, D. (2001), 'Vom Widerstandsrecht gegen den bischöflichen Stadtherrn. Ein Consilium Francesco Zabarellas für die Bürger von Trient (1407)', *Zeitschrift der Savigny Stiftung für Rechtsgeschichte*, CXVIII, KA LXXXVII, 307–85.

Luca da Penne, (1582), *Commentaria D. Lucae de Penna iuriscons. Clarissimi in Tres Posteriores Lib. Codicis Iustiniani. In quibus, & inter alia ab eo curiose observata multa, idque doctissime, ad cognitionem magistratuum & Praefecturarum Francorum, collegit & animadvertit, usumque antiquorum magistratuum Romanorum aptissime ostendit [...]* (Lugduni).

Maffei, D. (1956), *L'umanesimo giuridico* (Milan).

Martì Viladamor, F. (1995), *Noticia Universal de Cataluña de Francesc Marti Viladamor*, X. Torres(ed.) (Vic).

_____. (n.d.), *Noticia Universal de Cataluña*, Biblioteca de Catalunya, Fullets Bonsoms, 76 (Barcelona).

Panizza, D. (1981), *Alberico Gentili, giurista ideologo nell'Inghilterra elisabettiana* (Padua).

Quaglioni, D. (1983), *Politica e diritto nel Trecento italiano. Il 'De tyranno' di Bartolo da Sassoferrato (1314–1357). Con l'edizione critica dei trattati 'De Guelphis et Gebellinis', "De regimine civitatis' e 'De tyranno'* (Florence).

———. (1994), '"Fidelitas habet duas habenas". Il fondamento dell'obbligazione politica nelle glosse di Bartolo alle costituzioni pisane di Enrico VII', in G. Chittolini, A. Molho and P. Schiera (eds), *Le origini dello Stato. Processi di formazione statale in Italia fra medioevo ed età moderna* (Bologna), pp. 381–96.

———. (1999), '"Rebellare idem est quam resistere". Obéissance et résistance dans les glosses de Bartole à la constitution "Quoniam nuper" d'Henry VII (1355)', in : J.C. Zancarini (ed.), *Le Droit de résistance XIIe–XXe siècle* (Fontenay-St. Cloud), pp. 35–46.

———. (2003), Conclusioni, in A. De Benedictis and K.H. Lingens (eds), *Sapere, coscienza e scienza nel diritto di resistenza (XVI–XVIII sec.) – Wissen, Gewissen und Wissenschaft im Widerstandsrecht (16.–18. Jahrhundert)* (Frankfurt am Main), pp. 369–76.

Reinhard, W. (1999), *Geschichte der Staatsgewalt. Eine vergleichende Verfassungsgeschichte Europas von den Anfängen bis zur Gegenwart* (München).

Sbriccoli, M. (1974), *Crimen laesae maiestatis. Il problema del reato politico alle soglie della scienza penalistica moderna* (Milan).

Schorn-Schütte, L. (ed.) (2004), *Aspekte der politischen Kommunikation im Europa des 16. und 17. Jahrhunderts* (München).

Skinner, Q. (1978), *The Foundations of Modern Political Thought. The Age of Reformation* (Cambridge).

Spinoza, B. (1999), *Trattato politico*, testo e traduzione a cura di P. Cristofolini (Pisa).

———. (2000), *Ethics*, ed. and trans. by G.H.R. Parkinson (Oxford).

Suter, A. (1997), *Der schweizerische Bauernkrieg von 1653. Politische Sozialgeschichte – Sozialgeschichte eines politisches Ereignisses* (Tübingen).

Thompson, E.P. (1971), 'The Moral Economy of the English Crowd in the Eighteenth Century', *Past & Present*, 50, 76–136.

———. (1991), *Customs in Common* (London).

Ullmann, W. (1946), *The Medieval Idea of Law as Represented by Lucas de Penna. A Study in Fourteenth-Century Legal Scholarship* (London).

Walter, J. (1999), *Understanding Popular Violence in the English Revolution. The Colchester Plunderers* (Cambridge).

Waquet, F. (2002), *Latin or the Empire of a Sign. From the Sixteenth to the Twentieth Centuries*, trans. J. Howe (London and New York).

Part III: Images

Four images are objects of discussion in this section's four papers: the tree; the museum; heroism and sainthood; and Latin, as a language shared by scholars, professionals, and schoolchildren.

These are not the only images to which reference is made in this book's pages. Several others appear in various essays – from images of the body in the first section, to those of violence in the second. Many more could have been chosen, to which no reference is made in this book. We have, for example, avoided the rich theoretical discussions regarding images that, from the Byzantine era's iconoclastic clashes through those of the sixteenth century's religious Reformation, often emerged in theological and philosophical discourse. So have we also neglected the complex and intense discussions about the meaning of images from the writings of Franciscan and Dominican preachers in the thirteenth and fourteenth centuries, through those of Italian theorists in the fifteenth and sixteenth, to the echoes of these earlier discussions in the writings of distinguished twentieth century art historians and philosophers such as Ernst Gombrich and Arthur Danto. To these two more theoretical issues, one could add an almost infinite number of other images, very specific as the image of bread or that of light which we toyed with the idea of including in this volume, to somewhat more abstract, such as the powerful images of Odysseus (Ulysses), or Heracles (Hercules), or Aphrodite (Venus), each of which generated a discursive tradition of its own, from long before the Middle Ages to, arguably, our own days. The catalogue of such omissions could, indeed, be lengthy, but not especially useful. Better, here, to briefly suggest what function this section occupies in the context of our broader inquiry.

Our aim, then, is more modest. We offer, below, four suggestions of how certain images – in this case the four selected for systematic treatment – can be used to illustrate the emergence of four resilient discursive traditions in Europe. Some of these traditions had very long lives, those of the tree and of Latin, for example. Others were more circumscribed in time, and depended on their expression on more specific circumstances, the case of the museum being an example. The images of sainthood and heroism found specific expressions in the sixteenth and seventeenth centuries that are analysed, below, although the roots of such expressions can be traced back to much earlier times. Alongside each discursive tradition's long temporal dimension, there is also its geographic breadth. In nearly all instances each of these discourses drew on the contributions of participants from Poland to Italy, from Denmark to the Iberian peninsula. Discursive traditions were generated around images, as much as they were around notions of margins and of communities, explored, respectively, in this book's preceding sections.

Chapter 12

The Tree

Christiane Klapisch-Zuber

Trees have peopled the imagination of the Christian West. Several images have been used, reappearing in different versions, having to do with language or with visual aspects. Everybody knows the tree of life.[1] We meet this cosmic symbol from Mesopotamian antiquity, in the four corners of the world, and sometimes in much more elaborate forms than in Europe.[2] But the tree of life is not – except in some of its Christianized forms – specific to the popular culture of Europe's ancient societies. The trees of Eden, versions of the cosmic tree of life, open and close the Bible; their union with the redemptive tree of the cross fertilized medieval art and produced some of its finest inventions, but it cannot be said that in itself the tree of life is a founding figure of Europe's identity. It nourished its imagination, overlapping with other representations and influencing neighbouring images, but did not take a place as a dominant figure at the heart of the dreams of our traditional societies. Other trees have had an unexpected destiny, as, for instance, the tree of universal power Nebuchadnezzar dreamed of, the meaning of which Daniel explained to the king (Dan. 2, 7–13 and 4, 17–23): this tree that nourishes, gives shade and protects is another of those images or metaphors whose extensions in the rhetoric of power are still referred to today.[3]

Here, we shall mention a few other arboreal series. In the Christian West, and this is perhaps a difference from other, non-European cultures, the symbolic and metaphorical trees borrowed from the religious or popular repertoire continually interacted with the *arbor*, i.e. the tree-based diagrams widely used by medieval clerics and then by early modern scholars as they sought to explain through them the meaning of the world. The tree image that came to prevail became a tool of thought, a widely used conception in Europe until the nineteenth century. The *arbor*, the tree of life and the tree of power, to mention just three, thus offer different aspects of a metaphor; the exchanges between these have been repeated and mutually enriching, giving rise to a profusion of 'natural' trees, vivid figures of Western symbolism and rhetoric.

The Naturalization of the Diagrams

To approach the *arbor* of the monasteries, schools and universities is, then, to enter into the realm of arborescence, a mode of constructing thought that long dominated scientific and philosophical reflection; the most ancient examples preserved hark back to Boethius, and were reworked by Carolingian clerics.[4] Proceeding by successive subdivisions, such diagrams progress through successive branchings that find their origin in a trunk or common root. Their model is the *Divisio Philosophiae* or *Divisio Scientiae* that inspired reflections on the hierarchy of knowledge and the organization of the sciences pursued in the monasteries of late Antiquity or the High Middle Ages. Later, starting in the eleventh or twelfth centuries, they emerged in teaching, and never ceased thereafter to be enriched with new subdivisions, witnesses to the refinement of concepts and the diversification of human activity.

At the outset, let me insist on one point: the visual language that dominates scholastic teaching and genealogical presentations in the last two centuries of the Middle Ages, namely circles linked by lines, came to be shared by all of Europe. All clerics knew how to decipher it and use it. If the chronicles are to be believed, even the parishioners of the kingdom of France subjected to the English in the first third of the fifteenth century would have been able to understand the genealogical diagrams nailed to the doors of their churches by their English masters. The mendicant friars introduced this language into the heart of central Europe. The universal chronicles, a historical genre that enjoyed immense success from well before to well after the introduction of printing, appealed to these linked signs, as did dynastic histories, in their versions as genealogies; for their part, logicians, philosophers and theologians had systematic recourse to them in the declining Middle Ages, to the point of building, like their historian colleagues, such dense ramifications that the eye can no longer penetrate them or grasp their internal relationships.

This very simple baggage of medallions and connecting lines is not a self evident matter. For instance, to express genealogical links, Arab calligraphers enter the name in a band running the whole length between two branches, not in a medallion distinct from the network of lines; the individual is as it were himself the link with which the genealogy is constructed, and does not need to be distinguished otherwise in a personalized disk.

From the Carolingian age, the term applied to the Western diagrams, *arbor*, encouraged transfers of the metaphor into the visual sphere, the diagrams being decorated with various vegetable ornaments.[5] The diagram that expressed most strikingly this process of 'vegetalization' was the *arbor juris* or *arbor consanguinitatis*; those tables of kindred and affinity required by civil lawyers to regulate succession, and canon lawyers to prevent incest were characterized in their dominant version by a silhouette that vaguely recalls a tree. Early on, in the ninth and tenth centuries, they were adorned with a vegetable apparatus, before later being disguised as real trees (fourteenth century).[6] The precedence of language over image is here affirmed, with the same precocity as the glosses on the legal diagram going back to Isidore of Seville that encouraged development of the theme of branches and twigs.

In the course of the Middle Ages, the naturalization process spread to all types of *arbores*. However, the origins of this development are to be sought less in the direct suggestions of language or the arborescences of scholars than in the speculations of theologians and mystics; the range of images burdened with references to the tree of life, the tree of Jesse, the tree of the Cross, were inexorably enriched. Those trees were at first presented as natural trees, with the trunk coming from roots and the finest flowers at the top. Clerics and the devout drew on visual images of trees, which set out the mysteries of the faith, the stages of the Passion and Redemption, the symbolic correspondences between areas of knowledge and ages of life or humours, temperaments and elements, the symmetries between virtues and vices, etc. The tree of Jesse, not a genealogical tree of Christ properly speaking but an illustration of the Incarnation and the birth of the Church, became undoubtedly, from the twelfth or thirteenth century, one of the most widespread images in churches, and among those that most influenced the formation of a genealogical imagery dominated by trees. Taken literally, the figure of the ancestor lying down at the foot of the tree (Jesse, father of King David) and the various ancestors of Jesus, kings of Judah the artists brought on to the trunk leading to Christ or to the Virgin, offered a model for organizing kinship images that affected all later representations. Although, I repeat, the intention of the image was theological and eschatological, not strictly speaking genealogical, this personage of the ancestor as founder of a community or lineage was to meet with immense success in both monastic and lay circles.

Thus, genealogical diagrams, normally built from top to bottom, in their turn took the path of vegetalization, *ipso facto* undergoing an inversion of the direction for reading them. Artists became bolder in the late twelfth century, to the point of turning upside down the traditional diagram of the Carolingian dynasty or building up that of the Welfs, making them very early on into trees rooted in the earth. Around 1300, genealogical diagrams were brought into the vast family of other *arbores*, a word that began to be applied to them; thenceforth they underwent the same fate as other diagrams and were most often cast in the form of a tree. The undertaking was not easy, since the descending organization customary in the representation of lineages resisted this reversal. Thus, it was only towards the end of the fifteenth century that the figure of the genealogical tree as we know it became fully established, and set off to conquer Europe. The direct influence of the tree of Jesse on genealogical representations is in fact to be found rather late, in the fifteenth century much more than in the twelfth to fourteenth centuries, but helped to spread the image of the genealogical tree; in the branches we find the descendants of the founding father placed at the root. One might think that in the family and dynastic mentalities of the early modern period the success of such images, copied from the greatest houses down to the most bourgeois, was due to the projection into the future that henceforth eclipsed the concern to claim a glorious ancestry.

While adoption of an image of a real tree became widespread starting in the Renaissance, the genealogical diagram was not eliminated any more than the references to the tree of life or the trees of Paradise drove out the kindred-and-affinity diagrams drawn by parishioners under the guidance of their curates. The genealogical diagram remained the province of kinship experts, and kept its utility in all the preparatory work aimed at reconstructing the genealogical links in a kinship group or between two future spouses. By its luxuriance, however, the natural tree suggested more poetically the proliferation of descendants than a set of mere lines. The symbolic resonances of its spreading also made it an image of prestige, highlighting distinction and social success.

The fate of the actual genealogies of Jesus, drawn from the gospels of Matthew or Luke, also shows the growing grip in early modern times of the image of the tree. Since the ninth or tenth centuries, with the Mozarabic genealogies, representation by a diagram running horizontally from one page to another of a codex from Adam to Christ had prevailed.[7] Shortly before 1200, a Parisian cleric, Pierre de Poitiers, proposed a renewed version, following the pattern of a scroll deployed vertically, and this model prevailed until the age of printing.[8] But such diagrams did not as yet evoke natural trees in any way. John Speed (1552–1629), who in the early seventeenth century proposed a new version of the Bible genealogies by systematizing their graphical apparatus, still kept to diagrams, except for one natural tree representing the nations deriving from Noah through his three sons, which was taken up again in 1675 by Athanasius Kircher.[9] In ensuing decades, these figures accompanied many English editions of the scriptures.

People had thus become accustomed to presenting biblical genealogies or the lineage of Christ's ancestors solely by series of medallions or groups of personages. Here again, though, the recent prestige of the tree came to be felt and arboreal images multiplied. Finally, in the eighteenth century in particular, in Protestant countries, engravers ventured to present, starting with an Adam on the ground at the base of the trunk, escutcheons or medallions containing the names of Christ's ancestors scrolled around the trunk of a tree or climbing up the bark! Contrary to what Mary Bouquet suggests, this arrangement, where Adam is not shown lying down, conforms with the model of dynastic and lay genealogical trees that had become current at the time, more than with the tree of Jesse.[10] The appearance of the tree in the holiest genealogy points rather to both the abandonment suffered by the by now superannuated Jesse, and the popularization of the tree metaphor as a necessary figure for genealogy.

All-Purpose Trees

One of the functions of the *arbor* in the monastery schools and in scholastic teaching was to sort, classify and create hierarchies. Pierre de la Ramée, before 1572, was to bring to perfection this art of classification and distinction in examining problems of logic or dialectic, and to multiply *arbores* still further. After the Renaissance, the functions of the vegetalized *arbor* were no longer confined solely to moral values or the divisions of Science or Philosophy, but were applied to the world of social and political realities. Thus, in early modern times naturalization came to apply to all the areas of visual representation traditionally dominated by the arboreal diagram termed *arbor*. Not only did *arbores* theoretically or concretely represent human kinship, but trees of hierarchic concepts resulting from the Aristotelian *Divisio Philosophiae* and the *Divisio Scientiae* became endowed, after the end of the Middle Ages, with burgeoning leaves, and were often transformed straightforwardly into trees rooted in the earth. They allowed ever more complex diagrams to exist, offering links of medallions bearing concepts that multiplied in endless ramifications.[11] But having become vegetable, the *arbores* pursued an imperialist policy in the visualization of concepts, with the apogee coming in the early ages of printing.

Since the thirteenth century, arboreal images in fact welcomed every possible concept, idea and image, and adapted every possible reference to the structure of a real tree. Trees became the support for the most varied proofs, drawing partly on the symmetry of branches, partly on their arrangement in tiers and their hierarchy, partly on their ever-finer diversification right to the last twig, partly on a shifting, alternating reading, moving from bottom to top before going back down to the bottom again.[12] In the tree, anything goes in order to link up with memory, to give an ordered reading of nature and thought. The tree that preachers had used since the thirteenth century to organize their demonstrations, on the precept 'Praedicare est arborisare', came superabundantly to illustrate the treatises of humanist rhetoric printed in the Renaissance.[13] The tree was also to serve orthodoxy or power. The first is illustrated by the Parisian priest Artus Désiré, who, in his *Description de la Cité de Dieu*, which appeared in 1550 in Rouen, inserted an 'Arbre des héréticques'.[14] By contrast with the 'arbres du péché (trees of sin)' of medieval manuscripts, where the roots were mingled with various sins or the lack of faith, the 1550s draftsman was not much concerned with detailing the roots of the evil he was describing; instead, he took the suitable model of the tree of Jesse, that is, an iconographical schema already overexploited by the religious orders of the fifteenth and sixteenth centuries, but here duly demonized. For like Jesse, the grimacing Devil lies at the root of the trunk which at its summit bears the Antichrist framed by his modern messengers Melanchthon, Luther and Calvin; the three other branches are inhabited by fifteen or so historical heretics, all identified by a streamer bearing their name. This sums up Désiré's prophetic message: this genealogical tree of denials of the orthodox faith summarizes the links connecting the Devil to the Antichrist, with the numerous figures of heresy as foot soldiers.

As for power, in 1579 Charles Figon gave a very expressive illustration of its mechanisms of government. In his *Discours des Estats et Offices tant du gouvernement que de la justice et des finances de France*, Charles Figon published a real 'organization chart' *ante litteram*, a great 'Arbre des Estats et Offices de France' where he sought to bring out the relations and hierarchies among the various organs in the apparatus of the monarchical state. He follows their mutual dependencies in the branchings and the various tiers of fronds of a natural-type tree.[15] In terms of justice, he makes original use of the metaphor of the sap nourishing the great body of the royal state: to a crude rising sap he adds a descending sap which, in the form of appeals coming from those on trial and a chain of magistrates giving justice, descends back down towards the king, producing a sort of inverse arborescence within the first one.[16]

Figure 12.1 'Arbre des Estats et Offices de France'. Charles Figon, *Discours des Estats et Offices tant du gouvernement que de la justice et des finances de France*, Paris, 1579. Paris, Bibliothèque Nationale de France.

Orderings and Challenges

Apart from its descriptive and heuristic role, the tree was used in early modern times to reveal social or political hierarchies, and even to denounce conflicts that arose from them.[17] The draftsmen then had recourse to suggestions associated with the tiers of branches more than with those of forks and ramifications. Around 1300, Ramon Llull had *inter alia* designed an 'imperial tree', engraved in the 1515 Lyons edition, which reappears in the seventeenth-century editions. The branches of this tree, with the emperor as trunk, shelter the members of hierarchical and professional collectives: barons, knights, burghers, counsellors, prosecutors, judges, advocates, ambassadors, confessors and inquisitors.[18] While laying out the ordinary structures of society, the image here, as it were, holds itself in reserve; it displays but does not criticize. However, the levels of the branches can also serve as a frame for discreet social criticism: the illustrators of *L'Arbre des batailles* by Honoré Bonet in the fifteenth century sometimes showed social groups confronting each other on the different levels of a tree.[19]

These miniatures remained confined to restricted circles, whose members strove to overlook their polemical dimension, drawing only on the appeal to respect for the old norms of chivalry or for elites. Opposition and subversion were by contrast very much at the heart of the musings that tree images could arouse in early modern times. In the early sixteenth century, the social criticism buried in the foliage could become virulent, as shown by a woodcut probably by Hans Weiditz from the years before the Peasant War. The image conceals its polemical violence at the bottom and the very top of a huge tree.[20] The three principal levels of branches are peopled by representatives of the social groups, from manual workers all the way to sovereigns. The oppression and liberation of rural folk are evoked at the very bottom, where two peasants, crushed by the tree, are pulling themselves out from its roots, while at the top a third is resting and a fourth playing bagpipes. The sleeper is holding a pitchfork he could very well use as a weapon. The image is thus pregnant with conflict. Indeed, the war that a few years later (1525) the peasant world was to wage against its oppressors brought out the pitchforks and put the bagpipes away. The whole tree of society was shaken. Such a widespread image as the tree was thus able to become a weapon challenging the very order it was being asked to evoke before the reader's eyes. A century later Grimmelshausen's hero Simplicissimus, lost in the fury of the early seventeenth century wars, dreams one evening, all the while suffering from an empty belly, of trees peopled with old soldiers; the fierce struggle to ascend to the branch where food, wealth and authority accumulate leaves to those rejected at the root only with their hunger: 'nobodies like craftsmen, day labourers, especially peasants and others … since the whole weight of the tree pressed down on them and crushed them'.[21] This disturbing vision echoes Hans Weiditz's engraving. Another century and a half later we see revolutionary caricatures using *ad nauseam* the metaphor of the country bumkins supporting the whole weight of the body politic.[22] The tree has turned into a clumsy heap of the wealthy and profiteers and disappeared as such, but can still be discerned as a subtle watermark in these representations of society's hierarchies.

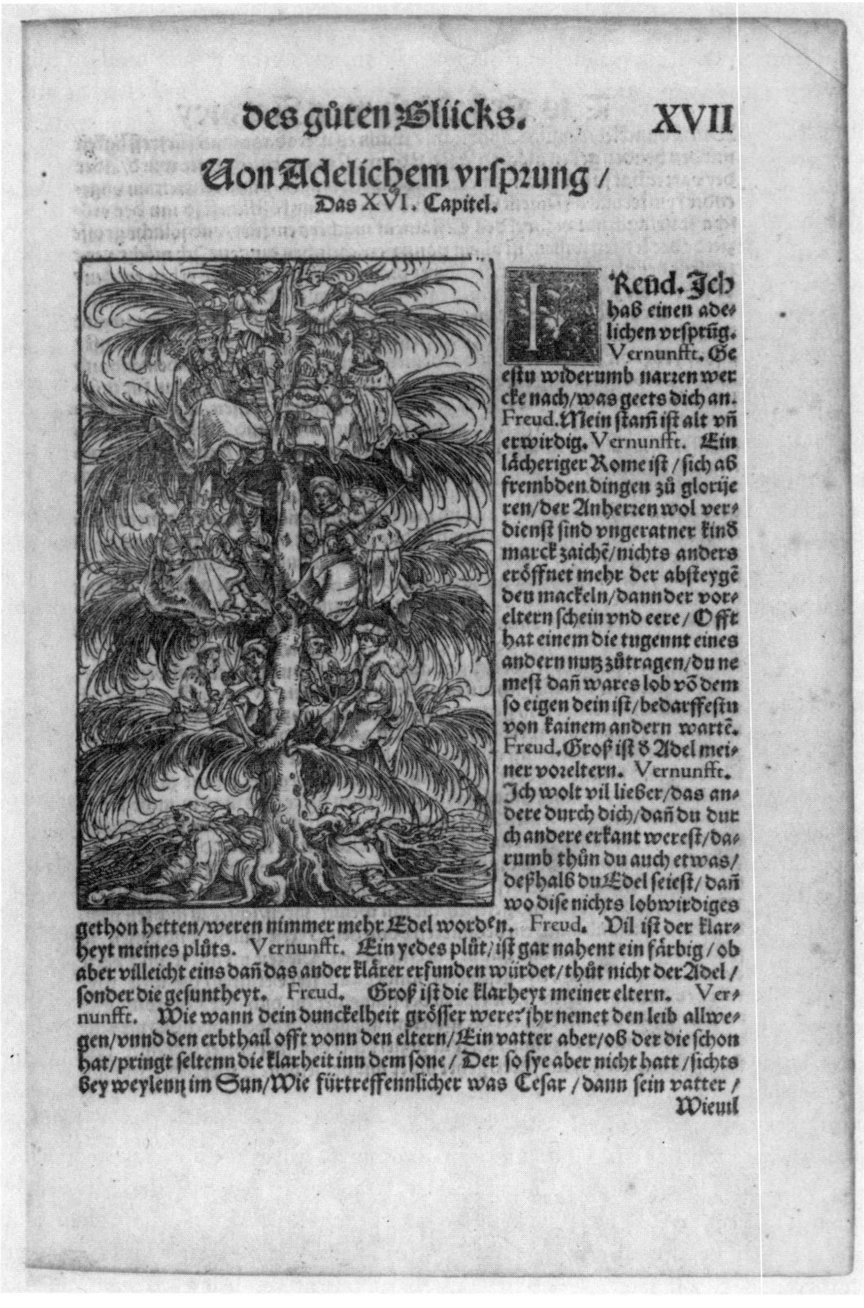
des gůten Glücks. XVII

Von Adelichem vrsprung / Das XVI. Capitel.

FReüd. Ich hab einen adelichen vrsprūg. Vernunfft. Se est widerumb narren wercke nach/was geets dich an. Freud. Mein stam̄ ist alt vñ erwirdig. Vernunfft. Ein lächeriger Rome ist / sich ab frembden dingen zů glorijeren/der Anherren wol verdienst sind vngeratner kind marck zaichē/nichts anders eröffnet mehr der absteygē den mackeln/dann der voreltern schein vnd eere / Offt hat einem die tugennt eines andern nutz zůtragen/du nemest dañ wares lob vō dem so eigen dein ist/bedarffestu von kainem andern wartē. Freud. Groß ist d Adel meiner voreltern. Vernunfft. Ich wolt vil lieber/das andere durch dich/dañ du durch andere erkant werest/darumb thůn du auch etwas/deßhalb du Edel seiest/dañ wo dise nichts lobwirdiges gethon hetten/weren nimmer mehr Edel wordē. Freud. Vil ist der klarheyt meines plůts. Vernunfft. Ein yedes plůt/ist gar nahent ein färbig / ob aber villeicht eins dañ das ander klärer erfunden würdet/thůt nicht der Adel / sonder die gesuntheyt. Freud. Groß ist die klarheyt meiner eltern. Vernunfft. Wie wann dein dunckelheit grösser were? Ihr nemet den leib allwegen/vnnd den erbthail offt vonn den eltern/Ein vatter aber/ob der die schon hat/pringt seltenn die klarheit inn dem sone / Der so sye aber nicht hatt /sichts bey weylenn im Sun/Wie fürtreffennlicher was Cesar / dann sein vatter / Wieuil

Figure 12.2 Hans Weiditz, 'Tree of social statuses', 1517. Petrarca, *Von der Arzney bayder Glück*, Augsburg, 1532, f. XVII. Paris, Bibliothèque Nationale de France.

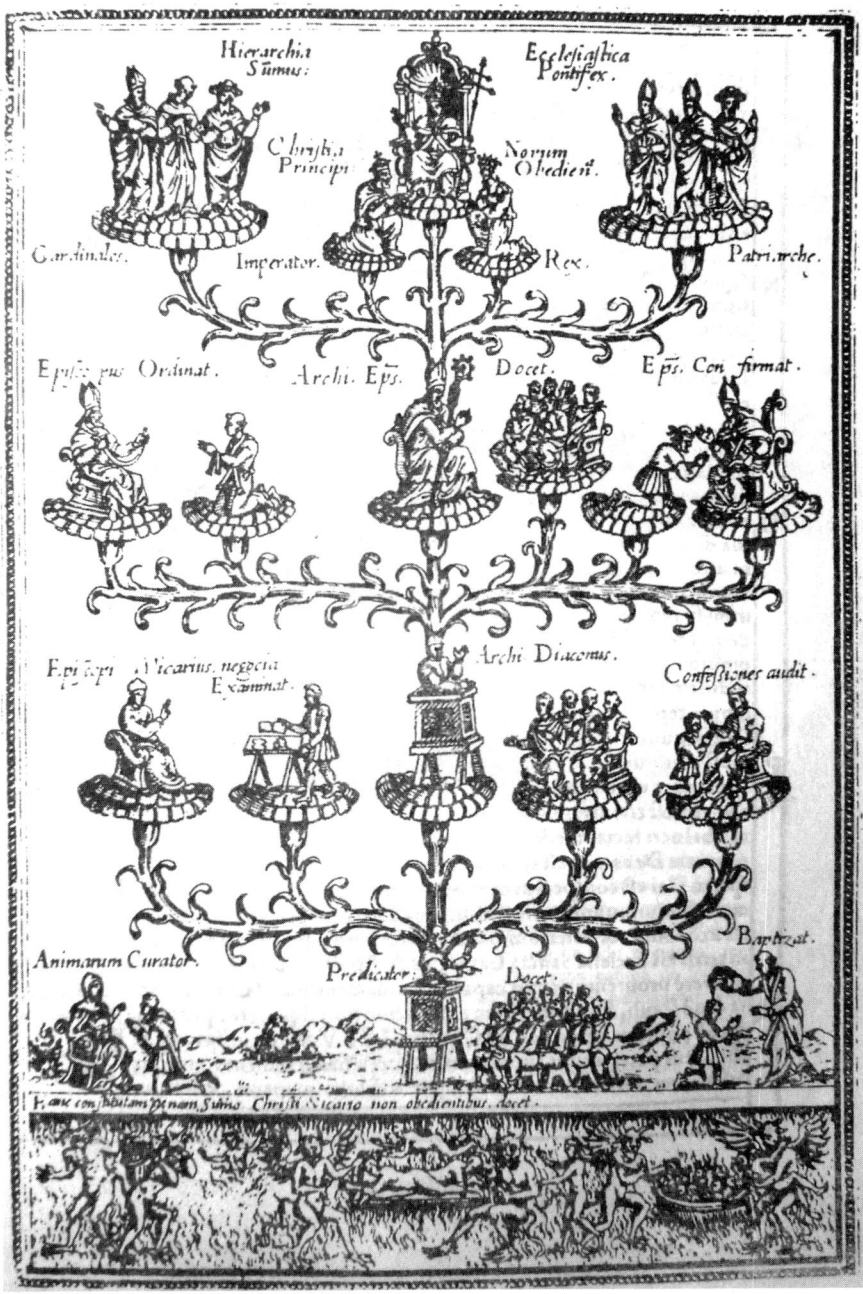

Figure 12.3 'Hierarchia Ecclesiastica'. Diego de Valadés, *Rhetorica christiana ad concionandi et orandi usum accommodata*, Perugia, 1579, p. 176.

The two contemporary trees of the 'temporal' and 'ecclesiastical hierarchies' that illustrate Diego de Valadés' *Rhetorica christiana* published in Perugia, are simpler and more schematic. They rise above a representation of hell in three tiers of dignitaries, up to the Emperor for the first hierarchy, up to the Pope for the second.[23] The householder is at the foot of one tree, and the simple curates and preaching friars at the other and both recall the context of the work; Diego is a Franciscan from Oaxaca in Mexico, born in 1533, and his image of the 'ecclesiastical hierarchy' recalls the evangelization and mass baptisms that marked the period of his youth, immediately after the conquest. Details in these images, deeply impregnated by Western tradition, also show the trace left by indigenous modes of representation. Another engraving in the work, in defence of the Indians and as a religious counterpoint to these unyielding expressions of the two powers, superposes two very Franciscan trees of the cross on two pillories where an adulterous pair of Indians are undergoing the most abominable tortures: the trees are the only salvation possible for the unfortunates close to being overwhelmed by the diabolical waves. We can see that Valadés, or his Mexican draftsmen, did not fully understand the iconographic models that inspired him.[24] Images like these are valuable; they let us grasp the intimate upheavals the 'colonization of the imagination' meant for the autochthonous masses, over and above the oppression and the destruction of traditional frameworks of indigenous society.[25] The discreetly critical view of the treatment given the Indians offered by Valadés in these engravings nicely conforms with other images and discourses circulating in the sixteenth and seventeenth centuries. It also interests us here particularly for conveying an explicitly negative connotation to plants of the most innocent appearance.

Genealogical Trees of Nations

In the age of absolute monarchies, the genealogical trees of sovereigns were, as it were, to sweep in their subjects, and the whole nation was called on to identify itself with the genealogy of its king. Sixteenth-century and seventeenth-century prints disseminated a tree iconography that passed on the discourses and diagrams of the medieval clerics defending the territorial claims of their lay masters. During the Hundred Years' War between France and England or the Wars of the Roses between York and Lancaster in England, or in the competition between the French monarchy and the Germanic Holy Roman Empire, genealogical argument had often extended to the seniority of a people's regional settlement and the antiquity of a line of succession.[26] Myths of national origin took over the tales of dynastic origins, thus constituting in the fifteenth century the inspiration for the politics of the emerging European nations. The tree of a royal house tended to become its kingdom's; the nation became a tree.

We can take as an example the fairly extravagant genealogical tree forming the central part of the 'Triumphal Arch', one of the great publishing enterprises of Emperor Maximilian, printed in 1517–1518. This huge image, three meters high, was engraved on over 200 woodblocks under the direction of Albrecht Dürer.[27] It was to form part of a set bringing it together with two other engraved series, the

Figure 12.4 A. Callais, 'Arbre généalogique des Valois et Bourbon', 1594. Paris, Bibliothèque Nationale de France, Cabinet des Estampes.

'Triumphal Cart' and 'Triumphal Procession'. In the middle of the triumphal arch, at the Emperor's feet, a long line of his ancestors and predecessors moves in a serpentine movement from Clovis, the first Christian ancestor claimed by the Habsburgs. This serpentine tree is rooted near three matrons called *Francia*, *Sycambria* and *Troia*, symbolizing the mythical origins of the Franks, as descendants of fugitives from Troy and founders of the kingdom of Sicambria. Maximilian claimed still older origins for his family than Clovis, but the 'triumphal arch' pedigree does not settle the debate brought by historians in the emperor's pay against the link between Trojans and Franks. The tree rooted behind *Francia* is certainly that of the House of Austria to which the spectators owe fealty; but neither the mythological nor the national goddess, who are there also to recall the historical roots of a nation, personifies the Empire properly speaking, nor its territory.

The 'allegorical tree of the houses of France and Navarre' illustrates a still more advanced stage of elaboration of a 'national' tree. For the sake of the common good, in the peace of Tours on 26 April 1589, the two rivals, Henri of Bourbon, king of Navarre, and Henri III of France, finally agreed that the divided kingdom would survive whole, and that the crown would revert to the Bourbon. One engraving then reflected the victory of the tree of France and Navarre over the claims of the Guises, and the numerous copies of it show how the print – as Maximilian I had foreseen - managed, alongside writing and discourse, to serve a political purpose.[28] After his coronation in 1594, Henry of Navarre, now Henri IV, benefited from a new version of the theme, conceived by Callais.[29] On all these engravings we see the ancient Saint Louis, ancestor of the two branches of Valois and Bourbon, lying on the ground; the lower half of his body becomes a tree, the tree of France; but this is a tree with a trunk inexorably divided over the course of ten or so generations. The duke of Guise, like a new Milo of Crotone, seeking to enlarge the gap in the trunk, is caught by his own game; with his hand imprisoned in the tree, he is about to be devoured by wolves. Only a little angel, 'Sacred Love', pulling the threads of the affair together in a literal sense, can manage to bring together the two branches: thanks to him, at the very top, Henri III finally passes the sceptre to Henri IV, like a runner passing a baton. '*Sic Francia divisa coalescet*': the division of the French kings' genealogical tree is here indeed the division of France itself; '*Francia divisa*' is restored in its integrity when the branches of the royal genealogy finally join together again in the sacred love of kinship. One could ask if the oak of Vincennes under which Saint Louis gave justice, and the tree of Liberty under which the citizens of the Revolution danced, and which the British caricatured,[30] were not the reflection, exalted by the republican tradition, of this tree of a pacified, integral nation whose ancestors were kings.

The genealogy of nations, and in particular that of Europe, whose ancestor medieval tradition sought in one of Noah's three sons, Japheth, was revisited as modern times advanced, and the figure of the tree incarnating it took on renewed life. Towards the end of the seventeenth century, a Swedish academic from Uppsala, Olaus Rudbeck, rehabilitated the myth of Atlantis, so as to oust the Jews from their role as God's chosen people.[31] For Rudbeck, Sweden was the true Atlantis, the cradle of history, and he deployed considerable efforts to prove that light had come to the

Greeks from the North. With a few etymological distortions, Rudbeck assimilated Greek gods and Gothic gods, as had previously been done with Greek gods and Hebrew patriarchs. The frontispiece of his work's first volume shows a map of the Eurasian continent with three trees, the roots of which the reader can follow back to the Middle East, to Noah crouching on Mount Ararat. While the liana-root of the accursed Ham is lost in the deserts of Africa, the tree of Shem, a vine, grows very high, up to the name 'Jesus', who irrigates the world with his blood. The third, the tree of Japheth, is a vigorous apple tree, with its root running more or less underground from Noah up to Sweden, where it grows; the trunk is engraved with the letters ATLAS. On the fruits are inscribed names of the legendary or historical kings of Sweden; but the apples that fall off bear the names of the nations of all Europe. 'The genealogy of the world is thus made to come from two stocks; the Hebrew stock and the Atlantic stock. The first is the axis of redemption, the second the axis of nations'.[32] On a later plate Rudbeck, surrounded by eleven figures (but without Herodotus, who did not recognize the Gothic nature of the Atlantes) displays with his scalpel, as in an anatomy lesson, the place of Sweden.[33] The Atlantis thesis aroused critical responses from Pierre Bayle, and even more stinging ones from Vico, though such scholars as Gian Rinaldo Carli subsequently took up the Atlantis myth on Italy's behalf.[34] By making Saturn the leader of the peoples of Atlantis, such national, imaginary or cosmological arguments brought up to current taste the local archaic traditions, with the Americas of the New World being introduced, by Carli, in to the old legendary canvas.[35]

Thus, around 1700, the trees of Noah's sons retained some demonstrative value; at least their author, Rudbeck, expected from them irresistible visual effects on readers in search of their origins. The image shows the Swedish apple tree of Japheth advancing underground towards the North, through the cold countries of Europe; silently it also made its way in the imagination of the Nordic listeners of Rudbeck's 'anatomy lesson of nations'. In the Age of Enlightenment, the tree continued to nourish a certain European self-awareness.

The Philosophers' Critique

Around that time, however, the tree aroused the most grating responses when it came to private genealogies. To the extent that the searches of new genealogists were helping to maintain monarchical society, especially by establishing the legitimacy of the second of its orders, the nobility, they came under the wrath of Enlightenment criticism. This criticism was even sharper than the groping versions of the sixteenth and seventeenth centuries.

By the mid eighteenth century voices were already taking on a tone of raillery at the lies of genealogy and its trees. The loudest one, heard throughout Europe, came from the Encyclopaedists. The article on genealogy in the French *Grande Encyclopédie*, seems, however, to hesitate between two attitudes; and seems in any case to have been written by two different hands.[36] To begin with, it calmly sets out the principles and objectives of the art, recalling its 'extreme importance for history', while deploring 'the absurdities of certain historians who through their adulation make the origins of houses or princes go back to heroic times', like the author who counted 'one hundred and eighteen generations without lacuna or break', obviously in the direct line, between Adam and Philip II, king of Spain. Then suddenly the tone changes, and the author launches on a diatribe attacking forgetfulness of unimportant ancestors in favour of the most prestigious ones: 'If we had the exact, true genealogy of each family, it is more than likely that no man would be admired nor despised on the ground of birth. There is scarcely a beggar on the streets not descended in direct line from some illustrious man, nor a single noble raised to the highest dignities of State, orders and chapters, without a number of obscure people among his ancestors'. The conclusion returns to more neutral tones. But the critique takes off again in the next section, on the 'genealogical tree'.[37] Basically, the Platonist argument that a king may descend from a slave or a slave from a king is revived here to mention the 'crowd of artisans and farmers' everyone has among his ancestors. The author then returns to the metaphor of the tree; it would take much cutting and pruning to show only 'a great minister of State or a famous soldier' and eliminate 'the honest artisan' at the tree's root. No genealogical tree is innocent; the very genre is fallacious.

The doubt which in the *Grande Encyclopédie* is cast on the forms of genealogy is extended even more radically to traditional representations of the structure of all knowledges. In reflecting on the best visual expression for the diversification of knowledge and techniques, the *philosophes* spared neither the metaphor nor the image of the tree. Here they had to deal with a strong tradition, already mentioned earlier, that drew its inspiration from the medieval *arbores scientiae*. Ramon Llull had inherited from medieval philosophy the tree diagrams that contained and ordered knowledge. His 'tree of science' with eighteen roots, half of them divine and referring to the creation, half of them logical and governing the world of knowledge, was the support for his 'great art' of the search for a 'universal science' or 'wisdom'; the Lyons edition of 1635, which is antedated to 1515, shows the influence his thought was still exercising in the early seventeenth century, and again offers engravings of these trees.[38] A more traditional representation of the tree structure of the disciplines is given by Pierre de la Ramée (or Ramus) and his disciples, in the second half of the sixteenth century, where the totality of human knowledge is organized in hierarchical order by distinctions and successive divisions.[39] In both Llull and La Ramée, the encyclopaedist idea expressed by the tree was meant to make God's wisdom shine. For an understanding of the links between the arts and the sciences detached from this divine wisdom, the chief link, however, is Francis Bacon (1561–1626), and the eighteenth-century encyclopaedists were repeatedly to acknowledge their debt to him.[40] Bacon had proposed to use the tree to bring out knowledge and order founded on the mental operations applied to objects: memory, imagination and reason would allow all arts and crafts to be organized, and as they were launched, past discoveries would lead to the invention of new ones; the catalogue had to remain open.[41] This was knowledge in expansion, a tree in full growth ... Diderot and d'Alembert were unsparing in their eulogies of this evolutionary aspect of Bacon's tree of knowledge as the engine for their own analyses.

But is the tree the best tool for analysis and exposition? The Encyclopaedists began by proclaiming exactly this, before, in highly instructive fashion, back tracking.[42] Their 'Diagrammatic System of Human Knowledge', i.e. the vast table in the form of a tree that opens the *Grande Encyclopédie*, takes over Bacon's tripartite scheme and splits knowledge according to the same major faculties of man: memory, reason and imagination. In 1749, the prospectus for the Encyclopaedia written by Diderot announced that the aim was to 'form a genealogical tree of all the sciences and all the arts, marking the origin of each branch of our knowledge, the links they have between them and the connection to the common stem'. Is the tree the proper metaphor? D'Alembert very soon corrected the ambition proclaimed in 1749. In 1750, in the 'Discours préliminaire' he states that 'the encyclopaedic order in no way assumes that all the sciences directly have to do with each other. They are branches that start from the same trunk, knowledge of human understanding. These branches often have no immediate link with each other, and several are joined by the trunk alone'. Insisting on the plurality of sciences more than on their totalization, the Encyclopaedists thus moved between 1750 and 1752 from representing the encyclopaedic system as a tree to showing it cartographically.[43]

Even to reject it, it is noteworthy that the most theoretical reflection cannot always do without the imagery of the tree when genealogical thought thrives. Descartes himself, moreover, had had recourse to the metaphor for his 'Arbre des sciences', a tree that was to be as foreign to Bacon's as to the Encyclopaedists': its roots were metaphysics, the trunk physics, and the branches that emerged from it, i.e. the other sciences, were reduced to three, namely medicine, mechanics and morals, the 'ultimate degree of wisdom'.

The *Grande Encyclopédie* did not repeat the silhouette or structure of a natural tree in its own initial table.[44] On the basis of a tradition that derived from medieval scribes, it preferred, like Pierre de la Ramée, lateral to vertical branching, since the abundance of notions to be introduced in each 'generation' made it impossible to enter them on a continuous line – in fact some medieval scribes ranked names or notions in columns where they derived from the same 'father' and belonged to the same 'family', and linked them by a leafy embrace since no one could forget that this was indeed what was then called an *arbor*;[45] and lateral human genealogies, of which a number of medieval examples are known, were often used in the seventeenth and eighteenth centuries. The Encyclopaedists, for their part, no longer took the rather futile trouble to disguise their structure as a tree. The other metaphors they favoured, primarily the geographical map, the *mappemonde*, took over from the tree, at least in their discourse, as it had already done in Bacon.[46]

But metaphors live long, and others took the risk in their stead. For example, Chrétien Roth ventured a few years later to draw a tree, incorporated in 1780 into the 'Table de l'Encyclopédie' of pastor Pierre Mouchon.[47] The title of the work, *Essai d'une distribution généalogique des sciences et des arts principaux*, emphasized the genealogical aspect of the classification of the sciences in the *Système figuré*, ignoring the cartographical metaphor that had been favoured by the authors of the Encyclopaedia, and was supposed to help one orient oneself in the multiple links among the sciences and the arts. In the end, Chrétien Roth scarcely persuades the reader that the tree offered more advantages than a mere tree structure. His image of vast foliage, beautiful as it may be, does not help one find one's way in the architecture of the branches; by comparison with the tree structure, Roth's tree gives the deceptive impression of wealth and vitality, but is no longer the tool for thought it had been, and unremittingly conveys a rigid image of the link between the sciences. Thus, even the aspect of the tree most prized since the thirteenth century, by both mystics and theologians or preachers, namely its profusion as a sign of spirit or fecundity, here remained without heuristic consequences. In seeking to say too much, the draftsman quite simply failed to draw out its simultaneously suggestive and clarificatory effects.

One of the last trees of knowledge, aimed at representing the advance of the human spirit or the concatenation of knowledge, thus becoming a mouthpiece for a genuine 'science of man' was Saint-Simon's;[48] however, like the encyclopaedia he had also contemplated, it was to remain a draft. The tree as analytical tool had undoubtedly used up much of its resources by the nineteenth century. Is it a totally obsolete figure? There is at least one area where its form has become a distinguishing feature and continues to prevail: genealogy. Though in the twentieth century new expository techniques have been added to its formal presence, it remains the central stereotype. Subject to greater polemic, the tree of the evolution of life, an unprecedented type of tree structure, was to nourish equally profound debate in the nineteenth and twentieth centuries.

The Strayings of Life

It was the German morphological scholar Ernest Haeckel (1834–1919), 'probably the keenest and most influential propagandist of evolution', who was most explicitly to transcribe the idea of phylogenesis into tree images. These were to become 'canonical images', still today charged with petrifying and restraining the scientific imagination through their implicit assumptions.[49] Haeckel's 'General Morphology of Organisms' (1866) offered a genealogical tree proper, recapitulating the evolution of life, but also a great number of tree structures.[50] Both the former and the latter 'show in exemplary fashion', writes Stephen Gould, 'how iconography reflects ideological blinkers'.

The most 'realistic' tree of the ones Haeckel published, then, represents the genealogy of man (*Stammbaum des Menschen*). It is manifestly shot through by a simplistic notion of progress which, through the diversification and succession of species from a common origin, ineluctably leads to the finest outcome of the evolution of life, namely man, just as the tree of Jesse led to Christ and the birth of the Church. It shows a series of branchings which, on the model of the genealogical tree, express the appearance of new branches, i.e. new species bearing characteristics differing from those of the branch from which they were separated. The tree is oriented upwards, and thus towards the human being, the genealogy it traces is indeed man's, and the history of life is primarily that of the human lineage. Haeckel's tree renders the species in a hierarchical order according to their place in the process of diversification, which according to him indicates the superiority of their more complex organization. Here, however, each appearance of a new species has the effect of marginalizing or even eliminating from the diagram the branch in relation to which it is individualized, as if evolution, in its aspect of diversification of species, could advance only by evicting previous forms of life in favour of later ones regarded as superior.[51] The limitations of the graphical choice of the tree as the support for evolution thus have to do with the fact that a spatial position in the image is assigned to the various forms of life in accordance with implicit value judgments.[52]

The many trees, or rather tree structures, filling Haeckel's book, and devoted to the major classes of living things, highlight the assumption that the greatest diversity is not an original situation, but the result of evolution, whereas this latter proceeds by decimation.[53] Haeckel's trees become more bushy and differentiated at their summits than closer to the bases of their trunks; they form cones, a visual structure which scientists found very difficult to eliminate, while subjecting it to distortions affecting the representation of the relative diversity of groups of species.

The image of the cone broadening out upwards like a tree long survived Haeckel. It has only recently been called into question.[54] The criticisms aimed at it evidently come from better knowledge of the various forms of life, in particular their dates. But it is also the very principle of representation inherited from genealogical thought that has been disputed: an ancestor, who is also dead, necessarily precedes the appearance and existence of a new form of life which *de facto* replaces it. The genealogical model of tree structure marked theories of the diversification of languages as well as of species. In Haeckel's time, August Schleicher applied Darwinian theories to the emergence of languages from an Indo-European *Ursprache*, tracing tree diagrams that resulted from the elimination of ancient languages in favour of more modern ones – tree structures which, like those inspiring the vision of evolution in Haeckel, gave the impression of a vigorous expansion that was predictable by the simple procedure of ramification.[55]

If all these 'canonical' images of evolution we find it hard to eliminate seem outdated in modern science, we, alongside Stephen Jay Gould, are entitled to ask about the other representations hidden deep within us that would have to be drawn on to give a visual account of chance and contingency, true motors of evolution, that the tree cannot, in its upward growth, give an account of. The failure of the genealogical tree as an expository structure since the Enlightenment encyclopaedists or as a heuristic guide in modern science cannot hide the fact that for nearly two millennia this figure satisfied Europeans' hunger for models of both logical and historical origins.

Translated by Iain L. Fraser

Notes

1. James (1966); Cook (1974). The tree is also a symbol of fecundity, going even to the point of engendering human beings; see Bacqué-Grammont (forthcoming); I thank the author for having allowed me to read this article before publication.
2. Winter (1986).
3. Peil (1993); Rigotti (1992).
4. On the 'tree' of Porphyry (a third-century neo-platonist) and the commentaries on his treatise on the *Isagoge* of Boethius, see Wirth (1989), pp. 61–78.
5. The *Arbor porphyriana* in a Vatican manuscript of the twelfth century and another one in Darmstadt; however, it was not until the fifteenth century that fully fledged trees were to be encountered. See Esmeijer (1973).
6. Schadt (1982).
7. Williams (1994).
8. Klapisch-Zuber (2000), pp. 121–38.
9. Speed (1635).
10. Bouquet (1996).
11. Wirth (1983).
12. For various late-medieval examples: trees of wisdom, trees of the ages of life, trees of the alphabet, etc., see Klapisch-Zuber (2000), pp. 209–12. For trees of the ages of life, see esp. Sears (1986), pp. 140–4, 151–3, 201–2.
13. On the arts of preaching and the Pseudo-Bonaventure, see Klapisch-Zuber (2000), pp. 216–17. On the trees of knowledge that set up series of associations, thus transforming the way of teaching such traditional subjects as rhetoric, see Bolzoni (1995).
14. Crouzet (1990), pp. 191–206, 228–30 and illustration.
15. Figon (1579). Le Roy Ladurie (1991) has very carefully analysed this 'arbre des estats et offices de France'.
16. Le Roy Ladurie (1991), p. 253.
17. Burke (1992).
18. Le Roy Ladurie (1991), p. 250.
19. While the illustrator of a manuscript kept in Chantilly keeps to fights between men-at-arms or knights, around 1470 Loyset Liédet, an artist from Bruges, sets out in tiers in a tree, not without malice, the representatives of various social statuses, down to women fighting on the lower level, giving great blows with distaffs.
20. This engraving of the tree of statuses by Hans Weiditz, circa 1517, was to be reprinted in the German translation of Petrarch (1532), fº XVII. See Weydt (1983).
21. Grimmelshausen (1990), pp. 49–52.
22. Niccoli (1979), many illustrations.
23. 'Hierarchia temporalis' and 'Hierarchia Ecclesiastica', engravings illustrating D. de Valadés (1579), p. 180 and p. 176. See Sartor (1992); Finzi and Morganti (1995); Bolzoni (1999).
24. For instance, the branches going downwards of the trees of the cross are hung with lianas on which are hanging twelve figures, believers or the apostles, showing a great misunderstanding of the essential role of scrolls or the Western form of corollas in genealogical trees, here transformed into little clouds! Valadés (1989), p. 497.
25. Gruzinski (1988), p. 238f; Gruzinski (1990).
26. For France, see Beaune (1985); Klapisch-Zuber (2000), pp. 187–206.
27. Laschitzer (1888). Tanner (1993).

28. Maître I.F. (1589).
29. Callais (1594).
30. Gillbray (1757–1815), 'The Tree of Liberty with the Devil tempting John Bull' (1798), coloured engraving where the apple tree has as its fruits murder, treason, atheism, but also the Whig club, democracy, the Age of Reason, etc.
31. Rudbeck (1679–1702). See Vidal-Naquet (1982) and (2000), ch. 1, pp. 29–83. See also Svenbro (1980).
32. Vidal-Naquet (1982), p. 48.
33. Vidal-Naquet (1982), p. 51.
34. Vidal-Naquet (1982), p. 52–3.
35. Vidal-Naquet (1982), p. 54. See the reconstitutions of pre-Roman history proposed by Villani (1990).
36. *La Grande Encyclopédie* (1751–1762), t. VII, p. 485. The most critical author is "D.J.".
37. *La Grande Encyclopédie* (1751–1762), t. VII, p. 485–6. D.J. concludes that 'it is amusement for a philosopher lost in a marsh'.
38. Llull (1635).
39. Chatelain (1996), esp. pp. 157–9.
40. On Llullian encyclopaedism and its heritage see Spallanzani (1982).
41. Chatelain (1996), p. 160–1.
42. Cernuschi (1996).
43. See the entry 'Encyclopédie' by Diderot, analysed by Cernuschi (1996), pp. 379–80.
44. 'Système figuré des connoissances humaines', *Grande Encyclopédie* (1751–1762), t. 1.
45. For examples see Evans (1980).
46. Chatelain (1996), pp. 160–2.
47. Mouchon (1780).
48. Seckel and Tesnière (1996), pp. 420–2, with a reproduction of the two 'Arbres de la connaissance de Bacon et de Saint-Simon', a plate taken from Saint-Simon (n.d.).
49. Gould (1991), p. 343.
50. Haeckel (1866).
51. Gould ([1999], pp. 63–73) likens these repeated expulsions to the procedures for representing geological eras which, since the nineteenth century, stopped showing invertebrates once they had reached vertebrates, or fish so as to favour exclusively land vertebrates, and so on, up to Man.
52. Thus, in almost caricature fashion, the insects, with nearly a million species, are relegated to a lower position on the side, and their branch breaks off with the 'appearance' of the vertebrates!
53. Gould ([1991], pp. 343–8), reproduces and analyses several of Haeckel's phylogenetic *Stammbäume*.
54. See the replacement evolutionary trees or bushes proposed by Gould (1991), pp. 39–42 and pp. 275–6.
55. Schleicher (1863); the last four pages show fine tree diagrams of languages on two foldouts; and Schleicher (1861). See also the evolutionist metaphor of the tree of religions in Renan (1947), vol. 5, pp. 1143–5 and p. 1513, and the commentary by Olender (1994).

References

Bacqué-Grammont, J-L. (forthcoming), 'En guise d'introduction: autour de trois compendium d'époque ottomane', in J-L. Bacqué-Grammont et al., *L'arbre anthropogène du Waqwaq, les femmes-fruits et autres zoophytes. Recherches sur un mythe à large diffusion dans le temps et l'espace.*

Beaune, C. (1985), *Naissance de la nation France* (Paris).

Bolzoni, L. (1995), *La stanza della memoria: modelli letterari e iconografici nell'età della stampa* (Turin).

Bolzoni, L. (1999), 'Les images du livre et les images de la mémoire : l'"Achille et l'Enea" de Lodovico Dolce et la "Rhetorica christiana" de Diego Valadés)', in M. Plaisance (ed.), *Le livre illustré italien au XVIe siècle* (Paris), pp. 151–76.

Bouquet, M. (1996), 'Family Trees and their Affinities: The Visual Imperative of the Genealogical Diagram', in *Journal of the Royal Anthropological Institute of London*, 2, pp. 43–66.

Burke, P. (1992), 'The language of orders in early modern Europe', in M.L. Bush (ed.), *Social Orders and Social Classes in Europe since 1500: Studies in Social Stratifications* (London and New York), pp. 1–12.

Callais, A. (1594), 'Arbre genealogique des Valois et des Bourbon', BNF, Cabinet des Estampes (Paris).

Cernuschi, A. (1996), 'L'arbre encyclopédique des connaissances. Figures, opérations, métamorphoses', in R. Schaer (ed.), *Tous les savoirs du monde. Encyclopédies et bibliothèques, de Sumer au XXIe siècle* (Paris), pp. 377–82.

Chatelain, J.-M. (1996), 'Du Parnasse à l'Amérique: l'imaginaire de l'encyclopédisme à la Renaissance et à l'Âge classique', in R. Schaer (ed.), *Tous les savoirs du monde. Encyclopédies et bibliothèques, de Sumer au XXIe siècle* (Paris), pp. 156–63.

Cook, R. (1974), *The Tree of Life: Symbol of the Centre* (London).

Crouzet, D. (1990), *Les Guerriers de Dieu. La violence au temps des troubles de religion (vers 1525–vers 1610)* (Paris).

Esmeijer, A. (1973), 'De VII liberalibus artibus in quadam pictura depictis. Een reconstructie van de arbor philosophiae van Theodulf van Orleans', in *Album amicorum J. G. van Gleder* (The Hague), pp. 102–13.

Evans, M. (1980), 'The Geometry of Mind', *Architectural Association Quarterly*, 12, 4, pp. 32–55.

Figon, C. (1579), *Discours des Estats et Offices tant du gouvernement que de la justice et des finances de France* (Paris).

Finzi, C. and A. Morganti (eds) (1995), *Un francescano tra gli indios: Diego Valades e la Rhetorica christiana* (Rimini).

Gillbray, J. (1798), 'The Tree of Liberty with the Devil tempting John Bull', coloured engraving published by H. Humphrey.

Gould, S.J. (1989), *Wonderful Life* (New York).

———. (1991), *La vie est belle. Les surprises de l'évolution* (French translation of *Wonderful Life* [1989]) (Paris).

———. (1999), 'Scale e coni: l'evoluzione ingabbiata dalle immagini canoniche', in O. Sacks, S.J. Gould, J. Miller, D.J. Kevles and R.C. Lewontin (eds), *Storie segrete della scienza* (Cles), pp. 49–81.

Grimmelshausen, H.J.C. von (1990), *Les aventures de Simplicissimus*, bk. I, chap. XV and XVI, trad. by J. Amsler (Paris).

Gruzinski, S. (1988), *La colonisation de l'imaginaire. Sociétés indigènes et occidentalisation dans le Mexique espagnol. XVIe–XVIIIe siècle* (Paris).

Gruzinski, S. (1990), *La guerre des images de Christophe Colomb à Blade Runner (1492–2019)* (Paris).

Haeckel, E. (1866), 'Systematischer Stammbaum des Menschen', in *Generelle Morphologie der Organismen, vol. II : Allgemeine Entwickelungsgeschichte der Organisme* (Berlin).

James, E.O. (1966), *The Tree of Life. An Archaeological Study* (Leiden).

Klapisch-Zuber, C. (2000), *L'Ombre des ancêtres. Essai sur l'imaginaire médiéval de la parenté* (Paris).

La Grande Encyclopédie (1751–1762) (Paris).

Laschitzer, S. (1888), 'Die Genealogie des Kaisers Maximilian I', *Jahrbuch der kunsthistorischen Sammlungen des allerhöchsten Kaiserhauses*, 7, pp. 1–200.

Le Roy Ladurie, E. (1991), 'L'Etat royal de Louis XI à Henri IV, 1460–1610', in *Histoire de France Hachette* (Paris), pp. 246–63.

Llull, R. (1635), 'Arbor scientiae', counterfeit edition of the Lyons one of 1515.

Maître I.F. (1589), 'Arbre allégorique de France et de Navarre', Bibliothèque Nationale de France, Cabinet des Estampes (Qb1. 1589) (Paris).

Mouchon, P. (1780), *Essai d'une distribution généalogique des sciences et des arts principaux*.

Niccoli, O. (1979), *I sacerdoti, i guerrieri, i contadini. Storia di un'immagine della società* (Turin).

Olender, M. (1994), *Les langues du Paradis. Aryens et Sémites, un couple providentiel* (Paris).

Peil, D. (1993), 'Der Baum des Königs. Anmerkungen zur politischen Baummetaphorik', in W. Euchner, F. Rigotti, P. Schiera (eds), *Il potere delle immagini. La metafora politica in prospettiva storica* (Bologna), pp. 33–65.

Petrarch (1532), *Von der Arzney bayder Glück* (Augsburg).

Rigotti, F. (1992), *Il potere e le sue metafore* (Milan).

Renan, E. (1947), *Oeuvres complètes*, H. Psichari (ed.) (Paris).

Rudbeck, O. (1679–1702), *Atlantica (Atland eller Manheim)*, 4 vols (Uppsala).

Saint-Simon, C.H. de Rouvroy, comte de (n.d.), *Esquisse d'une nouvelle encyclopédie, ou Introduction à la philosophie du XIXe siècle* (Paris).

Sartor, M. (1992), *'Ars dicendi et excudendi': Diego Valadés incisore messicano in Italia* (Padua).

Schadt, H. (1982), *Die Darstellungen der Arbores Consanguinitatis und der Arbores Affinitatis* (Tübingen).

Schleicher, A. (1861), *Compendium der vergleichenden Grammatik* (Weimar).

———. (1863), *Die Darwinsche Theorie und die Sprachwissenschaft. Offenes Sendschreiben an Herrn Dr Ernst Häckel* (Weimar).

Sears, E. (1986), *The Ages of Man. Medieval Interpretations of the Life Cycle* (Princeton).

Seckel, R.J. and V. Tesnière (1996), 'De Panckoucke à Queneau', in R. Schaer (ed.), *Tous les savoirs du monde. Encyclopédies et bibliothèques, de Sumer au XXIe siècle* (Paris).

Spallanzani, M. (1982), 'Sull'albero enciclopedico delle conoscenze: una classificazione del sapere tra Bacone e Descartes', *Rivista critica di storia della filosofia*, 3, 307–24.

Speed, J. (1635), *The Genealogies Recorded in the Sacred Scriptures According to Every Family and Tribe* (London).

Svenbro, J. (1980), 'L'idéologie gothisante et l'Atlantica' d'Olof Rudbeck', *Quaderni di storia*, 11, 121–56.

Tanner, M. (1993), *The Last Descendant of Aeneas. The Hapsburgs and the Mythic Image of the Emperor* (London and New Haven).

Valadés, D. de (1579), *Rhetorica Christiana ad concionandi et orandi usum accomodata* (Perugia); facsimile ed. and Spanish tr., Universidad Nacional Autònoma de México (1989), p. 417 and p. 407.

Vidal-Naquet, P. (1982), 'Hérodote et l'Atlantide: entre les Grecs et les Juifs. Réflexions sur l'historiographie du siècle des Lumières', *Quaderni di storia*, 16 (Bari).

————. (2000), *Les grecs, les historiens, la démocratie. Le grand écart* (Paris).

Villani, G. (1990), *Nuova cronica*, l. 1, chap. 1–10, G. Porta (ed.) (Parma), pp. 1–16.

Weydt, G. (1983), 'Der Standebaum. Zur Geschichte eines Symbols von Petrarca bis Grimmelshausen', *Simpliciana*, IV–V.

Williams, J. (1994), *The Illustrated Beatus: A Corpus of the Illustrations of the Commentary on the Apocalypse* (London).

Winter, U. (1986), 'Der "Lebensbaum" in der altorientalischen Bildsymbolik', in H. Schweizer (ed.), '... *Bäume braucht man doch!' Das Symbol des Baumes zwischen Hoffnung und Zerstörung* (Sigmaringen), pp. 57–88.

Wirth, J. (1989), *L'Image médiévale* (Paris).

Wirth, K.-A. (1983), 'Von mittelalterlichen Bildern- und Lehrfiguren im Dienste der Schule und des Unterrichts', in B. Moeller, H. Patze and K. Stackmann (eds), *Studien zum städtischen Bildungswesen des späten Mittelalters und der frühen Neuzeit* (Göttingen), pp. 256–370.

Chapter 13

From the Renaissance to the Enlightenment ... through Antiquity

The Beginnings of the European Network of Museums

Edouard Pommier

'For specialists, this collection should become a public school'. Thus can a remark in a letter dated 8 April 1589 from the Roman scholar Fulvio Orsini to Cardinal Odoardo Farnese concerning the antiquities collection of his illustrious family be loosely but faithfully translated. His concern was that the collection be conserved so as to remain accessible to a certain public, one we would term today the scholarly community. The same Fulvio Orsini had received a letter from the cardinal Granvelle a few years before, on 22 March 1581, explaining that, if the libraries and antiquities remained in Rome, the city would become a universal school attracting men of letters and artists.[1] The Farnese collection, therefore, could help Rome to accomplish its mission. Let us go back another half century to around 1525 to read the inscription on the panels inlaid in the walls of the courtyard of the Della Valle Palace dedicating the antiquities presented there to the happiness of all, the inspiration of painters and poets, the charms of leisure, the memory of ancestors and proposing them for imitation by posterity.[2]

These few citations reveal that, throughout the sixteenth century, Rome invented, if not the museum itself, then, at least, the identity of the institution such as we know it today; as a place of memory, a place of study and creation, a place of delectation, and as a place for the public, opened to all, before becoming the property of all. How did Rome invent the museum? How did that invention, which could not long remain the privilege of Rome alone, spread and diversify throughout Italy and certain parts of Europe? How did it achieve, by the end of the Enlightenment, a coherence that would be raised to the status of a paradigm for our epoch?

To summarize the invention of the museum in this way is, at the very least, to deform, if not to betray, a complex phenomenon that matured slowly in the mysterious realms of humanist consciousness. It was a period that witnessed a radical change in the perception of ancient sculptures, exposed to the gaze of men of letters and artists; a transformation that would see the 'political' images of the persecution of the Christians turned into representations of Roman grandeur and immoral images of sin taken as models by creators in their search for beauty.[3] The thesis forwarded in many scholarly works, moreover, that the Donation of Constantine, used since the Carolinian epoch to justify the temporal power of popes, was a simple forgery, gained wide acceptance by 1470. The search for a different form of legitimacy seems to have played an important role in the establishment of a new relation with Antiquity. The politics of Pope Sixtus IV would seem a brilliant symbol of this.[4]

The creation of the first public collection of Rome at the Capitol through the famous so-called donation of 15 December 1471 is a decisive moment[5] commemorated by a marble inscription displayed at the Palace of the Conservators that is worthy of imperial epigraphy and would merit being the first entry in a universal inventory of museums if one existed. We learn from the text that Pope Sixtus IV decided to 'restore' a certain number of bronze sculptures to the Roman people that testify to its past excellence and valour. 'Restore' is the essential word here whose meaning is reinforced by the attribution that follows 'to the Roman people from whom they originated'. This 'restoration' clearly marks the continuity of the history of Rome and the objects included in it incarnate the identity of the collectivity that is the 'Roman people'; so much so that the works to this day belong to the people's representatives, that is to say, the municipality of Rome. Sixtus IV did not intend to create a 'museum'; however, he did lay the foundations of the idea of the museum as the guardian of a municipal or national identity that was, therefore, public and perpetual. Such is the destiny, since 1471, of the *Capitoline She-Wolf*, fragments of the *Colossus*, the *Spinario*, the *Camillus*, the *Hercules*, the bas-reliefs of Marcus Aurelius' triumphal arch, the sculptures *Tiber* and *Nile* reunited between 1471 and 1517, and the *L.J. Brutus*, founder of the Roman Republic, which joined the others in 1564. The value of this first collection is not only assured by the historical and legendary past of these objects, but also by their installation on the hill of the Capitol, the traditional seat of the Roman Senate. Location and collection complement one another, and create a link underscored by the transfer of the statue of Marcus Aurelius from its place before the Basilica of Lateran ordered by Paul III in 1537.[6] Indeed, a medal stamped on that occasion bears the inscription '*Hanc petunt miracula sedem*'. An admirable oeuvre like the Marcus Aurelius required an emplacement like the Capitol, an assertion made explicit by the inscription Paul III had placed on the pedestal of the statue: '*Paulus III ... ut memoriae opt(imi) principi (s) consuleret patriaeq(ue) decora atq(ue) ornamenta restitueret, ex humiliore loco in aream Capitolinam transtulit ...*'. Once again, a 'restitution' to the sculpture's place of origin is evoked. It is surprising to note that, for the Pope, Bishop of Rome, the square before his Cathedral was considered less dignified than the place of the Capitol.

Following Sixtus IV who invented a prefiguration of the museum as eternal host to works of Antiquity that carry the memory of the Roman people, Julius II, his nephew, would trace a second path in 1506 that would also prove to be extraordinarily fruitful. The aim of Julius II was to collect, conserve and valorize works of Antiquity considered exemplary for the admiration of the public and the imitation of artists. This represented the culmination of a long progression that, one could say, symbolically began with Petrarch and was propelled by the irresistible attraction of works invested with the prestige of a lost perfection, that was conveyed by ancient literature, and whose traces it was necessary to recover. Vasari admirably evoked this aspiration in the introduction to the third part of his *Lives* when he spoke of waiting for a revelation that would be transmitted by the sculptures described by Pliny the Elder.[7] The fortuitous discovery of an exceptional group of works on 14 January 1506 – immediately identified as the *Laocoön* by Giuliano da San Gallo by placing them in relation to a passage of the *Natural History* and, in this way, inventing a fundamental method of art history[8] – provoked a decisive response from the Pope: he purchased and installed them in the courtyard of the Belvedere on the hill of the Vatican, which the Romans had dedicated to Apollo. Thus the hill devoted to beauty would take its place next to the hill devoted to history, making the Vatican the second museum pole of Rome after the Capitol. The arrival of the *Laocoön*, followed by *Apollo, Venus, Felix, Hercules,* and the *Rivers*, during Clement VII's pontificate of another *Venus* and, most notably, of the *Torso*, and, finally, during Paul III's of the *Hermes* would transform the courtyard of the Belvedere into a place of wonders, celebrated by chroniclers, poets and diplomats.[9] It was the '*Antiqua novitas*', according to the fortunate expression of Francisco de Holanda, Portuguese artist and theoretician of Flemish origin, whose Roman sojourn from 1538 to 1540 would allow him to record a precious image of these treasures.[10] If, as is likely, Julius II intended to display the mythical origins of Rome there, his plan would be hindered by the following reality: while the admirable statues evoked by Pliny the Elder would suddenly materialize, strikingly, the paintings of Book XXXV would remain absent.

As at the Capitol, we can speak of a kind of 'sacralization' inherent in the museum collection, which is manifested in the presentation of works – 'come una capella' – like saints in a niche;[11] such as those immediately proclaimed famous throughout the entire world for their beauty, works like the *Laocoön*,[12] so very coveted that the Pope himself hit upon the idea to give it away to King Francis I in 1516. Such works would become a source for the education of artists and installed at the Belvedere itself by Florentine sculptor Baccio Bandinelli in 1530 under the pompous name, destined to have a long career, of 'Academy'.[13] Thirty years later, Federico Zuccaro would realize a series of drawings dedicated to his brother Taddeo's initiatory voyage towards glory, that depicted him copying the *Laocoön*.[14] Sacralization, therefore, but also commercialization, as evidenced by the vulgarized castings in bronze of certain works like the *Apollo* or the *Torso*.[15]

With his brief of 28 November 1534, Paul III attempted to enact a policy of territorial protection, by imposing the principle of preliminary authorization for the removal of Antiquities from Rome. He thus discovered the intimate link between the invention of the institution of the museum and the notion of patrimony, even if the latter would long remain a theoretical wish.[16]

By conferring a new status on ancient art and proclaiming its political, historical, artistic and cultural importance before the entire world did Rome accomplish a unique gesture? Or would it set an example destined to be followed, that is to say, to bring about the creation of new Romes, according to Vasari's expression in his biography of Primaticcio,[17] where he referred to the copies cast from Roman Antiquities collected at Fontainebleau? The example of Rome, clearly, is to be found first and foremost in Rome itself, where collections of Antiquities presented in courtyards or even integrated into the architecture of palace facades multiplied, thus assuring their permanence, valorization, and publicity. This was the case, first, with the Palazzo Della Valle in 1525, under the direction of Lorenzo Lotti, a student of Raphael, followed by several more, including the Palazzo Maffei, Villa Giulia and Villa Medici.[18] In this way, according to Cassiodorus' image, the new Rome offered the spectacle of the 'people of statues' that ancient Rome had become, and that were almost as numerous as the living population.[19] Would this people cross the frontiers of the Holy Sea's territorial jurisdiction to migrate towards distant lands to be colonized?

This migration, which was to have enormous consequences, would, in fact, take place as early as the sixteenth century towards two hospitable lands, according to two different rhythms, and leading to two simultaneous conclusions. These were Venice and Munich.

Even though the history of Venice is intimately linked with ancient culture, the antiquity, monuments and statues, it is at once familiar and exterior to the Republic; it cannot pretend to form a legitimate part of Venetian identity. In Venice, like in most countries of Europe outside Italy, the presence of Greco-Roman antiquities did not have a political justification, only a cultural one; therefore, their appropriation could only be a cultural phenomenon. The process by which museums in the Roman style were disseminated is marked by a second characteristic: the passage of the museum from the status of private property to the status of public property, in the strongest sense of the word, that is, the property of a state that transcends those who govern it, the Republic becoming guarantor of the 'public nature' of its property. To understand this phenomenon it suffices to remember the role of two members of one of the most illustrious families of the Venetian oligarchy: the Grimani. Domenico, Patriarch of Aquileia assembled a collection in Rome that by the terms of his testament passed to the Republic in 1523. It would be installed in a room in the Doges' Palace where, at least, illustrious visitors, such as Henry III in 1574, could visit it. His nephew Giovanni, himself Patriarch of Aquileia, would assemble a much more important collection that he placed in a centrally located room with zenithal lighting in his Palace of Santa Maria Formosa. In 1587, he would finally ask the Senate to find a 'public place' for it where it could remain unified and accessible. The Senate proposed the anti-chamber of the Marciana Library where the collection was definitively installed in 1596, three years after Giovanni Grimani's death. This came to be known as the 'Statuario publico', a reference that underlined, as observed an

English voyager, the ownership of the state. The association of the collection with the library seems to reconstitute an ideal Alexandria, on a reduced scale, in the Palace of Sansovino presided over by the *Wisdom* of Titian.[20]

The creation of the 'Statuario publico' of Venice is, in itself, a considerable event because it represents the reproduction of the Roman model on the basis of a different legitimacy. While the museum served as a factor of political and cultural identity at the Capitol and the Belvedere, in Venice, it would become the conservatory of an Antiquity considered a patrimony that was common to all societies claiming kinship with its literary and artistic heritage. Tangible remnants of Antiquity could be possessed as a right even by peoples who were not its natural inheritors.

This is demonstrated by the creation, at nearly the same moment, of the first museum outside the Italian domain, in Munich. In Bavaria, the initiative would depart from the summit of the state. The Duke Albert V, who had transformed his state between Vienna and the Rheinland Bishoprics into a bastion of the Counter-Reformation, was determined to demonstrate his political power through the splendour of a culture of which Antiquity was an integral part. He began to constitute a collection that would express his '*virtus*' and '*liberalitas*' as early as 1560 through the intermediary of very active agents like Jacopo Strada. The collection was invested with a power, if not to make the Prince, then, at least, to flatter him. Albert V attached such importance to the presentation of his Antiquities, considered the natural cultural appendages of his political power, that he decided, in 1567, to build a palace especially reserved for this purpose. The 'Antiquarium' was finished in 1580.[21]

The creation of the 'Statuario publico' of Venice and the 'Antiquarium' of Munich were the simultaneous demonstration of an almost natural tendency towards the multiplication of the Roman model. Antiquity could not remain the monopoly of one city: its cultural importance was so great that it would give rise to a kind of network that would, in turn, augment its political importance.

At the same moment that Venice and Munich were transposing, in their own way, the model of the museum of Antiquity in the Roman style, Italy proposed another example, invented in Florence, which was also to prove extraordinarily fecund. While the new Rome was constituting itself as the legitimate heir of Ancient Rome, assuring continuity through the management of its monumental and artistic patrimony, Florence invented another patrimony composed of its own artistic creation, becoming conscious of producing an art that was equal, if not superior, to that of Antiquity. This 'modern' art, according to the term used by Cennino Cennini[22] around 1400, was an art that exalted its inventors, and Giotto first among them, as the 'lights of Florentine glory'. It was an art that would soon be held up as a paradigm for future generations on the same level as ancient art,[23] and also integrated into a founding history of Florentine identity, whose content was beginning to be assembled a century before the first edition of Vasari's masterpiece. The invention of the history of artists (1550) and the invention of the Academy of Arts (1563) conditioned and announced the invention of another form of museum, the museum of fine arts according to a terminology fixed in the eighteenth century. Florence would treat the Renaissance, whose glory she attributed to herself, as Rome would treat Antiquity, whose unique inheritor she proposed to be. As the public rushed 'in frenzied admiration', as Vasari put it,[24] to see the masterpieces that would multiply from 1500 on, and as artists came, as if on a pilgrimage, to the new sanctuaries decorated by Masaccio, Leonardo, Raphael and Michelangelo, it is not difficult to understand why Cosimo I de' Medici, veritable founder of the Tuscan state, and his successors would make every effort to constitute, by commissioning or buying, confiscating or extorting, a grand collection of 'modern' art, the first of its kind in Europe. The Medici had perfectly well understood that the grandeur of Florence henceforth rested on the radiance of its culture and not on adventurous wars of conquest. In 1584, Grand Duke Francis I decided to use the upper level of the 'Uffizi', built as a kind of administrative centre and completed twenty years before by Vasari, to house his collection. This arrangement associated a central room, the 'Tribuna', its cosmological decoration presiding over the most precious works, with the gallery, which, with its impressive extension of rooms that opened onto one of its sides, offered a space favourable for the accumulation of masterpieces.[25] Completed in 1591, this complex was celebrated in the first guide to Florence published that same year which announced its opening to the public.[26]

Intended for amateurs, who would come to admire the marvellous power of painting, and artists, who would find inexhaustible sources for study and inspiration, the Gallery of the Uffizi also served as a cornerstone of Florentine identity, inseparable from the renown attached to the city's role in the development of the arts since Giotto. Not by chance, the Grand Duke signed an edict as early as 1602 which established a principle of control, according to which the Academy was entrusted with the task of controlling the export of works of art from the Florentine territory, while also permanently and definitively banning the exportation of works of nineteen artists, listed by name in the edict's annex. This was an unheard of measure that proves the specifically patrimonial character of the creation of the first museum of fine arts and should be compared to similar measures taken in Rome following the creation of the first two public collections of Antiquities.[27] The simultaneous emergence of the museum and of protective legislation invites us to pose the same question we did concerning Rome: would Florence remain unique, or would its example inspire the creation of another, or several other, Florences?

Before attempting to provide parts of an answer, it is important to note that Italy disposed of the first 'network' of museums at the end of the XVI century with poles in Rome, Florence and Venice, completed by two other examples: first, the 'Museo' (the first to place the term on its façade) created on the border of Lake Como by Paolo Giovio in 1543 to accommodate a collection of portraits that, along with their descriptions, constituted a remarkable demonstration of remembering the past by reference to images of those who had been distinguished because of their political and military exploits or their intellectual creations;[28] and, second, the museum associated in 1618 with the Academy, created by the Bishop of Milan, Federico Borromeo, as early as 1613. This first network also provides the sketch of a typology of the institution.[29]

The development of the Italian model in no way follows a linear evolution and the example of the Antiquarium of Munich long remained isolated: the seventeenth century is a period of real institutional blockage. Yet, even then, some things did happen. The confirmation and multiplication of protective measures invented in 1534 by Paul III, bespoke, in Italy, the consolidation of the juridical foundations of the museum. We can assume that the repetition of such measures is the best evidence of their inefficiency, even though many anecdotes reveal that they were perceived as a bothersome reality for those who wished to 'extract' (as it was termed) artistic treasures from Rome.[30] Furthermore, recourse was made to the *fedecommesso* (entails), a principle of Roman law, according to which the owner of a collection of antiquities or paintings could in perpetuity oblige inheritors to maintain the unity and integrity of a collection, thus escaping, not only the common law of successions, but also the possibility that the collection might be placed on the market.[31] Only the Pope's intervention could exempt an inheritor from strict observance of the rule of *fedecommesso*. The collections of the great Roman families, like the Colonna, Doria, and Maffei, were subject to this strict disposition, which would appear to be of extraordinary interest for the development of the culture of the museum. It implied that the masterpieces of Antiquity and modern art were subject to a special juridical regime – *l'attache à perpétuelle demeure*, as one says in French law – which ordained the perpetual attachment of an inalienable collection to a certain place (in this case Rome) constituting *de facto* a museum. Such is the little known, but substantial, contribution of the seventeenth century to the history of the museum.

At the same moment, in the Germanic domain, we can see the flourishing of a literature that could quite simply be defined as 'museographical'. These works offered advice concerning the constitution and management of collections, and were often accompanied by lists of collections that could apparently be visited, principally in the German and Italian states.[32] This literature begins with the treatise of the Fleming Samuel Quiccheberg, published in 1565 in Munich where he served as counsellor to Duke Albert V, at the very moment when the latter would put together the collection that resulted in the creation of the Antiquarium.[33] This genre would reach its apogee with the treatise of L. Christoph Sturm, published in 1704 in Hamburg. In addition to highly pertinent advice concerning the display of works of art, it is notable because it gave priority to security and visibility over aesthetic effects. It also contained the grandiose plan for the ideal museum, that seems a transposition of the palatial plan par excellence: Versailles.[34]

Thus, the pause of the seventeenth century was not barren because it coincided with decisive progress concerning the juridical protection of collections and the development of a reflection on their conditions of operation, thus establishing the conceptual foundations of our institution.

As early as the first half of the eighteenth century, a pontifical policy building upon the accomplishments of the Renaissance would give the museum, as we know it today, its definitive form and invent a model that would be followed by all of Europe. The popes of the Enlightenment may not have been great theologians or politicians. Yet, they understood perfectly well that the only way to reinforce the glory of 'Roma Triumphans' and to consolidate Rome's status as the 'model of all cities' was by developing cultural action that was based on the idea of Rome's continuity from Antiquity to the Modern Age. Accompanied by the refinement of edicts that strengthened the protection of patrimony[35] and that led to the law of 5 January 1750, which extended these protections to 'modern' works and is the model for contemporary legislation, pontifical policy unfolded in three stages, the first of which dealt with the Capitol.

Around 1720, Clement XI strengthened the collection of the Palace of Conservators founded by Sixtus IV by renovating the courtyard with a decor of triumphal architecture that welcomed the imperial statue of victorious Rome flanked by captives.[36] In 1734, Clement XII decided to transform the disused Palazzo Nuovo, built by C. Rainaldi around 1650 in front of the Palace of Conservators, into a 'Capitoline Museum', which would house the increasing number of archaeological finds and, thus, become, as stated in the preface to the first volume of the 1750 catalogue, a barrier against the covetousness of foreigners.[37] The Museum of the Capitol, as it was thereafter known, was admired by scholars such as J.J. Barthélémy,[38] conservator of the Cabinet of Medals of the Royal Collection of France (letter of 1756), and Winckelmann,[39] and attracted young Roman and foreign artists and the amateurs of the Grand Tour. The third episode, which would have an enormous symbolic reach despite its fortuitous point of departure, occurred in 1748: G.B. Sacchetti, ruined inheritor of a beautiful collection of paintings constituted as early as 1630 and placed under the regime of the *fedecommesso*, was desperately seeking to escape the pursuit of his creditors. Benedict XIV very intelligently pronounced the dissolution of the *fedecommesso*; in compensation, Sachetti ceded part of his collection to the Pope and freely sold the rest. Placed at the Palace of the Conservators, the paintings of Sachetti, which would be joined in 1750 by those of Prince Gilberto Pio di Savoia, recovered in very similar circumstances, formed the Capitol's Picture Gallery,[40] which was opened to the public in 1749. In this way, Rome's first museum pole was formed, associating antiquities and modern art, on the hill that would remain the symbol of Rome's political tradition. The Vatican hill, whose collections had been neglected since the epoch of the Counter-Reformation, would be the theatre of comparable events 20 years later, prompted by the outbreak of archaeological discoveries linked to the development of excavations. Clement XIV liberated the antiquities gathered by his Renaissance predecessors from the sheds where they had been hidden since 1560 and had the courtyard of the Belvedere transformed, so they could be displayed in the shelter of a solemn portico. But it is his successor, Pius VI, who would take the decisive measure: that of attaching a veritable museum to Bramante's courtyard in order to receive new acquisitions, including those from the Mattei *fedecommesso* dissolved in 1770. Rooms specialized by theme (animal rooms, muses, etc.) converged on a solemn rotunda, raised as an imitation of the Pantheon, with a floor composed of an authentic Roman mosaic: the room of the Gods of Olympus.[41] Pius VI crowned his oeuvre with the installation of an art gallery, opened in 1789, which would make the Vatican hill symmetrical to the Capitol.[42]

Between 1750 and 1790, Rome imposed the universal model of the museum, associating collections from Antiquity with modern art in two architectural spaces. At the same time, the first Italian-wide network at the end of the sixteenth century was reinforced, though it is not possible to claim that it was a result of the Roman model's influence. Antiquities remained the foundation for a feeling of identity that was affirmed even in communities that were modest in terms of population, but animated by a patriotically inspired scholarship that found expression in the creation of museums. Such was the case in Cortona,[43] where notables created an 'Etruscan Academy' in 1726, devoted to the study and display of Etruscan artefacts, and, in light of the anxiety aroused by the coming extinction of the Medici dynasty and the problem of succession it posed, intended to affirm Tuscan identity and the continuity of a history that was even older than Rome's. Over the course of the century this Academy would gradually develop a museum around local archaeological discoveries. Such was also the case in Volterra,[44] where the municipal administration obtained a very strict regulation of archaeological excavations from the Tuscan government in 1744 and 1761, while several private collections given to the city, including that of the great historian Mario Granacci, permitted the opening of a museum in 1789 that would be installed in the Palazzo dei Priori, thus demonstrating the value of its symbolism for the sense of local identity.

Sometimes, scholarly considerations would take precedence over issues of identity. Such would be the case in Verona,[45] thanks to the action of the highly eminent historian Scipione Maffei, who, in light of his intention to create a museum of antiquities, assembled a series of inscriptions – some of which were local, but most originated in other regions of Italy – with the intention of conserving historical material. He wanted to give the institution, housed in an architecture of the Palladian tradition finished in 1740, a solid juridical base: it would be founded upon 'Jus comune', that is to say, public law. The collection, composed above all of inscriptions, would thus be protected against the claims of families and foreigners, whose covetousness posed a threat to Italy. At the same time, these collections, by being placed at the disposal of historians, would also serve the beneficio pubblico. If the protection of an 'identity' were at stake, it would be the identity of a community that was at once vaster than Tuscany or Volterra, but also more diffuse because its reference was to an Italy that was devoid of a politically unifying structure.

The decisive event that would structure the Italian museum network takes place in Naples and is very well known: it follows the fortuitous discovery in 1711 of Herculaneum, one of the cities destroyed by the catastrophe of Vesuvius in 79, and the beginning of systematic excavations, first, there in 1737, and, a few years later, extended to Pompeii.[46] The unprecedented importance of the discovery of paintings and objects of daily life would lead to the foundation in 1758 of a 'site museum' near the two cities in Portici, where a first attempt would be made to present the lifestyle of ancient Rome. Serving, therefore, at the same time, as a site museum and a museum of civilization, the museum founded at Portici was considered the personal property of the King and visits to it were highly restricted while awaiting the publication, extending over thirty-five years, of the luxurious volumes of the 'Antiquity of Herculaneum'. The creation of the museum was, moreover, preceded in 1755 by the publication of legislation regarding the protection and control of the antiquities.[47]

The Bourbon dynasty, which would install itself in Naples in 1734 and transform the kingdom into a veritable state, carried with it the magnificent Farnese collections it had inherited, which were finally presented between 1758 and 1764 in the royal residence of Capodimonte and made accessible for visits and study. At century's end, with the arrival of the antiquities of Rome's Farnese Palace and their proximity to the museum in Portici, Naples became a complete museum pole, fulfilling, around 1780, the promise of the grandiose plans regarding the unification in their capital of the Bourbon collections.

The rationalization of the museum was accomplished in Florence, whose example would be followed for nearly two centuries.[48] To begin with, this took place at a juridical level. Before her death the last Medici, Anna Maria Luisa, imposed in 1737, the obligation on the Habsburg-Lorraine dynasty, her inheritors by European consensus, to conserve for perpetuity the entire Medici collection in Florence as the property of the Tuscan state. This disposition was scrupulously respected by Francesco di Lorena and Pietro Leopoldo (1765–1791), who was a model of the enlightened Prince. In a meaningful gesture, the latter transferred the management of the museum from the Ducal House to the Ministry of Finance, marking, in this way, the passage of the property from the family to the state. Expanded and more precise protective legislation aimed to conserve ancient and modern patrimony in its place of origin. The Uffizi Gallery would become a museum of Renaissance painting and sculpture (a Renaissance that would reach back to the fourteenth century) and antiquities, ridding the collections of merely curious objects, which the century of the Enlightenment could no longer admire, either for aesthetic or scientific reasons.

In the Germanic domain the Italian model experienced an expansion that makes it possible to refer to the beginning of a European network of museums. Freed from the ravages of the wars of religion, and of French and Turkish wars, and stimulated by a multitude of centres of power, the territories of the Empire experienced an unprecedented cultural flourishing. To Princes in their quest for prestige, the Italian states offered the example of collections organized into museums in Rome, Florence, Milan and Naples, themselves among the principal attractions of the Grand Tour. Versailles, on the other hand, used the mirage of a policy of *grandeur* embodied in a monument that concentrated all the attributes of power, including the rich collections of paintings assembled by Louis XIV. These, nevertheless, remained 'private' property, aspiring to no more of a 'public' vocation than court festivals.

Following an often – uncertain chronology, the Age of Enlightenment in the Empire marks the passage from the collection to the museum. Two examples are prominent: Dresden and Vienna. In Saxony, as early as 1587, Duke Christian I had been encouraged by one of his counsellors who had travelled to Italy, G. Kaltemarckt, to follow the example of Florence.[49] In fact, through the early eighteenth century, one witnessed the phenomenon of the accumulation of precious objects, scientific instruments, machines (as befits a country whose industry knew a precocious development), family portraits, paintings – particularly Flemish and Dutch – bought according to what was available in the Amsterdam or Hamburg markets. The great turning point would occur with Augustus II (who reigned from

1694 to 1733). His sense of public interest inspired him to place his collections at the service of 'all those devoted to the progress of knowledge' and he would begin to distribute his works among distinct buildings organized in specialized departments (porcelain, scientific objects, decorative arts).[50] Augustus III (his successor who reigned until 1762) deserves credit for assigning a prominent place to the *beaux arts*. On the counsel of a brilliant Italian connoisseur, Francesco Algarotti, the sovereign desired to assemble a first-rate Italian collection. In 1745 after long secret negotiations, taking advantage of the financial troubles of the Duke d'Este, François III, he bought 100 masterpieces from the Modena collection,[51] installed the works the following year in specially fitted ancient stables, and inaugurated the collection at the end of 1746. Winckelmann, an assiduous visitor to the Gallery of Dresden before his departure for Rome, wrote an unfinished description and precisely characterized this event:[52] the fine arts had arrived in Dresden '*wie eine Fremde Kolonie*'. The desire to culturally appropriate already famous paintings from the schools of Lombardy, Venice and Bologna is clear. With this spectacular purchase, Italian painting became a common patrimony for the Europe of the Enlightenment, reinforced by the arrival, in 1754, of a Raphael bought from the Benedictines of San Sisto di Piacenza, taking advantage of their need for money. Economic laws thus began to impose the migration of masterpieces.[53]

The formation of the museum of Vienna took place over a much longer period than the museum of Dresden. The collection existed for a long time before the museum. Without relating all of the stages of its formation, it is necessary to recall its essential moment, brought about by a passionate amateur, the Archduke Leopold William (1614–1662), who began gathering a superb Italian collection, in particular Venetian (taking advantage of the lack of protection measures in Venice), and subsequently completing it during his sojourn in Brussels as governor of Flanders (from 1647 to 1656) with a Flemish collection of comparable quality.[54] Known by its inventories and publicized through the engravings and paintings of its 'conservator', David Teniers the Younger, this 'European' collection, which was perhaps the first of its kind after the ephemeral collection of Charles I of England, was admired by the Venetian specialist Marco Boschini,[55] who was glad to see Giorgione and Tintoretto, Titian and Veronese, presented in this 'temple of painting'. Left to the Emperor Leopold I, nephew of the Archduke, the collection was first installed in the apartments of the Hofburg and opened for artists' visits in 1773. Its transformation into a museum marks an important episode in the enlightened policy of Maria Theresa and Joseph II, who decided to transfer it to the disused palace of the Belvedere.[56] Inaugurated in 1780, Joseph entrusted the organization of the imperial museum to the engraver and scholar from Basel, Christian von Mechel,[57] who had spent a formative sojourn in Rome in the entourage of Winckelmann. Mechel, who had recently made a name for himself with the publication of a monumental catalogue of the collections of the Gallery of Dusseldorf in collaboration with the architect Nicolas de Pigage (1778), would set his mind to realize a 'systematic arrangement' that would turn the museum into a 'visible depository of the history of art' founded on the separation of paintings into 'schools': with the Italians divided by region according to a tradition that appeared at the end of the sixteenth century, accompanied by the ancient Flemish masters of the Low Countries, the Dutch and the Germans.

At the same moment that L. Lanzi arranged the paintings of the Uffizi to visibly 'trace' the history of painting, although, admittedly, the paintings displayed were almost exclusively Tuscan, Mechel created another museum of the modern age with an obvious cultural objective. The magnificent paintings of Velazquez were not hung: they remained in the private domain of the reigning family. The museum of the Belvedere did not visualize the dynasty's historical memory, but, rather, a plastic culture composed of the assimilation of Italian and Flemish elements, which still allowed the 'German patriot' to read with delight this inscription at the entry of the room: 'German School'.

The modernity of the museum is confirmed by the hostility it would arouse in certain circles. In fact, journals like the *Deutsches Museum* criticized an excessively scholarly or abstract disposition, which could not possibly be suitable for 'sensitive' men like artists.[58]

In Dresden and Vienna we witness, therefore, a phenomenon of the 'naturalization' of foreign art (essentially from Italy and Flanders), which had become a common heritage of European culture and welcomed in open museums. The vocation of other museums, like those of the Capitol and the Belvedere in Rome, or the Uffizi in Florence, was to maintain the works of Antiquity or those of the Tuscan school in their historical context. Antiquity remained, for certain German rulers, an element of culture in the tradition founded by Albert V at the end of the sixteenth century in Munich, as shown by the desire of Friedrich II, Landgrave of Hesse-Kassel, to erect an imposing building, finished in 1779 and considered one of the first manifestations of Neo-classicism in Germany, in order to house antiquities bought in Italy.[59]

In the 1830s, a scholar[60] who had compiled a catalogue of German collections wrote that the museum had become an 'affair of State', or, more literally, 'a necessity for the State'. The Age of Enlightenment had laid the foundations of this system with its two modalities: the Italian, with a profoundly patrimonial character, and the German, whose character was essentially cultural. At the end of the eighteenth century, the circle closes: the last director of fine arts of the French monarchy, the Count d'Angiviller, who presided over the innovative project for preparing the transformation of the Grand Gallery of the Louvre for the installation of the royal collections, at the end of 1788, wrote of his hope to see the Estates-General 'restore to Europe the enjoyment of her buried riches' through the realization of his project. Without knowing it, D'Angiviller spoke in the vein of Sixtus IV in 1471. It was not a question then of restoring a patrimony to the Roman people, but rather of placing it under the gaze of Europe, to 'communicate', to use an essential term of that epoch, the masterpieces of the Renaissance and Classicism to Europe as a whole.[61]

The museum became a great European design illustrated by images that manifest its common vocation and transport us back to the dreams of the sixteenth century evoked above. The images of the Capitoline Museum – like the engraving of

G.D. Campiglia (in the catalogue of Bottari) depicting students copying the *Dying Gladiator*,[62] or the design of Jean Grandjean depicting amateurs examining the *Antinous* [63] – illustrate the programme inscribed on the walls of the Della Valle Palace, and engraved on a medal displayed at the Society of Antiquities of Kassel in 1777 that showed Minerva explaining ancient pieces of art to a child in front of the façade of the Fridericianum Museum.[64] The engraving of J. Duplessis-Berteaux, in the *Voyage Picturesque* of Saint Non (1782), representing the solemn transfer of the antiquities of Herculaneum to the Museum of Naples, is an homage to Antiquity that seems to emerge directly from a Renaissance text and is all the more impressive as it is the image of a dream; the transfer never actually took place.[65] The allegory of Fischer on the creation of the Belvedere Museum in Vienna (1781) harks back to the myth of the temple of the arts that seemed to inspire the realization of the rooms of Pius VI at the Belvedere in Rome.[66]

These museums became theatres of social life, which was foremost that of the English nobility who stopped in Florence during the Grand Tour to visit the Museum of the Uffizi, as shown in the painting by J. Zoffany (1774) of the *Tribuna*. There the representation of a real museum merges with the representation of an ideal museum as the painter associates the painting masterpieces hung on that famous room's walls with ancient masterpieces presented in other rooms.[67] However, the social event held in the museum, might also prove premonitory, as is suggested by the painting of Bénigne Gagneraux, who represented the first public meeting of the Pope and the head of the Reform Church of Sweden, the beginning of a difficult dialogue.[68] On 1 January 1784, in the Room of the Muses, at the inauguration of the Vatican Museum, Pius VI met an illustrious tourist to Rome: Gustav III, King of Sweden. Presenting their exchange as purely 'fortuitous', as contemporary informers did, is a pious lie that cannot hide the event's exceptional significance. They were not, in effect, two sovereigns engaging in banal diplomatic banter, but, rather, the heads of the Catholic Church and the Lutheran Protestant Church of Sweden and one could thus speak of a first example of an ecumenical summit meeting. Contemporary correspondence reveals that the conversation began and continued thanks to a passion shared by the speakers: the Vatican Museum's spectacular collection of antiquities. Remarking the evident interest of the King of Sweden, the Pope proposed to serve as his guide and to 'lead him through all the rooms and explain to him what was worth, as an antiquarian would have done'. Some years after his return to Sweden, Gustav III would found a gallery of antiquities in Stockholm.[69]

More 'arranged' than 'fortuitous', the fact is that the meeting actually occurred. This is in itself significant because it demonstrates, in an unexpected way, how the museum of antiquities functioned as a space for dialogue and sociability. There is more. Gustav III was so impressed that some weeks later he would command a commemorative painting from French painter Bénigne Gagneraux who had established himself in Rome in December 1776 after receiving the Prix de Rome awarded by the Burgundian States.[70] Completed the following year, the painting would be shown at the Vatican before being sent to Sweden (where it would arrive in July 1786). Pius VI admired it so much that he would soon command a replica from the author.[71]

The creation of these two almost identical versions of the painting demonstrates the importance the protagonists attached to the meeting of 1 January 1784, and to their 'common' inauguration of the Vatican Museum. However, a further meaning can be read from the placement of figures adopted by Gagneraux. He places the Pope, who had extended an invitation for the visit, in front, with the King of Sweden preparing to follow him; on an intermediate level, on both sides of the opening that gives onto the 'rotunda', he places two of the most famous statues that are, in reality, found next door in the courtyard of the Belvedere: *Apollo* and *Antinous*.

Thanks to the liberty he thus takes with topographical truth, the painter gives a prominent role to the two sculptures: *Apollo* seems to preside over the scene and to give his benediction to the dialogue that is being launched, his attitude inspiring that of Pius VI, while Gustav III seems to be the living double of *Antinous*. The impression that the painting intended to transmit a solemn message is further reinforced by its spatial construction and the creation of an ambiance that makes one irresistibly think of Raphael's *School of Athens*, that temple of wisdom and knowledge at whose pinnacle stood the Church itself.

In this painting, desired by the two persons who would be that unwonted scene's heroes, the ancient statues seem at once to inspire and to be witness of the beginning of a public dialogue between the Catholic Church and one of the main churches issued from the Reform. Antiquity would thus become a source of tolerance and hope and would appear responsible for a kind of '*paideia*', to take an expression current in the Hellenistic epoch, that is, a mission of education and culture that would invest man with all of his '*humanitas*'. Antiquity was no longer exclusively the reference for a creation that must be continued, as the Academy taught, nor for a history that must be written, as Winckelmann proclaimed, but perhaps also for the promise of a reconciling irenicism after the dramatic lacerations that coincided with its exaltation at the apogee of the Renaissance. The museum had become the theatre of history.

Notes

1. Falguières (1988), pp. 245–6.
2. Falguières (1988), pp. 292–7.
3. Buddensieg (1983); Gramaccini (1996).
4. Black (1995).
5. Buddensieg (1983); Thoenes (1996).
6. Buddensieg (1969).
7. Vasari (1976), t. IV, pp. 6–8.
8. Settis (1999), pp. 110–11.
9. Daltrop,(1983) and (1985). Geese (1985–1986); Winner et al.(1998).
10. Deswarte-Rosa (1993).
11. Daltrop (1985).
12. Vasari (1976), t. V, p. 1984, pp. 245–6.
13. Goldstein (1996), p. 11.
14. On this cycle, see the catalogue of the last sale Christie's New York, 28 January 1999, pp. 70–80.
15. Schweikart (1993); Alison (1992).
16. Jestaz (1963).
17. Vasari (1976), t. VI, p. 144. Vasari writes: 'quasi una nuova Roma'.
18. Falguières (1988).
19. Cassiodorus, VII, 13.
20. *Lo statuario publico della Serenissima ...* (1997).
21. von Busch (1973), and Hamdorf (1992).
22. Cennini (1991), ch. 1, p. 18: 'Il quale Giotto rimutò l'arte del dipingere di Greco in latino e ridusse al moderno'.
23. Pommier (1995).
24. Vasari (1976), cf. note 7.
25. Heikamp (1964); Berti, (1967), and Barocchi and Ragioneri (1983).
26. Bocchi (1591), pp. 100–12.
27. Emiliani (1978), pp. 32–9.
28. Giovio (1999), pp. 112–79.
29. Jones (1992); Borromeo (1997).
30. Emiliani (1978), pp. 67–151.
31. Eiche (1983), pp. 353–9.
32. Berliner (1928).
33. Hajos (1958), pp. 151–6, and references to Giulio Camillo in Quiccheberg (1963), pp. 207–11; Falguières (1992).
34. Cf. Berliner (1928), pp. 336–8.
35. Emiliani (1978), pp. 96–108.
36. Liebenwein (1981) and Cushing Aikin (1980).
37. Fröhlich and Kunze (1998); Bottari (1750), t. I, p. XII.
38. Barthélémy (1972), p. 96.
39. Winckelmann (1952), t. I, letters of 7 December 1755 (p. 190) and of 29 January 1756 (p. 202).
40. Bocconi (1930), pp. 337–40.
41. Pietrangeli (1951–1952); Pietrangeli (1976–1977); von Steuben (1981); Howard (1990), pp. 142–153; Consoli (1996); Liverani (2000).
42. Pietrangeli (1995), pp. 205–19 and pp. 168–73; Abita (1998).

43. Barocchi and Gallo (1985); Morelli (1985); Harari (1998); Paolucci and Maetzcke (1992).
44. Caterni (1989).
45. Franzoni (1975–1976); Marchini (1972–1973); Mariani Canova (1975–1976); Sandrini (1982).
46. Fittipaldi (1995), pp. 275–96; *Civiltà del Settecento a Napoli* (1979), t. II, pp. 29–39 and 58–68; Fornari Scianchi and Spinosa (1995), pp. 80–93.
47. Emiliani (1978), pp. 227–41.
48. Gatti (1879); Meloni Trkulja (1979), pp. 9–13; Barocchi (1982); Casciu (2002).
49. Gutfleisch and Menzhausen (1989); Dubielzig (1990).
50. Seydewitz and Seydewitz (1957); Glaser (1980); Heres (1991).
51. Winkler (1989).
52. Winckelmann (1968), p. 29.
53. Pommier (2002).
54. Glaras (1967, 1968).
55. Boschini (1966),Vento I°, pp. 57–8.
56. Meijers (1995).
57. Wüthrich (1956).
58. Deutsches Museum, Leipzig, February 1783, pp. 182–185; Nicolaï (1784), t. IV, pp. 492–501.
59. Dittscheid (1995).
60. Klemm (1837), p. 135.
61. Pommier (2001).
62. Bottari (1750), t. III.
63. Grandjean (1780), Amsterdam, Rijksmuseum.
64. *Aufklärung und Klassizismus* …, (1979), Me. 9, pp. 186–187.
65. Saint Non (1782), t.1, pp. 54–5: Duplessis Berteaux, Transfert des antiquités du musée de Portici au palais des études de Naples.
66. Fischer, Allégorie de la création du Musée impérial (1781), Vienna, Belvedere Museum.
67. John Zoffany, La Tribuna, (c. 1772–1777), London, Royal collection.
68. Pommier (2000).
69. Bjurström (1992) (with a summary in English).
70. Bénigne Gagneraux, L'entrevue de Gustave III avec le pape Pie VI dans le musée Pio clementino au Vatican, 1785, Stockholm National Museum.
71. This version, 1786, is located in Prague, National Gallery. Cf. *Bénigne Gagneraux* (1756–1795), (1983), pp. 98–100.

References

Abita, M.F. (1998), 'La sfortunata storia delle prima "Galleria di quadri" di Pio VI in Vaticano: 1789–1797', *Ricerche di Storia dell'arte*, 66, 67–78.

Alison, A.H. (1992), 'The bronzes of Pier Jacopo Alari Bonacolsi, called Antico', *Jahrbuch der Kunsthistorischen Sammlungen in Wien*, LXXXVIII, 35–310.

Aufklärung und Klassizismus in Hessen-Kassel unter Landgraf Friedrich II. 1760–1785 (1979), Exhibition catalogue (Kassel).

Barocchi, P. (1982), 'La storia della galleria degli Uffizi e la storiografia artistica', in *Annali della Scuola normale superiore di Pisa* (classe di lettere e filosofia), série III, XII, 4 (Pisa), pp. 1411–1523.

Barocchi, P. and D. Gallo (eds), (1985), *L'Accademia Etrusca* (Milan).

Barocchi, P. and G. Ragioneri (eds), (1983), *Gli Uffizi. Quattro secoli di una galleria* (Florence).

Barthélémy, J. J. (1972), *Voyage en Italie* (1756) (Genève).

Bénigne Gagneraux (1756–1795). *Un pittore francese nella Roma di Pio VI* (1983), exhibition catalogue, the Borghese Gallery (Rome).

Berliner, R., (1928), 'Zur älteren Geschichte der allgemeinen Museumslehre in Deutschland', *Münchner Jahrbuch der bildenden Kunst*, V, 327–352.

Berti, L. (1967), *Il principe dello studiolo. Francesco I dei Medici e la fine del Rinascimento fiorentino* (Florence).

Bjurström, P. (1992), *Nationalmuseum 1792–1992* (Stockholm).

Black, R. (1995), 'The Donation of Constantine: A New Source for the Concept of Renaissance', in A. Brown (ed.) *Language and Images of Renaissance Italy* (Oxford), pp. 51–85.

Bocchi, F. (1591), *Le bellezze della città di Firenze* (Florence).

Bocconi, S. (1930), *Collezioni capitoline* (Rome).

Borromeo, F. (1997), *Musaeum*, G. Ravasi and P. Cigada (eds) (Milan).

Boschini, M. (1966), *La carta del navegar pitoresco* (Venezia 1660), A. Pallasacchini (ed.) (Venice and Rome).

Bottari, G. (1750), *Il museo capitolino* (Rome).

Buddensieg, T. (1969), 'Zum Statuenprogramm in Kapitolsplan Pauls. III', *Zeitschrift für Kunstgeschichte*, XXXII, 177–228.

_____. (1983), 'Die Statuenstiftung Sixtus IV, im Jahre 1471', *Römisches Jahrbuch für Kunstgeschichte*, XX, 33–73.

Busch, R. von (1973), *Studien zu deutschen Antiken-sammlungen des 16. Jahrhunderts* (Tübingen).

Casciu, S. (2002), 'Omaggio all'Elettrice Palatina, Anna Maria Luisa de'Medici', in *Bollettino 1996–2001, Amici di Palazzo Pitti* (Florence), pp. 4–8.

Cassiodorus, *Variorum libri XII* (A.G. Fridl ed.), Corpus Christianorum, series latina, XCVI, Turnholt, 1973.

Caterini, G. (1989), *Volterra, Museo Guarnacci* (Pisa).

Cennini, C. (1991), *Il libro dell'arte*, Mario Serchi. (ed.) (Florence).

Civiltà del Settecento a Napoli (1979), exhibition catalogue (Florence).

Consoli, G.P. (1996), *Il Museo Pio Clementino. La scena dell'antico in Vaticano* (Modena).

Cushing Aikin, R. (1980), 'Romae de Dacia Triumphantis: Rome and Captives at the Capitoline Hill', *The Art Bulletin*, LXII, 4, 583–92.

Daltrop, G. (1983), 'Zur Aufstellung antiker Statuen in der Villetta di Belvedere des Vatikans', *Boreas – Münstersche Beiträge zur Archäologie*, VI, 217–32.

Daltrop, G. (1985), 'Nascita e significato della raccolta delle statue antiche in Vaticano', in M. Fagiolo (ed.), *Roma e l'Antico nell'arte e nella cultura del Cinquecento* (Biblioteca internazionale di cultura, 17) (Rome), pp. 111–29.

Deswarte-Rosa, S. (1993), 'Prisca pictura et antiqua novitas', in *La visión del mundo clásico en el arte español* (Centro de Estudios Históricos, VI jornadas de Arte, 1992) (Madrid), pp. 118–31.

Dittscheid, H.C. (Les musées en Europe), *à la ville de l'ouverture du Louvre* (Actes du colloque du Musée du Louvre), Paris, 1995

Dubielzig, U. (1990), 'Ancient Art in Gabriel Kaltermarkt's Kunstkammer, Literary Sources of the Passages on Antiquity', *Journal of the History of Collections*, II, 1–6.

Eiche, S. (1983), 'On the dispersal of cardinal Bembo's collections', *Mitteilungen des Kunsthistorischen Instituts in Florenz*, XXVII.

Emiliani, A. (1978), *Leggi, bandi e provvedimenti per la tutela dei beni artistici e culturali negli antichi stati italiani 1571–1860* (Bologna).

Falguières, P. (1988), 'La cité fictive. Les collections des cardinaux, à Rome, au XVIe siècle', in *Les Carrache et les décors profanes*, Actes du colloque de l'École française de Rome (2–4 octobre 1986), Bibliothèque de l'École française de Rome, no.106 (Rome).

———. (1992), 'Fondation du théâtre ou méthode de l'exposition universelle. Les inscriptions de Samuel Quicchelberg (1565)', in *Les cahiers du Musée d'art moderne*, 40, 91–115.

Fittipaldi, A. (1995), 'Les musées à Naples au temps de Charles et de Ferdinand de Bourbon (1734–1799)', in E. Pommier (ed.), *Les musées en Europe à la veille de l'ouverture du Louvre* (Actes du colloque du Musée du Louvre, 1993) (Paris).

Fornari Scianchi, L. and N. Spinosa (eds) (1995), *I Farnese. Arte e collezionismo*, exposition Parma-Naples-Munich (Milan).

Franzoni, L. (1975–1976), 'L'opera di Scipione Maffei e di Alessandro Pompei per il Museo publico veronese', in *Atti e Memorie della Accademia di Agricoltura, Scienze e lettere di Verona*, serie VI, XXVII, pp. 193–218.

Fröhlich, T. and M. Kunze (1998), *Römische Antiken Sammlungen im 18. Jahrhundert* (exhibition catalogue from Wörlitz and Stendal) (Mainz).

Gatti, A. (1879), *Le gallerie e i Musei di Firenze. Discorso storico* (Florence).

Geese, U. (1985–1986), 'Antike als Programm. Der Statuenhof des Belvedere im Vatikan', in *Natur und Antike in der Renaissance*. Exhibition catalogue (Frankfurt), pp. 24–50.

Giovio, P. (1999), *Scritti d'arte. Lessico ed ecfrasi*, S. Maffei (ed.) (Pisa).

Glaras, K. (1967), 'Die Entstehung der Galerie des Erzherzoges Leopold Wilhelm', *Jahrbuch der Kunsthistorischen Sammlungen in Wien*, LXIII (N. F. XXVII), 40–63.

Glaras, K. (1968), 'Das Schicksal der Sammlungen des Erzherzoges Leopold Wilhelm', *Jahrbuch der Kunsthistorischen Sammlungen in Wien*, LXIV (N. I. XXVIII), 181–200.

Glaser, G. (1980), 'Das Grüne Gewölbe im Dresdner Schloss als Weiterentwicklung der barocken Architekturidee des Spiegelkabinetts, als Spezialmuseum und als Ausgangspunkt gegenwärtiger Museumsgestaltung', *Jahrbuch der staatlichen Kunstsammlungen Dresden*, XII, 7–67.

Goldstein, C. (1996), *Teaching Art. Academies and Schools from Vasari to Alpers* (Cambridge).

Gramaccini, N. (1996), *Mirabilia. Das Nachleben antiker Statuen vor der Renaissance* (Mainz).

Gutfleisch, B. and J. Menzhausen (1989), "How a Kunstkammer should be Formed". Gabriel Kaltemarckt's advice to Christian I of Saxony on the formation of an art collection, 1587', *Journal of the History of Collections*, I, 3–32.

Hajos, E.M. (1958), 'The Concept of an Engravings Collection in the Year 1565: Quicchelberg, Inscriptiones vei Tituli Theatri Amplissimi', *The Art Bulletin*, XL.

Hamdorf, F.W. (1992), 'Du "theatrum mundi" à la glorification des ducs de Bavière. Remarques sur les collections d'antiques à Munich, du XVIe au XVIIIe siècle', in A-F. Laurens and K. Pomian (eds), *L'Anticomanie. La collection d'antiquités aux XVIIIe et XIXe siècles* (Paris), pp. 39–48.

Harari, M. (1998), 'Toscanità: etruschita. Da modello a mito storiografico: le origine settecentesche', in *Xenia*, XV.

Heikamp, D. (1964), 'La tribuna degli Uffizi come era nel Cinquecento', *Antichità viva*, III, 11–30.

Heres, G. (1991), *Dresdner Kunstsammlungen im 18. Jahrhundert* (Leipzig).

Howard, S. (1990), 'The Antiquarian Handlist and the Beginnings of the Pio Clementino', in *Antiquity restored. Essays on the Afterlife of the Antique* (Wien).

Jestaz, B. (1963), 'L'exportation des marbres de Rome de 1535 à 1571', in *Mélanges d'Archéologie et d'Histoire* (École Française de Rome), LXXV, pp. 415–66.

Jones, P.M. (1992), *Federico Borromeo and the Ambrosiana. Art patronage and reform in seventeenth-century Milan* (Cambridge).

Klemm, G. (1837), *Zur Geschichte der Sammlungen für Wissenschaft und Kunst in Deutschland* (Zerbst).

Liebenwein, W. (1981), 'Der Portikus Clemens' XI und sein Statuenschmuck. Antikenrezeption und Kapitolsidee im frühen 18. Jahrhundert', in H. Beck, P. C. Bol, W. Prinz and H. von Steuben, *Antikensammlungen im 18. Jahrhundert* (Berlin), pp. 73–105.

Liverani, P. (2000), 'The Museo Pio Clementino at the Time of the Grand Tour', *Journal of the History of Collections*, XII, 2, 151–59.

Lo statuario publico della Serenissima. Due secoli di collezionismo d'antichità 1596–1797 (1997), exhibition catalogue (Venice).

Marchini, G. (1972–1973), 'Il Museum Veronese nell' edizione del Maffei e nei cataloghi successivi', in *Studi storici Veronesi Luigi Simeoni, XXII–XXIII*, pp. 257–303.

Mariani Canova, G. (1975–1976), 'Il Museo maffeiano nella storia della museologia', in *Atti e Memorie della Accademia di Agricoltura, Scienze e lettere di Verona*, série VI, XXVII, pp. 177–91.

Meijers, D.J. (1995), *Kunst als Natur. Die Habsburger Gemähle Galerie in Wien um 1800* (Vienna).

Meloni Trkulja, S. (1979), 'Istituzioni artistiche fiorentine 1765–1825. Dalla Regenza al granducato di Pietro Leopoldo', in F. Haskell (ed.), *Saloni, Gallerie, Musei e loro influenza sullo sviluppo dell'arte dei secoli XIXe–XXe* (Bologna).

Morelli, G. (1985), *Vetus Etruria … Il mito degli Etruschi nella letteratura Architectonica, nell'arte e nella cultura da Vitruvio a Winckelmann* (Florence).

Nicolaï, F. (1784), *Beschreibung einer Reise durch Deutschland und die Schweiz im Jahre 1781*, t. IV (Berlin).

Paolucci, A. and A.M. Maetzcke (1992), *Il museo dell' Accademia Etrusca di Cortona* (Firenze).

Pietrangeli, C. (1951–1952), 'Il museo Clementino Vaticano', in *Atti della Pontificia Accademia Romana d'Archeologia* (serie III) *Rendiconti*, XXVII, 1–2, pp. 87–109.

Pietrangeli, C. (1976–1977), 'I musei vaticani al tempo di Pio VI', in *Atti della Pontificia Accademia Romana d'Archeologia* (serie III) *Rendiconti*, XLIX, pp. 195–233.

———. (1995), *Scritti scelti di Carlo Pietrangeli* (Roma).

Pommier, E. (1995), 'Les débuts de l'histoire de l'art à Florence', in E. Pommier (ed.), *Histoire de l'histoire de l'art*, conférences du musée du Louvre, 1991–1993, t. I (Paris), pp. 13–46.

———. (2000), 'Diabolisation, tolérance, glorification? La Renaissance et la sculpture antique', in J.P. Barbe and J. Pigeaud (eds), *La Tolérance, Études littéraires*, XXXII, 1–2 (Québec), pp. 55–70.

———. (2001), 'Le projet du Musée royal (1747–1789)', in T.W. Gaehtgens, C. Michel, D. Rabreau and M. Schieder (eds), *L'art et les normes sociales au XVIIIe siècle* (Paris), pp. 185–209.

———. (2002), 'Le problème des biens artistiques dans le contexte des rapports de force entre les nations: aux origines 1750–1815', in *Mélanges de l'École Française de Rome* (Italie et Méditerranée), t. CXIV, 1, 1, pp. 59–73.

Quiccheberg, S. (1963), 'Inscriptiones vel tituli theatri amplissimi', in *Bibliothèque d'Humanisme et Renaissance*, XXV.

Saint Non, R. de (1782), *Voyage pittoresque ou description des Royaumes de Naples et de Sicile* (Paris).

Sandrini, A. (1982), 'Il Lapidarium Veronense e le origini dell'architettura museale', in *Studi storici Luigi Simeoni*, XXXII (Verona), pp. 153–160.

Schweikart, G. (1993), 'Zwischen Bewunderung und Ablehnung: Der Torso im 16 und 17 Jahrhundert', *Kölner Jahrbuch*, XXVI, pp. 27–47.

Settis, S. (1999), *Laocoonte. Fama e stile* (Rome).

Seydewitz, R. and M. Seydewitz (1957), *Das Dresdner Galerie Buch, Vierhundert Jahre Dresdner Gemäldegalerie* (Dresden).

Steuben, H. von (1981), 'Das Museo Pio-Clementino', in H. Beck, P.C. Bol, W. Prinz and H. von Steuben (eds), *Antikensammlungen im 18. Jahrhundert* (Berlin), pp. 149–61.

Thoenes, C. (1996), 'Sic Romae. Statuenstiftung und Marc Aurel, in *Ars Naturam adjuvans, Festschrift für Matthias Winner* (Mainz), pp. 86–99.

Vasari, G. (1976), *Le vite de'più eccellenti pittori, scultori ed architettori*, R. Bettarini and P. Barocchi (eds), vol. IV (Florence).

Winckelmann, J.J. (1952), *Briefe*, Walther Rehm and Hans Diepolder (eds) (Berlin).

_____ . (1968), *Gedanken über die Nachahmung der griechischen Wercke in der Mahlerey und Bildhauerkunst* (Dresde, 1755) in *Kleine Schriften, Vorreden, Entwürfe*, W. Rehm (ed.) (Berlin).

Winkler, J. (ed.) (1989), *La vendita di Dresda* (Modena).

Winner, M., B. Andrete and C. Pietrangeli (eds) (1998), *Il Cortile delle statue. Der Statuenhof des Belvedere in Vatikan* (Colloquium, Rome 1992) (Mainz).

Wüthrich, L.H. (1956), *Christian von Mechel, Leben und Werk eines Basler Kupferstechers und Kunsthändlers (1737–1817)* (Basel).

Chapter 14

Sainthood and Heroism
Images and Imagery in Sixteenth-century Europe

Denis Crouzet

We start with a preliminary observation. Peter Burke has shown that there was, from the years 1514–1523 onward, a curious phenomenon of 'crisis of canonization' that lasted until the late sixteenth century, with another peak between 1628 and 1658.[1] To explain this it is not enough to note the critical positions of Erasmus or of the Lutheran and Calvinist reformers. Nor that of Rabelais and his emblematic character Brother Jean des Entommeures – etymologically, the one that makes mincemeat of his enemies – grasping a cross to save the vineyard of Seuillé abbey from the sack planned by Picrochole's army; Brother John throws himself into the fight after calling on Saint Thomas, vowing to defend the property of the church, and shouting 'if I died there, should I not be a saint likewise?'.[2] These positions, denouncing the cult of the saints replacing that of Christ or satirizing the acquisition of sainthood through violence, certainly play a part. It is likely, though, that other considerations are important, having to do with the very understanding of sainthood and an alternative perception of the relation between sainthood and heroism. Sainthood prior to the reform crisis in the church, as conveyed by, for instance, the *Golden Legend* of Jacopo de Voragine, is strongly associated, apart from recognition of a 'power ... to act in favour of individuals or groups' and a holy *virtus* of mediation,[3] with the figure of a man or woman demonstrating the personification in themselves of the Good.[4] This personification may of course reach the point of martyrdom, an instant of heightened intensity in the fight with Evil. The heroism of saints, men or women, thus has to do with the image of transcendence attributed to them, making them move from the fact of an existence devoted to the honour of God to the point of a sacrificial offering and, in their lives and especially after their deaths, into the sphere of the marvellous and miraculous. Heroism, which is to be understood as a movement towards the heights of perfection, a movement carried along by the desire for death, has thus been one of the significant aspects of hagiographical writing.

A second preliminary datum deserves attention. Historians have noted that, starting in the thirteenth century, there was a significant break in hagiographical discourse, which gave only limited room to the saints of the twelfth and thirteenth centuries and preferred to focus representation on the 'ancient and traditional saints, most of them martyrs, who, though subjected by their persecutors to the most dreadful torments, had not denied God'.[5] The mysteries of the late fifteenth and early sixteenth centuries reflect this polarization around the theme of performance of a sacrifice, the theatricalization of suffering.[6] A world of blood and mutilations tends to typify the imagery and therefore the iconography of sainthood. Typically, the saint, in images and in theatricality, is in pain, expressing perfection through acceptance of suffering, even though the Church in the same period was occasionally attempting to react against this martyrological fascination by promoting a model of 'wise, doctrinal and clerical sainthood, perfectly incarnated by the great observant preachers of the fifteenth century: Saint Bernardino of Sienna and Saint Vincent Ferrer'.[7]

Be that as it may, the officialization of counter-reformation sainthood, as quantitatively studied by Peter Burke, seems to mark a break with or move away from this fascination. Only two of the fifty-five saints analysed died as martyrs. In its very choices and over and above any desire to take account of geographical, political or internal parameters within the church, Rome strove to value saints, men or women, who had lived in the imitation of saints of the past but not encountered the event of martyrdom. And everything suggests that this move or break was not an isolated fact; for in the case of the French wars of religion, faced with Jean Crespin's Calvinist *Martyrologue*, French Catholics did not manage to give any truly or massively effective reply, from the *Discours sur le saccagement des églises catholiques par les hérétiques anciens et nouveaux calvinistes... en l'an 1562* by Claude de Sainctes, though he tried to build a catalogue of priests and monks ferociously slain by the Huguenots, describing scenes that seem to repeat the martyrdoms of the early church, to the *Antimartyrologue ou verité manifestée contre les histoires des supposés martyrs de la religion pretendue reformée*, published only in 1622 by Jean Severt.

There was, then, a break we should ask ourselves about, since it shares in a shift in the set of images around which the European area was able to arrange a relative identity in its representation, in André Vauchez's expression, of a 'power' of communication, and thereby develop a coherent form for its desires, its wishes, and a way of modelling its imagery. This break clearly emerges from the French 'age of saints', in Benoît de Canfield's search to lose the self, in Pierre de Bérulle's 'sacrificial nihilism', in the practice of continual humiliation or contemplative quiet, but as from the sixteenth century it appears to be a European effort.[8] The French saints of the seventeenth century were pursuing the memory of the Spanish and Italian figures of sainthood of the sixteenth century. One question is called for in this connection. Does the effacement of sacrificial identity from among criteria of sainthood, both by the Church and by those living the experience of sainthood, lead to obscuring the link between sainthood and heroism, between sacral *virtus* and martyrdom? Or do we have to assume that early modern Europe, at a time when the idea and ideal of Christianity were being diluted, was marked by a deconstruction or recomposition, perhaps in some specific field of symbolization, of sacrificial heroism?

We shall, however, see that nothing here is simple, that when a heroic approach to sainthood is deconstructed to favour the production of a different heuristic approach, it is nonetheless true that in parallel or as a response it is appropriated or represented by some other imagery. Thus, there was a sort of dialogue between a dream of individual sainthood and an aspiration to collective sainthood, between two distinct sacrificial universes with shades of meaning, features and logics that have to be analysed and understood. This was at the very time when the all-embracing, dynamic idea of Christianity was being blurred.[9]

In the course of a long sixteenth century, through this dialogue that is reflected in breaks, conflicts and crises, it is perhaps a historically given identity of Europe that was being manufactured, by producing or challenging ways to attain salvation, in a play of meaning around images of heroism. The analysis has to begin by studying a saintly identity that is defined against the ideal of sacrificial heroism.

The Itineraries of Anti-heroic Sainthood

It should be noted at the outset that the relation between sainthood and heroism in sixteenth- and seventeenth-century Europe is part of an original paradox. An individual that the church after complex negotiation was to recognize and distinguish as a 'saint' was very often one whose lived experience entailed the deprivation of heroism, and for whom that experience had acted as a decisive impulse in a sacred quest. Several examples may be cited here that should allow us to understand that saintly heroism was reconstructed and modelled on a procedure of distortion or discarding, or even perhaps on anti-heroism.

Let us begin with Teresa of Avila in the account given in her autobiographical *Life*, written on the orders of her confessor. A desire for death is mentioned as marking Teresa's childhood after her mother's death at the age of 33. This desire was shared, 'at such a tender age', with her brother Rodrigo; it was underpinned by a sense of the exemplary nature of the martyrdom to which 'the saints were subjected for God'. Teresa says that it seemed to her that those saints' sufferings had let them purchase 'very cheaply the happiness of going to enjoy God'.[10] Childhood, starting from this perception of the ability to win eternity at the price of a single moment of sacrifice, was a period of sacrificial impatience that the whole rest of her life was to seek to restrain or to normalize through identification with the penitent figure of Mary Magdalene, but which at the time made her dream of 'enjoying as soon as possible the great joys of heaven that the books had described to me'.

It is here that the patterning of writing a penitent confession proves essential, by enabling two types of paths to be opposed. Teresa of Avila in fact reports that with her brother she had made a plan to leave as beggars for the 'country of the Moors', in order to suffer the agony of decapitation as early as possible. This desire for death is a wondrous thing stimulated by reading books showing that 'the pain and the glory are forever'. The 'path of truth' inscribed by God in Teresa's heart, in her own words, takes its origin in this aspiration to leave for another country, to go away so as to make a gift of herself to God; it is the path of 'courage': 'we would spend long moments talking about it, and we liked often to repeat: "forever! forever!"'.[11] There was a haste to meet eternity, an impatience to win salvation. Perhaps it was around this impossible dream that a complex arose, of a continuous fear of death, for there was a withdrawal from the path of wished-for death, a block of the desire. The experience of sainthood is here linked with the impossibility of heroic immediacy and perhaps with a form of concealed self-accusation. To paraphrase Michel de Certeau who sometimes insisted on the sense of guilt of a family of new Christians, she was inhabited by 'mourning',[12] a 'wound',[13] a nostalgia for a sort of lost paradise, unattained or unmerited. ... Or did Teresa at least want in her confession to evoke a personal history built on this theme?

As the writing moves towards to its close, the course traced in her *Life* brings Teresa to stress that the 'graces' and 'favours' she now felt her soul filled with, that 'immense beauty' that Christ has imprinted on her,[14] had finally brought her to 'no longer fear death, I who had been so afraid of it'.[15] The impossible sacrifice, refused or fled from, is depicted as making Teresa slip into an anguish against which mental prayer would be seen as a 'remedy'; an anguish at having had a fear of death that makes her live in a search for closeness to death, for a presence in herself of death itself, but a death that was always only lightly touched. The *Life* is then, the chronicle of a fundamental antagonism between non-realization of this wish to die, in physical suffering as brutal as it was intense, and death itself, which was unceasingly to torment for long and often atrociously Teresa, body and soul. For the desire for sacrificial death, in imitation of the sainted destinies of the past, led to an impossibility, to a checkmate, as it were dedicated to projecting itself into a continuum of bodily and spiritual pains that the *Life* has the purpose of recounting.[16] Ought one here perhaps not point to the gap that probably existed between the confession of faith that defines Christian martyrdom and the confession of faith that comprises Teresa's discourse on herself, and on her past, to the extent that the latter is structured around pain, a different pain?

Nor should the sphere of expansion of this desire for death be limited to an impossible sacrifice that would have implied a form of guilt and therefore melancholy. The way Teresa reconstructs her entry to the convent and then the period of her illness in her father's and her aunt's houses is significant. The theme of 'courage' comes in again, but with a different orientation. Violence is no longer the kind that comes from tortures inflicted by the enemies of God, but must henceforth come of itself. Everything here is swayed by the process of remembering the identification with and appropriation of sainthood. The important thing is, however, that violence far from disappears from past existence. On the contrary, she grasps it with extraordinary force, though in a different way than that of sacrificial immediacy. Teresa was to live in confrontation with violence, over a long period, and the relation between sainthood and heroism, though apparently checked by the impossibility of martyrdom, here becomes extremely dramatic, just because heroism has to do with what seems to be its opposite. This sharp contrast makes it hard for the saint to build her identity. The move towards experience of God's love, long and continually questioned, is structured by lengthy and intense bodily trials, symbolizing both the dream of martyrological death and its sublimation or transcendence in a prolonged interiorization: 'I remember, and I feel it is the truth, that when I went out of my father's house I suffered so much that I know not what can be worse when I die: one might have said that each of my bones was separating from the others; since I had not experienced that love of God that abolishes love for father and kin, I did so much violence to myself in everything, that had the Lord not helped me my considerations would in no way have been enough to keep me going. He gave me the courage to conquer myself ...'.[17] The important point in the writing here is showing that this experience is lived exactly as martyrological suffering, but it is herself that Teresa identifies as an executioner. It is a force that through suffering, and through an approach to death, seeks to stop her from going towards God. Inwardly, she lives through a sort of breaking on the wheel ... which she transcends with God's help, but in reality it is wished by God.

It is nonetheless the case that Teresa of Avila's confession is, as it were, haunted by an ambiguity in the relation to the foremost desire for death. As if permeated by certainty that it is in a long life that her dreamed-of movement towards 'forever' may, with difficulty, henceforth be accomplished, she aims at assurance that it is by the Lord's will that she has lived, throughout the years, in trials and in 'great droughts'.[18] Teresa's sacrificial heroism or rather anti-heroism is reconstructed as a form of painful communion with God; God, who in the words of Job gives men the good but also sends them evils: 'the Lord alone can know the unbearable torture I have felt. My tongue in ribbons, so much had I bitten it, my throat contracted with having swallowed nothing, and from the fact of my great weakness I choked, and not even water could go down. I had the impression of being all disarticulated: an immense confusion in my head. All curled up, rolled into a ball, that is what the torture of those days led to; I could move neither arm nor foot, nor hand nor head, no more than a dead person ...'.[19] The images the writing composes accumulate sufferings and repeat them. It is no longer death that is consecrated in martyrdom, but life itself. Life, that in this duration is conditional upon the experience of purification, is like martyrdom.

For there is no longer any question of a liberatory martyrdom that would immediately open up 'forever'. But the fight with the devil, with the illusions he employs, with the pains and the 'inward and outward troubles' to which he sometimes has recourse,[20] is thus bound to last throughout life.[21] And when illness is not there to make her body suffer horribly, Teresa of Avila asks God for it, as she did in 1538.[22] Being a saint then, is living in a time marked by vehement physical and spiritual attacks, facing the coming and going of violence in the self, in the body; while receiving love, once calm is regained, is like a 'great fire'.[23] A sequence of falls and risings: 'my life was extremely painful, since in prayer I saw my faults better. On the one hand God was calling me, on the other I followed the world. All the things of God contented me deeply, those of the world kept me bound ...'. There is fighting:

'I wished to live, well understanding that I was not living, but was fighting with a shadow of death'. The writing is, then, a weapon to defend herself against that shadow. But we have to see that under the appearances of a fight against evil, it is with God that the saint is fighting. For Teresa of Avila it was as it was for John of the Cross, namely, it is God who attacks, shatters, strikes and smites.[24]

The saint does not live through the immediacy of martyrdom; she lives and relives all the martyrdoms, of water, fire, air, the wheel, even going beyond martyrdom since she also enters the pains that adumbrate the most dreadful pangs of hell. That is, here she sets herself to move even beyond sainthood, since she undergoes sufferings the very saints were not given to suffer. She suffers what is reserved for the damned, or even more than what the damned endure. It is like a hell shut up within the hell reserved for her. For when a vision transports her to hell, it not only makes her see a world with an entrance that looks like a 'sort of very long, very narrow lane', with a space like an oven: 'very low, dark and narrow', with the ground swamped by muddy, pestilential water, crawling with 'little repellent reptiles'. It makes her see herself being placed in a hollow dug in the wall, very cramped. Especially, the figure of hyperbole is used to indicate that her martyrdom is more terrible than the most terrible pains of hell; everything she saw in that hell was 'delightful' to see by comparison with what she felt and continued to scare her long after, when she wrote the account of it: a fire burned her soul and intolerable pains tormented her. Tortures tore her apart: 'I did not see who was inflicting them on me', but she felt that she was being burned and torn. There is a 'someone' acting and at the origin of this absolute pain, that compels her to stay in this closed place where it is impossible for her to lie down or sit, with no light, with the walls shut in on themselves.[25] Interiorization, but in a paroxysm. In traditional hagiographical discourse martyrdom was the event that closed a life often marked by conversion and then exemplary conduct. Here, it invaded the whole of Teresa's life with rhythms of unheard-of, total violence, opening her up to sainthood, but only in the sphere of her subjectivity one may term 'anti-heroic'. There it is doubled in her penitential asceticism that becomes as it were the allegory of that desire to experience time differently.

Not long after this episode Teresa informed God of her great project, which as we know was to meet with mockery and resistance from part of the city of Avila. The very key to this desire for transcendence is given in the writing, which repeats an idea from Pedro de Alcántara. The heroic desire is rooted in the preliminary finding that 'the world is no longer capable of suffering so much perfection'. Again, in relation to the exemplary sainthood of the past, the theme arises of a complex that was subconsciously to lead to an alternative search. The 'great leaps of the saints' had been forgotten, and Teresa of Avila then wondered at the 'courage … God had given that holy man to go through bitter penitence for 47 years'.[26] There was a sort of romanticism to this sainthood, to be sought in the feeling of a lack of tension unable to reveal itself to itself, when in the course of a period of a paroxysm of trials ceaselessly repeated the will and the word of the Lord finally intervene. Then the 'fiction of the "interior castle" … does not have to do with a creation of an imaginary object but the opening of a space for the word, for the soul and for writing. It is a locus of speech, a world of the soul and a framework of discourse'.[27] This place is not one of violence but of love, a 'beautiful, delicious castle'[28] in the expression of Teresa of Avila herself. It is a little as if the 'forever' was arising if only for a moment....

In connection with early modern sainthood, Alphonse Dupront and Jean Delumeau were certainly able to speak of a process of interiorization of the myth of the crusade. Might it perhaps be better to speak of a search for a symbolic difference in phases, a strategy of gaps which meant that the sacrificial event of the sainthood of saints in 'great leaps' would take over the whole of life? It was an experience of specific sacrificial time that authorized Teresa of Avila to embark on the path of an unceasingly relived concentration of suffering. Here there is no loss or mythical impoverishment implying some 'grandiose introversion',[29] but on the contrary a hyperbolic recreation of heroism, seen as the negative of the martyrological heroism of the past. The hyperbole is all the greater since the suffering, starting again once it has been reduced, is relieved by fright at the perception of the soul's 'hardness',[30] and again by awareness that the *imitatio* of the saints, the practice of virtues of which they gave the example, is by no means enough.[31] Contemplating a little image of Christ 'all covered in sores' does not just suggest an evocation of the Redeemer's immense suffering 'for us', but plunges Teresa of Avila into 'regret' at 'having shown so little gratitude for those wounds that I felt my heart was breaking and I threw myself before him shedding floods of tears, begging him to strengthen me once and for all no more to offend him'. It is thus indeed within the self that the experience of suffering unfolds and lives on.[32] In any case it would be anachronistic to suggest an impoverishment or exhaustion of sacrificial tension. Everything now takes place in the interior sphere, and hence in the realm of the symbolic.

The first image of the impossible sacrifice comes in the writing when Teresa is pondering the 'cause that impelled me to establish such a tight rule' for the convent of Saint Joseph in Avila. This was at the time when she became aware of the troubles and misfortunes the Kingdom of France was undergoing, the ravages 'those Lutherans had made' that did not cease to proliferate. She emphasizes that she felt great sadness, that she wept 'before the Lord', imploring him to bring a remedy to these ills. Once again the theme of martyrological courage is introduced, but only to be immediately denied: 'I felt myself able give my life a thousand times to save one of the many souls being lost there'.[33] It was, she adds, because she could not realize her desire that she embarked on her work of establishing a 'tight' rule: 'seeing myself a woman and wretched, in the impossibility of being useful to the Lord's service as I would have wished, though he has so many enemies and so few friends, I therefore decided to do the very small thing that was within my reach'. This anti-heroism is accordingly to be understood as a different heroism, which under the obligatory discourse of humility through which the confession develops dissembles the logic of a symbolic power of accomplishment.

One must note the varied historiographical hypotheses about this new life, which extends even to moments of ecstasy, and is, henceforth, devoted to foundations. They emphasize on the one hand the pregnancy of chivalrous imagery, bringing Teresa of Avila to embark on the defence of the 'castle' of God, and they might then refer to the myth of the crusade. On the other hand they stress a 'self-dramatization' leading the saint to do in Spain what Cortés reported he planned to do in the New World, to work on the imagery of re-founding of an order of God, an order conforming to God's requirements. In any case, in her representation of herself in this *Life*, which is more a penitent confession than an autobiography,[34] one could not help distinguishing the 'heroic dimension' of a life thought of as an order of battle,[35] but it is a slanted dimension since it is established specifically on the impossibility of heroism, on a sublimated absence which is present in the self of absolute and continuous violence, of suffering.[36] To the point that one has to ask whether Teresa's experience, ultimately and over and above the retrospective justifications she gives herself with the figure of the inquisitor in the background, does not refer to a desire to locate the future field of combat within oneself, and does not testify to a dream to render the subject autonomous!

Another model must accordingly be brought in, appearing in certain texts of Ignatius of Loyola. Though chronologically earlier, he moves in the same direction, since he too evokes the dynamism of a construction-deconstruction of sainthood, proceeding from implementing an antinomic heroism. This model also goes through the experience of struggle against part of oneself.... The image of combat is thus present, a fight that leads the saint towards sainthood while suffering, while experiencing prolonged pain. And this fight is conceived of fundamentally as one against heroism, against the illusion of the various appearances and suggestions of heroism. There is, by contrast with Teresa of Avila, no longer a focus on a sacrificial desire that is impossible to accomplish, but a highlighting of the artificiality of that very desire.

Everything starts, then, from the representation of one of those weapons the 'enemy' uses, as written by Ignatius of Loyola, on 18 June 1536, in a letter to Teresa Rejadell: the vainglory that brings man to believe 'that there is in him much good and sanctity, setting him at a level above his merits'.[37] This is a posture of refusal, refusal of self-awareness, that is perhaps part of an Augustinian coming to awareness. The saint is a man who has to know he is exposed to 'arrows' and is therefore at the risk of dying for God if he imagines he is able to internalize some sainthood. Instead of having to bring him to a 'forever', the sacrificial dream is illusory and makes him incur condemnation. Death is prowling around him, especially since if he opposes the vainglory of humiliation and abasement of self he will also offer himself to it. For another of the enemy's weapons is the opposite of heroism, the 'false humility' that makes him consider that 'if he speaks of some grace accorded him by our Lord works, resolutions, desires he falls into the sin of another sort of vain glory, since he speaks to his own honour ...'. It thus makes him be silent about the benefits received from God.

The life of a servant of God is perilous, and that, as it were, summarizes the experience of the first part of Ignatius of Loyola's life. In *Saint Ignatius's own story as told to Luis González de Cámara*, the personal history is that of a 'great and vain desire to win honour' which is as it were slowly purified in the swing towards an inward heroism.[38]

Ignatius of Loyola starts by recounting how he had gone about to face a variant of the sacrificial heroism Teresa of Avila had dreamt of throughout her childhood and even still around 1560, which among the European nobility aimed at displaying to God and men a contempt for the world. Several expressions of the residue of that desire are enumerated. First, Ignatius of Loyola says that he was given up to the vanities of the world, taking pleasure only in the exercise of arms and thus in public exhibition of his courage, of his virtue. We know what followed: wounded in the leg, he was given up for lost by the physicians, and received the sacraments. Death did not want him, but it is important that heroism is nonetheless present in the imagery he recalls within himself. The account is here quite obviously symbolic. It aims to show how he strove to rid himself of an illusion. For a protuberance of flesh persisted on the wounded leg, and this time it was Ignatius of Loyola who required pain, who made it come to him when he took the decision to let himself be 'martyred by his own will'. Then comes the sequence of heroic desire to imitate the saints which accompanied his convalescence, when, as well as novels of chivalry, he read the *Vita Christi* of Ludolphus of Saxony and the *Golden Legend* of Jacopo de Voragine. He then wished, he confides, to imitate Saint Francis and Saint Dominic, pondering 'accordingly many difficult and painful things'.[39] It was at this point, then, that he developed the plan to go barefoot to Jerusalem, eating only herbs and performing the bodily penitences of the saints. This was still no more than a pilgrimage.

This path of the search for heroism in imitation, however, was given up, again symbolically, once he had taken the road to Montserrat, when he met a Moor who disputed that the Virgin could have conceived Christ while remaining a virgin. The Moor left him after having walked beside him, and it was at that moment that Ignatius of Loyola was seized by the desire to launch into his pursuit to 'give him some dagger blows for what he had said'.[40] But doubt also tormented him: 'an internal fight between obedience to the chivalrous code or heroic crusade, or the code of the Gospel'. It was to the mule he was riding that he left the choice which path to pursue: after the Moor, or on to Montserrat. This episode is intended in the biographical account to symbolize progress in the abandonment, commenced divinely, of violence as an act accomplished by God and able to lead up to sacrificing oneself. A new threshold had been crossed, though it was not enough to defeat the power of attraction of vainglory, the glory that has to see a man ready to sacrifice himself.

It was, then, 'our Lord' who made him take the direction of the Marian sanctuary of Montserrat, where he took further the break with the ideal of warlike or sacrificial heroism. Ignatius of Loyola confessed for three days in succession, dressed in 'the arms of Christ', i.e. a garment of rough cloth, took up a pilgrim's staff and a little water bottle, asked for his weapons, sword and dagger, to be hung up at the altar of Our Lady, and kept vigil the whole night, either standing or on his knees, before the altar dedicated to the Virgin, before departing secretly for Barcelona. This is theatre of deliberate abandonment of a heroic desire, with these new arms that are not arms, which testify above all to a desire for penitence. But this abandonment implies for him, now that he goes begging and hungry, no longer cuts his hair, lets his toenails and fingernails grow, a fight with himself which brings about a transfer towards specifically the heroism of refusing glory and its temptations. This heroism is the negative of the heroism of the challenge to death, all the more heroic because, not being marked by the inward martyrdom lived through by Teresa of Avila, it was nonetheless subjected to real trials. The hero reproduces in himself the image of Saint Anthony resisting temptation.

When he was at Manresa, it was indeed 'many times', as he was to write, that in the full light of day he might contemplate 'something' in the air close to him. This was an image of the vainglory coming back to prowl around him, as it were to fascinate him: 'it gave him much consolation, for it was very beautiful, extremely beautiful. He could not well distinguish what type of thing it was, but it seemed to him in a way that it had the form of a serpent and had many things shining like eyes, while not being that. He took much delight and was consoled at seeing this thing; and the more often he saw it the more his consolation grew; and when this thing disappeared from his sight, he felt displeasure'.[41] The saint could become a saint only after having been, as it were, cut in two between his desire for glory and his desire to fight that illusory glory by devoting himself to becoming a 'new soldier of Christ'. He was cut in two since he was tortured by doubts and scruples, since he wondered unceasingly at his ability to have confessed all his sins, to the point of contemplating suicide by throwing himself into a 'big hole'. He was cut in two since his visions of the Trinity or of Christ's humanity as a 'white body neither very large nor very small' arose. His story at that decisive moment comes from a set of images, the opposition between the light emanating from the 'thing' and this Christ that is not yet anything more than a white halo with a vague shape ...

There was more than just Jansenism to contribute to the 'demolition of the hero'.[42] At least, there had been a Jesuit 'pre-demolition'! What historians call the Cardoner enlightenment thus marks a step forward towards a break in this dissociated posture. The anguish at the death of God that flows from attachment to vainglory remains, but the vainglory itself is finally, despite its glittering temptations, identified as such. Heroism becomes the demoniac revealing itself, and shows itself up for what it is, the opposite of what Christ is. That is then like a conversion becoming real, at the end of a series of stages. The enlightenment comes about, significantly, near a church dedicated to Saint Paul, when while he is kneeling before a cross, the 'something with the many eyes' appears to Ignatius of Loyola. The vision is revelation, since the 'something' shows itself in a colour not so fine as usual. It was then that Ignatius of Loyola received the 'very clear awareness, with an assent of the will, that that was the devil'.[43] The heroism recomposed following this vision is indeed an anti-heroism, consisting then in living in the fear or the phobia of vainglory, to the point, once Ignatius of Loyola has resumed his march to Jerusalem, of not even daring to say what the goal of his pilgrimage is. He seeks to replace one sublimity by another, that of the man following Christ by ridding himself increasingly of his delusions, with that of ridding himself of himself.

True heroism in Ignatius's eyes further consists in rejecting the knowing oneself as, and wishing oneself to be, a just man, a saint, and in demanding, on the threshold of the death facing him during an illness, for the ladies present to cry out to him 'Sinner!' It is an awareness of the impossibility associated with humility. There is, then, a conflict that continues even once the image of death has been identified as the consolatory illusion of glory. It is a fight in oneself and against oneself, reflected, moreover, in a situation of suffering inwardness, in a 'great confusion and great pain because he felt he had not fully used the gifts and graces the Lord our God had communicated to him'.[44] But the desire for otherness that inspired him found its limits when, after visiting the holy places, he asked to be allowed to stay in Jerusalem to 'help souls' but the authorization was refused. He confides that he then understood that the divine will was not that he should remain in the Holy Land. Anti-heroic heroism then fully takes on the rejection of self, it is the gift of one's life to Christ 'to be useful to souls'.[45] Even if the inward path was different, in the last analysis for both Teresa of Avila and Ignatius of Loyola the reshaping of the experience of sainthood gravitates around the exposure of a crisis of heroism, a substitution of one heroism for another. The saint no longer wishes to be marked by the model of martyrological sacrifice, but is the person remaining after that temptation, finding in tribulations and perils a 'spiritual consolation', to use a term from Francis Xavier.[46] He accomplishes the sacrifice within himself.

Obviously, one ought not to conclude that the sixteenth century expelled the martyrological image from the sphere of the search for sainthood; it integrated it. One ought not, either, to deduce a break from the anti-heroic perspective desired by Ignatius of Loyola: there were the 123 priests executed in England between 1577 and 1603, among them Jesuits Edmund Campion and Robert Southwell, and several more. Through the missions in more or less remote lands, it is certain that there was in the Company of Jesus the appearance of a sacrificial recentring.[47] In the wake of the *Theatre of the Cruelties of Heretics in Our Time* by the Englishman Richard Verstegan, we have to cite *La peinture spirituelle* by Louis Richeome, published in 1611 at Lyons, bringing up the pitiful scenes of the 'Martyrs of those of this Company slain for the faith of Jesus Christ': starting with the 39 or 40 Fathers massacred by the pirate Jacques Sore, 'slaughtered lambs', while travelling to evangelize the lands of Brazil under the direction of Father Ignatius of Azevedo; 'behold these bodies consecrated to God, in their life, and victims given to God, in their death, floating upon the azure back of this dreadful element, and now appalled by the felony of these Tigers clothed in human skin'.[48] After the anti-heroic refusal of vainglory by Ignatius of Loyola, the theme of the similarity of the new martyrs with the martyrs of ancient times was here to be given more value. As Franck Lestringant has written, the *Peinture spirituelle* is an example of a publication with a 'remarkable yield of energy', conveying the horror of massacre in the certainty of victory.[49] The story is told in order to indicate that it can only be repeated, since from the example of the martyrs one has to conclude there is hope in the sowing of blood: 'thus, of old the Christians grew as they were buried and martyred, since as an ancient doctor says the blood of the martyr is the seed of the Christians and of the field of the Church of God'.

But as has been said, one must not leap to conclusions; since already in the years 1572–1585, Niccolò Circignani [Pomarancio] had painted in the church of Santo Stefano Rotondo in Rome a cycle of 32 frescos showing the first Christian martyrs. Again, the church of the English novices in Rome, Saint Thomas à Becket, was completed in 1583, with a set of paintings showing *inter alia* the death by torture of

Edmund Campion and the novices Sherwin and Briant. In this figurative rhetoric of horror[50] one has to see that despite appearances it undermines what might be an appeal to sacrificial heroism or to its resurgence. That heroism is still and again, by contrast with what one might expect, deconstructed. For in the tormented vision of Richard Verstegan or in the horrifying one of Pomarancio, 'the scenic space here gets in the way of identification'; it promotes in the spectator a response of rejection more than of painful, masochistic adherence to the agony of the tortured. For Verstegan, there is no longer a question of condescending to the corpse: instead of inciting his spectator to die stoically for the confession of the Catholic faith, he denounces a scandal and invites to the fight by all means against 'a murderous religion too plainly inspired by the devil...'.[51] There is no question here of glory acquired through death. The apparently martyrological sacrifice acts by way of pedagogy, has its meanings inverted, applies less as an act of heroism than as proof of the evil that lives in the enemies of God and makes them oppose God. Those who died atrociously died only to "help souls", to help them understand what evil is. The event thus counts as proof of the necessity not to stop endeavouring to lead or to bring back unbelieving souls to God, since not to know the true faith means to be inhabited by an immense Evil. It is, according to the objective early set for himself by Ignatius of Loyola, to 'help souls, never to stop helping them'.

Alternative Experiences

Things ought not to be left there. Accordingly, it will be in a different area from the one just analysed that we shall have to look for a phenomenon of symbiosis in sixteenth-century Catholic Europe between sainthood and heroism. On this view we have to start from 'informal' sainthood, from the sainthood towards which the faithful facing situations of denominational conflict were aiming. Here, the sacrificial theme forcibly emerges, as if a migration of heroism, parallel to the de-heroicization we have just seen, had been under way. One might in this connection take up again the analyses concerning the obsession with 'purity of blood' that affected the Kingdoms of Spain and was based on the image of a chosen people, inheritor of the Chosen People, and obliged to preserve the blood that guaranteed its being the agent of the advancement of time. But let us instead take the case of France in the years 1560–1598. That was the France that minted the imagery of Teresa of Avila, since it was the country that saw heresy attacking the faithful of the Roman Church. A great dream of sainthood was expressed there, but a sainthood where the saint was one only through the transfer of a collective tension.

Heroism comes back to the forefront, in the sense that it is the path whereby the Christian, whether king or subject, marks faith in the divine love, acknowledges being a creature made by God in His image and redeemed by Christ's sacrifice. Violence, and this is the important point stressed by Catholic preachers and polemicists denouncing the Calvinist peril, is a human obligation, since it is through it that the faithful regain the soteriological status of the Covenant and are able, on the Day of Judgment, to rank among the elect. It was to be a violence of God, that would immediately free the Catholic of the guilt of the very act of putting to death the impious. Tolerating the impious would mean calling down ever more divisions, and therefore ever more punishments upon oneself and on one's own people. Tolerating the other is criminal since the other is a seducer, liable to put to death the innocent souls that let themselves be tempted. Wars, like aggression, are called just, implacably just, since murdering a heretic is a justification, as being God's justice. Everything is as if the imagery of the crusade, of eschatological taking up the cross, of sacrificial desire, had been projected into the very area of religious conflict. The Kingdom of France was represented as a holy land to be liberated from the infidel menace, and texts were published exalting the fight against the Albigensians, calling on everyone to become a crusader, a righteous person, to the point of offering up their body to death in order that God's glory should finally cease to be offended.

What was needed was war, as bloody a massacre as possible, in order for God to come back to loving men with love, to pardoning them, in order for God to forget infidelity and the offence that had led him to punish the kingdom by dividing religion. God is first and foremost a God of wrath and jealousy. His justice must be accomplished, and every Christian is called on to become the right arm of God. Which amounts to saying that war is holy, and that the Christian who devotes himself to it is a 'warrior of God', offering himself up to die for a God who does not tolerate infidelities.

The righteous can do no other than rejoice in their violence, exercised against the disciples of Moloch, and '... will wash their hands in the blood of the wicked'. This lustration is to be the very sign, the testimony, that the Christian has entered into the sphere of the sanctity of giving his life to God.[52] Antoine de Mouchy refers to Exodus 32, glorifying the people who at the command of the elect of God took up the sword to root out those who had, in its own midst, broken the Covenant. The people had in violence again become the chosen people; sainthood had been regained in that heroism that consisted in putting to death the enemy of God: 'for Moses had said, consecrate yourselves today to the Lord, even every man upon his son, and upon his brother; that he may bestow upon you a blessing this day.'[53] 'Blessing' – the word is of capital importance. When, after the massacre of Vassy, François de Guise made his entry into Paris, paeans of glory were published, hymning him as the one who came in the name of God, the chosen one, the new David, the saint defending the Church. When his body was brought back to the capital in late March 1563, it was welcomed as the body of a martyr who had died for the faith. His sacrifice meant he was now sitting by the side of Christ, as do the priests and monks of whom it was related that they had been 'inhumanly' massacred and tortured by the religious warriors for having refused to abjure their faith. To die for the faith is to die into eternal life, it is to live eternally. Killing is not a sin, it is instead to love God, to go to meet a desire of God, to accomplish an innocent and pure gesture. This violence is innocent and pure since it is violence of subjection to the divine order. It defaces the heretics to designate them implacably as those of whom God has foretold that they would always separate themselves from him out of desire to satisfy their bodies. The violence is not only lawful, it is a duty, the duty that goes before all else, for as long as the reformers kept taking off their masks in their wars. The heretic had to be hunted down like an animal, and offered up to God's vengeance, had to die for the pleasure of God and the salvation of the Christians. And there really is a reconstruction of a heroism of sainthood, since God's faithful must not only be ready to sacrifice the body, but also abandon all worldly attachments, not hesitating, some preachers would even say, to put to death a son or a brother. Christ is also alleged, among many other citations, to have proclaimed: 'I shall persecute mine enemies, I have reached them, and shall never go back until they have been put to an end'.[54] The enemy of God, someone leaving a Church confirmed by tradition and by the very duration of its history as a divine institution, is anathema, is a stain that can be washed out only in blood. Yet this reconstruction of heroism is significantly imagined as participation in a mystical body, that of Christ.

For it was at the time of the Ligue, after the death of the Guise brothers, that this tension reached a height, or rather, came to be expressed in symbolic mechanisms. Paris, the new Jerusalem in winter 1589, was linked spiritually to Christ in the fight against the Antichrist King and in imploring divine violence. The penitent processions led by little children, earthly images of Christlike sainthood, ploughed through Paris to solicit divine vengeance and proclaim the turning over of a new leaf; in the mortification imposed on the body of all, in an inward crusade that conditioned the imminent outward crusade, the town set itself prophetically under the reign of Christ the King. Continuous prayers were said every week in a church in the capital, while the faithful also assembled in private houses around an oratory so that they too could take part in the establishment of a sacred time. In particular, as from January 1589 and for 55 days, Paris became a graveyard city, honouring in continuous ceremonies of affliction the two dead martyrs of Blois, duke Henri de Guise and his brother Cardinal Louis de Guise. Mourning moved around the parishes, marking the total permeation of the social by a spiritual experience of communion with the souls of the victims of the bloody tyrant of Blois. The martyrs of Blois were represented as saints, victims of the bloody tyranny of a new Herod, hastening to exterminate the Catholic religion and all those seeking to defend it. The whole community of Paris, in a mystical body of suffering united in prayer, assembled in churches before mortuary chapels containing effigies of the martyrs of Blois, in a heightened décor of lights and black cloth sown with tears of silver, aimed at exercising a power of ecstatic fascination or extreme attraction. The mourning was a mystic sharing in the suffering of those who had sacrificed themselves, a spiritual union through tears and prayer, an absorption in or merger with their desire for God that had led them to accept death, say the texts, that the true nature of an Antichrist king might finally be revealed and that the fight against the forces of Satan might truly begin. The desire for God became desire for death, a gift of oneself to Christ, absolute negation of sinful man in soteriological tension. The sainthood of those who had died innocent was called on to take possession of those who were still alive and had to say they too were ready to die for the glory of God.

It is significant to note, then, that this mourning ended on 25 February, a day marked by a symbolic event that was a sort of long-distance regicide: a tableau set up in the Grands-Augustins convent representing Henry III was burned. Subsequently, an image was set up of Christ seated at table at Emmaus with the two disciples met 'as a pilgrim after his resurrection', an image to express the need for Christ's suffering that he might enter into glory, but able also to evoke by the working of substitution the will to install the reign of Christ the King against a corrupt, antichristian temporal reign, the reign of a Christ living again because he found his own, willing to die as he had died. It was a sign that a whole city, a whole penitent people, were offering themselves to the Saviour whose coming was then prophesied to be imminent, offering themselves symbolically for sacrifice. For is to give oneself to the Saviour not first of all to wed his sacrifice, his wish to suffer on the Cross for the salvation of all? It was as if Paris had set itself in a magic circle of appeal to Christ, which the Parisians were still tracing by marching day and night in procession, in lasting penitential adoration.

The phantasm of violence was thus fixed upon a king henceforth responsible for the wrath of God having fallen upon men to the point of keeping going in the kingdom a civil war that was the very sign of divine punishment. The regicide could then later be perceived by the Ligue members as a 'miracle', with God himself having come to start his last fight against Antichrist and his legions of Abomination. God had 'taken the cause of the just into his hands'. It was a meeting of God with a whole people. The Dominican Clément was exalted as a 'saint' in Paris, a saint sent from and supported by God; his sacrifice had not just put an end to the tyrant's days, but saved the city of God, namely Paris. Violence and sainthood were synonyms, but it has to be seen that the system of representation tended to show the act of regicide, accomplished at a moment when everything seemed necessarily lost for Paris and therefore the kingdom, as a consequence of the tension of collective sainthood. It was, it was repeated and sung, because everyone had prayed to God, had declared to God their willingness to sacrifice themselves to preserve the threatened religion, that God had allowed a visionary Jacobin to emerge from Paris, to whom God's angel had appeared commanding him to deal a providential blow at the unjust King. This refers back to the very ideal upon which the Ligue had been founded. In its literalness, apart from claiming to have come out of direct divine inspiration, the Ligue was a union with God, with 'his substance and with his own flesh ... a union of conjunction and of very brotherly company with Jesus Christ'. It was the last recourse to enable earthly society to remake itself as a mystic body and triumph over the forces of eternal death that were assailing it and attracting it. It was holy, and it made each of its members into 'zealots', i.e. Christians in saintly tension in their absolute desire for sacrifice. It made Ligue members share in the Passion, in the commitment of each to take up within themselves the cross and follow the Christ, 'our captain', and that joining rid them of themselves, uniting them in the absolute essence of unity, which is God. Being united in the holy Ligue meant being in the One that is 'eternal and absolute... without beginning'.

Being in the Ligue also meant being remote from 'human nature', living a 'flaring up' of divine zeal. It also meant being guided by God, and this having the self seized by a transcendent *virtus* resulted for the Ligue member in 'so great a strength and power that those who feel its secret and divine flames are as it were eaten and devoured inwardly in their bowels and to the marrow of their bones, and so caught up in their souls that they know not what human reason dictates or proposes to them'. This 'zeal' is sainthood, an outcome of persuasion by the 'celestial spirit'. In August 1589 this imagery accomplished a work of appropriation of the traditional sacrificial fable. It made Jacques Clément into a saint repeating the saving acts of the Old Testament, but also made each Ligue member into a saint, a biblical chosen one sharing in the identity of a people reliving the exalted acts of the chosen people of the Bible. In Jacques Clément leaving penitent Paris it was the whole Catholic Union that was being represented as acting, or rather, it was Christ that was said to have been acting.

The failure of sacrificial heroism that marks the end of the adventure of the Ligue might necessarily lead to a reconstruction of a desire of sainthood. In like manner, the spirituality of the early seventeenth century will fashion its identity in a rupture with the dream of violence, and in another migration of heroism – in short, in another symbolical transfer. Once sacrifice lost its meaning with the victory of Henry of Navarre, once it proved impossible to accomplish, once the form of crusade it referred to lost its topicality, an accommodation had to be made. As Denis Richet has noted, it was in the milieu of the old Ligue members gravitating around Madame Acarie that there emerged 'the initial nucleus of the French Catholic reform'. It was for that nucleus to bring about 'a transfer of the failure·of the Ligue to the level of spirituality: what they had not been able to do in the world without shaking the foundations of a State they were deeply attached to, might it not be done in silence and in a small company?'[55] That is, just as had earlier been the case for Teresa of Avila or Ignatius of Loyola, a specifically different imagery of heroism was sought because a desire for death for God could not be realized.

We can see, then, the Roman Church in the sixteenth century going through two experiences of sainthood. The first turned round anti-heroization of the saint, calling in question the pursuit of images of sacrificial example and valuing a labour of penitence and faith accomplished in long periods of suffering and pain. In perhaps a dialectic type of process, the second experience exalted faith as a sacrificial duty, with an eye to a sainthood that was collective and was modelled on the image of the chosen people, holy because it wanted to be the body of Christ, holy because it obeyed a jealous God and called on Israel never to bow before impiety, holy to the point of martyrdom, to the point of holy war.

Clearly, the demonstration just suggested is incomplete; not only because it is based on an analysis of only the two paradigms of Spain and France, through case studies, but above all because it has left out the question of the relation between sainthood and heroism in the pieties of the rupture with Rome. But the same ambivalence can be found among the various reformation constructions.

With Luther it is certain that a much more radical destabilization of representations of sainthood came about, since it was seen as disconnected from imagery of pain.[56] Until around 1512–1513 Luther was likely living through an inward crisis in the face of a sainthood that was asking too much of him in relation to the sin that he felt increasingly more virulently within him. It was 'the Christian faith that makes us saintly and just before God'.[57] Sainthood was radically deprived of drama, starting from the fact that Luther insisted on man's perversion because of original sin, which made it impossible for him by himself to fight against the evil within him, and plunged him into a corruption from which he could not escape by his own strength. He cannot be a saint except in tension of sainthood. Sin is accordingly defined as 'the hydra with innumerable heads, a monster with a tough life, against which we fight until death in the Lernean swamp of this life'. It is a 'Cerberus barking unceasingly, an invincible Antaeus released upon earth'.[58] The saint is a saint only in the moving time of his life and in the death he deals to the old Adam that nonetheless remains always present in him:

> *We must suffer. Just as the barley that is made into beer and the flax that is made into cloth must undergo many trials before managing to be useful and serve the purpose for which they were sown, so too must Christians suffer much: they must be sown, harvested, threshed. The old Adam has to be killed before we can be magnified and glorified. If we are to arrive at blessedness and its splendours, we must first die and be killed (Luke, 24, 26).*[59]

Sainthood undergoes a fundamental dialectical reversal that looks like an alternative to the Catholic anti-heroism of the ensuing years. The link that follows upon the certainty of human injustice is that of the justice alone of God, which is first and foremost love. It was to be in the book of Psalms that the Wittenberg doctor's attention was to be grasped by a verse in Psalm XXXI: *in justitia tua libera me*, 'deliver me in thy righteousness'. Continuing on from Saint Augustine, Luther reads in that not the meaning of deliverance by a sudden, brutal judgment, but God's consent to treating as just, as a saint despite his sins, the soul that gives itself up to him in faith. Sainthood is inaccessible to man, who can only be sanctified.[60] By 'righteousness' what has to be understood is that God consents to justify the sinner who has faith in him, who places all his trust in his love. Faith can only be a *donum dei*. Being in faith and living in faith means being and living in the gratuitous righteousness of God. God's justice is the justice which in his mercy God bought for man by incarnating himself as his Son. In a letter of 8 April 1516 the Wittenberg doctor gives the key to this structure of his system: 'Learn to say to Christ: thou, Lord Jesus, thou art my justice, and I am thy sin. Thou hast taken on to thy account that which was mine, and thou hast given me that which was thine. Thou wished to be that which thou wast not, and thou hast given me that which I was not'.[61] Only the sacrifice of a God that had become man was capable of fully satisfying divine justice. In consequence of this sacrifice, God, who was a God of mercy, despite the unworthiness of human creatures lasting for all eternity, imputes to them the merits of Christ. He invests them with a justice that they have not gained. It is then essentially that the whole of mankind that is under the sign of the cross, through the very love of God, the whole of mankind that is perhaps potentially sainted, no longer an individual man or woman who has received an extraordinary gift of perfection. Sacrifice does not belong to the order of the sinful creature that is man, for sainthood belongs to God alone.

The decisive thing is the concept of passive justice, which is eminently liberating: through faith, man links up with the sole love and sole sainthood of Christ. There can no longer be any heroism in testifying to sainthood, since everything comes from and starts from God, even the oppression the tyrant subjects one to, which must be borne. All the same, man's freedom in Christ must be actively reflected on the one hand in belief in the unique value of God's word, and on the other by works that enable him to live in harmony with the God who has worked to redeem mankind. There must be action, for believers are not effectively justified by the sacrifice that the divine mercy has attributed to them. They are justified only virtually: *non justificati, sed justificandi*, they must for the whole of their lives always feel themselves to be sinners in order *ipso facto* to depend constantly on divine grace, to be ever receptive to the voice of the spirit, to know that through faith they must remember that they have to 'kill unbelief, scorn and hatred for God and any grumbling against the wrath, against the judgment of God or against anything he says or does'. Sainthood, if it thus ceases to have to do with the receipt of grace, if it ceases to imply the perfection of a gift, cannot be anything but 'sanctification'; if it seems accessible to any man who apprehends the mercy of a God gratuitously offering grace, it is nonetheless always incomplete until the instant of death, since it is structured around 'putting to death' sin within oneself, with a death that lasts forever. The devil remains always present, and is all the more present because the rediscovery of the Gospel cannot but provoke him to unchain himself. As Marc Lienhard analyses it, 'man does not become just in himself, in what he is and does. He is so in communion with Jesus Christ. That is how good works spring forth. That comes about to the extent that man believes, that is, holds to Christ'. It is only in death that the ambivalence ceases and sainthood can be realized. Even to the humanists who around 1520 saw him as an 'inspired angel of God', Luther reaffirmed the theme of incompleteness; he was a 'poor envelope of stinking flesh promised to the worms', he was merely a 'disciple of Christ' at the service of Holy Writ.[62] Sainthood is not a quality but a promise, oriented towards action which is the realization in this world of God's Law.

The fundamental thing, then, is that Luther deconstructs the relationship between sainthood and heroism not just by positing that nothing is ever definitive in the Christian life. Heroism is occulted since there are 'holy states' ranging from the pastor's charge to the prince's or the sovereign's, the judge's or the servant's, passing through fatherhood and motherhood: 'whoso well rules his house and raises up his children to the service of God is also in true sanctuary, he accomplishes a holy work and is in a holy order. The same is true where children and servants are obedient to their parents or their masters; that is also pure sainthood, and whoso is in that state is a true living saint upon earth'.[63] The saint is, then, one rendered just and saintly by divine imputation, one who has within himself faith, a divine work. But he always knows himself to be a sinner, he is always penitent, always just. He is one who lets Christ live within himself, lets him into himself 'through the Gospel', every word of which is 'full of sanctity': 'the soul of whomso holds to that Word with true faith is so united with it that the virtues of the Word become his. Thus, through faith, God's

Word gives the soul sainthood, righteousness and truth, filling it with every sort of good thing...'.[64] There is a communication of divinity at work, making the sainthood of the Christian and implying a real demarcation of Luther's sainthood from Catholic sainthood and the two paths it proposes, a fundamental moment opening up sainthood as a promise to an 'us' that repeatedly flows from the reformer's pen. Any idea of transcendence deriving from a sacrificial tension or an ascetic will is denied. As Max Weber wrote, everyday activity becomes the field for the accomplishment of man's vocation: 'the only way to live agreeably with God [is] exclusively to accomplish in this world duties corresponding to the place existence has assigned the individual in society (*Lebensstellung*), duties that thus become his "vocation" (*Beruf*)'.[65] The accomplishment of this vocation in works testifies to love of one's neighbour and responds to the will of God.[66] Consequently, Lutheran sainthood, since it is sanctification, brings about a move into an ethical posture.

It is true that this everyday sainthood through work on oneself was confronted by counter-systems that instead proposed a renewed link between sainthood and heroism. One example here is, of course, the thought of Thomas Müntzer, who said that the believer, brought by his faith to dissolve into the divine will, to merge with it, embarks on a 'movement of deification'.[67] This is a process of interiorizing the spirit associated with the experience of the just, 'once suffering and the Cross have rendered him empty',[68] while coinciding in the present with the emergence of a time of trials and of violence. God lives in the saints, to whom he has given prophecy, who must mobilize to take up the sword and fight with all their strength against an attack by Satan which is to be the last. 'A theology of the Spirit immanent in mankind and communicated at all times to the heart by a living Word'.[69] Heroism is brought back in as a synonym of sainthood or of election, since the elimination of the impious and of tyrants is willed by God. In order for the holy church to be truly restored, in order for a 'servant of God full of grace' to arise, in order to awaken Christians to the will of God. Then there will come a 'host of the elect' who, dressed by the living Christ, will rank themselves against the devil and his helpers.[70] This sainthood is a prophetic sainthood in which the Elect are possessed by God. The saint is then a new Daniel called to violence and to sacrifice. In a letter sent in 1525 to disciples in the little town of Allstedt, Müntzer encourages them to suffer for the love of God, under pain of being 'martyrs of the devil'; and in particular, he encourages them no longer to live except to smite the 'scoundrels', no longer to feel pity, so that at last a free people may have God as their only Lord. In the routing out of the impious which is the very condition for accomplishing the divine desire, in the certainty that God's power is at work within each one, a brotherhood of the elect of the last days will find its unity in the service of Christ: 'let them all be brothers and love each other as brothers'. As it were in counter position to Luther's sainthood of the quotidian, to his sainthood secularized into an ethic, Müntzer defines a revolutionary, messianic sainthood wishing through the most violent sacrificial commitment to prepare the reign of evangelical reconciliation, a sainthood of possession by the spirit; a heroic sainthood in which the spirit speaks and acts from within the pure man. In less hyperbolical fashion, the same antinomy is at work as in Catholicism, with rejection of heroism on one side, and the myth of sacrificial commitment on the other.

Anabaptist millenarianism was part of the same paradigm of separation and violence; in a world called on to undergo the times of divine wrath, God was glorified in Münster for having restored 'the community as it was in the beginning, and as befits the Lord's saints', a community of the elect purified of all the enemies of God and due to become the messianic Kingdom of Christ. To this community of the elect the Holy Spirit speaks, ordering them to speak and to draw up the combat of the last days. Here again, violence is intimately associated with sainthood: 'the glory of all the saints is to draw down vengeance' on the impious. Here again, shifting the saints into eschatological time opposes the Lutheran approach of sainthood uncompleted in the time of human life.

One might continue the analysis by examining the Calvinist conception of sainthood in its specific features.[71] In Calvin it is clear that the Christian's vocation rests on an ethical discipline filtered through the individual's conscience. His ideal of conduct calls for humility, temperance, modesty and so forth. Max Weber's this-world asceticism is thus a semantic shift, since the saint is the one who throughout his life refuses himself as saint. One might also, returning to the study of the path of de-heroicization of the saint, dwell on Benoît de Canfield's perfection of annihilation or on Saint Francis of Sales and his approach of a sainthood offered to all in 'cutting out and moving away from the things of the world, and at the same time an affection for God and union with the divine will', in the humility and sweetness of charity. This French sainthood lags chronologically behind Italy or Spain, but returns to some of the tensions that had earlier been activated.

All in all, however, it appears that the question of sainthood in Europe in the sixteenth century was indeed asked in terms of its relation with heroism, whether rejected or exalted, or rather whether misappropriated by a painful effect of symbolic transfer or re-appropriated in a move of eschatological tension. But over and above these distortions, there was in that Europe of the crisis of Christian unity and in its historical evolutions a line of force that thus shared imagery between two images of itself: the image of a fight outside itself and that of a fight within itself. To seek the identity of these images of Europe is ultimately to highlight the fact that, on chronologies that vary according to place and according to specific modes of resolution, these images gravitated around various types of desire for death.

Translated by Iain L. Fraser

Notes

1. Burke (1987); de Maio (1972); Poutet (1981).
2. Rabelais (1994), pp. 278–9.
3. Vauchez (1999), pp. 22–3.
4. Vauchez (1999), p. 61.
5. Vauchez (1999), p. 65.
6. Vauchez (1999, p. 65) notes that this aspect brings in the case of Saint Francis, through the emphasis placed on the stigmata.
7. Vauchez (1999), p. 218.
8. Bergamo (1992), p. 18. On Bérulle, see Morgain (1995) and (2002).
9. Crouzet (1998) and (1982).
10. Slade (1985), p. 80, notes that this theme is taken up in a dedicatory poem to Saint Catherine of Alexandria: here again the price paid for eternal glory is not dear, from scorpions to the wheel or hanging. See also Bilinkoff (1990).
11. Thérèse D' Avila (1964), p. 15.
12. Certeau (1982), p. 42.
13. Certeau (1982), p. 43.
14. Thérèse D'Avila (1964), p. 280.
15. Thérèse D'Avila (1964), pp. 285–7.
16. Slade (1985), p. 80.
17. Thérèse D'Avila (1964), pp. 22–5.
18. Thérèse D'Avila (1964), p. 27.
19. Thérèse D'Avila (1964), p. 36.
20. Thérèse D'Avila (1964), p. 221.
21. Thérèse D'Avila (1964), p. 212.
22. Slade (1985), p. 82.
23. Thérèse D'Avila (1964), p. 215.
24. Morel (1960), vol. III, p. 92.
25. Thérèse D'Avila (1964), p. 232.
26. Thérèse D'Avila (1964), p. 190.
27. Certeau (1982), p. 259, whose 'entrance way is prayer'.
28. Certeau (1982), p. 265.
29. Dupont (1987), p. 293.
30. Thérèse D'Avila (1964), 'Le Livre de vie', p. 62.
31. Thérèse D'Avila (1964), p. 83.
32. Bédouelle (2002), pp. 118–20, speaks in connection with Teresa of Avila of 'interiorized reformation'.
33. Thérèse D'Avila (1964), p. 364.
34. Slade (1985), pp. 2–5, talks of 'judicial confession' .
35. Certeau (1982), p. 43.
36. Slade (1985), p. 111.
37. Loyola (1991), pp. 642–6.
38. Loyola (1991), pp. 1011–73; the account was narrated between 1553 and 1555.
39. Loyola (1991), p. 1021.
40. Loyola (1991), pp. 1024–5.
41. Loyola (1991), p. 1029. See Beinaert (1964), pp. 303–7.
42. Bénichou (1948), pp. 155–80.

43. Loyola (1991), pp. 1034–5.
44. Loyola (1991), p. 1036.
45. Loyola (1991), p. 1062.
46 Cited in Didier (1992), p. 75.
47. Po-Chia Hsia (1998).
48. Lestringant (1995), pp. 29–31.
49. Lestringant (1995), p. 34.
50. Lestringant (1995), pp. 22–3.
51. Lestringant (1995), p. 27.
52. Lestringant (1995), p. 12.
53. Lestringant (1995), pp. 12–3.
54. Mouchy (1560), pp. 6–7.
55. Richet (1991), pp. 92–3.
56. Rapp (1981).
57. Luther (n.d.), p. 169.
58. Luther (n.d.), pp. 38–9.
59. Luther(1992), pp. 343–4.
60. Vogler (n.d.).
61. Strohl (1924), p. 72.
62. Cited in Lienhard (1999), p. 93.
63. 'Of Christ's supper' (1528), cited in Lienhard (1999), p. 206.
64. Luther (n.d.), p. 59.
65. Weber (1964), pp. 90–1 and Disselkamp (1994), pp. 86–9.
66. On the providential dimension of the 'objective order in which the individual has been set by God', see Disselkamp (1994), p. 99.
67. Schaub (1984), pp. 120–1.
68. Schaub (1984), p. 217.
69. Schaub (1984), p. 139.
70. Schaub (1984), p. 222.
71. On this point see, even if they are terribly schematic, the analyses by Walzer (1987).

References

Bédouelle, G. (2002), *La Réforme du Catholicisme (1480–1620)* (Paris).
Beinaert, L. (1964), 'L'expérience fondamentale d'Ignace de Loyola et l'expérience psychologique', in Cerf (ed.), *Expérience chrétienne et psychologique* (Paris).
Bénichou, P. (1948), *Morales du grand siècle* (Paris).
Bergamo, M. (1992), *La science des saints. Le discours mystique au XVIIe siècle en France* (Grenoble).
Bilinkoff, J. (1990), *The Avila of Saint Teresa. Religious Reform in a Sixteenth-Century City* (Ithaca).
Burke, P. (1987), 'How to be a Counter-Reformation Saint', in *The Historical Anthropology of Early Modern Italy. Essays on Perception and Communication* (Cambridge), pp. 48–62.
Certeau, M. de (1982), *La fable mystique XVIe-XVIIe siècle* (Paris).
Crouzet, D. (1982), 'Sur le concept de barbarie au XVIe siècle', in F. Autrand and N. Cazauran (eds), *La conscience européenne au XVe et au XVIe siècle. Actes du colloque international organisé à l'E. N. S. de jeunes filles no. 22* (Paris), pp. 106–126.

_____. (1998), 'Chrétienté et Europe: aperçus sur une sourde interrogation du XVIe siècle', in G. Soutou and J.Bérenger (eds), *L'ordre européen du XVIe au XXe siècle. Actes du colloque de l'IRCOM 15–16 mars 1996* (Paris), pp. 11-50.

De Maio, R. (1972), 'L'ideale heroica nei processi di canonizzazione della controreforma', in *Richerche di storia sociale et religiosa*, 2, pp. 139–160.

Didier, H. (1992), *Petite vie de saint François Xavier* (Paris).

Disselkamp, A. (1994), *L'éthique protestante de Max Weber* (Paris).

Dupront, A. (1987), *Du Sacré. Croisades et pèlerinages. Images et langages* (Paris).

Goguel, M. (n.d), *Luther* (Paris).

Lestringant, F. (ed.) (1995), *Le Théâtre des cruautés de Richard Verstegan (1587)* (Paris).

Lienhard, M. (1999), *Martin Luther. La passion de Dieu* (Paris).

Loyola, I. de (1991), *Ecrits*, Maurice Giuliani (ed.) (Paris).

Luther, M. (1992), *Propos de table*, Louis Sauzin (ed.) (Paris).

_____. (n.d.), 'Can men of war be in a state of grace?', 'The book of Christian freedom...', (original ed. 1526), in *Luther*, Maurice Goguel (ed.) (Paris).

Morel, G. (1960), *Le sens de l'existence selon saint Jean de la Croix*, 3 vols (Paris).

Morgain, S-M. (1995), *Pierre de Bérulle et les carmélites de France. Histoire d'une querelle (1583–1629)* (Paris).

_____. (2002), *La théologie politique de Pierre de Bérulle (1598–1629)* (Paris).

Mouchy, A. de (1560), *Response a quelque apologie que les hérétiques ces jours passés ont mis en avant sous ce tiltre: Apologie ou deffense des bons Chrestiens contre les ennemis de l'Eglise catholique* (Paris).

Po-Chia Hsia R. (1998), 'The Martyred Church', in R. Po-Chia Hsia, *The World of Catholic Renewal 1540–1770* (Cambridge), pp. 5–91.

Poutet, Y. (1981), 'La sainteté d'après le droit canon et les normes en usage pour les causes de béatification du Concile de Trente à nos jours', in *Histoire et sainteté. Actes de la Cinquième Rencontre d'Histoire religieuse tenue à Angers le vendredi 16 octobre et à Fontevraud le samedi 17 octobre 1981* (Angers), pp. 53–64.

Rabelais, (1994), *Gargantua, Edition critique sur le texte de l'édition publiée en 1535 à Lyon par François Juste*, Gérard Defaux (ed.) (Paris).

Rapp, F. (1981), 'La sainteté à la veille de la Réformation dans les Pays germaniques', in *Histoire et sainteté. Actes de la Cinquième Rencontre d'Histoire religieuse tenue à Angers le vendredi 16 octobre et à Fontevraud le samedi 17 octobre 1981* (Angers), pp. 37–52.

Richet, D. (1991), *De la Réforme à la Révolution. Etudes sur la France moderne* (Paris).

Schaub, M. (1984), *Müntzer contre Luther. Le droit divin contre l'absolutisme princier* (Paris).

Slade, C. (1985), *St. Teresa of Avila. Author of a Heroic Life* (Berkeley and Los Angeles).

Strohl, H. (1924), *L'épanouissement de la pensée de Luther de 1515 à 1520* (Strasbourg and Paris).

Thérèse D'Avila, (1964), *Œuvres complètes*, (ed.) Marcelle Auclair (Paris).

Vauchez, A. (1999), *Saints, prophètes et visionnaires. Le pouvoir surnaturel au Moyen Age* (Paris).

Vogler, B. (n.d.), 'Le concept de sainteté chez les réformateurs et dans la piété protestante', in *Histoire et sainteté. Actes de la Cinquième Rencontre d'Histoire religieuse tenue à Angers le vendredi 16 octobre et à Fontevraud le samedi 17 octobre 1981* (Angers), pp. 37–64.

Walzer, M. (1987), *La révolution des saints* (Paris).

Weber, M. (1964), *L'éthique protestante et l'esprit du capitalisme* (Paris).

Chapter 15

Latin

Françoise Waquet

In 1582 Pedro González wrote a short Latin autobiography. That is hardly surprising at the time of the triumphant Renaissance – except that this man was originally a 'savage': he was born around 1537 in the Canary Islands, then scarcely distinguished from America, so that the Canary Islanders, confused with the Indians, were still regarded as belonging to an inferior type of humanity. Additionally, his physical appearance made Pedro look less man than beast: he was hairy, and it was probably as a natural curiosity that he was given to King Henry II of France at the age of 10. At the French court Pedro became civilized: he dressed in Western style – he is shown in Aldrovandi's *Monstrorum historia* dressed as a gentleman – and by his own admission he 'abandoned his savage customs and learned the liberal arts and Latin'. Just as his clothing marked his integration into European civilization, at its highest level,[1] so the Latin in which he wrote his autobiography reflected another acculturation, that of the savage who had become fully human.[2]

Pedro González – originally the non-European, the Other – supplies in his *vita* an excellent introduction for grasping one of the constitutive dimensions of early modern Europe between the sixteenth and eighteenth centuries. His example displays the spread Latin then had, and invites us to reconstruct a common history made up of shared practices. It also shows that Latin was not then merely a language to write or speak; it was a sign, and a sign that makes sense. This brings us to interest ourselves in not just the use made of Latin but the status conferred upon it and the values it was seen as having. The distinction I am drawing here between uses and values is one of pure convenience; practices and discourses interact with each other, and it is the synergy of them that gave Europe a Latin coloration, which is here not that of philology.[3]

Throughout the early modern period and all over Europe, Latin occupied a considerable and sometimes even exclusive place. It constituted a familiar environment in the life of men at a time when both school and church spoke Latin. It was the 'general language' of scholars.[4] It had not insignificant usage in both government administrations and diplomacy. A few specific situations will give the measure of this Latinity, while supplying the proper nuances dictated by chronology and geography. They will also enable us to grasp the processes set going in order to justify Latin practices, when challenges and competitions emerged, when what had gone without saying became the object of explanation and justification; they brought out arguments, widely shared, that were far from being based on linguistic competence alone. Thus, as much as the language itself it was these legitimatory discourses that gave Europe, under the sign of Latin, a profound identity.

The school world of the *Ancien Régime* fully deserves its name of '*pays Latin*'. Not only was Latin taught there and school-children consumed stupefying amounts of it, but teaching was still given in Latin, and both pupil and teacher spoke Latin. In very general terms, this was true until the middle years of the eighteenth century: the monopoly of Latin was then broken by the use of vernaculars in teaching, and its status tended to be reduced to that of a written language. For a time even the very first learning – of reading – was in Latin, in Paris until the early eighteenth century, but in French rural schools or the Piedmont countryside until the end of the *Ancien Régime*. This very general picture has to be qualified both geographically and chronologically, if only in the light of the conquests of Humanism: while in Italy the pupils of Guarino of Verona were already fluent latinists, their little comrades in northern countries were still 'barbarians'.

Religious divisions were not a factor for differentiation in the academic order. Whether Catholic or Protestant, schoolboys, and even more those attending colleges in the sixteenth to eighteenth centuries everywhere did Latin, or more exactly everywhere followed teaching given in Latin. In Reformation countries the schools remained just as Latin, and the competition from the vernaculars was not significant – except for religious teaching – before the middle years of the eighteenth century. The Orthodox world too became coloured with Latin, a totally imported Latin. In the reign of Peter the Great, in a broad movement to bring Russia into the Europe of knowledge, schools modelled on the Jesuit colleges were set up, like the one in Kiev offering a classical *cursus*; it was on this model that establishments were subsequently reformed or founded, so that in 1750 there were in the Russian Empire 26 colleges offering education based on a Latin curriculum.

This Latin unified the European academic landscape the more since its learning was associated with a set of common practices. These were further promoted by the standardizing models, like the Jesuit colleges in the Catholic world, or in the Lutheran world, the pedagogical precepts of Melanchthon – the 'preceptor of Germany'. On the European scale itself, one is struck by the presence of the same authors, or more exactly the same works, over which generations of schoolboys laboured. A classical school canon, determined both by pedagogical reasons – the concern to keep to authors of the best Latinity and avoid texts that were too hard – and by moral reasons – the need not to bring texts that were too free before the eyes of children – was rapidly formed. Dominated by Cicero, it scarcely changed over time and remained very narrow: it was to retract still further between the seventeenth and eighteenth centuries, at least in France. Reading the same authors, schoolboys also used the same textbooks, especially in the sixteenth century when Despautère's grammar and Erasmus's *Colloquia*, to cite two examples, had enormous success. However, over time internationalization declined for religious reasons – there are works which while widely disseminated had a circulation confined to one religious block – and national ones with the use of the vernacular in textbooks. Finally, everywhere the teaching of Latin had and retained a moral component, either by giving children works where learning of Latin and moral precepts went hand in hand, or by bringing out the moral lesson to be drawn from the study of suitably chosen texts. This teaching also had religious scope where the pagan texts, judiciously commented on, served on the one hand to show the errors and superstitions of the ancients, and on the other the excellence of the Christian religion.

At higher level, in the universities, Europe displayed the same Latin dimension. The advance of the vernaculars was even slower and more timid there than in schools. The exception always cited of Thomasius giving his course in German at Halle in 1687 is, on the evidence, isolated. It was as a language spoken within university precincts that Latin first gave way, even though the obligation remained for students to use Latin in examinations – then oral. Teaching remained very much mostly in Latin throughout the *Ancien Régime*; it was only for the new sciences or special courses that in the eighteenth century some professors used the vernacular, such as Barbeyrac at Lausanne for natural law, Genovesi at Naples for political economy or those Spanish professors who, at Valencia, taught mathematics and physics presented as practical sciences to students intended for the occupations of agriculture, industry and commerce.

This common history of the European pedagogical world can still be seen even once the monopoly of Latin was challenged. It was, significantly, in the second half of the eighteenth century that challenge rose everywhere against the omnipresence of Latin, associated with very limited average performance. This chalenge generally aimed in no way at eliminating Latin from the *cursus*, but at reducing its place, sidelining it to the rank of written language, and at the same time developing the scholarly study of the vernaculars. It brought in turn the emergence of arguments in favour of the learning of Latin, and those arguments were everywhere similar. They aimed not at the practical linguistic skills one might obtain – in any case increasingly less useful for professional life – but at the inherent efficiency of an intellectual and moral nature which Latin, or at least its study, allegedly possessed: an exercise for the memory, a training for the reason, help with learning the vernacular languages, fruitful communing with the masterpieces of Antiquity. This was a stock of arguments on which the nineteenth and twentieth centuries abundantly drew. Performance in Latin was never invoked in support of learning, first because it was always on average mediocre – still more orally than in writing; second, because what counted was not to make Latinists; in other words, what mattered was less, increasingly less, to know Latin than to have learned it.

Pan-Latinism reigned not just in schools but also in the Catholic Church, and was fully sanctioned by the Council of Trent.[5] Until the 1540s, calls for Bible translations in modern languages and for a liturgy in the vernacular were launched

within the Church itself by theologians, in the name of a renewal of the religious life
– meeting with response among the simple faithful like the Florentine Gelli. But the
linguistic choices made by the Protestant reformers and their attacks against the grip
of Latin quickly rendered any display of interest in the vernacular suspect of heresy.
The decisions taken at Trent show this. At the various meetings of the Council, many
discussions were held on the language question in connection with the mass, the
administration of the sacraments and the translation of the Bible. To keep to the
mass, the definitive position was based on the very nature of the Eucharist – not a
memorial of Christ's sacrifice, but a sacrifice coming about independently of man's
disposal. In consequence the priest alone needed to understand, he alone was the
guarantor of comprehension, the bearer of the faith, which could, accordingly, be
expressed in the language hallowed by tradition, namely Latin. It was recognized that
the mass contains teaching (whereas for Protestants it is only teaching); therefore it
was accordingly appropriate to give the faithful an explanation in the vulgar tongue.
This was formalized in a text voted on 17 September 1562; it stated in particular: 'if
anyone says that the mass should be celebrated only in the vulgar tongue ... let him
be anathema'. The same principles were adopted for the sacraments: their
administration in Latin was to be followed by an explanation in the vernacular. Both
in this text and in the discussions preceding it, hardly any arguments were raised for
seeing special qualities in Latin: a sacred language of universal usage, guaranteeing
through its stability and dignity the conservation of the treasure of the faith. The
Council's task had been to define the doctrinal value of the mass as a true sacrifice.
The language question entered only insofar as it was grafted on to the dogma of the
mass. While the mass had not been linked absolutely with one language, nor a link
established between the vulgar tongue and heresy, defence against the Reformation
played a decisive part in the maintenance of Latin.

Until the Vatican II Council, the decisions taken at Trent remained in force in
the Catholic Church, which passed for the 'fortress of Latin'.[6] Any attempt to make
room – even minimally – for the vernacular languages not only failed, but was even
an occasion for building up arguments and enhancing apologetics in favour of Latin,
which was ultimately cast as a sacred language – something that it never was
theologically. To remain with the liturgy, it was left exclusively Latin, and the rare
attempts to introduce the vernacular – for instance at the Synod of Pistoia (1786) –
were always condemned by Rome. The Council had also insisted on the intellectual
training of the clergy; seminars were set up for purpose, where future priests received
Latin instruction. Results were not always up to expectations, and the lower clergy
had only very modest knowledge of Latin. Even in high places, performance was not
always what one might have expected: thus, during the stormy debates that took
place at the Sorbonne – the theological faculty of Paris – regarding the reception of
the bull *Unigenitus*, one of the doctors 'was reduced for his lack of Latin ... to
making himself understood by signs and gestures'.[7]

To qualify such a view of things, as customary it is simplistic, we shall recall on
the basis of three examples that the Protestant world was not one without Latin. The
early reformers, including Luther and Calvin, were also humanists, writing in both

the vulgar tongue and Latin. Between 1521 and 1570, no less than 58 complete Latin translations of the Bible were published in Latin by Protestant publishers and printers.[8] The training of pastors kept an important place, alongside theology, for the ancient languages, starting with Latin; Latin remained the language of the Protestant clergy, of theological debate, of synods and of visits, not counting, of course, numerous works of theology.

This last mention brings us into the world of knowledge, a world where Latin counted as the 'common language'.[9] Let us start with data from bibliographical statistics. We may stress from the outset that studies on printed output – which retain a national and even local character – have generally highlighted the conquests of the vernaculars, with Latin being studied rarely, and increasingly as one moves forward in time, only by default. In France Latin dominated until the 1560s, the date when the proportion turned round, definitively, in favour of French. In 1598–1600, the share of Latin in print was nearly 25%; it then stabilized around 20%, as shown by two studies done in 1644 (French production) and 1660 (Parisian production). A notable fall came in the second half of the seventeenth century, and in 1701 titles in Latin represented only 8.5% of Parisian print. The decline accelerated in the eighteenth century, and in 1764 output in Latin and foreign languages made up no. more than 4.5% of printed output in the kingdom. In Italy the development was to be slower. Latin kept a majority position throughout the sixteenth century (51.8%), though with a slight decline between the two halves of the century (from 55.4% to 50.2%). A clear decline can be seen in the following century, where printed Latin represented only 29.73% of output, though with an unequal distribution according to place: 21% in Venice, 50% in Rome, 56% in Padua, two cities where the Church and university were very much present. In German-speaking countries the decline of Latin was early, and from 1520 printing was mainly in German; but subsequently Latin, lastingly, regained its rights: until the 1680s, books traded at the Frankfurt fairs were mostly in Latin. Then the trend inverted, and the decline was continuous throughout the eighteenth century, though at a lower level than in France: in 1770 editions in Latin still accounted for 14.25%.

These percentages – though only indicative – give an overall view. Qualitative assessments allow us to clarify matters. For Paris, the work of Henri-Jean Martin has shown that Latin was used throughout the seventeenth century, and still in the eighteenth century, in three major sectors: theology, scholarly output and schoolbooks. In the second category, Latin is very much present in works of scholarship, medicine – with the turnaround here coming around 1685[10] – and law, despite a strong advance of French. The most solid and lasting bastion was to be school publishing – in line with Latin's quasi-monopoly in teaching. The share of Latin in works to do with learned culture emerges from the reviews appearing between 1728 and 1740 in a periodical whose very title indicates its nature, the *Bibliothèque raisonnée des ouvrages des savants de l'Europe*: 31% of books reviewed were in Latin. Even at the end of the eighteenth century, Latin still kept a not inconsiderable place in the Europe of medicine, if we are to believe the highly authoritative opinion of book professionals: in 1779 Gosse, a Geneva bookseller, said: 'everything medical is generally good in Latin. Spain, Portugal, Italy and even France do not reject it...'.[11] While Latin publishing was in manifest decline, it is nonetheless the case that it persisted in the scientific sphere, to the extent that the ancient tongue retained an essential role in a Europe where the vernaculars had not all yet, in the early eigteenth century, conquered full literary dignity, and where the learned public, though certainly not numerous, was geographically scattered.

Three types of publications are emblematic. Scholarly journals were mostly published in a vernacular. There were some appearing in Latin: 20% for the period 1665–1747; still, in the second half of the seventeenth century, we know of 14 new Latin titles between 1751 and 1760 and 13 between 1771 and 1780 for the German-speaking world alone, in the broad sense. Translations into Latin of works written in the vernacular were not lacking, even if, for reasons that the history of national literatures and languages can easily account for, attention has generally gone to the opposite phenomenon. They were, however, numerous, particularly for the seventeenth century and the start of the following one. Works in all disciplines were translated into Latin, and there were translations everywhere. However, it is clearly apparent that the Low Countries, Switzerland and Germany played a major role here: the dynamism of the Dutch presses, the mediating role played by Swiss booksellers, the presence at Geneva of skilled translator labour given the presence of refugee pastors, the existence in Germany and Central Europe of a still largely Latin market – all that explains for this area the development of a practice which, as elsewhere, still had to do, at the end of the seventeenth century, with the almost total lack of knowledge of living languages outside their frontiers, except for Italian and French. Medicine books that had only one or two editions in their original language had up to 8 or 10 in Latin; the same was true for religious polemic. Thus, for Pascal's *Lettres provinciales*, it was the Latin version produced by Nicole – six editions between 1658 and 1700 – that 'truly popularized the victorious pamphlet in Europe'.[12] In fact, it was to their Latin editions that some books and their authors owed a reputation going beyond their countries. The dissemination outside Italy of Galileo's *Dialogo dei due massimi sistemi* was based largely on the 1635 Latin translation. The success of Robert Boyle on the Continent is inseparable from the – extremely rapid – translation of his writings in Germany, Switzerland and Holland; moreover, it was not in English in Britain, but in Latin at Geneva that in 1677 the first collection of his works appeared, the *Opera Varia*, as well as, three years later, an expanded edition with new writings.

As the language of the Republic of Letters, Latin had as its allies the printers-booksellers who sought in this way to open up broader markets. They argued in favour of the ancient tongue for large-format books printed on fine paper and adorned with numerous plates, all splendid publications but also extremely costly, and, for obvious economic reasons, needing Europe-wide distribution; they thus pushed authors to accompany their text with a Latin translation. Thus, chiefly in the eighteenth century, and more specifically its first half, bilingual works appeared in such areas as scholarship, archaeology, botany, zoology, and anatomy, juxtaposing, in varied typographic presentations, texts in vernacular and in Latin.

Despite the rise of the vernaculars and then their predominance, Latin was retained in the world of science. Throughout the eighteenth century, many works continued to appear in Latin; to cite only major ones, the *Ars conjectandi* (1713) by Jacob Bernoulli I, the *Mechanica* (1736) and *Introductio in analysin infinitorum* (1748) by Leonhard Euler, the *Systema naturae* (first edition in 1735) by Linnaeus, or the *De viribus electricitatis in motu musculari* (1791) by Galvani.

Several factors operated to keep Latin as the language of science, starting with university education, which was until a late date given in Latin. This is, in fact, only one aspect, perhaps the most visible, of an environment heavily dominated by Latin. Newton, who gave his Cambridge courses and produced the bulk of his work in Latin, had a library containing more books in Latin than in English, and he annotated in Latin the Latin books he read. This last practice was probably natural to men who spent the better part of their time reading and writing in Latin. Reading, writing and speaking in Latin, and moreover in their specific research fields, scholars did not feel as strongly as one might imagine today the need to use the vernacular for their scientific publications. Even where they detached themselves from classical texts, even where lessons of commentary gave place to the teaching of experience, the weight of acquired habits, recourse to a specialized vocabulary, and taking the public into account, all go to explain why the vernacular did not impose itself all at once in the learned world. Still more, quite naturally, the major influence exercised by certain works that appeared in Latin played a part in maintaining the ancient language: the new concepts they conveyed were not always easily translatable, while they were in any case perfectly clear to the limited number of learned people who had to deal with them; this explains why, for instance, in eighteenth-century Italy, where the Tuscan tongue had conquered – for some time now – full literary dignity, the best Newtonian physics was written in Latin.

The first great learned works in modern languages commonly cited, Galileo's *Dialogo dei due massimi sistemi* and Descartes's *Discours de la méthode*, thus in no way mark the rout of Latin; moreover, both these authors published other writings of theirs in the ancient tongue, and for Descartes his most important ones. In fact, like many of his contemporaries, he could easily move from one language to the other and fit his language usage to the intended audiences; thus, his biographer Adrien Baillet notes in connection with the *Meditationes* that 'he felt it in no way appropriate to publish the work first in French as he had done with his Essays, but having written it chiefly for the learned and in both new and lofty style, he felt he had to speak their language and express himself in their way as far as possible'.[13]

One of the factors still helping to maintain Latin was the absence of vernacular languages for expressing knowledge. While there were countries where the modern languages early acquired literary dignity and were felt capable of conveying learned thought, there were others where till a late date Latin continued, in the absence of such a language of culture. This was the case for Finland. In the eighteenth century in that country, then belonging to Sweden, the language position was as follows: the people spoke Finnish, the aristocracy, clergy and urban middle classes spoke Swedish; but neither language was regarded as a language of culture. In these circumstances knowledge was expressed in Latin, and the situation remained the same well into the nineteenth century, when the only things published in Finnish were still religious works and writings of no great intellectual scope.

As the data of bibliographical statistics clearly show, the matter was played out between the seventeenth and eighteenth centuries; however, the change was neither radical, nor linear, nor monolithic. While the vernaculars won early in books with practical aims, the old tongue continued for theoretical writings. Thus, the law well shows a prevalence of Latin, as emerges from a count done on the basis of Italian output: of the 3,700 works printed between 1700 and 1800, 81% were in Latin, as against 19% in Italian; the proportion printed in the vulgar tongue was higher in the second half of the century – 31% as against 7% – and for editions of laws and statutes (52%) than for jurisprudence and doctrine (12%); *a contrario*, Latin remained the language of treaties, of exegetical works on the sources of civil law and of verdicts of supreme courts.

The Latin that was losing ground in publications – and the bibliographical statistics are unambiguous – was by no means eliminated from the world of knowledge: terminology bears its imprint. This emerges from translations into vernacular tongues of technical works. In Britain, the solution that prevailed in the sixteenth century was first to anglicize specific terms, either by adapting them by giving them an English ending or by making a literal translation; the Latin words for which there was no English equivalent were kept, accompanied by an explanation, or by putting a glossary at the end of the work; thus, some Latin 'untranslatables' entered into scientific English. However, between the sixteenth and eighteenth centuries many specialized vocabularies were developed in various vernaculars. Latin was often the basis for them. Thus, the anatomical nomenclature available to a French doctor in the eighteenth century was 'essentially Greco-Latin'. The Italian language bears the marks in its medical, or more specifically anatomical, vocabulary of a similar influence of Latin, which can be read through various chronological strata.

Remaining with terminology, there is one science which in early modern times developed entirely in Latin: botany. The sixteenth century had been marked by a trend to vernacularization dictated by the utilitarian and practical nature of the science. However, this venacularization brought a feeling of fragmentation of the discipline, and a consequent return to Latin, particularly marked as from the seventeenth century. The confusion brought by the custom of designating each plant by describing it by a fairly long phrase, and the divergences among botanists naming the same plant differently, were reduced only through the reform made by Linnaeus. We shall not here dwell on the binary system that was the basis for the new nomenclature nor on its adoption, which was in line with its usefulness. The success of this reform was also the success of Latin. Linnaeus ruthlessly rejected 'barbarous' terms, expressing a clear preference for the Latin names; he was also concerned to include names of Greek origin, since the Greeks had largely contributed to founding the discipline: these names were, however, Latinized, as were the names of celebrated botanists used as generic terms. Jussieu, who worked on the taxonomy of plants according to other criteria – a 'natural method' – remained faithful to Latin. Botany became a Latin science, to the point that in 1789 John Berkenhout was able to write: 'Those wishing to remain ignorant of the Latin tongue should stay away from the study of botany'.[14] And this science has remained Latin until today: it matters little that this technical Latin differed in many respects from Cicero's.

The reform carried out by Linnaeus served as a model in efforts made to give chemists a systematic nomenclature. In this discipline too confusion was great: terms varied to designate the same substance, chemists differed in the use of certain names, and in order to avoid ambiguity the usage had grown up of using long descriptive phases that were more definitions than names. The need for a systematic nomenclature became still more acute in the second half of the eighteenth century: new elements were then being discovered, compounds being prepared for the first time, and the area of 'pneumatic' chemistry opening up. Standardization was essential to the very progress of the discipline. Torbern Bergman, Professor at the University of Uppsala, gave a complete method of systematic nomenclature, in 1775–1784, strongly advocating the use of Latin: as the traditional language of the learned, it had the further advantage of being a dead language and thus sheltered from all change; starting from this common basis, translations could be made that would have the same references. Thus, the *lingua chimica* would be uniform everywhere. This choice is easy to understand: Bergman was a university professor and taught in Latin; the reference he used, Linnaeus's classification, was in Latin, and what is more, he had been Linnaeus's pupil; finally, his mother tongue, Swedish, was then unknown outside Sweden, and even in that country not a language of culture. This language choice was one of the points of disagreement with Guyton de Morvau: he in fact supported the vernacular tongue, specifically French. However, in the *Méthode de nomenclature chimique* (1787) to which he contributed, more specifically in the dictionary of new French terms, he included Latin equivalents: the old language remained a sure interpreter in exchanges among scientists. This viewpoint remained: when in the nineteenth century Berzelius had recourse to symbols to designate the chemical elements, he made them on the basis of their Latin names. Bergman had also proposed that the Latin names of all metals should end with *-um*; this principle was adopted, and remains in force today.

Many names and works have been cited to refute the simplistic equation often made between ancient and Latin, modern and vernacular. It is true that some of the emblematic authors of 'modernity' advocated the vernacular, or associated Latin with outdated knowledge. For Thomasius, it symbolized scholastic thought, or more generally 'the weight of now outdated modes of thought'.[15] Nonetheless Latin persisted, even from the pens of scholars that historiography has judged among the most modern. The point is that the old tongue played a part it was for long uniquely able to fill. It even seemed to be a recourse when the multiplication of vernaculars came to raise problems for scholars facing publications in languages they did not understand. Already in 1640, Marin Mersenne proposed the following solution: to create an 'excellent academy made up of 15 or 20 honest men of each nation, in each kingdom, to ensure the translation into the common language of Christian Europe, which is Latin, of what they judge worthy of that language, so that all may share it'.[16] A century later, when the difficulties had only increased, D'Alembert came back to the point in the *Discours préliminaire* of the *Encyclopédie*. But while approving the usage of writing everything in the vulgar tongue, he noted the drawbacks that had resulted. Latin seemed one recourse: 'Use of the Latin language, the ridiculousness of which we have shown in matters of taste, could not but be most useful in works of philosophy, where clarity and precision must be the whole merit, and only a universal conventional language is needed'. And he added: 'it would therefore be desirable to restore its usage: but there is no room for hope here'. The same desire and the same hope was expressed in the intellectual world of the nineteenth century and even the early twentieth century, faced with a modern Babel it was feared might be fateful to science.

Alongside printed output, the much more colossal mass of conserved archives attests the continuation of Latin in the government and administration of the States of early modern Europe. The dates of the shifts to the vernacular vary not only by country, but also according to the magistracies and the levels of administration. We shall confine ourselves to a few examples, pointing out from the outset that Latin lasted longer in Central Europe and in political units that brought together multilingual territories, that in these countries it was local government that first moved to the vernacular, and finally that elsewhere the official 'proclamation' of the vernacular did not *ipso facto* mean that the bureaucracies totally dropped the use of the ancient tongue.

Poland long remained faithful to Latin, and the petty nobility from which the administrative class was recruited remained strongly attached throughout the eighteenth century to the maintenance of the language. With the first partition of Poland (1772), Silesian and Polish territories came under the domination of Prussia. For their administration, the Prussian aristocracy, which like their prince had been won over to French, were induced to retain Latin in their training. Still in 1798, a minister of the King of Prussia was stressing that '...Latin was essential not just because of Roman law, but because of the new Polish territories where almost the whole educated class speaks Latin'.[17] 'Royal' Hungary, then united to the Empire, offers an example, as complex as it is interesting, of continuation of Latin in administration. In the seventeenth century five modern languages were spoken on its territory; it would, as Comenius noted in 1652, have been a veritable tower of Babel had not a sixth, Latin, acted as a common language. It is not surprising that the central government used it for the acts of the Diets – in no way implying that Latin was always spoken there – and for correspondence with Vienna; the King of Hungary, i.e. the Emperor, similarly used Latin in relations with his Hungarian subjects, as shown by the documents coming from the two bodies that were in relation with Hungary: the Hungarian Chancellery and the Court of Auditors. By contrast, Latin had by no means the same preponderant role in local government, where, as one moves down the levels, it disappears in favour of the vernaculars. Things worked this way until the late eighteenth century, when Joseph II – who nonetheless knew and even spoke Latin – decided with practical aims to Germanize the Hungarian administration and substitute German for Latin. The resistance was so strong that in 1790 he had to revoke his rescripts in this connection, and his successor had to restore the old usage.

Latin, in the use made of it in the Hapsburg monarchy, acted in the role of a third language, absolutely essential to governing a set of linguistically extremely diverse territories. The use made of it in diplomacy was very similar. While the principle of equality among States implies that there is no diplomatic language as such and that everyone is entitled to use his own language, Latin was nonetheless widely used in the Middle Ages and in the sixteenth century, by tacit convention. In 1640, the situation was as follows, as emerges from the usages of various governments in their correspondence with France: a number of states used French, several being themselves French-speaking; others used their own language, like the King of Spain, the Protestant Swiss cantons or the Italian states; finally, some wrote only in Latin, including the Emperor, the Elector of Saxony, the imperial city of Augsburg, the Hanseatic towns, and the Kings of Sweden, Denmark and Poland. France itself ordinarily used French in its diplomatic correspondence; but Latin was used to write to the Diet, to the Princes or states of the Empire when addressed collectively, to the chancellor of Poland. In both audiences and negotiations diplomats always took extreme care to respect the linguistic usages, using their own language or the conventional third language, namely Latin. Hence, for instance, the Imperial protestations when at Münster the French addressed the Princes of the Empire or their deputies documents in French or containing French: for the imperial Diets had the inviolable rule of communicating with foreign powers only in Latin. Any departure from established usage was presented as exceptional: at Utrecht the imperial envoy, though using French in discussions, carefully specified that this was in no way to constitute a precedent. Until the Treaty of Rastadt (1714) that 'consecrated' the arrival of French as a diplomatic language – since the Empire had agreed to sign the treaty in French – diplomatic exchanges had a considerable part for Latin. However, it did not stop being used after that date: many treaties were still written and signed in the language. France, despite the affirmation of French on the international scale, was no exception: thus the Versailles treaty (18 September 1735) between France and Poland regarding King Stanislas is in Latin. However, use of the traditional language tended to decline during the eighteenth century, and it remained chiefly a matter for the 'powers devoted to Latin', the Papacy, the religious orders or the Empire.

A command of Latin thus long remained necessary to the conduct of foreign policy. There were princes who had enough knowledge of it to conduct negotiations, like Charles XII of Sweden who, in 1701–1702, negotiated with the Poles in German but also in Latin. A fortiori, chancellery staffs, ambassadors and other diplomats had to have a good training in the subject. Some were even excellent Latinists. The Comte d'Avaux, who headed the French mission at the negotiations for the Peace of Westphalia, wrote and spoke Latin perfectly, even verging on purism: thus, he deleted the expression Sacra Majestas Christanissima, though highly honourable for the king of France, on the ground it was 'not good Latin'.[18] It is not surprising, then, that when the Treaty of Rastadt was being negotiated the Maréchal de Villars, who had no great confidence in his Latinity, called to his side the rector of the Strasbourg Jesuits. The problem was not only of pure Latinity; the need was to avoid using a word with an interpretation that might lead to consequences. All this explains why the training of diplomats long continued to give a place to Latin, even in a country like France where the vernacular tongue had since the sixteenth century been the language of administrative and jurisdictional acts, and while French was tending to prevail as a language of diplomacy. On the one hand some powers were continuing to produce documents in Latin, and on the other in cases where precedent and the verification of titles played an essential part it was necessary to have staff available capable of reading and understanding texts written in the old language. Very specifically, in the academy of politics set up in Paris in 1712, future diplomats were trained in Latin for both practical and obvious reasons. However, as one continues into the eighteenth century, Latin increasingly tended to give way to French, which reigned throughout the nineteenth century before in turn being out-competed by English. But even English has kept in its diplomatic and political vocabulary a number of Latin words and expressions attesting the major role Latin once played in relations among States.

A trip round the world of school, church, the Republic of Letters and national administration has brought out the Latin dimension Europe between the sixteenth and eighteenth centuries, where everywhere the same practices, based on the same justifications, were current. The common identity created was strengthened still further by largely shared social values that found their basis and expression in Latin.

Latin helped to 'class' people, to connote membership in society's elite, consecrating the gentleman. Its growing 'uselessness' for a number of activities went hand in hand with its affirmation as a social sign. This distinguishing quality emerges most especially from the 'desire' for Latin manifested by those not socially earmarked for it. Such aspirations were everywhere opposed, on the basis of a conservative view of society. While everyone ought to be 'brought up according to his status and in relation to the tasks he has to fulfil in society',[19] Latin was no use to the son of the peasant or the artisan, destined to spend his life behind the plough or in a shop; and for a merchant's son, arithmetic was worth more than Latin verse. Additionally, this learning of Latin risked being harmful not just for them but for the body politic as a whole. With Latin these children would take on ambitions above their status, which they would be quite unable to satisfy: and the risk was great that on reaching adulthood these men, now without status, might under the blows of disillusion and frustration embrace extreme ideas, or even tend towards rebellion. The rulers, reformers and pedagogues who in the eighteenth century agreed upon the need for elementary education for the people shared the same reservations regarding prolonged education, which would then be based on Latin. Examples could be taken from Britain, Prussia, Austria, France or the Italian states; I shall confine myself to Spain.

The Spanish reformers regarded Latin dangerous for the mass of the population as encouraging to chimerical aspirations. Ultimately it would lead to general weakening of the nation or even to revolt; for the moment, it was the cause of the economic evils affecting the country, by deviating labour that ought naturally to have gone to agriculture or the mechanical arts. Thus in 1747 Ferdinand VI limited the number of Latin schools, confirming an order of Philip IV in this connection. For already in the early seventeenth century Latin had been regarded by the 'arbitristas' as responsible for Spain's decadence: it took young people away from agriculture, crafts and trade in favour of ecclesiastical and administrative careers, considered unproductive in economic terms. The whole social balance was affected, and the nation's very existence was at stake. Already for Fernández de Navarrete (1621) the Latin schools, in the excessive number of 4000, in fact had their share in the decline of the kingdom's power: whereas an uneducated soldier would throw himself into the mêlée, one with a smattering of Latin would reflect, and let victory go.

It was in the name of the same view of society that women were not admitted to Latin. Since Providence had fixed roles proper to the sexes, a division ratified by nature, Latin, as the appanage of men, was *ipso facto* refused to women, 'shut up' both within the domestic space and in the use of the vulgar tongue. Latin and the knowledge that went with it would by arousing unheard-of ambitions turn women away from their duties and bring fateful consequences for the family, and ultimately for society as a whole. A moral reason was also invoked, expressed in a proverb current in the eighteenth century: 'a woman speaking Latin never ended well'.[20] The ancient languages, it was explained, contained obscenities one would not dare to say in modern languages; ignorance of Latin thus preserved women's innocence, and also kept them from licentious thoughts. With few exceptions women did not do Latin, and they had to await the twentieth century to have the same full access to it as boys.

Admission and exclusion strengthened the place of Latin in society and the role of 'honourable science' that was assigned to it. This was something Pedro González perfectly understood when he wrote his *vita* in Latin; and it matters little that the prose was scarcely Ciceronian. For this 'sign of wealth', to take up the analyses of sociologists,[21] was a male sign. The proof can be found by looking at a wonderful portrait of Pedro's daughter Antonietta.[22] Like her father, she was hairy, and like him, wore rich garments marking high status. But there is a difference that immediately leaps to the eye. An unfolded piece of paper she holds in her hand contains a short autobiography: these few lines are not in Latin but in Italian.

The social value and therefore prestige attached to Latin were paralleled by an element of power that men of the time were perfectly aware of. The now famous Menocchio testifies to this when he says 'the fact of speaking Latin is a betrayal of the poor, since at trials poor people do not know what is being said and are deceived, and if they want to say a couple of words, they need to have a lawyer'.[23] Unequal relations were established under the sign of Latin, in fact a range of practices which, having to do with prestige, authority and manipulation, brought reactions of admiration, submission or resignation. Latin was thus part of the instruments of power, strengthening them or even organizing them. One can find many traces of this in the legal and scientific worlds, but also in relations between the sexes as well as in the division which, in the churches, was made between the faithful and a clergy that knew Latin – even if not all that well.

A few examples taken from medicine will show how the system worked. Molière is read everywhere, in French or in translation. In two of his comedies, among the most famous – *Le malade imaginaire* and *Le médecin malgré lui* – he denounced the power that physicians, by their clothing and their Latin *galimatias*, exercised, though lacking any certain knowledge, over common mortals. The Latin words they spoke, though empty of knowledge, nonetheless acted upon their patients like charms. In the previous century the English playwright William Bullein had, in his *Dialogue Against the Fever Pestilence* (1564), using hollow and pompous Latin, denounced the hold exercised by physicians over the sick, which could readily be translated into hard cash.

The same process of a mystificatory Latin can occasionally be found from the pens of physicians themselves. Latin was a way to ensure their power over others, a tool of deception operating to their greater profit. 'The most perspicacious and wisest physicians', wrote Antonio Vallisnieri in 1722, 'know the weakness of their art, know how little knowledge they have of the true, indisputable, internal reasons for illnesses ... which is why they cunningly strive to cover up and hide all that under Greek, Arabic, Latin and barbarous words, unable to tolerate any sincere physician writing in the common tongue, for fear that the art, if understood by all, would lose credit, and they their profit'.[24] However, the same Antonio Vallisnieri wrote the consultations he gave in Latin: in those official documents, the ancient tongue shared in the acknowledged prestige of the physician, strengthening the authority of his opinion. This emerges also from the use, very discreet as it is, that William Buchan makes of Latin in his *Domestic Medicine* (1769). This work, which had enormous success, was part of an output of original writings and translations aimed at the health education of the population, while freeing them from the grip of charlatans. Buchan had written in English; however, on the reverse of the title page he placed two Latin quotations, from Cicero and Celsus, epigraphs certifying his professional competence and inviting the reader to trust fully in a text even if in the vulgar tongue.

The asymmetry of the doctor-patient relationship was further enhanced by the development of medical science, when it began to utilize increasingly technical language and have recourse to Latin. By the way, this shows the weakness of the common idea of a linear linguistic revolution running always from Latin towards the vernaculars. On this point the registers of the Bristol Infirmary, a hospital for the poor founded in 1737, are very eloquent. While the reports drawn up by the physicians had followed the patients' accounts and used their own words, in the latter third of the century they were based entirely on the physical diagnosis done by the practitioner. The report was then no longer written in ordinary language but in technical terms, and Latin replaced the vernacular. While in the late 1770s English was used in 70% of diagnoses, by the end of the century the proportion was totally reversed, Latin being used in 79% of cases. The patient no longer had a word to say, being reduced to a clinical case described in a language doubly unintelligible to him, because of its technical vocabulary and of the choice of language. The distance between doctor and patient was thus increased, a phenomenon not without practical consequences. The physician Thomas Beddoes noted in 1804 that the poor, rather than consulting hospital doctors, preferred to turn to their neighbours 'for they speak to the sick in their own language'.[25] Ultimately the gap was to become too great between the two, making the relation inoperative: the patient would be driven towards other, more intelligible authorities, even the very ones doctors wanted to guard them from: do-gooding but ignorant neighbours, or charlatans.

The latter, while remaining more directly accessible, had well understood the power Latin could confer. To ward off the prestige of the doctor and win the trust of others, they made great use everywhere of the ancient language. First, they baptised their remedies with it, such as *Elixir magnum stomachum, Pilulae in omnes morbos, Pilulae radiis solis extractae, Gremelli pulmonates, Panchimagogum febrifugum*, not to mention numerous though less picturesque *Elixir vitae, Aurum potabile or Aqua coelestis*, to remain with medicines sold in England.[26] They laced their speech with Latin words and adorned their brochures with Latin quotations, like the charlatan from Brittany who in 1786 had printed on a handbill he distributed *Nolite confidere verbis, sed factis* [trust not the words but the facts].[27] They had well understood that Latin attested a skill and produced the desired effect on others, as did those practising in Piazza Navona in Rome in the 1680s. 'I have seen some', wrote a French traveller, ' … who coming along loaded with several volumes in Greek or Latin, gave authority to what they were handing out to that ignorant populace using numbers of passages they did not understand themselves and that have neither rhyme nor reason, which did not fail to make so much impression on the hearers as to make them desert others, who beside these doctors of the public square appeared as nothing but mountebanks, jugglers and charlatans'.[28]

Latin thus acted as a tool of authority, or of coercion and manipulation, strengthening the prestige of those who knew it and incarnating a power that was the more absolute for being unintelligible. These observations will scarcely be surprising, referring as they do to a conception of power favoured by recent historiography, stated in terms of force, exclusion and prohibition. But by keeping to that one might forget that power is also protection of the weak by the strong, the duty on those having authority to exercise it for the good of others. This role was played by Latin: it was also intentionally used to preserve and protect. Much use was made of Latin to hide certain realities of a medical or sexual nature that might be able to shock. This usage was not confined to the privileged spheres of medicine and moral theology; it can be met with in writings in the most diverse disciplines and registers. Thus, Edward Gibbon used Latin in his *Decline and Fall of the Roman Empire* when he had to describe facts of a sexual nature like the 'vices' of the empress Theodora; called on to defend himself from the attacks of indecency some had levelled against him, he replied by brandishing inter alia the following argument: 'My English text is chaste, and all the licentious passages are left in the obscurity of a learned language'.[29] As a 'learned language' Latin automatically set the message in a context that was itself learned. It thus became nothing more than a code, a means of transmitting a quantity of technical information. It enabled one to say, and more especially write, things that had to be written though the moral standards of the times forbade saying them in everyday language.

In 1818 Joseph de Maistre defined Latin as 'the European sign'.[30] By this term he meant not some sort of language skill, which if one considers the average of the 'Latinate' was never very great. Instead he was taking note of the functions Latin had been allotted and the discourses that had underlain its uses. Each of these were to last right into the 1960s, updating in new contexts opinions and beliefs forged between the sixteenth and eighteenth centuries when Latin, Europe and Civilization shared one and the same vision.

Translated by Iain L. Fraser

Notes

1. On clothing as a mark of belonging to a community, see, in this volume, the article by G. Calvi.
2. I wish to thank Roberto Zapperi for telling me about the autobiography of Pedro González contained in a manuscript in the Lessing Rosenwald collection kept in the National Gallery of Arts in Washington. Pending publication of the study Zapperi has begun on Pedro González and his family, refer, specifically for the status of hairy people, to Zapperi (1985).
3. This article takes up many elements from my book *Le latin ou l'empire d'un signe, XVIe–XXe siècle* (Waquet [1999]) where specific references to the examples given here can be found. These are explicitly given in this article only for quotations or works explicitly cited.
4. The expression is from Bacon (1874), p. 434.
5. The fundamental work here is Schmidt (1950).
6. The expression is from Brunot (1967), who uses it for the eighteenth century alone, p. 67.
7. Gres-Gayer (1991), p. 213.
8. Gantet (1996), p. 144.
9. *Encyclopédie...* (1765), t. IX, *s.v.* 'Langue'.
10. Martin (1982) and (1984), p. 95 and p. 101.
11. Cited from Bonnant (1983), p. 71.
12. Sainte-Beuve quoted by Dubois (1980), t. I, p. 617.
13. Baillet (1972), vol. II, p. 107.
14. Stearn (1966), p. 6.
15. Blackall (1959), p. 13.
16. Mersenne (1970), p. 420.
17. Armstrong (1973), pp. 130–31.
18. Brunot (1966), p. 393.
19. Bernis (1878), t. I, p. 20.
20. N.C. (1718), p. 28.
21. I am here referring to the analyses by Veblen on classical studies (1970), pp. 259–64; and by Bourdieu (1982).
22. This portrait, by Lavinia Fontana, is kept in the Musée des Beaux-Arts, Blois.
23. Ginzburg (1976), p. 12.
24. Scotti Morgagni (1976), p. 158.
25. Fissell (1991), p. 106.
26. Names taken from Porter (1989), p. 107.

27. Ramsey (1989), p. 136.
28. Connors and Rice (1991), pp. 76–7.
29. Gibbon (1994), p. 69.
30. Maistre (1841), p. 136.

References

Armstrong, J.A. (1973), *The European Administrative Elite* (Princeton).

Bacon, F. (1874), *Works. Volume XIV* (London).

Baillet, A. (1972), *La vie de Monsieur Des-Cartes* (Hildesheim, New York) (orig. ed.: Paris, 1691).

Bernis, F.J.P., cardinal de (1878), *Mémoires et lettres*, F. Masson (ed.) (Paris).

Blackall, E.A. (1959), *The Emergence of German as a Literary Language, 1700–1715* (Cambridge).

Bonnant, G. (1983), 'La librairie genevoise dans les Provinces-Unies et les Pays-Bas méridionaux jusqu'à la fin du XVIIIe siècle', in *Genava*, XXXI.

Bourdieu, P. (1982), *Ce que parler veut dire. L' économie des échanges linguistiques* (Paris).

Brunot, F. (1966), *Histoire de la langue française des origines à nos jours. Tome V. Le français en France et hors de France au XVIIe siècle* (Paris).

_____. (1967), *Histoire de la langue française des origines à nos jours. Tome VII. La propagation du français en France jusqu'à la fin de l'Ancien Régime* (Paris).

Connors, J. and L. Rice (eds) (1991), *Specchio di Roma barocca. Una guida inedita del XVII secolo* (Rome).

Dubois, E.T. (1980), 'La polémique autour des "Lettres Provinciales": quelques réflexions concernant l'utilisation respective du latin et du française', in J.-C. Margolin (ed.), *Acta conventus neo-latini turonensis. Tours, 6–10 septembre 1976. 3e Congrès international d'études néo-latines* (Paris).

Encyclopédie ou Dictionnaire raisonné des sciences, des arts et des métiers, par une société de gens de lettres...(1765) (Paris).

Fissell, M.E. (1991), 'The Disappearance of the Patient's Narrative and the Invention of Hospital Medicine', in R. French and A. Wear (eds), *British Medicine in an Age of Reform* (London and New York).

Gantet, C. (1996), 'La religion et ses mots. La Bible latine de Zurich (1534) entre la tradition et l'innovation', in *Zwingliana*, XXIII.

Gibbon, E. (1994), *My Life and Writings. Illustrated from his Letters, with Occasional Notes and Narrative by John Lord Sheffield*, A.O.J. Cockshut and S. Constantine (eds) (Keele).

Ginzburg, C. (1976), *Il formaggio e i vermi. Il cosmo di un mugnaio del '500* (Turin).

Gres-Gayer, J.M. (1991), *Théologie et pouvoir en Sorbonne. La faculté de théologie de Paris et la Bulle Unigenitus, 1714–1721* (Paris).

Martin, H.-J. (1982), 'Classements et conjonctures', in H.-J. Martin and R. Chartier (eds), *Histoire de l'édition française. Tome I. Le livre conquérant. Du Moyen Âge au milieu du XVIIe siècle* (Paris).

_____. (1984), 'Une croissance séculaire', in H.-J. Martin and R. Chartier (eds), *Histoire de l'édition française. Tome II. Le livre triomphant* (Paris).

Mersenne, M. (1970), *Correspondance... IX. Janvier 1642–27 décembre 1642*. C. de Waard (ed.) (Paris).

Maistre, J. de (1841), *Du pape* (Paris) (orig. ed.: 1819).

N.C. (1718), *Les femmes savantes ou Bibliothèque des dames qui traite de sciences qui conviennent aux dames, de la conduite de leurs études, des livres qu'elles peuvent lire et de l'histoire de celles qui ont excellé dans les sciences* (Amsterdam).

Porter, R. (1989), *Health for Sale. Quackery in England, 1660–1850* (Manchester).

Ramsey, M. (1989), *Professional and Popular Medicine in France, 1770–1830* (Cambridge).

Schmidt, H.A.P. (1950), *Liturgie et langue vulgaire. Le problème de la langue liturgique chez les premiers Réformateurs et au Concile de Trente.... Traduction du néerlandais* (Rome).

Scotti Morgagni, S. (1976), 'Latino e italiano nel primo Settecento. Note in margine a una lettera inedita di A. Vallisnieri a L.A. Muratori', in *Rendiconti dell'Istituto lombardo. Classe di lettere e scienze morali e storiche*, 110.

Stearn, W.T. (1966), *Botanic Latin. History, Grammar, Syntax, Terminology and Vocabulary* (London).

Veblen, T. (1970), *Theory of the Leisure Class* (Paris) (orig. ed.: 1899).

Waquet, F. (1999), *Le latin ou l'empire d'un signe, XVIe–XXe siècle* (Paris), (English ed.: London, 2001).

Zapperi, R. (1985), 'Arrigo le velu, Pietro le fou, Amon le nain et autres bêtes: autour d'un tableau d'Agstino Carrache', in *Annales E.S.C.*.

French Abstracts. Résumés en Français

Crypto-identités. Turcs, Chrétiens et Juifs déguisés

Giovanni Ricci

Dans cet essai, est considéré le sujet des crypto-identités, non pas en termes abstraits ou universels, mais plutôt en le liant à un dossier spécifique et mineur quoique très ramifié, celui du déguisement ethnico-religieux dans l'Europe des premiers Temps Modernes. Il s'agit d'analyser la typologie du déguisement en prenant en compte les relations réciproques entre les trois grandes religions du Livre. Précisons cependant que l'on exclut de l'analyse les renégats, les convertis, les moriscos, les marranes, les nouveaux Chrétiens, qui ne sont pas déguisés – ils seraient bien plutôt des revêtus – et qui posent d'autres problèmes déjà bien connus. Encore, les déguisements étudiés ici (soit des acquisitions de vêtements d'autrui) ne sont pas ceux qu'on tolère au Carnaval, mais ceux qui sont pratiqués tout au long de l'année et donc illicites. Notre dossier nous éloigne du monde des idées et nous plonge parmi des hommes qui se livrent à des gestes matériels, souvent rapaces ou malhonnêtes. Pourtant, on soupçonne que cette dimension, pétrie de quotidienneté, ait contribué à engendrer, au fil du temps, un discours sophistiqué concernant l'identité individuelle. Dans la perspective choisie, l'identité serait le fruit d'une évolution inattendue que la formule suivante résume: des crypto-identités au sens littéral de 'cachées' (inventées et un peu malhonnêtes), aux identités 'crypto-', au sens littéral aussi d'invisibles (privées et un peu sincères). Il en sortirait donc un fragment d'image de l'Europe à la généalogie bien sûr moins noble que d'autres déjà explorées, un fragment toutefois en action et pas du tout ignoble dans certaines de ses issues.

Ségrégation, migration et récupération de l'Orient dans l'Europe méditerranéenne au début de l'époque moderne. Le cas de l'Espagne sémitique

André Stoll

Ses rapports conflictuels avec son pluriséculaire passé à dominante sémitique (arabo-musulmane et sépharade), incarné par les descendants morisques et judéoconvers de son propre 'Orient de l'intérieur', rendent l'Espagne impériale de la Première Modernité (XVIe-XVIIe s.) paradigmatique par son attitude de rejet et de récupération face à cet Autre nommé Orient. Et cela plus que toute autre des civilisations de l'Occident européen, et non seulement des civilisations chrétiennes à partir des Croisades. L'analyse critique des mythes de fondation des sociétés méditerranéennes anciennes, qui se réclament elles-mêmes d'une ascendance (proche-)orientale, montre en effet que, paradoxalement, elles définissent leur supériorité morale et civilisatrice comme le fruit d'une coupure radicale avec la civilisation orientale déchue qui leur a pourtant donné naissance. C'est dans la fabulation 'maurophile' élaborée à l'époque du roi absolu Philippe II, que l'on découvre des analogies étonnantes entre l'impériale Cordoue des Maures et la souveraine République de Carthage selon l'*Énéide*. Conformément au mythe gréco-romain de l'ascendance phénicienne de la divine Europe, mais sans recourir à la même dénomination, ces deux florissantes Républiques se définissent ainsi tacitement comme des sociétés 'orientales d'Occident' ou 'd'Europe', qui marquent clairement leur supériorité civilisatrice par rapport à celles du Proche-Orient de leurs origines. L'imaginaire 'maurophile' des générations romantiques contribuera de son côté à creuser encore le fossé discursif entre cet Orient 'européen' et l'autre, assimilé désormais à despotisme, obscurantisme et décadence.

Genre et corps

Giulia Calvi

Cet article éclaire quelques aspects de la façon dont les relations entre les hommes et les femmes, ainsi que la représentation symbolique du masculin et du féminin, contribuent à construire une image de l'Europe. En privilégiant l'approche de l'anthropologie historique, l'analyse vise à repérer les stratégies discursives et visuelles qui construisent les identités de genre par le biais de marquages visibles, comme le corps et le vêtement, et à travers les éléments constitutifs de la relation hétérosexuelle, soit les usages matrimoniaux et les comportements domestiques. La relation entre les genres, telle qu'elle apparaît dans ses formes historiques, permet de distinguer les minorités ethniques, linguistiques et religieuses, de tracer les frontières, de repérer des permanences de longue durée à l'intérieur des différentes aires européennes. À des formes tendanciellement hégémoniques de représentations communes aux régions occidentales s'opposent des pratiques, traditions, cultures diffuses dans le Nord scandinave et dans les régions caucasiennes et orientales. De cette représentation des relations de genre ressort une image de l'Europe hétérogène, composite et non linéaire.

Magie et sorcellerie

Stuart Clark

Au début de la modernité, la démonologie avait un caractère paneuropéen et exprimait des façons de penser et d'écrire qui étaient partagées par les gens cultivés à travers tout le continent. Les concepts de magie et de sorcellerie qu'elle adoptait devinrent des armes culturelles servant à marginaliser ceux qui n'étaient pas dans la prétendue pureté des religions européennes. Les résultats apparaissent clairement dans des pays comme le Brésil, le Pérou et le Mexique, où les religions indigènes étaient condamnées pour sorcellerie. Une forme culturelle, imaginée en Europe, était de la sorte instrumentalisée afin de distinguer des valeurs et des institutions européennes et créer une idéologie continentale. En même temps, à l'intérieur de l'Europe, d'autres missionnaires allaient christianisant les populations en maniant la même rhétorique. 'Otras Indias!', tel était leur slogan. Si donc de la colonisation se dégage une image de l'Europe, on rencontre la même image dans les rapports domestiques des églises face aux religions marginales.

Une république de marchands?

Francesca Trivellato

D'après le concept de cosmopolitisme que nous héritons des lumières, les échanges économiques érodent progressivement les différences ethniques et religieuses, et la logique du profit serait vecteur de tolérance. Dans cet article, on soutient qu'au cours de l'age moderne, la société mercantile européenne voit s'étendre ses propres frontières, mais que, au XVIIIe siècle, il s'agissait de tout autre chose qu'une entité indifférenciée dans laquelle l'intérêt économique se substituait aux formes identitaires et aux discriminations. En outre, s'il est vrai que de nouvelles infrastructures et des instruments légaux et de crédit facilitèrent les échanges commerciaux sur de longues distances, et en particulier les échanges entre des agents séparés par des barrières géographiques et culturelles, l'intégration des marchands resta liée à des procès d'interactions informelles et de communication entre diverses communautés mercantiles. Les lettres commerciales eurent un impact décisif sur ces procès parce que la standardisation progressive de leur langage consentit le développement d'une grammaire des obligations dont la signification légale et conceptuelle était compréhensible dans une pluralité de contextes. Le rôle et la position des marchands juifs Sépharades dans l'Europe occidentale révèlent la complexité du discours et des pratiques du cosmopolitisme et leurs contradictions. Comme minorité discriminée dans l'Europe chrétienne et privée d'un état propre, ceux-ci furent malgré tout la diaspora mercantile qui remporta les plus grands succès et qui parvint à constituer des alliances commerciales durables avec des non-juifs. Comme groupe le plus acculturé et le plus intégré de la diaspora juive en Europe, les riches marchands Sépharades d'Amsterdam, Livourne, Venise, Londres, Hambourg et Bordeaux néanmoins maintenaient des liens étroits avec des parents dans l'empire ottoman et adoptaient des formes de parentèle (bigamie incluse) difficilement conciliables avec l'image conventionnelle de la modernisation liée au discours du cosmopolitisme européen.

Une communauté scientifique européenne: échanges et amitié chez les premiers historiens naturalistes modernes

Florike Egmond

Considérer de près la formation de l'histoire naturelle en tant que nouveau champ de l'expertise scientifique au début de l'Europe moderne contribue à éclaircir les questions concernant la façon dont la science en Europe parvint à un caractère spécifiquement européen, quel rôle cela joua dans la construction d'une identité européenne, comment cela a même pu contribuer à un phénomène reconnu comme proprement européen : la Révolution Scientifique. On ne se concentre pas, dans cet essai, sur l'histoire des idées (scientifiques) mais sur les pratiques, la construction d'un nouveau champ du savoir et les conséquences de telles pratiques au regard de la formation d'une communauté scientifique européenne.

L'un des plus grands botanistes européens, Carolus Clusius (1526–1609), fut une figure clé dans la formation de ce nouveau terrain de l'expertise scientifique, comme auteur, traducteur, chercheur, directeur d'un jardin botanique, illustrateur, conseillé de collectionneurs, protégé d'aristocrates et de princes, maître de jeunes scientifiques et illustrateurs, correspondant avec des centaines d'informateurs et experts à travers l'Europe. Dans cet article, on se concentre sur ses réseaux et sa correspondance. La correspondance de Clusius ne reflète pas seulement le renouvellement des pratiques et des idées scientifiques, mais fait aussi paraître comment les échanges d'honneurs et de dons caractéristiques de l'ancien style de sociabilité ont influencé l'interaction d'experts venant de différents pays, contribuant ainsi à façonner un nouveau style européen de l'échange scientifique et une communauté européenne des naturalistes.

La Galaxie des Cours

Rita Costa Gomes

Dans les cours européennes des époques médiévales et modernes, l'utilisation d'un 'langage' commun, conçu en dehors des catégories et des traditions du républicanisme ou de la scolastique, a conduit au développement de traditions discursives spécifiques. Les cours royales dans leur ensemble, qu'elles soient princières ou ecclésiastiques, semblent constituer une galaxie composée de corps ayant à la fois des caractéristiques diverses et un haut degré de similarité interne. Dans de telles configurations humaines, plus ou moins densément distribuées dans les différents pays européens, sont produits et circulent des discours qui ont trait à la reproduction du pouvoir et à ses 'secrets'. Caractérisées par la présence du monarque, par le groupe humain qui entoure et réalise cette présence, et finalement en tant que place ou siège mobile du pouvoir souverain, les cours européennes sont le lieu d'une réflexion sur la valeur de la proximité physique du courtisan avec la personne royale, réflexion qui aboutit à des concepts précis. On propose ici d'explorer trois exemples de provenance diverse qui permettent de voir comment les traditions discursives concernant le rapport entre la figure souveraine et le courtisan finissent par impliquer une opposition tranchante entre individu et société.

Les rites de passage et le grand Tour.

Robert Wokler

À partir de la moitié du XVIIe siècle jusqu'à la Révolution Française, le Grand Tour était conçu comme une sorte d' 'université itinérante' visant à compléter l'éducation des gentilshommes et de leur fournir un contact direct avec les réalisations de la civilisation européenne à une époque où bien des universités étaient dominées par des clercs sectaires. Un tel voyage à travers l'Europe était rendu possible par la situation de paix relative et de prospérité qui suivit les guerres de religion. Loisirs, richesse, instruction, et nouvelles routes et canaux, tout cela contribuait à rendre possible cette expérience. Principalement d'Angleterre et du Nord protestant, mais parfois aussi de France, les voyageurs séjournaient à Rome et dans d'autres destinations du sud d'Europe pour inspecter les racines classiques et les antiques monuments de la civilisation. En Europe centrale et de l'Ouest, ils cherchaient davantage à apprécier les réalisations architecturales et artistiques des cultures modernes. En Suisse, ils étaient attirés par les paysages d'un état de nature vierge des ravages des activités humaines. Dans tous les coins de l'Europe, ils étaient frappés par la variété et les différences des modes de vie indigènes. Archéologues et historiens, plutôt que candidats au Grand Tour, allaient en Grèce à l'époque des Lumières, et l'Espagne était plutôt rarement visitée par eux. Dans la mesure où le Grand Tour était considéré comme une sorte de cours de civilisation européenne, il était marqué par l'ambition des voyageurs de gommer les frontières politiques, mais elles furent reconstruites par suite de la Révolution française, puis par le traité de Versailles qui manifesta l'ethos des Etats nations modernes plutôt que l'esprit cosmopolite du Grand Tour.

Citoyenneté et métier de l'Etat

Janet Coleman

Cette contribution commence par la question suivante: comment la citoyenneté était-elle diversement définie et mise en pratique pendant l'époque dite 'pré-moderne', soit dans une période allant de la synthèse augustinienne concernant l'expérience historique de l'Etat impérial romano-chrétien jusqu'au XVIIIe siècle, en passant par le Moyen Age scolastique et la Réforme ? En révélant certains éléments de continuité dans les images du citoyen européen et celles des Etats qui définissent l'appartenance légitime à la totalité sociale, on en vient à contester ce que l'on pense communément aujourd'hui : soit qu'il y a une conception de l'Europe, proprement univoque et moderne, laquelle serait le résultat de l'âge des Lumières. Il ne s'agit pas d'une question portant sur l'espace géographique mais sur une expérience historique. L'investigation porte sur les discours juridiques et théologiques et ceux de la théorie et de la pratique politique, à travers la longue durée.

Les auteurs tenus pour représentatifs dans chacun de ces domaines, apprécient diversement l'extension et la nature des facultés humaines jugées nécessaires pour se gouverner, et par conséquent jugent diversement la fonction de l'Etat. On présente d'abord ce qu'il en est de la relation entre citoyen et Etat à travers le *Corpus juris Civilis* de Justinien. Puis on examine la pénétration de cette conception impériale romaine dans la théologie chrétienne augustinienne qui présente l'Etat comme ce qui assure la concorde entre les citoyens. Mais c'est le débat scolastique entre néo-augustiniens et néo-aristotéliciens sur les moyens de réaliser le bien commun qui apparaît comme jetant les bases des débats futurs concernant la capacité des hommes, qu'elle soit ou non naturelle, à préférer l'amour du bien commun à l'amour de soi. Ce débat se reflète dans les procédures post-scolastiques d'excommunication comme dans les procédures publiques visant à maintenir la réputation des personnes accédant aux charges publiques et des citoyens. Il est suggéré que l'Europe, en tant qu'expérience historique, est intrinsèquement traversée par les conflits spirituels et politiques internes au christianisme, conduisant à deux orientations antagonistes de la citoyenneté et de l'Etat. Non seulement catholiques et protestants, mais encore libéraux et communautariens conservent les thèmes apparus dans les débats opposant néo-augustiniens et scolastiques néo-aristotéliciens, dont découlent les efforts persistant en vue de discerner les membres légitimes et d'exclure les autres, pour le maintien de la paix, de la sécurité, voire de l'identité collective. Nombres d'aspects de l'Etat européen moderne et de ses citoyens maintiennent des caractéristiques dont les origines restent 'pré-modernes'. Qu'ils se révèlent directement présents ou reconfigurés sous d'autres formes, on ne comprend pas sans eux une certaine laïcité contemporaine.

Les images de la loi en Europe: à la recherche de traditions communes

Pietro Costa

Est-ce que nous pouvons supposer l'existence d'un tissu juridique européen dans la période allant du Moyen Age à l'affirmation de la Modernité ?

Le phénomène du *jus commune* – la *interpretatio* du droit romain, une *interpretatio* qui commence dans le Moyen Age et se prolonge jusqu'à l'essor des codifications modernes – semble nous donner une réponse facile. Le *jus commune* est pourtant un phénomène complexe et il faut évaluer soigneusement le rapport entre le jus commune et la multiplicité des institutions politiques particulières. Le *jus commune* semble être en effet, plutôt qu'un ordre juridique commun, une tradition culturelle partagée, un paradigme, dans le sens kuhnien du terme. Les caractéristiques de ce paradigme sont les suivantes : la détermination d'un texte prescriptif (le *Corpus Iuris* de Justinien, en premier lieu), la considération du droit romain comme '*ratio scripta*', l'attribution à l'*interpretatio* d'une dimension créative, l'idée que le juriste doit et peut dévoiler les caractéristiques essentielles de l'ordre en général.

Le paradigme lié à l'*interpretatio* du *jus commune* n'est pourtant pas la seule tradition juridique partagée entre le Moyen Age et la Modernité. Une autre tradition se développe à partir d'un paradigme différent : la théorie de la loi naturelle (et des droits naturels). C'est le paradigme qui soutient la rhétorique réformatrice du XVIIIe siècle, fondée sur l'opposition entre l'existence et l'essence, entre les régimes politiques et sociaux existants et les modèles déontologiques imposés par la nature même.

Résister à la violence publique; actions, droit, émotions.

Angela De Benedictis

Les images de rébellion et les portraits de rebelles qui peuplent l'histoire et l'historiographie de l'Europe de la fin du Moyen Age à l'époque moderne forment une séquence au bout de laquelle se dresse le monopole du recours à la force légitime de l'Etat du prince ; ce recours étant entendu comme la nécessaire conclusion des condamnations répétées des actes de violence injustifiable que commettaient les sujets contre leur prince. À ce tableau général, en répond un autre qui présente des images dans lesquelles les sujets estimaient, à juste titre, pouvoir résister à la violence publique exercée par le prince lorsque celui-ci, au lieu d'incarner la justice, la négligeait et agissait contre le droit.

Sont présentées synthétiquement les situations de 'rébellion' et de 'révolte', entre la moitié du XIVe siècle et la fin du XVIIIe siècle, sur le territoire florentin, dans la principauté épiscopale de Trente, en Catalogne et en Suisse, sur la 'terre sans frontières' située entre le monde rhénan et les Pays Bas. La lecture de certains textes fondamentaux de la réflexion juridique qui, sur cette longue période, avaient diversement analysé et défini le *crimen rebellionis*, permet d'observer jusqu'à quel point la justification de la rébellion, en tant que résistance licite à la violence publique de l'injustice du prince et non en tant que crime, demeure constante et continue. À la suite des dernières interprétations du *Tractacus politicus* de Spinoza, on cherche à mettre en évidence comment une telle justification devint constitutive d'un discours politique qui s'opposa explicitement à la nouvelle théorie politique sur l'obéissance inconditionnelle des sujets. Si la violence du prince comportait. en puissance l'anéantissement de ses sujets, ces derniers pouvaient réagir par la violence: il s'agissait d'une résistance nécessaire afin d'affirmer leur propre existence.

L'arbre

Christiane Klapisch-Zuber

L'image de l'arbre a occupé une place importante dans la pensée occidentale de l'époque prémoderne et moderne, les origines de ses usages scientifiques étant à chercher dans les figures généalogiques et philosophiques (*Divisio philosophiae*) médiévales. La réflexion sur la hiérarchisation des concepts dérive ainsi d'une très longue expérience d'exposition discursive et elle en a hérité les techniques graphiques. Reportées sur le terrain de l'analyse sociale et politique, les figures d'arbres ont également servi depuis la Renaissance des propos polémiques ou de critique sociale, la propagande politique et la théorie politique. Depuis la fin du XVIIIe siècle, elles ont enfin soutenu l'idée d'évolution, mais, reportant trop fidèlement la pensée généalogique dans les processus du vivant, elles ont abouti à des impasses qui n'ont été dénoncées que dans les dernières décennies.

De la Renaissance aux Lumières en passant par l'Antiquité

Les débuts du réseau européen des Musées

Edouard Pommier

L'Italie de la Renaissance invente le Musée, sous deux modalités : à Rome, le musée consacré aux antiquités, considérées comme des signes d'identité et de mémoire ou comme des témoignages de la perfection exemplaire de la sculpture grecque; et à Florence, le musée consacré aux œuvres de l'art 'moderne', qui s'épanouit à partir de 1500 et devient à son tour une référence pour les artistes.

Le modèle italien inspire la création, à Munich, à la fin du XVIe siècle, du premier musée d'antiquités au nord des Alpes. Ce modèle se renforce au XVIIIe siècle, avec le développement des deux pôles romains du Capitole et du Belvédère, associant antiquités et peinture 'moderne'. Il suscite l'apparition, dans les états de l'Empire, d'un premier réseau européen dans lequel la société éclairée retrouve les éléments d'une communauté de culture, fondée sur le partage du même patrimoine archéologique et artistique. A la veille de la rupture de 1789, la France de l'Ancien Régime lance à son tour un projet qui sera arrêté, puis repris sous une autre forme par la Révolution.

Le musée est une invention léguée par l'Italie de la Renaissance à l'Europe des Lumières, qui en fait une illustration originale, et encore très vivante aujourd'hui, de sa conscience historique.

Sainteté et héroïsme: images et imaginaires dans l'Europe du XVIe siècle

Denis Crouzet

Il y eut, tout au long du XVIe siècle, comme une mise en crise de la sainteté jusqu'alors primordialement mise en imaginaire à travers le paradigme du sacrifice. La vie sainte fut repensée par Thérèse d'Avila ou Ignace de Loyola comme un antihéroïsme. Elle fut une vie marquée par des agressions spirituelles et physiques véhémentes, qui étaient intérieurement vécues dans la constatation désabusée que le monde n'était 'plus capable de souffrir les nombreuses perfections' assumées par les saints et les saintes du passé. Dans un autre axe, Luther témoigna aussi d'une conscience de l'inaccessibilité. Le réformateur souligna que la sainteté héroïque et sacrificielle des temps anciens, qui exprimait la perfection d'un *donum Dei*, était désormais inatteignable par la créature irrémédiablement souillée par le péché originel. La sainteté devint une fin que, dans la quotidienneté, le croyant devait promouvoir , elle était une série d''Etats saints' qui concernaient autant la charge du pasteur que celle du souverain, du juge, du père ou de l'artisan... Mais à cette synchronie dans le refus d'un système d'images s'oppose, comme par réaction, une tension héroïque et dramatique, supportée par une certitude eschatologique, qui porta certains croyants à chercher à réaliser, de manière immédiate, le sacrifice de soi. Une certitude qui se trouva mise en représentation en deux séquences différentes; d'abord dans le millénarisme anabaptiste des années 1525–1535, et ensuite, dans l'exclusivisme de certains ligueurs français. La sainteté était définie comme un état donné par Dieu à ceux qui s'engageaient à combattre jusqu'à la mort pour l'avènement du règne du Christ. C'est-à-dire que l'histoire du XVIe siècle européen peut apparaître comme traversée par un combat d'images, comme un conflit d'images gravitant autour de la relation de la personne croyante à l'héroïsme, à la mimésis martyrologique.

Latin

Françoise Waquet

Un parcours dans le monde de l'école, de l'Église, du savoir et de l'administration montre à l'évidence la dimension latine qui fut celle de l'Europe entre les XVIe et XVIIIe siècles; partout eurent cours de mêmes pratiques appuyées sur de mêmes discours. L'identité commune qui se créa, se renforça encore de valeurs sociales largement partagées qui trouvèrent dans l'usage de cette langue leur fondement et leur expression. Rien d'étonnant qu'on ait vu dans le latin le 'signe européen'.

Index of Names and Places

Related Titles of Interest

THE EUROPEAN PUZZLE
The Political Structuring of Cultural Identities at a Time of Transition
Edited by Marion Demossier

The twin concepts of "Culture" and "Identity" are inescapable in any discussion of European Integration and yet over the last ten years their meaning has become increasingly contested. By combining an anthropological and political perspective, the authors challenge the traditional boundaries within the issue of the construction of Europe. In the first part, historians and anthropologists from various national traditions discuss the process of the construction of Europe and its implications for cultural identities. The second section examines a number of topics at the core of the process of Europeanization and presents up-to-date information on each of these issues: political parties, regions, football, cities, the Euro, ethnicity, heritage and European cinema. Emphasis is be placed on the political structuring of cultural identities by contrasting top-down and bottom-up processes that define the tensions between the unity and diversity of the European Community.

Marion Demossier is a senior lecturer in French and Anthropology at the University of Bath.

Summer 2007. 224 pages, bibliog., index.
ISBN 1-57181-626-7 Hb $75.00/£45.00
ISBN 1-84545-371-9 Pb $25.00/£15.00

LANGUAGES OF CIVIL SOCIETY
Edited by Peter Wagner

The past two decades have witnessed a revival of the concept of 'civil society'. From East Central Europe to Latin America and East Asia to the recent calls for a 'European civil society' and a 'global civil society', the concept signifies the need for national and supra-national forms of civic commitment against both unjustified state domination and neo-liberal marketization. Reviewing the long history of the concept, its use in various regional contexts and its place in critical political theory, this book takes comprehensive stock of these debates and asks about the potential of the concept of civil society in guiding political transformations towards fuller understandings of liberty and democracy.

Peter Wagner is Professor of Social and Political Theory at the European University Institute, Florence, and Professor of Sociology at the University of Warwick

Available. 264 pages, bibliog., index
ISBN 1-84545-118-X Hb $75.00/£42.00
ISBN 1-84545-119-8 Pb $25.00/£17.50
Volume 1 of European Civil Society

Berghahn Books, Inc. 150 Broadway, Suite 812, New York, NY 10038, USA

Berghahn Books, Ltd. 3 Newtec Place, Magdalen Rd. Oxford OX4 1RE, UK

orders@berghahnbooks.com   www.berghahnbooks.com

Related Titles of Interest

CONFLICTED MEMORIES
Europeanizing Contemporary Histories
Edited by Konrad Jarausch and Thomas Lindenberger

Despite the growing interest in general European history, the European dimension is surprisingly absent from the writing of contemporary history. In most countries, the historiography on the 20th century continues to be dominated by national perspectives. This volume focuses on the development of a shared conception of recent European history that will be required as an underpinning for further economic and political integration so as to make lasting cooperation on the old continent possible. It tries to overcome the traditional national framing that ironically persists just at a time when organized efforts to transform Europe from an object of debate to an actual subject have some chance of succeeding in making it into a polity in its own right.

Konrad H. Jarausch is director of the Zentrum für Zeithistorische Forschung Potsdam and Lurcy Professor of European Civilization at the University of North Carolina in Chapel Hill. **Thomas Lindenberger** is project leader at the Zentrum für Zeithistorische Forschung Potsdam and teaches at Potsdam University. He is currently directing a DFG funded research group on "Mass Media in the Cold War" at the ZZF Potsdam

Spring 2007. 304 pages, bibliog., index
ISBN 1-84545-284-4 Hb $85.00/£50.00
Volume 3 of Contemporary European History

FOUNDATIONS OF NATIONAL IDENTITY
From Catalonia to Europe
Josep Llobera

"Llobera is analytical and engaged in about equal measures, exploring new opportunities for national identities within the emerging structural framework of the European Union...Llobera's engaged and original book is a welcome addition to the macro-anthropology of European nationalisms, raising old questions with a new twist and combining, surprisingly successfully, the roles of anthropologist and national chronicler." **JRAI**

Since it emergence in the 19th century in response to feudalism, nationalism has been a mixed blessing. Originally seen as a positive force, often enough it has resulted in warfare and persecution of minorities, so much so that, over time, it has been considered a social evil whose apparent decline has been greeted as a positive development. The author disputes this or rather, he maintains that the picture that emerges is more complex: nationalism is not disappearing but has taken on a different form. What we are experiencing is an increasing autonomy of ethnonations, i.e. nations without a state, in the wake of a weakening of the multinational states and the transfer of their sovereignty upwards, in the case of Europe to the federation of the European Union, and downwards to the "ethnonations."

Josep R. Llobera is Visiting Professor of Anthropology at University College London and at the Universitat Pompeu Fabra in Barcelona.

Available. 320 pages, bibliog., index
ISBN 1-84545-042-6 Pb $25.00/£14.95
ISBN 1-57181-612-7 Hb $75.00/£50.00
Volume 19 of New Directions in Anthropology

Berghahn Books, Inc. 150 Broadway, Suite 812, New York, NY 10038, USA

Berghahn Books, Ltd. 3 Newtec Place, Magdalen Rd. Oxford OX4 1RE, UK

orders@berghahnbooks.com   www.berghahnbooks.com